Learning Through Visual Displays

A Volume in
Current Perspectives on Cognition, Learning, and Instruction

Series Editors:
Gregory Schraw, *University of Nevada*
Matthew T. McCrudden, *Victoria University of Wellington*
Daniel Robinson, *Colorado State University*

Current Perspectives on Cognition, Learning, and Instruction

Gregory Schraw, Matthew T. McCrudden, and Daniel Robinson, Series Editors

Learning Through Visual Displays

edited by

Gregory Schraw
University of Nevada

Matthew T. McCrudden
Victoria University of Wellington

and

Daniel Robinson
Colorado State University

Information Age Publishing, Inc.
Charlotte, North Carolina • www.infoagepub.com

Library of Congress Cataloging-in-Publication Data

Learning through visual displays / edited by Gregory Schraw, University of
Nevada, Matthew McCrudden, Victoria University of Wellington and Daniel
Robinson, Colorado State University.
pages cm. -- (Current perspectives on cognition, learning, and
instruction)
ISBN 978-1-62396-233-3 (paperback) -- ISBN 978-1-62396-234-0 (hardcover) --
ISBN 978-1-62396-235-7 (ebook) 1. Visual learning. 2. Cognition. 3.
Learning, Psychology of. I. Schraw, Gregory J. editor of compilation. II.
McCrudden, Matthew T. editor of compilation. III. Robinson, Daniel R. editor
of compilation.
LB1067.5.L43 2013
371.33'5--dc23

                                                              2013004595

Printed in the United States of America

CONTENTS

SECTION IV: USING VISUAL DISPLAYS TO IMPROVE RESAERCH

SECTION I

INTRODUCTION

CHAPTER 1

VISUAL DISPLAYS AND LEARNING

Theoretical and Practical Considerations

**Gregory Schraw,
Matthew T. McCrudden, and Daniel H. Robinson**

ABSTRACT

We provide a rationale for this volume, summarize each of the chapters, discuss general design principles for visual displays, and make four recommendations for future research. We state five goals for the volume. A summary of each chapter is provided and linked to these goals. We also discuss five information-processing functions of visual displays, including schema activation, reduction of cognitive load, provision of new information, conceptual integration, and promotion of deeper conceptual understanding and transfer to new settings. Each of these functions is discussed in detail within the chapters included in the volume. We conclude with four recommendations for future research.

Learning Through Visual Displays, pp. 3–19
Copyright © 2013 by Information Age Publishing

This volume addresses the design, instructional application, and theoretical conceptualization of visual displays, which we define as graphic representations of information communicated to learners. Visual displays can stand alone or be included with other forms of media (e.g., written text, video presentation) to create a multimedia instructional message. We assume that a visual display may be included within, or external to, an instructional message, or used in some hybrid manner. The main reason to include a display is to increase cognitive efficiency by reducing information processing load, distributing load over multiple channels, and to highlight salient information (Hoffman & Schraw, 2010). Visual displays have been shown to increase surface, deeper and transfer learning (e.g., Mayer, 2005; Robinson & Kiewra, 1995).

GOALS

We undertook this volume to address five goals. *One goal* is to advance the field with respect to micro- and macrotheory about visual displays. By microtheory, we mean a theory which explains the design and use of a specific type of display such as concept maps or tree diagrams. By macrotheory, we mean a theory that ties together all manner of visual displays such as notes, maps, hierarchical graphs, and animations under a single umbrella that identifies domain-general design and instructional principles. While we do not expect to resolve these issues in the current volume, we hope to begin to address them so that additional research and theory may benefit.

A *second goal* is to identify general design principles that can help instructional designers build better visual displays and match the strengths of a particular display to specific learning contexts (Smith, Best, Stubbs, Archibald, & Roberson-Ray, 2002). There is a surprisingly small amount of research and theory in this area in our opinion. However, a variety of authors have proposed general principles such as efficiency (Lane & Sandor, 2009; Sweller, 1999), accuracy (Tufte, 2001), visual guidance (Hegarty, Canham, & Fabrikant, 2010; Lane & Sandor, 2009) and structural coherence (Latour, 1990; Tufte, 2001). Efficiency refers to designs that minimize mental computations and information processing load that do not contribute to learning and memory (Hoffman & Schraw, 2010; Mayer, this volume). Accuracy refers to designs that convey their intended meaning and facilitate similar interpretations across users (Smith et al., 2002). Visual guidance refers to designs that highlight important and relevant information and make it easier to integrate this information (Lane & Sandor, 2009). Structural coherence refers to design properties that make clear the individual components in a visual display, the relationship among those components, and a description of the process that is being modeled (Tufte, 2001).

Related to general design principles, Lane and Sandor (2009) provide three general suggestions for constructing effective distributional and trend graphs based on previous research (Kosslyn, 1993; Tufte, 2001) that are applicable to all visual displays. One is to limit the amount of information in the representation to only what is needed. Doing so helps to reduce overall cognitive load and complexity. A second is to highlight important information by making it the visual focal point, including interpretative notes if necessary, and eliminating unnecessary information. A third is to enhance the overall efficiency of the visual display by using the type of representation that is best suited to convey the desired information and support a correct conclusion about the data. For example, a matrix is best-suited to convey compare-and-contrast information (Jairam, Kiewra, Kauffman, & Zhao, 2012).

In addition, Schraw and Paik (this volume) summarize common features of visual displays (Eichelberger & Schmid, 2009; Graham, Kennedy, & Benyon, 2000; Larkin & Simon, 1987; Latour, 1990; Morse & Lewis, 2000). One is that displays reduce the amount of information to a more manageable amount, which promotes cognitive economy (Lane & Sandor, 2009; Kosslyn, 1993). A second is that visual displays organize or summarize information in a manner that enables the viewer to readily grasp the intended big conceptual picture (Slough, McTigue, Kim, & Jennings, 2010; Tufte, 2001). A third is that displays attract and channel the viewer's attention to the most salient aspect of the information (Mayer, 2005; Vekiri, 2002). Fourth, visual displays foster inference-generation by highlighting the significant interrelationships among component variables (Heer, Bostock, & Ogievetsky, 2010). Last, displays provide an explicit visual model that can be used as an internalized mental model of events or processes, or used as a retrieval structure in memory to facilitate recall or future learning (Slough et al., 2010).

A *third goal* of this volume is to present reviews of representative research. Schraw and Paik (this volume) present a typology that includes eight general types of visual displays. We recruited experts in each of these areas to provide state-of-the-art updates. Although, we were unable to address all of the categories (e.g., maps); section three of this volume includes chapters that partially or completely address seven of the eight categories shown in the Schraw and Paik typology. These chapters also provide valuable references to recent reviews and meta-analyses of different categories of visual displays.

A *fourth goal* is to identify how well-designed visual displays can improve information processing. Several ways in which displays can improve processing are discussed in detail in section two of the volume in the context of cognitive load theory (Low, Jin & Sweller, this volume) and multimedia learning theory (Mayer, this volume). We discuss five ways in which well-designed visual displays improve information processing later in this chapter. These include activating existing schemata, reducing the cognitive load of information, promoting integration between a text and visual displays or across individual features within the display, providing new information that a text alone cannot provide, promoting transfer to new learning situations, and increasing deeper comprehension and especially the construct of integrated mental models of the situation presented in the text and/or visual display. We note as well that many of the chapters included in this volume discuss these five aids to learning in detail.

A *fifth goal* is to identify gaps in the literature and pressing concerns for future research. We have already commented above on the lack of cohesive research in visual displays, especially in areas such as geographical maps, causal diagrams, and hierarchies that are used frequently in the classroom and textbooks. We believe more research and theory is needed in at least four areas, including the development of a comprehensive typology of visual displays, a set of display-general design principles that govern all displays, as well as a set of display-specific principles. Below, we also discuss the need for a general intervention sequence for teaching students of all ages how to interpret and use visual displays, as well as a call for more intervention research that carefully evaluates the effect of instruction and display use on shallow, deeper, and transfer learning.

SUMMARY OF CHAPTERS

The 15 following chapters are arranged into four sections. Section I includes four chapters which collectively address conceptual and theoretical frameworks for understanding the structure and use of visual displays. Section II includes eight chapters that examine different types of visual displays in detail, including a discussion of the structure of displays, ways in which they affect learning, and suggestions for designing and using displays in the future. Section III includes three chapters that focus on analyzing and reporting test information and data.

Section I

In Chapter 2, Schraw and Paik discuss a variety of instructional visual displays, which they organize into a typology of visual displays. They summarize research, instructional interventions, and effects on learning for each of the eight different types of displays. These include signals within a text, notes, networks, sequences, hierarchies, distributions, maps and animations. The eight types of visual displays are compared regarding similar and unique features and several examples within each of the categories are discussed. The authors describe four ways that visual displays affect learning, including helping learners to focus on important information by selecting and highlighting the most relevant concepts, reducing the amount of information and organizing it in a manner that reveals the most important relationships and complex processes among concepts, instantiating external information into internal mental models that improve comprehension of important information, and reducing extraneous cognitive load associated with learning a large amount of complex information. They make several conclusions related to classroom instruction, (a) displays of all types are ubiquitous in textbooks and classroom instruction, (b) that most students experience difficulty reading and interpreting visual displays, (c) there is far too little formal instruction on reading, interpreting, and generating graphs, and (d) instruction helps to improve reading, interpreting and constructing displays, but especially when students lack relevant knowledge and spatial reasoning skills. The authors also discuss six unresolved issues germane to future research and theory development.

In Chapter 3, Low, Jin, and Sweller explore the instructional consequences of logical relations between multiple sources of information, where logical relations refer to the physical manner in which multiple pieces of information are related to one another. Their work is situated within cognitive load theory (CLT) that argues that human cognition is limited by innate physiological architecture in sensory, working, and long term memory (Sweller, 1999). These limits, coupled with the fact that experts possess large stores of knowledge, lead to a variety of phenomena such as the split-attention, redundancy, modality and transient information effects described in the chapter. The bulk of the chapter focuses on the conditions under which various CLT effects can be obtained. Low et al. argue that the split-attention, modality, and redundancy effects depend heavily on the logical relation between the various sources of information. Specifically, many of these effects can be explained based on the extent to which multiple sources of information are intelligible on their own.

In Chapter 4, Mayer describes a cognitive theory of multimedia for understanding the role of visual displays in learning. This theory states that learning is enhanced when individuals use both visual and auditory channels, optimize the use of limited processing capacity through strategic processing, and identify ways to process information at a deeper level to promote better memory and transfer of learning to new situations. Mayer summarizes three principles of instructional design that enhance learning. These including increasing the coherence of information by eliminating extraneous and redundant information, increasing spatial contiguity by placing text next to corresponding visual information, and signaling essential information. The chapter concludes with three goals for future research. These include the need to better understand design principles that enhance learning, to identify situations where instructional strategies are most effective, and explain the underlying cognitive mechanism by which learners construct deeper meaning. This chapter is especially helpful because it presents an integrated theory of learning based on information principles that can be used to design and implement a wide variety of instructional strategies.

In Chapter 5, Kalyuga discusses the role of knowledge and working memory on learning from visual displays using CLT as a theoretical framework for understanding the effects of prior knowledge on learning. He argues that expert knowledge is the single most important constraint on learning, and that knowledge differences between experts and novices lead to differential effects of instruction and use of visual displays. Different instructional formats may impose more or less cognitive load on learners as a function of working memory capacity and different types of knowledge. Indeed, the chapter explores the consequences of the expertise reversal effect (ERE), which refers to the interactions between the effectiveness of different instructional designs and levels of learner expertise or prior knowledge. The ERE predicts that novice learners benefit more from instructional guidance than experts, whereas too much support may impose unnecessary cognitive load on experts. The chapter considers three strategies for reducing the negative effect of the ERE on experts. One is to utilize two different modalities such as visual and auditory systems to better distribute cognitive load. A second strategy is to integrate visual information within visual displays to eliminate redundancy. A third strategy is to break apart especially complex displays into simpler units that reduce interactivity and cognitive load. Kalyuga concludes that the design of visual displays needs to take into account the trade-off between level of knowledge and the limits of human cognitive architecture. Expert knowledge compensates for limited architecture, whereas instruction helps to compensate with novices.

Section II

Section II focuses on instructional applications. In Chapter 6, Crooks and Cheon examine a number of issues related to computerized note taking (CNT). They argue that CNT provides an instructional method that attempts to combine the cognitive benefits of note taking (essential processing) with the cognitive benefits of graphic organizers (generative processing) to increase learning from e-text during online instruction. The chapter begins with a review of traditional note taking in which they discuss the encoding and external storage functions of paper-and-pencil notes. This is followed by a discussion of computer-based note taking and the *passivity hypothesis*, which states that computer-based cutting and pasting of notes decreases learning due to the ease of the cut and paste function. Disabling, restricting, or expediting the copy-paste function are discussed as interventions aligned with the passivity hypothesis, whereas partial computer-based note taking and prompting self-regulation are discussed as interventions aligned the *excessive-demands hypothesis,* which states that the cut-paste decreases learning due to the demand it imposes on limited cognitive resources. The authors conclude that findings from both lines of research supported their respective hypotheses. Overall, they suggest the literature supports the excessive demands hypothesis and propose that the passivity hypothesis results from a lack of essential processing among students lacking the metacognitive skills to appropriately use the copy-paste feature.

In Chapter 7, Nesbit and Adesope examine the theory, research, and design of concept maps, which they define as diagrams that represent concepts as labeled nodes and represent relationships between the concepts as labeled links that connect the nodes. They discuss several different varieties of concept maps and also examine conditions under which a diagram would not be considered a true concept map. They discuss a meta-analysis of 55 studies that examined concept maps that found that construction of a concept map during study significantly increased learning. The authors provide seven different reasons why concept maps may promote better learning, These include dual coding, but especially advantages due to dual-coding of information in semantic and visual channels, and deeper processing attributable to the integration among concepts in a concept map. Using pre-constructed concept maps also increases learning, especially when they are used before, during and after the learning cycle. Individuals with low prior knowledge may benefit most from using concept maps. The authors also discuss how concept maps may be used as web-based navigational tools and for assessment purposes. The chapter concludes with several suggestions for future research that examine how concept maps affect study time, depth of processing, and the construction of mental models that facilitate later retrieval.

In Chapter 8, van Meter and Firetto discuss the use of a general drawing strategy to promote deeper representational understanding and learning. The authors describe the *generative theory of drawing construction* (GTDC; van Meter & Garner, 2005), which provides a theoretical model of the cognitive processes underlying drawing. The GTDC explains drawing according to the cognitive processes of selection, organization and forced integration, and makes use of processing in both visual and verbal channels in memory. The GTDC also is discussed in relation to existing learning theories and the facilitation of self-regulated learning skills. The model focuses on three general skills that include setting standards for performance, applying (strategic) operations, and monitoring goal progress. Each phase holds specific implications for learners' effective use of the drawing strategy. They provide an excellent review of relevant research that focuses on the role of drawing in support of self-regulation and link this to their discussion of the GTDC. The authors conclude with a variety of suggestions for testing the GTDC in future research.

In Chapter 9, Renkl and Schwonke consider a number of instructional support strategies that help learners use static (i.e., displays that do not change over time) visual displays more effectively. These include direct (e.g., cuing, self-explanation prompts) and indirect (e.g., proving advance information about the purpose and structure of the display) procedures. The goal of these instructional activities is to promote deeper structural learning, especially an integrated conceptual understanding of the information, in addition to surface retention and learning. The authors also review a variety of strategies that are consistent with current models of self-regulated learning, including active integration procedures, a strategy script, and guided picture processing. They conclude with three general instructional principles, including a focus on deeper structural learning activities, incorporating scaffolding strategies to assist learning, and providing specific learning goals that enable students to judge the relevance of information and focus their attention at an optimal level. This chapter is especially useful as a model of how to implement abstract design principles into teachable learning strategies that enhance deeper understanding.

In Chapter 10, Dexter and Hughes discuss the use of graphic organizers as aids for teaching academic content to students with a learning disability (LD). They provide a definition of graphic organizers (GOs), which include a variety of visual displays such as timelines, venn diagrams, summary matrices, and taxonomies. They summarize four different theoretical frameworks which help to explain the ways in which GOs facilitate understanding and are linked to learning problems due to limited working memory resources and inability to link prior knowledge with new information. These include theory of subsumption, assimilation theory, the visual argument hypothesis, and dual coding theory. Collectively, these theories suggest that learners benefit from GOs because they activate schemata, help learners organize complex information, make implicit relationships explicit, and reduce cognitive load. Indeed, a review of relevant research and meta-analyses by the authors indicates that use of

GOs improve both surface and transfer learning. The authors draw several important instructional conclusions, including that GOs help LD students more than others, help low-knowledge students more than others, and improve deeper learning in all students.

In Chapter 11, Poliquin and Schraw investigate the effects of a 20-minute instructional intervention on subsequent understanding of a causal diagram. The authors provide a review of previous research using causal diagrams, as well as their general structural properties. Then they describe an experiment in which college undergraduates were taught to interpret a causal diagram and were asked to transfer these skills to understanding when a different text that describes a complex causal process. Specifically, college undergraduates in a training group received an instructional sequence on the structure, component variables, use, and conclusions related to a seven-variable causal model displayed in a two-dimensional diagram. Participants in the training and no-training groups then studied a 1,700-word text without a diagram and completed a variety of learning tasks. Participants in the training group had higher text recall, generated more predictor variables and produced more types of styles with greater clarity in their self-generated drawings, and had more short-answer responses than participants in the no-training group. These findings supported the *causal explication hypothesis*, which states that training which facilitates comprehension of a causal diagram also helps individuals understand the causal structure of a text even when a causal diagram of the text is not present and the text is unrelated to the training diagram. Based on these findings, Poliquin and Schraw suggest that a brief, instructional intervention helps individuals to understand causal diagrams and to transfer those interpretation skills to understanding the causal structure of an unrelated text. They also discuss several implications of their findings and the extent to which comparable training with other types of visual displays may have similar effects.

In Chapter 12, Höffler, Schmeck, and Opfermann compare differences in individual processing in static and dynamic visual representations. The authors review the role of working and long-term memory, as well as the benefits of dual-channel processing within the information processing system. These structural properties are described in terms of three current theories of multimedia learning. The authors argue in favor of simultaneous visual and semantic processing of complex information in order to better distribute cognitive load. The chapter considers a variety of different types of visual representations, comparing static and dynamic representations in particular, and discussing in detail the conditions under which both types facilitate learning. The role of prior knowledge and cognitive style are considered as well. The authors describe the expert reversal effect in which instructional activities that benefit low-knowledge learners usually do not benefit high-knowledge learners. In contrast, the role of cognitive style (i.e., visualizers vs. verbalizers) was inconclusive. Several possible hypotheses are compared regarding the effect of spatial ability, although the authors note that too few empirical studies have been conducted to draw a valid conclusion. The chapter concludes with a discussion of best instructional practices related to the use of visual representations.

In Chapter 13, Andriessen and Baker consider the theory and instructional uses of argument diagrams, which they define as visual representations of interlinked claims, arguments and counterarguments that can be created and modified by small groups of students interacting on the same screen. They discuss at length the structure of arguments and describe software that enables groups of learners to construct ongoing arguments in a collaborative fashion. They compare four different types of learning outcomes associated to the use of argument diagrams in collaborative learning contexts, including knowledge acquisition within a particular domain: improving collaboration by participating in joint argument design, knowledge management by sharing information in a network, and knowledge construction as a shared group activity. These learning outcomes are not mutually exclusive, but indicate the main focus of learning goals of students, the instructional design by teacher or researcher as well as the assessment of the outcomes. The authors argue for scripted instruction in the use of argument maps to assure that learners use them properly and efficiently. They conclude that research on argument maps should take into account the type of learning that is at stake, which will thus determine the methodology applied for experimentation and analysis.

Section IV

Section IV addresses how visual displays may be used to organize, report, and interpret research data. In Chapter 14, Olafson, Feucht, and Marchand examine how visual displays may be used in qualitative research. They provide a brief comparison of the use of visual displays in quantitative and qualitative research and discuss at length the use of computer software to generate visual summaries of data. A detailed comparison is made between the processes (e.g., scoring data, generating codes) and products (e.g., conclusions, themes, models) of qualitative analyses. They distinguish among three levels of qualitative analysis, including the text, table and graphic level. These distinctions are used to propose a 3 (text, table, graphic) x 2 (process, product) matrix that compares the uses of six different types of qualitative visual displays. Much of the chapter explains and provides examples of how computer software such as Atlas.ti can be used to create visual displays for the processes and products of qualitative analysis. The chapter concludes with a summary of six common analytic and interpretive processes. This chapter is important because it codifies six different uses of visual displays into a typology that can be used for instructional and data-analytic purposes. Each of these six types of displays is illustrated with an example. In addition, the authors compare the relative strengths and weaknesses of using different data-analysis techniques and reporting strategies. It also raises a question whether a comparable two-dimensional matrix might be created to classify displays used in quantitative research.

In Chapter 15, Pastor and Finney discuss the use of visual displays for enhancing the interpretation and reporting of quantitative research. They discuss four ways in which visual displays facilitate cognition, including the reduction of cognitive load, linking and organizing information, creating new meaning that is not conveyed in text or numbers alone, and building a conceptual bridge between novel and familiar information. They argue that coupling visual and verbal information not only reduces load, but promotes a deeper understanding of information because learners make the effort to coordinate the two non-redundant sources of information. The bulk of the chapter illustrates in detail how three complex statistical modeling procedures can use visual displays to enhance learning these procedures, as well as understanding the main conclusions suggested by the data output. The authors conclude with a discussion of four possible reasons that high-quality displays are not used in journals more often. They argue that none of these reasons justify the exclusion of potentially helpful displays both in the classroom and when reporting data in research reports. This chapter makes three important contributions to quantitative analysis by describing how visual displays enhance understanding, providing strategies for using displays in the classroom and publications, and identifying possible reasons why displays are not used more frequently despite their beneficial properties.

In Chapter 16, Foley and Buckendahl conclude the volume with a broad discussion of how visual displays may be employed to enhance the design and development of assessments. They describe a 10-step sequence of test development in which each step contributes in some way to test validity. Each step in the cycle is discussed in detail and illustrated with a variety of visual displays that serve two purposes, including helping viewers better understand the role of validity in testing and illustrating each step in a practical instructional manner so lay experts can implement the activities in each step of the test development process. The authors provide a wide array of visual displays that illustrate the purpose and implementation of test development activities in each step. Collectively, they provide examples of most of the eight categorized visual displays shown in Schraw and Paik (this volume). In addition, they discuss the usefulness of visual displays when training nonexperts to understand each of the 10 steps and associated activities in the testing process. They conclude with three general recommendations for the use of visual displays in the test development and validation process. One is to explore the use of visual displays throughout the test development and validation process to reduce the cognitive burden for subject matter experts (SMEs) and increase interpretability for consumers of test results. A second is to evaluate the effectiveness of different data visualizations in various testing contexts to assess their effectiveness on experts and novices. A third is to disseminate the utility of different visual displays to the broader testing community.

FIVE INFORMATION PROCESSING FUNCTIONS

The chapters summarized above collectively suggest five important information-processing functions of visual displays. These include activating schemata, reducing cognitive load, providing new information, promoting integration and transfer, and fostering deeper comprehension.

Activating schemata refers to two related activities, including instantiating existing schemata via a visual display that helps learners understand text information and providing a template for a new schema that provides an organization framework for understanding remembering information (Radvansky, 2006). Previous research suggests that schema activation facilitates processing in a variety of ways, but especially making information processing faster and less effortful (Mayer, this volume).

A second information-processing function of visual displays is to reduce cognitive load (Low et al., this volume; Paas, Renkl, & Sweller, 2003). Cognitive load may occur during learning due to intrinsic, extraneous, or germane variables (Sweller, 2012). Visual displays help reduce cognitive load in at least two ways. One way is by using two separate information-processing channels devoted to visual and conceptual processing respectively. Research indicates that each channel possesses a separate pool of cognitive resources, thereby increasing an individual's total information processing capacity. A second way is to increasing the efficiency of processing within each channel by providing visual scaffolding prior to and during the learning task. This may be especially helpful for low-knowledge learners who benefit more than high-knowledge experts from advance organizers and visual displays that provide conceptual scaffolding (Kalyuga, this volume; Renkl & Schwonke, this volume).

A third information-processing function is that visual displays frequently provide new information that is not included in the text explicitly or is difficult to present in words rather than pictures. For example,

Poliquin and Schraw (this volume) discuss several advantages of causal diagrams when learning about complex causal relationships among variables. Perhaps the biggest advantage is the explicit conceptual model that is presented in a causal diagram that shows the type of relationship among variables, as well as the magnitude and direction of the variable. In most cases, the conceptual framework conveyed by a causal diagram, a concept map (Nesbit & Adesope, this volume), or a confirmatory factor-analytic model (Pastor & Finney, this volume) is extremely difficult to describe in words compared to a visual display.

A fourth function is that visual displays promote integration of information in text as well as transfer to new learning environments. Regarding integration, research summarizes in section two of this volume shows that matrix notes (Crooks & Cheon, this volume) and pictures (van Meter & Firetto, this volume) enhance integration and learning. Höffler et al. (this volume) discuss how both static and animated pictures provide better integration by conveying a sequence of activities, while Olafson et al. provide examples in Tables 14.1 and 14.2 of how visual displays provide an exhaustive summary of all possible process-product combinations in qualitative data analysis. Simlarly, Foley and Buckendahl (this volume) show how a single diagram reveals a multicomponent sequence of activities that collectively provide data in support of a validty argument in educational testing environments.

A number of chapters also discuss the role of visual displays in transfer of diagramming and interpretation skills to a new learning environment. For example, Poliquin and Schraw (this volume) conducted an experiment in which college students who received a structured lesson on the structure and interpretation of causal diagrams spontaneously transferred this knowledge to understanding a different text that included an implicit causal model within it, but was studied without an external visual display of the causal model. Students were better able to remember information and recall direct and indirect effects among variables. In addition, many of the chapters in this volume support two benefits related to transfer of skills. One is that knowledge of how to construct and interpret visuals displays, such as matrix notes (Crooks & Cheoan, this volume) and maps (Clark et al., 2008), increases. A second is that using different types of visual displays to interpret information and construct an integrated conceptual framework of the domain increases as well (De Simone, 2007; van der Merr, 2012).

A fifth information-processing function is that visual displays often increase deeper comprehension by facilitating the construction of explicit conceptual frameworks or mental models. By conceptual frameworks, we mean an integrated schematic understanding of the components and relationships within a domain that might be captured within a sophisticated concept map, hierarchical tree diagram, typology, or distributional display. Understanding the conceptual structure of a domain is essential to expert problem solving and self-regulation of learning (Holyoak & Morrison, 2005). By mental model, we mean an integrated process-model of complex phenomena that might be captured in sequential displays such as causal diagrams (Poliquin & Schraw, this volume), timelines, flowcharts, and argument maps (Andriessen & Baker, this volume). Zwann and Madden (2004) discuss a variety on mental models and procedural situation models, as well as information processing variables that constrain them. Both the construction of mental models and making inferences based on these models has been shown to enhance decoding, translating, interpreting and evaluation of learning during information processing (Schonborn & Anderson, 2010).

RECOMMENDATIONS FOR FUTURE RESEARCH

The chapters included in this volume suggest four general recommendations for future research. One is to explore a general theory of visual displays that includes a comprehensive typology. Schraw and Paik (this volume) developed an eight-category typology that classified visual displays in terms of their instructional purpose. However, as they acknowledge, their typology does not address a comparison of underlying structural features of displays or a discussion of how these features may impose information processing constraints on learning. They note that other displays exist in the literature even though there is very little agreement among these typologies. We believe that the development of a comprehensive classification system that enables researchers to classify different types of displays based on structure and function would make it easier to understand common and unique features of displays and how these features affect learning.

A second recommendation is to develop a set of design principles for constructing and disseminating displays in textbooks or multimedia outlets. We assume there are general characteristics of displays such as the efficiency (Hoffman & Schraw, 2010; Lane & Sandor, 2009), accuracy (Tufte, 2001), visual guidance (Hegarty et al., 2010) and structural coherence (Tufte, 2001) properties described above. However, we also assume it is reasonable to identify both display-general and display-specific structural properties. An example of the former is a minimization principle in which a display is limited to its essential components. An example of the latter is a hierarchical inclusion principle in which some displays (e.g., tree diagrams, map diagrams) specify how some actions or components are included within other categories. We note within the context of the present volume that little work has been done in this regard and presents a significant obstacle in our opinion to a general design theory of visual displays.

A third recommendation is to generate and validate a general instructional sequence for teaching learners how to use and apply visual displays. Like design principles, there is a paucity of instructional studies in the literature and no integrated discussions of general instructional principles for visual displays. One consequence is that displays tend to be microdeveloped and studied in isolation. Nevertheless, extent studies show robust gains for both surface and deeper learning (Abrami et al., 2008; De Simone, 2007; Liben, 2009; McCrudden, Magliano, & Schraw, 2011; Schwonke, Berthold, & Renkl, 2009; van der Merr, 2012) following instruction. Even simple instructional interventions of 10 to 15 minutes may significantly alter the extent to which students of all ages use displays to increase learning (Mautone & Mayer, 2007; Schwonke et al., 2009).We propose that researchers identify several plausible instructional sequences and test the effectiveness of all of them in a comparative setting. We envision at least two key issues to investigate. One is a clear specification of steps in the instructional sequence. A second is the amount of time, training, practice and feedback allocated at each step in the sequence.

A fourth recommendation is to increase the amount of basic instructional research that compares the utility of different types of displays, or multiple displays, to one another. This research should include four levels of learning outcomes to achieve optimal effectiveness, including shallow, deep, conceptual, and transfer types of outcomes. Some or all of these outcomes have been used previously in studies (e.g., Mayer, this volume; Poliquin & Schraw, this volume; Renkl & Schwonke, this volume). In this framework, shallow processing refers to measures of factual recognition or recall. Deep learning refers to understanding concepts, relationships among concepts, or assumptions implicit in the to-be-learned information. Conceptual outcomes focus on the "big picture" that is captured in schemata and mental models. Relevant measures are discussed in Schraw and Robinson (2011). Transfer refers to how a skill or conceptual understanding acquired in one setting may generalize to a different setting. Researchers have investigated both near- and far-transfer learning outcomes (cf. Mayer, this volume). We believe that both are appropriate as research outcomes in order to establish the "generalizability" of instructional effects for different types of visual displays. We also suggest that researchers incorporate three recommendation made by Foley and Buckendahl (this volume) when evaluating the effectiveness of visual displays in the test development and validation process. These include using visual displays throughout the test development and validation process to reduce the cognitive burden on test developers, evaluate the effectiveness of different data visualizations in various testing contexts, and disseminate the results of such inquiries to the broader research community.

REFERENCES

Abrami, P. C., Bernard, R. M., Borokhovski, E., Wade, A., Surkes, M. A., Tamim, R., & Zhang, D. (2008). Instructional interventions affecting critical thinking skills and dispositions: A stage 1 meta-analysis. *Review of Educational Research, 78,* 1102-1134.

Clark, D., Reynolds, S., Lemanowski, V., Stiles, T, Yasar, S., Proctor, S., Lewis, E., Stromfors, C., & Corkins, J. (2008). University students' conceptualization and interpretation of topographic maps. *International Journal of Science Education, 30,* 375-406.

De Simone, C. (2007). Applications of concept mapping. *College Teaching, 55,* 33-27.

Eichelberger, H., & Schmid, K. (2009). Guidelines on the aesthetic quality of UML class diagrams. *Information and Software Technology, 51,* 1686-1698.

Graham M., Kennedy, J., & Benyon, D. (2000). Towards a methodology for developing visualizations. *International Journal of Human-Computer Studies, 53,* 789-807.

Heer, J., Bostock, M., & Ogievetsky, V. (2010). A tour through the visualization zoo. *Communications of the ACM, 53,* 59-67.

Hegarty, M., Canham, M. S., & Fabrikant, S. I. (2010). Thinking about the weather: How display salience and knowledge affect performance in a graphic inference task. *Journal of Experimental Psychology: Learning, Memory, and Cognition, 36,* 37-53.

Hoffman, B., & Schraw, G. (2010). Conceptions of efficiency: Applications in learning and problem solving. *Educational Psychologist, 45,* 1-14.

Holyoak, K. J., & Morrison, R. G. (2005). Thinking and reasoning: A reader's guide. In K. J. Holyoak & R. G. Morrison (Eds.), *The Cambridge handbook of thinking and reasoning* (pp. 1-9). Cambridge, England: Cambridge University Press.

Jairam, D., Kiewra, K. A., Kauffman, D. F., & Zhao, R. (2012). How to study a matrix. *Contemporary Educational Psychology, 37,* 128-135.

Lane, D. M., & Sandor, A. (2009). Designing better graphs by including distributional information and integrating words, numbers, and images. *Psychological Methods, 14,* 239–257.

Larkin, J. H., & Simon, H. A. (1987). Why a diagram is (sometimes) worth 10,000 words. *Cognitive Science, 11,* 65-100.

Latour, B. (1990). Drawing things together. In M. Lynch & S. Woolgar (Eds.), *Representation in scientific practice* (pp. 19-68). Cambridge, MA: MIT Press.

Mayer, R. E. (Ed.). (2005). *The Cambridge handbook of multimedia learning.* New York, NY: Cambridge University Press.

Liben, L. S. (2009). The road to understanding maps. *Current Directions in Psychological Science, 18,* 310-315.

Kosslyn, S. M. (1993). *Elements of graphic design.* New York, NY: Freeman.

Mautone, P. D., & Mayer, R. E. (2007). Cognitive aids for guiding graph comprehension. *Journal of Educational Psychology, 99,* 640-652.

McCrudden, M. T., Magliano, J., & Schraw, G. (2011). The effects of diagrams on online reading processes and memory. *Discourse Processes, 48,* 69-92.

Morse, E., & Lewis, M. (2000). Evaluating visualizations: using a taxonomic guide. *International Journal of Human-Computer Studies, 53,* 637-662.

Paas, F., Renkl, A., & Sweller, J. (2003). Cognitive load theory and instructional design: Recent developments. *Educational Psychologist, 38,* 1-4.

Radvansky, G. 2006). *Human memory.* Boston, MA: Pearson.

Robinson, D. H., & Kiewra, K. A. (1995). Visual argument: Graphic organizers are superior to outlines in improving learning from text. *Journal of Educational Psychology, 87,* 455-467.

Schonborn, K. J., & Anderson, T. R. (2010). Bridging the educational research-teaching practice gap: Foundations for assessing and developing biochemistry students' visual literacy. *BAMBED, 38,* 347-354,

Schraw, G., & Robinson, D. H. (2011). Conceptualizing and assessing higher order thinking skills. In G. Schraw & D. Robinson (Eds.), *Assessment of higher order thinking skills* (pp. 1-15). Greenwich, CT: Information Age Publishers.

Schwonke, R., Berthold, K., & Renkl, A. (2009). How multiple external representations are used and how they can be made more useful. *Applied Cognitive Psychology, 23,* 1227-1243.

Slough, S. W., McTigue, E. M., Kim, S., & Jennings, S. M. (2010). Science textbooks use of graphical representation: A descriptive analysis of four sixth grade science texts. *Reading Psychology, 31,* 301-325.

Smith, L. D., Best, L. A., Stubbs, D. A., Archibald, A. B., & Roberson-Ray, R. (2002). Constructing knowledge. The role of graphs and tables in hard and soft psychology. *American Psychologist, 57,* 749-761.

Sweller, J. (1999). *Instructional design in technical areas.* Camberwell, Australia: ACER Press.

Sweller, J. (2012). Human cognitive architecture: Why some instructional procedures work and others do not. In K. Harris, S. Graham, & T. Urdan (Eds.), *APA Educational Psychology Handbook* (Vol. 1, pp. 295-325). Washington, DC: American Psychological Association.

Tufte, E. R. (2001). *The visual display of quantitative information* (2nd ed.). Cheshire, CT: Graphics Press.

van der Meer, J. (2012): Students' note-taking challenges in the twenty-first century: Considerations for teachers and academic staff developers. *Teaching in Higher Education, 17,* 13-23.

Van Meter, P., & Garner, J. (2005). The promise and practice of learner-generated drawing: Literature review and synthesis. *Educational Psychology Review, 17,* 285-325.

Vekiri, I. (2002). What is the value of graphical displays in learning? *Educational Psychology Review, 14,* 261-312.

Zwann, R. A., & Madden, C. J. (2004). Updating situation models. *Journal of Experimental Psychology: Learning, Memory and Cognition, 30,* 283-288.

SECTION II

THEORETICAL FRAMEWORKS

CHAPTER 2

SOME INSTRUCTIONAL CONSEQUENCES OF LOGICAL RELATIONS BETWEEN MULTIPLE SOURCES OF INFORMATION

Renae Low, Putai Jin, and John Sweller

ABSTRACT

In many curriculum areas, multiple sources of information may or may not be required during learning. Visual sources of information, such as diagrams, may be used in conjunction with spoken or written text, for example. Over the last few decades, many researchers have used cognitive load theory as a guide for investigating the instructional consequences of various permutations of different sources of information. One of the major but rarely considered findings is that the logical relationship between sources of information is critical to the instructional consequences and instructional recommendations. How we should organize a diagram and text, for example, depends on the logical relations between the diagram and text with different logical relations leading to very different instructional recommendations. The instructional consequences are vastly different depending on whether diagrammatic information associated with textual information is intelligible in isolation. These issues will be discussed with respect to several cognitive load theory effects along with the instructional implications that flow from those effects.

Learning Through Visual Displays, pp. 23–45

INTRODUCTION

Over the last few decades, a substantial and important literature has developed concerned with relations between various modes of information during instruction. Presenting information in visual form such as diagrams, pictures, animations or 3D real life in association with either spoken or written text have contributed to the literature base (e.g., Mayer, 2009). The bulk of this work has been concerned with the instructional consequences of various physical permutations of visual and textual information. While such work is critical, there is another factor that is equally critical: the manner in which information is physically presented, which concerns the logical relations between different sources of information. Logical relations indicate the manner in which two sources of information such as, for example, a diagram and related text, refer to each other. Logical relations can impact heavily on the instructional consequences of physical relations between information sources where physical relations indicate the physical layout or design of multiple sources of information. The instructional consequences of the same physical relation between two seemingly similar sources of information can be totally reversed depending on their logical relation. For example, the manner in which diagrams should be presented with text, including the physical layout, not only depends on the fact that diagrams and text are being used, but also on the manner in which the diagram and text refer to each other, such as the logical relation between the particular diagram and particular text.

There is a paucity of literature associated with the instructional consequences of the logical relations between multiple sources of information. Since much of the literature that is available is associated with cognitive load theory, we will begin by discussing that theory.

Cognitive Load Theory

Cognitive load theory (CLT) is an instructional theory derived from our knowledge of the evolutionary bases of human cognitive architecture and the instructional consequences that flow from that architecture. A key aspect of the theory is the relation between long-term memory and working memory, and how instructional materials interact with this cognitive system. The theory suggests that learning happens best under conditions that are aligned with human cognitive architecture. The structure of human cognitive architecture is apparent through the results of experimental research. Basically, the human cognitive architecture comprises three essential components: sensory memory, working memory, and long-term memory (Atkinson & Shiffrin, 1968).

Sensory memory is the temporary storage of information brought into the central nervous system through the senses and typically lasts for a very brief period. Working memory is generally regarded as "a processing resource of limited capacity involved in the preservation of information while simultaneously processing the same or other information" (Swanson, 1999, p. 986). In contrast, long-term memory can store immeasurably large amounts of information for a potentially unlimited duration. The contents of long-term memory are sophisticated structures that permit us to perceive, think, and solve problems as single entities rather than as a group of rote learned facts. These structures, known as schemata, are what permit us to treat multiple elements as a single element. They are the cognitive structures that make up our knowledge base (Sweller, 1988). Schemata are acquired over a lifetime of learning, and may have other schemata contained within them. For learning to occur, information contained in instructional material must first be processed by working memory. For schema acquisition to occur, instruction should be designed to reduce working memory load so information may be processed in working memory and added to information in long term memory. CLT is concerned with techniques for reducing working memory load in order to facilitate the changes in long-term memory associated with schema acquisition. The theory has many implications in the design of learning materials which must, if they are to be effective, keep unnecessary cognitive load of learners at a minimum during the learning process.

As previously mentioned, CLT has been associated with cognitive principles from the perspective of evolutionary psychology (Sweller, 2011, 2012; Sweller, Ayres, & Kalyuga, 2011). This evolutionary framework of human cognitive architecture is summarized as follows: There are two categories of knowledge: biologically primary and biologically secondary (Geary, 2007, 2008, 2012). Biologically primary knowledge is the knowledge that we have evolved to acquire over many thousands of generations, such as language comprehension, acquisition, and production, which are essential for humans as a species. This long-term evolution enables us to acquire these skills simply by being immersed in a language-rich environment. In contrast, biologically secondary knowledge, such as literature, mathematics and science, has only recently been required as cultural knowledge. Therefore, although we may be able to acquire this type of knowledge that has been accumulated during the relatively short period of civilization, we have not explicitly evolved to acquire such knowledge. Biologically secondary knowledge is typically taught in educational institutions or by experts. At least some assistance and considerable personal effort are needed to acquire biologically secondary knowledge.

The distinction between biologically primary and secondary knowledge can be seen with respect to language acquisition. We have evolved to learn to listen and speak our native language and so, for example, do not need to be taught how to organize our tongue, lips, breath and voice in order to speak. We have not evolved to learn to read and write and need to be explicitly taught in educational institutions. CLT applies to biologically secondary knowledge.

There are five basic principles that can be used to describe the human information processing system from the perspective of evolution by natural selection (Sweller et al., 2011; Sweller & Sweller, 2006). These five principles apply equally to the information structures that underlie evolution by natural selection and human cognition. In this chapter, only the relation of the principles to human cognition will be discussed.

1.   The *information store* principle states that long-term memory contains a very large store of information governing most human cognitive activity. The information store holds schemata, the building blocks of knowledge, discussed above. Schemata can be used automatically or under conscious control.

2.   The *borrowing and reorganizing* principle states that the bulk of information in long-term memory is obtained by borrowing information from other individuals by imitating them (Bandura, 1986), listening to what they say or reading what they write. This information is reorganized when combined with preexisting information held in long-term memory.

3.   The *randomness as genesis* principle states that although most of the information in long-term memory is borrowed from others, creativity occurs when a learner randomly generates a problem-solving move and tests its effectiveness.

4.   The *narrow limits of change* principle states that large-scale, dramatic, random changes are likely to cause traumatic effects on the functionality of long-term memory and thus the limited capacity of working memory ensures small, incremental changes in long-term memory to maintain the relative stability of the cognitive system.

5.   The *environmental organizing and linking* principle states that whereas the amount of information from sensory memory that can be processed by working memory is limited, the amount of information from long-term memory organized as schemata that can be processed by working memory has no known limits. As a consequence, once material is organized and stored in long-term

memory, the limitations of working memory disappear when dealing with that material (Ericsson & Kintsch, 1995). The environmental organising and linking principle provides the ultimate justification for the human cognitive system. It suggests that the purpose of instruction is to store organized information in long-term memory that then can be used to efficiently process material from the environment.

On the basis of the human cognitive architecture outline above, in order to promote effective changes to long-term memory, information should be presented explicitly in a manner that reduces any unnecessary load on working memory (extraneous cognitive load) and at the same time directs working memory resources to information that is intrinsic to the task at hand (intrinsic cognitive load). Intrinsic cognitive load is imposed by the degree of interactivity of essential elements of information. If there are many interacting elements that are intrinsic to the task, intrinsic cognitive load is high. This load can be reduced by knowledge held in long-term memory because knowledge allows many interacting elements to be considered as a single element. Extraneous cognitive load is imposed by the degree of element interactivity due to the manner in which instructional material is presented. If instructional material requires learners to unnecessarily process numerous interacting elements of information, extraneous cognitive load will be high (Sweller, 2010). This load can be reduced by reformatting the different sources of information that constitute the instructional material.

CLT has generated many controlled, experimental studies indicating that some instructional presentations minimise cognitive activities that are unnecessary to learning so that cognitive resources can be freed to concentrate on essential activities. In essence, CLT proposes to use limited working memory effectively and efficiently during teaching and learning, seeks to eliminate the violations of instructional principles based on human cognitive architecture, and attempts to aid learners in their schema acquisition according to their expertise and other characteristics. The particular CLT effects relevant to this chapter and discussed below are the split-attention, redundancy, modality and transient information effects.

Over the last few decades, many researchers have used CLT to hypothesize the instructional consequences of various permutations of different sources of information. An important finding associated with this bulk of work is that the logical relations between different sources of information can impact instructional effectiveness.

Some Logical Relations Between Multiple Sources of Information

Consider the diagrams and text of Figures 2.1 and 2.2. With a similar physical layout, the relation between diagram and text appears identical in the two figures. In both cases we have a diagram and some text underneath that refers to the diagram. It is easy to assume that any instructional implications that apply to the information of Figure 2.1 also apply to the information of Figure 2.2 In fact the logical relations of the textual information to the diagram differs markedly in the two figures and in conjunction with CLT summarized above, that difference has substantial instructional consequences.

In Figure 2.1, for a novice in this area, the geometry statements are probably essential to an understanding of the information contained in the figure. In turn, the statements are completely unintelligible without reference to the figure. As a consequence, there is a strong degree of dependence between the figure and the statements. The statements refer to the figure and the figure provides meaning to the statements. In that sense, they are mutually dependent and that dependence is a critical factor in instructional design. Critically, in order to understand the information, at various points, both the diagram and the text must be considered simultaneously because they are unintelligible in isolation. It may be desirable to organize instruction in a manner that facilitates learners' ability to process both sources of information simultaneously.

The need to consider both the diagram and text simultaneously has working memory implications. Based on CLT as discussed above, there is very likely to be a heavy working memory load, and that working memory load needs to be considered when designing instruction. Details concerning the instructional design implications will be provided below in the discussion of the split-attention, modality, transient, element interactivity and expertise reversal effects.

In contrast to Figure 2.1, the diagram and text of Figure 2.2, while apparently similar in terms of physical layout, have an entirely different logical relation. Learning how the blood flows in the heart, lungs, and rest of the body results in a very different set of relations between the diagram and statements to learning how to solve the geometry problem of Figure 2.1. For most learners, the diagram of Figure 2.2 is entirely self-contained in that what needs to be learned can be learned with no reference to the text. The text merely repeats much of the information contained in the diagram. In fact, depending on a learner's knowledge of anatomy, the text also may be learned independently of the diagram.

The relative independence of the diagram and text of Figure 2.2 compared to Figure 2.1, and the fact that the text essentially repeats

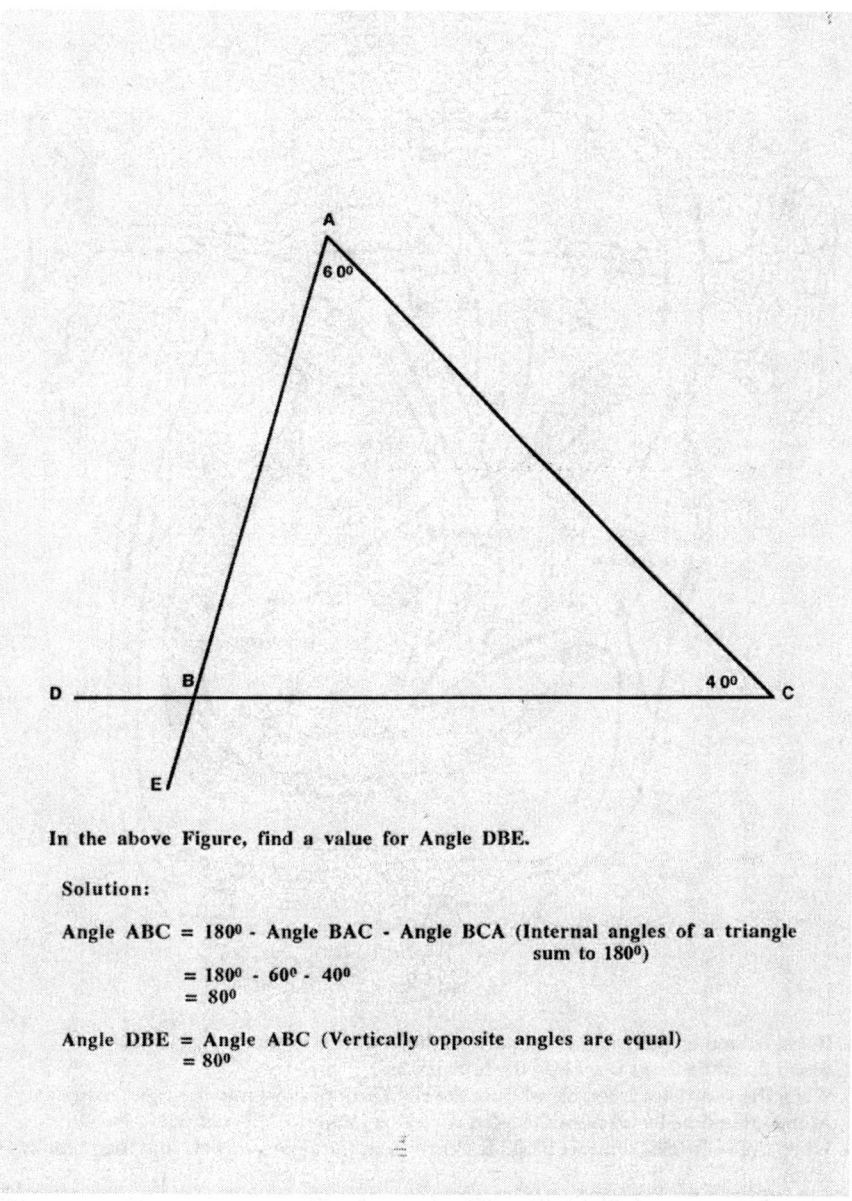

In the above Figure, find a value for Angle DBE.

Solution:

Angle ABC = 180⁰ - Angle BAC - Angle BCA (Internal angles of a triangle
                                                                    sum to 180⁰)

          = 180⁰ - 60⁰ - 40⁰
          = 80⁰

Angle DBE = Angle ABC (Vertically opposite angles are equal)
          = 80⁰

Figure 2.1.   A conventional, split-attention geometry example.

Diagram indicating flow of blood through the heart, lungs and body

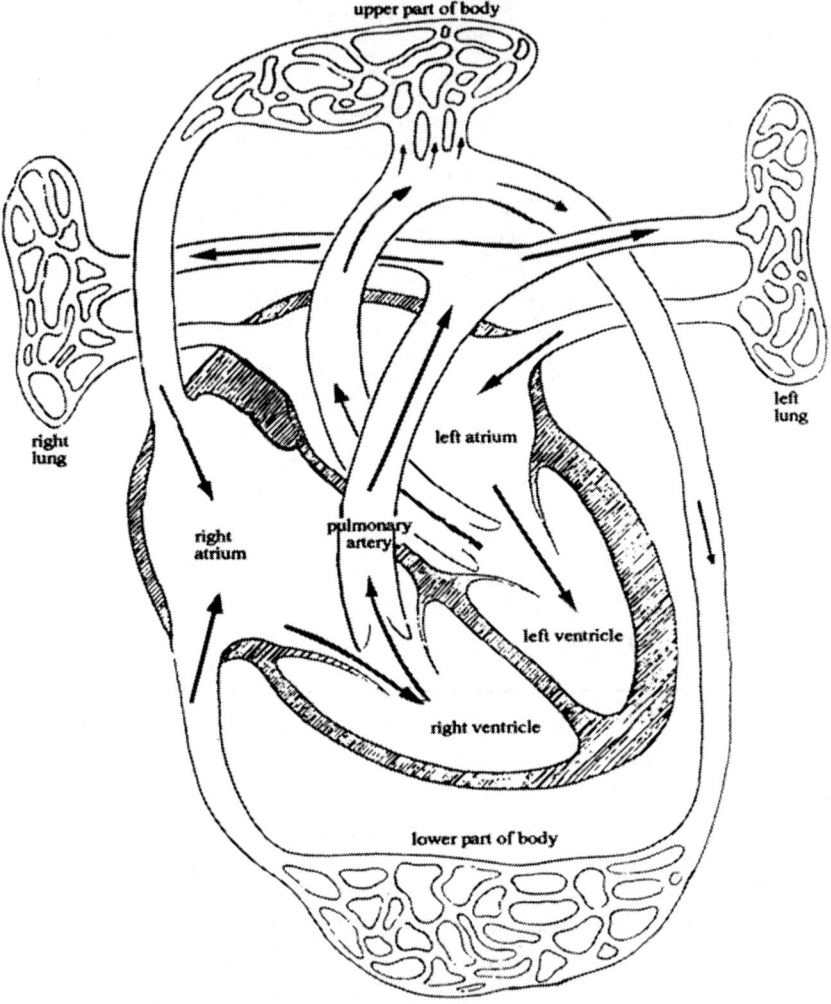

1. Blood from the upper and lower parts of the body flows into the right atrium.
2. Blood from the lungs flows into the left atrium.
3. When the ventricles relax, blood from the right atrium flows into the right ventricle.
4. At the same time blood from the left atrium flows into the left ventricle.
5. When the ventricles contract blood is forced from the right ventricle into the pulmonary artery
6. Blood is also forced from the left ventricle into the aorta.
7. The blood entering the pulmonary artery supplies the lungs.
8. The blood entering the aorta is pumped back to the body.

Figure 2.2.   A conventional, redundant biology example.

much of the information of the diagram rather than explaining some aspects of the diagram also has CLT implications and so instructional implications. While learners may attempt to process the diagram and text simultaneously in working memory, they do not have to. What needs to be learned is intelligible by just considering the diagram alone without any reference to the text. While considering the diagram and text simultaneously is essential when attempting to understand and learn the information contained in Figure 2.1,. considering the diagram and text of Figure 2.2 simultaneously is unnecessary and indeed, may merely have the effect of increasing extraneous cognitive load. From an instructional design perspective, it may be preferable to organize instruction in a manner that discourages learners from considering the diagram and text of Figure 2.2 simultaneously rather than making it easier to consider both simultaneously as suggested for the information of Figure 2.1. Comparing Figures 2.1 and 2.2, the logical relations between the diagram and the text are more important than the similar physical layout. The sections below concerned with the redundancy, transient, element interactivity and expertise reversal effects discuss the relevant instructional implications associated with the differing logical relations of the information of Figures 2.1 and 2.2.

The Split-Attention Effect

Split-attention occurs when multiple sources of information are physically or temporally separate from each other, making it impossible to attend to both simultaneously. This creates a problem because a learner must attend to both sources of information simultaneously in order to establish logical relations between them, which is necessary for understanding the material. However, when physically or temporally disparate, each source is unintelligible in isolation, at least for learners with low prior knowledge. The diagram and text of Figure 2.1 provide an example of the required logical relations. They are physically separate, cannot be understood in isolation and so must be mentally integrated in order for the information to be understood.

The working memory load imposed by the need to mentally integrate disparate sources of information may interfere with learning. If the need to mentally integrate disparate sources of information is obviated by, for example, physically integrating the sources of information, extraneous cognitive load should be reduced and learning enhanced. Figure 2.3 provides an example of the information of Figure 2.1 in physically integrated format. A comparison of the formats of Figures 2.1

and 2.3 with an advantage to the integrated format of Figure 2.3 provides an example of the split-attention effect.

The split-attention was initially reported by Tarmizi and Sweller (1988), who used geometry worked examples in their attempt to replicate the effectiveness of worked examples in learning algebra (Cooper & Sweller, 1987; Sweller & Cooper, 1985) and in other mathematics-related domains (Zhu & Simon, 1987). Contrary to their expectation, using worked examples did not produce better learning outcomes than using conventional problem-solving strategies in their initial geometry experiment. Apparently, the requirement to mentally integrate the two sources of information (diagram and textual solutions) due to the format of the worked examples imposed an increase in cognitive load that prevented cognitive resources being used for learning. When diagrams and statements required to understand the diagrams are physically separate, as normally occurs in conventionally structured geometry worked examples (Figure 2.1), working memory resources must be expended to mentally integrate the two sources of information, reducing the effectiveness of worked examples. In subsequent experiments, when the format of presenting geometry worked examples was altered to an integrated version in which statements were physically integrated with the diagram (Figure 2.3), learning was enhanced. The integrated format alleviated the extraneous cognitive load imposed by the requirement to split-attention between diagrams and text, freeing working memory resources to attend to processes that facilitated learning.

Tarmizi and Sweller's (1988) findings have led to a number of studies that have extended the split-attention effect to the learning of coordinate geometry (Sweller, Chandler, Tierney, & Cooper, 1990), physics (Ward & Sweller, 1990), material designed for training of electrical apprentices (Chandler & Sweller, 1991), and learning in a computer environment (Sweller & Chandler, 1994; Chandler & Sweller, 1996). Similarly, Mayer and his research associates have demonstrated that split-attention could also occur with temporal separation, thus leading to an unnecessary extraneous cognitive load (Mayer & Anderson, 1991, 1992; Mayer & Sims, 1994; Moreno & Mayer, 1999). In the area of language learning, Yeung, Jin, and Sweller (1998) found that the integrated format, which combined explanatory notes with reading passages, reduced the cognitive load related to vocabulary search and facilitated the process of reading comprehension for young native speakers as well as inexperienced learners of English as a second language (ESL). More recently, Hung, Sweller, and Jin (2009) found that reducing split-attention facilitated learning by undergraduate geography students studying ESL.

The split-attention effect has implications for displaying information in a multimedia context where there will inevitably be at least two sources

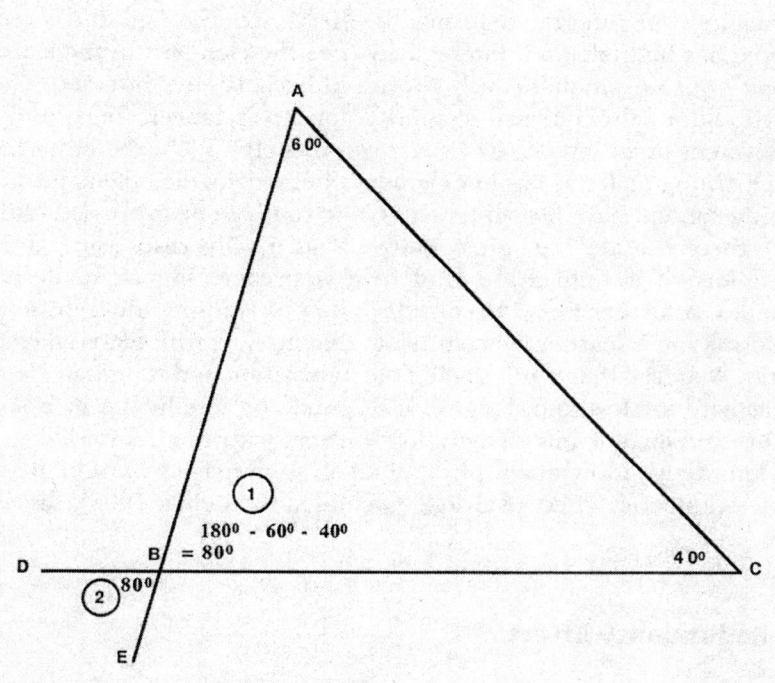

Figure 2.3.   A physically integrated geometry example.

of information. Research suggests that multiple sources of information need to be integrated into an optimal format to minimize extraneous cognitive load. However, those sources of information must be complementary to each other rather than merely repetitions of the same information (see next section on the redundancy effect). In addition, as pointed out by Sweller and Chandler (1994), compared to a nonintegrated display of information, an integrated format is effective only when the learning material has high element interactivity (i.e., the elements in the learning content must be simultaneously processed because they interact). Under this condition, the intrinsic cognitive load is relatively high and the employment of an integrated format can be helpful. On the other hand, if the learning material has low element interactivity (i.e., elements in the learning content have little interaction and thus can be processed individually), there is a low intrinsic cognitive load. In this case, using an integrated format is unlikely to lead to a noticeable impact on learning outcomes. A further factor to consider when integrating different sources of information is learner characteristics that interact with material characteristics. Material that is not intelligible in isolation and is high in element interactivity for low knowledge learners may be intelligible in isolation and low in element interactivity for learners with more knowledge. For high knowledge individuals, physical integration may be harmful because of the redundancy effect (Kalyuga, Chandler, & Sweller, 1998), discussed next.

The Redundancy Effect

The redundancy effect occurs when additional information presented to learners results in negative rather than positive effects on learning. Figure 2.2 includes a diagram with redundant text. It should be noted that redundancy is sometimes defined as referring to identical information presented in different forms; however, within a CLT framework it is usually more broadly defined as any additional, unnecessary information. While the physical relation between the diagram and text of Figure 2.2 is identical to the physical relation of the diagram and text of Figure 2.1, the logical relations are very different. In the case of Figure 2.1, both sources of information are critical to understanding for a learner with low prior knowledge. In the case of Figure 2.2, the diagram is intelligible in isolation and the text is merely a textual repetition of the information contained in the diagram. The diagram can be understood independently of the text. The text is redundant, requires working memory resources to process it and learning may be enhanced by eliminating it (Chandler & Sweller, 1991).

In the current era of multimedia display environments, it is not unusual for an instructor or a web-based course designer to consider presenting the same information in different forms or displaying additional detailed information to enhance learning, assuming that such additional information will not produce negative learning outcomes. However, CLT suggests the possibility of negative effects due to redundancy. Because working memory is extremely limited in terms of its capacity and duration, when learners are exposed to material containing the same information in multiple forms or present unnecessary elaborations, their cognitive functioning can be impaired and their learning process may be negatively affected. For instance, to teach pupils to learn a noun, say, the name of an animal (elephant), a teacher can write the word on a flashcard or on a whiteboard and read it (presenting information in both visual and audio forms). One may further assume that it is a good idea to show pupils a flashcard containing both the word and picture and at the same time provide the pronunciation. Such instruction sounds more "interesting" and more "informative", and can be easily accomplished using modern information technology. However, controlled experiments designed to test the effect of adding pictures to words when learning to read have indicated that reading outcomes are superior using written words plus sounds rather than presenting written words, pictures, and sounds simultaneously (Miller, 1937; Solman, Singh, & Kehoe, 1992; Torcasio & Sweller, 2010). This phenomenon can be explained by assuming that adding pictures to the presentation of written words and sounds is redundant, and that redundancy can have a negative impact on the effective use of limited working memory to process and transfer information to long-term memory. Redundancy imposes an extraneous cognitive load.

The redundancy effect has been demonstrated in a number of studies (Mayer, Heiser, & Lonn, 2001; Sweller, 2005). In one study, a series of experiments was carried out to test the redundancy effect in a computer course (Sweller & Chandler, 1994; Chandler & Sweller, 1996) in which the learners were divided into two groups. Participants in one group worked on a computer with the assistance of a computer manual that combined text with diagrams. Participants in the other group simply learned using the computer manual either on a screen or in hard-copy but did not actually work on a computer. Because the act of working on the computer was largely irrelevant to the real task of understanding the program, participants in the first group who had to work on a computer could not use working memory efficiently to transfer the knowledge of programming into their long-term memory. In other words, the computer work was redundant and occupied working memory resources that otherwise could be used by learners to assimilate the appropriate information. In another series of experiments on the use of computer manuals, researchers reported that computer manuals with minimized explanatory text were more effective and user-friendly than conventional manuals (Carroll, 1990; Carroll, Smith-Kerker, Ford, & Mazur-Rimetz, 1987). The minimized manuals summarized the more wordy and detailed conventional manuals. Similarly, researchers have found that a summarized text was superior to a full text (in which some parts may be redundant) in terms of learning outcomes (Mayer, Bove, Bryman, Mars, & Tapangco, 1996; Reder & Anderson, 1980, 1982).

In research on learning English as a foreign language (EFL), Hirai (1999) noticed that, for less proficient Japanese EFL learners, their listening rate was far behind their reading rate. Diao and Sweller (2007) and Diao, Chandler and Sweller (2007) thus proposed that, if novice EFL learner were exposed to both auditory and visual information for reading comprehension, such an audio-visual presentation might result in a redundancy effect. They tested this hypothesis and found that the Chinese EFL learners who were exposed to simultaneous presentations of spoken and written text had a higher mental load and produced lower test scores in both word decoding and reading comprehension in comparison with those who were given written information only. In a similar vein, Kalyuga, Chandler, and Sweller (2004) found that the simultaneous presentation of written and spoken text during a presentation imposes an extraneous cognitive load. Learning was enhanced by presenting in one modality only.

As is the case with the split-attention effect, the redundancy effect has been demonstrated in a variety of contexts. It should be noted that it is not just diagrams and redundant text that can be used to demonstrate the redundancy effect. While diagrams are frequently more intelligible than the equivalent text, there are instances where any one of diagrams, the presence of equipment, or auditory information have been found to be redundant (see Sweller, 2005 for experimental evidence). CLT can be used to provide guidance on the conditions that determine redundancy and hence what material is likely to be redundant. For instance, in deciding whether text should be added to a diagram, the instructional designer needs to consider several factors. Is the diagram intelligible on its own? If so, the text may be redundant. Does the text provide essential information? If so, it is not likely to be redundant and should be retained.

Another factor to consider is learner expertise. Whether information is high in element interactivity and whether it is intelligible on its own depends largely on the learner. Information that is intelligible for more expert learners may not make sense to novices who require additional explanatory material. In short, whether or not additional material is redundant can be determined by considering the cognitive load implications of that material in the context of learner expertise.

From the perspective of the current chapter, the logical relation between the multiple sources of information is critical. If sources of information can be understood in isolation, the manner in which instruction is designed should be very different to the treatment of sources of information that rely on each other for intelligibility.

The Modality Effect

Controlled studies on the split-attention effect and the redundancy effect demonstrate that the limitations of working memory can be overcome by formatting instructional materials in a manner that minimizes extraneous cognitive load so that cognitive resources can be released to attend to processes useful for learning. The manner in which instruction should be reformatted depends on the logical relations between the sources of information. The negative consequences of split-attention can be alleviated by physical integration of disparate sources of information. The negative consequences of redundancy can be alleviated by eliminating redundant information. The differing instructional implications flow directly from the differing logical relations between sources of information.

The consequences of extraneous cognitive load can also be alleviated by expanding effective working memory capacity as demonstrated by controlled studies on the modality effect (see Low & Sweller, 2005, Mayrath, Nihalani, & Robinson, 2011). The modality effect occurs when information presented in a dual mode (visual and auditory) is more effective than when the same information is presented in a visual or auditory mode alone. Again, whether the modality effect is obtained depends on the logical relations between the sources of information. The modality effect can only be obtained under conditions in which the split-attention effect occurs. The multiple sources of information must be unintelligible in isolation and rely on each other for intelligibility. The effect will not be obtained in which the redundancy effect occurs, such as when a diagram and spoken text are redundant. Redundant spoken text can be expected to have exactly the same negative consequences as redundant written text. In both cases, redundancy will consume scarce working memory resources and impact negatively on learning performance. Where textual information is essential for understanding, then presenting it in spoken rather than written form may be beneficial.

Mousavi, Low, and Sweller (1995) tested for the modality effect in educational settings, in which geometry problems and related instructions were used. As usually occurs in the case of geometry (see Figure 2.1), the diagrams and text relied on each other for intelligibility. There were two information presentation conditions: audio-visual and visual-visual. In the audio-visual presentation, diagrams were given as visual information and the related text was provided as audio input, whereas in the visual-visual presentation, both diagrams and associated text were in a visual format. The data obtained from this series of experiments demonstrated that learners in the audio-visual group performed much better than did those in the visual-visual group.

From a CLT perspective, the modality effect can be explained by assuming that the memory load due to a picture with written text presentation induces a high load in the visual working memory system because both sources of information are initially processed in this system. In contrast, the diagram and narration version induces a lower load in visual working memory because auditory and visual information are each initially and subsequently processed in their respective systems. Therefore, the total load induced by this version is spread between the visual and the auditory components in the working memory system. In other words, the use of audio and visual information may not overload working memory if its capacity is effectively expanded by using a dual-mode presentation compared to a single-mode presentation.

This basic modality effect was subsequently confirmed in a number of studies. For instance, Tindall-Ford, Chandler, and Sweller (1997) reported increased effective working memory and improved learning outcomes under audio-visual conditions in comparison with visual-visual conditions. They obtained the effect using electrical engineering materials in which the information was high in element interactivity but as predicted, failed to obtain the effect using low element interactivity material. As was the case for geometry, the multiple sources of information were unintelligible in isolation. Adopting the scale recommended by Paas and van Merriënboer (1993), Tindall-Ford and colleagues found that the participants' self-reported cognitive load was lower under audio-visual conditions than visual-visual conditions for learning such material. Applying the modality principle, Jeung, Chandler, and Sweller (1997) reported improved learning outcomes by using visual indicators to highlight the most complex parts of information in the spoken text. In an industrial training course, beginners' learning experience was enhanced using dual-mode presentations (Kalyuga, Chandler, & Sweller, 2000).

Using web-based or computer-aided instructional design, Mayer and his colleagues (Mayer & Moreno, 1998; Moreno & Mayer, 1999; Moreno, Mayer, Spires, & Lester, 2001) tested the modality effect in a number of courses. In general, they found that students learned more when scientific explanations were given as pictures plus narration (or spoken text) than under the condition of pictures together with on-screen text. According to Mayer's (2005) interpretation, when learners are dealing with pictures and related on-screen text, their visual channel may become overloaded while their auditory channel is unused. When words are narrated or the spoken text is provided, the learners can use their auditory channel to process such information, and the visual channel will deal with the pictures only. The redistribution of information flow can lead to enhanced multimedia learning. When the information contained in a picture is too complex, simultaneous presentation of corresponding auditory information may still be beyond the capacity of working memory. In this case, a sequencing method can be used to reduce cognitive load (Schnotz, 2005). For instance, the picture can be presented before its related text (Kulhavy, Stock, & Caterino, 1994).

In line with CLT, Brünken, Steinbacher, Plass, and Leutner (2002) replicated the modality effect in two different multimedia learning environments. In this study, they used a dual-task approach to measure cognitive load in which performance on a visual secondary reaction time task was taken as a direct measure of the cognitive load induced by multimedia instruction. Brünken and associates found that the differences in the learning outcome demonstrated by the modality effect were related to different levels of cognitive load induced by the different presentation formats of the learning material. Specifically, they found that an emphasis on visual presentation of material resulted in a decrement on a visual secondary task, indicating an overload of the visual processor. In a subsequent study, Brünken, Plass, and Leutner (2004) again reproduced the modality effect while measuring cognitive load using a dual-task methodology. In this study, the secondary task was auditory instead of visual and there was a decrement in performance on the auditory secondary task when the primary task placed an emphasis on the auditory processor. Again, in all of these demonstrations of the modality effect, the multiple sources of information relied heavily on each other for intelligibility.

Although most studies on the modality effect demonstrated the effect, there have been exceptions. Tabbers, Marten, and van Merriënboer (2004) found a reverse modality effect. A reverse modality effect occurs when visual-only information is superior to audio-visual information. Tabbers et al. found that visual-only instructions were superior to audio-visual instructions under self-paced conditions. They suggested time was available for the transfer of critical information from working memory to long-term memory so eliminating effects due to a working memory overload. Nevertheless, Wouters, Paas and van Merriënboer (2009) did not obtain a modality effect under self-paced conditions in which high school students viewed computer-presented animated models with either written or spoken text. More recently, Schmidt-Weigand, Kohnert, and Glowalla (2010) obtained some limited evidence for a modality effect. They examined university students' visual attention during an animation and did not obtain an overall modality effect under self-paced or system-paced conditions, although there was an advantage on a visual memory test (where participants had to provide answers as illustrations drawn on paper) for the spoken text condition in comparison with the written text condition. Failures to obtain the modality effect can be attributed to the transient information effect, discussed next.

The Transient Information Effect

Leahy and Sweller (2011) hypothesized an important condition under which the modality effect will not be obtained or will be reversed. Under most conditions, while written information is permanent, spoken information is relatively transient. A written statement can be returned to indefinitely and so is permanent. A spoken sentence may be lost once it has been spoken and so is transient. Because of its transient nature, there may be no advantage to presenting lengthy, complex, unfamiliar information in a dual-modality form. Trying to remember previous information that has now disappeared, while processing current information, may overload working memory. In contrast, if the information is written rather than spoken, it does not disappear and we can return to earlier information thus reducing the working memory load.

This hypothesis was tested over two experiments with primary school students who were presented with either audio/visual or visual only instructions. In the first experiment, participants who received visually-presented text and a diagram had better performance than participants who received audio text and a diagram, a finding that is inconsistent with previous data on the modality effect. In the second experiment, when both the auditory and visual test instructions were reduced in length, the group with audio/visual instructions performed better than the group with visual only instructions, demonstrating a conventional modality effect. Taken together with previous findings on modality effects, Leahy and Sweller's (2011) initial work on the transient information effect have the following instructional implication: When verbal information can be presented in relatively small, simple chunks, it should be provided in auditory form along with other visual information; however, if the verbal information is long and complex, it should be presented in visual form so that if need be, it can be reaccessed.

CONCLUSIONS

This chapter has been concerned with some of the conditions under which various CLT effects can be obtained. We have emphasized the importance of logical relations between multiple sources of information. The distinction between the conditions under which the modality and split-attention conditions will be obtained and the conditions under which the redundancy effect will be obtained need to be carefully noted. The three effects depend heavily on the logical relation between the various sources of information.

The logical relations that we have considered can be summarized in the following way. The split-attention and modality effects only can be obtained when the various sources of information are unintelligible in isolation and must be integrated before they can be understood. Thus, a diagram and text such as a geometry diagram and an explanation can be used to demonstrate the split-attention or modality effects because a statement such as Angle ABC is unintelligible without reference to a diagram. The statement and diagram should be physically integrated or presented in dual-modality form in order to reduce extraneous cognitive load and facilitate learning. With respect to the modality effect, if the verbal material is lengthy and complex, it should not be presented in auditory form. A written only presentation is preferable so that learners can easily refer back to relevant information. In contrast to the conditions relevant to the split-attention and modality effects, if diagrams or text are intelligible in their own right and simply redescribe each other, physical integration or the use of dual-modality presentations will not be of benefit and indeed, may increase extraneous cognitive load and reduce learning. Elimination of redundancy will reduce extraneous cognitive load and facilitate learning and so is called for under such conditions.

The cognitive load effects discussed in this chapter were generated by hypotheses that flow from CLT. The theory is based on a human cognitive architecture with a working memory that is limited in capacity yet crucial to learning. Any instructional procedure that imposes a heavy extraneous cognitive load is likely to be ineffective. In order to reduce extraneous cognitive load, information should be presented in integrated rather than split-source format, dual-modality rather than visual-only form, with redundant information eliminated. The major point we have emphasized in this chapter is that whether information should be restructured from a split-attention format into an integrated format, or whether it should be presented in dual-modality rather than single-modality form or eliminated due to redundancy, does not just depend on the physical format of the information. It depends also on the logical relations between the various instructional elements.

REFERENCES

Atkinson, R. C., & Shiffrin, R. M. (1968). Human memory: A proposed system and its control processes. In K. W. Spence & J. T. Spence (Eds.), *The psychology of learning and motivation* (Vol. 2, pp. 89-195). Oxford, England: Academic Press.

Bandura, A. (1986). *Social foundations of thought and action: A social cognitive theory.* Englewoods Cliffs, NJ: Prentice Hall.

Brünken, R., Steinbacher, S., Plass, J. L., & Leutner, D. (2002). Assessment of cognitive load in multimedia learning using dual-task methodology. *Experimental Psychology*, *49*, 109-119.

Brünken, R., Plass, J. L., & Leutner, D. (2004) Assessment of cognitive load in multimedia learning with dual task methodology: Auditory load and modality effects. *Instructional Science, 32*, 115-132.

Carroll, J. M. (1990). *The Nurnbergfunnel: Designing minimalist instruction for practical computer skill.* Cambridge, MA: MIT Press.

Carroll, J. M., Smith-Kerker, P., Ford, J., & Mazur-Rimetz, S. (1987). The minimal manual. *Human-Computer Interaction, 3*, 123-153.

Chandler, P., & Sweller, J. (1991). Cognitive load theory and the format of instruction. *Cognition and Instruction, 8*, 293-332.

Chandler, P., & Sweller, J. (1996). Cognitive load while learning to use a computer program. *Applied Cognitive Psychology, 10*, 151-170.

Cooper, G., & Sweller, J. (1987). The effects of schema acquisition and rule automation on mathematical problem-solving transfer. *Journal of Educational Psychology, 79*, 347-362.

Diao, Y., Chandler, P., & Sweller, J. (2007). The effect of written text on learning to comprehend spoken English as a foreign language. *American Journal of Psychology, 120*, 237-261.

Diao, Y., & Sweller, J. (2007). Redundancy in foreign language reading comprehension instruction: Concurrent written and spoken presentations. *Learning and Instruction, 17*, 78-88.

Ericsson, K. A., & Kintsch, W. (1995). Long-term working memory. *Psychological Review, 102*, 211-245.

Geary, D. (2007). Educating the evolved mind: Conceptual foundations for an evolutionary educational psychology. In J. S. Carlson & J. R. Levin (Eds.), *Psychological perspectives on contemporary educational issues* (pp. 1-99). Greenwich, CT: Information Age Publishing.

Geary, D. (2008). An evolutionarily informed education science. *Educational Psychologist, 43*, 179-195.

Geary, D. (2012). Evolutionary Educational Psychology. In K. Harris, S. Graham & T. Urdan (Eds.), *APA Educational Psychology Handbook* (Vol. 1, pp. 597-621). Washington, DC: American Psychological Association.

Hirai, A (1999). The relationship between listening and reading rates of Japanese EFL learners, *Modern Language Journal, 83*, 367-384.

Hung, H. C. M., Sweller, J., & Jin, P. (2009). *Split attention in reading comprehension for ESL/EFL.* Köln, Germany: Verlag VDM.

Jeung, H., Chandler, P., & Sweller, J. (1997). The role of visual indicators in dual sensory mode instruction, *Educational Psychology, 17*, 329-343.

Kalyuga, S., Chandler, P., & Sweller, J. (1998). Levels of expertise and instructional design. *Human Factors, 40*, 1-17.

Kalyuga, S., Chandler, P., & Sweller, J. (2000). Incorporating learner experience into the design of multimedia instruction. *Journal of Educational Psychology, 92*, 126-136.

Kalyuga, S., Chandler, P., & Sweller, J. (2004). When Redundant On-Screen Text in Multimedia Technical Instruction Can Interfere With Learning. *Human Factors, 46*, 567-581.

Kulhavy, R. W., Stock, W. A., & Caterino, L. C. (1994). Reference maps as a framework for remembering text. In W. Schnotz & R. W. Kulhavy (Eds.), *Comprehension of graphics* (pp. 153-162). Amsterdam: Elsevier Science B. V.

Leahy, W., & Sweller, J. (2011). Cognitive load theory, modality of presentation and the transient information effect. *Applied Cognitive Psychology, 25*, 943-951.

Low, R., & Sweller, J. (2005). The modality principle in multimedia learning. In R. E. Mayer (Ed.), *The Cambridge Handbook of Multimedia Learning* (pp. 147-158). New York, NY: Cambridge University Press.

Mayer, R. E. (2005). Cognitive theory of multimedia learning. In R. E. Mayer (Ed.), *The Cambridge Handbook of Multimedia Learning* (pp. 31-48). New York, NY: Cambridge University Press.

Mayer, R. E. (2009). *Multimedia learning* (2nd ed.). New York, NY: Cambridge University Press.

Mayer, R. E. & Anderson, R. (1991). Animations need narrations: An experimental test of a dual-coding hypothesis. *Journal of Educational Psychology, 83*, 484-490.

Mayer, R. E. & Anderson, R. (1992). The instructive animation: Helping students build connections between words and pictures in multimedia learning. *Journal of Educational Psychology, 84*, 444-452.

Mayer, R. E., Bove, W., Bryman, A., Mars, R., & Tapangco, L. (1996). When less is more: Meaningful learning from visual and verbal summaries of science textbook lessons. *Journal of Educational Psychology, 88*, 64-73.

Mayer, R. E., Heiser, J., & Lonn, S. (2001) Cognitive constraints on multimedia learning: When presenting more material results in less understanding. *Journal of Educational Psychology, 93*, 187-198.

Mayer, R. E. & Moreno, R. (1998). A split-attention effect in multi-media learning: Evidence for dual processing systems in working memory. *Journal of Educational Psychology, 90*, 312-320.

Mayer, R. E. & Sims, V. K. (1994). For whom is a picture worth a thousand words? Extensions of a dual-coding theory of multimedia learning. *Journal of Educational Psychology, 86*, 389-401.

Mayrath, M., Nihalani, P., & Robinson, D. (2011). Varying tutorial modality and interface restriction to maximize transfer in a complex simulation environment. *Journal of Educational Psychology, 103*, 257-268.

Miller, W. (1937). The picture clutch in reading. *Elementary English Review, 14*, 263-264

Moreno, R., & Mayer, R. E. (1999). Cognitive principles of multimedia learning: The role of modality and contiguity. *Journal of Educational psychology, 91*, 358-368.

Moreno, R., Mayer, R. E., Spires, H. A., & Lester, J. C. (2001). The case for social agency in computer-based multimedia learning: Do students learn more deeply when they interact with animated pedagogical agents? *Cognition and Instruction, 19,* 177-214.

Mousavi, S., Low, R., & Sweller, J. (1995). Reducing cognitive load by mixing auditory and visual presentation modes. *Journal of Educational Psychology, 87,* 319-334.

Paas, F., & Van Merriënboer, J. (1993). The efficiency of instructional conditions: An approach to combine mental-effort and performance measures. *Human Factors, 35,* 737-743.

Reder, L. & Anderson, J. R. (1980). A comparison of texts and their summaries: Memorial consequences. *Journal of Verbal Learning and Verbal Behaviour, 19,* 121-134.

Reder, L. & Anderson, J. R. (1982). Effects of spacing and embellishment on memory for main points of a text. *Memory and Cognition, 10,* 97-102.

Schmidt-Weigand, F., Kohnert, A., & Glowalla, U. (2010). A closer look at split visual attention in system- and self-paced instruction in multimedia learning. *Learning and Instruction, 20,* 100-110.

Schnotz, W. (2005). An integrated model of text and picture comprehension. In R. E. Mayer (Ed.), *The Cambridge Handbook of Multimedia Learning* (pp. 49-69). New York, NY: Cambridge University Press.

Solman, R., Singh, N., & Kehoe, E. J. (1992). Pictures block the learning of sight words. *Educational Psychology, 12,* 143-153.

Swanson, H. L. (1999). What develops in working memory? A life span perspective. *Developmental Psychology, 35,* 986-1000.

Sweller, J. (1988). Cognitive load during problem solving: Effects on learning. *Cognitive Science, 12,* 257-285.

Sweller, J. (1994). Cognitive load theory, learning difficulty, and instructional design. *Learning and Instruction, 4,* 295-312.

Sweller, J. (2005). The redundancy principle. In R. E. Mayer (Ed.), *Cambridge handbook of multimedia learning* (pp. 159-167). New York, NY: Cambridge University Press.

Sweller, J. (2010). Element interactivity and intrinsic, extraneous and germane cognitive load. *Educational Psychology Review, 22,* 123-138.

Sweller, J. (2011). Cognitive load theory. In J. Mestre & B. Ross (Eds.), *The psychology of learning and motivation: Cognition in education* (Vol. 55, pp. 37–76). Oxford, England: Academic Press.

Sweller, J. (2012). Human Cognitive Architecture: Why some instructional procedures work and others do not. In K. Harris, S. Graham, & T. Urdan (Eds.), *APA Educational Psychology Handbook* (Vol. 1, pp. 295-325). Washington, DC: American Psychological Association.

Sweller, J., Ayres, P., & Kalyuga, S. (2011). *Cognitive load theory.* New York, NY: Springer.

Sweller, J., & Chandler, P. (1991). Evidence for cognitive load theory. *Cognition & Instruction, 8,* 351-362.

Sweller, J. & Chandler, P. (1994). Why some material is difficult to learn. *Cognition and Instruction, 12,* 185-233.

Sweller, J., Chandler, P., Tierney, P., & Cooper, M. (1990). Cognitive load as a factor in the structuring of technical material. *Journal of Experimental Psychology: General, 119,* 176-192.

Sweller, J., & Cooper, G. (1985). The use of worked examples as a substitute for problem solving in learning algebra. *Cognition and Instruction, 2,* 59-89.

Sweller, J., & Sweller, S. (2006). Natural information processing systems. *Evolutionary Psychology, 4,* 434-458.

Tabbers, H. K., Martens, R. L., & van Merriënboer, J. (2004). Multimedia instructions and cognitive load theory: Effects of modality and cueing. *British Journal of Educational Psychology, 74,* 71-81.

Tarmizi, R., & Sweller, J. (1988). Guidance during mathematical problem solving. *Journal of Educational Psychology, 80,* 424-436.

Tindall-Ford, S., Chandler, P., & Sweller, J. (1997). When two sensory modes are better than one. *Journal of Experimental Psychology: Applied, 3,* 257-287.

Torcasio, S. & Sweller, J. (2010). The use of illustrations when learning to read: A cognitive load theory approach. *Applied Cognitive Psychology, 24(5),* 659-672.

Ward, M., & Sweller, J. (1990). Structuring effective worked examples. *Cognition and Instruction, 7,* 1-39

Wouters, P., Paas, F., & van Merriënboer, J. J. (2009). Observational learning from animated models: Effects of modality and reflection on transfer. *Contemporary Educational Psychology, 34,* 1-8.

Yeung, A. S., Jin, P., & Sweller, J. (1998). Cognitive load and learner expertise: Split-attention and redundancy effects in reading with explanatory notes. *Contemporary Educational Psychology, 23,* 1-21.

Zhu, X., & Simon, H. (1987). Learning mathematics from examples and by doing. *Cognition and Instruction, 4,* 137-166.

CHAPTER 3

FOSTERING LEARNING WITH VISUAL DISPLAYS

Richard E. Mayer

ABSTRACT

The design of visual displays with words should be based on evidence-based principles. Three principles for reducing extraneous processing during learning (i.e., cognitive processing that does not support an instructional goal) are coherence (reduce extraneous material), spatial contiguity (place printed words near corresponding part of visual display), and signaling (highlight essential material). Three principles for managing essential processing during learning (i.e., cognitive processing needed to mentally represent the presented material) are segmenting (break material into parts), pretraining (familiarize learners with key terms), and modality (put words in spoken form). Three principles for fostering generative processing (i.e., deeper cognitive processing aimed at making sense of the material) are personalization (use conversational style), embodiment (have instructors use human-like gesture), and voice (use human speech rather than machine speech). Boundary conditions for each principle are based on a cognitive theory of how people learn.

Learning Through Visual Displays, pp. 47–73
Copyright © 2013 by Information Age Publishing
All rights of reproduction in any form reserved.

INTRODUCTION TO VISUAL DISPLAYS IN EDUCATION

A visual display in education is any visual representation intended for communication with a learner, including static visual representations (such as illustrations, photos, graphs, diagrams, and maps) and dynamic visual representations (such as animations and videos). Visual displays are commonly used in instructional media such as textbooks, slide presentations, face-to-face tutorials, online lessons, and computer games. For example, approximately half the space in textbooks is devoted to visual displays (Mayer, 1993; Mayer, Sims, & Tajika, 1995).

An annotated visual display contains both a visual representation (which can be called graphics, visuals, or pictures[1]) and a verbal representation (such as printed or spoken words). Examples include animation with accompanying spoken text and illustrations with embedded printed text. Not all annotated visual displays in education are equally effective, so instructors need research-based principles for how to design annotated visual displays that promote learning (Mayer, 2009, 2011a). In this chapter, I examine research-based principles for the design of annotated visual displays in education.

For example, consider the explanation of the water cycle shown in Figure 3.1. The purpose of this annotated visual display is to help the learner build a mental model of how the water cycle works, which would be reflected in the ability to apply what was learned to solve problems in new situations. Figure 3.1 may look like a nicely rendered visual display that presents the information in an appealing way, but in taking a cognitive science viewpoint I see serious problems with it.

What is wrong with Figure 3.1 as an instructional device? Let me count the ways. First, it contains a large amount of extraneous material that can distract the learner, such as gratuitous use of many colors that serve no instructional purpose, detailed rendering of features that would be better presented in more schematic form, and inclusion of several different types of fancy arrows when one streamlined style would be less complicated. Processing of this extraneous material creates extraneous cognitive processing in the learner, which may supplant cognitive processing needed to mentally represent the material. In short, Figure 3.1 violates what I have called the *coherence principle*, which calls for minimizing extraneous material (Mayer, 2005a, 2009). Figure 3.2 shows how the water cycle can be represented in a way that is more consistent with the coherence principle.

Second, Figure 3.1 presents a long caption at the bottom of the screen, which forces the learner to scan back and forth between the words and the relevant part of the graphic. The cognitive load involved in scanning back and forth between corresponding words and graphic elements is a form

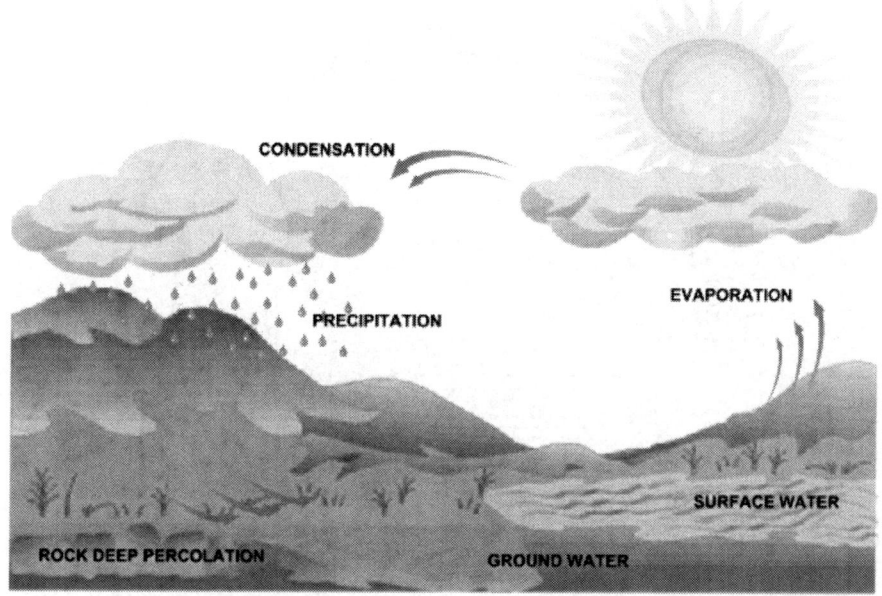

Distillation has been an essential part of nature since the earth began. The heat of the sun evaporates water from the earth's surface into the atmosphere, leaving impurities behind. As the vapor cools, it condenses into clouds and falls back to earth as rain or snow, which eventually flows onto the surface of the earth.

Figure 3.1.   What's wrong with this visual display about the water cycle?

of extraneous processing—cognitive processing that does not serve the instructional goal. In short, the figure violates what I have called the *spatial contiguity principle*, which calls for placing printed text segments next to the corresponding part of the graphic (Mayer, 2005a, 2009). Figure 3.3 shows how the water cycle can be represented in a way that is more consistent with the contiguity principle (and the coherence principle).

Third, Figure 3.1 lacks a useful title or pointers to guide the learner's processing of the graphic. The lack of signaling (or cueing) for where to look at the visual display can create extraneous processing in which the learner wastes cognitive resources by looking all around the figure in a disorganized way. Devices such as headings and pointers that number the steps in the water cycle process can be called signaling (or cueing) because they signal to the learner (or cue the learner) where to look on the page or screen. In short, Figure 3.1 violates what I have called the *signaling principle*, which calls for highlighting the essential material in a lesson

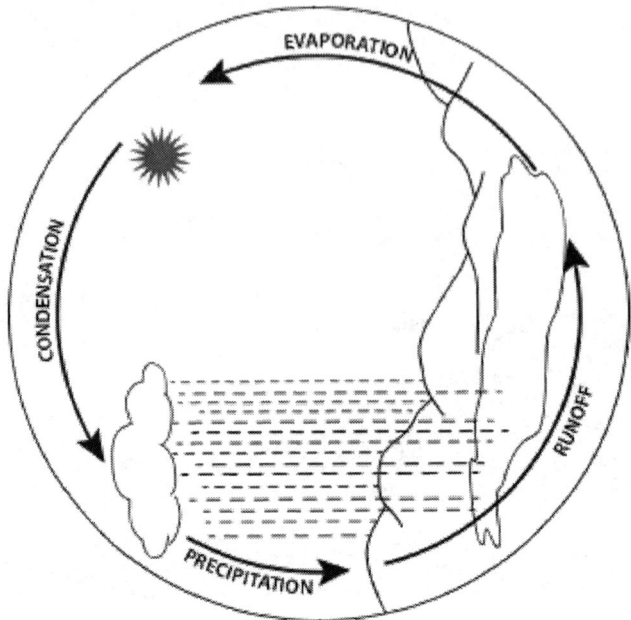

Distillation has been an essential part of nature since the earth began. The heat of the sun evaporates water from the earth's surface into the atmosphere, leaving impurities behind. As the vapor cools, it condenses into clouds and falls back to earth as rain or snow, which eventually flows onto the surface of the earth.

Figure 3.2.   Applying the coherence principle to a visual display about the water cycle

(Mayer, 2005a, 2009). Figure 3.4 shows how to add signals in the form of (a) a title or heading so the learner knows which parts of the graphic to attend to and (b) numbering of the text segments so the learner knows the order in which to look at the parts of the graphic.

Fourth, interpretation of Figure 3.1 requires that the learner know the meaning of key technical terms such as "condensation" or "distillation." Novices are unlikely to know what those words mean, which can force them to allocate so much cognitive processing to figuring out what the words mean that little processing capacity remains for building a mental model of the water cycle. A solution to this problem is to provide pre-training in the names and characteristics of the key components in the water cycle, such as a prior visual display that clearly describes each key component. This approach is shown in Figure 3.5, and is consistent with what I have called the *pretraining principle* (Mayer, 2005b, 2009), which

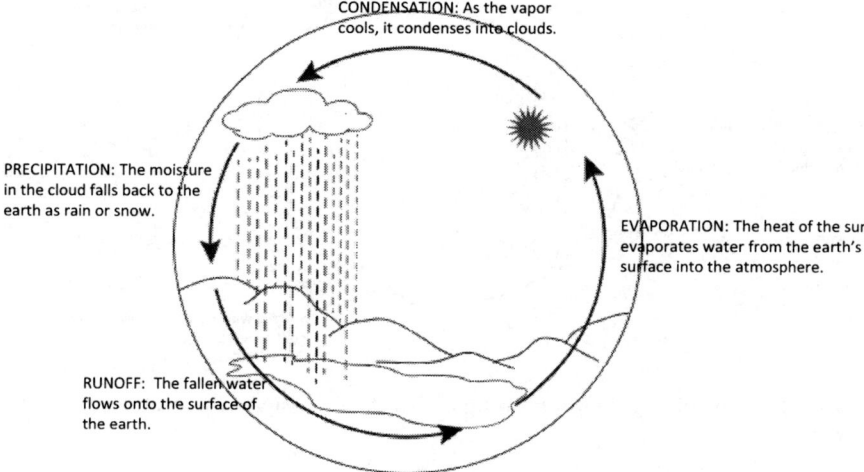

Figure 3.3. Applying the spatial contiguity principle to a visual display about the water cycle

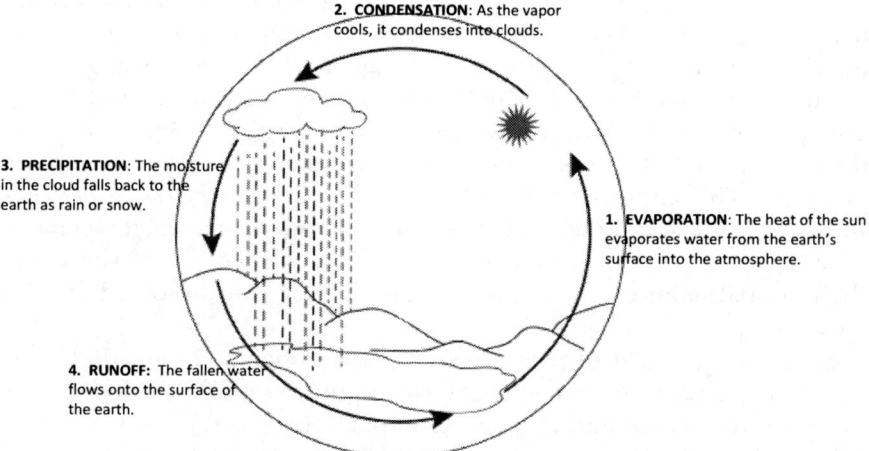

Figure 3.4. Applying the signaling principle to a visual display about the water cycle

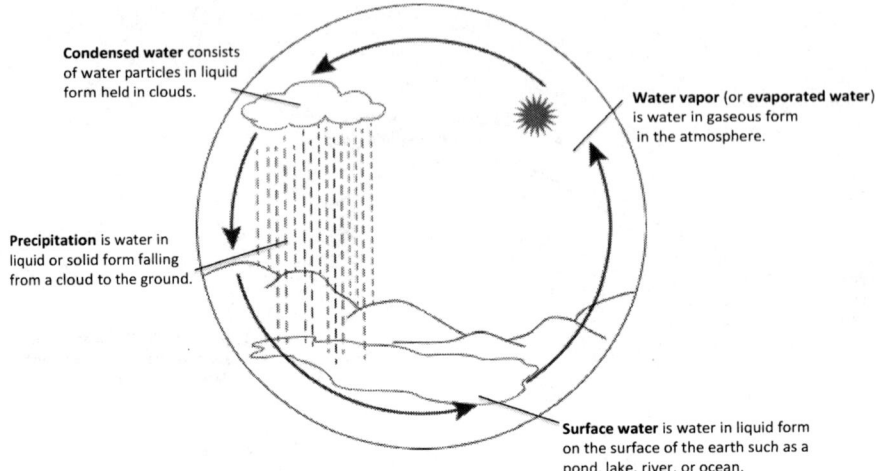

Figure 3.5.   Applying the pretraining principle to a visual display about the water cycle.

calls for providing pretraining in the names and characteristics of key terms in a lesson.

Fifth, if the learners are extreme novices, the amount of essential information on the screen or page may be overwhelming, even when extraneous material has been removed and essential material has been highlighted. To help the learner manage cognitive processing of the essential material, it might be useful to add the steps in the water cycle one at a time, as is shown the series of frames in Figure 3.6. In this way, the learner can fully process one step in the cycle before moving on to the next one. This approach is based on what I call the *segmenting principle*, which calls for breaking a complex lesson into manageable segments (Mayer, 2005b, 2009). Segmenting may be particularly important what the essential material is complex for the learner and presented at a fast pace.

Sixth, if the visual display can be narrated such as in a slideshow or in an online narrated presentation, it might be useful to minimize the words on the screen and instead accompany the visual display with spoken words (as exemplified in Figure 3.7). When a lot of printed words and complicated graphics are presented, the learner's visual channel may become overloaded so some of the essential material is missed. Using spoken words can offload some of the processing demand from the learner's visual channel to the verbal channel, thereby effectively creating more capacity for essential processing (i.e., it frees up capacity in visual working memory to be used for processing the pictorial mate-

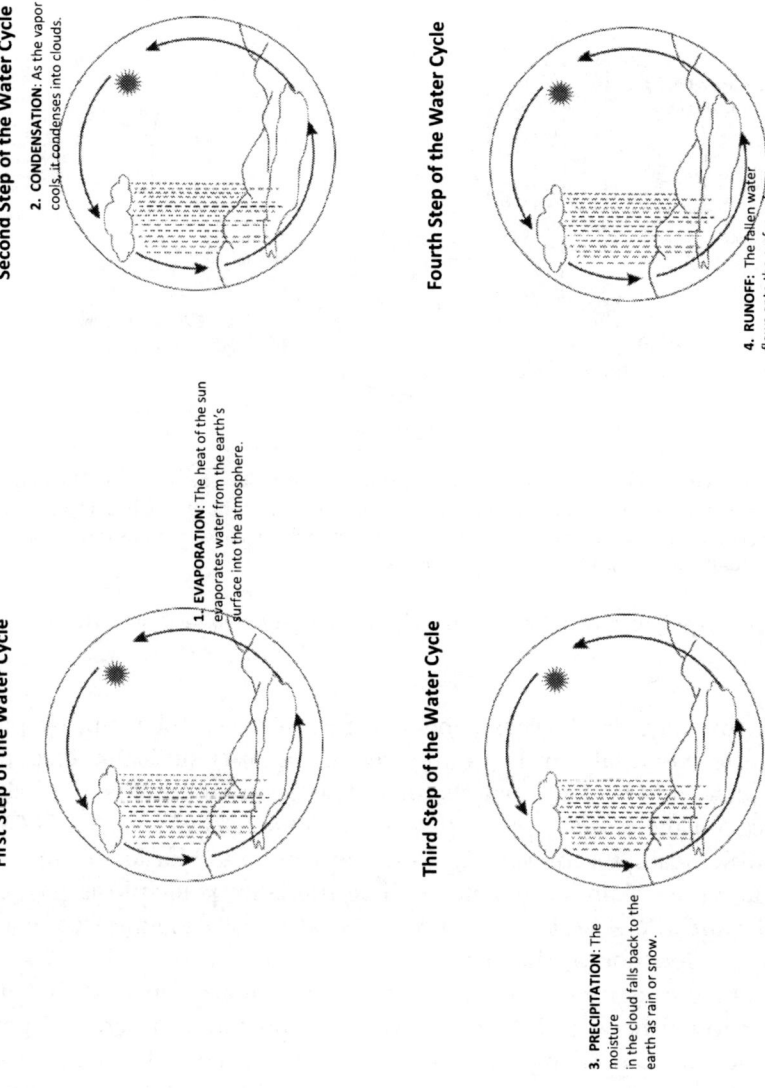

First Step of the Water Cycle

1. EVAPORATION: The heat of the sun evaporates water from the earth's surface into the atmosphere.

Second Step of the Water Cycle

2. CONDENSATION: As the vapor cools, it condenses into clouds.

Third Step of the Water Cycle

3. PRECIPITATION: The moisture in the cloud falls back to the earth as rain or snow.

Fourth Step of the Water Cycle

4. RUNOFF: The fallen water flows onto the surface of the earth.

Figure 3.6. Applying the segmenting principle to a *visual display* about the water cycle.

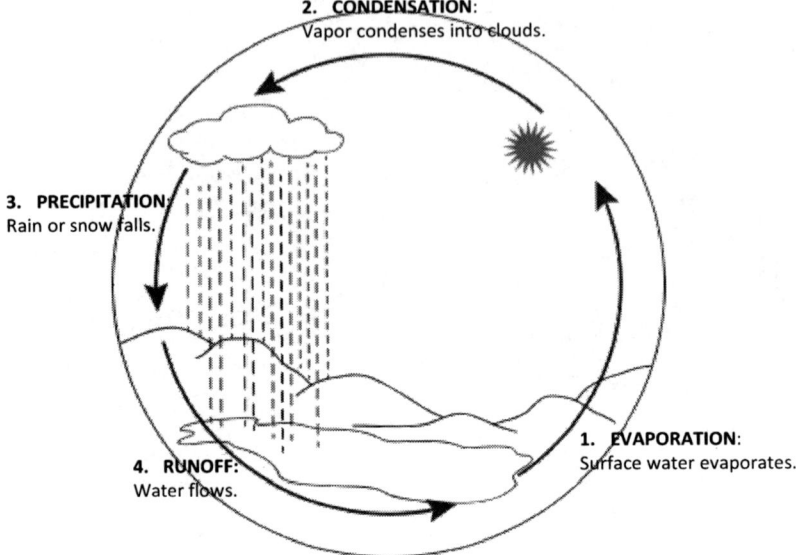

Spoken: "Distillation has been an essential part of nature since the earth began. The heat of the sun evaporates water from the earth's surface into the atmosphere, leaving impurities behind. As the vapor cools, it condenses into clouds and falls back to earth as rain or snow, which eventually flows onto the surface of the earth."

Figure 3.7.   Applying the modality principle to a visual display about the water cycle.

rial). In this way, the learner can manage essential processing by processing the essential words in the verbal channel and the essential graphic elements in the visual channel. This technique is based in what I have called the *modality principle* (Low & Sweller, 2005; Mayer, 2005b, 2009), which calls for presenting words in a multimedia lesson in spoken form rather than printed form. The modality principle is particularly relevant when the lesson is presented at a fast pace and the words are easily understood by the learner.

Seventh, the learner may lack motivation to make sense of the presented material because the lesson seems off-putting. To better engage the learner, we can change the wording from formal style to conversational style as is shown in Figure 3.8. People try harder to make sense of an explanation (i.e., engage in generative processing) when they feel a social partner is communicating with them (Mayer, 2005c). Using social cues such as conversational style is intended to prime a social stance in the learner, which can lead to greater effort to make sense of the lesson.

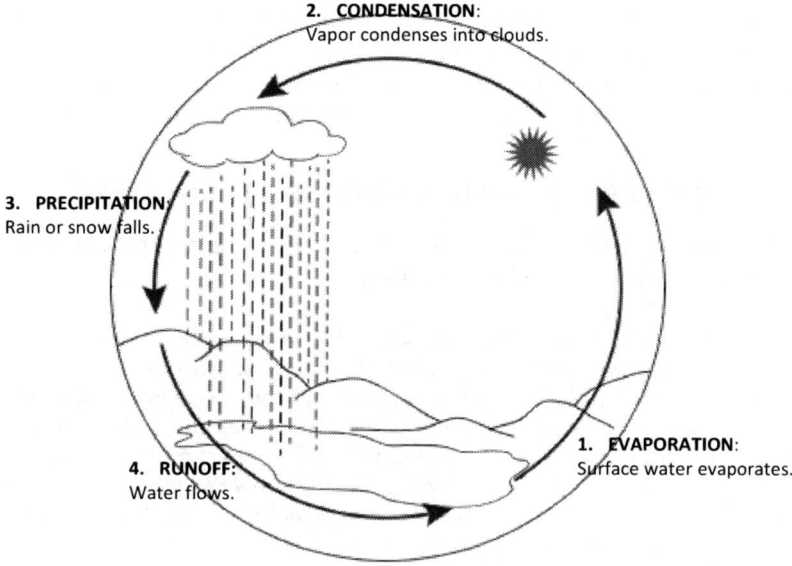

2. **CONDENSATION**: Vapor condenses into clouds.

3. **PRECIPITATION**: Rain or snow falls.

4. **RUNOFF**: Water flows.

1. **EVAPORATION**: Surface water evaporates.

Spoken: "As you hike along a trail you come to your pond. The heat of the sun above you evaporates water from your pond, as you feel the humid air rising. As the vapor from your pond cools in the atmosphere, it condenses into clouds. The moisture in your cloud falls back to earth as rain or snow, which eventually flows back into your pond."

Figure 3.8.   Applying the personalization principle to a visual display about the water cycle.

In short, the *personalization principle* calls for presenting printed or spoken words in conversational style (Mayer, 2005c, 2009).

Finally, consider a situation in which the water cycle slide is explained by someone talking about it, such as an instructor delivering a slideshow presentation or an online lesson presented by an onscreen pedagogical agent. The *embodiment principle* suggests that people learn more deeply when the instructor or onscreen agent uses humanlike gesture, facial expression, eye contact, and body movement (Mayer & DaPra, 2012). The *voice principle* suggests that people learn more deeply when the words are spoken in a human voice rather than a machine-generated voice (Mayer, 2005c, 2009). Both of these approaches are intended as social cues that prime a social stance in the learner, leading to motivation to exert effort to make sense of the material.

How can we use annotated visual displays to help promote deep learning of instructional material? This is the motivating question for this chapter. In the remainder of this chapter, I present the case for annotated visual displays in education, a theoretical framework for understanding how people learn with annotated visual displays, research-based principles for how to design annotated visual displays that help people learn better, and a discussion of future directions for research on annotated visual displays that support student learning.

THE CASE FOR VISUAL DISPLAYS IN EDUCATION

Consider the following explanation of how a bicycle tire pump works (in which I have italicized the key sentences):

> Bicycle tire pumps vary in the number and location of the valves they have and in the way air enters the cylinder. Some simple tire pumps have the inlet valve on the piston and the outlet valve at the closed end of the cylinder. A bicycle tire pump has a piston that moves up and down. Air enters the pump near the point where the connecting rod passes through the cylinder. *As the rod is pulled out, air passes through the piston and fills the area between the piston and the outlet valve. As the rod is pushed in, the inlet valve closes and the piston forces air through the outlet valve.*

If you are like most people in a study by Mayer and Gallini (1990), you are able to remember a few steps in the process when asked to give an explanation, but you are not able to answer transfer questions such as explaining why the pump might not work or how to make it more efficient.

However, now consider the two frames in Figure 3.9, containing the same words as the last two sentences of the pump text and containing line drawings of the pump before and after the handle is pushed down. Mayer and Gallini (1990) found that seeing the visual display along with the words greatly improves your transfer performance (e.g., by one standard deviation). Overall, across 11 experimental comparisons described in Mayer (2009), students performed better on a transfer test after studying words and corresponding visuals rather than words alone, yielding a median effect size of 1.39, which is considered a large effect. This work is the basis for the *multimedia principle*, which is the idea that people learn more deeply from words and corresponding visuals than from words alone.

The multimedia principle provides the rationale for including appropriate visual displays along with corresponding words in educational communications. When the goal is to promote retention and transfer in learners, there is clear and consistent evidence for including visual displays (Fletcher & Tobias, 2005; Mayer, 2009, 2011a). However, not all visual displays are equally effective in promoting deep learning, so in the following two sections I explore a research-based theory of how people learn with visual displays and research-based principles for how to design visual displays for effective instruction.

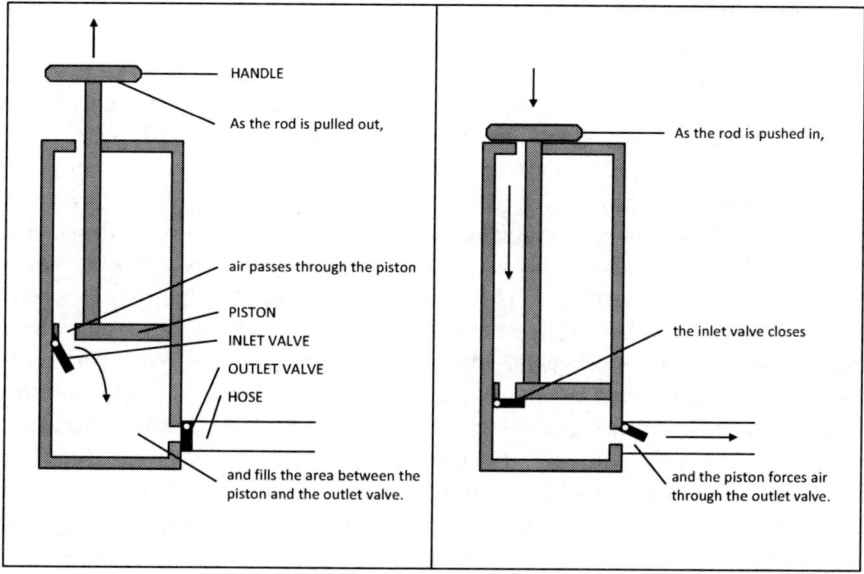

Figure 3.9.   An annotated visual display about how bicycle tire pumps work.

HOW PEOPLE LEARN WITH VISUAL DISPLAYS

The science of learning is concerned with developing a research-based theory of how people learn (Mayer, 2011b; Sweller, Ayres, & Kalyuga, 2011). Figure 3.10 shows the cognitive theory of multimedia learning (Mayer, 2009), which offers a research-based theory of learning that is relevant to how people learn with visual displays.

The cognitive theory of multimedia learning is based on three principles from research in cognitive science: the *dual channels principle*, the *limited capacity principle*, and the *active processing principle*. The dual channels principle is the idea that humans possess separate channels for processing visual and verbal information (Paivio, 1986, 2007). In Figure 3.10, the verbal channel is represented in the top row and the visual channel is represented in the bottom row. The limited capacity principle is the idea that people are able to actively process only a few elements in each channel at any one time (Baddeley, 1999; Sweller, 1999, 2005). In Figure 3.10, the bottleneck in each channel occurs in the box labeled *working memory*. Finally, the active processing principle is idea that meaningful learning occurs when the learner engages in appropriate cognitive processing during learning, including attending to relevant incoming information, mentally organizing it into a coherent cognitive representation, and mentally connecting it with other representations and relevant knowledge from long-term memory (Mayer, 2009; Wittrock, 1989). In Figure 3.10, active cognitive processing is indicated by the arrows labeled *selecting, organizing*, and *integrating*.

Figure 3.10 shows the aspects of the architecture of the human information processing that are most relevant to learning with visual displays: three memory stores (represented as boxes for sensory memory, working memory, and long-term memory), three cognitive processes (represented as arrows for selecting, organizing, and integrating), and three kinds of cognitive representations (within each box). The left most box represents an instructional lesson containing visual displays with words. The second box represents *sensory memory*, which can briefly hold exact sensory copies of visual images impinging in the eyes and auditory images impinging on the ears. If the learner attends to the fleeting visual and auditory images (as indicated by the *selecting words* and *selecting images* arrows), some of the information is transferred to the third box (labeled *working memory*) where the material is held as words and pictures and then organized (as indicated by the *organizing words* and *organizing images* arrows) into coherent representations (which I call *verbal models* and *pictorial models*). The right most box is *long-term memory*, which contains the learner's storehouse of knowledge. During meaningful learning, prior knowledge is activated in long-term memory and transferred to working memory where it is integrated with incoming information (as indicated by the *integrating* arrow) and verbal and pictorial material are integrated as well (also indicated by the *integrating* arrow).

In short, meaningful learning depends on the learner being able to engage in the processes of selecting, organizing, and integrating within a cognitive system that has limited capacity in working memory and separate channels for visual and verbal information.

HOW INSTRUCTIONAL DESIGN PRINCIPLES CAN IMPROVE LEARNING WITH VISUAL DISPLAYS

The science of instruction is concerned with understanding how to help people learn (Mayer, 2011b). Table 3.1 lists three demands on the learner's limited processing resources during learning that are relevant for instructional design: *extraneous processing, essential processing*, and *generative processing*. Extraneous processing occurs when the learner engages in cognitive processing during learning that does not support the instructional goal (i.e., no selecting, organizing, or integrating). Essential processing occurs when the learner mentally represents the presented material in working memory during learning (i.e., selecting relevant

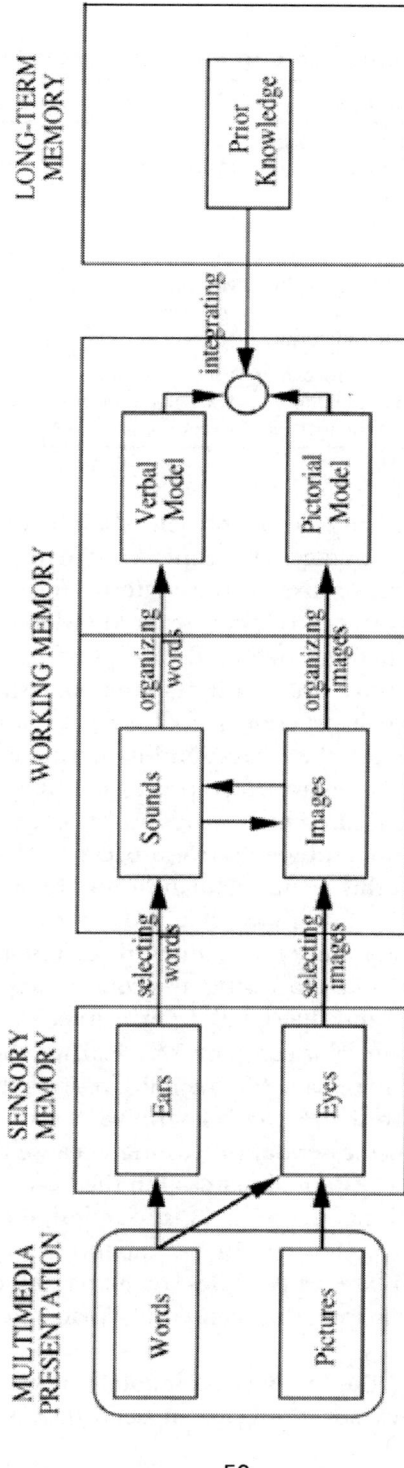

Figure 3.10.   A cognitive theory of learning from words and visuals.

Table 3.1. Three Demands on Cognitive Resources During Learning

Type	Description	Cause	Design Implication
Extraneous processing	Cognitive processing that does not support the instructional goal	Caused by poor instructional design	Reduce extraneous processing
Essential processing	Cognitive processing needed to mentally represent the presented material	Caused by the complexity of the material	Manage essential processing
Generative processing	Cognitive processing aimed at making sense of the material	Caused by the learner's motivation to exert effort	Foster generative processing

information and organizing it as presented). Generative processing occurs when the learner engages in deeper cognitive processing during learning aimed at making sense of the material (i.e., reorganizing the material and integrating it with relevant prior knowledge).

First, when the instructional materials are poorly designed, learners may waste precious cognitive processing resources on aspects of the lesson that do not support the instructional goal, such as scanning back and forth between a caption and the corresponding part of a visual display. In this case the amount of extraneous processing may overwhelm the learner's cognitive system, thereby leaving insufficient capacity to engage in the essential processing and generative processing that are needed for meaningful learning. In this scenario, an appropriate instructional design goal is to redesign the lesson in ways that reduce extraneous processing. In an expanded discussion below, I examine three research-based principles for reducing extraneous processing: the coherence principle, the spatial contiguity principle, and the signaling principle.

Second, when the material is complex for a learner, the need to engage in essential processing necessary for mentally representing the essential material may overwhelm the learner's cognitive system. In this case, it is not appropriate to reduce essential processing because the learner needs to mentally represent the essential material in the lesson. In this scenario, an appropriate instructional design goal is to redesign the lesson in ways that manage essential processing. In an expanded discussion below, I examine three research-based principles for managing essential processing: the pretraining principle, the segmenting principle, and the modality principle.

Third, in some cases the learner has mentally represented the essential material but chooses not to engage in deep processing even though cognitive processing capacity is available. I attribute this situation to a lack of motivation by the learner to engage in generative processing—that is, deeper processing of the essential material. In this scenario, an appropriate instructional goal is to redesign the lesson in ways that foster generative processing. In an expanded discussion below, I examine three research-based principles for fostering generative processing: the personalization principle, the embodiment principle, and the voice principle.

Table 3.2 summarizes the research evidence for three principles of instructional design aimed at the learner's reducing extraneous processing during learning (Mayer, 2011a). For each principle, Table 3.2 lists the number of experimental comparisons in which students learned with a lesson that implemented the principle (experimental group) versus students who learned with an otherwise identical lesson that did not implement the principle (control group). The dependent measure is performance on a transfer test in which the learner must use the information in a new situation to solve a problem or answer a question. For each principle, Table 3.2 also lists the median effect size, which is based on subtracting the transfer test score of the control group from the transfer test score of the experimental group and dividing by the pooled standard deviation (Cohen, 1988).

First, the coherence principle is that people learn more deeply when extraneous material is eliminated from the lesson. As shown in the first row of Table 3.2, the coherence principle as upheld across 14 experiment tests, yielding a median effect size of 0.97, which is in the high range. For example, students performed better on transfer tests when seductive details (i.e., interesting but irrelevant facts and graphics) were deleted from an illustrated text (Harp & Mayer, 1997, Experiment 1; Harp & Mayer, 1998, Experiments 1, 2, 3, and 4) or a narrated animation (Mayer, Heiser, & Lonn, 2001, Experiment 3) on lightning formation; students performed better on transfer tests if extraneous words were eliminated from lessons containing printed text and illustrations on ocean waves

Table 3.2.   Three Principles for Reducing Extraneous Processing

Principle	Description	Number of Tests	Median Effect Size
Coherence	Reduce extraneous material	14	0.97
Spatial contiguity	Place printed words near corresponding part of visual display.	13	1.08
Signaling	Highlight essential material.	6	0.52

(Mayer & Jackson, 2005, Experiments 1a and 1b) or lightning (Mayer, Bove, Bryman, Mars, & Tapangco, 1996, Experiments 1, 2, and 3), or lessons containing narration and animation on ocean waves (Mayer & Jackson, 2005, Experiment 2); and students performed better on transfer tests when background music was deleted from computer-based narration and animation on lightning (Moreno & Mayer, 2000a, Experiment 1) or brakes (Moreno & Mayer, 2000a, Experiment 2).

The theoretical idea behind the coherence principle is that eliminating extraneous processing allows the learner to have more cognitive capacity available for essential processing and generative processing. The coherence principle is consistent with using schematic drawings rather than highly realistic drawings, using color sparingly rather than including many different colors in a visual display, using a consistent style of arrows rather than many different kinds, and using words and video that focus on the essential material rather than words and video that portray interesting but extraneous details. In each case, the essential point can be made with a minimum about of detail.

Second, the spatial contiguity principle is that people learn more deeply when printed words are placed next to corresponding parts of the visual display. As shown in the second row of Table 3.2, across 13 experimental comparisons, the median effect size was 1.08, which is in the large range. Support for the spatial contiguity principle comes from 13 experimental comparisons involving paper-based lessons on lighting (Mayer, Steinhoff, Bower, & Mars, 1995, Experiments 1, 2, and 3), brakes (Mayer, 1989, Experiment 2), the heart (Chandler & Sweller, 1991, Experiment 6), engineering (Chandler & Sweller, 1991, Experiment 1; Chandler & Sweller, 1992, Experiment 1; Tindall-Ford, Chandler, & Sweller, 1997, Experiment 1), and mathematics (Sweller, Chandler, Tierney & Cooper, 1990, Experiment 1); and computer-based lessons on lightning (Moreno & Mayer, 1999, Experiment 1), pumps (Bodemer, Ploetzner, Feuerlein, & Spada, 2004, Experiment 1), statistics (Bodemer, Ploetzner, Feuerlein, & Spada, 2004, Experiment 2), and physics (Kester, Kirschner, & van Merrienboer, 2005, Experiment 1). Recent reviews of the spatial contiguity effect (Ayres & Sweller, 2005; Ginns, 2006) have also found strong supporting evidence, but the spatial contiguity principle may apply most strongly for low-knowledge learners (Kalyuga, 2005), when the material is complicated (Ayres & Sweller, 2005), and when the learner places the words next to graphics through interactivity (Bodemer, Ploetzner, Feuerlein, & Spada, 2004).

Third, the signaling principle is that people learn more deeply when essential material in a lesson is highlighted. As shown in the third row of Table 3.2, the signaling principle was supported across six experimental tests, yielding a median effect size of 0.52, which is a medium-sized effect.

Transfer test performance was higher for signaled versus nonsignaled lessons across six experimental comparisons involving a computer-based multimedia lesson on how airplanes achieve lift (Mautone & Mayer, 2001, Experiments 3a and 3b) and paper-based lessons on lightning (Harp & Mayer, 1998, Experiment 3a) and biology (Stull & Mayer, 2007, Experiments 1, 2, and 3), yielding a median effect size of $d = 0.52$. There is preliminary evidence that signaling may be more effective when the display is complex (Jueng, Chandler, & Sweller, 1997) and when it used sparingly (Stull & Mayer, 2007).

Table 3.3 summarizes the research evidence for three principles of instructional design aimed at managing the learner's essential processing during learning (Mayer, 2011a), including a description of each principle, along with the number of experimental tests and median effect size for each. The top row of Table 3.3 describes the segmenting principle—the idea that people learn more deeply when a complex visual display is broken down into manageable segments that the learner can digest. In nine experimental comparisons, students who received segmented lessons performed better on transfer tests than did students who received continuous lessons, yielding a median effect size of $d = 0.82$, which is a large effect. For example, the segmenting principle was found in computer-based multimedia lessons on electric motors (Mayer, Dow, & Mayer, 2003, Experiments 2a and 2b), lightning (Mayer & Chandler, 2001, Experiment 2), geography (Mautone & Mayer, 2007, Experiment 2), chemistry (Lee, Plass, & Homer, 2006, Experiment 1), and probability problem solving (Gerjets, Scheiter, & Catrambone, 2006, Experiments 1a and 1b); and a paper-based mathematics lesson (Ayres, 2006, Experiments 1a and 2a). The theoretical justification is that the learner is better able to completely process the visual display and accompanying words when the material is presented in a series of bite-size chunks.

Table 3.3. Three Principles for Managing Essential Processing

Principle	Description	Number of Tests	Median Effect Size
Segmenting	Break material into manageable segments.	9	0.82
Pretraining	Provide pretraining in names and characteristics of key terms.	10	0.88
Modality	Use spoken words rather than printed words.	32	0.88

The second row of Table 3.3 describes the pretraining principle, in which people learn more deeply from annotated visual displays when they receive pretraining in the names and characteristics of the key concepts in the lesson. In 10 experimental comparisons, students who received pretraining performed better on transfer tests after a multimedia lesson than did students who did not, yielding a median effect size of $d = 0.88$, which is a large effect. The pretraining principle has been supported in studies involving computer-based presentations on brakes (Mayer, Mathias, & Wetzell, 2002, Experiments 1 and 2), pumps (Mayer, Mathias, & Wetzell, 2002, Experiment 3), statistics (Kester, Kirschner, & van Merrienboer, 2004, Experiment 1), and electronics (Kester, Kirschner, & van Merrienboer, 2006, Experiment 1); computer-based simulation games in geology (Mayer, Mautone, & Prothero, 2002, Experiments 2 and 3); and paper-based multimedia lessons on mathematics (Clarke, Ayres, & Sweller, 2005, Experiment 1a) and electrical engineering (Pollock, Chandler, & Sweller, 2002, Experiments 1 and 2). The theoretical rationale is that learners can devote more cognitive resources to building connections among the key concepts in the lesson if they already know what the key concepts mean.

The third line in Table 3.3 summarizes the modality principle, in which people learn better from a visual display with words when the words accompanying the visual display are in spoken form rather than printed form. In 36 experimental comparisons—the most of any principle—people tended to learn better from multimedia lessons that contained spoken words rather than printed words, yielding a median effect size of $d = 0.88$, which is a large effect. The modality effect has been tested by comparing computer-based multimedia lessons with recorded voice or onscreen text (Atkinson, 2002, Experiments 1a, 1b, and 2; Craig, Gholson, & Driscoll, 2002, Experiment 2; Harskamp, Mayer, Suhre, & Jansma, 2007, Experiments 1 and 2a; Jeung, Chandler, & Sweller, 1997, Experiments 1, 2, and 3; Kalyuga, Chandler, & Sweller, 1999, Experiment 1; Kalyuga, Chandler, & Sweller, 2000, Experiment 1; Mayer, Dow, & Mayer, 2003, Experiment 1; Mayer & Moreno, 1998, Experiments 1 and 2; Moreno & Mayer, 1999, Experiments 1 and 2; Tabbers, Martens, & van Merrienboer, 2004, Experiment 1), paper-based multimedia lessons with tape-recorded voice or printed text (Leahy, Chandler, & Sweller, 2003, Experiment 1; Mousavi, Low, & Sweller, 1995, Experiments 1, 2, 3, 4, and 5; Tindall-Ford, Chandler, & Sweller, 1997, Experiments 1, 2, and 3), and computer-based multimedia simulation games with spoken or onscreen text (Moreno & Mayer, 2002, Experiments 1a, 1b, 1c, 2a, and 2b; Moreno, Mayer, Spires, & Lester, 2001, Experiments 4a, 4b, 5a, and 5b; O'Neil, Mayer, Herl, Thurman, & Olin, 2000, Experiment 1). Similarly, strong support for the modality effect has been reported in recent reviews (Ginns, 2005; Low & Sweller, 2005; Mayer, 2005b). However, there is preliminary evidence that the modality principle is strongest when the material is complex for the learner (Tindall-Ford, Chandler, & Sweller, 1997) and when the pace is fast and not under learner control (Tabbers, Martens, & van Merrienboer, 2004). The theoretical rationale is that when people pay attention to printed words they are not paying attention to the visualization because the two visual presentations compete for the same limited resources, so using spoken text allows the learner to free up capacity by using the auditory channel to complement the visual channel.

Table 3.4 summarizes the research evidence for three principles of instructional design aimed at fostering generative processing during learning (Mayer, 2011a), including a description, number of experimental tests, and median effect size for each. The top row of Table 3.4 summarizes the evidence for the personalization principle—the idea that people try harder to understand a lesson when the words are in conversational style rather than formal style. In 11 experimental comparisons, students performed better on a transfer test when the words in a multimedia lesson were in conversational style (e.g., using "I" and "you") rather than in formal style (e.g., using third person), yielding a median effect size of $d = 1.11$, which is a large effect. The personalization effect was found in learning about lightning in a computer-based multimedia presentation (Moreno & Mayer, 2000b, Experiments 1 and 2), the human respiratory system in a computer-based multimedia presentation (Mayer, Fennell, Farmer, & Campbell, 2004, Experiments 1, 2, and 3), botany in a multimedia game (Moreno & Mayer, 2000b, Experiments 3, 4, and 5; Moreno & Mayer, 2004, Experiments 1a and 1b), and engineering in a multimedia game (Wang, Johnson, Mayer, Rizzo, Shaw, & Collins, 2008, Experiment 1). The rationale is that social cues such as conversational speech prime a social stance in learners, in which they try harder to comprehend what a communication partner is saying. This idea is consistent with Reeves and Naas' (1996) media equation theory in which people have a natural tendency to treat media, such as computers, like real people.

The second row of Table 3.4 shows the research evidence for the embodiment principle, in which students learn more deeply when the instructor or onscreen agent displays human-like gesturing rather than no gesturing. In three experimental comparisons, students performed better on a transfer test after viewing a slideshow on how solar cells work in which an onscreen agent engaged in human-like gesturing, facial expressions, eye gaze, and body movement than when the on-screen agent stood still, yielding a median effect size of $d = 0.92$, which is a large effect (Mayer & DaPra, 2012, Experiments 1, 2, & 3). The theoretical rationale is that when the instructor displays social cues, the students are more likely to accept the instructor as a social partner and therefore try harder to make sense of the communication. In short, people are more

Table 3.3.   Three Principles for Fostering Generative Processing

Principle	Description	Number of Tests	Median Effect Size
Personalization	Put words in conversational style rather than formal style.	11	1.11
Embodiment	Have instructors use human-like gesturing rather than no gesturing.	3	0.92
Voice	Use human speech rather than machine speech.	3	0.78

likely to treat onscreen agents like real people if the agents display human-like movements (Cassell, Sullivan, Prevost, & Churchill, 2000).

The third row of Table 3.4 shows the research evidence for the voice principle, in which people learn better when spoken text involves a human voice rather than a machine generated voice. In three experimental comparisons involving computer-based lessons on lightning (Mayer, Sobko, & Mautone, 2003, Experiment 2) and mathematics word problems (Atkinson, Mayer, & Merrill, 2005, Experiments 1 and 2), students performed better on transfer tests from multimedia lessons with human voice rather than machine voice, yielding a median effect size of $d = 0.78$, which is a large effect. The rationale is that human voice is a social cue that primes a social stance in learners in which they try harder to understand what their communication partner is saying. Nass and Brave (2005) argue that humans are "wired for speech" (p. 1), and provide evidence that appropriate human voice can activate a human-computer relationship.

FUTURE DIRECTIONS FOR RESEARCH ON VISUAL DISPLAYS THAT SUPPORT STUDENT LEARNING

Modern research on visual displays that support student learning can be traced back to research on the beneficial role of illustrations in text beginning in the 1980s (Fleming & Levie, 1993; Mandl & Levin, 1989; Schnotz & Kulhavy, 1994; Willows & Houghton, 1987). The advent of computer-based communication technology has expanded the focus to include the role of visuals in all kinds of multimedia instruction, ranging from slideshows to online lessons to narrated animations and videos to serious games (Mayer, 2005d, 2009, 2011a).

The current state of research on multimedia instruction has produced a collection of research-based principles for how to design instruction containing words and visuals and has produced research-based theories of how people learn from words and visuals (Mayer, 2005d). Four important goals for future research are to grow the research base, to distinguish boundary conditions, to refine an underlying theory, and to develop effective methodologies.

First, an important goal is to continue to build an empirical research base concerning evidence-based principles for the design of instruction involving words and pictures. In an influential analysis of educational research, Shavelson and Towne (2002) emphasized the need for replication as a guiding principle of educational research. In particular, it would be useful to examine whether existing principles can be extended into realistic educational environments such as classroom learning or online learning in real courses. In addition, it would be worthwhile to expand the research base to include principles concerned with motivation and metacognition.

Second, an important goal is to examine the conditions under which design principles tend to be most (or least) effective, in order to establish boundary conditions for each principle. These boundary conditions should include the type of material, type of learners, and type of learning environment. For example, do the principles apply equally well for learning conceptual knowledge and cognitive strategies as for learning cognitive procedures and facts, for learners with low and high levels of prior knowledge, and for various computer-based learning environments such as virtual reality and intelligent tutoring systems? Design principles are not intended to be immutable laws, but rather should be consistent with the cognitive theories of learning which suggest when principles should be most (or least) effective.

Third, another important goal is to contribute to a cognitive theory of learning. The focus should be on better specifying the mechanisms by which learners build cognitive representations from words and visuals, and on including the role of motivational processes (e.g., the learner's beliefs about learning) and metacognitive processes (e.g., the learners monitoring and control of learning processes). This direction is consistent with one of Shavelson and Towne's (2002) guiding principles of educational research, which calls for linking research with relevant theory.

Fourth, methodologies are needed that better investigate the effects of instructional methods on cognitive processing during learning, including physiological methods such as eye-tracking and cognitive neuroscience methods such as event related potentials (ERP) and functional magnetic resonance imaging (fMRI). Although fMRI-based research has not yet had a major impact on educational psychology, research using eye-tracking methodology is beginning to make useful contributions. This direction is consistent with another one of Shavelson and Towne's (2002) guiding principles of educational research, which calls for using appropriate research methods. When the goal is to determine what causes instructional effectiveness, experimental research designs are recognized as the method of choice (Phye, Robinson, & Levin, 2005; Shavelson & Towne, 2002).

Overall, the field has enjoyed encouraging success over the past 20 years in producing evidence-based principles for the design of instruction with words and visuals and in building research-based theories of how people learn with words and visuals. If research progresses along the lines suggested in this section, the next decades promise to bring significant advances both to educational practice and to educational theory.

ACKNOWLEDGMENTS

Preparation of this chapter was supported by Grant N000140810018 from the Office of Naval Research. Part of this chapter is based on the research review reported in Mayer (2011b). Correspondence concerning this chapter should be sent to Richard E. Mayer, Department of Psychological and Brain Sciences, University of California, Santa Barbara, CA 93111. E-mail: mayer@psych.ucsb.edu

NOTE

1.   I use the terms, graphics, visuals, and pictures interchangeably with the term, visual displays.

REFERENCES

Atkinson, R. K. (2002). Optimizing learning from examples using animated pedagogical agents. *Journal of Educational Psychology, 94,* 416-427.

Atkinson, R. K., Mayer, R. E., & Merrill, M. M. (2005). Fostering social agency in multimedia learning: Examining the impact of an animated agent's voice. *Contemporary Educational Psychology, 30,* 117-139.

Ayres, P. (2006). Impact of reducing intrinsic cognitive load on learning in a mathematical domain. *Applied Cognitive Psychology, 20,* 287-298.

Ayres, P., & Sweller, J. (2005). The split attention principle in multimedia learning. In R. E. Mayer (Ed.), *The Cambridge handbook of multimedia learning* (pp. 135-146). New York, NY: Cambridge University Press.

Baddeley, A. D. (1999). *Human memory.* Boston, MA: Allyn & Bacon.

Bodemer, D., Ploetzner, R., Feuerlein, I., & Spada, H. (2004). The active integration of information during learning with dynamic and interactive visualisations. *Learning and Instruction, 14*, 325-341.

Cassell, J., Sullivan, J., Prevost, S., & Churchill, E. (Eds.). (2000). *Embodied conversational agents.* Cambridge, MA: MIT Press.

Chandler, P., & Sweller, J. (1991). Cognitive load theory and the format of instruction. *Cognition and Instruction, 8,* 293-332.

Chandler, P., & Sweller, J. (1992). The split-attention effect as a factor in the design of instruction. *British Journal of Educational Psychology, 62*, 233-246.

Clarke, T., Ayres, P., & Sweller, J. (2005). The impact of sequencing and prior knowledge on learning mathematics through spreadsheet applications. *Educational Technology Research and Development, 53*, 15-24.

Cohen, J. (1988). *Statistical power analysis for the behavioral sciences.* Mahwah, NJ: Erlbaum.

Craig, S. D., Gholson, B., & Driscoll, D. M. (2002). Animated pedagogical agents in multimedia educational environments: Effects of agent properties, picture features, and redundancy. *Journal of Educational Psychology, 94*, 428-434.

Fleming, M., & Levue, W. H. (Eds.). (1993). *Instructional message design* (2nd ed). Englewood Cliffs, NJ: Educational Technology Publications.

Fletcher, J. D., & Tobias, S. (2005). The multimedia principle. In R. E. Mayer (Ed.), *The Cambridge handbook of multimedia learning* (117-134). New York, NY: Cambridge University Press.

Gerjets, P., Scheiter, K., & Catrambone, R. (2006). Can learning from molar and modular worked examples be enhanced by providing instructional explanations and prompting self-explanations? *Learning and Instruction, 16*, 104-121.

Ginns, P. (2005). Meta-analysis of the modality effect. *Learning and Instruction, 15*, 313-332.

Ginns, P. (2006). Integrating information: A meta-analysis of spatial contiguity and temporal contiguity effects. *Learning and Instruction, 16*, 511-525.

Harp, S. F., & Mayer, R. E. (1997). The role of interest in learning from scientific text and illustrations: On the distinction between emotional interest and cognitive interest. *Journal of Educational Psychology, 89*, 92-102.

Harp, S. F., & Mayer, R. E. (1998). How seductive details do their damage: A theory of cognitive interest in science learning. *Journal of Educational Psychology, 90*, 414-434.

Harskamp, E., Mayer, R. E., Suhre, C., & Jansma, J. (2007). Does the modality principle for multimedia learning apply to science classrooms? *Learning and Instruction, 18*, 465-477.

Jeung, H., Chandler, P., & Sweller, J. (1997). The role of visual indicators in dual sensory mode instruction. *Educational Psychology, 17*, 329-433.

Kalyuga, S. (2005). Prior knowledge principle in multimedia learning. In R. E. Mayer (Ed.), *The Cambridge handbook of multimedia learning* (pp. 325-338). New York, NY: Cambridge University Press.

Kalyuga, S., Chandler, P., & Sweller, J. (1999). Managing split-attention and redundancy in multimedia instruction. *Applied Cognitive Psychology, 13*, 351-371.

Kalyuga, S., Chandler, P., & Sweller, J. (2000). Incorporating learner experience into the design of multimedia instruction. *Journal of Educational Psychology, 92*, 126-136.

Kester, L., Kirschner, P. A., & van Merrienboer, J. G. G. (2004). Timing of information presentation in learning statistics. *Instructional Science, 32*, 233-252.

Kester, L., Kirschner, P. A., & van Merrienboer, J. J. G. (2005). The management of cognitive load during complex cognitive skill acquisition by means of computer-simulated problem solving. *British Journal of Educational Psychology, 75*, 71-85.

Kester, L., Kirschner, P. A., & van Merrienboer, J. J. G (2006). Just-in-time information presentation: Improving learning a troubleshooting skill. *Contemporary Educational Psychology, 31*, 167-185.

Leahy, W., Chandler, P., & Sweller, J. (2003). When auditory presentations should and should not be a component of multimedia instruction. *Applied Cognitive Psychology, 17*, 401-418.

Lee, H., Plass, J. L., & Homer, B. D. (2006). Optimizing cognitive load for learning from computer-based science simulations. *Journal of Educational Psychology, 98*, 902-913.

Low, R, & Sweller, J. (2005). The modality principle in multimedia learning. In R. E. Mayer (Ed.), *The Cambridge handbook of multimedia learning* (pp. 147-158). New York, NY: Cambridge University Press.

Low, R., & Sweller, J. (2005). The modality principle in multimedia learning. In R. E. Mayer (Ed.), *The Cambridge handbook of multimedia learning* (pp. 147-158). New York, NY: Cambridge University Press.

Mandl, H., & Levin, J. R. (Eds.). (1989). *Knowledge acquisition from text and pictures.* Amsterdam, The Netherlands: Noth-Holland.

Mautone, P. D., & Mayer, R. E. (2001). Signaling as a cognitive guide in multimedia learning. *Journal of Educational Psychology, 93*, 377-389.

Mautone, P. D., & Mayer, R. E. (2007). Cognitive aids for guiding graph comprehension. *Journal of Educational Psychology, 99*, 640-652.

Mayer, R. E. (1989). Systematic thinking fostered by illustrations in scientific text. *Journal of Educational Psychology, 81*, 240-246.

Mayer, R. E. (1993). Illustrations that instruct. In R. Glaser (Ed.), *Advances in instructional psychology* (Vol. 4, pp. 253-284). Hillsdale, NJ: Erlbaum.

Mayer, R. E. (2005a). Principles for reducing extraneous processing in multimedia learning: Coherence, signaling, redundancy, spatial contiguity, and temporal contiguity principles. In R. E. Mayer (Ed.), *The Cambridge handbook of multimedia learning* (pp. 183-200). New York, NY: Cambridge University Press.

Mayer, R. E. (2005b). Principles for managing essential processing in multimedia learning: Segmenting, pretraining, and modality principles. In R. E. Mayer (Ed.), *The Cambridge handbook of multimedia learning* (pp. 169-182). New York, NY: Cambridge University Press.

Mayer, R. E. (2005c). Principles of multimedia learning based on social cues: Personalization, voice, and image principles. In R. E. Mayer (Ed.), *The Cambridge handbook of multimedia learning* (pp. 201-212). New York, NY: Cambridge University Press.

Mayer, R. E. (Ed.). (2005d). *The Cambridge handbook of multimedia learning.* New York, NY: Cambridge University Press.

Mayer, R. E. (2009). *Multimedia learning* (2nd ed). New York, NY: Cambridge University Press.

Mayer, R. E. (2011a). Instruction based on visualizations. In R. E. Mayer & P. A. Alexander (Eds.), *Handbook of research on learning and instruction* (pp. 427-445). New York, NY: Routledge.

Mayer, R. E. (2011b). *Applying the science of learning.* Upper Saddle River, NJ: Pearson.

Mayer, R. E., Bove, W., Bryman, A., Mars, R., & Tapangco, L. (1996). When less is more: Meaningful learning from visual and verbal summaries of science textbook lessons. *Journal of Educational Psychology, 88,* 64-73.

Mayer, R. E., & Chandler, P. (2001). When learning is just a click away: Does simple user interaction foster deeper understanding of multimedia messages? *Journal of Educational Psychology, 93,* 390-397.

Mayer, R. E., & DaPra, C. S. (2012). An embodiment effect in computer-based learning with animated pedagogical agents. *Journal of Experimental Psychology: Applied, 18,* 239-252.

Mayer, R. E., & Gallini, J. K. (1990). When is an illustration worth ten thousand words? *Journal of Educational Psychology, 82,* 715-726.

Mayer, R. E., & Jackson, J. (2005). The case for conciseness in scientific explanations: Quantitative details can hurt qualitative understanding. *Journal of Experimental Psychology: Applied, 11,* 13-18.

Mayer, R. E., Dow, G., & Mayer, R. E. (2003). Multimedia learning in an interactive self-explaining environment: What works in the design of agent-based microworlds? *Journal of Educational Psychology, 95,* 806-813.

Mayer, R. E., Fennell, S., Farmer, L., & Campbell, J. (2004). A personalization effect in multimedia learning: Students learn better when words are in conversational style rather than formal style. *Journal of Educational Psychology, 96,* 389-395.

Mayer, R. E., Heiser, H., & Lonn, S. (2001). Cognitive constraints on multimedia learning: When presenting more material results in less understanding. *Journal of Educational Psychology, 93,* 187-198.

Mayer, R. E., Mathias, A., & Wetzell, K. (2002). Fostering understanding of multimedia messages through pre-training: Evidence for a two-stage theory of mental model construction. *Journal of Experimental Psychology: Applied, 8,* 147-154.

Mayer, R. E., Mautone, P., & Prothero, W. (2002). Pictorial aids for learning by doing in a multimedia geology simulation game. *Journal of Educational Psychology, 94,* 171-185.

Mayer, R. E., & Moreno, R. E. (1998). A split-attention effect in multimedia learning: Evidence for dual processing systems in working memory. *Journal of Educational Psychology, 90,* 312-320.

Mayer, R. E., Sims, V., & Tajika, H. (1995). A comparison of how textbooks teach mathematical problem solving in Japan and the United States. *American Educational Research Journal, 32,* 443-460.

Mayer, R. E., Sobko, K., & Mautone, P. D. (2003). Social cues in multimedia learning: Role of speaker's voice. *Journal of Educational Psychology, 95*, 419-425.

Mayer, R. E., Steinhoff, K., Bower, G., & Mars, R. (1995). A generative theory of textbook design: Using annotated illustrations to foster meaningful learning of science text. *Educational Technology Research and Development, 43*, 31-43.

Moreno, R., & Mayer, R. E. (1999). Cognitive principles of multimedia learning: The role of modality and contiguity. *Journal of Educational Psychology, 91*, 358-368.

Moreno, R., & Mayer, R. E. (2000a). A coherence effect in multimedia learning: The case for minimizing irrelevant sounds in the design of multimedia messages. *Journal of Educational Psychology, 92*, 117-125.

Moreno, R., & Mayer, R. E. (2000b). Engaging students in active learning: The case for personalized multimedia messages. *Journal of Educational Psychology, 92*, 724-733.

Moreno, R., & Mayer, R. E. (2002). Learning science in virtual reality multimedia environments: Role of methods and media. *Journal of Educational Psychology, 94*, 598-610.

Moreno, R., & Mayer, R. E. (2004). Personalized messages that promote science learning in virtual environments. *Journal of Educational Psychology, 96*, 165-173.

Moreno, R., Mayer, R. E., Spires, H. A., & Lester, J. C. (2001). The case for social agency in computer-based teaching: Do students learn more deeply when they interact with animated pedagogical agents? *Cognition and Instruction, 19*, 177-213.

Mousavi, S. Y., Low, R., & Sweller, J. (1995). Reducing cognitive load by mixing auditory and visual presentation modes. *Journal of Educational Psychology, 87*, 319-334.

Nass, C., & Brave, S. (2005). *Wired for speech*. Cambridge, MA: MOT Press.

O'Neil, H. F., Mayer, R. E., Herl, H. E., Niemi, C., Olin, K., & Thurman, R. A. (2000). Instructional strategies for virtual aviation training environments. In H. F. O'Neil & D. H. Andrews (Eds.), *Aircrew training and assessment* (pp. 105-130). Mahwah, NJ: Erlbaum.

Paivio, A. (1986). *Mental representations: A dual-coding approach*. Oxford, England: Oxford University Press.

Paivio, A. (2007). *Mind and its evolution: A dual-coding approach*. Mahwah, NJ: Erlbaum.

Phye, G. D., Robinson, D. H., & Levin, J. (Eds.). (2005). *Empirical methods for evaluating educational interventions*. San Diego, CA: Elsevier Academic Press.

Pollock, E., Chandler, P., & Sweller, J. (2002). Assimilating complex information. *Learning and Instruction, 12*, 61-86.

Reeves, B., & Nass, C. (1996). *The media equation*. New York, NY: Cambridge University Press.

Schnotz, W., & Kulhavy, R. W. (Eds.). (1994). *Comprehension of graphics*. Amsterdam, The Netherlands: North-Holland.

Shavelson, R. J., & Towne, L. (Eds.). (2002). *Scientific research in education*. Washington, DC: National Academy Press.

Stull, A., & Mayer, R. E. (2007). Learning by doing versus learning by viewing: Three experimental comparisons of learner-generated versus author-provided graphic organizers. *Journal of Educational Psychology, 99,* 808-820.

Sweller, J. (1999). *Instructional design in technical areas.* Camberwell, Australia: ACER Press.

Sweller, J. (2005). Implications of cognitive load theory for multimedia learning. In R. E. Mayer (Ed.), *Cambridge handbook of multimedia learning* (pp. 19-30). New York, NY: Cambridge University Press.

Sweller, J., Ayres, P., & Kalyuga, S. (2011). *Cognitive load theory.* New York, NY: Springer.

Sweller, J., Chandler, P., Tierney, P., & Cooper, M. (1990). Cognitive load and selective attention as factors in the structuring of technical material. *Journal of Experimental Psychology: General, 119,* 176-192.

Tabbers, H. K., Martens, R. L., & van Merrienboer, J. J. G. (2004). Multimedia instruction and cognitive load theory: Effects of modality and cueing. *British Journal of Educational Psychology, 74,* 71-81.

Tindall-Ford, S., Chandler, P., & Sweller, J. (1997). When two sensory modalities are better than one. *Journal of Experimental Psychology: Applied, 3,* 257-287.

Wang, N., Johnson, W. L., Mayer, R. E., Rizzo, P., Shaw, E., & Collins, H. (2008). The politeness effect: Pedagogical agents and learning outcomes. *International Journal of Human Computer Studies, 66,* 96-112.

Willows, D. M., & Houghton, H. A. (Eds.). (1987). *The psychology of illustration: Volume 1, Basic research.* New York, NY: Springer-Verlag.

Wittrock, M. C. (1989). Generative processes of comprehension. *Educational Psychologist, 24,* 345-376.

CHAPTER 4

KNOWLEDGE AND WORKING MEMORY EFFECTS ON LEARNING FROM VISUAL DISPLAYS

Slava Kalyuga

ABSTRACT

Research studies in expert-novice differences in learning conducted over the last several decades have demonstrated that learners' knowledge base is a single most important cognitive characteristic that influences their learning and performance. Recent studies within a cognitive load framework have found that instructional presentation formats that are effective with novice learners could become ineffective for more proficient learners (the expertise reversal effect). The major design implication of these studies is the need to tailor presentation formats to levels of learner expertise in a task domain. This chapter reviews major empirical findings associated with the expertise reversal effect in areas of multimedia learning that use various visual displays and their implications for the design of adaptive displays.

Learning Through Visual Displays, pp. 75–96

Most of research in improving the design of instructional presentations (including visual displays) is usually conducted with novice learners who do not possess substantial prior knowledge in the specified domain. This is not surprising as novices are most in need of instruction. Nevertheless, instruction still is likely to be required by more advanced learners too. Cognitive studies of expert-novice differences indicate that prior knowledge is the most important learner characteristic that influences learning processes. The research studies described in this chapter suggest that instructional design methods and techniques for more advanced learners may differ substantially from those suitable to novices. For example, as learners acquire more expertise in a specific domain, the information or activities that previously were essential may become redundant and cause increased, but unnecessary cognitive load.

Accordingly, many research studies conducted within a cognitive load framework have demonstrated that instructional representation formats that are effective with novice learners can become ineffective for more proficient learners due to cognitive activities that consume additional working memory resources (the expertise reversal effect; see Kalyuga, 2007; Sweller, Ayres, & Kalyuga, 2011 for recent overviews). The effect is explained by the added cognitive load that more knowledgeable learners may experience due to processing instructional components that are redundant for them (as compared to processing instructional components that are not redundant). When learners must reconcile the demands of externally-provided information with existing internal knowledge-based guidance, they may be distracted from fluent execution of appropriate cognitive processes. As a consequence, presentation formats lead to different instructional outcomes for learners who have different levels of task-specific expertise. The major design implication of this effect is that instructional presentation formats should be tailored to the learner's level of expertise in a task domain. This chapter reviews major empirical findings associated with the expertise reversal effect in areas of multimedia learning that use various visual displays and their implications for the design of adaptive representations.

COGNITIVE ARCHITECTURE AND HUMAN LEARNING

According to cognitive load theory, two major components of our cognitive architecture that are critical to learning are long-term memory and working memory (for a more comprehensive overview of this architecture and cognitive load theory, see Sweller et al., 2011; also Sweller, Low, & Jin, this volume). Several decades of research in cognitive science starting from the pioneering studies by de Groot (1946/1965) and Chase and

Simon (1973) in chess expertise clearly demonstrated the significance and the critical role of the knowledge base in long-term memory in most of human cognitive activities including learning (e.g., Bransford, Brown, & Cocking, 1999; Sweller et al., 2011). This organized knowledge base could be conceptualized as generic knowledge structures (schemas) representing concepts and procedures that allow us to categorize problem situations and effectively govern our behavior.

Working memory is another major component of our cognitive architecture that, according to the above model of human cognitive architecture, represents a mechanism that limits the scope of immediate simultaneous changes to the knowledge base in long-term memory that may potentially inhibit its functionality. Working memory is also associated with conscious processing of information within the focus of attention. Its processing capacity and duration are severely limited when dealing with novel information (Baddeley, 1986; Cowan, 2001; Miller, 1956). In most models of working memory, it has two partially independent channels for processing visual and auditory information. Accordingly, the capacity of each of these channels is limited to only several units of information at a time.

From the perspective of these characteristics of human cognitive architecture, the importance of the learner organized knowledge base is primarily determined by its ability to effectively reduce the capacity limitation of working memory by encapsulating many elements of information into higher-level chunks that could be treated as single units in working memory (Ericsson & Kintsch, 1995). Experts and more experienced learners heavily rely on this mechanism in managing their cognitive load (in addition to another critical mechanism of automating basic procedures to the point at which they do not require any controlled conscious processing).

In evolutionary educational psychology (e.g., Geary, 2007, 2008), knowledge is divided into two major types: biologically primary knowledge that we have evolved to acquire rapidly without much conscious effort (e.g., basic skills in speaking and listening a common form of our native language, using general problem solving heuristics, or establishing function-structure relations in different objects we use), and biologically secondary knowledge that we have not evolved to acquire in this way (e.g., writing and reading skills, or knowledge of mathematics and science we usually learn at schools and universities; see Sweller et al., 2011; Sweller et al., this volume). A similar (though not interpreted directly in evolutionary terms) division between intuitive and explicit knowledge is also proposed in dual-process theories of reasoning in developmental psychology that make a distinction between intuitive and analytical thinking (e.g., Barrouillet, 2011; Evans, 2011). The first type of processing is fast, high capacity, independent of working memory, and could be related to the above primary knowledge, while the second type is slow, low capacity, heavily dependent on working memory and could be related to the above secondary knowledge.

However, regardless of specific conceptualizations of intuitive/primary knowledge, there is a consensus in the above fields that this knowledge is learned early and unintentionally by being involved in appropriate activities, and that it is largely inaccessible to conscious control and use minimal (if any) working memory resources. Accordingly, cognitive processes involved in learning intuitive/primary and explicit/secondary knowledge are different. This distinction may have important implications for visual displays that depict either primary/intuitive or secondary/explicit types of knowledge. In education, most visual displays require the use of secondary knowledge, and cognitive load theory is primarily concerned with managing cognitive load involved in learning this type of knowledge. Considering levels of learner expertise is critical for selecting optimal instructional designs for visual displays in such knowledge domains.

EXPERTISE REVERSAL EFFECT

The expertise reversal effect refers to the interactions between the effectiveness of different instructional designs and levels of learner expertise (or prior knowledge). If novice learners have to simultaneously process many new elements of information in working memory, the corresponding instructional design may result in a potential cognitive overload. To reduce this load, special instructional design techniques have been suggested in cognitive load theory (e.g., eliminating split attention by closely integrating different parts of presentations, using several different modalities for presenting different components of instruction, or providing additional detailed instructional guidance).

However, if such instructional techniques are used with more experienced learners who already have an adequate relevant knowledge base to deal with the original information, these learners may be forced to unnecessarily co-refer and reconcile the corresponding components of their knowledge base and the additionally provided information. These processes may distract these learners from fluently executing already learned procedures and taking the advantage of their knowledge base. More importantly, such processes may impose additional cognitive load that would reduce working memory resources available for further learning (e.g., making generalizations or refining and strengthening available knowledge structures). This mechanism has been suggested to explain the expertise reversal effect in cognitive load theory (see Kalyuga, 2007; Kalyuga & Renkl, 2010, Sweller et al, 2011, for recent overviews).

Thus, according to this mechanism, there are two general types of instructional conditions that may cause unnecessary (extraneous) cognitive load resulting in an expertise reversal effect. In the first type of condition, less experienced learners may be hindered by limited instructional guidance, whereas more experienced learners may benefit from limited instructional guidance. Alternatively, in the second type of condition, extensive instructional guidance may hinder more experienced learners because relating and cross-referencing the overlapping internal and external representations of the same information may impose an additional extraneous load, whereas less experienced learners may benefit from extensive instructional guidance.

The relative effectiveness of different instructional formats may reverse as levels of learner expertise increase. Instructional design formats that have been effective with low-knowledge individuals can lose their effectiveness and even have negative consequences as these learners become more experienced in the domain. For more knowledgeable learners, the provision of the same information as for novices may become redundant and relatively ineffective. In other words, presenting experienced learners with detailed information that they do not need any more may hinder their performance relative to other similar experienced learners who have not been presented with such detailed instructions. The presentation formats that are optimal for novices may hinder relative performance of more experienced learners.

The major instructional design implication of this effect is the need to dynamically tailor specific instructional techniques and presentation formats to changing levels of learner expertise. The following sections of this chapter will review the available empirical findings associated with this effect that are relevant to the design of visual displays, particularly in different multimedia and hypermedia learning environments.

REDUCING COGNITIVE LOAD IN VISUAL DISPLAYS

An essential advantage of pictorial representations over verbal representations is their capability to provide a more direct access to information that is represented in a more compact and cognitively economical and efficient way (Larkin & Simon, 1987). In pictorial representations, much of the needed information is presented at a single location and little search is required as each element is close to other related elements. In contrast to verbal information that usually needs to be processed sequentially, elements of visual information can be encoded simultaneously. Pictorial representations may therefore reduce cognitive load imposed by intrinsically complex materials compared to the equivalent verbal information (e.g., Carlson, Chandler, & Sweller, 2003), and thus enable learners to redirect their cognitive resources towards solving complex tasks. Pictures may also act as external memory aids; thus, also reducing the demand on cognitive resources (Hegarty & Just, 1993). However, instructional advantages of diagrams may depend on learners' prior domain-specific knowledge and experience. Less knowledgeable learners may have difficulty in inferring meaning from purely symbolic representations because in the absence of prior knowledge, their cognitive processes would be restricted by the severely limited capacity of their working memory.

Visual Displays With Onscreen or Narrated Text

If related visuals and text that require each other for understanding are physically or temporally separated, then integrating them may require cognitive processes of visual search-and-match or temporal maintenance in working memory, resulting in increased extraneous cognitive load. Physically-embedded or temporally-synchronized representations may reduce or eliminate this load and enhance learning (split-attention effect; e.g., Mayer & Gallini, 1990; Sweller, Chandler, Tierney, & Cooper, 1990). However, this may not be the case for more knowledgeable learners for whom this embedded or synchronized information may not be needed, but is still processed. Eliminating such redundant representations could be more effective than including them because there is no benefit to processing them.

The dual-channel processing assumption of cognitive theory of multimedia learning (see Mayer, this volume) may explain why combining pictures and concurrent spoken words has an advantage over printed or onscreen words only. In this case and also when textual information is embedded into diagrams, the advantages of pictorial representations effectively extend to the combined materials. However, the instructional benefits of diagrams may depend on learners' knowledge and expertise in a specific domain. For example, unnecessary (extraneous) cognitive load can be reduced if learners have prior knowledge of the abstract representational conventions used in a specific representational system, and therefore do not need to engage in search-and-match processes while looking for their meaning (Lowe, 2003). Highly knowledgeable learners may comprehend a textual segment alone and a diagram alone and do not need both being presented. These learners are also able to reduce their cognitive load by switching less often between processing the text and the diagram and holding representations with fewer chunks in working memory due to available knowledge base (Hegarty & Just, 1989).

Graphics-enhanced instructional explanations and spatially integrated pictorial and verbal instructional representations can improve learning outcomes for students with low prior knowledge levels, but not for those with higher prior knowledge levels (individual differences principle, Mayer, 2009). The advantages of multimedia presentations can disappear as levels of learner knowledge increase. For more knowledgeable learners, some sources of pictorial and verbal information may be redundant. Processing such redundant information and integrating it with available knowledge structures in long-term memory may consume cognitive resources that become unavailable for productive learning. Therefore, eliminating such redundant information could be a better design decision when dealing with more experienced learners.

Support for this claim can be found in a series of longitudinal studies on the effectiveness of computer-based visual displays in which technical apprentices were intensively trained from novice to more expert states in specific engineering areas (Kalyuga, Chandler, & Sweller, 1998, 2000, 2001). Levels of learner performance and cognitive load were monitored at different stages along the way to investigate changes in the relative effectiveness of different design methods.

In the first study, Kalyuga et al. (1998) used instructional materials that included electrical wiring diagrams with textual on-screen explanations. The study demonstrated that physically integrated formats with sections of text embedded directly into diagrams were effective for novices as compared to a split-source format (a split-attention effect in cognitive load theory). However, as learners acquired more knowledge in the domain, integrated formats became much less effective. After extensive training in the domain, the effectiveness of the integrated diagram and text format decreased significantly while the effectiveness of a diagram alone condition increased. Thus, more experienced technical apprentices learned new versions of a familiar class of wiring diagrams more effectively from the diagrams alone rather than from diagrams with integrated detailed explanations. Additional instructional explanations were redundant for these learners and generated extraneous cognitive load. Accordingly, subjective ratings of cognitive load indicated that sole diagrams were easier to process for more knowledgeable learners, whereas less knowledgeable learners found it easier to process the integrated format.

The second study investigated the modality effect. According to the modality effect in cognitive load theory, using visual representations with narrated rather than on-screen textual explanations enhances student learning (Mayer, 1997; Mayer & Moreno, 1998; Mousavi, Low, & Sweller, 1995; Tindall-Ford, Chandler, & Sweller, 1997). For more knowledgeable learners, however, narrated explanations may become redundant and reduce learning effectiveness similar to physically embedded on-screen text. Kalyuga et al. (2000) trained technical apprentices to read charts that are used to set up cutting machines. Both single- and dual-modality presentations were used. When a leaner clicked on a button that corresponded to a procedural step, an explanation of this step was delivered either as an auditory narration through headphones (i.e., dual-modality format) or displayed as an identical visual text next to the diagram (i.e., single-modality format, Figure 4.1). Replacing on-screen textual explanations with corresponding narrated explanations was beneficial for novice learners (thus demonstrating a modality effect). Interactive diagram-only presentations (that provided student-controlled on-screen highlights of lines, numbers and other components of the chart) were less effective for these inexperienced learners.

Following the initial (pretraining) learning phase, all learners went through a series of common intensive training sessions and became more experienced in the task domain. When they had to learn more advanced types of charts using different experimental instructional formats (Figure 4.2), the advantage of auditory narrations disappeared, and the interactive diagram-only presentation format became more beneficial than the diagram with narrated or on-screen explanations, and learners reported less perceived cognitive load. Thus, as expertise levels increased, the advantage of the narrated diagrams over a diagram-alone condition disappeared, and eventually reversed compared to the pattern of results obtained earlier with novice learners.

The third study investigated the worked examples effect. Kalyuga et al. (2001) compared displayed worked examples on writing switching equations for relay circuits with exploratory-based instructions in which learners had to construct a suitable circuit first and then write an equation for it. The worked examples group initially outperformed the exploratory group, but as the level of learner expertise increased after a series of training sessions, the exploratory group eventually outperformed the worked examples group. Kalyuga, Chandler, Tuovinen, and Sweller (2001) had similar findings, which showed that the advantages of displaying worked examples on how to program industrial equipment (with program steps directly embedded into the relay circuits close to corresponding elements) over learning by solving the programming problems on their own (the worked example effect) disappeared as trainees acquired more knowledge in the domain.

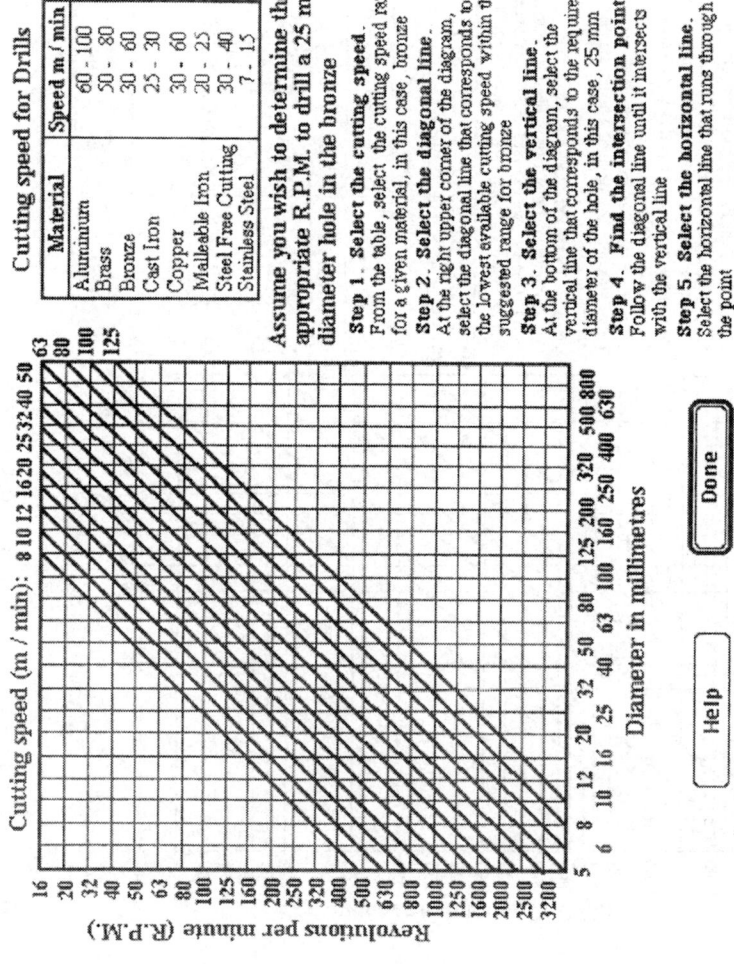

Cutting speed for Drills

Material	Speed m / min
Aluminium	60 - 100
Brass	50 - 80
Bronze	30 - 60
Cast Iron	25 - 30
Copper	30 - 60
Malleable Iron	20 - 25
Steel Free Cutting	30 - 40
Stainless Steel	7 - 15

Assume you wish to determine the appropriate R.P.M. to drill a 25 mm diameter hole in the bronze

Step 1. Select the cutting speed.
From the table, select the cutting speed range for a given material, in this case, bronze

Step 2. Select the diagonal line.
At the right upper corner of the diagram, select the diagonal line that corresponds to the lowest available cutting speed within the suggested range for bronze

Step 3. Select the vertical line.
At the bottom of the diagram, select the vertical line that corresponds to the required diameter of the hole, in this case, 25 mm

Step 4. Find the intersection point.
Follow the diagonal line until it intersects with the vertical line

Step 5. Select the horizontal line.
Select the horizontal line that runs through the point

Step 6. Read off the R.P.M.
By following the horizontal line to the left, we can read off the appropriate R.P.M.

Help   Done

Figure 4.1.   Single-modality format presented to novice learners.

83

Assume you wish to determine the appropriate R.P.M. to finish a 16 mm diameter high speed tough steel workpiece

Step 1. Select a given material. From the table, select a given material (tough steel).

Step 2. Select the angular line. At the right border of the diagram, select the angular line that corresponds to the suggested cutting speed for finishing tough steel

Step 3. Select the vertical line. At the bottom of the diagram, select the vertical line which corresponds to a given diameter (16 mm)

Step 4. Find the intersection point. Follow the angular line until it intersects the vertical line

Step 5. Read off the R.P.M. By moving horizontally from the intersection point to the left, we can read off the appropriate R.P.M. for the 16 mm tough steel workpiece

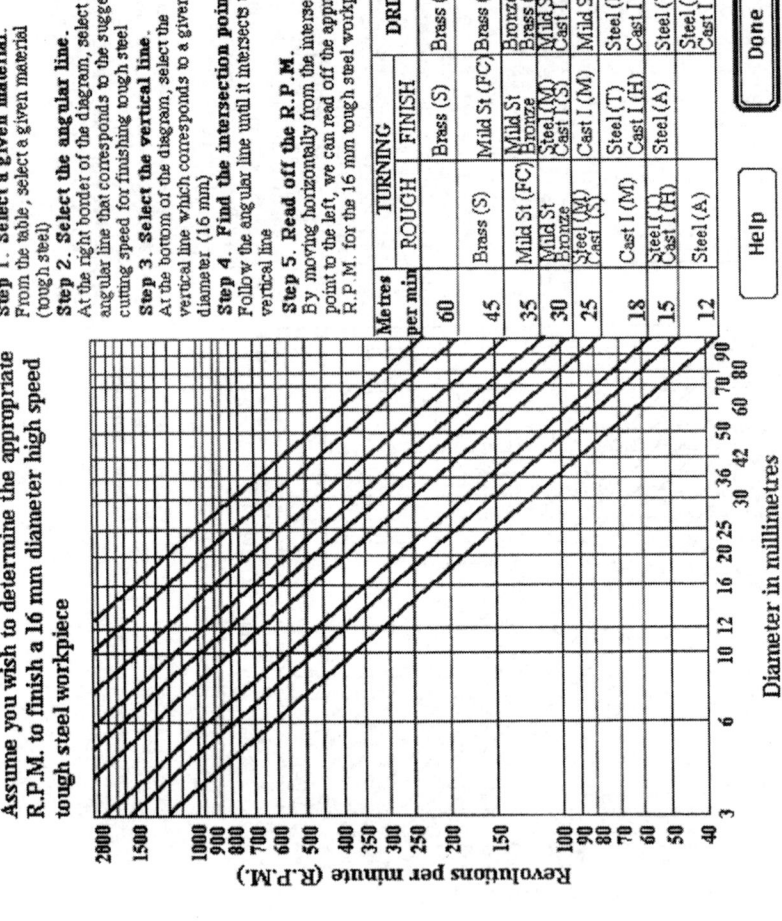

Metres per min	TURNING		DRILL
	ROUGH	FINISH	
60		Brass (S)	Brass (S)
45	Brass (S)	Mild St (FC)	Brass (M)
35	Mild St (FC)	Mild St Bronze	Bronze Brass (H)
30	Mild St Bronze	Steel (M) Cast I (S)	Mild St (FC) Cast I (S)
25	Steel (M) Cast (S)	Cast I (M)	Mild St
18	Cast I (M)	Steel (T) Cast I (H)	Steel (M) Cast I (M)
15	Steel (T) Cast I (H)	Steel (A)	Steel (T)
12	Steel (A)		Steel (A) Cast I (H)

Help   Done

Revolutions per minute (R.P.M.)

Diameter in millimetres

Figure 4.2.   Single-modality format presented to more experienced learners.

Pictorial Representations in Language Instruction

Chinese characters are examples of pictorial representations in a language domain. In order to complement them with phonetic information, a phonic transcription system called *pinyin* is usually used in instructional materials. Also, characters are often presented with both pinyin and verbal pronunciations concurrently. However, Lee and Kalyuga (2011) demonstrated that such concurrent presentations improved learning of pronunciation only for relatively more advanced learners. For novices, no differences were found between pinyin with pronunciation and pronunciation-only conditions. For these learners, visual pinyin in addition to pronunciation could have imposed additional cognitive load that eliminated any potential learning gains. For more experienced learners, a *pinyin* with pronunciation condition outperformed the pronunciation only format. The more experienced learners had sufficient knowledge to be able to use the additional information without adding more cognitive load.

REDUCING VISUAL COGNITIVE LOAD IN INTERACTIVE DYNAMIC VISUALIZATIONS

Interactive dynamic visualizations are most commonly implemented as instructional simulations and animations. Their use in education (especially in science education) has increased significantly in recent years; however, there is not yet strong evidence of improved students' learning outcomes. Recent research suggests that although dynamic visualizations can enhance learning under some conditions (Schnotz & Rasch, 2005; Tversky, Morrison, & Betrancourt, 2002), static visualizations may result in better learning outcomes under different conditions (Schnotz, Böckheler, & Grzondziel, 1999). From a cognitive load perspective, a major reason for lower than expected instructional effectiveness of dynamic visualizations is that they are not always consistent with limitations of our cognitive system (Plass, Homer, & Hayward, 2009). Under some conditions, dynamic visualizations may significantly increase cognitive load experienced by the learners resulting in decreased learning outcomes.

Simulations

Failures of some instructional simulations to demonstrate clear instructional advantages could be attributed to potentially high levels of working memory load related to the representation of the content of the visual information and how well this representation supports relevant cognitive processes and assists in managing visual cognitive load. Representational formats for input parameters and levels of instructional guidance could be important factors that may differentially influence effectiveness of simulations for learners with various levels of prior knowledge in a task domain.

Complementing traditional symbolic (e.g., verbal and numerical) representational formats for input parameters used in instructional simulations with iconic (pictorial) versions may enhance instructional effectiveness of simulations, especially for novice learners (Lee, Plass, & Homer, 2006). Iconic representations contain concrete graphics to represent the various elements of the physical environment (e.g., flames to represent temperature, weights to represent pressure, locks in open or closed states to show the variable or fixed parameters instead of traditional radio-buttons; see Figure 4.3 for an example). In another dimension, traditional exploratory-based simulations could be complemented by

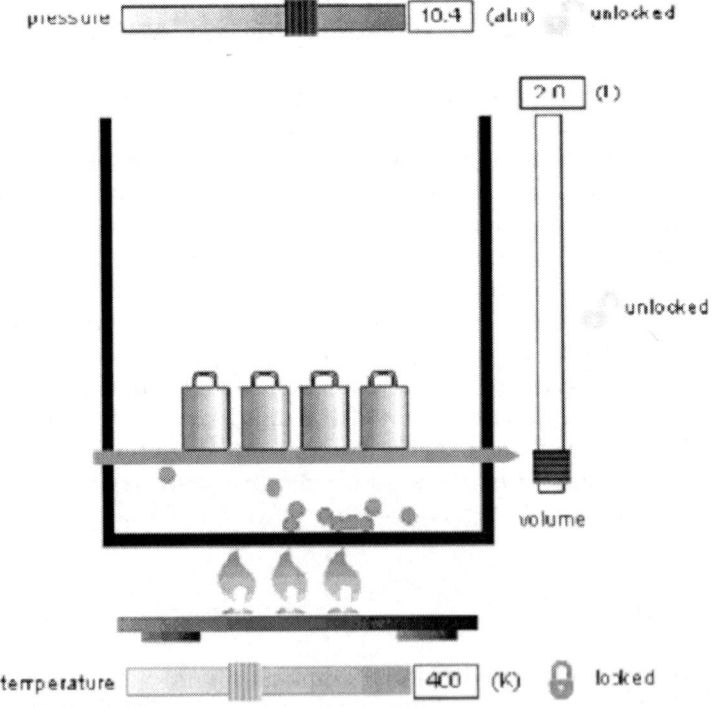

Figure 4.3.   Visual display with iconic information representations in a gas laws simulation.

worked-out versions of simulations as a form of incorporating components of instructional guidance into simulated learning environments.

There has been empirical data obtained from studies that compared
different formats of simulations for learning gas laws in high-school
chemistry to support these assumptions (Homer & Plass, 2010; Kalyuga &
Plass, 2007; Lee, Plass, & Homer 2006). Even though adding iconic representations to symbolic information leads to a visually more complex display and requires some additional processing resources, such iconic
representations can alleviate the need to interpret and store meanings of
symbolic information in working memory, thus delivering overall cognitive benefits. The added iconic representations externally-represent information that the learners would otherwise have to hold internally in their
working memory, and help to better relate new information to their prior
knowledge. Therefore, a display with a higher visual complexity and additional representations still could be less difficult to understand.

Lee et al. (2006) investigated an interaction between the above two
different modes of visual representations in the gas law simulation for
middle-school chemistry students and different levels of learners' prior
science knowledge. They found that while novice learners benefited from
the added iconic representations, more experienced learners learned
better from symbolic-only representations. It is likely that iconic
representations were redundant for these learners and could interfere with
their knowledge-based cognitive processes. Similar results were obtained
by Homer and Plass (2010) in web-based simulations of the kinetic theory
of gas. They found that adding iconic representations to the simulation
only facilitated learning for low prior knowledge students. It should be
noted that Lee et al. (2006) demonstrated an expertise reversal effect only
with interactive simulations that had manageable levels of complexity
(intrinsic cognitive load), at least for more knowledgeable learners (for
example, simulations that involved only two parameters at a time). For
high complexity materials that involved many interactive parameters and
generated excessive levels of intrinsic cognitive load for all participants (for
example, gas simulations in which all three parameters were considered
simultaneously), iconic representations were beneficial for all learners.

Animations

From a cognitive load perspective, continuous animations could be
cognitively demanding for novice learners due to high levels of transitivity of these information presentations. Novice learners could benefit more
from studying a set of equivalent static diagrams. On the other hand,
more experienced learners may benefit from animations since they can

handle the transitivity of animations due to their available knowledge structures. For example, while learners with higher levels of prior knowledge showed better results after studying animated procedural examples in transforming graphical representations of linear and quadratic functions in mathematics, less knowledgeable learners performed significantly better after studying sets of static representations demonstrating main steps of the transformations on a single screen (Kalyuga, 2008a).

Using animated and static representations of the relation of time to the Earth's rotation, Schnotz and Rasch (2005) demonstrated that relatively low-experienced students learned more from static representations, while there were no differences for high-experience students. In another experiment, Schnotz and Rasch also compared simple animations with interactive animations that allowed students to manipulate parameters. Results indicated that higher knowledge students learned more from interactive animations, while low-knowledge learners benefitted more from simple simulations. From a cognitive load perspective, interactive animations (simulations) could impose excessive cognitive load on inexperienced learners, while more knowledgeable students could benefit from this format, guided by their available prior knowledge structures without experiencing cognitive overload.

Web-Based Representations

Low prior knowledge learners may experience cognitive overload when dealing with unstructured web-based (hypertext and/or hypermedia) representations. They may need to devote most of their cognitive capacity to searching for relevant elements of information preventing them from building appropriate knowledge structures. These learners may learn better from more structured representations or interactive presentations with restricted levels of interactivity (Shapiro, 1999; Shin, Schallert, & Savenye, 1994).

The structure of representations may be an important factor determining the effectiveness of interactive visual displays for learners at different levels of expertise. For example, Shapiro (1999) found that interactive overviews as a tool for organizing and structuring presented material in hypermedia-based learning was more beneficial for novices than for learners with higher levels of prior knowledge in the domain. It was suggested that the need to process unnecessary sources of information could cause the effect (another possible explanation could be that the structure of the overviews was incompatible with these learners' available knowledge structures resulting in additional working memory resources spent on reconciling these two sources of information). These results correspond to earlier conclusion of Eylon and Reif (1984) who found that presenting hierarchically structured material benefited low ability learners but not high ability learners.

Web-based, nonlinear hypertext concept maps may have different levels of structure. Well-structured maps demonstrate explicitly the hierarchy of relations between concepts. On the other hand, unstructured maps may show only the network of relations without an explicit hierarchy. Amadieu, van Gog, Paas, Tricot, and Marine (2009) compared these two types of concept maps in the area of biology and demonstrated that low prior knowledge students learned more conceptual knowledge from the structured format, while there was no difference for high prior knowledge learners. Also, both types of learners indicated less cognitive load when learning from the structured maps. In a related study, Amadieu, Tricot, and Marine (2009) also demonstrated that free recall of the material for low prior knowledge learners was better following the hierarchical structure. However, high prior knowledge learners demonstrated better recall after studying the unstructured maps. It was suggested that the information provided by the hierarchical structure was redundant for these learners and imposed an extraneous cognitive load that inhibited further learning.

Spreadsheets

Breaking displays of complex information with high levels of element interactivity (high intrinsic cognitive load) into a set of isolated representations and ignoring relations between these components during the initial stages of learning may artificially reduce element interactivity and the initial cognitive load for a low-knowledge learner. At a later stage, the partial schemas and representations acquired during this initial stage, may allow more efficient building of more comprehensive schemas with complex interactions between elements (the isolated-interacting elements effect; Pollock, Chandler, & Sweller, 2002). Such isolated-elements learning tasks followed by fully interacting elements instruction may benefit low-knowledge learners, but not learners with higher levels of prior knowledge in the domain, thus demonstrating an expertise reversal effect.

Blayney, Kalyuga, and Sweller (2010) compared two instructional formats for training accountants using interactive spreadsheet-based representations of information. In one of these formats (isolated-interactive elements format), learners had to accomplish a complex calculation using a staged approach by calculating a partial result in one cell first, then using it in another cell to complete the procedure. In another format (fully interactive elements format), learners had to complete the whole procedure using a single cell. According to the isolated-interactive elements effect in cognitive load theory, working memory load could be reduced by initially presenting elements of information sequentially in an isolated form without reference to other elements followed by a fully interactive form in the next instructional phase. The results of this study demonstrated that only novice learners benefited from this instructional method. More experienced learners benefited from the fully interacting elements instruction using complex single-cell formulas from the beginning. Their available relevant knowledge structures allowed them to avoid potential cognitive overload. However, when these experienced learners were presented the sequential, isolated elements instructional format, they had to use additional cognitive resources on cross-referencing the redundant for them simplifications with their available knowledge, thus increasing extraneous cognitive load.

When using spreadsheets as instructional tools in teaching specific subjects, instruction in the required new spreadsheet skills and techniques is sometimes presented in an integrated form at the same time as instruction is specific subject concepts. Such integrated formats are expected to provide required technical support just-in-time, save time, and make instruction more efficient. However, Clarke, Ayres, and Sweller (2005) demonstrated that in learning mathematics, the integrated format benefited only relatively more experienced students who already had some basic skills in using spreadsheets. Less experienced students benefited more from the sequential condition in which instructions on how to use spreadsheets were provided prior to applying this knowledge in learning mathematics. Measures of cognitive load using subjective ratings indicated that concurrently presented information on spreadsheet applications and mathematics overloaded novice learners.

TAILORING VISUAL DISPLAYS TO LEVELS OF LEARNER EXPERTISE

The expertise reversal effect implies that presentation formats in visual displays need to be tailored to current levels of learner expertise and, accordingly, adjusted as these levels change during learning. Of course, an important condition for developing such adaptive displays is the availability of assessment tools that can diagnose levels of learner expertise rapidly and in real time. A possible approach to such rapid assessment of expertise could be based on observing how learners begin dealing with briefly presented tasks in specific areas. For example, in the first-step diagnostic method (Kalyuga, 2006c; Kalyuga & Sweller, 2004), students have to rapidly indicate their first step towards solution of a briefly presented task (e.g., solving an algebra problem). More experienced learners would use their well-learned knowledge for solution procedures to skip some immediate starting steps and rapidly switch to doing intermediate and more advanced steps of the solution as their first steps. On the other hand, less experienced learners may only be able to perform a very first immediate step according to the procedure, if they have learned it before, or start random search for a solution step. Alternatively, students could be briefly presented with potential solution steps (at the initial, intermediate, and advanced stages of the solution) and asked to rapidly verify their correctness (a rapid verification method; Kalyuga, 2006b, 2008b).

The rapid diagnostic methods were used in adaptive tutorials in algebra (Kalyuga & Sweller, 2004, 2005) and vector addition motion problems in kinematics (Kalyuga, 2006a). The tutorials provided instructional formats that were optimal for learners with different levels of expertise as measured by ongoing rapid assessment methods. Depending on the outcomes of such assessments, the learner proceeded to the next learning stage or was required to repeat the same stage and then take the test again. Similar adaptation strategies based on measuring learner performance and/or ratings of cognitive load have been realized within the cognitive load framework in training air traffic controllers (Salden, Paas, Broers, & van Merriënboer, 2004; Salden, Paas, & van Merriënboer, 2006).

An alternative to the above system-controlled approach to tailoring representation formats to learner levels of expertise is a learner-controlled approach. With this approach, learners themselves select the formats they believe are appropriate at their current level of understanding. However, there has not been any empirical evidence obtained that supports the effectiveness of learner control in selecting learning tasks and presentation formats (Chung & Reigeluth, 1992; Niemec, Sikorski, & Walberg, 1996). From a cognitive load perspective, novice learners could be cognitively overloaded by the selection process and require assistance. Therefore, the learner-controlled approach may only be effective for learners who have sufficient prior knowledge of the domain, thus indicating a possibility of an expertise reversal effect in relation to the degree of learner control over presentation formats. An adaptive guidance approach based on continuous monitoring of learners progress and providing them with individually tailored recommendations for the selection of learning tasks and activities has been successfully used by Bell and Kozlowski (2002). A similar approach could possibly be applied for optimizing representational formats in visual displays.

CONCLUSION

The design of visual displays needs to take into account our current knowledge of human cognitive architecture. High levels of working memory load may inhibit learning from such displays, and levels of learner prior knowledge should be considered as an important factor influencing their effectiveness. Acquiring knowledge base in a specific task domain may reduce a potential working memory overload and enhance learning. As learner experience in the domain increases, limited duration and capacity of working memory could become less important because many relevant schematic representations may already be held in long-term memory.

Some established information display design principles are in agreement with cognitive load effects. For example, according to the proximity compatibility principle, when two or more sources of information must be mentally integrated, parts of the information should be displayed close together. The principle of multiple resources requires using different modalities such as audition and vision (Wickens, Lee, Liu, & Gordon-Becker, 2003). Levels of learner (user) domain-specific knowledge represent an important factor determining conditions of applicability of these principles.

Visuals such as pictures and diagrams are cognitively efficient information representations. They usually require less search processes since their elements are located close to other related elements. Integrated verbal and visual representations and dual-modality formats also retain these benefits. However, their instructional benefits depend on levels of learner domain-specific knowledge or expertise. More knowledgeable learners may benefit more from single-modality pictorial-only representations.

According to the expertise reversal effect, and in contrast to our common intuition, the information presentation formats that are optimal for novices may inhibit learning for more experienced learners. Their already available knowledge structures may require integration with displayed (and redundant for these more knowledgeable learners) information thus imposing an unnecessary extraneous cognitive load and eliminating or even reversing a positive learning effect. This chapter reviewed empirical findings associated with the expertise reversal effect in various information presentation formats used in visual displays. The interactions between different formats of visual displays and levels of learner expertise have been found with a wide variety of representational contexts including mathematics, science, engineering, programming, accountancy, language and others. Participants ranged from primary school to university levels.

One common condition of applicability of this effect is a sufficiently high level of element interactivity (or complexity of the material). Simple presentations with low levels of element interactivity are unlikely to demonstrate any significant expert-novice differences. At the other end of the complexity spectrum, excessively high levels of element interactivity may also prevent such differences, since very complex materials may impose excessively high levels of cognitive load for all learners.

The main instructional implication of the expertise reversal effect is the need to tailor visual displays to changing levels of learner expertise in order to optimize use of working memory resources. Ideally, changes in the learner domain-specific knowledge base need to be dynamically monitored and specific presentation formats tailored accordingly. Adaptive visual displays may enhance learning and performance by providing appropriate representations of information that are tailored to learners' current knowledge base and available cognitive resources. Truly effective displays should be adaptive to a range of learner cognitive characteristics to provide personalized interactions and displays of information.

REFERENCES

Amadieu, F., Tricot, A., & Marine, C. (2009). Prior knowledge in learning from a non-linear electronic document: Disorientation and coherence of the reading sequences. *Computers in Human Behavior, 25*, 381-388.

Amadieu, F., van Gog, T., Paas, F., Tricot, A., & Marine, C. (2009). Effects of prior knowledge and concept-map structure on disorientation, cognitive load, and learning. *Learning and Instruction 19*, 376-386.

Baddeley, A. D. (1986). *Working Memory.* New York: Oxford University Press.

Barrouillet, P. (2011). Dual-process theories and cognitive development: Advances and challenges. *Developmental Review 31*, 79-85

Bell, B. S. & Kozlowski, S. W. J. (2002). Adaptive guidance: Enhancing self-regulation, knowledge, and performance in technology-based training. *Personnel Psychology, 55*, 267-306.

Blayney, P., Kalyuga, S., & Sweller, J. (2010). Interactions between the isolated-interactive elements effect and levels of learner expertise: experimental evidence from an accountancy class. *Instructional Science, 38*, 277-287.

Bransford, J. D., Brown, A. L., & Cocking, R. R. (Eds.). (1999). *How people learn: Mind, brain, experience, and school.* Washington, DC: National Academy Press.

Carlson, R., Chandler, P., & Sweller, J. (2003). Learning and understanding science instructional material. *Journal of Educational Psychology, 95*, 629-640.

Chase, W. G., & Simon, H. A. (1973). Perception in chess. *Cognitive Psychology, 4*, 55-81.

Chung, J., & Reigeluth, C. M. (1992). Instructional prescriptions for learner control. *Educational Technology, 32*, 14-20.

Clarke, T., Ayres, P., & Sweller, J. (2005). The impact of sequencing and prior knowledge on learning mathematics through spreadsheet applications. *Educational Technology Research and Development, 53*, 15-24.

Cowan, N. (2001). The magical number 4 in short-term memory: A reconsideration of mental storage capacity. *Behavioral and Brain Sciences, 24*, 87-114.

De Groot, A. (1965). *Thought and choice in chess*. The Hague, Netherlands: Mouton. (Original work published 1946).

Ericsson, K. A., & Kintsch, W. (1995). Long-term working memory. *Psychological Review, 102*, 211-245.

Evans, J. S. B. T. (2011). Dual-process theories of reasoning: Contemporary issues and developmental applications. *Developmental Review, 31*, 86-102

Eylon, B., & Reif, F. (1984). Effects of knowledge organization on task performance. *Cognition and Instruction, 1*, 5-44.

Geary, D. C. (2007). Educating the evolved mind: Conceptual foundations for an evolutionary educational psychology. In J. S. Carlson & J. R. Levin (Eds.), *Psychological perspectives on contemporary educational issues* (pp. 1-99). Greenwich, CT: Information Age Publishing.

Geary, D. C. (2008). An evolutionarily informed education science. *Educational Psychologist, 43*, 179-195.

Hegarty, M., & Just, M. A. (1989). Understanding machines from text and diagrams. In H. Mandl & J. Levin (Eds.), *Knowledge acquisition from text and picture* (pp. 171-194). Amsterdam, The Netherlands: North Holland.

Hegarty, M., & Just, M. A. (1993). Constructing mental models of machines from text and diagrams. *Journal of Memory and Language, 32*, 717-742.

Homer, B. D., & Plass, J. L. (2010). Expertise reversal for iconic representations in science visualizations. *Instructional Science, 38*, 259-276.

Kalyuga, S. (2006a). Assessment of Learners' Organized Knowledge Structures in Adaptive Learning Environments. *Applied Cognitive Psychology, 20*, 333-342.

Kalyuga, S. (2006b). Rapid assessment of learners' proficiency: A cognitive load approach. *Educational Psychology, 26*, 613-627.

Kalyuga, S. (2006c). Rapid cognitive assessment of learners' knowledge structures. *Learning and Instruction, 16*, 1-11.

Kalyuga, S. (2007). Expertise reversal effect and its implications for learner-tailored instruction. *Educational Psychology Review, 19*, 509-539.

Kalyuga, S. (2008a). Relative effectiveness of animated and static diagrams: An effect of learner prior knowledge. *Computers in Human Behavior, 24*, 852-861.

Kalyuga, S. (2008b). When less is more in cognitive diagnosis: A rapid assessment method for adaptive learning environments. *Journal of Educational Psychology, 100*, 603-612.

Kalyuga, S., Chandler, P., & Sweller, J. (1998). Levels of expertise and instructional design. *Human Factors, 40*, 1-17.

Kalyuga, S., Chandler, P., & Sweller, J. (2000). Incorporating learner experience into the design of multimedia instruction. *Journal of Educational Psychology, 92*, 126-136

Kalyuga, S., Chandler, P., & Sweller, J. (2001). Learner experience and efficiency of instructional guidance. *Educational Psychology, 21*, 5-23.

Kalyuga, S., Chandler, P., Tuovinen, J., & Sweller, J. (2001). When problem solving is superior to studying worked examples. *Journal of Educational Psychology, 93*, 579-588.

Kalyuga, S., & Plass, J. (2007, July 6-8). Managing cognitive load in instructional simulations. In M. B. Nunes & M. McPherson (Eds.), *Proceedings of the IADIS International Conference E-Learning* (Vol. pp. 27-34). Lisbon, Portugal: International Association for Development of the Information Society (IADIS) Press.

Kalyuga, S., & Renkl, A. (2010). Expertise reversal effect and its instructional implications: Introduction to the special issue. *Instructional Science, 38*, 209-215.

Kalyuga, S., & Sweller, J. (2004). Measuring knowledge to optimize cognitive load factors during instruction. *Journal of Educational Psychology, 96*, 558-568.

Kalyuga, S., & Sweller, J. (2005). Rapid dynamic assessment of expertise to improve the efficiency of adaptive e-learning. *Educational Technology Research and Development, 53*, 83-93.

Larkin, J. H., & Simon, H. A. (1987). Why a diagram is (sometimes) worth ten thousand words. *Cognitive Science, 11*, 65-99.

Lee, C. H., & Kalyuga, S. (2011). Effectiveness of on-screen pinyin in learning Chinese: An expertise reversal for multimedia redundancy effect. *Computers in Human Behavior, 27*, 11-15.

Lee, H., Plass, J. L., & Homer, B. D. (2006). Optimizing cognitive load for learning from computer-based science simulations. *Journal of Educational Psychology, 98*, 902-913.

Lowe, R. K. (2003). Animation and learning: Selective processing of information in dynamic graphics. *Learning and Instruction, 13*, 157-176.

Mayer, R. E. (1997). Multimedia learning: Are we asking the right questions? *Educational Psychologist, 32*, 1-19.

Mayer, R. E. (2009). *Multimedia learning*. Cambridge, MA: Cambridge University Press.

Mayer, R., & Gallini, J. (1990). When is an illustration worth ten thousand words? *Journal of Educational Psychology, 82*, 715-726.

Mayer, R., & Moreno, R. (1998). A split-attention effect in multimedia learning: Evidence for dual-processing systems in working memory. *Journal of Educational Psychology, 90*, 312-320.

Miller, G. A. (1956). The magical number seven, plus or minus two: Some limits on our capacity for processing information. *Psychological Review, 63*, 81-97.

Mousavi, S. Y., Low, R., & Sweller, J. (1995). Reducing cognitive load by mixing auditory and visual presentation modes. *Journal of Educational Psychology, 87*, 319-334.

Niemec, P., Sikorski, C., & Walberg, H. (1996). Learner-control effects: A review of reviews and a meta-analysis. *Journal of Educational Computing Research, 15*, 157-174.

Plass, J. L., Homer, B. D., & Hayward, E. O. (2009). Design factors for educationally effective animations and simulations. *Journal of Computing in Higher Education, 21*, 31-61.

Pollock, E., Chandler, P., & Sweller, J. (2002). Assimilating complex information. *Learning and Instruction, 12*, 61-86.

Salden, R. J. C. M., Paas, F., Broers, N. J., & van Merriënboer, J. J. G. (2004). Mental effort and performance as determinants for the dynamic selection of learning tasks in air traffic control training. *Instructional Science, 32*, 153-172.

Salden, R. J. C. M., Paas, F., & van Merriënboer, J. J. G. (2006). Personalized adaptive task selection in air traffic control: Effects on training efficiency and transfer. *Learning and Instruction, 16*, 350-362

Schnotz, W., Böckheler, J., & Grzondziel, H. (1999). Individual and co-operative learning with interactive animated pictures. *European Journal of Psychology of Education, 14*, 245-265.

Schnotz, W., & Rasch, T. (2005). Enabling, facilitating, and inhibiting effects of animations in multimedia learning: Why reduction of cognitive load can have negative results on learning. *Educational Technology Research and Development, 53*, 47-58.

Shapiro, A. M. (1999). The relationship between prior knowledge and interactive overviews during hypermedia-aided learning. *Journal of Educational Computing Research, 20*, 143-167.

Shin, E. C., Schallert, D. L., & Savenye, W. C. (1994). Effects of learner control, advisement, and prior knowledge on young students' learning in a hypertext environment. *Educational Technology Research and Development, 42*, 33-46.

Sweller, J., Ayres, P., & Kalyuga, S. (2011). *Cognitive load theory*. New York, NY: Springer.

Sweller, J., Chandler, P., Tierney, P., & Cooper, M. (1990). Cognitive load and selective attention as factors in the structuring of technical material. *Journal of Experimental Psychology: General, 119*, 176-192.

Tindall-Ford, S., Chandler, P., & Sweller, J. (1997). When two sensory modes are better than one. *Journal of Experimental Psychology: Applied, 3*, 257-287.

Tversky, B., Morrison, J. B., & Betrancourt, M. (2002). Animation: Can it facilitate? *International Journal of Human-Computer Studies, 57*, 247-262.

Wickens, C. D., Lee, J., Liu, Y., & Gordon-Becker, S.E. (2003). *An introduction to human factors engineering* (2nd ed.) Upper Saddle Hill, NJ: Prentice Hall.

CHAPTER 5

TOWARD A TYPOLOGY OF INSTRUCTIONAL VISUAL DISPLAYS

Gregory Schraw and Eugene Paik

ABSTRACT

This chapter discusses a variety of *instructional visual displays* (IVD), which is defined as a graphic representation of relationships. This definition is intended to capture the essential characteristics of the "graphic displays" discussed in this volume. In this introductory chapter, we present an IVD typology consisting of eight categories: signals; notes; networks; sequences; hierarchies; distributions; maps and spatial proximity; and animations. Our typology reflects an initial attempt to understand the feature space of common instructional displays. We view this typology as the first step toward a unified theory of instructional visuals, which provides (1) a parsimonious causal explanation how changes in IV affect learning; and (2) a basis for a prescriptive theory (e.g., design principles) that would allow us to efficiently create and/or modify IVDs to bring about desired learning outcomes. We summarize four common properties of displays in our typology and discuss six emergent issues that require additional research.

Learning Through Visual Displays, pp. 97–129
Copyright © 2013 by Information Age Publishing
All rights of reproduction in any form reserved.

INTRODUCTION

The purpose of this chapter is to present a typology of visual displays for instructional purposes. We define an instructional visual display (IVD) as a visual representation used to convey a set of relationships. An IVD may be associated with a verbiage (e.g., included within the text, appended to the text, or made accessible thru some adjunct link) or as a stand-alone display that is independent from any text. By typology, we mean a classification of IVDs into different categories based on common properties and purpose. There are different criteria one might use to create an IVD typology. Our IVD typology focuses on those visual features that encode salient relationships (e.g., order, inclusion/exclusion) among elements in the display. Our typology is intended to provide a framework for relating the different types of IVD discussed in this volume.

There is a surprisingly small amount of research on the design, use, and instruction of IVDs given their ubiquity in textbooks, journals, and popular magazines. Some IVDs such as geographical maps, temporal sequences, and causal diagrams are especially underresearched given their prevalence and importance. In our view, there is a general dearth of research on the design and instructional use of specific types of IVDs, as well as a broader theoretical understanding of what aspects of IVDs have the greatest impact on learning.

Several recently developed typologies exist. Desnoyers (2011) described a hierarchical taxonomy of displays based on Linnean principles that distinguished three classes of displays based on their information and content. Heer, Bostock, and Ogievetsky (2010) presented a five-category system based on the communicative purpose of displays found commonly in science texts. Morse and Lewis (2000) reviewed several different taxonomic approaches used to classify the task demands among different types of displays. Rodriguez and Dimitrova (2011) proposed a four-category system based on the communicative purpose of the IVDs.

Several observations are worth noting about these typologies in the larger context of this volume. One is that classification systems tend to be discipline-specific and focus on displays common within that discipline while excluding displays not common to that discipline. A second is that the existing categorization systems have little in common with one another in terms of organizational scheme such as number of categories or levels of complexity within the system. In the four cases cited above, the organizational frameworks do not resemble one another at all. A third observation is that none of these existing typologies seem to provide an adequate organizational framework for discussing and comparing the

IVDs in this volume because they include structurally different types of displays in a single category or omit important types of displays.

Despite the lack of an agreed upon typology of IVDs, it is clear that most or all displays possess at least five common features (Eichelberger & Schmid, 2009; Graham, Kennedy, & Benyon, 2000; Larkin & Simon, 1987; Latour, 1990; Morse & Lewis, 2000). One is that displays reduce the amount of information to a more manageable amount, thereby promoting cognitive economy (Lane & Sandor, 2009; Kosslyn, 1993). Summary tables, for example, usually attempt to make comparisons across four or five dimensions that affect the topics beings summarized. Second, displays are intended to organize or summarize information in a manner that enables the viewer to readily grasp the intended big conceptual picture (Slough, McTigue, Kim, & Jennings, 2010; Tufte, 2001). Third, displays are intended to draw the viewer's attention to the most salient aspect of the information (Mayer, 2005; Vekiri, 2002). For example, time series diagrams illustrate how data changes over time. Fourth, IVDs facilitate inference-generation by highlighting the significant interrelationships among component variables (Heer et al., 2010). Fifth, IVDs often provide an explicit visual model that can be used as an internalized mental model of events or processes, or used as a retrieval structure in memory to facilitate recall or future learning (Slough et al., 2010). These models may be tentative in nature, as when a student constructs an initial concept maps that links related concepts, or they may be stable as a when a student studies a geographical map of countries in western Europe that may not change for decades.

We suggested above that there is no single unifying conceptual typology in the research literature; nor is there as much empirical research as one would hope for regarding the design and instructional effectiveness of IVDs. Nevertheless, it is widely believed that IVDs that possess some or all of the five features summarized in the preceding paragraph promote better understanding with less effort (Larkin & Simon, 1987). In particular, several theoretical models described within and beyond this volume suggest that IVDs improve learning due to separate visual and semantic processing channels that increase total cognitive capacity and help to distribute the cognitive load of information across these channels (Kalyuga, Chandler, & Sweller, 2000; Mayer, 2005; Schnotz, 2002; Vekiri, 2002).

Instructional research using different IVDs is limited, as suggested above. Fortunately, previous studies that have included formal instruction about the purpose and interpretation of IVDs show robust gains for both surface and deeper learning (Abrami et al., 2008; De Simone, 2007; Liben, 2009; McCrudden, Magliano, & Schraw, 2011; Schwonke, Berthold & Renkl, 2009; van der Merr, 2012). Research indicates that students of all ages, including college students, experience difficulty using IVDs. One reason is that half of the graphics included in textbooks are either decorative or unrelated semantically to the text itself (Slough et al., 2010). Nevertheless, simple instructional interventions appear to ameliorate the difficulties of using and learning from IVDs, so that even a 10 to 15 instructional sequence may significantly alter how students allocate attention while studying IVDs, their ability to integrate information within an IVD with corresponding text, and how well they remember text and visual information (Mautone & Mayer, 2007; Schwonke et al., 2009).

Research also suggests that experts in a domain of study engage in two especially important interpretative activities when using IVDs that may help beginning students engage in deeper learning given instruction. One activity is constructing an integrated mental model to test assumptions about the phenomenon of interest. A second activity is making inferences about what the information in the display means within the broader context of the domain of knowledge they are attempting to model (Roth & Bowen, 2001). These two general skills (i.e., *mental model construction* and *inference generation*) can be mapped to the four more narrowly defined cognitive processes of decoding, translating, interpreting and evaluating IVDs (Schonborn & Anderson, 2010).

The remainder of this chapter includes three sections. The first section provides a typology that considers eight different types of IVDs. We generated this typology based on previous categorization schemes in research articles (Desnoyers, 2011; Heer et al., 2010), books (Jonassen, Beissner, & Yacci, 1993; Kosslyn, 1993), textbooks in a variety of disciplines such as science and the social sciences, and professional journals that use IVDs to inform the reader. The eight types of displays provide a broader set of categories than other classification systems that we encountered; thus, this framework may be more inclusive, although we assume it is not exhaustive. Representative examples of many different displays included in our typology appear in most chapters in this volume. The second section discusses implications for learning and future research using IVDs. We focus on six topics, including the need for a unifying framework for IVDs, a better understanding of common and unique information processing demands of each type of display, whether some types of displays are better suited to particular communicative arguments, effective instructional strategies, the role of person characteristics such as spatial ability and knowledge, and a discussion of domain-general and domain-specific design principles when constructing IVDs. We stress that different types of IVD require dedicated instruction to be used effectively. The third section concludes with main findings of the paper and a discussion of four themes from our review of the literature.

EIGHT TYPES OF INSTRUCTIONAL VISUAL DISPLAYS

This section provides a typology based on eight categories of IVDs. Our typology is intended to provide the broadest possible organizational framework for the different types of IVDs discussed in this volume. Figure 1 lists these displays and examples within each category. Our typology is based upon a review of chapters in this volume, previous typologies (Desnoyers, 2011; Heer et al., 2010; Morse & Lewis, 2000; Rodriguez & Dimitrova, 2011; Slough et al., 2010), and electronic searches using key terms such as *graphics, displays, representations, organizers* with qualifiers such as *adjunct, graphic, spatial,* and *visual.* We reiterate that the typology in Figure 5.1 is not intended to be exhaustive either within or between categories.

Our chief criterion for the eight categories in Figure 5.1 was to sort IVDs on the basis of their instructional purpose. Each time a display is used instructionally, either in isolation or in combination with other information, it is intended to convey an understanding of how information within the display is interrelated and related to complementary text information. The visual relationships among units of information in the display convey meaning about their order, sequence and importance. The visual structures may also indicate more complex relationships. The purpose of each display is to present relationships among units of information, and how the information collectively presents one potential organization model.

Table 5.1 provides definitions, general instructional purposes, and examples for different types of IVDs in each of the eight categories. All of

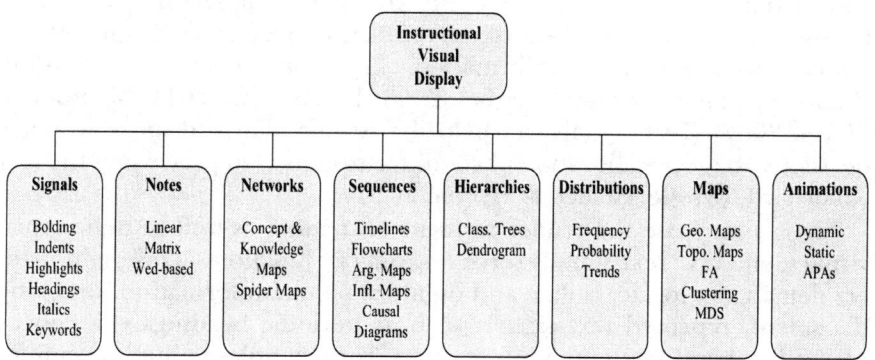

Note: Class. Trees = classification trees. FA = Factor analysis. MDS = multidimensional scaling. APAs = animated pedagogical agents.

Figure 5.1.   Eight types of IVDs (and within-category examples).

the categories in Figure 5.1 have multiple entries. Most of these entries are defined and discussed in detail in one or more of the chapters in this volume. We draw on these definitions in our chapter to maintain consistency. In addition, we discuss later in this chapter the adequacy of these definitions, as well as the need for additional criteria that can be used to categorize IVDs into categories.

For present purposes, we note that the eight categories are not intended to be mutually exclusive of one another. One source of overlap is the shared assumption that all types of IVDs aid learning by providing an organized graphic summary of important information. This information may be redundant with information in text or auditory form. Later in this chapter we address whether redundancy affects the usefulness of a display and the extent to which different types of displays are redundant and useful to the learner as well.

Signals

The term *text signal* refers to visual devices used to direct the reader's attention to particular portions of text or a visual display. Text signals can be used to provide the reader metatext information such as the organizational structure of the text (Lorch, Lemarié, & Grant, 2011). Text signals can be implemented using a wide variety of formatting techniques (e.g., indentations, bolding and highlighting, italics) and auxilary text (e.g., preview statements, summaries, underlining, headings). Even certain verbiage within the text (e.g., directive phrases like *in conclusion*; connective words that promote inferences such as *before, after,* and *because*) have been classified as text signals (Cain & Nash, 2011). Text signals are common in expository text and typically increase recall, the speed and efficiency of text search, organization of information, and conceptual understanding (Lemarié, Lorch, Eyrolle, & Virbel, 2008; Lorch et al., 2011; Mautone & Mayer, 2007). Text signals can help the reader plan and make strategic decisions about the allocation of cognitive resources in processing the text (Cauchard, Eyrolle, Cellier, & Hyona, 2010).

Signals may cue the reader to focus on textual as well as non-textual visual elements. Text signals serve a variety of functions. They help readers demarcate, locate, isolate and organize textual information. In a long document, repeated text signals such as periodic headings can convey hierarchical and sequential information. For example, multiple headings are used to signify the main sections of this chapter, while bolded headings are used to divide each section into distinct subsections.

Research on text signals was common during the 1980s. More recently, visual signaling techniques have been a focus of multimedia research,

Table 5.1.   A Summary of the Definition, Purpose and Examples of Different Types of IVDs

Type of Display	Definition	Instructional Purpose	Examples
Signals	Visual devices used to direct the reader's attention to particular portions of text or a visual display.	Highlight important information and organizational features of a text.	Bolding. Underlining. Italics. Highlighting. Headings. Indentations.
Notes	An external organized record of information.	Organize important information during study to enhance encoding, storage and retrieval.	Linear. Matrix. Web-based.
Networks	Node-link representations that connect concept nodes to one another via links labeled relationships	Condense, reorganize, and elaborate on information to create an integrated conceptual understanding.	Concept, knowledge, spider, and definition maps.
Sequences Hierarchies	Relationships among ordered events over time	Model a system's events over time. Show directional and causal relationships between variables.	Timelines. Flowcharts. Argument and influence maps. Causal diagrams.
	Ordered categorical relationships among concepts or ordered pathways between one event and another.	Classify objects. Show ordered inclusion in a taxonomy. Partition a set of events. Model a chain of ordered events.	Classification trees. Dendrograms.
Distributions	Show the density, variability, or trends in data.	Understand the statistical properties of distributions. Describe data. Illustrate trends.	Normal distribution. Regression lines. Trends across time or conditions.
Maps and Spatial Proximity	Relationships among objects within a coordinate system, spatial contiguity, similarity, or proximity between two or more objects.	Model physical environments using scaled representations. Show scaled relationship or distance between variables.	Geographical and topological maps. Multidimensional scaling. Cluster analysis. Venn and pie diagrams.
Animations	A series of changing pictures or images that show movement or moment-to-moment change in a dynamic process.	Illustrate a dynamic process. Explicate a problem-solving procedure. Use animated agents as tutors.	Animated images. Animated pedagogical agents.

albeit under different labels such as *highlighting, cueing,* and *directive animation* (De Koning Tabbers, Rikers, & Paas 2009; Höffler & Leutner, 2007; Schnotz & Lowe, 2008). One difference between text signals and directive animations is that text signals are essentially static signals that do not change over time. In contrast, multimedia research has focused primarily on visual signals such as animations that change over time. We opine that this change in focus did not stem from any significant advances in our understanding of learning or teaching. Rather, it simply reflects the affordances of the available technologies (i.e., pen and paper prior to 1980s; MacIntosh and Windows/PC soon thereafter) during the times of the research. Be that as it may, text signals and directive animations share a common purpose. They are both technologies that utilize visual signals to improve learning. We refer to this class of technologies as *signals.* While text signals and directive animations may share a common purpose, there is one issue which directive animation research addresses that text signal research did not: multiplicity of sensory channels. Multimedia presentations may include auditory elements (e.g., aural narration, background music, sound effects) as well as visual elements (e.g., written text and graphs). The presence of information across multiple sensory channels raises the issue of how information across those channels are cognitively integrated. Jeung, Chandler, and Sweller (1997) theorized that visual signals (e.g., electronic blinking) that help the learner identify the visual referents of auditory narrations would enhance learning. They argued that highlighting the referents of aural narration could help the learner integrate auditory and visual information more efficiently by reducing cognitive demands associated with visually searching for the referents of the auditory narration. A number of studies have produced results consistent with Jeung et al.'s *highlighting theory.* Indeed, we are aware of no documented evidence that is inconsistent with the theory, nor are we aware of any substantive theoretical advancements beyond the theory in signals research.

Notes and Tabular Comparisons

Notes are perhaps the most common type of visual display used by students. Note-taking may be defined as the act of creating a record of organized information (Kauffman, Zhao, & Yang, 2011). Previous research suggests that notes have both an encoding and an external storage function (Kiewra, 1989; Kobayashi, 2005, 2006). Studies show that notes taken at the time of learning have a positive effect on organization and storage of information in long-term memory, while notes used at a later time have a positive effect on the retrieval and reorganization of information, as well as integrating previously learned information with new information to create a deeper understanding of text information (Bohay, Blakely, Tamplin, & Radvansky, 2011; Kauffman et al., 2011). Recent reviews and meta-analyses suggest that the encoding function of notes may have little impact on learning, whereas the combined effect of encoding and review of notes has a significant positive impact on learning compared to a control group or review-only group (Kobayashi, 2006). In addition, providing instructor's notes increases the effects of note-taking more than pre-training or verbal instructions only. This is believed to be attributable to the thoroughness and organization of instructor's note. In contrast, Hartley (2002) found that note-taking had little effect on learning and retention in nonacademic settings such as courtroom or counseling sessions.

The note-taking literature distinguishes, between *linear* and *matrix* notes that may be presented in a traditional paper format or as web-based notes. Linear notes are arranged in a hierarchical or list-like order, usually based on the chronological presentation of information in a text. For example, linear notes of the preceding paragraph might read as follows:

1. Definition of note-taking
2. Encoding and retrieval functions
3. Summary of recent reviews

    (a) Joint effect of encoding and retrieval study on learning
    (b) Effect of instructor's notes

Linear notes are one-dimensional in nature based on the order of information. Although it is possible to make comparisons across different information in linear notes, it is difficult to systematically compare information as it is in matrix notes.

Matrix notes utilize two or more dimensions to better compare and contrast information in a tabular format (Kauffman & Kiewra, 2010). In a typical two-dimensional set of matrix notes, with one dimension compares different categories of information (e.g., religions), while a second dimension contrasts those categories using the same set of variables (e.g., the existence of god, afterlife, or grace). Crooks and Cheon (this volume, Figure 8.1) provide an example of a two-dimensional matrix that compares different types of large cats (e.g., lion, panther) across a variety of variables (e.g., habitat, range, hunting behavior). Olafson, Feucht, and Marchand (this volume, Tables 15.1 and 15.3) compare and contrast different aspect of qualitative research processes and products using matrix displays. Similarly, Table 5.1 in this chapter compares the eight types of IVDs with respect to definition, purpose and examples. Using a two-dimensional set of matrix notes enables learners to make comparisons easier and to integrate information more completely (Robinson & Kiewra, 1995).

Web-based notes may include either linear of matrix-type displays that are presented to students using web-based applications. Students may also take notes using an empty note-taking shell (Kauffman et al., 2011), by cutting and pasting using a computer-based tool (Igo, Bruning, & McCrudden, 2005; Igo, Bruning, McCrudden, & Kauffman, 2003), or using partial (e.g., summary) or complete (e.g., verbatim) notes created by the instructor (Crooks & Katayama, 2002; Katayama & Crooks, 2001, 2003; Robinson et al., 2006). Generally, web- and computer-based notes are most effective when students are given a partially completed template and are then asked to complete the template with their own self-generated notes. There is no clear cut evidence that web-based notes are better; however, it may be easier to use and manipulated information in web-based settings that increases learning.

From an instructional standpoint, even college students are poor at taking notes and benefit from instruction (van der Merr, 2012). Ironically, many studies that have investigated note-taking do not actually teach students how to construct linear or matrix notes. Studies that teach note-taking typically focus on the encoding and external storage function of notes, a comparison of linear, matrix and computer notes, how to extract important information from a text into notes, and strategies for organizing information. Results consistently reveal that teaching students how to take different types of notes improves the note-taking process, as well as surface and deeper learning (Harati & Khomeini, 2011; Tsai & Wu, 2010; van der Merr, 2012).

Networks

Network displays consist of node-link representations that connect labeled nodes to one another via links denoting relationships (Nesbit & Adesope, 2006). Networks include explicit links between units of information that are implicit in linear and matrix notes. A distinction is made in the literature between concept maps and knowledge maps, where the former connect individual concepts or larger conceptual units to one another, while the later connect factual units (Jonassen et al., 1993; Novak & Gowan, 1985). Semantic and thematic maps consist of networks that link information in a text or themes by labeled relationships that describe the relationship between nodes. Definition maps link a key work to a definition, examples and words like it. Spider maps consist of a main idea as the center of the map once it is connected to subordinate concepts (Jonassen et al., 1993). All of these types of network diagrams work using the same principle of identifying a main concept and linking it to related concepts in a manner that promotes integrated conceptual understanding of an important concept.

The most common type of network display is a concept map. The typical concept map asks students to identify key information, link it explicitly with a named relationship (through an action word such as *is related to*), using arrowheads to indicate directionality (De Simone, 2007). Concept maps may be directional or non-directional, provided they are based on a core concept as the central starting point with links radiating outward to related concepts. Nesbit and Adesope (this volume) shows a concept map of climate change processes that distinguish between saline internal and external factors that cause significant climate change. Concept maps and other related techniques help learners to elaborate on an important concept and link the concept to other related concepts.

Network maps, which show the relationship among important nodes in a network, are also common in technical literature. Figure 5.2 shows a simple network map of the structure of the U.S. government, including the judicial, legislative, and executive branches. Like concept maps, network maps identify a main concept and link it to important supporting concepts. Network maps provide detailed organizational information about information related to the main concept. For example, in Figure 5.2, the network shows the relationship of three independent branches of the Federal government, as well as sub-branches of government within each of the three primary branches. Nevertheless, networks with explicit links may require inferences about important relationships. For example, in Figure 5.2, the conclusion that the three branches of government are independent of one another must be inferred.

De Simone (2007) described two instructional uses of concept mapping. One is to teach concept mapping as an external representational system to help students select, organize, and elaborate important concepts in a unit of study. This use of concept maps helps learners synthesize large amounts of information into smaller, better organized networks. The second is to use the external representation as extensions to internal representations (i.e., mental models) of a complex system (Wouters, Paas, & van Merriënboer, 2008). There are two advantages to this method, including less time allocated to constructing an external representation, and greater elaboration and integration to construct the internal representation. De Simone argued that both instructional uses may become more efficient when electronic software is used to create and modify concept maps. Doing so saves time and effort during the revision process, increases learning compared to a control group, introduces a variety of available software programs to students, and enables students and instruction to share

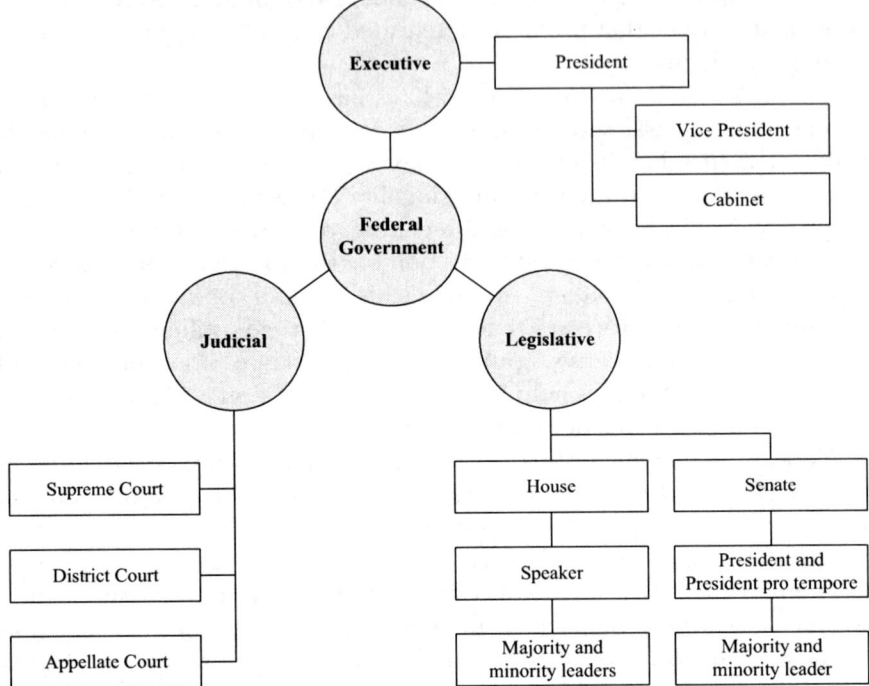

Figure 5.2.   A network diagram of the three branches of the United States federal government

information with other students, but especially those at a distance, more easily (Nesbit & Adesope, 2011).

More recently, Simon (2010) summarized four advantages of concept network maps during instructional planning. One is to identify the most relevant ideas to include in the curriculum. *Curriculum concept maps* do so by representing explicit concepts and relationships about a particular knowledge domain, and therefore provide greater curricular cohesion (Novak & Gowan, 1985). A second concerns how to sequence topics in the curriculum. Simon argues that while concept maps do not specify the sequence in which topics must be taught, they highlight a series of "valid sequences" that help educators evaluate the sequencing of topics. A third advantage considers the linkage between curriculum and texts. Curriculum concept maps may be especially helpful when there is no textbook that covers the knowledge domain, or when multiple texts and readings are used that otherwise are difficult to integrate. A fourth advantage is that network displays provide greater clarity when preparing examination and evaluation questions, in part because they highlight salient information and relationships, and in part because they provide a visual guide as to which concepts are most important and need to be assessed.

A recent meta-analysis of concept and knowledge maps reported four key findings (Nesbit & Adesope, 2006). On is that low-ability students may benefit more than high-ability learners when using concept maps. This may be due to the added value of an external representation and strategy instruction that compensates for low background knowledge or information processing skill. Second, concept maps appear to be equally effective when used by a single individual or in a peer-assisted group, although groups typically generate more sophisticated concept maps (Kwon & Cifuentes, 2009). Third, individual difference variables such as intelligence and spatial ability did not play a significant role in the use or potential benefit of concept maps. However, in more recent research that used hierarchical displays such as tree diagrams, prior knowledge was found to be a highly significant moderator of learning (Schwonke et al., 2009). For this reason, novices should be provided with adequate knowledge prior to constructing concept and knowledge maps. Fourth, concept maps appear to promote learning for central ideas more than peripheral ones. This likely is due to the fact that concept maps and network displays in general operate from the design principle of including the main concept in the center of the diagram and working outward. Overall, concept and knowledge maps were found to be more effective at promoting learning and transfer compared to lectures, reading without visual aids, or class discussions.

Sequences

Sequences represent a set of temporally ordered events. The ordering of the events are encoded in directed links called relationships. Linear notes and networks also represent ordered relationships; however, they differ from sequences in that they are not restricted to temporal ordering. For example, the ordering of linear notes are often based on the order in which information is presented in a text. While the relationships in sequences always imply some temporal order, the ordering may be causal or noncausal in nature.

At least five different types of sequential relationships have been reported in the literature, including timelines, flowcharts, argument diagrams, influence diagrams, and causal diagrams. Timelines convey a sequence of events over one or more past-to-present chronological timelines. Timelines increase learning, especially when comparing understanding within and between multiple timelines (e.g., events in world history, and the history of art and psychology simultaneously (Korallo, Foreman, Boyd-Davis, Moar, & Coulson, 2012). Flowcharts provide a visual representation of the operations in a multistep process. Although flowcharts share common structural elements with concept and network maps, they differ in at least two ways. One is that they also convey specific information about the temporal order between nodes, while a second is that nodes in a concept map represent concepts rather than states, dates or processes (e.g., Figure 10.2 in Van Meter & Firetto, this volume). Flowcharts increase learning of factual information, as well as creating better conceptual understanding of the relationships between elements in the flowchart (Davidowitz & Rollnick, 2005). Argument diagrams provide a visual representation of a logical argument as well as its non-linear and multidirectional structure (van Amelsvoort, Andriessen, & Kanselaar, 2008). Influence diagrams are visual models for representing complex decision-making processes using directional pathways among a variety of nodes that represent constraints and decision-making choices (Bielza, Gomez, & Shenoy, 2011). Finally, causal diagrams use arrows to depict directional cause-and-effect relationships among sequenced events (McCrudden, Schraw, Lehman, & Poliquin, 2007). Research indicates that all of these displays improve learning and deeper understanding, especially following instruction that helps learners understand the structure of displays and use them to make inferences.

Several different types of sequential displays are discussed in this volume, including argument diagrams in Andriessen and Baker (this volume) and causal diagrams in Poliquin and Schraw (this volume). We do not discuss these displays now because they are discussed in detail in upcoming chapters. However, we note three general characteristics of sequential displays. One is that sequences are temporally ordered using either a timeline or by describing a sequence that is time sensitive (e.g., x occurs before y, which occurs before z). This enables sequential diagrams to situate events in time, order events, and describe the relationship between events at the same time or across time. A second characteristic is that sequences specify directional or causal relationships explicitly in which one variable influences another. Third, sequences are effective at modeling a complex process or dynamic system in order to better understand how systems change and the dynamic interplay among variables within the system. For example, Zhang (2008) illustrates how causal diagrams may be used to model ancestral relationships and the role of genotype and ancestral behaviors on proximal (e.g., smoking) and distal (e.g., lung cancer) indicators.

Studies in a wide variety of disciplines consistently show that students need instruction to make effective use of sequential IVDs, but to improve deep learning. For example, Vella (2011) found that a simple coloring technique used to identify historical changes increased learning at levels of conceptual difficulty. Korallo et al. (2012) found that timelines presented in virtual computer environments increased learning more than traditional booklet timelines even though both conditions increased learning compared to no supplemental timelines. One explanation of this outcome was that the computer environment better integrated the timeline with text information. Canter and Atkinson (2010) reported that flowcharts facilitated the learning and necessary adaptations associated with adaptive management programs and that flowcharts help to develop an holistic perspective on management choices. Practice using and interpreting flowcharts also increased learning substantially (Davidowitz & Rollnick, 2005; Michael & Hartley, 1991). Argument diagrams likewise promote deeper learning and better arguments, provided that student are given instruction in how to use and interpret diagrams, but especially in how to label and understand labeled relationships in the diagram (Andriessen & Baker, this volume; van Amelsvoort et al., 2008). Instruction with causal diagrams increases both surface and deeper learning (McCrudden et al., 2007; McCrudden, Schraw, & Lehman, 2009), but also has a significant positive impact on the construction and sophistication of causal schemata that appear to generalize beyond the specific learning tasks of a study (Kemp, Goodman, & Tenenbaum, 2010; Jonassen & Ionas, 2008). Thus, teaching specific information using a causal diagram may help students better understand the nature and entailments of causality in a more general sense.

Hierarchies

Hierarchies show ordered categorical relationships among concepts (e.g., a taxonomy) or ordered pathways between one event and another (e.g., a decision tree). Hierarchies often include sequential information; however, they also include information about the generality of a category of information that subsumes categories or events within it. Hierarchical displays may be used for a variety of purposes, including to classify a large set of data or variables into discrete categories, to show qualitatively different levels of complexity as in a taxonomy, or to show all possible pathways and outcomes in a set of hypothetical events.

We distinguished between two classic examples of hierarchical displays which we refer to as *classification trees* and *dendrograms*. Classification trees are used to partition a domain of information into discrete, ordered subsets as in Figure 5.3, which shows different types of knowledge in long-term memory. In this example, semantic knowledge may be partitioned into increasingly finer-grained units such as schemata, concepts embedded within a schema, facts embedded within a concept, and propositions embedded within facts (Schraw, 2006). In contrast, a dendrogram depicts a hierarchical clustering of events or objects into an exhaustive partition of outcomes. Dendrograms include a variety of similar representations techniques based on the common method of subdividing one node into two or more nodes, including game and probability trees, cladograms, decision trees, hierarchical clustering methods, and parse trees. A simple dendrogram appears in Figure 7.1 of Renkl and Schwonke (this volume), which shows an exhaustive partition of the probability of 20 discrete outcomes.

Jonassen et al. (1993) highlight several strengths and weaknesses of hierarchical displays. One strength is that hierarchical displays partition a more-inclusive set into smaller subsets. For example, Figure 5.1 shows that the set of IVDs may be partitioned into smaller sets with unique properties that help learners focus on selected types of knowledge within a much larger display. Second, most hierarchical diagrams are easy to construct and use and do not require special training beyond orienting instructions. Third, hierarchical diagrams may provide a broad conceptual framework of a domain of knowledge or set of events that is easier to display visually than to describe in words. For this reason, hierarchies can be thought of as a special type of concept map, where all the relationships are restricted to "consists of." Unlike other IVDs such as concept maps,

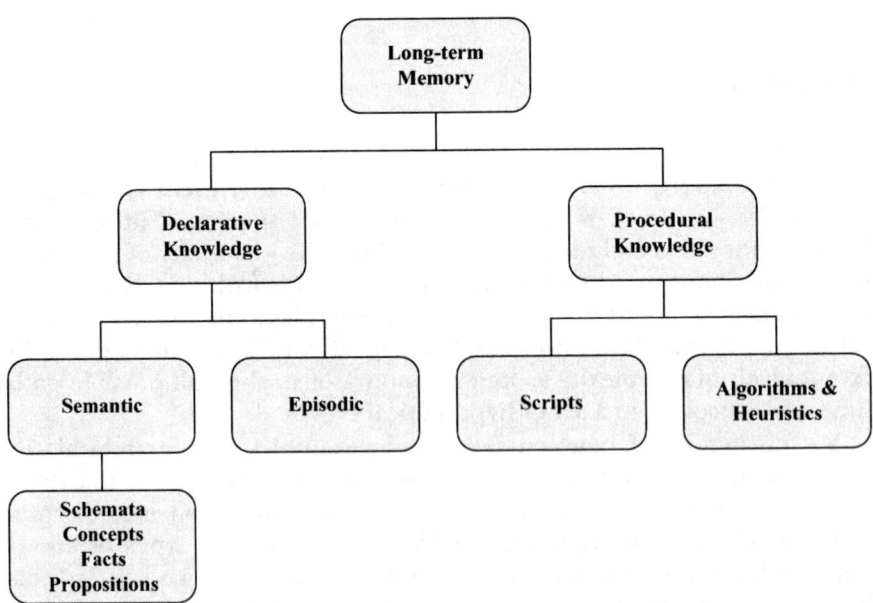

Figure 5.3   Partial classification of knowledge in long-term memory.

hierarchical IVDs typically do not explicitly display information about the type of relationships because all the relationships are of the same type (i.e., *X* is subordinate of *Y*).

There are surprisingly few instructional studies using hierarchical diagrams compared to other types of IVDs. Of those we located, all suggested that a wide variety of hierarchical displays appear in educational contexts and that students receive little or no instruction about how to use or create them. In a sample of high school biology texts, Catley and Novick (2008) found that most textbooks used a variety of hierarchical displays, that many displays intended to illustrate evolutionary processes were inaccurate, and that texts and classroom instruction provided no explicit instruction in how to use and interpret the diagrams. Also, some displays were more difficult than others. For example, a number of misconceptions occurred when students were asked to create cladograms (i.e., a representation that shows which taxonomy have branched from common ancestors) to map evolutionary processes (Halverson, Pires, & Abell, 2011; Meir, Perry, Herron, & Kingsolver, 2007). These included incorrect mapping of time, misunderstanding of species relationships based on map proximity, mistaking map nodes for evolutionary changes, and misinterpreting a straight line as an indicator of no evolutionary change. Glazer (2011) identified an additional 12 common problems with graph interpretation related to these misconceptions.

One study also reported that some types of IVDs may promote more or deeper learning than others. Dabbagh and Denisar (2005) compared hierarchical displays (i.e., a tree diagram) to a heterarchical display (i.e., a network diagram) and found greater learning and transfer for the network group. They attributed this finding to the fact that networks provided explicit links between nodes and that network typically focused on a concept of central importance, which was situated at the center of the network display. Collectively, these studies indicated that hierarchical displays are common, but may be more difficult to understand than other types of displays. Studies that included high school and college students revealed that even older students in advanced science classes experienced trouble understanding them, even though this may be attributable to the amount and unfamiliarity of content knowledge.

Distributions and Trend Graphs

Distributional displays show the frequency or probability of an event over a range of scores. For this reason, they share a number of characteristics with sequential displays and spatial proximity displays such as pie diagrams discussed below. However, one important purpose of distributional displays is to show a change in data or a trend over time as a function of one or more variables such as the likelihood of an outcome in a normal distribution given a specific sample mean or variance.

Trend line graphs show the relationship between one variable across levels of a second variable. Both distributions and trend graphs are common in statistics, mathematics, and science textbooks. For example, Figure 14.1 in Pastor and Finney (this volume) used linear regression trendlines to show the difference between high-motivation and low-motivation subgroups as a function of age and time. Distributions and trend graphs appear to be better at summarizing data, showing trends, and showing points and patterns, whereas tables are better for understanding point estimates such as means and standard deviations (Jarvenpaa & Dickson, 1988; Lane & Sandor, 2009). Nevertheless, most IVDs in psychology journals consist largely of bar charts, frequency tables, and pie diagrams rather than distributions (Lane & Sandor, 2009). We discuss these below under the category of spatial proximity diagrams.

Distributional displays provide important information about score density, variability, and skewness and kurtosis. A comparison among different distributional families also helps students understand statistical modeling and the behavior of data (Wagner, 2007). For example, it is common in beginning statistics classes to transform a normal distribution of raw scores into a standard normal diction of z scores. The use of overlapping distributions also is helpful for illustrating effect size, the likelihood of type I and II errors, and statistical power (Kirk, 1994). Trend graphs complement distributional information and are especially well suited for showing changing trends and interactions between variables across different experimental condition. Unfortunately, misunderstanding trend lines is a common problem among students in the sciences, including college students (Glazer, 2011).

Lane and Sandor (2009) provided three general suggestions for constructing effective distributional and trend graphs based on previous research (Kosslyn, 1993; Tufte, 2001) that are applicable to other IVDs. One is to limit the amount of information in the representation to only what is needed; that is, to eliminate any extraneous information. A second is to highlight important information using signaling techniques. A third is to select the type of representation that is best suited to convey the desired information so that the desired conclusions are drawn from the data). These strategies help to reduce the complexity and, thereby, the cognitive demands of the IVDs.

Maps and Spatial Proximity Diagrams

A map shows the scaled spatial relationships among coordinates within a specified locale, while spatial contiguity displays show the similarity or proximity between two or more objects. Maps provide a geographical or topological representation of a place (e.g., North American cities or a star atlas) or system (e.g., an electrical circuit or bus routing system), providing over 50 interpretable dimensions of information (e.g., contour, coordinates, distance, latitude) depending on the type of map (Gillen, Skryzhevska, Henry, & Green, 2010). Geographical maps are ubiquitous in geography and science textbooks, and appear in many popular magazines. One common type of display is a geographical density map that shows the concentration of services such as popular restaurants or cell phone coverage in a designated area. Maps are used frequently to provide information about the relative proportion of language, religion, ethnicity, occupation and weather features in different regions of a locale. They also are accessible via Internet sites and cell phone GPS systems to virtually all adults with even minimal technological access.

Geographical and topological maps are both symbolic and spatial in nature and require the learner to decipher spatial relationships among its symbolic components (Liben, 2009). Students must understand that symbolic marks on a surface stand for environmental features (e.g., elevation) and how representational space (e.g., scale) is used to depict a larger environmental space. Many people receive limited formal instruction on how to use and interpret maps, which leads to poor map reading skills. Limited instruction is compounded in part by age-linked abilities to perform symbolic and spatial map reasoning (Liben, 2009; Liben & Downs, 1993), as well as instructional texts that frequently address fewer than 50% of common map interpretation terms (Gillen et al., 2010). One particular problem is that younger students fail to learn cognitive translation skills which enable them to generate a two-dimensional schematic representation of a three-dimensional environment. Given these difficulties, research shows that formal instruction improves learning and map use, but especially when accompanied by explicit self-explanation of map features and the use of reasoning skills needed to perform map translation (Clark et al., 2008; Kastens & Liben, 2007). Even college students experience these problems and find it significantly easier to translate and navigate when maps are present during the navigation task (Schwartz, Verdi, Morris, Lee, & Larson, 2007). Although spatial ability is related to map understanding, studies consistently show that instructional training helps to improve understanding and map use above and beyond the effect of spatial ability (Clark et al., 2008).

Many types of charts, diagrams and graphs are similar to traditional maps in that they reveal spatial proximity between variables. Important differences exist, however. One is that maps represent the distance between objects in Euclidean space while abstract graphs may plot variables in terms of abstract concepts such as time or "student engagement."

Pie diagrams, venn diagrams, and histograms are good examples of proximity measures. Proximity also may be modeled in two-dimensional space using multidimensional scaling and clustering techniques (Jonassen et al., 1993). These techniques typically rely on the use of a Euclidean distance measure to scale data points in two or three dimensions based on distance from each other. Commonly used statistical examples include factor analysis, cluster analysis, and multidimensional scaling.

Animations

An animation may be defined as a series of changing pictures or images that show movement or moment-to-moment change in an ongoing process (Höffler & Leutner, 2007). Researches have compared the effect of animations and static visualizations and found that animations yield consistent positive effect on learning compared to static images when they are directive (i.e., provides signaling support for accompanying narration). While the meta-analysis of relative instructional efficacies of static and dynamic images by Höffler & Leutner (2007) indicated that representational animation (i.e., animation that depict the dynamic behavior of dynamic systems) showed that the studies included in the meta-analysis aggregated to a moderately positive effect on learning, more recent animation effect studies (e.g., Paik & Schraw, 2012; Mayer, Hegarty, Mayer, & Campbell, 2005; Schnotz & Rasch, 2005) indicate that cognitive effects of animation may be more complex. Schnotz and Rasche (2005) have argued that animation can enable or facilitate individuals to mentally visualize the behavior of dynamic systems that they would be unable to or have difficulty with only static images. Mayer et al. (2005) have argued that animation has the potential to diminish the germane cognitive processes by eliminating the need to mentally simulate the behavior of system being presented. An animation also may provide an external model that can be used to construct an internal mental representation or model of a complex system or process. However, studies consistently find that animations are more effective with high-knowledge learners and individuals with high working memory capacity (cf. Höffler, Schmeck, & Opfermann, this volume).

Spatial ability and prior knowledge are especially important moderators of animation effectiveness (Ruiz, Cook, & Levinson, 2009). Höffler & Leutner (2011) found that high spatial ability learners outperformed low ability students when learning from static pictures, while there was no difference due to ability when learning from animations. A meta-analysis of animation effects reported that animation improves learning compared to static pictures and that this effect was sometimes stronger for low spatial ability learners. One possible explanation is that animation reduces cognitive load with respect to constructing a mental sequence and therefore may help learners with fewer cognitive resources or lower spatial ability (Ke, Lin, Ching, & Dwyer, 2006). Another explanation is that animation can have different metacognitive influences across among learners. Paik and Schraw (2012) showed that replacing static images with animations induced different forms of illusion of understanding. In high proficient learners, animation induced the pessimistic form (i.e., animation learners were more pessimistic than static image learners when the effects of learning was statistically removed). In contrast, animation induced the optimistic form with low proficient learners. Animations and static graphics also are more effective for individual with prior knowledge or those who receive pretraining, in part, due to strategic allocation of attentional resources (Cook, Wiebe, & Carter, 2007; Wouters et al., 2008). Use of animated pedagogical agents and tutors enhance learning as well, due in part to the their ability to provide relevant background knowledge, simulate learning strategies, reduce cognitive load, provide instructional models, and integrate multiple sources of information into a single conceptual model (Reed, 2005; Woo, 2009).

Researchers have proposed a number of design guidelines for using animations and animated pedagogical agents (Plass, Homer, & Hayward, 2009). One common recommendation is to use animations to promote self-explanation via targeted prompts (de Koning, Tabbers, Rikers, & Paas, 2010). Wouters et al. (2008) proposed three general guidelines that included managing the complexity of subject matter, eliminating obstacles due to poor design that obstruct learning, and helping learners to engage in the active and relevant processing of subject matter. Reducing the complexity of material and organizing to-be-learned information decrease cognitive load. In addition, providing relevant background knowledge, pretraining, and increasing student motivation helps learners to utilize their processing capacity more effectively.

SUMMARY

The typology in Figure 5.1 attempts to classify a wide array of commonly used IVDs based on the instructional purpose of the representation. We created eight nonmutually exclusive categories in an attempt to summarize the key properties and instructional uses of different types of displays. We view our typology as a starting point regarding how to define, classify, and investigate different types of IVDs. Table 5.1 provides general definitions and examples of eight types of displays and subtypes within each category.

At a broader level, all of the displays in Figure 5.1 facilitate learning in four ways. One is that they help learners focus on important information by selecting and highlighting the most relevant concepts in an otherwise large amount of to-be-learned information. IVDs do so by signaling and winnowing information into representations that eliminate redundant and superfluous information and organize remaining information based on the most important concepts and interrelationships among concepts (De Simone, 2007; Höffler & Leutner, 2007; Jonassen et al., 1993; Mayer, 2005, this volume). Reducing large amounts of information into smaller, well-organized displays enables learners to focus their attention on the most important relationships among main concepts (Mautone & Mayer, 2007; Schnotz, 2002; Vekiri, 2002).

A second way that IVDs improve learning is that they reduce and organize information in a manner that reveals the most important relationships and complex processes among concepts. These relationships often must be inferred from a single text or multiple sources of information that the learner is expected to integrate and interpret on their own. Unfortunately, research indicates that even college students are poor at interpreting complex external graphs and representations on their own and benefit significantly from formal instruction and feedback from experts (de Koning et al., 2010; Nesbit & Adesope, 2006; Plass et al., 2009). Nevertheless, scaffolded instruction significantly improves students' ability to read, interpret and construct graphs of all types. Research also suggests that even brief instructional interventions provide substantial benefits when using a variety of IVDs (Harati & Khomeini, 2011; Kauffman et al., 2011; Lorch et al., 2011; Nesibt, this volume; Poliquin & Schraw, this volume).

A third instructional benefit of displays is that they help learners to instantiate external information into internal mental models that improve comprehension of important information and subsequent reasoning about that information (Jonassen & Ionas, 2008; Kemp et al. 2010; Kosslyn, 1993; Reed, 2005). One of the greatest challenges of learning is to extract important information from external representations, organize that information into an integrated conceptual model, and represent that model internally in long term memory in a manner that promotes subsequent learning and critical thinking about the information (Abrami et al., 2008; Dunbar & Fugelsang, 2005; Glazer, 2011; Halpern, 2007; Johnson-Laird, 2004). Research suggests that IVDs help learners internalize mental models and use these models to think critically about complex phenomena, provided novices receive adequate instruction that includes step-by-step strategies and informational feedback (CITES; Novak & Gowan, 1985; Poliqun & Schraw, this volume).

A fourth benefit is that well-designed IVDs reduce extraneous cognitive load associated with learning a large amount of complex information (Kalyuga et al., 2000; Plass et al., 2009; Sweller, 1999; Wouters et al., 2008). Cognitive load may be reduced in two complementary ways, either by reducing the total amount of information through elimination of unimportant and redundant information, or by distributing load across different linguistically-based versus spatially-based modalities (Schnotz, 2002; van Merriënboer & Sweller, 2005). Research shows that verbal and spatial channels utilize independent limited-capacity cognitive resources; thus, distributing load across these channels has the effect of increasing total processing capacity.

In addition, Glazer (2011) summarized a number of personal and situational factors that affect learning from IVDs, including the learner's prior knowledge and spatial skill, as well as a host of characteristics related to the size and complexity of the display. Each of these is discussed in greater detail in other chapters in this volume (Höffler, Schmeck, & Opfermann; Kalyuga; Low et al.; Mayer; Renkl & Schwonke). These studies overwhelmingly indicate that students of all ages and skill levels experience difficulty understanding displays. For this reason, Glazer recommended a three-step instructional sequence in which learners are taught to read and extract data from graphs, to make inferences using graphs about the meaning and implications of the data in the graph, and how to create graphs to convey thematic information and trends that is consistent with other researchers (Roth & Bowen, 2001; Wainer, 1992). These strategies have been shown to help learners adjust to personal and situational factors that decrease the effectiveness of learning.

Consistent with Glazer (2011), our review suggests four conclusions related to classroom instruction of IVDs. One is that displays of all types are ubiquitous in textbooks and classroom instruction, especially at high school and college classrooms. It is unclear based on a literature review whether some types of displays are more common or difficult to understand than others. However, it is clear that all types are relatively common, especially in the sciences, and that even college students find it difficult to interpret complex IVDs (Catley & Novick, 2008; Lane & Sandor, 2009). A second conclusion is that many students experience difficulty reading and interpreting IVDs, including otherwise highly self-regulated college students (Davidowitz & Rollnick, 2005; Glazer, 2011; Gillen et al., 2010). A third is that there is far too little formal instruction on reading, interpreting, and generating graphs. Indeed, most studies that examined student understanding did not include a formal instructional component of any type. It appears that most students in most types of classes throughout their schooling are expected to acquire visual literacy skills on their own. A fourth conclusion is that instruction helps to improve reading, interpreting and constructing IVDs, but especially when students lack relevant knowledge and spatial reasoning skills. Our review suggests that the interpretation of displays is especially difficult and fraught with error, which improves markedly given even limited instruction (Davidowitz & Rollnick, 2005; De Simone, 2007; Liben, 2009; Schwonke et al., 2009; van der Meer, 2012).

SIX ISSUES FOR FUTURE THEORY AND RESEARCH

Figure 5.1 shows eight categories in a descriptive typology of IVDs. Our goal thus far in this chapter has been to categorize displays discussed in this volume into different categories to highlight the different structural properties and purposes of commonly used IVDs. No doubt our typology could be expanded upon in terms of categories and types of displays. In addition, questions arise about the similar and unique features of displays shown in Figure 1 that we did not address. In this section, we identify six issues for future research that must be addressed in order to develop a comprehensive design and instructional framework for IVDs.

The most pressing issue to address in our opinion is to develop a comprehensive theoretical framework of IVDs that guides design and instruction. A number of authors have considered categorization schemes (Desnoyers, 2011; Heer et al., 2010; Jonassen et al., 1993; Morse & Lewis, 2000; Rodriguez & Dimitrova, 2011) and general design principles of IVDs (Lane & Sandor, 2009; Kosslyn, 1993; Tufte, 2001). Unfortunately, existing typologies have little in common, nor has there been a systematic comparison of different typologies to identify common and unique categorization principles. One suggestion is to conduct a review and comparative analysis of typologies to identify criteria that might be used to construct a comprehensive typology. This type of analysis may reveal a large assortment of criteria that could be used to develop a typology. Ideally, a careful analysis would winnow the set of criteria in order to develop a comprehensive typology, or provide an argument why a narrow set of criteria is not attainable.

A second issue is to identify common and unique information processing demands across different categories in the typology or even across different types of displays within a category. Theories of information processing efficiency such as cognitive load theory (Sweller, 1999) and multimedia learning theory (Mayer, 2005) have developed a variety of principles (e.g., expert reversal effect; modality effect) that constrain the use of limited cognitive resources while processing complex visual and auditory information. Presently, it is not clear whether these principles apply to the same extent across different types of IVDs. By the same token, little is known about the relative cognitive demand of different types of IVDs. Some may require specific processing skills or strategies that others do not. For example, distributional displays probably require e degree of probabilistic reasoning that is unnecessary when viewing geographical maps. Some may require a specific type of reasoning as well. For example, complex causal displays may require learners to reasoning about direct and indirect causality in a way that is not necessary when using notes or concept maps.

A third issue is to investigate whether some types of displays are better suited to particular communicative arguments. For example, causal diagrams are ideally suited to convey causality among a set of variables in a way that matrix notes are not. We assume that each category in Figure 5.1 and each type of display within that category has specific features that make it best suited for conveying certain types of information (cf. Jonassen et al., 1993). Although the uniqueness of each type of display seems obvious, there has been very little comparative research that has examined whether some displays communicate information more effectively than others, either in terms of processing time, or amount of learning. One possible benefit of this research would be to identify specific features of a display (e.g., a timeline) that could be added to a different display (e.g., a geographical map) to create a hybrid display that meets two or more instructional purposes.

A fourth issue is to develop a better instructional technology for improving understanding from IVDs (Pettersson, 2010). Research supports four conclusions thus far, including: (a) students of all ages do not use displays optimally (van der Meer, 2012), (b) some displays are easier to understand and promote learning more than others (Nesbit & Adesope, 2006), (c) prompts and self-explanation facilitate the use of displays (de Koning, 2010; Clark et al., 2008), and (d) IVDs often increase both shallow and deeper learning (Bohay et al., 2011; McCrudden et al., 2007; Vella, 2011). Notwithstanding these conclusions, little is known about how instructional strategies are affected by IVDs. One especially important instructional question is how to teach learners to use IVDs in a manner that optimizes deeper conceptual processing.

A fifth issue is to develop a better understanding of the role of individual variables when using IVDs. Two types of variables have been discussed in the literature, including prior knowledge and spatial ability. Research confirms that IVDs are more effective with individuals with high knowledge and high spatial ability (Höffler et al., this volume; Renkl & Schwonke, this volume). One explanation is that both of these dimensions provide information processing advantages that allow learners to focus more resources on the display itself, thereby increasing learning. In contrast, individuals with low knowledge or low spatial ability learn less when provided with displays. Although there is agreement that knowledge and spatial ability increase learning, it is less clear whether they interact with one another, or are affected by self-efficacy to use IVDs. More research is needed about the moderating effect of individual characteristics such as knowledge, spatial ability, and reasoning skills, as well as motivational variables such as interest and self-efficacy.

A sixth issue is to develop and investigate a set of guiding design principles for constructing IVDs. Very few studies have done so empirically, although there are a number of authors who have provided general design principles (Jonassen et al., 1993; Lane & Sandor, 2009; Kosslyn, 1993, Tufte, 2001). Currently, it is unclear whether there are a set of domain-general (i.e., *universal*) design principles that guide the construction and use of all types of displays, or if some displays have domain-specific (i.e., *encapsulated*) design principles. Most principles that we identified appeared to be universal in nature. Some principles appeared in the literature using a variety of different names even though they referred to the same design principle. We identified four principles that we refer to as *interpretative fidelity, visual guidance, structural coherence*, and *efficiency*. Interpretative fidelity occurs when a displays conveys the designer's intended meaning (Kosslyn, 1993; Lane & Sanders, 2009). Visual guidance occurs when the structure of information or signals within the display guides the learner through the comprehension process (Hegarty, Canham, & Fabrikant, 2010). Structural coherence occurs when the components of the display and the processes or contents they describe are aligned clearly (Tufte, 2001). Efficiency occurs when a visual display includes only what is necessary in a visual array that minimizes mental computations and cognitive load (Mayer, 2005; Sweller, 1999). These principles are not intended to be exhaustive. Rather, we argue that researchers should propose and validate a comprehensive set of design principles that include the four principles described here. Researchers also should distinguish between universal versus encapsulated principles and determine which of these principles have the greatest impact on usability and learning.

CONCLUSIONS

This chapter proposed an eight-category typology of IVDs. We argued that each type of display has a somewhat unique instructional purpose even though all types of displays share at least four common properties that facilitate learning. These include helping learners identify important information, organize information, incorporate external information in a display into an internalized mental model, and reduce extraneous cognitive load by distributing information. No doubt a better articulated theory of IVDs could expand on this list.

We also discussed six issues that must be addressed in future research to improve the design and use of IVDs. These included the need for a unifying framework for IVDs, a better understanding of common and unique information processing demands of each type of display, investigating whether some types of displays are better suited to particular communicative arguments, effective instructional strategies, the role of person characteristics such as spatial ability and knowledge, and a discussion of domain-general and domain-specific design principles when constructing IVDs. Implicit within this discussion was the assumption that an overarching theory of IVDs is needed to better understand how and why they improve learning. We argued that existing theories of multimedia learning focus on the type of resources that learners use to process information and general learning principles that affect the use of resources. However, these theories do not address structural differences per se among different types of IVDs; nor is it clear what type of information processing demands each type of displays imposes on learners.

Although there have been several meta-analyses on specific types of IVDs such as concept maps (Nesbit & Adesope, 2006) and animations (Höffler & Leutner, 2007), there has not been a meta-analysis that cuts across the eight categories shown in Figure 5.1. A similar argument can be made for previous literature reviews that have focused on specific types of IVDs (Bohay et al., 2011; Hartley, 2002) with the exception of Glazer (2011). Nevertheless, our review of the literature for this chapter suggests four broad themes based on empirical findings. One is that displays frequently increase learning by helping individual to select and organize salient information. A second is displays may reduce cognitive load and processing effort because they provide higher-level organization and integrate of information, complex relationships, and processes prior to or during study. A third is that all types of IVDs require dedicated instruction to be used effectively, even among otherwise self-regulated college students. A fourth is that well-designed displays work best, but especially those that are presented contiguous to text information, are not overly redundant, provide explicit representation of otherwise implicit relationships and processes, and provide close alignment between the type of display and the intended learning outcome.

It is clear from our review that a wide variety of IVDs are used commonly in classroom situations. It also is clear that teachers and text designers believe that IVDs enhance learning—an assumption that may not be true among low-knowledge or low-ability learners. Far more research and theory are needed to construct a unified understanding of the role of IVDs. We suggest at minimum an effort to construct a theory of displays, an integrated typology, guidelines for using displays in texts and classroom instruction, and a set of general and display-specific design principles.

REFERENCES

Abrami, P. C., Bernard, R. M., Borokhovski, E., Wade, A., Surkes, M. A., Tamim, R., & Zhang, D. (2008). Instructional interventions affecting critical thinking skills and dispositions: A stage 1 meta-analysis. *Review of Educational Research, 78*, 1102–1134.

Bielza, C., Gomez, M., & Shenoy, P. P. (2011). A review of representation issues and modeling challenges with influence diagrams *Omega, 39*, 227-241.

Bohay, M., Blakely, D. P., Tamplin, A. K., &. Radvansky, G. A. (2011). Note-taking, review, memory, and comprehension. *The American Journal of Psychology, 124*, 63-73.

Cain, K., & Nash, H. M. (2011). The influence of connectives on young readers' processing and comprehension of text. *Journal of Educational Psychology, 103*, 429-441.

Canter, L., & Atkinson, S. F. (2010). Adaptive management with integrated decision making: An emerging tool for cumulative effects management. *Impact Assessment and Project Appraisal, 28*, 287-297.

Catley, K. M., & Novick, L. R. (2008). Seeing the wood for the trees: An analysis of evolutionary diagrams in biology textbooks. *BioScience, 58*, 976-989.

Cauchard, F., Eyrolle, H., Cellier, J. M., & Hyona, J. (2010). Vertical perceptual span and the processing of visual signals in reading. *International Journal of Psychology, 45*, 40-47.

Clark, D., Reynolds, S., Lemanowski, V., Stiles, T, Yasar, S., Proctor, S., ... Corkins, J. (2008). University students' conceptualization and interpretation of topographic maps. *International Journal of Science Education, 30*, 375–406.

Cook, M., Wiebe, E . N., & Carter, G. (2007). The influence of prior knowledge on viewing and interpreting graphics with macroscopic and molecular representations. *Science Education, 92*, 848-867.

Crooks, S. M., & Katayama, A. D. (2002). Effects of study note format on the comprehension of electronic text. *Research in the Schools, 9*, 21-32.

Dabbagh, N., & Denisar, K. (2005). Assessing team-based instructional design problem solutions of hierarchical versus heterarchical web-based hypermedia cases. *Educational Technology Research & Development, 53*, 5-23.

Daley, B. J., & Torre, D. M. (2010). Concept maps in medical education: an analytical literature review. *Medical Education, 44*, 440-448.

Davidowitz, B. & Rollnick, M. (2005). Development and application of a rubric for analysis of novice students' laboratory flow diagrams. *International Journal of Science Education, 27*, 43-59.

De Koning, B. B., Tabbers, H. K., Rikers, R. M. J. P., & Paas, F. (2009). Towards a framework for attention cueing in instructional animations: Guidelines for research and design. *Educational Psychology Review*, 21, 113-140.

De Koning, B., B., Tabbers, H. K., Rikers, R. M. J., & Paas, F. (2010). Learning by generating vs. receiving instructional explanations: Two approaches to enhance attention cueing in animations. *Computers & Education, 55*, 681-691.

De Simone, C. (2007). Applications of concept mapping. *College Teaching, 55*, 33-27.

Desnoyers, L. (2011). Toward a taxonomy of visuals in science communication. *Applied Theory, 58*, 119-134.

Dunbar, K., & Fugelsang, J. (2005). Scientific reasoning and thinking. In K. Holyoak & R. Morrison (Eds.), *The Cambridge handbook of thinking and reasoning* (pp. 705-726). Cambridge, England: Cambridge University Press.

Eichelberger, H. & Schmid, K. (2009). Guidelines on the aesthetic quality of UML class diagrams. *Information and Software Technology, 51*, 1686-1698.

Gillen, J., Skryzhevska, L., Henry, M. C. & Green, J. (2010). Map interpretation instruction in introductory textbooks: A preliminary investigation. *Journal of Geography, 109*, 181-189.

Glazer, N. (2011). Challenges with graph interpretation: a review of the literature. *Studies in Science Education, 47*, 183-210.

Graham M., Kennedy, J., & Benyon, D. (2000). Towards a methodology for developing visualizations. *International Journal of Human-Computer Studies, 53*, 789-807.

Halpern, D. F. (2007). The nature and nurture of critical thinking. In R. J. Sternberg, H. L. Roediger & D. F. Halpern (Eds.), *Critical thinking in psychology* (pp. 1-14). Cambridge, England: Cambridge University Press.

Halverson, K. L., Pires, C. J., & Abell, S. K. (2011). Exploring the complexity of tree thinking expertise in an undergraduate systematics. *Science Education, 95*, 794-823.

Harati, N. A., & Khomeini, I. (2011). Fostering lecture note takers' autonomy through strategies-based instruction. *Modern Journal of Language Teaching Methods, 1*, 53-65.

Hartley, J. (2002). Notetaking in Non-Academic Settings: A Review. *Applied Cognitive Psychology, 16*, 559–574.

Heer, J., Bostock, M., & Ogievetsky, V. (2010). A tour through the visualization zoo. *Communications of the ACM, 53*, 59-67.

Hegarty, M., Canham, M. S., & Fabrikant, S. I. (2010). Thinking about the weather: How display salience and knowledge affect performance in a graphic inference task. *Journal of Experimental Psychology: Learning, Memory, and Cognition, 36*, 37-53.

Höffler, T. N, & Leutner, D. (2007). Instructional animation versus static pictures: A meta-analysis. *Learning and Instruction , 17*, 722-738.

Igo, L. B., Bruning, R. B., & McCrudden, M. T. (2005). Exploring differences in students' copy-and-paste decision making and processing: A mixed-methods study. *Journal of Educational Psychology, 97*, 103-116.

Igo, L. B., Bruning, R. B., McCrudden, M., & Kauffman, D. (2003). Infogather: A tool for gathering and organizing information from the Web. In R. Bruning, C. Horn, & L. PytlikZilling (Eds.), *Web based learning: What do we know? Where do we go?* (pp. 57-77). Greenwich, CT: Information Age Publishing.

Jarvenpaa, S., & Dickson, G. W. (1988). Graphics and managerial decision making: Research based guidelines. *Communications of the ACM, 31,* 764-774.

Jeung, H., Chandler, P., & Sweller, J. (1997). The role of visual indicators in dual sensory mode instruction. *Educational Psychology, 17,* 329-343.

Jonassen, D. H., Beissner, K., & Yacci, M. (1993). *Structural knowledge: Techniques for assessing, conveying,and acquiring structural knowledge.* Hilsdale, NJ: Lawrence Erlbaum.

Jonassen, D. H., & Ionas, I. G. (2008). Designing effective supports for causal reasoning. *Educational Technology Research and Development, 56,* 287-308.

Johnson-Laird, P. N. (2004). Mental models and reasoning. In J. Leighton & R. Sternberg (Eds.), *The nature of reasoning* (pp. 169-201). Cambridge, England: Cambridge University Press.

Kalyuga, S., Chandler, P., & Sweller, J. (2000). Incorporating learner experience into the design of multimedia instruction. *Journal of Educational Psychology, 92,* 126-136.

Kastens, K. A., & Liben, L. S. (2007). Eliciting self-explanations improves children's performance on a field-based map skills task. *Cognition and Instruction, 25,* 45-74.

Katayama, A. D., & Crooks, S. M. (2001). Examining the effects of notetaking format on achievement when students construct and study computerized notes. *The Learning Assistance Review, 6,* 5-23.

Katayama, A. D., & Crooks, S. M. (2003). Online notes: Differential effects of studying complete or partial graphically organized notes. *Journal of Experimental Education, 71,* 293-312.

Kauffman, D. F., & Kiewra, K. (2010). What makes the matrix so effective: An empirical test of indexing, extraction, and localization effects. *Instructional Science, 38,* 679-706.

Kauffman, D. F., Zhao, R., & Yang, Y. (2011). Effects of online note taking formats and self-monitoring prompts on learning from online text: Using technology to enhance self-regulated learning. *Contemporary Educational Psychology, 36,* 313-322.

Ke, F., Lin, H., Ching, Y., & Dwyer, F. (2006). Effects of animation on multi-level learning outcomes for learners with different characteristics: A meta-analytic assessment and interpretation. *Journal of Visual Literacy, 26,* 15-40.

Kemp, C., Goodman, N. D., & Tenenbaum, J. B. (2010). Learning to learn causal models. *Cognitive Science, 34,* 1185-1243.

Kiewra, K. 1989. A review of note-taking: The encoding-storage paradigm and beyond. *Educational Psychology Review 1,* 147-172.

Kirk, R. E. (1994). *Experimental design: Procedures for the Behavioral sciences* (2nd ed.). Belmont, CA: Brooks-Cole.

Kobayashi, K. (2005). What limits the encoding effect of note-taking? A meta-analytic examination. *Contemporary Educational Psychology, 30,* 242-262.

Kobayashi, K. (2006). Combined effects of note-taking and reviewing on learning and the enhancement through interventions: A meta-analytic review. *Educational Psychology: An International Journal of Experimental Educational Psychology, 26,* 459-477.

Korallo, L., Foreman, N., Boyd-Davis, S., Moar, M., & Coulson, M. (2012). Can multiple "spatial" virtual timelines convey the relatedness of chronological knowledge across parallel domains? *Computers & Education, 58,* 856-862.

Kosslyn, S. M. (1993). *Elements of graphic design.* New York, NY: Freeman.

Kwon, S. Y., & Cifuentes, L. (2009). The comparative effect of individually-constructed vs. collaboratively-constructed computer-based concept maps. *Computers & Education, 52,* 365-375.

Lemarié, J., Lorch, R. F., Jr., Eyrolle, H., & Virbel, J. (2008). SARA: A text-based and reader-based theory of signaling. *Educational Psychologist, 43,* 27-48.

Lane, D. M., & Sandor, A. (2009). Designing better graphs by including distributional information and integrating words, numbers, and images. *Psychological Methods, 14,* 239-257.

Larkin, J. H., & Simon, H. A. (1987). Why a diagram is (sometimes) worth 10,000 words. *Cognitive Science, 11,* 65-100.

Latour, B. (1990). Drawing things together. In M. Lynch & S. Woolgar (Eds.), *Representation in scientific practice* (pp. 19-68). Cambridge, MA: MIT Press.

Liben, L. S. (2009). The road to understanding maps. *Current Directions in Psychological Science, 18,* 310-315.

Liben, L. S., & Downs, R. M. (1993). Understanding person–space–map relations: Cartographic and developmental perspectives. *Developmental Psychology, 29,* 739-752.

Lorch, R., Lemarié, J., & Grant, R. (2011). Signaling hierarchical and sequential organization in expository text. *Scientific Studies of Reading, 15,* 267-284.

Mautone, P. D., & Mayer, R. E. (2007). Cognitive aids for guiding graph comprehension. *Journal of Educational Psychology, 99,* 640-652.

Mayer, R. E. (2005). Principles for reducing extraneous processing in multimedia learning: Coherence, signaling, redundancy, spatial contiguity, and temporal contiguity principles. In R. E. Mayer (Ed.) *The Cambridge handbook of multimedia learning* (pp. 183-212). Cambridge, England: Cambridge University Press.

Mayer, R. E., Hegarty, M., Mayer, S., & Campbell, J. E. (2005). When static media promote active learning: Annotated illustrations versus narrated animations in multimedia instruction. *Journal of Experimental Psychology: Applied, 11,* 256-265.

McCrudden, M. T., Schraw, G., Lehman, S., & Poliquin, A. (2007). The effect of causal diagrams on text learning. *Contemporary Educational Psychology, 32,* 367-388.

McCrudden, M. T., Magliano, J., & Schraw, G. (2011). The effects of diagrams on online reading processes and memory. *Discourse Processes, 48,* 69-92.

Meir, E., Perry, J., Herron, J. C., & Kingsolver, J. (2007). College students' misconceptions about evolutionary trees. *The American Biology Teacher, 9,* 71-76.

Michael, D., & Hartley, J. (1991). Extracting information from flowcharts and contingency statements: The effects of age and practice. *British Journal of Educational Technology, 22,* 84-98.

Morse, E., & Lewis, M. (2000). Evaluating visualizations: using a taxonomic guide. *International Journal of Human-Computer Studies, 53,* 637-662.

Nesbit, J. C., & Adesope, O. O. (2006). Learning with concept and knowledge maps: A meta-analysis. *Review of Educational Research, 76,* 413-448.

Nesbit, J. C., & Adesope, O. O. (2011). Learning from animated concept maps with concurrent audio narration. *The Journal of Experimental Education, 79,* 209-230.

Novak, J. D., & Gowin, D. B. (1985). *Learning how to learn.* New York, NY: Cambridge University Press.

Paik, E. S., & Schraw, G. (2012). Learning with animation and illusions of understanding. *Journal of Educational Psychology.* Advance online publication. doi:10.1037/a0030281

Pettersson, R. (2010). Information design–principles and guidelines. *Journal of Visual Literacy, 29,* 167-182.

Plass, J. L., Homer, B. D., & Hayward, E. O. (2009). Design factors for educationally effective animations and simulations. *Journal of Computers in Higher Education, 21,* 31-61.

Reed, S. K. (2005). From research to practice and back: The animation tutor project. *Educational Psychology Review, 17,* 55-82.

Robinson, D. H., & Kiewra, K. A. (1995). Visual argument: Graphic organizers are superior to outlines in improving learning from text. *Journal of Education Psychology, 87,* 455-467.

Robinson, D. H., Katayama, A. D., Odom, S., Beth, A., Hsieh, Y. P., & Vanderveen, A. (2006). Increasing text comprehension and graphic note-taking using a partial graphic organizer task. *Journal of Educational Research, 100,* 103-111.

Rodriguez, L., & Dimitrova, D. N. (2011). The levels of visual framing. *Journal of Visual Literacy, 30,* 48-65.

Roth, W. M.. & Bowen, G. M. (2001). Professionals read graphs: a semiotic analysis. *Journal for Research in Mathematics Education, 32,* 159-194.

Ruiz, J. G., Cook, D. A., & Levinson, A. J. (2009). Computer animations in medical education: a critical literature review. *Medical Education, 43,* 838-846.

Schnotz, W. (2002). Commentary: Towards an integrated view of learning from text and IVDs. *Educational Psychology Review, 14,* 101-120.

Schnotz, W., & Lowe, R.K. (2008). A unified view of learning from animated and static graphics. In R. K. Lowe & W. Schnotz (Eds.), *Learning with animation. Research implications for design* (pp. 304-356). New York, NY: Cambridge University Press.

Schonborn, K. J., & Anderson, T. R. (2010). Bridging the educational research-teaching practice gap: Foundations for assessing and developing biochemistry students' visual literacy. *BAMBED, 38,* 347-354.

Schnotz, W., & Rasch, T. (2005). Enabling, facilitating, and inhibiting effects of animations in multimedia learning: Why reduction of cognitive load can have negative results on learning. *Educational Technology Research and Development, 53,* 47-58.

Schraw, G. (2006). Knowledge: Structures and processes. In P. Alexander & P. Winne (Eds.), *Handbook of educational psychology* (2nd ed., pp. 245-264). San Diego, CA: Academic Press.

Schwartz, N. L., Verdi, M. P., Morris, T., Lee, T. R., & Larson, N. K. (2007). Navigating web-based environments: Differentiating internal spatial representations from external spatial displays. *Contemporary Educational Psychology, 32,* 551-568.

Schwonke, R., Berthold, K., & Renkl, A. (2009). How multiple external representations are used and how they can be made more useful. *Applied Cognitive Psychology, 23*, 1227-1243.

Simon, J. (2010). Curriculum changes using concept maps. *Accounting Education: An International Journal, 19*, 301-307.

Slough, S. W., McTigue, E. M., Kim, S., & Jennings, S. M. (2010). Science textbooks use of graphical representation: A descriptive analysis of four sixth grade science texts. *Reading Psychology, 31*, 301-325.

Sweller, J. (1999). *Instructional design in technical areas.* Camberwell, Australia: ACER Press.

Tsai, T., & Wu, Y. (2010). Effects of note-taking instruction and note-taking languages on college EFL students' listening comprehension. *New Horizons in Education, 58*, 120-132.

Tufte, E. R. (2001). *The visual display of quantitative information* (2nd ed.). Cheshire, CT: Graphics Press.

van Amelsvoort, M., Andriessen, J. & Kanselaar, G. (2008). How students structure and relate argumentative knowledge when learning together with diagrams. *Computers in Human Behavior, 24*, 1293-1313.

van der Meer, J. (2012): Students' note-taking challenges in the twenty-first century: Considerations for teachers and academic staff developers. *Teaching in Higher Education, 17*, 13-23.

van Merriënboer, J. J. G., & Sweller, J. (2005). Cognitive load theory and complex learning: recent developments and future directions. *Educational Psychology Review, 17*, 147-177.

Vekiri, I. (2002).What is the value of graphical displays in learning? *Educational Psychology Review, 14*, 261-312.

Vella, Y. (2011). The gradual transformation of historical situations: Understanding change and continuity through colors and timelines. *Teaching History, 144*, 116-123.

Wagner, C. H. (2007). Standard distributions: One graph fits all. *Teaching Statistics, 29*, 54-56.

Wainer, H. (1992). Understanding graphs and tables. *Educational Researcher, 21*, 14-23.

Woo, H. L. (2009). Designing multimedia learning environments using animated pedagogical agents: factors and issues. *Journal of Computer Assisted Learning, 25*, 203-218.

Wouters, P., Paas, F., & van Merriënboer, J. J. (2008). How to optimize learning from animated models: A review of guidelines based on cognitive load. *Review of Educational Research, 78*, 645-675.

Zhang, J. (2008). Causal reasoning with ancestral graphs. *Journal of Machine Learning Research, 9*, 1437-1474.

SECTION III

USING VISUAL DISPLAYS TO ENHANCE LEARNING

CHAPTER 6

STATIC AND DYNAMIC VISUAL REPRESENTATIONS

Individual Differences in Processing

Tim N. Höffler, Annett Schmeck, and Maria Opfermann

ABSTRACT

The benefits of visual representations that are added to (written or spoken) words to enhance learning are beyond doubt and have been well-established throughout educational research in the last two decades. In this regard, the preceding chapters have introduced and discussed the cognitive foundations for learning with different kinds of visual representations and the ways they can be used throughout different learning scenarios. This chapter adds another aspect to this overall view by addressing when and why dynamic representations are beneficial for learning and whether they are in any way superior to static pictures. Moreover, we focus on whether such learning effects differ with respect to different conditions as well as different learner characteristics, such as prior knowledge, cognitive style and spatial ability. We conclude that different visual representations may be more useful in specific situations; however, using any visual representation is preferable to none at all.

Learning Through Visual Displays, pp. 133–163
Copyright © 2013 by Information Age Publishing
All rights of reproduction in any form reserved.

INTRODUCTION

Imagine that you are a popular sports coach and asked to give a presentation on successful techniques in high jumping, or that you are a biology teacher and want to explain the processes of mitosis and meiosis to your students. How would you give such presentations? Would you only *talk* about what you would like to explain? Probably not - within a few minutes, your audience would ask you to *show* them examples of what you are trying to explain. Thus, you would very likely include visual representations in your presentation from the beginning. Now consider the examples above - what kind of representations would you use? Would you show a series of static pictures in which different states of the cell division process are shown or of a high jumper successfully jumping over a two-metre bar? Or would you show an animation depicting an entire scene? And would the visual representations you show be concrete, that is, photographs or microscope recordings, or more abstract, where the form is in drawings or comic-like animations? Finally, would you decide differently depending on *whom* you are expected to explain these things to?

The *general* assumption that adding pictures to (written or spoken) words can enhance learning has been investigated in several research areas in the past few decades and has led to a number of well-supported theories (e.g., dual coding theory, Paivio, 1986; cognitive theory of multimedia learning, Mayer, 2009; integrated model of text and picture comprehension, Schnotz, 2005; cognitive load theory, Sweller, 2010), some of which are described in other chapters of this book (Low, Jin, & Sweller, this volume; Mayer, this volume; Renkl & Schwonke, this volume). Most of these theories are based on models of human cognitive architecture, specifically, the structure and processing limitations of working memory. A brief summary of these models as well as an explanation of the overall benefits of the use of visual representations to enhance text comprehension is given in the following section. Apart from this general assumption on the learning benefits of visual representations in general, however, there still exists a considerable amount of controversy regarding the question of which kind of representations should be used and the extent to which this choice depends on the contents to be learned and the individual learner characteristics. These aspects will be discussed in the main sections of this chapter. In particular, we will focus on advantages and disadvantages of static versus dynamic visual representations under different conditions and their relation with individual learner characteristics such as prior knowledge, cognitive style and spatial ability. The chapter concludes with recommendations for future design of learning materials.

WHY LEARNING (OFTEN) WORKS BETTER WHEN VISUAL REPRESENTATIONS ARE ADDED TO TEXT

The question of why several forms of visual representation can foster meaningful learning has been addressed in numerous studies and several well-supported theories (compare the preceding chapters of this book (Low et al., this volume; Mayer, this volume). Most of these theories are based on dual channel assumptions of the human mind and its constraints on information processing. More specifically, working memory is assumed to be limited with regard to the amount of information it can process at a single time (Baddeley, 1992). This information can consist of verbal and/or pictorial representations, which are either processed in a visual or auditory sensory channel (Paivio, 1986), depending on the modality of the representations. Both sensory channels are considered to be limited with regard to the amount of information they can process in parallel. Information that has been processed in both channels is available in order to be selected for further processing, which takes place in different subsystems of the working memory. According to Baddeley (1992), working memory consists of three substructures—the phonological loop responsible for processing verbal information, the visuo-spatial sketchpad for handling visuo-spatial information, and an executive control structure that coordinates these two subsystems. Both the phonological loop and the visuo-spatial sketchpad are able to keep only a certain amount of information active for further processing.

Based on Baddeley's (1992) multicomponent view, the cognitive theory of multimedia learning (CTML; Mayer, 2005, 2009) states that enriching text with visual representations helps learners gain a deeper understanding during instruction. In other words: "Students learn better from words and pictures than from words alone" (*multimedia principle*; Mayer, 2009, p. 223). This is based on the assumption that words and pictures are qualitatively different with regard to the information they contain and are processed in independent channels in memory. That is, words and pictures convey qualitatively different types of information contents because of the different channels in which they are processed (Mayer, 2009). This multimedia effect could be shown in several paper-based as well as computer-based studies (e.g., Moreno & Valdez, 2005; Plass & Jones, 2005; Schwamborn, Thillmann, Leopold, Sumfleth, & Leutner, 2010; Schwamborn, Thillmann, Opfermann, & Leutner, 2011).

In line with this, the integrated model of text and picture comprehension (Schnotz, 2005) also proposes different information processing channels for textual and pictorial information. Further, the model assumes that each sensory modality is responsible for processing their respective inputs on a *perceptual level*, which refers to the information transfer between the environment and working memory, including not only visual and auditory, but also haptic and other sensory channels that can support the initial processing of words and pictures. On a *cognitive level*, a verbal and a visualization channel are assumed. Verbal selection processes lead to a propositional text base, and verbal organization processes result in a text-based mental model. Similarly, pictorial selection processes lead to an image base, and pictorial organization processes result in a picture-based mental model. While verbal organization processes take place in the verbal part of working memory, the pictorial organization processes are localized in the pictorial part of working memory (Baddeley, 1992; Chandler & Sweller, 1991). The text-based model and the picture-based model are then integrated in a one-to-one mapping process. During this mapping process, elements of the text-based model are mapped to elements of the picture-based model, and vice versa. Similarly, relations within the text-based model are mapped to relations within the picture-based model and vice versa. Integration requires that components of the text-based model and corresponding components of the picture-based model are simultaneously activated in working memory.

In contrast to the CTML, the integrated model states that "only one mental model is constructed that integrates information from different sources from the beginning" (Schnotz, 2005, p. 59). The benefits of pictures in addition to text are based on this integrative assumption, that is, "students learn better from words and pictures than from words alone under the condition that verbal and the pictorial information are simultaneously available in working memory" (Horz & Schnotz, 2008, p. 50).

Finally, according to Ainsworth's (1999, 2006) DeFT (design, functions, tasks) framework for learning with multiple representations, multiple representations, including pictures and text, have three key functions in benefiting learning. First, these multiple representations support complementary cognitive processes, as when "learners can choose to work with the representation that best suits their needs" (Ainsworth, 2006, p. 188). Second, multiple representations constrain interpretation options, thereby preventing inaccurate interpretations. Third, they promote a deeper conceptual understanding when learners can abstract information from representations, extend knowledge they have with regard to one representation to other representations, and relate representations to each other without fundamentally reorganizing their knowledge. In short, according to these theories, different kinds of visual representations can *enrich* understanding of textual information, given that learners can mentally connect these two different sources of information. However, the learning benefits of visual representations depend strongly on the *type of visual information* provided. This will be the focus of the next section.

TYPES OF VISUAL REPRESENTATIONS THAT CAN BE USED TO SUPPORT MEANINGFUL LEARNING

One important distinction between different types of visual representations is that they can be either instructional (i.e., with the goal to immediately support learning) or decorative (i.e., serving a rather esthetic, thus possibly motivational, purpose). In the following sections we will mainly focus on instructional visual representations, which presumably enhance learning to a greater extent than decorative representations because the latter often lack relevant informational content. For instance, Clark and Mayer (2003) emphasize that *explanative* visual representations should be used for multimedia learning, whereas *decorative* visual representations do not contain additional information that fosters deeper cognitive processes and might even hinder learning; a claim that is consistent with Mayer's (2009) *coherence principle* (CTML). Similarly, in a recent meta-analysis, Höffler and Leutner (2007) found the mean effect size of *representational* animations in contrast to static pictures was significantly superior to the mean effect size of *decorational* animations in contrast to static pictures. They adapted Carney and Levin's (2002) terminology, who also include *organizational* (providing a structural framework), *interpretational* (clarifying difficult text) and *transformational* (including memory enhancing components) as further functions of pictures (see also Levin, 1981). Whatever terminology is used —decorative visual representations do not directly support the construction of an elaborated mental model of the information to be learned. The main goal of instructional representations is to help the learner build an adequate mental model for understanding the learning topic. Depending on the situation and requirements, this mental model can either be dynamic or static. Both static pictures and animations can promote the construction of either static or dynamic mental models (cf. Schnotz & Lowe, 2008). Static pictures (especially series of static pictures) can be the basis for dynamic models (Hegarty, 1992), and animations can trigger a static mental model. Schnotz and Lowe (2008) give the example of a video clip which explains how a complex building is composed from its parts, which illustrates how animations may yield a static mental model.

Different Ways to Distinguish Instructional Visual Representations

There are a number of approaches to classify instructional visual representations (e.g., Niegemann et al., 2008; Schnotz, 2005; Weidenmann,

1993). One important approach has been made by Schnotz (2005), who distinguishes descriptive and depictive representations. Descriptive (propositional) representations can be defined by the comparison to *symbols* which describe an idea or concept but are not structurally similar. The symbols ♀ and ♂, for instance, can be found on bathroom doors and represent "female" and "male," respectively. However, they bear no structural similarity to a woman or a man (note that Schnotz also subsumes text under his conception of descriptive representations; for instance the word "shark," which does not have any similarity with the fish itself). According to Schnotz (2005), such descriptive representations are more suitable to convey abstract knowledge. In contrast, depictive representations can be defined as comparable to *icons* because they show similarities or other structural commonalities of their respective referents. They contain more information and are thus suitable to convey concrete knowledge at a glance as well as support the drawing of inferences. In this regard, Niegemann et al. (2008) further distinguish between realistic pictures (such as the photograph or the drawing of a man and a woman on the bathroom door), analogy pictures (for instance, depicting working memory and its limited capacity as a bottle that can only be filled to a certain point, see above; Baddeley, 1999) and logical pictures (for instance diagrams and graphs).

Now recall the earlier examples on teaching high jumping and biological processes. When you present such topics to a large group that is unfamiliar with these topics, you could use realistic or depictive representations (Niegemann et al., 2008; Schnotz, 2005). But you might still be unsure whether to show one or more static pictures depicting different scenes of a successful jump or the cell division, or whether your audience would learn more if you showed a dynamic representation, that is, a video or an animation. However, if you were a math teacher and wanted to explain the Pythagorean theorem to your students, you probably would not have this dilemma. In that case, showing the drawing of a rectangular triangle with squares above the two legs and the hypotenuse, that is, one single static picture (cf. Figure 6.1), would suffice.

In such cases, the contents you teach mainly consist of *facts* or theorems. In contrast, much of the knowledge students have to learn at school or university refer to *processes* (i.e., *dynamic* contents), such as our high jumping or biology examples. Whenever such processes or other dynamic contents are the focus of learning, animations might enhance learning (Münzer, Seufert, & Brünken, 2009), because crucial information about motions is explicitly provided. Thus, in the following sections we will focus on the use of static and dynamic visual representations.

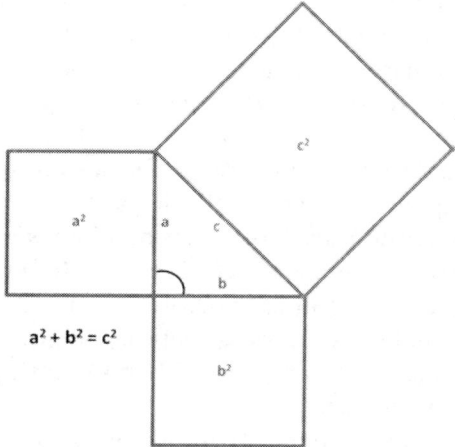

Figure 6.1.   A static picture explaining the Pythagorean theorem.

Static and Dynamic Visual Representations

Are animations generally superior to static pictures when it comes to learning and understanding dynamic processes? This issue has been addressed in a number of studies; yet no conclusive statement can be made at this point (for overviews, see Höffler & Leutner, 2007; Tversky, Morrison, & Bétrancourt, 2002) because the more effective option is dependent on the circumstances, as will be shown in the following sections. Similar to static pictures, animations have different advantages and disadvantages that come into play depending on the learning scenario. For instance, in the high jumper example, an animation might show the motion *as a whole* and is thus a more complete representation of what has to be learned, whereas a series of static pictures might only show different stages of this motion. Thus, to understand how the jumper really moves, or for imitating this movement oneself (for instance in a sports lesson), an animation might be the better choice. On the other hand, dynamic representations are *transient*; that is, while the animation continues, relevant information cannot be seen anymore (Mayer & Chandler, 2001). In order to understand the process as a whole (in this case jumping), the individual steps must all be retained in working memory. This might lead to increased extraneous cognitive load in terms of cognitive load theory (CLT; Low et al., this volume; Sweller, 2010; Sweller, van Merriënboer, & Paas, 1998; van Merriënboer & Sweller, 2005). In such a case, animations are not necessarily beneficial for learning. A series of static pictures, on the other hand, might be better suited to highlight pivotal steps in certain dynamic processes (Catrambone & Seay, 2002; Hegarty, Kriz, & Cate, 2003). For instance, when watching animations of the mitosis or meiosis processes of cell division, it might be harder to detect the transitions from the prophase to the metaphase to the anaphase and so on. These, however, can easily be shown by exemplary static pictures or frames taken out of an animation such as in Figure 6.2. Additionally, it has been shown that learners tend to make inaccurate causal assumptions when watching animations, in particular abstract animations (cf. Tversky, Heiser, Mackenzie, Lozano, & Morrison, 2008). Abstract symbols representing molecules, or in our example, chromosomes during mitosis, might easily be seen as intentionally pushing or chasing each other. Obviously, this can lead to problematic misconceptions.

Another possible disadvantage of animations and videos is that watching a dynamic visual representation "does not necessarily invite cognitive engagement, but permits completely passive viewing" (Höffler & Schwartz, 2011, p. 1718). An animation might lead to deceptive clarity, an illusion of understanding (Rebetez, Bétrancourt, Sangin, & Dillenbourg, 2010), as learners need not carry out necessary active integration processes of the underlying concepts (Schnotz & Rasch, 2008) and might thus be underwhelmed (Lowe, 2004).

In summary, research has thus far revealed mixed results that speak either in favor of animations (e.g., Catrambone & Seay, 2002; Münzer et al., 2009; Spotts & Dwyer, 1996; Yang, Andre, & Greenbowe, 2003; for an overview see Höffler & Leutner, 2007), or question their general superiority over static pictures (e.g., Imhof, Scheiter, & Gerjets, 2011; Lewalter, 2003; Mayer, Hegarty, Mayer, & Campbell, 2005; Swezey, 1991; Tversky et al., 2002). Therefore the next section will detail the conditions under which static or dynamic visual representations can foster learning. We start with a short definition of what can be understood as static or dynamic.

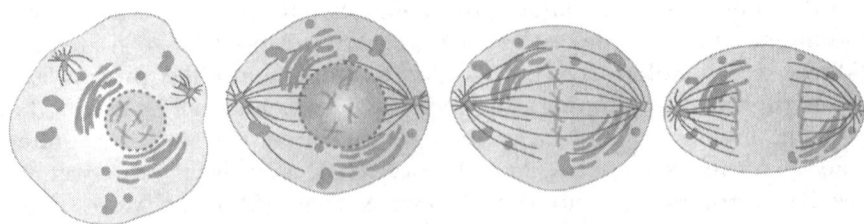

Figure 6.2.   Exemplary states of the mitosis process.

WHAT CAN BE UNDERSTOOD AS STATIC OR DYNAMIC?

Imagine looking at three or four pictures depicting states of a high jumper's movement in a book or in a slideshow. You might classify these as *static* visual representations. In addition, if shown the previously mentioned animation of a high jumper or a movie in cartoon form, you would probably call these *dynamic* visual representations. But how would you classify, for instance, a flip-book with 50 consecutive pictures of the high jumper that you flip through rapidly so that it looks as if the person is really jumping (cf. Figure 6.3)?

Researchers have defined *animation* as a series of rapidly changing (computer screen) representations that suggest some kind of movement to the viewer (Rieber & Kini, 1991). That is, a series of pictures or frames that *simulate* movement, which is actually not taking place.

Ploetzner and Lowe (2012) as well as Imhof, Jarodzka, and Gerjets (2009) constructed a systematic characterization of animations in order to be able to analyse animations comparatively. Ploetzner and Lowe identified four main dimensions of animations (i.e., how an animation is *presented* and arranged, the level of *user control* over time line and presentation of the animation, *scaffolding* in terms of cues and prompts to support the learner, and *configuration* of the animation in terms of setting and execution) with several subdimensions. Moreover, they aimed at "inspiring the development of new types of animations as well as the investigation of their educational effectiveness" (Ploetzner & Lowe, 2012, p. 792).

Just like static pictures, animations can provide external models for mental representations, for instance, by compensating for learners' insufficient aptitudes or skills to imagine motions or dynamic processes as a whole (Schnotz & Lowe, 2008). In terms of animations as an enrichment to

Source: Image used with permission from Rolf Dober; http://www.sportpaedagogik-online.de

Figure 6.3.   A series of consecutive static pictures depicting the correct sequence of motions for high jumping. In this case, all 14 pictures have been merged into one picture.

textual information, Mayer and Moreno (2002) state that all basic principles of the CTML (in former articles called generative theory of multimedia learning) apply to learning with animations in a similar way as they do to learning with static pictures. The authors show this explicitly for the multimedia principle, the contiguity principle, the coherence principle, the modality principle, the redundancy principle, and the personalization principle. In terms of the CLT (Sweller et al., 1998), well-designed static pictures or animations can thus take extraneous cognitive load off learners' working memory and free capacities for schema construction and learning processes related to germane cognitive load (i.e., load involved in schema construction). This might be especially important in learning scenarios where the intrinsic cognitive load (i.e., multiple interacting elements) is high, for example when the topic to be learned is very complex, or when little prior knowledge exists.

Are Animations Always Better?

With regard to the benefits of animations versus static pictures, and in addition to the above mentioned aspects, Höffler and Leutner (2007) in their meta-analysis argued that animations can help learners mentally visualize a process or a procedure, thus reducing cognitive load compared to a situation in which the process or the procedure must be reconstructed from a series of static pictures. Furthermore, static pictures may contain more or less abstract signaling cues like arrows or highlighting, which need to be interpreted and integrated with the pictorial and textual information. Thus, cues carry the inherent danger of imposing even more cognitive load onto working memory, which in case of a cognitive overload could lead to misconceptions and therefore to a deficient mental model (Lewalter, 1997). On the other hand, Höffler and Leutner also emphasize the above mentioned transient nature of animations and the difficulty of retaining information no longer available when the respective frames have disappeared (Hegarty, 2004). Overall, the meta-analysis conducted by Höffler and Leutner showed a rather positive pattern of results in favor of animations. Of the 26 studies they analyzed, animations (note that these were all noninteractive animations) outperformed static pictures with a mean effect size of Cohen's $d = 0.37$ (95% confidence interval $0.25 - 0.49$). The authors emphasized, however, that this overall result should be viewed in light of potentially moderating variables, especially since it seems to contradict other studies that did not provide evidence for a general advantage of animations on learning (e.g., Bétrancourt & Tversky, 2000; Mayer et al., 2005). In the following section, we will focus on individual learner characteristics that determine how well different people learn from different kinds of visual representations. In subsequent sections we discuss some of these moderator variables and examine potential influences that refer to the instructional design of the animations.

INSTRUCTIONAL DESIGN OF ANIMATIONS: WHERE IS THE IMPACT?

One aspect that contributes quite clearly to the question of whether animations have a beneficial effect on learning is the content shown in the animation. Depictive animations proved far more superior to static pictures than decorative animations. In other words, animations foster learning especially when the content of the to-be-learned information is explicitly depicted in the respective animation. For instance, when the topic is primarily the *motion* of something, animations may be the preferred method compared to static pictures. Examples include the procedure for bandaging a hand (Michas & Berry, 2000), or the motions of electrons inside a flashlight battery (Yang, Andre, & Greenbowe, 2003). One interpretation of these findings is that depictive animations facilitate the generation of a mental model of the motion to be learned by providing a *prototype*: "An animation is likely to be useful when the learning material entails motion, trajectory or change over time so that the animation helps to build a mental model of the dynamics" (Bétrancourt & Tversky, 2000, p. 326). Yet, animations that only served decorative purposes in the studies reported (for instance, animated pedagogical agents), did not have an additional benefit for learning and sometimes even hindered knowledge acquisition. This is consistent with the *coherence principle* by Mayer (2009). In other words, decorative animations seem to be kind of *seductive details* (Harp & Mayer, 1998) that distract learners with interesting and unimportant details and draw learners' attention from the actual content to be learned. In addition, the motivational effects often accredited to decorative visual representations (cf. Lenzner, Schnotz, Müller, & Horz, 2006; Niegemann et al., 2008; but cf. Clark & Feldon, 2005 for a contrary opinion) do not seem to counteract this disadvantage.

Another aspect that needs to be taken into account is the kind of knowledge expected to be acquired in a specific learning situation. Höffler and Leutner (2007) in their meta-analysis found greater benefits of animations on procedural-motor knowledge compared to problem-solving knowledge or declarative knowledge, whereby the difference between the latter two failed to reach statistical significance. One should, however, view these results with care, as the difference between procedural-motor knowledge and problem-solving knowledge could at least partly be traced back to the fact that all effect sizes pertaining to procedural-motor knowledge were exclusively based on representational visual representations, while effect sizes concerning problem-solving knowledge were based on representational as well as decorative visual representations.

Nevertheless, van Gog, Paas, Marcus, Ayres, and Sweller (2009) innovatively linked this result with findings from neuroscience: A so-called mirror neuron system (cf. Rizzolatti & Craighero, 2004) seems to be located in several areas of the human brain which is activated, among other functions, when observing motor sequences carried out by others. Generally, similar brain areas are activated when actions are observed or actually executed (see Figure 6.4). Therefore, the system supports the ability to *imitate* and to *understand* action. Van Gog et al. (2009) argue that because of the biologically evolved mirror neuron system, dynamic representations "should be most effective for learning tasks that involve human movement, because such visual representations automatically trigger an effortless process of embodied simulation by the mirror neuron system" (p. 25). And, indeed, the above stated result of the meta-analysis of Höffler and Leutner (2007) seems to suggest just that—tasks that require procedural-motor knowledge were best learned with animations (see also Ayres, Marcus, Chan, & Qian, 2009). Referring to our high-jumping and biology examples, animations thus should be more helpful when teaching high jumping than when teaching meiosis and mitosis—because the evolution is on our side, having made our brains especially useful when it comes to imitating action.

In sum, there is evidence for the superiority of animations when learning procedural-motor knowledge. Similar results, however, might have been expected for animations when conveying problem-solving knowledge, which can also be regarded as procedural knowledge, in this case on a cognitive level (e.g., Mayer & Moreno, 2002). But the results of the meta-analysis did not provide further evidence backing this common

Figure 6.4.   Mirror neurons are activated when observing motions made by others. Similar brain areas are activated when actions are observed or actually executed.

assumption—in many cases, static pictures seem to suffice to learn not only simple facts, but even to gain deeper understanding. Making an animation video-based or computer-based also has an impact on the learning efficiency of animations and refers to the level of realism. Would you rather use a video of a real high jumper or a schematic, black-and-white animation (cf. Figure 6.5) to teach the most efficient way to jump over the bar? It depends, right? A video of real human movement might better trigger the mirror neuron system (see above; although the system also seems to be triggered by anthropomorphic actions, see Gazzola, Rizzolatti, Wicker, & Keysers, 2007) and might provide a positive boost to learners' motivation (although such an impact on motivation does not necessarily translate into learning, cf. Schnotz & Lowe, 2008). The schematic animation, however, has the advantage of focusing on the essential parts and not containing unnecessary (*seductive*) details which might shift learners' attention.

In this regard, the meta-analysis of Höffler and Leutner (2007) provided—unsatisfactorily—mixed results. While at first glance, video-based animations seemed superior to computer-based ones, the advantages of highly realistic (video-based) animations could, at least to a certain extent, be attributed to a statistical confound due to with the role of animations (representational vs. decorative) in which all video-based animations were representational, whereas a substantial portion of the computer-based animations were decorative. Thus, compared to learning with static pictures, using animations with lower levels of realism does not necessarily lead to less optimal learning, which is consistent with Tversky et al.'s (2002) statement "animations should lean toward the schematic and away from the realistic" (p. 258). In so doing, learners should have the ability to concentrate on essential contents of the animation—"sufficiently complex

 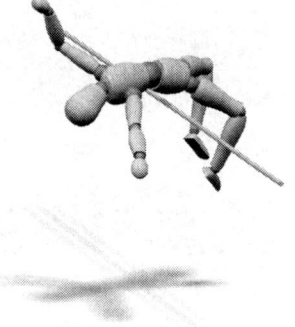

Figure 6.5.   Highly realistic and schematic pictures illustrating high jumping.

to convey the important information within it, yet simple enough to be easily understood" (Milheim, 1993, p. 173; see also Lowe, 1999, 2003).

These mixed results are also supported by more recent findings of Imhof, Scheiter, and Gerjets (2011), who varied the degree of realism and the kind of visual representations in a learning scenario where students had to acquire knowledge on the locomotion patterns of fish. While the degree of realism did not contribute significantly to learning success, animations generally outperformed sequentially shown static pictures. This effect, however, disappeared when animations were compared to the same series of simultaneously shown static pictures (Figure 6.6).

In the latter case, students could possibly better comprehend the transitions from one locomotion step to the next. In addition, compared to the sequentially shown static pictures, they have to keep less information active in working memory (because all pictures were shown on one page, and they could look at preceding steps again once they had looked at following steps). Thus, the imposed cognitive load might still have left enough capacity for schema construction and for building the mental model of the whole locomotion (which, in turn, was shown entirely by the respective animation). These findings are also in line with Rieber (1990, 1994), who concluded that animations should highlight only crucial aspects of a topic. In his study, a "chunking-strategy" was used that aimed to break animations into discrete steps so new information was presented step-by-step. Rieber also used animations with a low level of realism and noted that his chunking-strategy would be only one of several possibilities of cueing in animations. Following Tversky et al. (2002), such a cueing strategy could include narrations, arrows or graphic accentuations. This has, for instance, been taken up by Münzer et al. (2009), who let students learn about processes related to the synthesis of adenosine triphosphate

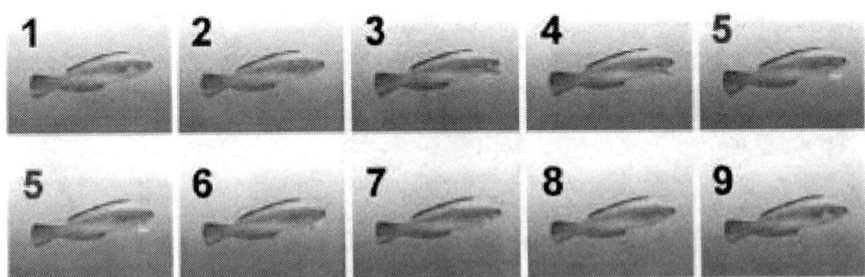

Source: Image used with permission from Birgit Imhof.

Figure 6.6.   Series of simultaneously shown static pictures depicting motions of fish used in the study of Imhof et al. (2011).

(ATP) in cells by means of either providing (1) a series of static pictures showing essential states of this process, (2) an enriched static pictures condition, in which pictures showing intermediate steps in the process were added and where arrows in the pictures indicated the motion of the elements, or (3) animations showing the whole process at once. Results showed that animations as well as enriched static pictures were superior to "normal" static pictures when it came to the acquisition of process knowledge (i.e., knowledge about the processes illustrated by the visual representations), whereas no differences were found regarding structure knowledge (regarding the spatial configuration of the elements of the visual representations). In line with the previous considerations, explicit information on aspects of *motion* helped especially when this kind of knowledge had to be acquired.

This latter finding contradicts the results of the meta-analysis by Höffler and Leutner (2007), who found that instructional animations were generally superior to static pictures regardless of whether static pictures were enriched in some way or not. For instance, the presence or absence of annotated text in animations and pictures did not account for differences with regard to learning because the superiority of animations to static pictures did not vary significantly in such cases. Moreover, the effect size in favor of animations did not vary significantly depending on the presence or absence of signaling cues such as arrows and highlighting in static pictures. In terms of this missing effect for enriched static pictures, the authors argue that pointing out the most important elements, as within—nontransient—static pictures might be unnecessary. The viewers normally have sufficient time to find these elements by themselves. Yet, cues might have been expected to play an important role in learning with animations to avoid missing critical aspects due to the transient nature of animations, thus placing high demands on working memory capacity (Ainsworth & VanLabeke, 2004). Nevertheless, as results are still mixed and neither the meta-analysis nor recent research provides conclusive evidence for such a hypothesis, further research is needed in this respect.

All in all, research thus far has not revealed—and probably never will reveal—a definitive answer to whether static or dynamic visual representations are generally more suitable for learning. Tversky et al. (2002) did not find animations to be superior to static pictures, yet argued that if they were to do so, it would be because there was more information available in animations than in static pictures. Höffler and Leutner (2007) reported a general advantage of animations irrespective of the instructional design of the visual representations which was used in the 26 studies they reviewed.

Coming back to our high jumping and mitosis/meiosis examples, you might still not be able to decide whether to show your audience a video of someone jumping, or from a cell division under a microscope, whether you would prefer a cartoon-like animation, or if (a series of) static pictures would best suit your needs. Maybe for your final decision, you would consider additional factors—for example, probably, *who* you are actually supposed to talk to. This brings us to the second big issue that has attracted research interest regarding the discussion about static versus dynamic pictures: the individual learner characteristics that learners bring along when confronted with a specific learning scenario. In the following section, we focus on those characteristics which stand in closest connection to learning with visual representations, namely spatial ability, cognitive style, and prior knowledge.

INDIVIDUAL DIFFERENCES: WHO BENEFITS FROM WHAT?

A main reason for the lack of unambiguous recommendations for either static or dynamic visual representations might be their varying effectiveness for different types of learners. Probably one of the most investigated learner characteristics (not only with regard to the learning efficiency of animations) is the prior knowledge that learners have before they are exposed to a certain learning situation. In this regard, the *expertise reversal effect* (Kalyuga, 2007; Kalyuga, this volume; Kalyuga, Ayres, Chandler, & Sweller, 2003) states that "instructional techniques that are highly effective with inexperienced learners can lose their effectiveness and even have negative consequences when used with more experienced learners" (Kalyuga et al., 2003, p. 23). This assumption has also been taken up by Mayer (2009), who states in his *individual differences principle* that design effects might be stronger for low prior knowledge learners than for high prior knowledge learners. In other words, the benefits of multimedia learning materials depend on learners' prior knowledge in that adding visual representations to a text might be especially helpful for low prior knowledge learners, whereas it may hinder learning for high prior knowledge learners, because in such cases, the danger of presenting redundant information might occur.

The role of prior knowledge for learning with multimedia materials also depends on the amount of learner control when interacting with a specific learning scenario. In this regard, Opfermann (2008) found a high level of learner control in a multimedia learning environment on probability (featuring worked examples, animations, and self-pacing) was not more helpful than structured and system-controlled presentations of the information, and even hindered knowledge acquisition for low prior knowledge learners. Such findings can be explained in part by learners' disorientation (cf. "lost in hyperspace"; Conklin, 1987), which may lead to cognitive overload because when learners have the freedom to decide what to learn at any point of time, they may not be able to pick out the relevant aspects without sufficient prior knowledge.

The Role of Cognitive Style for Learning With Animations

The *cognitive style* of learners is another potentially crucial aspect that comes to mind for learning with animations versus static pictures. Cognitive style is defined as a stable attitude that determines individuals' modes of perceiving, remembering, thinking, and problem solving (Messick, 1976). This factor, closely related to (and occasionally used synonymously with) *learning style* (e.g., Kirby, Moore, & Schofield, 1988), or *individual learning preferences* (e.g., Plass, Chun, Mayer, & Leutner, 1998), refers to findings that with regard to multimedia instructional materials, some people tend to choose visual material rather than verbal material and describe themselves as visual learners (*visualizers*), while others describe themselves as verbal learners (*verbalizers*; e.g., Jonassen & Grabowski, 1993; Mayer & Massa, 2003). In the following, we use the term cognitive style to refer to this phenomenon (for an overview, see Kozhevnikov, 2007).

While Plass et al. (1998) found that in general, and consistent with the CTML (Mayer, 2009), enriching text with pictures or animations led to better learning outcomes than text alone, their study (see Figure 6.7 for a screenshot) also revealed an aptitude-treatment interaction (ATI) effect in which learning success was substantially impaired if pictures or animations were missing, but only for visualizers. The authors concluded that visualizers profit considerably from visual material, whereas verbalizers depend far less on visual material. Riding and Douglas (1993) also reported an ATI-effect when confronting visualizers and verbalizers with either text plus pictures or text plus text. In this study, visualizers performed better with the text-plus-pictures condition, whereas verbalizers were better with the text-plus-text condition. However, Massa and Mayer (2006) did not find this effect. Thus, it is not clear whether verbalizers rely mainly on the textual parts of a multimedia instruction. As with many other ATI-effects, results are inconsistent and few (Biggs, 2001; Cronbach, 2002).

With regard to the role of cognitive style, not only for learning with visual representations in general, but concerning our distinction between static pictures and animations, Höffler, Prechtl, and Nerdel (2010) noted that up to that point in time, not much research had been conducted explicitly addressing this issue. The authors assumed that as the distinction between static and dynamic pictures is clearly visual, "a highly or less

Source: Image used with permission from Jan Plass.

Figure 6.7.   Screenshot of the learning environment used in Plass et al's (1998) study.

developed visual style should play a more pronounced role than a visual versus verbal style" (Höffler et al., 2010, p. 480). In line with Salomon's (1979) *supplantation theory*, which states that dynamic external representations can compensate for insufficient aptitudes or skills to imagine motions internally, they see animations as explicit external representations of a process and deem such external models as useful to help learners with a less developed visual style (who report to think less in pictures and use less mental images) develop adequate mental representations. Accordingly, animations could possess a compensatory illustrative power for learners with less pronounced visual styles or skills (Lewalter, 1997).

   In contrast, Höffler et al. (2010) noted that such a compensatory effect, while found for learners with low spatial ability (cf. next section), had not yet been shown for cognitive styles. Therefore, they investigated whether a compensatory effect of animations for "less developed visualizers" (who think less in pictures and use less mental images) could be found in a learning environment focusing on primary reactions in photosynthesis (see Figure 6.8). Their results revealed an interaction between highly developed and less developed visualizers when comparing animations and static pictures. Highly developed visualizers had better results regarding comprehension when learning with static pictures (and significantly outperformed less developed visualizers), while for less developed visualizers, it made no difference whether they learned with animations or static pictures. Interestingly, highly developed visualizers performed worse with animations than with static pictures. One possible explanation might be the transitory nature of animations discussed earlier in this chapter which could have produced a higher extraneous cognitive load. An alternative explanation can be derived from the work of Schnotz and Rasch (2005), who reported inhibiting effects of animations on learners who would otherwise be able to perform the mental simulation of a process by themselves. These results suggested that the facilitating effect of the external support decreased their ability to perform relevant cognitive processes on their own. In addition, less developed visualizers could not benefit from animations significantly. Thus, animations might not be able to effectively compensate for the presumed lack of less developed visualizers to work with visual material by providing them with an adequate dynamic mental model.

Overall, when it comes to learning with animations, results on the moderating role of cognitive style are rather inconclusive. Although the study of Höffler et al. (2010) found an interaction between cognitive style

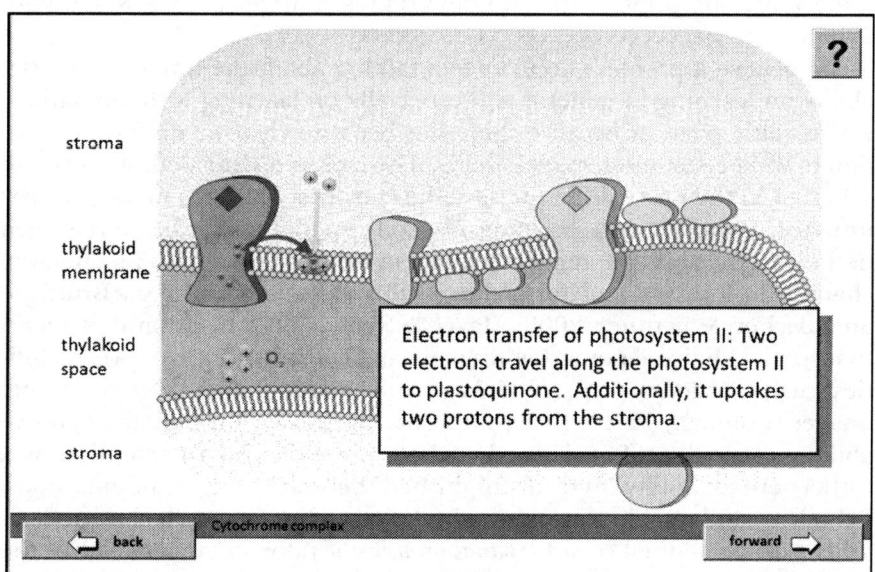

Figure 6.8.   Screenshot used in the static version of Höffler et al.'s (2010) study.

and the type of visual representations provided, their results speak in favor of static pictures, as neither of the two groups of learners learned better with animations. As only a few research studies have been conducted so far, more studies should be carried out to validate these findings. In addition, the authors emphasize that cognitive style might not be the deciding factor when it comes to learning with animation, and that in studies investigating the role of cognitive style for learning with animation or static pictures, *spatial ability* should be taken into account as there seems to be evidence that different types of visualizers rely on their levels of spatial ability (Kozhevnikov, Hegarty, & Mayer, 2002). Our next section will focus on spatial ability and its influence on learning with animations.

The Role of Spatial Ability for Learning With Animations

Quite early on the idea of spatial ability as a possible moderator between the instructional design of visual representations and learning success was put forward. One example was Mayer's (2005, 2009) individual differences principle, which states that besides low prior knowledge learners, learners with high spatial ability also benefit from multimedia presentations. The rationale behind this assumption is that students with high spatial ability, when presented with visual information, can better retain this information in their working memory, and thus learn better when words are presented with visual representations (Mayer & Moreno, 1998).

We believe a problem occurs when talking about the impact of spatial ability on learning in general and especially on learning with animations versus static pictures because there has been no clear or uniform definition of what constitutes spatial ability. The lack of a clear definition is also reflected in the many different ways the construct has been measured. For instance, in multimedia learning research, spatial ability has often been defined as the ability to mentally rotate or fold objects and to imagine the changes in location and form due to this manipulation (e.g., Brünken, Steinbacher, & Leutner, 2000; Mayer & Sims, 1994). In general, it seems that spatial ability is not a one-dimensional construct but comprises abilities such as generating, retaining, and manipulating abstract visual images (Lohman, 1979). In a comprehensive review on human cognitive abilities, Carroll (1993) defined spatial ability or visual perception as a rather broad ability and distinguished between five sub-dimensions, namely spatial visualization, spatial relations, closure speed, closure flexibility, and perceptual speed. *Spatial visualization*, for instance, involves the ability to imagine spatial movements of objects and shapes (Hegarty & Waller, 2004). An example of a spatial visualization test is the paper fold-ing test developed by Ekstrom, French, Harman, and Dermen (1976). Ten items show successive pictures of two or three folds made to a square sheet of paper. The final picture in the sequence shows the folded paper with a hole stamped through it. The students have to choose among five pictures the one that shows how the stamped sheet would look when fully opened (cf. Kozhevnikov, Motes, & Hegarty, 2007). The second factor, *spatial relations*, refers to the ability to perceive spatial patterns or maintain orientation with respect to objects in space. Those two subdimensions of spatial ability, spatial visualization and spatial relations, are considered to be the most demanding on executive functioning (Miyake, Friedman, Rettinger, Shah, & Hegarty, 2001), and therefore potentially the most meaningful when learning with dynamic representations. What is more, in contrast to the other three factors identified by Carroll (1993), they require mental transformations, which are known to be important constraints on visual processing. The third and fourth factor, *closure speed* and *flexibility of closure*, constitute the speed to apprehend and identify visual patterns in spite of perceptual distractions. The fifth factor, *perceptual speed*, is defined as the speed needed to find known visual patterns, make comparisons, and carry out other simple tasks involving visual perception.

With regard to the impact of spatial ability on learning with animations, Hegarty (2005) assumes that spatial ability enhances learning because learners with high spatial ability benefit from learning with animations, while learners with low spatial ability do not. This assumption has also been called the *ability-as-enhancer hypothesis* (Huk, 2006; Mayer & Sims, 1994; Plass, Chun, Mayer, & Leutner, 2003). However, there is still little empirical evidence supporting this hypothesis—and even fewer studies which compared animations and static pictures regarding the influence of spatial ability. Although the results of Mayer and Sims (1994) supported the ability-as-enhancer hypothesis, they have to be viewed carefully because the authors used two animations that differed in the type of verbal narration and are thus not likely 100% comparable. Providing some support for the hypothesis, Isaak and Just (1995) found a main effect for spatial ability in that high-spatial-ability learners viewing an animation were less susceptible to an optical illusion.

Several authors thus argue in favor of quite the opposite, the so called *ability-as-compensator hypothesis* (Höffler, 2010; Höffler & Leutner, 2011; Lee, 2007). This hypothesis states that high spatial ability learners could compensate for less than optimal visual representations like, for example, static pictures for a dynamic process (by mentally animating the process). Likewise, learners with low spatial ability might benefit from animations because they provide an external representation of a process or procedure that helps learners to build an adequate mental model that would be more difficult to construct using static pictures (Hays, 1996). Animations might therefore act as a "cognitive prosthetic" for learners with low spatial ability (Hegarty & Kriz, 2008). This assumption was supported by findings from Lee (2007), Höffler and Leutner (2011), and Stebner, Lebens, Wirth, and Opfermann (2009), who found that in the domain of chemistry, learners with high spatial ability were able to compensate for the lack of information in static compared to dynamic visual representations. A meta-analytic review (Höffler, 2010) and another recent empirical study (Lee & Shin, 2012) also supported these findings.

CONCLUSIONS: CAN WE GIVE RECOMMENDATIONS FOR THE DESIGN OF VISUAL REPRESENTATIONS?

Coming back to the beginning of our chapter, let us suppose that you are still to decide which kind of presentation you would like to give to the students. It might already have become clear that this decision cannot be made easily and that there is no panacea-like recommendation in which one *perfect instructional design* can be applied to all learners in all different learning situations. Whether you want to use static pictures, animations, or a video obviously depends on the contents you want to convey to learners such as facts (in this case, static pictures might be sufficient) or processes (which might be more comprehensible when conveyed by means of animations) as well as on the individual learner characteristics such as prior knowledge, cognitive style and spatial ability the learners bring along. The only aspect that you would be quite sure about after having read this book and this chapter would be to include some kind of visual representations in your talk. Pictures that are added to text are more beneficial for learning than text alone (Mayer, 2009), a statement that is based on the dual-channel assumption of the human memory system. If we process verbal and visual information in different channels (Baddeley, 1999; Paivio, 1986), it makes sense to use them both instead of overloading one channel. In addition, because words and pictures are qualitatively different regarding the information they contain, they can complement, but not substitute for one another (Mayer, 2009). In this regard, when you explain the optimal turn the body of the high jumper should make the moment his feet leave the ground, it is much easier to understand if you add one or more picture(s) to your presentation instead of just describing this turn with words.

With regard to the *type* of visual representation you should use to complement your textual explanations, the situation gets a little trickier. In accordance with the distinction by Weidenmann (1993), or the coherence principle by Mayer (2009), it might be advisable to use informational (instructional) representations if you want the students to understand and learn the contents instead of just motivating them. That is, you would probably show decorative representations (such as the funny video mentioned above) *at the beginning of the talk* to stimulate your learners' interest. During the presentation itself, however, instructional representations, such as animations showing successful jumps or (series of) static pictures showing essential points of the movement of a successful high jumper should be used.

Now the question still remains whether you should prefer static pictures, animations or even show a "real" video to your audience. We believe the best answer to this question still seems to be "it all depends". Although Münzer et al. (2009) state that when *dynamic contents* (e.g., processes such as a high jump) are to be learned, animations should be preferred, research has shown that their benefits interact with several other aspects. If you want your learners to *understand* the jumping process as a whole, you might prefer not to show an animation, because its transient nature would make it difficult for the learner to retain the single steps simultaneously in working memory. In this case, it would be better to show a series of static pictures depicting key movements of a successful jump because individual learner characteristics as spatial ability and cognitive style might constrain the type of visual representation you should use. On the other hand, if you wanted your audience to *learn how to jump*; that is, to imitate the movement, it would be better to show the process as a whole so that not only the key movements, but also the transitions in between, can be viewed *as a whole*.

Once you have decided about whether to use static or dynamic representations, you would, however, be free to choose the level of realism of the representations. One might argue that realistic animations might better trigger the mirror neuron system (see above), and thus might lead to a more accurate imitation of the movement. An alternative view is that a movie of a real high jumper could include seductive details (e.g., visible details of the audience in the background or a certain attractiveness of the high jumper; etc.; cf. Figure 6.5), which you could avoid in an animation. As found by Imhof et al. (2011) or by Höffler and Leutner (2007) in their meta-analysis, research still provides mixed results on this question.

Apart from the *pure instructional design* of your presentation, another aspect to consider is your audience and their individual learner characteristics. Different learners profit differently from dynamic or static visual representations (as summarized in Table 6.1). Of course, if your audience is completely unknown to you (for instance, if you are invited to give your talk as an external guest), it would be rather difficult to find out about cognitive styles or spatial abilities of the people. You might, however, be able to guess something about their prior knowledge. Are they familiar with the topic? Will your audience consist of experts, or be mixed, or

**Table 6.1.   Brief Summary of Main Research Findings
Concerning Interplay of Learning Characteristics and
Type of Visual Representation**

	Prior Knowledge	*Cognitive Style*	*Spatial Ability*
Static images	Usually sufficient for high prior knowledge learners; potentially generating too much cognitive load for low prior knowledge learners.	Some evidence that highly developed visualizers (who report to think much in pictures) learn better with static pictures than with animations.	The higher the learner's spatial ability, the better are his/her learning results when learning with static pictures.
Dynamic representation (animations)	Generally recommendable for learners with both high and low prior knowledge, though redundant information can hinder learning for high prior knowledge learners (expertise reversal effect)	When the visual style is not as pronounced (tending towards a verbal style), animations and static pictures seem to be equally good for learning – but animations are not better.	Animations seem to be able to act as "cognitive prosthetic" for learners with low spatial ability (so that they don't have to visualize the process mentally and thus learn better than with static pictures).

include novices regarding sports and high jumping? In the latter cases, you might want to include more instructional help in your presentation by highlighting the direction of the motions with additional arrows. However, such information would be redundant and thus cause extraneous load for learners with higher prior knowledge.

Spatial ability and cognitive style are important constraints that affect the type of visual representation being used. For high spatial ability learners or those with a highly developed visual style (the "visualizers"), static pictures might work as well as animations, because these learners are better able to grasp the information provided in the pictures and draw inferences regarding dynamic aspects by themselves. However, for learners with low spatial ability, or those with a less developed cognitive style, animations might be the preferred method, because in this case, learners would be provided with external representations of the processes and procedures (e.g., the movements in a jump) and would not have to build up adequate mental models all by themselves.

It should be noted that the individual learner characteristics we have been referring to in this chapter should not be viewed as being exhaustive. There are several other characteristics (e.g., epistemological beliefs;

metacognitive and self-regulatory abilities; motivation) that can play a substantial role as moderators (cf. Gerjets & Hesse, 2004; Schraw, Dunkle, & Bendixen, 1995) or mediators (cf. Davis, Bagozzi, & Warshaw, 1989; Opfermann, 2008) between the instructional design of a learning environment, strategies and activities deployed during learning as well as cognitive load and learning outcomes. These, however, were not part of this chapter which focused on learner characteristics that have a special impact on learning with visual representations (compared to learning in general).

One strategy for taking individual learner characteristics and the differential benefits of static versus dynamic pictures into account would be to make instructional design features *optional* during learning. That is, one could provide several kinds of visual representations from which the learners could choose from, depending on their individual preferences, characteristics, but also learning progresses. This kind of adaptive learning is assumed to be more beneficial for heterogeneous groups of learners compared to a completely pre-structured learning environment, which cannot take all of the above mentioned aspects into account (cf. Schnotz, Heiß, & Eckhardt, 2005).

In general, neither static nor dynamic visual representations are superior to one another regarding learning success, nor are there specific learning scenarios in which it is optimal to use only one. Much depends on the specific group of learners. The benefits of visual representations depend on many interacting factors, especially the type of information, and it would be a real challenge to take them all into account when preparing your talk or other learning materials. We believe there is still much room for further research in order to give more differentiated recommendations for the design of visual representations.

ACKNOWLEDGMENTS

The authors would like to thank Cornelia Gerigk for proofreading and correcting the English text and Sabrina Hilz for her valuable help in drawing Figure 6.2.

REFERENCES

Ainsworth, S. E. (1999). A functional taxonomy of multiple representations. *Computers and Education, 33*, 131-152.

Ainsworth, S. E. (2006). DeFT: A conceptual framework for considering learning with multiple representations. *Learning and Instruction, 16*, 183-198.

Ainsworth, S., & VanLabeke, N. (2004). Multiple forms of dynamic representation. *Learning and Instruction, 14*, 241-255.

Ayres, P., Marcus, N., Chan, C., & Qian, N. (2009). Learning hand manipulative tasks: When instructional animations are superior to equivalent static representations. *Computers in Human Behavior, 25*(2), 348-353.

Baddeley, A. (1992). Working memory. *Science, 255*, 556-559.

Baddeley, A. (1999). *Essentials of human memory.* Hove: Psychology Press.

Bétrancourt, M., & Tversky, B. (2000). Effect of computer animation on users' performance: A review. *Travail-Humain, 63*, 311-329.

Biggs, J. (2001). Enhancing learning: A matter of style or approach? In R. J. Sternberg & L. Zhang (Eds.), *Perspectives on thinking, learning, and cognitive style* (pp. 73-102). Mahwah, NJ: Erlbaum.

Brünken, R., Steinbacher, S. & Leutner, D. (2000). Räumliches Vorstellungsvermögen und Lernen mit Multimedia [Spatial ability and learning with multimedia]. In D. Leutner, & R. Brünken (Eds.), *Neue Medien in Unterricht, Aus- und Weiterbildung: Aktuelle Ergebnisse empirischer pädagogischer Forschung* [New media in education: Recent results of empirical pedagogical research] (pp. 37-46). Münster, Germany: Waxmann.

Carney, R. N., & Levin, J. R. (2002). Pictorial illustrations still improve students' learning from text. *Educational Psychology Review, 14*, 5-26.

Carroll, J. B. (1993). *Human cognitive abilities.* New York, NY: Cambridge University Press.

Catrambone, R., & Seay, A. F. (2002). Using animation to help students learn computer algorithms. *Human Factors, 44*, 495-511.

Chandler, P., & Sweller, J. (1991). Cognitive load theory and the format of instruction. *Cognition and Instruction, 8*, 293-332.

Clark, R. E., & Feldon, D. F. (2005). Five common but questionable principles of multimedia learning. In R. E. Mayer (Ed.), *Cambridge Handbook of Multimedia Learning* (pp. 97-115). Cambridge, England: Cambridge University Press.

Clark, R. C., & Mayer, R. E. (2003). *E-Learning and the science of instruction.* San Francisco, CA: Jossey-Bass/Pfeiffer.

Conklin, J. (1987). Hypertext: An introduction and survey. *IEEE Computer, 20*(9), 17-41.

Cronbach, L. J. (Ed.). (2002). *Remaking the concept of aptitude: Extending the legacy of Richard E. Snow.* Mahwah, NJ: Erlbaum.

Davis, F. D., Bagozzi, R. P., & Warshaw, P. R. (1989). User acceptance of computer technology: A comparison of two theoretical models. *Management Science, 35*, 982-1003.

Ekstrom, R. B., French, J. W., Harman, H. H., & Dermen, D. (1976). *Manual for kit of factor-referenced cognitive tests.* Princeton, NJ: Educational Testing Service.

Gazzola, V., Rizzolatti, G., Wicker, B., & Keysers, C. (2007). The anthropomorphic brain: The mirror neuron system responds to human and robotic actions. *NeuroImage, 35*, 1674-1684. doi:10.1016/j.neuro image.2007.02.003.

Gerjets, P., & Hesse, F. W. (2004). When are powerful learning environments effective? The role of learning activities and of students' conceptions of educational technology. *International Journal of Educational Research, 41*, 445-465.

Harp, S. F., & Mayer, R. E. (1998). How seductive details do their damage: a theory of cognitive interest in science learning. *Journal of Educational Psychology, 90*, 414-434.

Hays, T. A. (1996). Spatial abilities and the effects of computer animation on short-term and long-term comprehension. *Journal of Educational Computing Research, 14*, 139-155.

Hegarty, M. (1992). Mental animation: Inferring motion from static diagrams of mechanical systems. *Journal of Experimental Psychology: Learning, Memory and Cognition, 18*, 1084-1102.

Hegarty, M. (2004). Dynamic visualizations and learning: Getting to the difficult questions. *Learning and Instruction, 14*, 343-351.

Hegarty, M. (2005). Multimedia learning about physical systems. In R. E. Mayer (Ed.), *The Cambridge handbook of multimedia learning* (pp. 447-465). Cambridge, England: Cambridge University Press.

Hegarty, M., Kriz, S., & Cate, C. (2003). The roles of mental animations and external animations in understanding mechanical systems. *Cognition and Instruction, 21*, 325-360.

Hegarty, M., & Kriz, S. (2008). Effects of knowledge and spatial ability on learning from animation. In R. Lowe & W. Schnotz (Eds.), *Learning with animation: Research implications for design* (pp. 3-29). Cambridge, England: Cambridge University Press.

Hegarty, M., & , D. (2004). A dissociation between mental rotation and perspective-taking spatial abilities. *Intelligence, 32*, 175-191.

Höffler, T. N. (2010). Spatial ability: Its influence on learning with visualizations – a meta-analytic review. *Educational Psychology Review, 22*, 245-269.

Höffler, T. N. & Leutner, D. (2007). Instructional animation versus static pictures: A meta-analysis. *Learning and Instruction, 17*, 722-738.

Höffler, T. N., & Leutner, D. (2011). The role of spatial ability in learning from instructional animations—Evidence for an ability-as-compensator hypothesis. *Computers in Human Behavior, 27*, 209-216.

Höffler, T. N., Prechtl, M., & Nerdel, C. (2010). The influence of visual cognitive style when learning from instructional animations and static pictures. *Learning and Individual Differences, 20*, 479-483.

Höffler, T. N.. & Schwartz, R. (2011). Effects of pacing and cognitive style across dynamic and non-dynamic representations. *Computers & Education, 57*, 1716-1726.

Horz, H., & Schnotz, W. (2008). Multimedia: How to combine language and visuals. *Language at Work, 4*, 43-50.

Huk, T. (2006). Who benefits from learning with 3d models? The case of spatial ability. *Journal of Computer-Assisted Learning, 22*, 392-404.

Imhof, B., Jarodzka, H., & Gerjets, P. (2009). Classifying instructional visualizations: A psychological approach. *Image, 10*, 99-123.

Imhof, B., Scheiter, K., & Gerjets, P. (2011). Learning about locomotion patterns from visualizations: Effects of presentation format and realism. *Computers & Education, 57*, 1961-1970.

Isaak, M. I., & Just, M. A. (1995). Constraints on the processing of rolling motion: The curtate cycloid illusion. *Journal of Experimental Psychology: Human Perception and Performance, 21,* 1391-1408.

Jonassen, D. H., & Grabowski, B. L. (1993). *Handbook of individual differences, learning, and instruction.* Hillsdale, MI: Erlbaum.

Kalyuga, S. (2007). Expertise reversal effect and its implications for learner-tailored instruction. *Educational Psychology Review, 19,* 509-539.

Kalyuga, S., Ayres, P., Chandler, P., & Sweller, J. (2003). The expertise reversal effect. *Educational Psychologist, 38,* 23-31.

Kirby, J. R., Moore, P., & Schofield, N. (1988). Verbal and visual learning styles. *Contemporary Educational Psychology, 13,* 169-184.

Kozhevnikov, M. (2007). Cognitive styles in the context of modern psychology: Toward an integrated framework. *Psychological Bulletin, 133,* 464-481.

Kozhevnikov, M., Hegarty, M., & Mayer, R. E. (2002). Revising the visualizer–verbalizer dimension: Evidence for two types of visualizers. *Cognition and Instruction, 20,* 37-77.

Kozhevnikov, M., Motes, M., and Hegarty, M. (2007). Spatial visualization in physics problem solving. *Cognitive Sciences, 31,* 549-579.

Lee, H. (2007). Instructional design of web-based simulations for learners with different levels of spatial ability. *Instructional Science, 35,* 467-479.

Lee, D. Y. & Shin, D.-H. (2012). An empirical evaluation of multi-media based learning of a procedural task. *Computers in Human Behavior, 28*(3), 1072-1081.

Lenzner, A., Schnotz, W., Müller, A., & Horz, H. (2007, August). *Emotional and motivational effects of decorative pictures in knowledge communication.* Paper presented at the annual meeting of the European Association for Research on Learning and Instruction (EARLI). Budapest, Hungary.

Levin, J. R. (1981). On functions of pictures in prose. In F. J. Pirozzolo & M. C. Wittrock (Eds.), *Neuropsychological and Cognitive Processes in Reading* (pp. 203-228). New York, NY: Academic Press.

Lewalter, D. (1997). *Lernen mit Bildern und Animationen: Studie zum Einfluss von Lernermerkmalen auf die Effektivität von Illustrationen* [Learning with pictures and animations: A study about the influence of learner characteristics on the efficiency of illustrations]. Münster, Germany: Waxmann.

Lewalter, D. (2003). Cognitive strategies for learning from static and dynamic visuals. *Learning and Instruction, 13,* 177-189.

Lohman, D. F. (1979). *Spatial ability: A review and reanalysis of the correlational literature.* (Technical Report No. 8). Stanford, CA: Stanford University.

Lowe, R. K. (1999). Extracting information from an animation during complex visual learning. *European Journal of Psychology of Education, 14,* 225-244.

Lowe, R. K. (2003). Animation and learning: Selective processing of information in dynamic graphics. *Learning and Instruction, 13,* 157-176.

Lowe, R. K. (2004). Interrogation of a dynamic visualization during learning. *Learning and Instruction, 14,* 257-274.

Massa, L., & Mayer, R. E. (2006). Testing the ATI hypothesis: Should multimedia instruction accommodate verbalizer-visualizer cognitive style? *Learning and Individual Differences, 16,* 321-335.

Mayer, R. E. (2005). (Ed.). *Cambridge Handbook of Multimedia Learning*. Cambridge: Cambridge University Press.

Mayer, R. E. (2009). *Multimedia learning* (2nd ed.). Cambridge, MA: Cambridge University Press.

Mayer, R. E., & Chandler, P. (2001). When learning is just a click away: Does simple user interaction foster deeper understanding of multimedia messages? *Journal of Educational Psychology, 93,* 390-397.

Mayer, R. E., Hegarty, M., Mayer, S., & Campbell, J. E. (2005). When static media promote active learning: Annotated illustrations versus narrated animations in multimedia instruction. *Journal of Experimental Psychology: Applied, 11,* 256-265.

Mayer, R. E., & Massa, L. (2003). Three facets of visual and verbal learners: Cognitive ability, cognitive style, and learning preference. *Journal of Educational Psychology, 95,* 833-841.

Mayer, R. E., & Moreno, R. (1998). A split-attention effect in multimedia learning: Evidence for dual processing systems in working memory. *Journal of Educational Psychology, 90,* 312-320.

Mayer, R. E., & Moreno, R. (2002). Aids to computer-based multimedia learning. *Learning and Instruction, 12,* 107-119.

Mayer, R. E. & Sims, V. K. (1994). For whom is a picture worth a thousand words? Extensions of a dual-coding theory of Multimedia. *Journal of Educational Psychology, 86,* 389-401.

Messick, S. (1976). Personality consistencies in cognition and creativity. In S. Messick (Ed.), *Individuality in learning* (pp. 4-23). San Francisco, CA: Jossey-Bass.

Michas, I. C., & Berry, D. C. (2000). Learning a procedural task: Effectiveness of multimedia presentations. *Applied Cognitive Psychology, 14,* 555-575.

Milheim, W. D. (1993). How to use animation in computer-assisted-learning. *British Journal of Educational Technology, 24,* 171-178.

Miyake, A., Friedman, N. P., Rettinger, D. A., Shah, P., & Hegarty, M. (2001). How are visuospatial working memory, executive functioning, and spatial abilities related? A latent-variable analysis. *Journal of Experimental Psychology, 130,* 621-640.

Moreno, R., & Valdez, A. (2005). Cognitive load and learning effects of having students organize pictures and words in multimedia environments: The role of student interactivity and feedback. *Educational Technology Research and Development, 53,* 35-45.

Münzer, S., Seufert, T., & Brünken, R. (2009). Learning from multimedia presentations: Facilitation function of animations and spatial abilities. *Learning and Individual Differences, 19,* 481-485.

Niegemann, H. M., Domagk, S., Hessel, S., Hein, A., Hupfer, M., & Zobel, A. (2008). *Kompendium multimediales Lernen* [Compendium for multimedia learning]. Heidelberg, Germany: Springer.

Opfermann, M. (2008). *There's more to it than instructional design: The role of individual learner characteristics for hypermedia learning.* Berlin, Germany: Logos.

Paivio, A. (1986). *Mental representations: A dual coding approach.* Oxford, England: Oxford University Press.

Plass, J. L., Chun, D., Mayer, R. E., & Leutner, D. (1998). Supporting visualizer and verbalizer learning preferences in a second language multimedia learning environment. *Journal of Educational Psychology, 90*, 25-36.

Plass, J. L., Chun, D., Mayer, R. E., & Leutner, D. (2003). Cognitive load in reading a foreign language text with multimedia aids and the influence of verbal and spatial abilities. *Computers in Human Behavior, 19*, 211-220.

Plass, J. L., & Jones, L. C. (2005). Multimedia learning in second language acquisition. In R. E. Mayer (Ed.), *Cambridge Handbook of Multimedia Learning* (pp. 467-488). Cambridge, England: Cambridge University Press.

Ploetzner, R., & Lowe, R. (2012). A systematic characterisation of expository animations. *Computers in Human Behavior, 28*, 781-794.

Rebetez, C., Bétrancourt, M., Sangin, M., & Dillenbourg, P. (2010). Learning from animation enabled by collaboration. *Instructional Science, 38*, 471-485.

Riding, R. J., & Douglas, G. (1993). The effect of cognitive style and mode of presentation on learning performance. *British Journal of Educational Psychology, 63*, 297-307.

Rieber, L. P. (1990). Using computer animated graphics with science instruction with children. *Journal of Educational Psychology, 82*, 135-140.

Rieber, L. P. (1994). *Computers, graphics, and learning.* Madison, WI: Brown and Benchmark.

Rieber, L. P., & Kini, A. S. (1991). Theoretical foundations of instructional applications of computer-generated animated visuals. *Journal of Computer-Based Instruction, 18*, 83-88.

Rizzolatti, G., & Craighero, L. (2004). The mirror-neuron system. *Annual Review of Neuroscience, 27*, 169-192.

Salomon, G. (1979). *Interaction of media, cognition, and learning: an exploration of how symbolic forms cultivate mental skills and affect knowledge acquisition.* San Francisco, CA: Jossey-Bass.

Schnotz, W. (2005). An integrated model of text and picture comprehension. In R. E. Mayer (Ed.), *Cambridge Handbook of Multimedia Learning* (pp. 49-69). Cambridge, England: Cambridge University Press.

Schnotz, W., Heiß, A., & Eckhardt, E. (2005). *Wann sind Lernhilfen in hypermedialen Lernumgebungen erfolgreich?* [When is learning support in hypermedia learning environments successful?] In A. Schütz, S. Habscheid, W. Holly, J. Krems, & C. G. Voß (Eds.), *Neue Medien im Alltag: Befunde aus den Bereichen Arbeit, Lernen und Freizeit* (pp. 189-203). Lengerich, Germany: Pabst Science.

Schnotz, W., & Lowe, R. (2008). A unified view of learning from animated and static graphics. In R. Lowe, & W. Schnotz (Eds.), *Learning with animation: Research implications for design* (pp. 304–356). Cambridge, England: Cambridge University Press.

Schnotz, W., & Rasch, T. (2005). Enabling, facilitating, and inhibiting effects of animations in multimedia learning: Why reduction of cognitive load can have negative results on learning. *Educational Technology. Research and Development, 53*, 47-58.

Schnotz, W., & Rasch, T. (2008). Functions of animations in comprehension and learning. In R. K. Lowe, & W. Schnotz (Eds.), *Learning with animation: Research implications for design* (pp. 93-113). New York, NY: Cambridge University Press.

Schraw, G., Dunkle, M. E., & Bendixen, L. D. (1995). Cognitive processes in well-defined and ill-defined problem solving. *Applied Cognitive Psychology, 9,* 523-538.

Schwamborn, A., Thillmann, H., Opfermann, M., & Leutner, D. (2011). Cognitive load and instructionally supported learning with provided and learner-generated visualizations. *Computers in Human Behavior, 27,* 89-93.

Schwamborn, A., Thillmann, H., Leopold, C., Sumfleth, E., & Leutner, D. (2010). Der Einsatz von vorgegebenen und selbst generierten Bildern als Textverstehenshilfe beim Lernen aus einem naturwissenschaftlichen Sachtext [The use of presented and learner-generated pictures as aid for comprehension in science text learning]. *Zeitschrift für Pädagogische Psychologie, 24,* 221-233.

Spotts, J., & Dwyer, F. M. (1996). The effect of computer-generated animation on student achievement of different types of educational objectives. *International Journal of Instructional Media, 23,* 365-375.

Stebner, F., Lebens, M., Wirth, J., & Opfermann, M. (2009, March). *Learning from animations and static pictures: The impact of spatial ability and cognitive load.* Paper presented at the Cognitive Load Conference, Open University of the Netherlands, Heerlen, NL.

Sweller, J. (2010). Element interactivity and intrinsic, extraneous, and germane cognitive load. *Educational Psychology Review, 22*(2), 123-138.

Sweller, J., van Merriënboer, J. J. G., & Paas, F. W. C. (1998). Cognitive architecture and instructional design. *Educational Psychology Review, 10,* 251-296.

Swezey, R. W. (1991). Effects of instructional strategy and motion presentation conditions on the acquisition and transfer of electromechanical troubleshooting skill. *Human Factors, 33,* 309-323.

Tversky, B., Bauer-Morrison, J., & Bétrancourt, M. (2002). Animation: Can it facilitate? *International Journal of Human-Computer Studies, 57,* 247-262.

Tversky, B., Heiser, J., Mackenzie, R., Lozano, S., & Morrison, J. (2008). Enriching animations. In R. Lowe & W. Schnotz (Eds.), *Learning with animation: Research implications for design* (pp. 263–285). Cambridge, England: Cambridge University Press.

Van Gog, T., Paas, F. G. W. C., Marcus, N., Ayres, P., & Sweller, J. (2009). The mirror neuron system and observational learning: Implications for the effectiveness of dynamic visualizations. *Educational Psychology Review, 21*(1), 21-30.

Van Merriënboer, J. J. G., & Sweller, J. (2005). Cognitive load theory and complex learning: Recent developments and future directions. *Educational Psychology Review, 17,* 147–177.

Weidenmann, B. (1993). Informierende Bilder. [Informational pictures.] In B. Weidenmann (Ed.), *Wissenserwerb mit Bildern* [Knowledge acquisition with pictures]. (pp. 9.-58). Bern, Switzerland: Hans Huber.

Yang, E. M., Andre, T., & Greenbowe, T. Y. (2003). Spatial ability and the impact of visualization/animation on learning electrochemistry. *International Journal of Science Education, 25,* 329-349.

CHAPTER 7

STATIC VISUAL DISPLAYS FOR DEEPER UNDERSTANDING

How to Help Learners Make Use of Them

Alexander Renkl and Rolf Schwonke

ABSTRACT

Visual displays are frequently used to enrich learning materials, with the intention to help learners develop deeper understanding. However, learners often fail to use such additional external representations productively. A variety of instructional support procedures was therefore developed and tested. One typical restriction of such procedures (e.g., integrated format, color coding) is that they do not adequately address the structural (i.e., deep) level of learning domains. Against this background, we tested ways to support learners' processing of visual displays and their integration with other information sources on the structural level. Direct procedures support the integration of visual displays with other information sources by corresponding self-explanation prompts. A more indirect procedure is to provide "instructions for use", whereby the learners are informed of the functions for gaining understanding that visual displays have. Overall, our findings suggest that typical instructional support procedures for processing visual

Learning Through Visual Displays, pp. 165–186

displays should be supplemented by procedures that direct the learners' attention to the structural level. We conclude with three general instructional principles drawn from our work.

Imagine that you read a book and you came to a phrase such as "As Figure 1 clearly shows, ...". You are astonished that you fail to see a figure, and you begin to scan the preceding and following pages. After finding the figure, you have to reread the passage in order to remember what exactly Figure 1 was supposed to illustrate. After rereading the passage and looking at the figure, Figure 1 still does not "clearly show" you anything. You put some effort in finding overlapping contents between the text and the figure. Although you are sure that the figure is supposed to relate to the text passage, you must work hard to see how the figure supports the arguments in the text. You have finally managed to figure out what the author was trying to communicate while feeling relieved that you are not incapable of understanding what the author had claimed to be obvious. As you continue reading you fervently hope that there will be no further references to figures in the remaining text.

Unfortunately, I imagine that all of us have had similar experiences in which a figure was added to a text to clarify things that did not necessarily increase the accessibility of the information. In these situations, the learner is challenged to find some correspondence between the text and visual display on the surface level, and after having identified some overlapping, further reflect on the two information sources and their interrelations in order to arrive at a deeper understanding on the structural level. The goal of this chapter is to develop several general instructional principles on how to support learners in the use of visual displays, and in particular, understanding information on the structural level.

We shall first specify the types of visual displays to be considered, followed by a discussion of the strengths and weaknesses of visual displays when they are used in conjunction with other information sources. Given that visual displays may not always facilitate learning, we describe typical instructional support procedures that attempt to remedy this problem. Against the background that these support procedures insufficiently address the structural (i.e., deep) level of learning domains, we discuss some of our own research on procedures that aim to induce processing on the structural level. We compare our support procedures to related approaches. Finally, we propose three recommendations on how to support learners to make productive use of visual displays.

STATIC VISUAL DISPLAYS FOR DEEPER UNDERSTANDING

There is a variety of different types of visual displays (e.g., realistic and schematic pictures, animations) with different (intended) functions of such displays (e.g., decorative or mnemonic) and different potential effects (e.g., motivation, fact retrieval, comprehension) (see Schraw, McCrudden, & Robinson, this volume). Against this background, generalized claims on learning from visual displays are probably "overstretched" (see also Vekiri, 2002). In this chapter, we will focus on static visual displays, which we define as pictures, graphics, flowcharts, and so on, that do not change over time.

Static visual displays can be added to other information sources to promote deeper understanding of the learning contents. For example, Figure 7.1 shows a screenshot from a learning environment in which one of the researchers' main goals was to include tree diagrams to promote deeper understanding of probability equations. Among others, the learners should integrate the multiplication sign of the equation and the ramifications of the pictorial tree diagram to understand the underlying structure; that is, that the multiplication sign stands for the inclusion of all possible combinations represented by the 20 branches in the pictorial tree diagram.

With reference to the taxonomy of Levin (1981), we can roughly state that we focus on visual displays that have an interpretational function; that is, visual displays that help learners clarify otherwise difficult to understand information from other informational sources, such as text or mathematical equations. Such an interpretational function differentiates from other functions, as postulated by Levin: decorational function (i.e., making materials more appealing by visuals that have no or hardly any relation to the contents), representational function (i.e., pictures "mirroring" text contents), organizational function (i.e., provision of a structural framework for the text content), and transformational function (i.e, provide a mnemonic aid for retrieving text information later on) (see also Carney & Levin, 2002; Levin, Anglin, & Carney, 1987).

The DeFT framework (Ainsworth, 2006) provides another prominent taxonomy of display types and corresponding functions. The core of this framework is the differentiation between different instructional functions of multiple external representations: (1) The *complementary function* has two subcategories that describe that different representations (e.g., text and pictures) can provide different information or stimulate different learning activities. (2) The *constraining function* refers to a better understanding of a domain resulting from the use of one representation (e.g., pictures) to constrain the interpretation of a second representation (e.g., text). A more familiar representation can be used to facilitate the interpretation of a less familiar one. Alternatively, the interpretation of one repre-

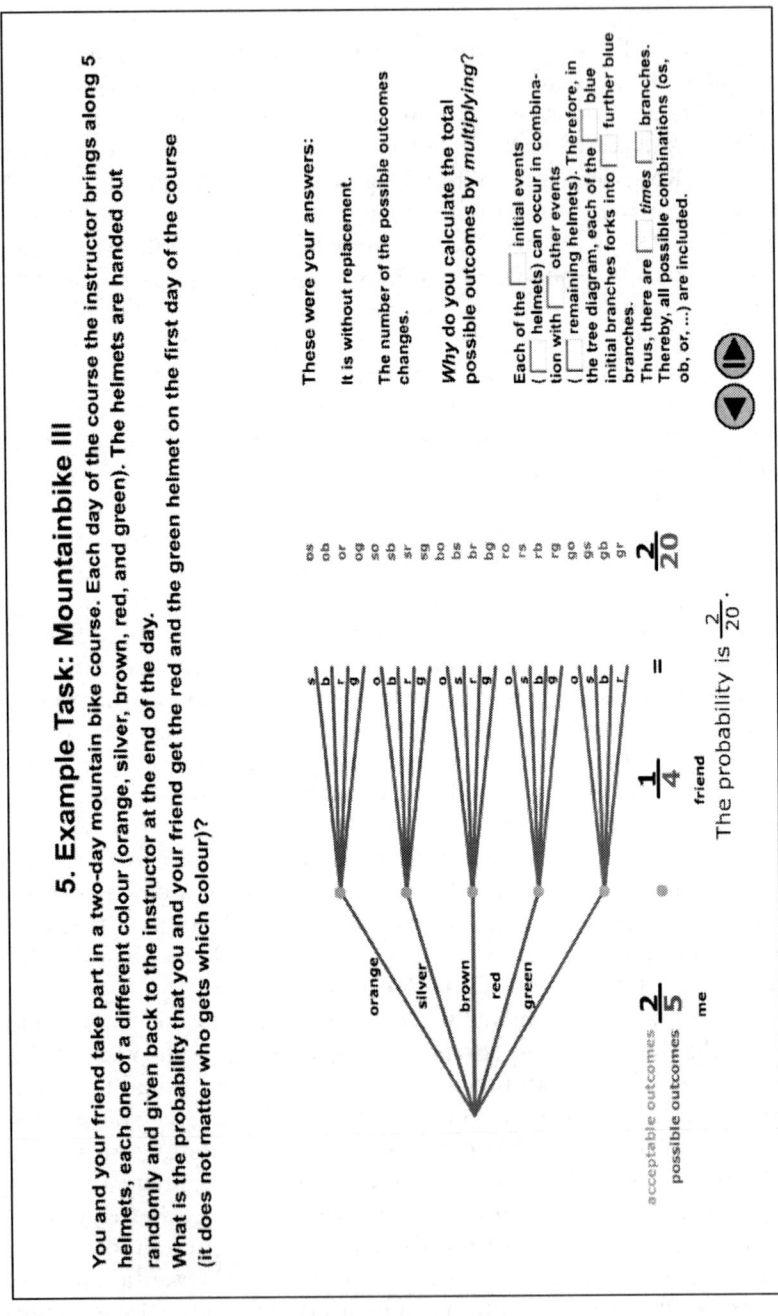

Figure 7.1. Screenshot from a learning environment with worked examples from the domain of probability.

sentation is constrained by the inherent property of a second representation; for example, pictures are usually more specific than text (e.g., whereas a text might say that a car parked beside a motorbike, a picture "says" on which side). (3) The *construction function* means that learners can gain deeper understanding when they integrate information from different representations (e.g., text and pictures; see also Schnotz, 2005). Such an integration process leading to deeper understanding usually includes abstraction from the surface features of the information sources (e.g., specific objects and numbers) to the underlying structure in terms of conceptual integration. As already specified, abstracting from the superficial specifics when integrating the multiplication signs and ramifications in a probability tree diagram (see Figure 7.1) can lead to deeper understanding.

In this chapter, we focus on the construction function. Although this function describes the valuable potential of visual displays added to other information sources, this potential does not always come to bear.

VISUAL DISPLAYS: POTENTIAL AND PITFALLS

A wide variety of studies supports the assumption that learning can be fostered when visual displays are added to other information sources (e.g., Carney & Levin, 2002; Mayer, 2009b; Levin et al., 1987; Vekiri, 2002). With respect to the design of visual displays to foster understanding, Mayer's cognitive theory of multimedia learning is one of the most prominent references (for a similar theory see Schnotz, 2005). Mayer (e.g., 2003, 2009b, this volume) postulated a *multimedia effect* in which learners learn more deeply from multimedia messages consisting of words and pictures than from more traditional modes of communication involving words alone.

However, there are also numerous studies demonstrating that visual displays do not necessarily foster learning (e.g., Ainsworth, 2006; Mayer, 2003; Schnotz, 2011). The reasons visual displays do not help can be related to the design of the learning materials (e.g., Mayer & Moreno, 2003) or to learners' processing difficulties (e.g., Ainsworth, 2006; Weidenmann, 1989). Both factors are of course related, for example, when it is difficult for learners to see the correspondences between a text and a visual display due to poor instructional design whereby both information sources are presented on different book pages, as described in the introductory example to this chapter (e.g., Mayer & Moreno, 2003; Renkl, 2011; Tarmizi & Sweller, 1988).

Specific learning difficulties can be associated with a number of factors. One of the most important is that the learners are unfamiliar with a certain type of visual display (e.g., box plot), meaning they cannot interpret it easily or correctly. This could be viewed as a lack of visual literacy, definable as skills in understanding and using visuals and the willingness to do so (Ausburn & Ausburn, 1978; Peeck, 1993). However, even if learners are familiar with the type of visual display, they sometimes ignore visuals or process them only very briefly and superficially (e.g., Peeck, 1993; Schüler, Scheiter, Rummer, & Gerjets, 2012; Weidenmann, 1989). They may attend to salient but relatively irrelevant details (e.g., Lowe, 2003), and even when they attend to relevant elements, they often cannot or do not integrate the information in visual displays with the other informational sources in order to gain deeper understanding (Ainsworth, 2006; Seufert & Brünken, 2004). For this reason, we discuss procedures that help learners integrate visual displays with other information sources in the next section.

TYPICAL SUPPORT PROCEDURES

Support procedures for processing visual displays added to other informational sources have been researched extensively within the framework of cognitive load theory (e.g., Sweller, Ayres, & Kalyuga, 2011; Sweller, Low, & Jin, this volume; Sweller, van Merriënboer, Paas, 1998) and Mayer's cognitive theory of multimedia learning (e.g., Mayer, 2009b, this volume; Mayer & Moreno, 2003). The main assumption of both of these theories is that learning is often suboptimal because learners are confronted with extraneous demands that do not contribute to the acquisition of the information's main conceptual contents. Typical examples of extraneous demands results from the presentation of unimportant and distracting information (i.e., seductive details) or from the nonintegrated provision of related information sources (cf. the introductory example to this chapter). Such extraneous demands can distract the learners from the deeper, integrated understanding of information because cognitive overload interferes with schema construction processes. Accordingly, typical instructional support procedures aim to reduce extraneous demands mainly in the three ways we describe below.

One instructional strategy is to enhance the presentation of information to improve integration. Text and visual displays are learned better when they are spatially integrated (*integrated format*) instead of being presented as two separate information sources (*split-attention format*). If information is presented in separate sources, learners must often engage in extensive visual search and storage processes in an effort to interrelate the different information sources. Such search processes increase extraneous load or processing (Mayer & Moreno, 2003; Tarmizi & Sweller, 1988) that does not support and can even hinder deep content-related processing (i.e., germane load or generative processing). One way to improve the integration of different information sources such as visual displays and text or equations is to spatially integrate them by, for example, writing the size of an angle in a geometry example directly into the line drawing (Sweller et al., this volume). Physical integration of this type makes cognitive resources available so that deep content-related processing can occur. Indeed, various studies show that such a facilitation of integration substantially enhances learning outcomes (Mayer & Moreno, 2003; Mwangi & Sweller, 1998; Renkl, 2011; Tarmizi & Sweller, 1988; Ward & Sweller, 1990).

A second way to support learners is to rely on the *modality effect* (Mayer & Moreno, 2003; Mousavi, Low, & Sweller, 1995; for a meta-analysis see Ginns, 2005). If a visual display is combined with text, learning is superior if textual information is presented in an auditory rather than visual format. Although the explanation of this effect differs somewhat between authors (e.g., Ginns, 2005; Schüler et al., 2012), a typical account is that the auditory presentation of text allows simultaneous processing of a text and a visual display (i.e., while listening to the text, the eyes can look at the corresponding elements in the visual display). If the text is presented in a written format, the learner must engage in the extraneous activity of searching for related informational elements. From an instructional standpoint, exploiting the modality principle helps learners to reduce extraneous demands and thus learn information with less effort.

A third strategy to reduce extraneous demands and enhance learning outcomes is to use *color coding* (e.g., Kalyuga, Chandler, & Sweller, 1999; Keller, Gerjets, Scheiter, & Garsoffky, 2006). For example, Ozcelik, Karakus, Kursun, and Cagiltay (2009) provided visual displays showing synapses that complemented text. They used the same colors for corresponding elements in both information sources (e.g., calcium ions in blue, sodium ions in purple, etc.). The corresponding colors in a visual display and a text help the learners to see "what belongs to what" and relieve them from the extraneous demand of visual searching. From an instructional standpoint, color coding links similar information in a manner that reduces processing effort.

Several other strategies that reduce extraneous load have been described elsewhere, including cues in the form of visual pointers (e.g., Mautone & Mayer, 2001), the flashing of corresponding elements (e.g., Bartholomé & Bromme, 2009), or blurring temporarily irrelevant areas while the crucial areas (e.g., relevant parts of the human body when learning to diagnose epileptic seizures; e.g., Jarodzka et al., 2012) remain sharp. They all primarily reduce extraneous demands and thereby create positive conditions for deeply processing the learning materials. However, they do not prompt or support deep processing directly (e.g., Bartholomé & Bromme, 2009; Berthold & Renkl, 2009), and in fact it is questionable whether learners use the cognitive capacity they have gained by reducing extraneous demands for deep processing (cf. Renkl, 1997). We thus discuss strategies to promote deeper learning below.

SUPPORTING LEARNING ON SUPERFICIAL AND STRUCTURAL LEVELS

The support procedures presented in the previous section primarily help learners notice "what elements in a visual display belong to what elements in other information sources." However, mapping on the superficial level does not guarantee mapping on the structural level (cf. Seufert & Brünken, 2004). Let us again refer to Figure 7.1. A learner might infer that the multiplication sign in the equation corresponds to the ramifications in the pictorial tree diagram. This knowledge does not, however, assure that the learner becomes aware that the multiplication (sign) stands for the inclusion of all possible combinations represented by the 5 x 4 (= 20) branches in the pictorial tree diagram (structural aspect). That is, learners have to integrate visual displays and other representations on a structural level in order to gain deep conceptual understanding (cf. Seufert & Brünken, 2004).

Against this background, it makes sense to develop and test instructional procedures that support the structural integration of visual displays with other information sources, perhaps in combination with more surface-oriented support. In the following we describe several studies from our lab that tried to support structural integration in different ways. One *direct approach* is to employ self-explanation prompts that explicitly encourage the learners to interrelate different representations on the structural level. A second, more *indirect approach* is to provide the learner with advance information about the instructional function of visual displays.

Direct Approach

Roy and Chi (2005) concluded that self-explanations foster conceptual understanding when multiple representations have to be integrated at a deeper level. Nevertheless, they did not directly test the helpfulness of self-explanation prompts for integrating multiple representations. Other authors have raised doubts about this assumption. For example, Sweller (2006) and Kalyuga (2010) argued that the demand to self-explain complex materials (e.g., materials consisting of text and visual displays) may take cognitive load over the limits. Thus prompting self-explanations may be ineffective or even have detrimental effects.

Consistent with the overload hypothesis, we found in a pilot study on the domain of probability that learners had difficulties with self-explanation prompts that tried to guide the integration of text, visual displays, and equations (see Berthold, Eysink, & Renkl, 2009). When we used open self-explanation prompts (e.g., "Why do you calculate the total acceptable outcomes by multiplying?" see Figure 7.1), the learners had severe problems in providing adequate and correct answers. As a consequence, we examined in relevant research whether stronger instructional assistance is more beneficial than open self-explanation prompts.

Assisting self-explanation prompts (Berthold et al., 2009). Berthold et al. tested the effects of three conditions: *Assisting self-explanation prompts* that helped learners to integrate multiple representations on a conceptual level, *open self-explanation prompts*, and *no self-explanation prompts*. In a computer-based learning environment on probability, learners studied eight worked examples including a text presenting the problem formulation, a tree diagram (i.e., a graphical, visual solution), and an equation (i.e., solution with mathematical symbols). Participants were 62 psychology students (mean age of about 25 years). All conditions were supported on the superficial level by employing a combined color coding and flashing procedure. This type of superficial help that made it easier for the learner to figure out "what belongs to what" in the different representations (see Figure 7.1) was provided to reduce extraneous demands (Sweller et al., 1998; Mayer, 2009a) and thereby to save cognitive capacity for productive self-explanation.

Berthold et al. (2009) used assisting self-explanation prompts of the following type: "Why do you calculate the total acceptable outcomes by multiplying?" In the first example of each pair of isomorphic examples, assistance was provided in the form of fill-in-the-blank self-explanations (e.g., "There are ___ times ___ branches. Thereby, all possible combinations are included," see Figure 7.1). In the subsequent isomorphic examples, this assistance was faded out. The answers had to be typed into corresponding text boxes. In the condition with open self-explanation prompts, the learners got self-explanation prompts without any additional support (e.g., open answer to "Why do you calculate the total acceptable outcomes by multiplying?").

Note that both the assisting self-explanation prompts and open prompts put an emphasis on integrating the visual displays and equations to each other on a structural level. For example, the prompt "Why is there a 4 in the denominator of the second single experiment, even though there are 20 branches in the tree diagram?" referred to the equation ("the

4 in the denominator") *and* to the visual display ("20 branches in the tree diagram"). When reacting to this prompt, the learners had to relate the denominator of the equation to the corresponding branches of the pictorial tree diagram. In so doing, they could understand that the "4" corresponds to the number of remaining events of one initial branch. As there were five initial branches, five times four (i.e., 20) branches are included. In the control group without self-explanation prompts, the learners studied the same worked examples as in the other two conditions. the only difference was that the learners were just provided with a text box in which to take notes. They received no prompts.

Berthold et al. (2009) found that both types of self-explanation prompts fostered conceptual knowledge as compared to the control group. Furthermore, assisting self-explanation prompts had additional effects on conceptual understanding in comparison to open self-explanation prompts. The effect on conceptual understanding was mediated by self-explanations, as assessed by the entries in the text boxes. These self-explanations not only related solution steps to underlying principles, they also explicated the rationale of the principles (e.g., "For the denominator, there are five *times* four branches. Thus each of the five first branches of the tree diagram forks out in four further branches as each of the five first events can occur in combination with one of the four remaining events"). For procedural knowledge, both prompt types were effective as compared to the control group; the two prompt types did not significantly differ from each other.

These results showed that both prompt types supported the acquisition of procedural knowledge. For increasing conceptual knowledge, self-explanation prompts worked best because they support the learners in generating self-explanations about the reason a principle works in a particular situation. The overall pattern of results suggests that using self-explanation prompts provides an effective way to foster the integration of visual displays with other information sources. Employing assisting self-explanation prompts is especially useful when high-quality self-explanations and conceptual understanding are the main instructional goals.

Combining superficial and structural support (Berthold & Renkl, 2009). A restriction of the study by Berthold et al. (2009) was that it just tested the effects of support procedures on the structural level ("on the top" of superficial support). Due to their study design (i.e., superficial support was provided in each condition), Berthold et al. could not test whether there are additive effects of superficial support and structural support. It is also conceivable that these types of support interact. If superficial support procedures do not "take away" unnecessary load (Sweller, 2006; see also de Koning, Tabbers, Rikers, & Paas, 2011), the learners might be overwhelmed by the demands to follow the structural support procedures (Kalyuga, 2010).

Berthold and Renkl (2009) varied both types of support by employing a computer-based learning environment almost identical to that of Berthold et al. (2009). Some of the learners received assisting self-explanation prompts that were more or less identical to those used by Berthold et al. In addition, within a 2 x 2 design (N = 85 high-school students of approximately 16 years), the presence of superficial support (in the form of combined color coding and a flashing procedure) was varied (note that the actual experimental design of Berthold and Renkl was more comprehensive; as their findings on the additional conditions are not relevant here, we restrict our discussion to the 2 x 2 "subdesign"). They found that both superficial and structural support fostered conceptual understanding. These effects were additive (i.e., no interaction effect). Note that the effect size was medium for superficial help (η^2 = .07) and strong for structural help (η^2 = .16). We can tentatively assume that focusing learners on the structural aspects produces greater gains in learning. For procedural knowledge, all effects failed to reach the 5% level of statistical significance.

In conclusion, both superficial and structural support procedures have additive effects, with the latter help being probably more effective. Hence, a practical consequence is to recommend less exclusive reliance on the usual forms of superficial support procedures. It seems better to use both types of support with special emphasis on structural support procedures. On the theoretical level, the present results confirm the position of Roy and Chi (2005), who claimed that self-explanations are very helpful when conceptual understanding is the most important outcome from studying multiple representations (e.g., visual displays in combination with text and equations). There is less support for the assumption of decreased learning due to cognitive overload as postulated by Sweller (2006) and Kalyuga (2010). Rather, in most studies, self-explanation demands did not overwhelm learners when confronted with complex materials.

Indirect Approach

Self-explanation prompts try to directly elicit structural alignments between visual displays and text or equations. As already shown, such prompts should include assisting features in order to best support the learners. However, such assisting prompts are laborious to develop, are not generic (i.e., applicable to a wide range of contents), and they must be integrated into a specific learning environment. It is therefore worthwhile exploring more parsimonious support procedures that foster integration between visual displays and other information sources on a structural level.

Informing learners about the function of visual displays (Schwonke, Berthold, & Renkl, 2009). One such procedure is to inform the learners about the function that visual displays have in certain materials, hoping that the learners will then use the visual displays in the manner intended by the instructional designer. The idea of informing the learners about the function of visual displays resulted from a pilot study by Schwonke et al. (2009, Study 1; $N = 16$ students of psychology), who used a slightly modified version of the learning environment of Berthold and Renkl (2009)—more specifically, the version with superficial support (i.e., color coding), but without the structural support (i.e., no self-explanation prompts). Once the learners had worked on the examples from probability, Schwonke et al. implemented a stimulated recall procedure. The learners saw an animation of their gazes (i.e., gaze replay) on the first and last worked example, and they were asked to verbalize what they had been thinking while studying these examples. This type of stimulated recall procedure usually provides rich verbal data (van Gog, Paas, Merriënboer, & Witte, 2005). Schwonke et al. analyzed the learners' utterances with a coding scheme constructed on the basis of the DeFT framework in which the coding categories corresponded to the various cognitive functions of multiple representations as proposed by Ainsworth (2006). Our scheme consisted of three main categories: complementary function, constraining function, and construction function. We tested the extent to which the learners perceived the functions while working on examples containing multiple representations. The analysis of the learners' verbal protocols revealed that the students had little awareness of any type of function. A simple remedy to this problem is to simply tell the learners about the instructional design idea ("instructions for use"; Renkl, Berthold, Große, & Schwonke, in press).

Schwonke et al. (2009, Study 2) tested the effects of informing learners about how to use a visual display in the context of other information sources on learning outcomes. They briefly explained that there are two solutions procedures – tree diagrams (visual display) and equations—and that the tree diagrams should be used to gain an understanding on how the arithmetic equations are related to the problem formulations (see Figures 7.2 and 7.3). For this purpose, we used the metaphor of a bridge ("... the tree diagrams 'build' a bridge between the problem texts and the equations..."). This instruction consisted just of an enrichment of one introductory screen that oriented the learners about the upcoming type of learning tasks in the form of worked examples. In addition, a line drawing of a bridge shortly popped up between the single worked examples as a reminder.

Thirty psychology students were randomly assigned to the "informed" condition and a control condition (introductory screen without instruc-

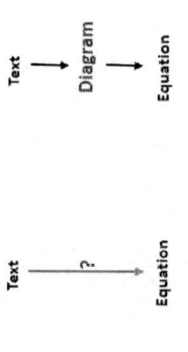
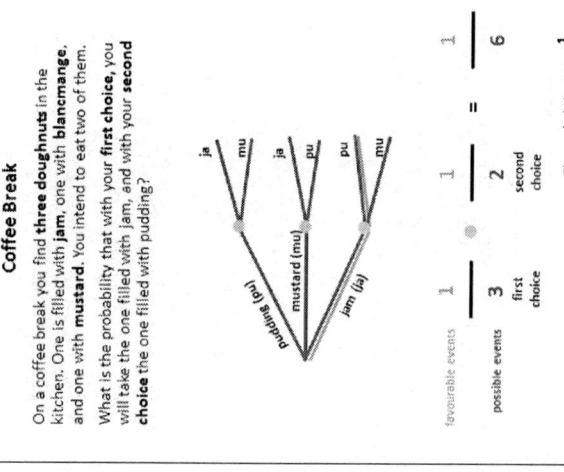

Figure 7.2. Screenshot of the instruction for the "informed" group (Schwonke et al., 2009) with information on the functions of the visual display (translated from German).

Illustration of the upcoming examples

On the following screen pages you will find some examples of completely solved problems, similar to the one on the right.

The problems always consist of a problem text, a tree diagram, and an equation.

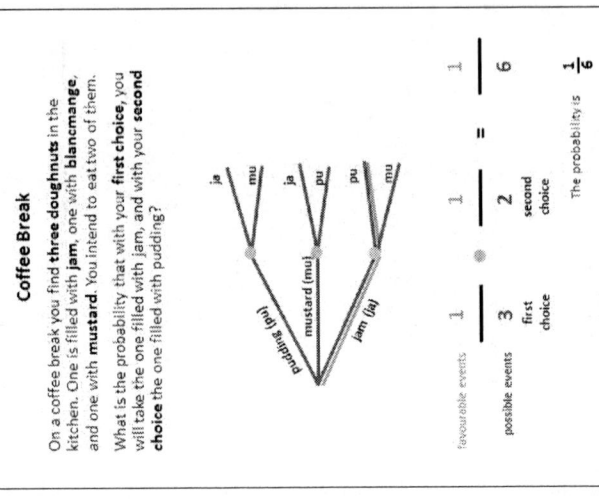

Coffee Break

On a coffee break you find **three doughnuts** in the kitchen. One is filled with **jam**, one with **blancmange**, and one with **mustard**. You intend to eat two of them.

What is the probability that with your **first choice**, you will take the one filled with jam, and with your **second choice** the one filled with pudding?

favourable events

$$\frac{1}{3} \cdot 1 \cdot 1 = \frac{1}{2} \cdot \frac{1}{6}$$

possible events

first choice   second choice

The probability is $\frac{1}{6}$

Figure 7.3.   Screenshot of the instruction for the control group (Schwonke et al., 2009) with no information on the functions of the visual display (translated from German).

tions for the use of the visual displays and without "reminding" line drawings). Eye-tracking data were recorded to gain insight into learning processes. The instruction condition produced better learning outcomes (as assessed by a post-test that included problems requiring conceptual understanding and procedural knowledge), yet there were no differences in learning time. This effect was also mediated by altering the attention patterns of students with different levels of prior knowledge, as assessed by eye-tracking (e.g., preventing learners with high prior knowledge from neglecting the tree diagrams; for details see Schwonke et al., 2009). These results suggested that a brief and parsimonious intervention provides metacognitive knowledge about the use of the visual display that led to substantial improvements in learning.

Informing about how to deal with multiple information sources and tools (Schwonke, Ertelt, Aleven, Salden, and Renkl, 2012). In a recent study, Schwonke et al. (2012) informed learners about how to manage the complexity of multiple information resources (visual displays in from of geometry diagrams, problem text etc.) and multiple tools (e.g., hints, glossary) in the intelligent tutoring system "Cognitive Tutor" (Koedinger & Corbett, 2006). More specifically, we tested the effects of a cue card providing some form of metacognitive knowledge about what to do with all these elements. The provision of such a cue card reduced learning time by about 20% in comparison to the control condition. In addition, learners with low prior knowledge also profited from the cue card with respect to learning gains (i.e., better conceptual understanding). As the cue card employed in this study was not specific to visual displays (but generally suggested ways to deal with different information sources and tools), we conclude that instruction that positively affects metacognitive awareness or self-regulation may indirectly improve learning from visual displays even when there is no direct intervention to improve understanding of the display itself.

In summary, the findings by Schwonke et al. (2009, 2012) demonstrate that letting learners know what to do with visual displays when integrating them with other information sources enhances learning. One important advantage of such an intervention is that it is very parsimonious and may reduce learning time (Schwonke et al., 2012).

Conclusions. The present findings on informing learners how to best utilize and integrate information from text and adjunct visual displays can be related to models of self-regulated learning (SRL) such as the four-stage model of SRL (e.g., Winne & Perry, 2000). Those authors differentiate between (a) knowledge about cognitive conditions (e.g., knowledge of study tactics and strategies, domain knowledge) and (b) knowledge about task conditions (e.g., knowledge about instructional cues, time, and social context). Knowledge provided by the instructional interventions about the most effective use of displays refers to the task-conditions category. Unfortunately, empirical studies on self-regulated learning have not put strong emphasis on this type of knowledge up to now. For this reason, we believe that the results of Schwonke et al. (2009, 2012) suggest modifications to this "not-so-well" researched aspect of the four-stage model of SRL. Specifically, models should take into account that self-regulatory knowledge may be provided externally through simple orienting instructions.

Nevertheless, an important restriction of the present evidence arises from the type of learners that participated in the studies. It might well be that informing learners about the functions of visual displays and what to do with them is sufficient for advanced learners with relatively good learning prerequisites (e.g., university students). Such information might lead to greater efficiency in that it activates prior knowledge which then helps them use their cognitive resources more strategically (production deficiency; Flavell, Beach, & Chinsky, 1966). However, younger learners might not possess the necessary prior knowledge or processing strategies in their repertoire (i.e., mediation deficiency), leading to a less effective intervention.

In addition, a study by Skuballa, Schwonke, and Renkl (2012) points to another important restriction attributable to limited working memory capacity. They used an informing procedure to support learners when studying a narrated animation that was rather complex. The animation showed several simultaneously working subsystems of a parabolic trough power plant. Skuballa et al. found that the intervention was detrimental for learners with low working memory capacity. Although untested currently, we assume that informational instructions about how to best utilize visual displays, which have to be kept in mind during learning, may overwhelm the limited memory capacity of (at least some) learners if the learning materials are too complex.

Finally, it is also unclear whether the effect of informing learners prior to the study phase can also be found in other domains employing other types of visual displays. Consider biomedical learning, for example. In a study by McCrudden, Schraw, Lehman, and Poliquin (2007) a diagram explicated the important causal relations from a text on the effects of space travel on the human body. In such cases, it might be obvious—at least to more advanced learners such as university students—what the function of the visual display is. Hence, there might be no need for an "informing" intervention. However, consistent with our research, it may be the case that learners with little prior knowledge or those unfamiliar with specific types of visual displays such as causal diagrams may experience difficulty that may be ameliorated by instruction as described above.

In summary, when presenting visual displays to learners in order to foster their understanding, they might not always know why the displays are provided and what to do with them. In these cases, informing the learners about the displays' function may help. Such instruction on visual displays may also contribute to the development of the learners' visual literacy. However, future research is necessary to determine the boundary conditions of an "informing" effect as found in the studies by Schwonke et al. (2009, 2012).

COMPARISON TO RELATED INSTRUCTIONAL APPROACHES

We note more generally that there is other research, aside from the studies presented here, on instructional approaches that focus on deeper learning from visual displays. These studies have examined active integration (e.g., Bodemer, Plötzner, Feuerlein, & Spada, 2004), strategy scripts (e.g., Bartholomé & Bromme, 2009; Kombartzky, Plötzner, Schlag, & Metz, 2010), and instructions for picture processing (Peeck, 1993). In general, they show that fostering the processing of visual display added other representations on the structural level to foster deeper understanding. In the following, we shortly discuss these approaches.

The first instructional approach is *active integration*, which was developed by Bodemer and colleagues (Bodemer et al., 2004; Bodemer, Plötzner, Bruchmüller, & Häcker, 2005). Instead of providing an integrated format, the learners actively integrated text and visual displays. For example, the learners started with a split-attention presentation of a pump and textual captions. Their task was to produce an integrated format by "drag and drop." The assumption was that active integration leads to an increase in germane load (Sweller et al., 1998) which corresponds to processing at the structural level. As predicted, in most experiments conducted by Bodemer et al., active integration led to better learning outcomes than when information was presented in an integrated format. Unfortunately, there are no specific data on the extent to which learners rely on surface cues or on structural considerations when actively integrating. Nevertheless, the superiority of active integration over presented integrated formats with respect to measures of understanding (Bodemer et al.) suggests that structural considerations can actually be elicited by active integration demands.

A second instructional approach, *strategy script*, was developed by Schlag, Plötzner, and colleagues (Kombartzky et al., 2010; Schlag & Plötzner, 2011) to help learners process and integrate text and visual displays (for a similar approach see Bartholomé & Bromme, 2009). With a strategy script, the learners are presented with a number of suggestions on how to process the different information sources, both on the superficial and structural levels (as described in this chapter). With respect to the integration of text and visual displays, learners are instructed to describe in written form the relations between the visual elements and verbal explanation in their own words. In several experiments, Schlag, Plötzner, and colleagues have observed positive effects on measures of understanding, suggesting that the integration of text and animation was actually fostered on the structural level. However, it is important to recall that the control groups processed text and animation with no support at all (see Kombartzky et al., 2010; Schlag & Plötzner, 2011). Hence, it is unclear to what extent the strategy script adds value to surface-oriented support.

Third, Peeck (1993) discussed a variety of *instructions for picture processing* that vary in their specificity, ranging from global hints to paying attention to pictures, to specific guidelines on how to process pictures (e.g., to complete a picture). Some of these instructions (e.g., label a picture; cf. active integration) clearly have the potential to direct the learners to the structural level. The "instruction for use" intervention by Schwonke et al. (2009) is somewhat different from the options presented by Peeck, as it provides explicit (metacognitive) knowledge about the instructional function of the visual displays. For this reason, further research is needed to test whether this type of metacognitive knowledge (Renkl et al., 2012) really has an added value to the options discussed by Peeck.

In conclusion, the instructional approaches discussed in this section also suggest that it is sensible to go beyond the surface level when supporting learners to make use of visual displays presented together with other information sources. It is currently unclear what specific strengths and weaknesses the different methods have; thus, further studies are needed that compare the different instructional methods with respect to the learning processes they elicit and to the pattern of learning outcomes they yield.

CONCLUSIONS

We have discussed the role that prior knowledge and limited working memory resources play on learning from visual displays in this chapter, as well as constraints imposed from a variety of extraneous variables. We propose that the negative effects of these constraints can be reduced or even eliminated by using a variety of easy to implement instructional strategies. We summarize the potential benefits of these strategies in the form of three general instructional principles:

1. *Include the structural level when supporting learners' use of visual displays.* Typical instructional procedures for supporting learners in the use of visual displays (e.g., integrated format, color coding) do

not directly address the structural level. Hence, it makes sense to additionally support the learners in considering structural aspects (e.g., by corresponding self-explanation prompts). Otherwise the learners may just determine "what belongs to what" without deepening their understanding by "semantically" (i.e., structurally) integrating visual displays with other representations so that a deeper understanding evolves.

2. *Provide special assistance for learners' considerations on the structural level.* For most learners, it is rather demanding to go beyond the surface level to the structural level in order to deepen their understanding. It is therefore sensible to not only direct the learners' attention to the structural level (see principle 1) but also to provide support for productive processing (e.g., by assisting self-explanation prompts). Without such support, the learner might be unable to produce elaborated and correct self-explanations. Poorly elaborated or incorrect self-explanations do not lead to enhance learning outcomes, and they may even be detrimental.

3. *Use informed instruction instead of "Easter-egg pedagogy."* In many classrooms and learning environments, a type of "Easter-egg pedagogy" is employed: the learners are not informed what they should learn and what they are expected to do in order to reach this goal —similar to parents having their children look for hidden eggs on Easter Sunday. It is, however, important that learners (a) know about the intended purpose of visual displays and the intent of the instructional designers when they include visual displays in learning materials and (b) know how to use the visual display in the manner intended by the instructional designers. Instead of letting the uninformed learners guess what to do, as in Easter-egg pedagogy, it makes sense to inform them about the function and intended use of visual displays. Informing learners heightens the probability that they will use the visuals in a way that deepens understanding, as was the instructional designer's intent.

REFERENCES

Ainsworth, S. E. (2006). DeFT: A conceptual framework for considering learning with multiple representations. *Learning and Instruction, 16*, 183-198.

Ausburn, L. J., & Ausburn, F. B. (1978): Visual literacy: Background, theory and practice. *Innovations in Education & Training International, 15*, 291-297.

Bartholomé, T., & Bromme, R. (2009) Coherence formation when learning from text and pictures: What kind of support for whom? *Journal of Educational Psychology, 101*, 282-293.

Berthold, K., Eysink, T. H., & Renkl, A. (2009). Assisting self-explanation prompts are more effective than open prompts when learning with multiple representations. *Instructional Science, 37,* 345-363.

Berthold, K., & Renkl, A. (2009). Instructional aids to support a conceptual understanding of multiple representations. *Journal of Educational Psychology, 101,* 70-87.

Bodemer, D., Plötzner, R., Bruchmüller, K., & Häcker, S. (2005). Supporting learning with interactive multimedia through active integration of representations. *Instructional Science, 33,* 73-95.

Bodemer, D., Plötzner, R., Feuerlein, I., & Spada, H. (2004). The active integration of information during learning with dynamic and interactive visualisations. *Learning and Instruction, 14,* 325-341.

Carney, R., & Levin, J. R. (2002). Pictorial illustrations still improve students learning from text. *Educational Psychology Review,* 14, 5-26.

De Koning, B. B., Tabbers, H. K., Rikers, R. M. J. P., & Paas, F. (2011). Improved effectiveness of cueing by self-explanations when learning from a complex animation. *Applied Cognitive Psychology, 25,* 183-194.

Flavell, J. H., Beach, D. R., & Chinsky, J. M. (1966). Spontaneous verbal rehearsal in a memory task as a function of age. *Child Development, 37,* 283-299.

Ginns, P. (2005). Integrating information: A meta-analysis of the spatial contiguity and temporal contiguity effects. *Learning and Instruction, 16,* 511-525.

Jarodzka, H., Balslev, T., Holmqvist, K., Nyström, M., Scheiter, K., Gerjets, P., & Eika, B. (2012). Conveying clinical reasoning based on visual observation via eye-movement modelling examples. *Instructional Science, 40,* 813-827.

Kalyuga, S. (2010). Schema acquisition and sources of cognitive load. In J. Plass, R. Moreno, & R. Brünken (Eds.), *Cognitive load theory and research in educational psychology* (pp. 48-64). New York, NY: Cambridge University Press.

Kalyuga, S., Chandler, P., & Sweller, J. (1999). Managing split-attention and redundancy in multimedia instruction. *Applied Cognitive Psychology, 13,* 351-371.

Kombartzky, U., Plötzner, R., Schlag, S., & Metz, B. (2010). Developing and evaluating a strategy for learning from animations. *Learning and Instruction, 20,* 424-433.

Keller, T., Gerjets P., Scheiter, K., & Garsoffky, B. (2006). Information visualizations for knowledge acquisition: The impact of dimensionality and color coding. *Computers in Human Behavior, 22,* 43-65.

Koedinger, K. R., & Corbett, A. T. (2006). Cognitive tutors: Technology bringing learning sciences to the classroom. In R. K. Sawyer (Ed.), *The Cambridge handbook of the learning sciences.* New York, NY: Cambridge University Press.

Levin, J. R. (1981). On functions of pictures in prose. In F. J. Pirozzolo & M. C. Wittrock (Eds.), *Neuropsychological and cognitive processes in reading* (pp. 203-228). New York, NY: Academic Press.

Levin, J. R., Anglin, G. J., & Carney, R. N. (1987). On empirically validating functions of pictures in prose. In D. M. Willows & H. A. Houghton (Eds.), *The psychology of illustration: I. Basic Research* (pp. 51-85). New York, NY: Springer.

Lowe, R. K. (2003). Animation and learning: Selective processing of information in dynamic graphics. *Learning and Instruction, 13,* 157-176.

Mautone, P. D., & Mayer, R. E. (2001). Signaling as a cognitive guide in multimedia learning. *Journal of Educational Psychology, 93,* 377-389.

Mayer, R. E. (2003). The promise of multimedia learning: Using the same instructional design methods across different media. *Learning and Instruction, 13,* 125-129.

Mayer, R. E. (2009a). Constructivism as a theory of learning versus constructivism as a prescription for instruction. In S. Tobias & T. M. Duffy (Eds.), *Constructivist Instruction: Success or failure?* (pp. 184-200). New York Routledge.

Mayer, R. E. (2009b). *Multimedia learning* (2nd ed.). New York, NY: Cambridge University Press.

Mayer, R. E., & Moreno, R. (2003). Nine ways to reduce cognitive load in multimedia learning. *Educational Psychologist, 38,* 43-52.

Mousavi, S. Y., Low, R., & Sweller, J. (1995). Reducing cognitive load by mixing auditory and visual presentation modes. *Journal of Educational Psychology, 87,* 319-334.

Mwangi, W., & Sweller, J. (1998). Learning to solve compare word problems: The effect of example format and generating self-explanations. *Cognition and Instruction, 16,* 173-199.

McCrudden, M. T., Schraw, G., Lehman, S., & Poliquin, A. (2007). The effect of causal diagrams on text learning. *Contemporary Educational Psychology, 32,* 367-388.

Ozcelik, E., Karakus, T., Kursun, E., & Cagiltay, K. (2009). An eye-tracking study of how color coding affects multimedia learning. *Computers and Education, 53,* 445-453.

Peeck, J. (1993). Increasing picture effects in learning from illustrated text. *Learning and Instruction, 3,* 227-238.

Renkl, A. (1997). Learning from worked-out examples: A study on individual differences. *Cognitive Science, 21,* 1-29.

Renkl, A. (2011). Instruction based on examples. In R. E. Mayer & P. A. Alexander (Eds.), *Handbook of research on learning and instruction* (pp. 272-295). New York, NY: Routledge.

Renkl, A., Berthold, K., Große, C. S., & Schwonke, R. (in press). Making better use of multiple representations: How fostering metacognition can help. In R. Azevedo & V. Aleven (Eds.), *International handbook of metacognition and learning technologies.* New York, NY: Springer.

Roy, M., & Chi, M. T. H. (2005). The self-explanation principle in multimedia learning. In R. E. Mayer (Ed.), *Cambridge handbook of multimedia learning* (pp. 271–287). Cambridge, UK: Cambridge University Press.

Schlag, S. & Plötzner, R. (2011). Supporting learning from illustrated texts: Conceptualizing and evaluating a learning strategy. *Instructional Science, 39,* 921-937.

Schnotz, W. (2005). An integrated model of text and picture comprehension. In R. E. Mayer (Ed.), *Cambridge handbook of multimedia learning* (pp. 49-69). Cambridge, England: Cambridge University Press.

Schnotz, W. (2011). Colorful bouquets in multimedia research: A closer look at the modality effect. *German Journal of Educational Psychology, 25,* 269-276.

Schüler, A., Scheiter, K., Rummer, R., & Gerjets, P. (2012). Explaining the modality effect in multimedia learning: Is it due to a lack of temporal contiguity with written text and pictures? *Learning and Instruction, 22*, 92-102.

Sweller, J., van Merriënboer, J. J. G., & Paas, F. G. (1998). Cognitive architecture and instructional design. *Educational Psychology Review, 10*, 251-296.

Schwonke, R., Berthold, K., & Renkl, A. (2009). How multiple external representations are used and how they can be made more useful. *Applied Cognitive Psychology, 23*, 1227-1243.

Schwonke, R., Ertelt, A., Otieno, C., Renkl, A., Aleven, V., & Salden, R. (2013). Metacognitive support promotes an effective use of instructional resources in intelligent tutoring. *Learning & Instruction, 23*, 136-150.

Seufert, T., & Brünken, R. (2004). Supporting coherence formation in multimedia learning. In P. Gerjets, P. Kirschner, J. Elen, & R. Joiner (Eds.), *Instructional design for effective and enjoyable computer-supported learning* (pp. 138-147). Tübingen, Germany: Knowledge Media Research Center.

Skuballa, I. T., Schwonke, R., & Renkl, A. (2012). Learning from narrated animations with different support procedures: Working memory capacity matters. *Applied Cognitive Psychology, 26*, 840-847.

Sweller, J. (2006). The worked example effect and human cognition. *Learning and Instruction, 16*, 165-169.

Sweller, J., Ayres, P., & Kalyuga, S. (2011). *Cognitive load theory.* New York, NY: Springer.

Tarmizi, R., & Sweller, J. (1988). Guidance during mathematical problem solving. *Journal of Educational Psychology, 80*, 424-436.

van Gog, T., Paas, F., Van Merriënboer, J. J. G., & Witte, P. (2005). Uncovering the problem-solving process: Cued retrospective reporting versus concurrent and retrospective reporting. *Journal of Experimental Psychology: Applied, 11*, 237-244.

Vekiri, I. (2002). What is the value of graphical displays in learning? *Educational Psychology Review, 14*, 261-312.

Ward, M., & Sweller, J. (1990). Structuring effective worked examples. *Cognition and Instruction, 7*, 1-39.

Weidenmann, B. (1989). When good pictures fail: An information-processing approach to the effect of illustrations. In H. Mandl & J. R. Levin (Eds.), *Knowledge acquisition from text and pictures* (pp. 157-171). Amsterdam, The Netherlands: Elsevier.

Winne, P. H., & Perry, N. E. (2000). Measuring self-regulated learning. In M. Boekaerts, P. Pintrich, & M. Zeidner (Eds.), *Handbook of self-regulation* (pp. 531-566). Orlando, FL: Academic Press.

CHAPTER 8

STRATEGIES FOR NOTE TAKING ON COMPUTER-BASED GRAPHIC ORGANIZERS

Steven M. Crooks and Jongpil Cheon

ABSTRACT

In this chapter we examine empirical evidence concerning the effectiveness of computer-based graphic organizer (CGO) note taking. CGO note taking is a computer-based instructional method that attempts to combine the cognitive benefits of note taking (essential processing) with the cognitive benefits of graphic organizers (generative processing) to increase learning from e-text during online instruction. Research investigating CGO note taking has been generally unsuccessful without behavioral interventions to improve the process (e.g., restricted copy-paste note taking). Interestingly, these interventions have ensued from conflicting hypotheses concerning the cognitive processes involved in CGO note taking—some studies claiming the method is too passive (passivity hypothesis) and other studies claiming the method is too demanding (excessive demands hypothesis). Disabling, restricting, or expediting the copy-paste feature were identified as interventions aligned with the passivity hypothesis, whereas partial CGO note taking and prompting self-regulation were identified as interventions aligned the excessive-demands hypothesis. In general, findings from both lines of

Learning Through Visual Displays, pp. 187–221
Copyright © 2013 by Information Age Publishing

research supported their respective hypotheses. However, the literature supports the excessive demands hypothesis and suggests that the passivity hypothesis results from a lack of essential processing among students lacking the metacognitive skills to appropriately use the copy-paste feature.

In U.S. higher education, online course enrollments are growing much faster than total course enrollments. Allen and Seaman (2011) found that from 2002-2010 the compound annual growth rate for online enrollments was over eight times that of total enrollments (18.3% vs. 2.1%). They also found that during this time period the percentage of total college students enrolled in at least one online course grew from less than 10 percent to over 30%.

Notwithstanding the proliferation of online learning, higher education institutions report that less than one-third of faculty accepts the value and legitimacy of an online education (Allen & Seaman, 2011). One factor contributing to this lack of acceptance appears to be the perception that online learning lacks the interactive capabilities of the traditional classroom (Hattangdi, Jha, & Ghosh, 2010; Kelsey & D'souza, 2004). Of the three types of distance education interaction identified by Moore (1989) (i.e., learner-content, learner-instructor, and learner-student), learner-content interaction (i.e., direct intellectual interaction with the instructional content) appears to provide the most promise in terms of improving learner achievement. This was the conclusion reached by Bernard et al., (2009) in a recent meta-analysis of the experimental literature in distance education. Their findings revealed that efforts toward improving the quality of learner-content interaction made a larger difference in learner achievement than efforts to improve learner-learner or learner-instructor interaction (Bernard et al., 2009). These findings suggest that research focused on improving the quality of learner-content interaction in online learning may be an effective means of not only improving student achievement in online learning, but also of improving faculty perceptions of this burgeoning mode of instructional delivery.

Understanding ways to improve learning from electronic text (e-text) is an important area of research related to learner-content interaction in online learning, particularly since e-text is the primary means of delivering online instructional content. In fact, over 90% of U.S. universities offering online learning programs rely on some form of e-text to deliver course content (Jones, Warren, & Robertson, 2009). While students prefer reading print text (Annand, 2008; Buzzetto-More, Sweat-Guy, & Elobaid, 2007; Woody, Daniel, & Baker, 2010), e-text provides some significant advantages that remain largely unexploited in online learning. For example, e-text can be modified (e.g., font face, size, and color), enhanced (e.g., embedded definitions), rearranged, and embellished (e.g., links to graphics). Anderson-Inman and Horney (2007) refer to these alterations of e-text as *supported e-text*, which they define as "text that has been altered to increase access and provide support to learners" (p. 153). The purpose of supported e-text is to enrich e-text with additional text or graphical resources to improve understanding of the original text (Anderson-Inman & Horney, 2007).

One promising form of supported e-text for online learning is note taking on a computer-based graphic organizer (CGO). The purpose of this chapter is to review current research on the effectiveness of various interventions used to improve the implementation of this form of supported e-text. We begin with a historical review of note taking and graphic organizer research; we then discuss current research that explores the use of computers to enhance note-taking strategies with graphic organizers. We then review various behavioral interventions designed to overcome some of the limitations of CGO note taking. Each intervention is classified according to the hypothesis that appears to have inspired the development of the intervention: (a) CGO note taking is too *passive* (passivity hypothesis) or (b) CGO note taking is too *demanding* (excessive demands hypothesis). Our focus is on how different types of CGO note taking improve learning from a cognitive processing perspective.

REVIEW OF RESEARCH ON NOTE TAKING

Note taking refers to the process of recording information from a source material (e.g., lecture, book, computer screen, observed action) while concurrently listening, studying, or observing (Piolat, Olive, & Kellogg, 2005). While most commonly associated with academic settings, note taking is also frequently employed in domestic and professional situations as well (Hartley, 2002; Sellen & Harper, 2002). Note taking has been identified as one of the first cognitive technologies (Makany, Kemp, & Dror, 2009) to aid learning, memory, and problem solving (Piolat et al., 2005). Researchers have identified two primary functions of note taking: (a) a process function: encoding and (b) a product function: external storage. The following sections review the research associated with these functions within the context of note taking while listening and reading.

The Process and Product Functions of Note Taking

Forty years ago, DiVesta and Gray (1972) suggested that note taking serves as a mechanism for encoding information and/or as a mechanism for external storage for later study or reference. The encoding function suggests that the actual process of recording notes, without reviewing them, is beneficial for learning; the external storage function suggests that the product of note taking (recorded notes) is beneficial for review and/or reflection (Boch & Piolat, 2005; Kiewra, 1989). The encoding and storage (i.e., review) functions have provided the framework for hundreds of studies exploring the effects of note taking while listening or reading (for reviews see Hartley, 1983; Kiewra, 1985, 1989; Kobayashi, 2005, 2006; Ryan, 1982).

The Encoding Effect. Several years ago, Hartley (1983) and Kiewra (1985) conducted independent reviews of the encoding function of note taking. They identified a combined 61 studies that compared the performance of students who took notes during lecture, without reviewing them, to the performance of students who did not take notes during lecture. Their findings revealed a note-taking encoding effect in 35 studies (57%), no effect in 23 studies (38%), and a reverse-encoding effect in three studies (5%) (Kiewra, 1989). More recently, Kobayashi (2005) conducted a meta-analysis of 57 studies that compared note taking to no note taking and found a small, positive encoding effect ($ES = .26$). Taken together, these finding provide modest evidence that note taking is beneficial for learning, even without reviewing the notes.

From a cognitive processing perspective, theorists have explained the encoding effect by suggesting that note taking may affect any of four cognitive processes: attention, mental effort, organization, and/or generation. In terms of attention, note taking has been found to increase attention to important information in a lecture (Einstein, Morris, & Smith, 1985; Kiewra, Mayer, Christensen, Kim, & Risch, 1991) and to sustain attention to learning material over an extended period of time (Peverly & Sumowski, 2012). Students also report attention directing benefits as one of the primary reasons they take notes (Van Meter, Yokoi, & Pressley, 1994).

Concerning mental effort, Peper and Mayer (1978) proposed the mental effort hypothesis, which is similar to Craik and Lockhart's (1972) levels of processing principle. This view suggests that the cognitive demands of note taking require deep mental processing or effort, with deeper levels being associated with more stable and elaborate memory traces (Bretzing & Kulhavy, 1979; Igo, Bruning, & McCrudden, 2005a; Kiewra, 1985). Research supports the notion that note taking is a cognitively demanding task, requiring the simultaneous coordination of complex language processing activities within a severely limited working memory system (Peverly, 2006; Piolat et al., 2005). In fact, Piolat et al. (2005), found that note taking was more demanding on working memory than either learning or comprehension. While note taking clearly requires significant mental effort, it is also important to note that a significant amount of the mental effort in note taking is extraneous to learning (Piolat et al., 2005; Rickards, 1998).

According to the organization hypothesis, note taking enhances encoding by helping learners develop internal connections among propositions, main ideas, and themes inherent in the source material (Einstein, Morris, & Smith, 1985). However, some researchers have suggested that the encoding process does not necessarily affect the internal organization of ideas because note taking does not involve organizing a new text, only recording an already organized one (Benton, Kiewra, Whitfill, & Dennison, 1993). Furthermore, the linear nature of most note-taking practices (e.g., outlines, lists) limits the internal organization of ideas through a lack of localization; that is, related ideas are spatially separated, concealing their relationships (Jairam, 2009; Kauffman & Kiewra, 2010). This suggests that organization is more likely a function of note reviewing than note taking.

Finally, Peper and Mayer (1978, 1986) proposed the generative processing hypothesis, which suggests that learners associate noted information with prior knowledge, thereby facilitating far-transfer tasks. This hypothesis is consistent with Wittrock's (1974) generative model of learning and Slamecka and Graf's (1978) generation effect. The generative model of learning suggests that instructional interventions that encourage associations between new information and memory facilitate recall and understanding; the generation effect refers to the finding that learners remember more information that they have generated than information that was generated by others. However, as with the organization hypothesis, some researchers have suggested that because of the cognitive demands of note taking, generative processing is more likely a result of note reviewing than note taking (see Kiewra, 1989).

The Review Effect. The benefits of note review have historically been examined by comparing the performance of learners who review their notes with those not permitted to review their notes (Kiewra, 1989). Hartley (1983) and Kiewra (1985) independently reviewed a combined 32 studies of the review function and found a review effect in 24 studies (75%) and no effect in eight studies (25%). No studies found review to be inferior to no review. Kobayashi (2006) conducted a meta-analysis comparing learners who took notes and reviewed them (note taking plus review) to learners who either (a) did not take notes or review them (12 studies) or (b) did not take notes but could mentally review the material before a test (18 studies). His findings revealed a medium to large note taking plus review effect in both comparisons, $(ES = 75, ES = .77$, respectively). These findings show strong support for the benefits of combining the note-taking process with a note-review period. In fact, the review effect appears to be stronger than the encoding effect alone. For instance, Kiewra et al. (1991) found that learners who did not even attend a lecture, but reviewed borrowed notes (review only), scored significantly higher on a conceptual-relations test than did learners who took notes but did not review them (encoding only). From a cognitive processing perspective, note review appears to help learners organize information (DiVesta & Gray, 1972), remember related (but unnoted) information (Rickards & Friedman, 1978), strengthen weak memory traces, and promote generative processing (Kiewra, 1989).

Cognitive load theory (Sweller, 1988; Sweller & Chandler, 1991) is a useful framework for conceptualizing the cognitive processes associated with the encoding and review functions note taking. Cognitive load theory concerns the way limited cognitive resources are used during an instructional task. Mayer (2009) identifies three types of cognitive load: (a) extraneous processing, (b) essential processing, and (c) generative processing. Extraneous processing, caused by poor instructional design or poor learner strategies, is detrimental to learning because it engages working memory resources in ways unrelated to the instructional objectives (Mayer, 2011). Essential and generative processing are important to accomplishing the instructional objectives. Essential processing refers to cognitive processing required to represent material in working memory, while generative processing refers to cognitive processing required to organize new material and integrate it with prior knowledge (Mayer, 2009). Our review of note taking suggests that the cognitive processes associated with the encoding function of note taking (i.e., attention and mental effort) are roughly analogous to Mayer's notion of essential processing, whereas the cognitive processes associated with the *review* function (organization and generation) are analogous to generative processing.

COMBINING GRAPHIC ORGANIZERS, NOTE TAKING, AND COMPUTERS

Researchers have recently begun to study the educational potential of combining the cognitive benefits of note taking with the cognitive benefits of studying a graphic organizer (GO) by having students take notes on a GO template. The goal of these studies has been to explore the additive potential of these two successful instructional techniques. We first provide an overview of GOs and related research and then discuss how note taking and GOs have been combined in both print and computer-based environments (i.e., CGO note taking).

As with note taking, GOs have been used to support learning from expository text. GOs are adjunct aids to text that use the spatial arrangement of words to communicate concept relations in two dimensions rather than one (Robinson & Kiewra, 1995) (see Figure 8.1). GOs have been found to be more effective than linear organizers (e.g., outlines, lists) for helping students learn concept relations (Kauffman & Kiewra, 2010; Robinson & Kiewra, 1995). The effectiveness of GOs is usually attributed to the fact that text concept relations and hierarchies are explicitly communicated by the spatial location of words within the organizer (Jairam, Kiewra, & Kauffman, 2012; Robinson, Corliss, Bush, Bera, & Tomberlin, 2003). This two-dimensional arrangement of text concepts enables learners to more easily compare relationships across concept attributes than with linear adjuncts. The benefits of studying GOs as adjunct aids have been observed with both print-based (Kiewra, Kauffman, Robinson, Dubois, & Staley, 1999; Robinson & Kiewra, 1995; Robinson & Schraw, 1994) and computer-based instruction (Robinson et al., 2003).

The cognitive benefits of GOs can be explained from the perspective of cognitive load theory. A linear organizer imposes more extraneous processing than a GO because learners must use limited working memory resources to search for concept relations (a task not directly related to the instructional objectives) that are made more explicit in a GO. That is, the two-dimensional arrangement of a GO reduces extraneous processing and facilitates generative processing. Therefore, note taking on GOs is essentially an attempt to combine the essential processing benefits of note taking with the generative processing benefits of GOs.

Paper-Based GO Note Taking

A typical study combining note taking with GOs consists of providing students with an expository text passage along with one or more skeletal GO templates on separate sheets of paper. A typical skeletal GO template consists of an empty matrix with column (main topics) and row (repeatable subtopics) headings designed to guide the note-taking process. While studying the text passage, students take notes by writing information contained in the text into the appropriate matrix cells. Studies comparing the effectiveness of skeletal GO note taking (while studying print text) to either outline or freeform note taking have not produced the same positive results observed when these methods (i.e., note taking and studying a GO) have been studied independently (Katayama & Robinson, 2000; Kauffman, 2004; Kiewra, Dubois, Christensen, Kim, & Lindberg, 1989). Interestingly, some positive findings favoring GO note taking over other note taking formats have been observed in lecture note taking studies. However, these positive findings have not been consistent (for a review see Kiewra, 1991).

The lack of significant achievement effects in paper-based GO note taking have been explained by the high cognitive demands required of the GO note-taking process. For example, Kiewra et al. (1989) postulated that GO note taking requires a high degree of selective attention, leaving students with few cognitive resources for understanding concept relations. Apparently, the extraneous and essential processing demands of GO note taking prevent students from realizing the generative processing benefits of the GO (i.e., facilitating understanding of concept relations). This explanation is supported by the success of GO note taking in studies including an intervention condition (e.g., partially completed GO template) designed to relieve some of the cognitive demands of the note-taking process (Katayama & Robinson, 2000).

CGO Note Taking

More recently, researchers have explored the effectiveness of CGO note taking. In CGO note taking, the computer screen is typically divided into frames, with one frame containing an e-text passage and the other frame containing a matrix note taking framework (i.e., CGO). Most CGO studies have employed a horizontal split-screen format, with the top frame containing the e-text and the bottom frame containing the skeletal CGO (see Figure 8.1). The e-texts and accompanying CGOs employed as treatment materials in the published literature have varied considerably in subject area, number, and size. For instance, e-texts have covered subject areas such as psychology, geology, and English writing, and ranged in length from 762 words to 3,500 words. CGOs accompanying a particular e-text have also varied in number (from 1 to 8) and in size (from 4 to 78 cells).

As with paper GO note taking, the CGO note taking research has failed to show the effectiveness of combining these study methods without some type of behavioral intervention to improve the note-taking process (Crooks & Katayama, 2002; Igo, Bruning, McCrudden, & Kauffman 2003; Katayama & Crooks, 2001). Similar to paper GO note taking, the insignificant results observed from nonintervention (i.e., skeletal) CGO note taking have been attributed to the cognitive demands of the process (Crooks & Katayama, 2002). However, in addition to the demands of the process, researchers have identified an attribute of the CGO note-taking medium—the copy-paste feature—as another significant problem limiting the effectiveness of CGO note taking (Igo, Bruning, & McCrudden, 2005a). Somewhat paradoxically, however, the copy-paste feature is purported to make the process too passive as opposed to too demanding. Copy-paste note taking appears to promote minimal mental effort because the ease associated with the process does not require students to be selective and thoughtful in their note-taking decisions. Fortunately, the

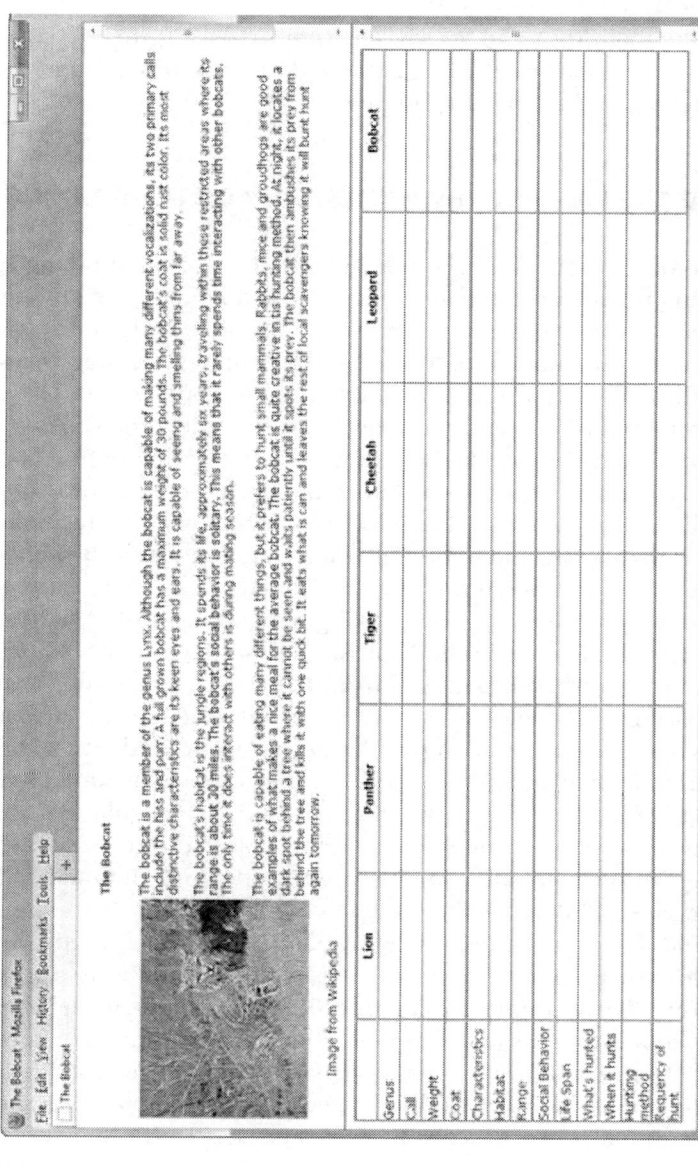

Source: Adapted from "Helping Students SOAR to Success on their Computer: A Mixed Methods Approach to Investigate and Test an Integrated Study Strategy System for Online Prose," Jairam (2009, p. 191).

Figure 8.1.   An example of a CGO.

computer affords the ability to intervene and/or scaffold the CGO note-taking process in ways not possible in paper-based note taking. In the remaining sections of this chapter we discuss these two seemingly contradictory hypotheses for the lack of success of CGO note taking (i.e., too passive vs. too demanding) and review research exploring the effectiveness of various computer-based interventions designed to overcome the limitations inherent in these two hypotheses.

ADDRESSING THE PASSIVITY HYPOTHESIS IN CGO NOTE TAKING

The failure to combine the learning benefits of GOs and note taking in CGO note-taking research is often attributed to the tendency of many students to ineffectively use the copy-paste feature included with most computer application programs (Igo, Bruning, McCrudden, & Kauffman, 2003; Igo et al., 2005a; Igo, Riccomini, Bruning, & Pope, 2006). Given the choice to copy-paste or type their notes, most students prefer to copy-paste. In fact, one study found that 80% of general education high school students chose to copy-paste, rather than type, their notes at the computer (Igo et al., 2003). Other studies have shown that this preference for copy-paste note taking is evident among college students as well (Bauer, 2008). However, the educational problem associated with copy-paste note taking relates to how it is typically used during note taking, rather than an inherent flaw with the feature itself. That is, most students resort to passively copying large, verbatim passages from the source text rather than being more selective in their copy-paste decisions (Igo et al., 2005a). Selectivity in copy-paste note taking is characterized by students taking the time to carefully analyze and evaluate text ideas before making copy-paste decisions. Selectivity is characteristic of high self-regulation and essential cognitive processing; less selectivity is characterized by surface text processing, indiscriminant copy-paste decisions, and minimal self-regulation (Igo et al., 2005a, 2005b; Nesbit et al., 2006).

Several studies have shown that many students lack the self-regulation skills to use the copy-paste feature to enhance essential processing during CGO note taking. For example, Igo et al. (2003) compared the achievement of high-school students asked to read an online text and take notes in either a CGO or in a computer notepad. The computer notepad used in their studies (and in the other studies reviewed in this chapter) was similar to a conventional word processing program (see Figure 8.2 for an example of a computer notepad). In the Igo et al. studies, both groups were given the option to either type or copy-paste their notes. In two studies (Experiments 3 & 4), using different online texts, students using the notepad did as well as those using the CGO on fact and concept-relations tests. That is, note taking in a CGO was no more effective than free-form note taking in a computer notepad. After analyzing the students' notes, the authors concluded that the advantages of the CGO were not realized because most students superficially processed the text by indiscriminately copying and pasting large, verbatim text passages. The students apparently did not realize the benefits of the CGO because the copy-paste function used in these studies did not encourage selectivity and deep cognitive processing.

Crooks and Katayama (2002) conducted two similar studies comparing the performance of college students who took notes in a CGO with those who took notes on either a blank sheet of paper (Experiment 1) or in a computer notepad (Experiment 2). In both studies, students using the computer were given the option to either copy-paste or type their notes. Similar to Igo et al. (2003), conventional note taking (either on paper or in a computer notepad) was as effective as CGO note taking on fact,

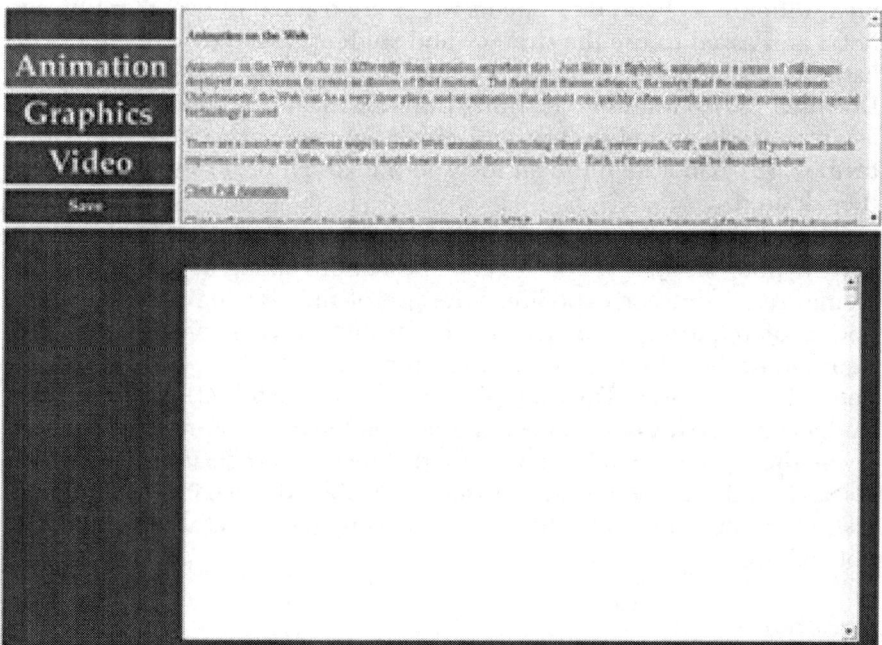

Source: Adapted from "Factors Influencing the Effectiveness of Note Taking on Computer-Based Graphic Organizers," by S. M. Crooks, D. R. White, and L. Barnard, 2007, *Journal of Educational Computing Research, 37*(4), p. 377. Copyright 2007 by the Baywood Publishing Company, Inc.

Figure 8.2.   An example of a computer notepad.

concept-relations, and transfer tests. Although the authors did not analyze the notes, the results are consistent with previous research and support the notion that the benefits of combining note taking and GOs in CGO note taking are often not realized when students have the option to copy-paste their notes.

One advantage of computer-based note taking is the option it affords instructional designers to manipulate the use of specific data entry modes (e.g., copy-paste, typing) through direct behavioral intervention (Bauer, 2008). These options are not available during conventional note taking with paper, where instructors are limited to less direct interventions (e.g., pretraining, giving verbal instructions) with the hope that students will apply the strategies during independent study. However, indirect interventions have been shown to be less effective than direct interventions (Kobayashi, 2005, 2006), especially as a means of changing a persistent behavior like verbatim note taking (Kiewra, 1984). The ineffectiveness of indirect interventions has been evident in free-form computer (i.e., notepad) note taking as well. For example, Quade (1996) found no achievement differences between students who were trained to take paraphrased notes and asked to use the strategy and students asked to take either verbatim notes or notes of their choosing. Similarly, Ramsay, Sperling, and Dornisch (2010) found no learning differences among groups of students asked to study an online text and either (a) summarize main ideas in a textbox, (b) elaborate on main ideas in a textbox, or (c) study the text as they desired.

Three behavioral interventions that have been used to address the passivity hypothesis associated with copy-paste note taking have involved disabling, restricting, or expediting the use of the copy-paste feature. The notion of requiring students to use effective study strategies that they would not otherwise choose has proven successful in free-form computer note-taking research. For example, Armel and Shrock (1995) found that students required to take notes in a notepad learned more than students given the option to take notes. In the next three sections, we review research and form some conclusions about the effectiveness of disabling, restricting, or expediting the use of the copy-paste feature during CGO note taking.

Disabling the Copy-Paste Feature

We identified three CGO studies in which note-taking format was an independent variable (CGO vs. notepad) and data entry mode (i.e., typing) was held constant (Igo et al., 2003; Kaufmann, Zhao, & Yang, 2011). Each study *required* college students to type their notes in either a computer notepad or a CGO. The results showed that the CGO groups outperformed the notepad groups on cued fact recall and concept-relations tests (Igo et al., 2003; Kaufmann et al., 2011, Experiment 2) as well as procedure and application tests (Kaufmann et al., 2011, Experiment 2). One study also found that the CGO group outperformed the notepad group on a test assessing the recognition of "knowledge of facts and relationships among those facts"[1] (Kaufmann et al., 2011, Experiment 1, p. 316). However, one study showed no significant differences on a fact recognition test (Igo et al., 2003). An analysis of the notes in each study revealed that the CGO groups recorded notes that were more complete (Kaufmann et al., 2011, Experiments 1 & 2) and of a higher quality (mostly paraphrases, see Igo et al., 2003) than the notepad groups.

We identified two other CGO note-taking studies that took an opposite approach to the three studies just reviewed. Instead of manipulating note-taking format, these studies manipulated the data entry mode (i.e., typing vs. copy-paste) and held note-taking format (CGO) constant (Igo et al., 2006; Katayama, Shambaugh, & Doctor, 2005). Katayama et al. (2005) studied college students required to either type or copy-paste their notes into a CGO and found that typing was superior to copy-paste on a transfer test, but not on a fact-recognition test. The researchers did not analyze the notes.

Igo et al. (2006) conducted a similar comparison with middle school learning disabled (LD) students using a Latin square design. Each student took notes in a CGO on three separate text passages, using a different data-entry mode (typing, copy-paste, and writing) for each text. The writing condition involved taking notes (using pencil or pen) on a paper GO. Their findings showed that copy-paste notes were superior to both typed and written notes on a fact recognition test; whereas written notes (in the paper matrix) were superior to copy-paste notes on a cued fact recall test, although this finding could not be replicated after a 4-day delay. The researchers did not include any measures of higher-order learning (e.g., transfer). A qualitative analysis showed that the LD participants preferred to copy-paste their notes, and that, regardless of their data entry mode (typing, copy-paste, or writing) they took mostly verbatim notes. They also concluded that the LD participants struggled to encode text ideas during CGO note taking.

In summary, four of the five studies reviewed provide evidence that CGO note taking is more effective when students are *required* to type their notes. This conclusion was supported in the studies comparing the performance of students required to type in either a CGO or a computer notepad. In each study, the CGO groups outperformed the notepad groups on tests of fact recall, concept relations, procedural calculations, and application (Igo et al., 2003; Kaufmann et al., 2011). None of these results were found in similar studies providing students the option to copy-paste their notes (e.g., Crooks & Katayama, 2002; Igo et al., 2003, Experiments 4 & 5). In addition, when copy-paste was directly compared to typing in a CGO, students required to type outperformed those required to copy-paste on a transfer test (Katayama et al., 2005). Apparently, some prior attempts at CGO note taking failed because students misused the copy-paste tool, resulting in a lack of essential processing. On the other hand, typing likely facilitated essential processing by encouraging a deeper processing of the text as evidenced by the more complete and personalized forms of their notes (Igo et al., 2003; Kaufmann et al., 2011).

The success of typing in a CGO is particularly interesting given that previous note-taking studies involving handwritten GO notes have resulted in minimal success (Katayama & Robinson, 2000; Kiewra et al., 1989). This suggests an interesting question, "Why is typing in a CGO more effective than writing on a paper GO?" This question is especially interesting given that in the CGO studies just reviewed the students were required to read from a computer screen—a process that has been shown to be slower and more effortful than reading from paper (Olive, Favart, Beauvais, & Beauvais, 2008). There are at least two answers to this question that suggest that typing notes requires less extraneous processing than writing notes.

First, typing is a more fluent transcription method than writing (Christensen, 2004). Even poor typists (e.g., hunt-and-peck) can maintain speeds around 30 wpm, whereas handwriting speeds (while copying) average around 20 wpm (Brown, 1988; Card, Moran, & Newell, 1983). Considering that transcription speed has been shown to be the best predictor of text note quality (even more so than reading comprehension), typing should have a significant advantage over writing during note taking (Peverley & Sumowski, 2012). The superior transcription fluency of typing should result in a greater automaticity of word production and enable students to allocate more working-memory resources toward quality note production (Peverley & Sumowski, 2012). A second related reason that typing may be more effective than writing during GO note taking is that CGOs typically integrate the source text and the note-taking tool within one screen, enabling students to maintain visual focus on a single surface (i.e., computer screen) while simultaneously reading and taking notes (Bauer, 2008). On the other hand, when writing notes on paper, students are required to split their attention between two visual surfaces, the source text and the matrix. This process involves holding to-be-noted text in a limited working memory until it is written (a relatively slow transcription method) in the appropriate matrix cell. The different processes involved in note writing versus note typing may explain the success of compulsory typing during CGO note taking.

It is also important to note that the studies just reviewed suggest that the benefits of typing do not extend to fact recognition performance (Igo et al., 2003, Experiment 5; Katayama et al., 2005). In fact, there is evidence that copy-paste may be superior to typing for recognizing facts (Igo et al., 2006). This is likely due to the verbatim form of most copy-paste notes. The finding that verbatim note taking facilitates fact recognition is consistent with conventional note-taking studies involving reading electronic text (Quade, 1995, 1996) and listening to a lecture (Carter & Van Matre, 1975; Peper & Mayer, 1986). This finding is perhaps best explained by the encoding specificity principle which states that the best retrieval cues are those that exactly duplicate a previously encoded memory trace (Tulving, 1983). From this perspective, verbatim notes are likely to be more effective than personalized notes (e.g., summary, paraphrase, etc.) for fact recognition because recognition items (e.g., multiple choice) contain retrieval cues that directly correspond to memory traces created from verbatim note taking. On the other hand, the studies just reviewed, and other research involving conventional notes from text (Slotte & Lonka 1999a, 1999b), suggest that verbatim notes are ineffective for promoting higher-order learning outcomes (e.g., application, or understanding concept relationships).

From a cognitive load perspective, the superiority of typing over copy-paste during CGO note taking is surprising considering that typing requires more extraneous processing. The copy-paste process utilizes computer memory to offload much of the extraneous processing required when typing notes into a CGO. While typing notes involves less extraneous processing than writing notes (as previously discussed), typing still requires students to engage in what Mayer and Moreno (2003) referred to as representational holding: "holding a mental representation in working memory over a period of time" (p. 45). When typing notes, students must (a) select text from a source material, (b) mentally select and hold a segment of this text in verbal working memory, (c) sequentially transfer this text segment from working memory to the computer (one letter at a time) before it is forgotten, and (d) repeat this process until the entire original text selection is recorded in the CGO. In contrast, copy-paste note taking eliminates the need for representational holding by offloading this task to computer memory. During copy-paste note-taking students need only (a) select text from a source material, (b) copy the text into computer memory, and (c) paste the entire text into the CGO.

From the standpoint of cognitive load theory, our review of copy-paste verses typing in CGO note taking presents a theoretical conundrum: "Why is a process that requires more extraneous processing (i.e., typing) more effective than a process that requires less extraneous processing (i.e., copy-paste)?" One answer to this question pertains to the insufficient mental effort hypothesis discussed previously. That is, the relative simplicity and ease of the copy-paste process appears to promote minimal mental effort among students lacking in motivation or metacognitive skill. Unfortunately, for these students, the copy-paste process not only reduces extraneous processing, but also essential and generative processing (Mayer, 2009). This has prompted note-taking researchers to investigate ways to use the copy-paste feature to help students direct working memory resources previously used for extraneous processing (i.e., representational holding in traditional note taking) toward essential and generative processing. One fruitful line of research in this regard involves restricting the amount of text that can be copied during CGO note taking.

Restricting the Copy-Paste Feature

Recent research has suggested that the effectiveness of copy-paste note taking can be improved if students use the additional time and cognitive resources afforded by this technique for essential processing. Studies conducted by Igo and Kiewra (2007) with high-achieving college (Experiment 1) and high school (Experiment 2) students appear to support this idea. The high achievers in their experiments demonstrated considerable metacognitive skill by using the copy-paste feature in a more selective and strategic manner than the lower achievers in previous studies (Igo et al., 2003). High achievers (presumably possessing considerable metacognitive skill) appear to be able to use the copy-paste feature more effectively than low achievers during CGO note taking. This finding suggests an interesting question for instructional technologists, "How can lower (or even regular) achievers be helped to use the copy-paste feature more effectively in CGO note taking?" This question has important implications for CGO note taking because most students are not higher achievers and they prefer to copy-paste rather than type.

Restricted copy-paste note taking is a behavioral intervention that has been investigated as a means of improving student performance during CGO note taking. The intent of this intervention is to encourage deeper text processing by requiring students to be more selective and evaluative in their note-taking decisions. Various terms have been used to describe hypotheses supporting restricted CGO note taking[2]—we use the term *restriction hypothesis* in this chapter (Igo, Kiewra, & Bruning, 2008). While the terminology has varied, the underlying theoretical support for each hypothesis has been the levels-of-processing theory (Craik & Lockhart, 1972), the notion that deeper processing leads to more durable memory traces. The restriction hypothesis predicts that restrictions on the amount of information that can be pasted in a CGO will encourage students to be more selective and evaluative in their decisions (Igo et al., 2008), thereby promoting more essential processing.

Igo and colleagues (Igo et al., 2003; Igo et al., 2005a; Igo et al., 2007; Igo et al., 2008) conducted five CGO note-taking studies comparing the effectiveness of restricted versus unrestricted copy-paste note taking on three learning measures: (a) cued fact recall, (b) concept recognition, and (c) relational inferences. One of the studies also included fact recognition (Igo et al., 2005a). The participants in four of the studies were college students and the remaining study involved high school students (Igo et al., 2007, Experiment 2). Each study contained a restricted condition that limited the amount of information that could be pasted into each cell of a CGO to seven words. One of the studies included two additional conditions that restricted pasting to 14 and 21 words (Igo et al., 2008). Each study also included an unrestricted condition with no pasting limits. The ability to type was disabled in each study; however, students were free to copy text verbatim (text appearing together in the text) or to personalize their notes by coping words from different areas of the text, as long as their notes did not exceed any word limitations placed on their particular condition (i.e., restricted conditions).

The results from the five studies were mixed. The restriction hypothesis was supported in two studies (Igo et al., 2003; Igo et al., 2005a) and rejected in the remaining studies. In the studies supporting the restriction hypothesis, the seven-word restriction groups outperformed the unrestricted groups on all learning measures except fact recognition. In two of these studies rejecting the restriction hypothesis (Igo et al., 2007, Experiments 1 & 2) there were no significant differences between groups on any learning measures. In the remaining study (Igo et al., 2008) there were no significant differences between the unrestricted group and the 7-word restriction group; however, the unrestricted group unexpectedly outperformed the additional restricted groups (14-word and 21-word) on the fact and inference tests.

Fortunately, subsequent analyses of the students' notes in four of the studies (Igo et al., 2005a; Igo et al., 2007, 2008), enabled the researchers to draw some conclusions from these somewhat puzzling findings. Two trends were evident from their analyses. First, quantitative analyses of the notes in all four studies showed that within the unrestricted groups, there was an inverse relationship between the number of words pasted and learning achievement. That is, among the students given free rein to copy and paste at will, those who pasted more words learned less than those who pasted fewer words. Second, interviews with unrestricted participants in two of the studies (Igo et al., 2005a; Igo et al., 2008) revealed a relationship between selectivity in copy-paste decisions and depth of cognitive processing. In general, less selective students (i.e., copious pasters) described shallower processing activities than more selective students. These trends suggest a linkage between the metacognitive behavior of selectivity (characterized by less, but more mindful, pasting) and greater depth of processing and achievement. This is consistent with previous research showing that more selective learning behavior is associated with greater depth of processing (Nesbit et al., 2006).

The relationships discovered in the analyses discussed above help explain why the restriction hypothesis was supported in two of the studies, but not in the remaining studies. An analysis of the notes in one of the studies supporting the restriction hypothesis (Igo et al., 2005a) showed that, consistent with the first trend, group differences in note quantity were inversely related to group differences in posttest performance. More specifically, the lower-performing unrestricted group pasted mostly verbatim notes containing six times as many words ($M = 42$ words per cell) as the notes of the higher-performing restricted group ($M = 7$ words per cell). Furthermore, evidence for the second trend was found from interview data linking lack of copy-paste selectivity (unrestricted group) with shallow cognitive processing and greater selectivity (restricted group) with deep cognitive processing. Since no note analysis was reported in the other study supporting the restriction hypothesis (Igo et al., 2003, Experiment 6), it is not possible to determine whether similar patterns existed in that study; however, given the similarities in the participants, it seems plausible that support for the restriction hypothesis resulted from deeper cognitive processing in the restricted groups due to their more selective and evaluative copy-paste decisions.

Analyses of students' notes from the studies rejecting the restriction hypothesis (Igo et al., 2007; Igo et al., 2008) revealed smaller group differences in note quantity than the differences in the study supporting the hypothesis (Igo et al., 2005a). While the restricted groups pasted about the same amount of information as their counterparts in Igo et al. (2005a) ($M = 6.80$ words per cell), the unrestricted groups pasted about half as many words as their counterparts ($M = 23$ words vs. $M = 42$ words). These data show that, in studies rejecting the restriction hypothesis, the unrestricted participants used much more selectivity in their copy-paste decisions (i.e., they pasted fewer words) than they did in studies supporting the restriction hypotheses (Igo et al., 2005a).

Clearly, students who choose, of their own volition, to exercise copy-paste selectivity experience similar learning benefits as do students who are forced (i.e., constrained by the software) to be selective. From a practical standpoint, however, many students do not appear to have the metacognitive skill to use the copy-paste feature to make selective note-taking decisions. Consistent with this observation is the fact that the low performing unrestricted groups in previous studies (Igo et al., 2003, 2005a) consisted of regular college students, whereas the high-performing unrestricted groups in most previous studies (Igo et al., 2007) consisted of "high achieving" students, in both college (Experiment 1) and high school (Experiment 2). It seems logical to assume that the high achievers in these studies possessed the metacognitive skill necessary to use the copy-paste feature in a strategic and selective manner, whereas the "regular" students in Igo et al., (2005a, 2006, Experiment 6) did not.

Finally, in terms of fact recognition performance, the findings from Igo et al., (2005) echo the findings from the required typing studies reviewed earlier (Igo et al., 2003, Experiment 5; Igo et al., 2006; Katayama et al., 2005). The results of those studies showed that the verbatim nature of unrestricted copy-paste note taking was not detrimental to (and may even increase) performance on fact recognition tests. Not surprisingly, this finding appears to have been replicated in the context of restricted CGO note taking. Just as unrestricted copy-paste note taking was at least as effective as typing for fact recognition, it was also as effective as restricted copy-paste note taking (Igo et al., 2005a). Taken together, these findings add further support for the application of the encoding specificity principle to CGO note taking.

Expediting the Copy-Paste Feature

Four CGO note-taking experiments have explored two different methods of expediting the copy-paste note-taking process: click-and-paste (Jairam & Kiewra, 2010) and drag-and-drop (Robinson, Katayama, Odom, Beth, Hsieh, & Vanderveen, 2006).[3] Although these methods were not the variables under investigation in these experiments, they were utilized as methods of recording notes in the context of comparing CGO note taking to other note formats. Rather than address the passivity inherent in selecting notes during copy-paste note taking, these techniques bypass this issue by providing students with preselected notes. In effect, these techniques enable students to devote more time to note review than to note taking. For example, Jairam and Kiewra (2010) employed the click and paste method in a computer-based study comparing CGO note taking to free-form note taking (i.e., notepad), along with three other computer note-taking conditions. The notepad group was permitted to copy-paste and/or type as they chose. Students in the CGO note-taking group were required to use the click-and-paste method. This method involved clicking on pre-selected text segments (e.g., [lions roar]) within an online text, after which the text segments were automatically "pasted" into the appropriate cell of a CGO. The text segments (i.e., notes) were set off from the rest of the text with brackets;

this removed the need for students to use any selectivity or evaluation in terms of note-taking decisions. The students simply clicked on the bracketed text and the notes immediately appeared in the CGO for later study. In both conditions, the note-taking tool (i.e., notepad or CGO) was displayed within the same screen as the online text. The results showed that the CGO group outperformed the notepad group on tests measuring concept relationships and fact recognition.

Robinson et al. (2006) conducted two quasi-experimental studies (with intact classrooms) and one true experiment with college students who either studied paper GOs prepared by their instructor or took notes in CGOs. All three studies exposed the participants to several versions of the treatment materials (11 to 18 GOs) for several weeks (5 to 15 weeks). Students in the paper GO groups were given several complete GOs corresponding to chapters in their course textbook; students in the CGO groups studied the chapter material by completing the GOs on the computer. In the CGO conditions, students took notes by dragging-and-dropping virtual note cards into the appropriate cell of a partially completed GO. This task required students to make evaluative judgments concerning which GO cell best matched the content on the note card. However, the students were not required to make note-selection decisions as the notes were prepared by the instructor beforehand. The results showed that CGO groups outperformed the notepad groups on several recognition tests covering the textbook content.

The success of these methods (i.e., click-and-paste & drag-and-drop) may seem puzzling considering that the success of the previous methods reviewed was attributed to greater depth of processing during note selection and recording. That is, the effectiveness of both required typing and restricted copy-paste CGO note taking was attributed to the greater essential processing these methods encourage via selectivity and evaluation in note-taking decisions. However, the methods reviewed here required minimal cognitive processing during note taking. For example, the click-paste method simply required students to click bracketed words within an online text; students were not required (in fact, they could not) be selective and evaluative with respect to either note selection or note recording. Similarly, the drop-drag method did not require selective and evaluative decision making during note selection (i.e., notes were already provided), only during note recording.

The success of these methods is perhaps best explained by the extensive time allocated for note review (Jairam & Kiewra, 2010) and the additional opportunities given for encoding (Robinson, et al., 2006). For example, Jairam and Kiewra (2010) provided participants as much time for note reviewing as they did for note taking (20 minutes for each). Additionally, these phases were carefully controlled so that participants could

not take notes during note review and vice versa; therefore, each participant was ensured a relatively substantial amount of time for note review.
In the studies by Robinson et al., (2006) students were encouraged to take
their own GO notes on paper before completing the CGO task. This likely
provided students with substantial opportunities for essential processing
before they participated in the note-recording task.

ADDRESSING THE COGNITIVE DEMANDS OF CGO NOTE TAKING

Another common explanation for the lack of success in CGO note taking
is that the cognitive demands of this method are too high and leave few
resources for understanding concept relations (Kiewra, 1989). More specifically, combining the demands of note taking with the demands of
studying a GO requires a high degree of selective attention that may mitigate the advantages that have been observed when these methods are
studied separately (Kiewra et al., 1989). Partial CGO note taking and self-
regulation prompts are two interventions that have attempted to lessen
the demands of this process.

Partial CGO Note Taking

One attempt to address the cognitive demands of CGO note taking is to
provide students with a partially completed GO template. This approach
purports to reduce cognitive load by providing students with note-taking
templates that are partially filled with provided notes (typically 50%) (see
Figure 8.3). The provided notes function as cognitive scaffolds to guide and
model the note taking process and lessen the burden imposed on working
memory. Studies investigating this approach have consistently shown that
it promotes deeper learning (usually measured by an application test) than
conventional note taking or studying a complete CGO provided by the
instructor, irrespective of the data input method (i.e., typing or copy-paste).

Eight studies have been published comparing the effects of partial
CGO note taking to other note-taking formats (Crooks & Katayama,
2002; Katayama & Crooks, 2003; Katayama & Crooks, 2001; Robinson et
al., 2006). Four of these experiments compared partial CGO note taking
to conventional note taking (Crooks & Katayama, 2002; Katayama &
Crooks, 2001). The conventional note-taking materials consisted of a
computer notepad in three of the experiments, and a sheet of paper in
the remaining experiment (Crooks & Katayama, 2002, Experiment 1).

The results showed that the Partial CGO groups outperformed the
conventional groups on all three transfer tests given (Crooks & Katayama,

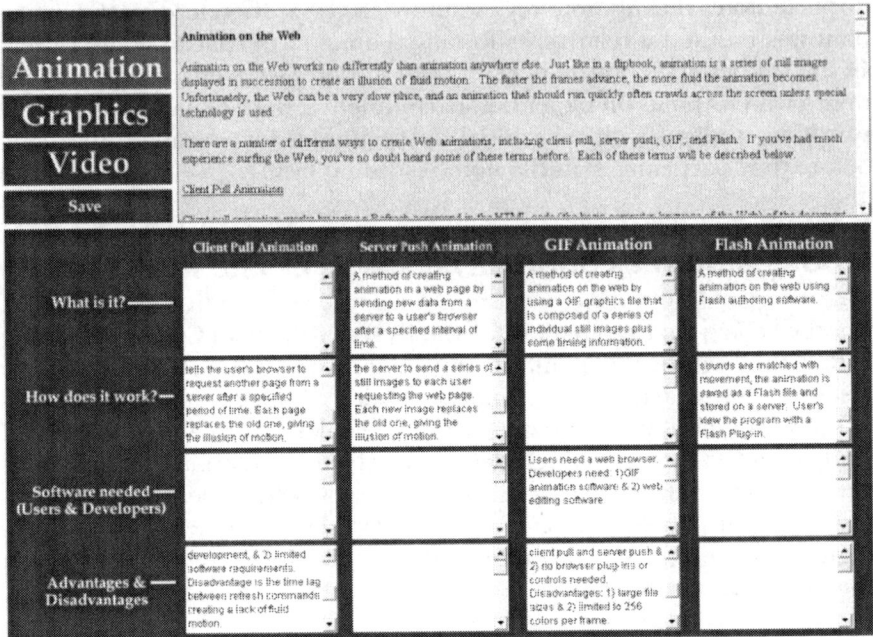

Source: Adapted from "Factors Influencing the Effectiveness of Note Taking on Computer-Based Graphic Organizers," by S. M. Crooks, D. R. White, and L. Barnard, 2007, *Journal of Educational Computing Research, 37*(4), p. 377. Copyright 2007 by the Baywood Publishing Company, Inc.

Figure 8.3.   An example of a partial CGO note-taking framework.

2002, Experiment 2; Katayama & Crooks, 2001, Exp. 1 & 2), but only one of 3 cue-recall tests (Crooks & Katayama, 2002, Experiment 1), and none of three fact recognition tests. Interestingly, the significant transfer results were obtained in spite of the fact that all four studies allowed the participants to copy-paste (or type) their notes, an option that was previously shown to be ineffective in three of these studies that compared skeletal CGO note taking (not partial) with conventional note taking (Crooks & Katayama, 2002; Katayama & Crooks, 2001, Experiment 1). These studies suggest that, compared to conventional note taking, partial CGO note taking may have advantages over skeletal CGO note taking.

Four other experiments compared partial CGO note taking to studying a competed CGO provided by an instructor (Katayama & Crooks, 2003; Robinson et al., 2006). In the only study including a transfer test, the partial CGO group outperformed the compete group; however, there were no significant differences on the cued fact recall or the fact recognition tests (Katayama & Crooks, 2003). In the remaining three studies, the Partial CGO groups once again surpassed the complete groups (who studied complete paper GOs) on several recognition tests given throughout a semester-long course (Robinson et al., 2006).

These results supply evidence that providing students with a partially completed CGO reduces the cognitive demands of CGO note taking enabling students to combine the depth of processing benefits of note taking with the concept relations benefits of a GO. Partial notes appear to function as cognitive scaffolds to help students deal with the cognitive demands of CGO note taking. These scaffolds appear to provide both quantitative and qualitative benefits. In quantitative terms, providing 50 percent of the notes in a CGO cuts the amount of required note taking in half. This obviously reduces the demands of the process and may enable students to devote cognitive resources to understanding concept relations (Kiewra et al., 1989; Katayama & Robinson, 2000). In qualitative terms, partial notes appear to guide or model note-taking behavior for students. For instance, Crooks, White, and Barnard (2007) found that students provided with summary notes, in half of the cells of a CGO, took more summary notes in the remaining cells than did students provided with verbatim notes. The summary notes taken by these students were not only more concise, but they were also judged to be of higher quality (i.e., more interconnected) than the notes taken by students given verbatim notes. The authors concluded that students tend to mimic provided notes in their own note-taking behavior.

Self-Regulation Prompts in CGO Note Taking

The cognitive demands of CGO note taking are further complicated by the fact that students are notoriously poor at self-regulating (i.e., managing, directing, and controlling) their learning activities (Schraw, Kauffman, & Lehman, 2002; Zimmerman & Schunk, 2007). This variable is especially important to consider in online learning settings where students are often required to complete challenging learning tasks (e.g., CGO note taking) with minimal guidance and support. One important aspect of effective self-regulation involves the use of cognitive strategies that promote deep learning (Pintrich, 1995), such as building associations among ideas in a text passage (Mayer, 2008). Building associations is a generative process that has been shown to increase understanding and retrieval of encoded information (Mayer, 1996). Unfortunately, students rarely use association strategies (e.g., taking spatial or graphic notes) when studying text-based material; instead, they focus on one idea at a time and organize information in lists or outlines (Jairam & Kiewra,

2010). Because the nature of many online learning activities requires a high degree of self-regulation, interventions designed to facilitate self-regulation such as building associations are critical (Kauffman, 2004).

Cognitive strategy prompts. As previously indicated, a primary benefit of learning from GOs pertains to building effective associations among related ideas in a GO. Building associations assists with the cognitive process of organization and is primarily a generative process (Mayer, 2010). However, many students may not have the self-regulation skills to spontaneously use association strategies without some type of intervention. To address this problem in CGO note taking, Jairam and Kiewra (2010) developed an association intervention designed to help students focus their attention on key associations in an online text. This intervention was made available to students after they finished inserting notes into a CGO. Students then learned associations by selecting association buttons (14 total) listed next to the CGO. When an association button was selected two events simultaneously occurred. First, an association was displayed in text below the CGO (e.g., "Wildcats that have the most weight live the longest"). Second, the relevant CGO cells were color highlighted to visually cue the association between related ideas in the matrix. In essence, this intervention prompted students to use a cognitive strategy that facilitates generative processing. Furthermore, the intervention guided the students' specific application of the strategy to help them exploit the full benefits of the GO as a study tool.

Jairam and Kiewra (2010) found that students studying CGO notes with the association intervention outperformed students studying CGO notes without the intervention on a concept relations test. Interestingly, the opposite result occurred on a fact recognition test; students not using the association intervention outperformed students who used the intervention. The intervention appeared to help students learn concept relations at the expense of learning to recognize facts. The authors reasoned that time spent focusing on learning relationships diminished the time available to learn facts (Jairam & Keiwra, 2010). This finding underscores the importance of matching desired learning outcomes (e.g., fact learning vs. relationship learning) with a suitable instructional intervention.

Metacogntive prompts. Another important aspect of self-regulation in learning is metacognition: the awareness of, and the ability to monitor, one's progress toward the attainment of learning goals (Bruning, Schraw, Norby, & Ronning, 2004; Eggen & Kauchak, 2007). Whereas self-regulation of cognitive strategies involves skill in using effective strategies, metacognition includes the ability to monitor the use of cognitive strategies to accomplish a learning goal. Unfortunately, many students lack the metacognitive skill to monitor their learning progress and apply needed changes to their study strategies or to seek remediation. Studies have shown that even when college students have the capacity to self-monitor, they rarely do so when studying online text unless they are prompted (Kauffman, 2004; Kauffman, Xun, Kui, & Ching-Huei, 2008). Again, the inability to monitor one's learning is particularly detrimental in online settings characterized by minimal feedback and instructional support.

Prompting students to monitor and/or reflect on their learning has been successfully applied in online learning environments (Azevedo, Guthrie, & Seibert, 2004; Azevedo, Moos, Greene, Winters, & Cromley, 2008; Kauffman, 2004; Kauffman et al., 2008; Kramarski & Mizrachi, 2006). For example, Kramarski and Mizrachi (2006) compared the performance of students who studied mathematics online or face-to-face, and either did or did not receive metacognitive prompts designed to encourage reflection on the e-text content (e.g.,"What is the problem/task all about?"). Their results showed that those studying with metacogntive prompts outperformed those studying without prompts. Of particular interest, however, was the finding that among students receiving prompts, the online students outperformed the face-to-face students. In a GO note-taking study, Kauffman (2004) studied the effects of metacognitive prompts designed to encourage self-monitoring in students studying a Web-based e-text while taking notes on a paper GO or on a sheet of paper (freeform). His findings showed that students receiving prompts outperformed students not receiving prompts on a fact recognition test. Interestingly, the application test results revealed a note-taking format by self-monitoring interaction. Among students taking notes on a GO, those receiving prompts scored higher than those not receiving prompts. However, among students taking free-form notes, those receiving prompts did not outperform those not receiving prompts.

The studies just reviewed suggest two hypotheses that relate to the potential effectiveness of using metacognitive prompts during CGO note taking. First, the evidence suggests that metacognitive prompts are a viable method for promoting metacognitive thinking while independently studying e-text. In fact, prompts may be more effective in this context than in a face-to-face setting (Kramarski & Mizrachi, 2006). Second, metacognitive prompts appear to be an effective means of encouraging metacognitive monitoring during note taking, especially GO note taking (Kauffman, 2004).

Kauffman et al. (2011) (Experiment 2) tested both of these hypotheses in a CGO note-taking study in which students either received or did not receive self-monitoring prompts encouraging them to review their notes at specific points while studying an e-text. Students either took notes in a CGO, a computer-based structured outline, or a notepad. The results revealed that students receiving self-monitoring prompts collected more notes and scored higher on a cued recall test than students not receiving self-monitoring prompts. Particularly interesting, however, were the application test results; consistent with Kauffman (2004), the prompts increased application test performance for the CGO note-taking group, but not the outline and notepad groups. The authors attributed this later finding to the superior perceptual enhancement of notes in a CGO as opposed to the often incoherent organization of more conventional notes. The perceptual enhancement provided by the CGO purportedly helped students locate e-text information that needed to be noted. The authors concluded that self-monitoring prompts are only effective for facilitating note taking if students are given a note-taking structure (e.g., CGO) that enhances their ability to recognize deficiencies (e.g., incomplete or missing notes) related to the prompts.

The Jairam and Keiwra (2010) CGO note-taking study reviewed earlier also included a metacognitive prompts condition. This condition included practice test questions designed to help students monitor their understanding of the e-text. The practice questions consisted of fact (e.g., "What is the average lifespan of the cheetah?") and concept relations (e.g, "How does the range of jungle cats compare to the range of plains cats?") questions. The questions were accessed by selecting buttons listed next to the CGO. When a practice question button was selected the question was displayed in text below the CGO. When students answered a fact question the answer appeared in the appropriate matrix cell. When students selected a relations question, the relationship referenced in the question was color highlighted in the relevant CGO cells to visually cue the association (the highlighting was identical to the association intervention discussed earlier). The results showed that students receiving practice question prompts in conjunction with a CGO outperformed students receiving a CGO alone, a computer-based structured outline, or a notepad on fact and concept relations texts. Practice questions appear to be another form of self-monitoring prompt that helps students apply effective study strategies.

SUMMARY

In this chapter we have examined empirical evidence concerning the effectiveness of combining two instructional methods (i.e., note taking and GOs) to improve learning from e-text, the most common means of content delivery in online courses today (Jones, Warren, & Robertson, 2009). A review of the note-taking literature revealed that both the process (i.e., encoding) and the product (i.e., of note review) of note taking are beneficial. From a cognitive processing perspective, the research suggests that the encoding function primarily involves essential processing (i.e., attention and mental effort), while the review function mainly involves generative processing (i.e., organization and generation) (DeLeeuw & Mayer, 2008). A review of GO research suggested that this method promotes generative processing (Mayer, 2010) by helping students learn concept relations (an organization process).

Research attempting to combine the cognitive benefits of note taking and GOs using paper materials revealed that this combination of methods was largely unsuccessful without some type of behavioral intervention (i.e., partial GO note taking). This lack of success was attributed to the high cognitive demands of GO note taking. Similar results were found in CGO note taking studies; however, the lack of success of these studies was attributed to conflicting hypotheses—some studies claiming the process was too passive and other studies claiming it was too demanding. Nonetheless, these contrasting hypotheses have produced two interesting lines of research featuring behavioral interventions designed to address the cognitive limitations inherent in their respective hypotheses. For example, disabling, restricting, or expediting the copy-paste feature were identified as interventions addressing the passivity hypothesis, whereas partial CGO note taking and prompting self-reflection were presented as interventions addressing the demanding hypothesis.

In general, findings from both lines of research supported their respective hypotheses. That is, the success of copy-paste interventions designed to increase selectivity and evaluation in note-taking decisions seemed to support the passivity hypothesis and the success of partial CGO note taking and self-regulation prompts seemed to support the demanding hypothesis.

THEORETICAL IMPLICATIONS

In this section we address the dynamic tension created by the conflicting hypotheses discussed above. That is, "How can the CGO note-taking process be both too passive *and* too demanding at the same time?"

The passivity hypothesis is an attempt to explain the results of CGO note-taking studies employing the copy-paste feature available with most computer-application programs. As mentioned earlier, the copy-paste feature facilitates note recording by eliminating the need for some extraneous processing (i.e., representational holding); however, it also appears to reduce essential and generative processing among students lacking the metacognitive skill to select important (i.e., essential) notes for further processing (Igo et al., 2003). This suggests that students lacking awareness of their learning needs may be disadvantaged by an instructional tool that, to be used effectively, *requires* metacognitive monitoring. Put simply, students lacking knowledge of the mental effort required to make effective note-selection decisions are likely to misuse a tool that does not require much effort.

On the other hand, behavioral interventions that require typing (Igo et al., 2003; Kaufmann et al., 2011), restrict copy-paste decisions (Igo et al., 2005a) , or prompt metacognitive monitoring during note taking (Kauffman et al., 2011) appear to induce students to invest needed mental effort during note selection, a primary component of essential processing (Mayer, 2010). These interventions also appear to promote generative processing as evidenced by superior application test performance (DeLeeuw & Mayer, 2008). Increased generative processing was likely due to the superior notes (i.e., less verbose, more efficient, and higher quality) generated from these interventions that were subsequently available for comparing concept relations during note review; reviewing concise, high quality CGO notes has been shown to increase application test performance more than reviewing verbose notes (Crooks et al., 2007).

Ironically, this interpretation reconciles the passivity and excessive demands hypotheses by suggesting that cognitive demand is central to both hypotheses. Contrary to being too passive, it appears that CGO note taking is quite metacognitively demanding, and copy-paste passivity may simply result from ignorance of these demands among those lacking the metacognitive monitoring ability to invest the necessary mental effort. This is evident from CGO note-taking studies showing that students lacking metacognitive ability fare poorly with the copy-paste tool, while students possessing metacognitive ability fare well (Igo & Kiewra, 2007).

Further support for the excessive demands hypothesis is provided by studies employing self-regulation interventions (i.e., cognitive and metacognitive prompts) during note review. These interventions appeared to promote generative processing by prompting students to study concept relations through explicit statements, visual cues, and practice questions (Jairam & Keiwra, 2010; Kauffman et al., 2011). The success of these interventions show that students benefit from direct interventions designed to facilitate generative processing. The implication is that generative processing does not automatically occur during CGO note taking due to the self-regulatory demands of the process.

INSTRUCTIONAL IMPLICATIONS

Educators and instructional designers should consider the CGO note-taking interventions discussed in this chapter as a viable means of supporting learning from e-text. Some of the interventions appear to primarily facilitate the attention and mental effort needed for essential processing during note selection (e.g., required typing and restricted copy-paste), while others tend to facilitate the internal organization needed for generative processing during note review (e.g., cognitive strategy and metacognitive prompts). In all cases, however, these techniques have been shown to be effective in helping students learn from e-text.

Because the copy-paste feature has the potential to encourage superficial cognitive processing among low-achieving students, educators should consider restricting, disabling, or expediting this function during CGO note taking. The click-and-paste (Jairam & Kiewra, 2010) and drag-and-drop (Robinson et al., 2006) methods seem less promising for promoting essential processing; however, they may be an effective way to provide a complete set to notes for review. To circumvent the cognitive demands of CGO note taking, educators should consider partial notes and/or prompts. Both of these methods have been proved effective and are relatively easy to implement.

Finally, our review shows the value of viewing the computer as a cognitive tool to engage and facilitate cognitive processing, rather than as simply an instructional delivery device (Jonassen, 2006). This view has enabled researchers to successfully develop behavioral interventions to circumvent the limitations associated with CGO note taking. Cognitive tools (e.g., copy-paste feature) applied in this way can function as intermediaries between students and learning goals by enabling them to dedicate more cognitive resources to essential and generative processing.

NOTES

1. Because two learning outcomes were combined in this test, it was not possible to determine which learning outcome (or perhaps both) was significantly affected by use of the CGO.
2. Igo and colleagues have used the terms *cognitive engagement* hypothesis (Igo et al., 2005a), *depth hypothesis* (Igo et al., 2006), *depth of processing hypothesis* (Igo & Kiewra, 2007), and *restriction hypothesis* (Igo et al., 2008).
3. These terms are descriptive of the note selection and recording processes used by the researchers. The terminology is ours, not the authors referenced.

REFERENCES

Allen, I. E., & Seaman, J. (2011). *Going the distance: Online education in the United States, 2011*. Babson Park, MA: Babson Survey Research Group.
Anderson-Inman, L., & Horney, M. (2007). Supported eText: Assistive technology through text transformations. *Reading Research Quarterly, 42*(1), 153-160.

Annand, D. (2008). Learning efficacy and cost-effectiveness of print versus e-book instructional material in an introductory financial accounting course. *Journal of Interactive Online Learning, 7*(2), 152-164.

Armel, D., & Shrock, S. A. (1996). The effects of required and optional computer-based notetaking on achievement and instructional completion time. *Journal of Educational Computing Research, 14*, 329-344.

Azevedo, R., Guthrie, J. T., & Seibert, D. (2004). The role of self-regulated learning in fostering students' conceptual understanding of complex systems with hypermedia. *Journal of Educational Computing Research, 30*, 87-111.

Azevedo, R., Moos, D. C., Greene, J. A., Winters, F. I, & Cromley, J. G. (2008). Why is externally-facilitated regulated learning more effective than self-regulated learning with hypermedia? *Educational Technology Research and Development, 56*, 45-72.

Bauer, A. (2008). *Designing note-taking interfaces for learning.* (Unpublished doctoral dissertation). Carnegie Mellon University, Pittsburgh, PA USA.

Benton, S. L., K. A. Kiewra, J. M. Whitfill, & R. Dennison. (1993). Encoding and external-storage effects on writing processes. *Journal of Educational Psychology 85*(2), 267-280.

Bernard, R. M., Abrami, P. C., Borokhovski, E., Wade, C. A., Tamim, R. M., Surkes, M. A., & Bethel, E. C. (2009). A meta-analysis of three types of interaction treatments in distance education. *Review of Educational Research, 79*(3), 1243-1289.

Boch, F., & Piolat, A. (2005). Note taking and learning: A summary of research. *The WAC Journal, 16*, 101-113.

Bretzing, B. H., & Kulhavy, R. W. (1979). Notetaking and depth of processing. *Contemporary Educational Psychology, 4*, 145-153.

Brown, C. M. (1988). *Human-computer interface design guidelines.* Norwood, NJ: Ablex.

Bruning, R., Schraw, G. J., Norby, M., & Ronning, R. R. (2004). *Cognitive psychology and instruction* (4th ed.). Upper Saddle River, NJ: Prentice Hall.

Buzzetto-More, N., Sweat-Guy, R., & Elobaid, M. (2007). Reading in a digital age: e-books: are students ready for this learning object? *Interdisciplinary Journal of Knowledge and Learning Objects, 3*, 239-250.

Card, S. K., Moran, T., & Newell, A. (1983). *The psychology of human-computer interaction.* Hillsdale, NJ: Lawrence Erlbaum Associates.

Carter, J. F., & Van Matre, N. H. (1975). Notetaking versus note having. *Educational Psychology , 67*, 900-904.

Christensen, C. (2004). Relationship between orthographic-motor integration and computer use for the production of creative and well-structured written text. *British Journal of Educational Psychology, 74*, 551-564.

Craik, F., & Lockhart, R. (1972). Levels of processing: A framework for memory research. *Journal of Verbal Learning and Verbal Behavior, 11*, 671-684.

Crooks, S. M., & Katayama, A. D. (2002). Effects of study note format on the comprehension of electronic text. *Research in the Schools, 9*, 21-32.

Crooks, S. M., White, D., & Barnard, L. (2007). Factors influencing the effectiveness of note taking on computer-based graphic organizers. *Journal of Educational Computing Research, 37*(4), 369-391.

DeLeeuw, K. E., & Mayer, R. E. (2008). A comparison of three measures of cognitive load: Evidence for separable measures of intrinsic, extraneous, and germane load. *Journal of Educational Psychology, 100,* 223-234.

DiVesta. F. J., &Gray, S. G. (1972). Listening and note taking. *Journal of Educational Psychology, 64,* 278-287

Einstein, G. O., Morris, J., & Smith, S. (1985). Note-taking, individual differences, and memory for lecture information. *Journal of Educational Psychology, 77,* 522-532.

Eggen, P., & Kauchak, D. (2007). *Educational Psychology, Windows on Classroom* (7th ed.). Upper Saddle River, NJ: Merril Prentice Hall.

Hartley, J. (1983). Notetaking research: Resetting the scoreboard. *Bulletin of the British Psychological Society, 36,* 13-14.

Hartley, J. (2002). Note taking in non-academic settings: A review. *Applied Cognitive Psychology, 16,* 559–574. doi:10.1002/acp.814.

Hattangdi, A., Jha, S., & Ghosh, A. (2010). A literature review of the perceptions of faculty about technology enabled distance education. *International Journal of Arts and Sciences, 3*(18), 379-390.

Igo, L. B., Bruning, R. B., McCrudden, M., & Kauffman, D. F. (2003). InfoGather: Six experiments toward the development of an online, data-gathering tool. In R. Bruning, C. A. Horn, & L. M. Pytlik-Zillig (Eds.), *Web-based learning: What do we know? Where do we go?* (pp. 57–77). Greenwich, CT: Information Age.

Igo, L. B., Bruning, R., & McCrudden, M. T. (2005a). Exploring differences in students' copy and paste decision making and processing: A mixed-method study. *Journal of Educational Psychology, 97*(1), 103-116.

Igo, L. B., Bruning, R., & McCrudden, M. T. (2005b). Encoding disruption associated with copy and paste note taking. In L. M. Pytlik-Zillig, M. Bodvarsson, & R. Bruning (Eds.), *Technology-based education: Bringing researchers and practitioners together* (pp. 107-119), Greenwich, CT: Information Age.

Igo, L. B., Riccomini, P. J., Bruning, R., & Pope G. (2006). How should middle school students with LD take web-based notes: A mixed methods study. *Learning Disability Quarterly, 29*(2), 112-121.

Igo, L. B., & Kiewra, K. A. (2007). How do high-achieving students approach web-based, copy and paste note taking? Selective pasting and related learning outcomes. *Journal of Advanced Academics, 18*(4), 512-529.

Igo, L. G., Kiewra, K. A., & Bruning, R. (2008). Individual differences and intervention flaws. *Journal of Mixed Methods Research, 2*(2), 149-168.

Jairam, D. (2009) *Helping students SOAR to success on their computer: A mixed methods approach to investigate and test an integrated study strategy system for online prose* (Doctoral dissertation). Retrieved from ProQuest Dissertations and Theses database (AAT 3350255).

Jairam, D., & Kiewra, K. A. (2010). Helping students soar to success on computer: an investigation of the SOAR study method for computer-based learning. *Journal of Educational Psychology, 102*(3), 601-614.

Jairam, D., Kiewra, K. A., Kauffman, D. F., & Zhao, R. (2012). How to study a matrix. *Contemporary Educational Psychology, 37,* 128-135.

Jonassen, D. H. (2006). Modeling with technology: Mindtools for conceptual change. Columbus, OH: Merill/Prentice Hall.

Jones, J. E., Warren, S., & Robertson, M. (2009). Increasing student discourse to support rapport building in web and blended courses using a 3D online learning environment. *Journal of Interactive Learning Research, 20*(3), 269-294.

Katayama, A. D., & Crooks, S. M. (2001). Examining the effects of notetaking format on achievement when students construct and study computerized notes. *The Learning Assistance Review, 6,* 5-23.

Katayama, A. D., & Crooks, S. M. (2003). Online notes: Differential effects of studying complete or partial graphically organized notes. *Journal of Experimental Education, 71*(4), 293-312.

Katayama, A. D., Shambaugh, R. N., & Doctor, T. (2005). Promoting knowledge transfer with electronic note taking. *Teaching of Psychology, 32,* 129-131.

Katayama, A. D., & Robinson, D. H. (2000). Getting students partially involved in notetaking using graphic organizers. *Journal of Experimental Education, 68,* 119-133.

Kauffman, D. F. (2004). Self-regulated learning in web-based environments: Instructional tools designed to facilitate self-regulated learning. *Journal of Educational Computing Research, 30*(1&2), 139-161.

Kauffman D. F., Xun G., Kui X., & Ching-Huei C. (2008). Prompting in web-based environments: supporting selfmonitoring and problem solving skills in college students. *Journal of Educational Computing Research 38,* 115-137.

Kauffman, D. F., & Kiewra, K. A. (2010). What makes a matrix so effective? An empirical test of the relative benefits of signaling, extraction, and localization. *Instructional Science, 38,* 679-705.

Kauffman, D. F., Zhao, R., & Yang, Y. S. (2011). Effects of online note taking formats and self-monitoring prompts on learning from online text: Using technology to enhance self-regulated learning. *Contemporary Educational Psychology, 36,* 313-322.

Kelsey, Kathleen D. and Alan D'souza (2004) Student motivation for learning at a distance: Does interaction matter? *Online Journal of Distance Learning Administration, 7*(2), Retrived from http://www.westga.edu/~distance/ojdla/summer72/kelsey72.html

Kiewra, K. (1991). Aides to lecture learning. *Educational Psychologist, 26,* 37-53.

Kiewra, K. A. (1984). Acquiring effective notetaking skills: an alternative to professional notetaking. *International Reading Association, 27*(4), 299-302.

Kiewra, K. A. (1985). Investigating note taking and review: A depth of processing alternative. *Educational Psychologist, 20,* 23–32.

Kiewra, K. A. (1989). A review of note-taking: The encoding storage paradigm and beyond. *Educational Psychology Review, 1,* 147-172.

Kiewra, K. A., Dubois, N. F., Christensen, M., Kim, S., & Lindberg, N. (1989) A more equitable account of the note-taking functions in learning from lecture and from text. *Instructional Science, 18,* 217-232.

Kiewra, K. A., Kauffman, D. F., Robinson, D. H., DuBois, N. F., & Staley, R. K. (1999). Supplementing foundering text with adjunct displays. *Instructional Science, 27*(5), 373-401.

Kiewra, K. A., Mayer, R. E., Christensen, M., Kim, S., & Risch, N. (1991). Effects of repetition on recall and note-taking: Strategies for learning from lectures. *Journal of Educational Psychology, 83*(1), 120-123.

Kobayashi, K. (2005). What limits the encoding effect of note-taking? A meta-analytic examination. *Contemporary Educational Psychology, 30*, 242-262.

Kobayashi, K. (2006). Combined effects of note-taking/reviewing on learning and the enchancement through interventions: A meta-analytic review. *Educational Psychology, 26*(2), 459-477.

Kramarski, B., & Mizrachi, N. (2006). Online discussion and self-regulated learning: Effects of instructional methods on mathematical literacy. *Journal of Educational Research, 99*(4), 218-230.

Makany, T., Kemp, J., & Dror, I. E. (2009). Optimising the use of note-taking as an external cognitive aid for increasing learning. *British Journal of Educational Technology, 40*(4), 619-635.

Mayer, R. E. (1996). Learning strategies for making sense out of expository text: The SOI model for guiding three cognitive processes in knowledge construction. *Educational Psychology Review, 8*, 357-371.

Mayer, R. E. (2008). *Learning and Instruction.* Upper Saddle River, NJ: Pearson.

Mayer, R. E. (2009). Constructivism as a theory of learning versus constructivism as a prescription for instruction. In S. Tobias & T. M. Duffy (Eds.), *Constructivist instruction: Success or failure?* (pp. 184-200). New York, NY: Routledge.

Mayer, R. E. (2010). Seeking a science of instruction. *Instructional Science, 38,* 143-145.

Mayer, R. E. (2011). *Applying the science of learning.* Upper Saddle River, NJ: Pearson.

Mayer, R. E., & Moreno, R. (2003). Nine ways to reduce cognitive load in multimedia learning. *Educational Psychologist, 38*(1), 43-52.

Moore, M. G. (1989). Three types of interaction. *The American Journal of Distance Education, 3*(2), 1-6.

Nesbit, J. C., Winne, P. H., Jamieson-Noel, D., Code, J., Zhou, M., MacAllister, ... & Hadwin, A. (2006). Using cognitive tools in gStudy to investigate how study activities covary with achievement goals. *Journal of Educational Computing Research, 35*(4), 339-358.

Olive, T., Favart, M., Beauvais, C., & Beauvais, L. (2008). Children's cognitive effort and fluency in writing: Effects of genre and of handwriting automatisation. *Learning and Instruction, 19*, 299-308.

Peper, R. J., & Mayer, R. E. (1978). Note-taking as a generative activity. *Journal of Educational Psychology, 70*, 514-522.

Peper, R. J., & Mayer, R. E. (1986). Generative effects of note-taking during science lectures. *Journal of Educational Psychology, 78*, 34-38.

Peverly, S. T. (2006). The importance of handwriting speed in adult writing. *Developmental Neuropsychology, 29*, 197-216.

Peverley, S. T., & Sumowski, J. F. (2012). What variables predict quality of text notes and are text notes related to performance on different types of tests? *Applied Cognitive Psychology, 26*, 104-117.

Pintrich, P. R. (1995). Understanding self-regulated learning. In P. R. Pintrich (Ed.), *Understanding self-regulated learning* (pp. 3-12). San Francisco, CA: Jossey-Bass.

Piolat, A., Olive, T., & Kellogg, R. T. (2005). Cognitive effort during note taking. *Applied Cognitive Psychology, 19*, 291-312.

Quade, A. M. (1995). A comparison of on-line and traditional paper and pencil notetaking methods during computer-delivered instruction. *Proceedings of the Annual National Convention of the Association for Educational Communications and Technology*, Anaheim, CA, 452-458.

Quade, A. M. (1996). An assessment of retention and depth of processing associated with notetaking using traditional pencil and paper and an on-line notepad during computer-delivered instruction. *Proceedings of Selected Research and Development Presentations at the 1996 National Convention of the Association for Educational Communications and Technology*, Indianapolis, IN, 560-570.

Ramsay, C. M., Sperling, R. A., & Dornisch, M. M. (2010). A comparison of the effects of students' expository text comprehension strategies. *Instructional Science, 38*, 551-570.

Rickards, J. P., & Friedman, F. (1978). The encoding versus the external storage hypothesis in note taking. *Contemporary Educational Psychology, 3*, 136-143.

Robinson, D. H., Corliss, S. B., Bush, A. M., Bera, S. J., & Tomberlin, T. (2003). Optimal presentation of graphic organizers and text: A case for large bites? *Educational Technology Research & Development, 51*(4), 25-41.

Robinson, D. H., Katayama, A. D., Odom, S., Beth, A., Hsieh, Y. P., & Vanderveen, A. (2006). Increasing text comprehension and graphic note-taking using a partial graphic organizer task. *Journal of Educational Research, 100*, 103-111.

Robinson, D. H., & Kiewra, K. A. (1995). Visual argument: graphic organizers are superior to outlines in improving learning from text. *Journal of Educational Psychology, 87*(3), 455-467.

Robinson, D. H., & Schraw, G. (1994). Computational efficiency through visual argument: do graphic organizers communicate relations in text too effectively? *Contemporary Educational Psychology, 19*, 399-415.

Ryan, M. T. (1982). Effects of paraphrase notetaking on prose learning. (Doctoral dissertation, University of Connecticut, 1981). *Dissertation Abstracts International, 42*(09), 3921A (UMI No. 820356).

Schraw, G., Kauffman, D., & Lehman, S. (2002). SRL theory. In J. Levin (Ed.), *Encyclopedia of cognitive science*. London, England: Macmillan.

Sellen, A. J., & Harper, R. H. R. (2002). *The myth of the paperless office*. Cambridge, MA: MIT Press.

Slamecka N. J., & Graf, P. (1978). Generation effect—delineation of a phenomenon. *Journal of Experimental Psychology: Human Learning and Memory 4*(6), 592-604.

Slotte, V., & Lonka, K. (1999a). Review and process effects of spontaneous note taking on text comprehension. *Contemporary Educational Psychology, 24*, 1-20.

Slotte, V., & Lonka, K. (1999b). Spontaneous concept maps aiding the understanding of scientific concepts. *International Journal of Science Education, 21*, 515-531.

Sweller, J. (1988). Cognitive load during problem solving: Effects on learning. *Cognitive Science, 12,* 257-285.

Sweller, J., & Chandler, P. (1991). Evidence for cognitive load theory. *Cognition and Instruction, 8,* 351-362.

Tulving, E. (1983). *Elements of episodic memory.* Oxford, England: Oxford University Press.

Van Meter, P., Yokoi, L., & Pressley, M. (1994). College students' theory of note taking derived from their perceptions of note taking. *Journal of Educational Psychology, 86,* 323–338.

Wittrock, M. C. (1974). Learning as a generative process. *Educational Psychologist, 11*(2), 87-95.

Woody, W. D., Daniel, D. B. & Baker, C. A. (2010). E-books or textbooks: Students prefer textbooks. *Computers & Education, 55,* 945-948.

Zimmerman, B. J., Schunk, D. H. (2007). Motivation: An essential dimension of self-regulated learning. In D. H. Schunk & B. J. Zimmerman (Eds.), *Motivation and self-regulated learning: Theory research and applications* (pp. 1-30). Bristol, PA: Taylor & Francis.

CHAPTER 9

STRATEGY TRAINING WITH CAUSAL DIAGRAMS TO IMPROVE TEXT LEARNING

Anne Poliquin and Gregory Schraw

ABSTRACT

We examined whether a 20-minute instructional intervention on under-standing a causal diagram (i.e., training phase) affected text understanding when reading a different text without a causal diagram (i.e. generalization phase). College undergraduates in a training group received an instructional sequence on the structure, component variables, use, and conclusions related to a seven-variable causal model displayed in a two-dimensional diagram. Participants in the training and no-training groups then studied a 1,700-word text without a diagram and completed a variety of learning tasks. Participants in the training group had higher text recall; generated more predictor variables and produced more types of styles with greater clarity in their self-generated drawings, and had more short-answer responses than participants in the no-training group. These findings supported the causal explication hypothesis, which states that training which facilitates comprehension of a causal diagram also helps individuals under-stand the causal structure of a text even when a causal diagram of the text is not present and the text is unrelated to the training diagram. We concluded

Learning Through Visual Displays, pp. 223–246
Copyright © 2013 by Information Age Publishing
All rights of reproduction in any form reserved.

that a brief, instructional intervention helped individuals to understand causal diagrams and to transfer those interpretation skills to understanding the causal structure of an unrelated text.

A causal diagram is a visual display that uses directional arrows to explain cause and effect relationships between two or more variables (McCrudden, Schraw, Lehman, & Poliquin, 2007). Causal diagrams may be used to help learners understand the complex implicit or explicit relationships between events described in a text (Oestermeier, & Hesse, 2000; Waldmann & Hagmayer, 2005). Implicit causal relationships in a text are especially difficult because the learner must infer them. However, even a text that carefully describes explicit causal relationships may be difficult to understand due to the complexity of the relationships and the learner's unfamiliarity with causal diagrams, diagrammatic reasoning, and knowledge about the entailments of causal relationships in general (Jonassen & Ionas, 2008; Olivier, 2001).

This study investigated the effect of strategy instruction on understanding and learning causal relationships in a text in which a complex causal system is described. This question is important for two reasons. One reason is that learners can find it difficult to understand causal arguments (Foster, 2010; Wolff, 2007); yet adjunct visual displays help them to do so (McCrudden, Magliano, & Schraw, 2011). Helping learners to understand causal diagrams is an important component in the development of visual literacy (Reed, 2006; Yeh & Cheng, 2010). According to Jonassen and Ionas (2008), causal relations are more complex than learners realize because learners must be able to articulate a variety of component variables and the nature of their causal relationship. The present research explored the utility of a simple instructional protocol to do so. A second reason is that it is unclear what aspects of causal relationships are most difficult to understand and remember. For example, it is unclear whether individuals find it more difficult to understand indirect versus direct causal effects in a text or diagram. Similarly, it is unclear whether causal diagrams affect surface (i.e., recall of text segments) and deeper (i.e., an integrated mental representation of the causal model) processing to the same extent. This study examined a variety of learning outcomes to assess the impact of causal diagrams on text understanding, thereby providing a better test of existing theory. It also informs theoretical differences among different types of diagrams they may be used to improve learning or to as outcome measures of learning (Ainsworth, 2006; Carifio & Perla, 2009; Umoquit, Tso, Burchett, & Dobrow, 2011).

Causality and Causal Entailments

Causal reasoning is an essential intellectual skill that undergirds higher-order thinking such as problem solving, critical thinking, hypothetical reasoning, and making accurate inferences (Dunbar, & Fugelsang, 2005; Inch & Warnick, 1998; Johnson-Laird, 2004; Klauer & Phye, 2008; Kuhn, 1991; Larkin & Simon, 1987). Jonassen and Ionas (2008) define causality as "the relationship that is ascribed between two or more entities where one incident, action, or the presence of certain conditions determines the occurrence or nonoccurrence of another entity, action, or condition" (p. 292). They also summarize three core entailments of causal reasoning cited in previous research:

1. The cause and effect must be contiguous in space and time.
2. The cause must be prior to the effect.
3. There must be a constant relationship between the cause and effect.

These entailments specify that the cause and effect must co-occur, that the cause must take place temporally before the effect, and that there is evidence of a causal relationship between them such that removing the cause will remove the effect. Jonassen and Ionas (2008) also discuss a fourth entailment in complex models in which learners must assess the necessity and sufficiency of each cause on each effect. Failure to understand each of these entailments may lead to poor causal reasoning (Steyvers, Tenenbaum, Wagenmakers, & Blum, 2003; Thagard, 2000).

Causal reasoning is poor even in college students who often fail to make causal arguments based on the four entailments described above or to support each entailment with genuine causal evidence (Kuhn, 1991; Kuhn & Dean, 2004). Jonassen and Ionas (2008) summarized three instructional methods to improve understanding causal relationships. One is direct instruction that conveys causal relationships by helping individuals understand the three entailments above, as well as component variables in a causal argument. A second is the use of diagrams or simulations in which learners view causal relationships as a static or non-static representations. A third method is modeling of causal relationships using a variety of interactive tools based on expert systems. Unfortunately, as they note, few studies have investigated these instructional methods, nor have direct comparisons of the three methods been made.

Understanding Causal Diagrams

A typical causal diagram has several salient informational features that enhance learning, including component variables, direct and indirect causal effects, null effects, and an integrated explanatory model. Component variables include each variable specified in the causal model. For example, there are seven variables in the model shown in Figure 9.1, including gender, money for food, diet, exercise, overall fitness, age, and amount of sleep. Typically, variables at the left of the model that have causal effects on other variables are called *exogenous* or *upstream* variables. Variables at the right that are acted upon by other variables are called *endogenous* or *downstream* variables. Variables that appear between the path between upstream and downstream variables are called *mediating* variables because they potentially have a mediating effect between upstream and downstream variables.

Upstream and mediating variables may have direct or indirect effects on downstream variables. A *direct effect* represents an unmediated causal effect between one upstream variable and a downstream variable. For example, exercise has a direct effect on fitness in Figure 9.1. An *indirect effect* represents a three-variable or more relationship in which variable 1 causes a change in variable 2, which causes a change in variable 3. Thus, variable 1 has an indirect causal effect on variable 3. For example, money for food affects diet, which affects fitness in Figure 9,1. In addition, a variable may have a *null effect* in which it is unrelated to other variables. For example, money for food is unrelated to exercise in Figure 9.1.

The overall interaction of all the variables in a causal system illustrates an *integrated explanatory model*. The model not only provides information

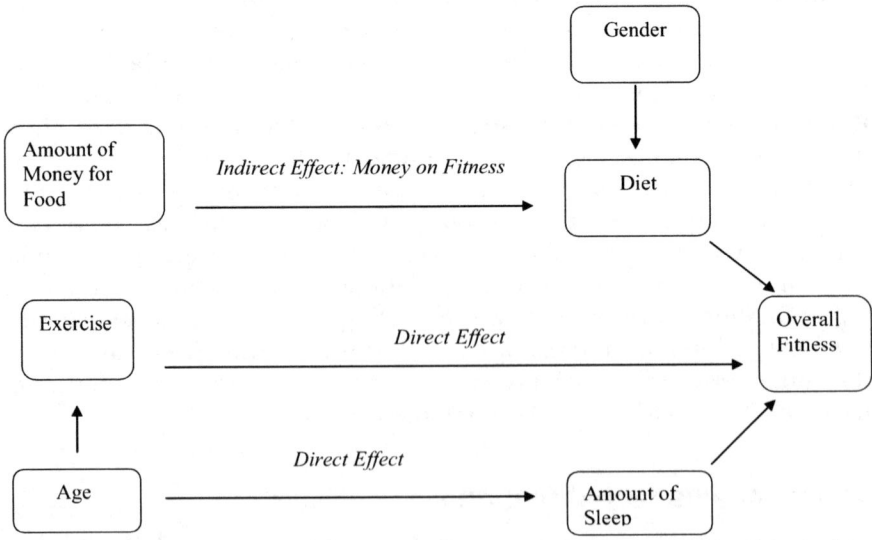

Figure 9.1.   Causal diagram of factors that affect overall fitness.

about how each variable is related to other variables, but also how the variables function in an integrated manner as a system of variables that explains complex causal processes. Explanatory models are used extensively in social science research to explain complex causal relationships and processes. In addition, there are well-known statistical modeling techniques that may be used to construct and test the "goodness of fit" of these models (Kline, 2005).

Previous Research

Causal diagrams appear frequently in textbooks and in professional journals, especially in research studies that utilize structural equation models of complex causal phenomena (Jonassen & Ionas, 2008; Kline, 2005). Oestermeier and Hesse (2000) identified 27 different categories of verbal causal arguments that occur in everyday language, many of which can be represented in causal diagrams like the one shown in Figure 9.1. Kemp, Goodman, and Tenebaum (2010) described a variety of causal schemata that individuals use to represent causal models in memory and use these models to engage in causal reasoning. Many of these schemata are examples of the 27 verbal causal arguments described by Oestermeier and Hesse (2000). Yet despite the frequency with which individuals encounter causal diagrams and arguments on a regular basis, there have been extremely few studies that have examined either the effect of causal diagrams on learning, or instructional interventions that help students understand causal diagrams.

By far the most common type of research on causal relationships and causal reasoning are studies that have investigated the representation of causal schemata in memory. This research indicates that both younger (Gopnik et al., 2004) and older learners (Kemp et al., 2010; Wolff, 2007) construct causal representations of real-life phenomena and use these representations to make judgments about the world, even though some of the causal representations they construct lead to inappropriate understanding and causal explanations (Chi, Roscoe, Slotta, Roy & Chase, 2012). A variety of other researchers have examined the structural representation and retrieval of causal schemata (Waldmann & Hagmayer, 2005), as well as probabilistic explanations of how these models are used to make causal inferences and decisions (Zhang, 2008).

A number of studies have investigated learning while using diagrams that include causal relationships but are not true causal diagrams as described above. These studies consistently support the conclusion that diagrams of all types improve understanding of noncausal and causal relationships that occur implicitly or explicitly within a text (Cromley,

Snyder-Hogan, & Luciw-Dubas, 2010; Larkin & Simon, 1987; Marinos, 2010; Shah & Hoeffner, 2002; Schnotz, 2002; Schnotz & Bannert, 2003; Vekiri, 2002; Winn, 1991). For example, O'Donnell (1993) found that a knowledge map which included causal information about steps in nervous system reactions improved performance on a speeded sentence completion task for declarative knowledge. DiCecco and Gleason (2002) reported that visual displays that show causal relationships provide the learner with a visual representation of the implicit structure and important connections of a text in a meaningful way. Gattis and Holyoak (1996) found that graphs provided external instantiations of mental representations that helped people to better understand causal relationships. Mautone and Mayer (2007) and Shah, Mayer, and Hegarty (1999) reported similar findings when comparing the effects of different types of graphical aids on text comprehension. Collectively, these studies found that diagrams help learners identify potential causal relationships and understand them better than individuals who do not use diagrams.

Two studies have examined learning while using causal diagrams such as Figure 9.1. McCrudden et al. (2007) conducted two experiments using a single-cause, multiple-outcomes diagram that described the causal effects of zero-gravity on human physiology during space travel. Experiment I found that learners in the diagram and no-diagram conditions did not differ with respect to memory for main ideas, but that individuals in the causal diagram condition better understood the five causal sequences in the text even when study time was controlled. This effect was replicated and extended to additional measures of deeper conceptual understanding by McCrudden, Schraw, and Lehman (2009). Experiment 2 examined learning when one studied the text only and a second group studied the causal diagram only. There were differences between the groups in terms of recall or understanding of the five causal sequences. These findings were interpreted as support for the *causal explication hypothesis*, which states that which states that causal diagrams improve comprehension by explicitly representing the causal structure described in a text in an integrated visual format.

A follow-up study by McCrudden et al. (2011) conducted three experiments to further investigate the effects of causal diagrams on processing and recall of text information. In Experiment 1, participants either studied or did not study a causal diagram before reading a text. Those who studied the causal diagram were given four minutes to do so. Results showed those who studied the diagram read diagram-relevant sentences faster and remembered more diagram-relevant information. This finding indicated that even a brief period of causal diagram study facilitated learning. Experiment 2 replicated the first experiment with the exception that individuals in the no-diagram condition read the passage twice. Once again, those who studied the diagram read diagram-relevant sentences faster and remembered more diagram-relevant information even when the no-diagram groups was assessed using the second reading of the text. This finding indicated that multiple study occasions did not eliminate the positive effects of the causal diagram. Experiment 3 used think-alouds in addition to recall and reading times to examine whether those in the diagram condition constructed more inferences while reading. Although the recall findings replicated Experiments 1 and 2, the two groups did not differ in terms of five different types of inference generation scores. This finding suggested that diagrams did not increase deeper processing in the diagram group. Rather, the diagrams explicated the causal structure implicit within the information in a manner that allowed those in the diagram group to process information with less effort, yet remember the information better.

Overall, the studies described above support the following conclusions: (a) there are many different types of causal arguments that occur in language and written text, (b) individuals construct causal schemata that enable them to evaluate information and make inferences about causal relationships, (c) many different types of diagrams support causal reasoning, and (d) studying a causal diagram that presents an explicit representation of a causal structure that is implicit or explicit in a text can increase learning efficiency (e.g., a higher ratio of learning to time spent studying).

The Present Study

The present study made several predictions based on the *causal explication hypothesis* (McCrudden et al., 2007), which states that causal diagrams improve comprehension by explicitly representing the causal structure described in a text in an integrated visual format. We trained participants to understand a causal diagram in a training phase. We then examined whether this training helped participants to generate a better understanding of causal relaationships when reading an unfamiliar text without a causal diagram during a generalization phase. On this view, prereading training of causal relationships using a causal diagram provides explicit knowledge about the role of upstream and downstream variables in causal relationships, as well as information about direct and indirect effects. Causal diagram training also should help learners construct causal relationships during or after reading, either as a conceptual mental representation or as a self-generated drawing. This hypothesis is consistent with research that found that visual training improved geometric and spatial reasoning on a subsequent visual performance transfer task (Walker, Winner, Hetland, Simmons, & Goldsmith, 2011).

We tested a scripted instructional intervention designed to improve understanding of causal relationships in a causal diagram. We hypothesized that instruction using the diagram would generalize to a better understanding of the causal relationships in a science text even when the reader did not study a causal diagram of those specific relationships either before or while reading the text. Individuals in the training group received a 20-minute instructional intervention on the components of a casual diagram and how to use the diagram to make inferences about the relationships among variables. Individuals then read a science text entitled *Improving Science Education* without an adjunct causal diagram. A no-instruction group read the same text under the same conditions, but without the causal diagram training. Learning was assessed using free recall of text segments, generation of themes, drawings of the causal relationships made during reading, essays about the main themes and claims in the text, and four short-answer questions that focused on the purpose of a causal diagram and the text's main conclusions.

We predicted that the causal diagram training would generalize to a better understanding of the causal relationships in the text and better understanding of the text's themes and conclusions based on those relationships. We expected the training group to outperform the no-training group on each of the outcome measures.

METHODS

Participants

Sixty-two undergraduate students from introductory educational psychology classes at a large university participated in the study. Participants were randomly assigned to one of two conditions, including the training and no-training groups.

Materials

Materials consisted of a packet of printed materials organized in a 9 x 12 manila envelope. Each packet contained a cover sheet with informed consent and a brief description of the study, a 1,700-word text entitled *Improving Science Education,* which provided a summary of predictors of science achievement (see Appendix A). Each booklet also contained an instruction sheet that asked them to draw a casual diagram while they read, a free recall test, an essay question in which the participants were asked whether they thought the research described in the text was important and what the main conclusions were, and four short questions related to the main points in the text.

Procedure

The training group received instruction in how to read and understand the causal diagram in Figure 9.1. The instruction sequence took approximately 20 minutes and included three main phases based on Scevak, Moore, and Kirby (1993). The *orientation phase* explained why causal diagrams are important and their strengths and weaknesses compared to other types of visual displays. The *informational phase* explained the flow of information in a causal diagram, as well as direct and indirect effects. The *integration phase* discussed how to identify themes and make inferences using a causal diagram. Each phase included simple examples from Figure 9.1 (e.g., the direct effect between exercise and fitness) and a real-world example (e.g., the indirect effect from fast driving to accidents to higher insurance rates). The instruction also discussed the flow of information in the causal chain, the role of arrows, and the relevance of spatial placement of variables.

Following the training, both groups were asked to create a causal diagram while they read the text, including direct and indirect effects. They were instructed to try to include all of the variables listed and to show their relationship to other variables. After the story was read and the diagram was completed, participants were given 15 minutes to complete a free recall task of the text. Participants next were given 15 minutes to write an essay that asked them to indicate whether they thought the research on improving science education was important. Specifically they were told, "Please state whether it is important or unimportant, and tell us why you thought so. Try to link this research to your own school experiences. In addition, comment on whether you personally support this kind of research (e.g., does it contribute to society as a whole)?"

Both groups next responded to four short answer questions that were designed to assess inferences and deeper processing derived from the text and or prior knowledge. The four short answer questions stated "In this part we want you to answer the short questions below. Please use complete sentences. (1) What is a structural model and how do researchers test it? (2) What is a direct effect? How does it differ from an indirect? effect? Give an example from the text for each. (3) Can you think of other variables that were not included in this research that should be? Explain why they are important. (4) What main conclusions can we draw from this article?" These questions were designed to show whether the participants could accurately answer the key issues from the text and furthermore extend their knowledge into preexisting conceptions about science.

Scoring

The 1,700-word text on *Improving Science Education* was broken down into 102 segments that each conveyed a separate idea unit. Each idea unit was scored once even if it was duplicated in the recall responses. Either verbatim or paraphrased recall was accepted using criteria from Lehman and Schraw (2002). Units that were relevant to more than one segment were attributed to whatever segment was closer in context or particular word use. For example, if the word *foundation* was used in the recall, then it would be matched to the segment that also used that word rather than others segments similar in context. One point was awarded to each segment. Thematic recall was also recorded when broad statements about the text were made that did not specifically match any of the 102 segments. For example, a theme would be "They need to go on trips to observe scientists." Intrusions were incorrect or irrelevant statements. These were scored as a "one" if an intrusion occurred and compared to determine whether the two groups differed on this dimension.

The causal diagrams were scored based on categories represented by the drawings. We sorted drawings into outline form, causal diagrams that resembled the practice diagram and a broad category that included tree diagrams, matrices and flow charts. Diagrams also were scored for clarity and the number of direct and indirect effects. A holistic score was applied to each diagram. Causal diagrams from the treatment group were expected to be clearer, more accurate and contain more correctly identified direct and indirect effects (see Appendix B).

The essays were scored with a holistic rubric on several dimensions. The overall quality was scored using a three-point scale (i.e., high, medium, low). Each essay also was scored for broad themes inferred from the text or resulting from the essay's questions about relating the research to their own experiences. The claim score was based on the number of individual causal arguments and supporting evidence that the reader produced.

The short answer questions were scored by assigning points to each possible response. Question one (i.e., What is a structural model and how do researchers use it?) has two points for describing a structural model and how scientists use it. The second question (i.e., What is a direct effect? How does it differ from an indirect effect?) was scored with three points, one to describe a direct effect, one for an indirect effect and one for a sample of each. Question number three (i.e., Can you think of other variables that were not included in this research that should be?) was awarded a 1 or a 0, rather than track the number of variables that might be listed. Question four (i.e., What main conclusions can we draw from this article?) asked the participant what the main conclusions are from the story. This was scored on a scale of zero to two, indicating no response or poor and two indicating one or more of the important conclusions.

After a data-scoring training session, the first author scored all of the outcomes measures with the second author, in which complete agreement was reached on 20 practice protocols. Ambiguous or uncertain scores were resolved in conference with both authors.

RESULTS

Means and standard deviations for each parametric outcome score are shown in Table 9.1. Nonparametric scores based on ranks are included in the text below. Parametric tests were conducted on interval and ratio scale scores, including the number of claims, holistic quality of answers, thematic recall. We conducted non-parametric tests (the Mann-Whitney U) to measure the clarity, number of styles and amount of data reported in the drawing measures. All statistical significance tests were conducted at the $p = .05$ level unless otherwise noted.

Recall

Results of the recall test yielded three scores, including the total number of idea units recalled from 102 possible units, the number of themes generated during recall, and the number of intrusions. The difference between the training and nontraining groups using the total recall score was significant, $t (60) = -2.57$. Table 9.1 revealed that the mean of the training group was 1.96 idea units higher than the nontraining group. The t-tests for the theme and intrusion scores did not differ significantly from one another, in part, because these scores were rare and close to zero in both groups. We concluded that the training resulted in significantly better recall of idea units for the training group.

Drawings

The drawings were examined for factual information as well as evidence that the training impacted conceptual understanding of causal diagram construction. A rubric was created to measure a series of variables that were assessed using parametric and non-parametric statistics. Of par-

Table 9.1.   Means and Standard Deviations for All Outcome Measures

Outcome Measure	Training (N = 31)		Nontraining (N = 31)	
	Mean	Standard Deviation	Mean	Standard Deviation
Recall				
Total Segments	7.19	3.70	5.22	2.09
Themes	.10	.30	.13	.42
Intrusions	.03	.18	.13	.34
Drawings				
Direct Effect	3.90	.53	3.68	.945
Indirect Effect	2.94	.35	2.74	.855
Predictors	4.71	1.00	3.90	1.97
Essays				
Themes	2.35	1.90	2.74	1.78
Claims	3.39	1.64	3.39	2.40
Intrusions	.03	.18	.13	.03
Short Answers				
Question 1	1.58	.62	.94	.81
Question 2	2.71	.64	2.13	1.05
Question 3	.71	.46	.77	.56
Question 4	1.71	.52	1.52	.62
Total	6.32	2.03	5.29	1.90
Inferences	.10	.30	.10	.30

ticular importance in determining whether a successful diagram was created were the idea units, including the four direct effect variables, the three indirect effect variables, and the five predictor variables. Means and standard deviations are reported in Table 9.1.

Separate t-tests were conducted on correctly identified direct effects, indirect effects, and predictor variables. No significant differences were found between the training and no-training group for the direct effect, $t (60) = -1.156$, or the number of indirect effects, $t (60) = -1.162$. In contrast, the predictor variable score reached significance, $t (60) = -2.028$. These findings suggested that training helps individuals remember more predictors of academic achievement, but does not help them remember whether predictors are direct or indirect effects.

Mann-Whitney U tests for interval ranks were conducted to measure clarity, number of different types of styles, and amount of information in the drawings as outlined in the drawing rubric (see Appendix A). For clarity, participants in the training group had higher scores (mean rank = 40) than participants in the no-training group (mean rank = 23), Mann-Whitney U = 217. For styles, participants in the training group had lower scores, with a mean rank of 22.50 than participants in the no-training group with a mean rank of 40.50, Mann-Whitney U = 201.50. This finding indicated that the no-training group used a wider variety of styles than the training group; however, the training group produced more appropriate causal diagrams that resembled prototypical causal diagrams like Figure 1. Finally, the amount-of-data score revealed significant differences between the training (mean rank = 26) and the no -training group (mean rank =37), Mann-Whitney U = 310.00. These results indicated that the no-training group included more non-critical information in their drawings compared to the training group. Overall, the training group produced better drawings of the causal relationships described in the text than the no-training group. This finding was consistent with findings discussed in Van Meter and Firetto (this volume).

Essay

The rubric assessed four essay dimensions, including themes, thematic statements, number of intrusion errors, and overall. Scores for these measures were analyzed using t-tests. Results indicated that there were no significant differences between the training and no-training groups on any of these measures.

In addition, a Mann-Whitney U test was conducted on the overall score for essay quality. The holistic score was generated by ranking the holistic quality of the essay as being high medium or low. The mean rank for the training group was 34.03; the mean rank for the non-training group was 28.97, which was not statistically significant, $p > .20$. These findings showed that causal diagram training had no effect on the length or quality of the essay.

Short Answers

Results from the short answer test created six separate scores, including individual scores for questions 1 through 4, a composite score for questions 1 through 4, and an inference score. The composite score was expected to be the most important measure of the effectiveness of training on performance as this score provides the most reliable estimate of overall performance. The difference between the training and no-training groups for the composite score was significant, $t(60) = -2.062$, indicating that training was effective (see Table 9.1 for mean and individual scores). Individual t-tests on each of the four questions revealed that the training group outperformed the no-training group on questions 1 and 2, but not on questions 3 and 4. The t-tests for the number of inferences generated within the short answers were not significant.

DISCUSSION

This study tested a scripted instructional intervention designed to improve understanding of causal relationships in a causal diagram. Causal relationships appear frequently in scientific and technical text, and often are implicit and difficult to understand (Chi et al., 2012; Kline, 2005; Steyvers et al., 2003). We hypothesized that instruction using the training diagram would generalize to a better understanding of the causal relationships in a science text even when the reader did not study a causal diagram. Specifically, we tested whether instruction to understand causal relationships in a text with an adjunct diagram during the training phase helped participants learn to identify causal relationships in a different text without the use of a diagram during the generalization phase. We assumed that the training would help participants develop strategies to construct an initial causal relationship schema that would generalize to other texts with causal relationships.

We made several predictions based on the *causal explication hypothesis* (McCrudden et al., 2007), which states that causal diagrams improve comprehension by explicitly representing the causal structure described in a text in an integrated visual format. An extension of this explication hypothesis is that training individuals to understand causal relationships using one causal diagram can enhance comprehension of a subsequent text with a causal structure in the absence of a causal diagram. That is, training individuals to comprehension even when an adjunct diagram of the text's causal structure is not present during reading. On this view, prereading training of causal relationships using a causal diagram provides explicit knowledge about the role of upstream and downstream variables in causal relationships, as well as information about direct and indirect effects. Causal diagram training also should help learners construct causal relationships during or after reading, either as a conceptual mental representation or as a self-generated drawing.

We predicted that the causal diagram training would generalize to better understanding of the causal relationships in the text and better understanding of the text's themes and conclusions based on those relationships. Learning was assessed using free recall of text segments, generation of themes, drawings of the causal relationships made during reading, essays about the main themes and claims in the text, and four short-answer questions that focused on the purpose of a causal diagram and the text's main conclusions. We expected the training group to out-perform the no-training group on each of these measures.

Results showed that the training group had higher text recall; gener-ated more predictor variables, types of styles, and had better clarity in self-generated drawings; and provided a greater number of composite short answer responses than the no-training group. These findings sup-ported the causal explication hypothesis, which states that training which facilitates comprehension of a causal diagram also helps individuals understand the causal structure of a text even when a causal diagram of the text is not present and the text is unrelated to the training diagram. The two groups did not differ in terms of recall for the number of direct and indirect effects, in part because recall was good in both groups.

These findings are important for two reasons. One is that a short train-ing session helped college students understand the basic structure of causal relationships as displayed in a causal diagram. This is important because many students are unfamiliar with causal diagrams and experi-ence difficulty trying to understand them (Foster, 2010; Olivier, 2001; Wolff, 2007). A second reason is that a brief training session with a causal diagram generalized to understanding the causal relationships described in an expository text, even when individuals do not study a diagram of the causal structure. This finding is consistent with research that found that visual training improved geometric and spatial reasoning on a subsequent visual performance transfer task (Walker et al., 2011). Although not tested in this study, diagram training could be delivered to students quite easily via a streamed tutorial that students could view on their own before read-ing information with a complex causal structure (Jonassen & Ionas, 2008).

We believe that causal diagram instruction may facilitate better understanding of causal relationships in a text in at least three ways. One is to provide a better understanding of the individual components in a causal diagram; specifically, upstream, downstream, and mediating variables. A second way is to help readers distinguish among direct, indirect, and noneffects. This is helpful because many learners do not have a clear understanding of causal effects and complex causal path-ways (Jonassen & Ionas, 2008). A third was is to help in make accurate inferences about the specific nature of causal relationships in a text and the extent to which causal relationship support plausible conclusions about the main ideas and implications of the text (McCrudden et al., 2007, 2011).

In addition, the training is valuable because students often avoid using a strategy that could be helpful because they do not know how to proceed. Often a study strategy that involves the production of a visual display is avoided due to a lack of comfort or assumption that the display must be perfect, symmetrical and pleasing (Scevak et al., 1993; Shah & Hoeffner, 2002). The training was successful in part because the causal diagram provided a concrete example and predesigned elements such as arrows, which presumably alleviated concerns over the "look" of the diagram. Training students to understand causal diagrams may help them to create and use diagrams that improve their learning with less design anxiety.

Future Research

Our findings suggest several questions for future research that have not been addressed in this or previous studies. One is whether causal diagram training like that used in the present study affects better understanding and reduced processing time when studying a second unrelated diagram. We believe that diagram training will generalize to both increased understanding and faster processing of new diagrams, consistent with previous research that reported faster reading times after studying a causal diagram (McCrudden et al., 2011). Causal diagram training also may help learners understanding the four entailments of causal effects described above and to better understanding direct and indirect causal effects in general (Steyvers et al., 2003), as well as to better understand a variety of causal schemata (Kemp et al., 2010).

A second question concerns whether causal diagram training leads to deeper conceptual understanding of an unrelated causal diagram. Although the present research used essays and short answers, we did not include a measure of deep conceptual understanding. In addition, while research suggests that learners learn more from a text after viewing a causal diagram; there was no evidence of differences in the type or number of inferences made in the diagram versus no-diagram group (McCrudden et al., 2011). This finding should be replicated following causal diagram training. In addition, it is possible that learners who receive the training may construct more sophisticated mental models of the complex causal structure in the text, generate more or better inferences, and be better able to use evidence to support causal inferences (Dunbar & Fugelsang, 2005; Klauer & Phye, 2008; Kuhn & Dean, 2004).

A third question concerns the efficacy of the causal diagram training on younger students. The present study investigated the diagram training with college students; however, middle and high-school students routinely read scientific passages that include complex causal relationships. We conjecture that causal diagram training may be even more effective for younger learners because they are generally less-skilled at reading expository text that include causal relationships, less-knowledgeable about the structure of causal relationships, and less-able to construct explicit representations of the implicit causal structure within diagrams (Gopnik et al., 2004). We predict that causal diagram training would enable younger and less-skilled readers to use limited cognitive resources in a more efficient manner that is directed at better recall and higher conceptual understanding.

SUMMARY AND CONCLUSIONS

This study tested the causal explication hypothesis' claim that a brief training session would improve understanding of causal relationships in a text, even when a causal diagram is not provided and the training is conducted using an unrelated topic. Results supported a very robust generalization effect in which the training improved recall, drawings of the causal structure within the text, and a variety of short-answer responses about the text. Our findings strongly supported the causal explication hypothesis which states that even limited training yields significant increases in learning. Given replication and extension of this finding, we believe the 20-minute training provides a very effective instructional training intervention to improve learning and long-term understanding of causal relationships.

APPENDIX A

IMPROVING SCIENCE EDUCATION

What makes someone good at science? It was once thought that being a good science student was the domain or boys, or perhaps "exceptionally smart boys." But recent studies indicate that girls do just as well in science if given the same encouragement and training. Moreover, students do not need to be whiz kids to excel at science. Rather, they need parental support, a good understanding of basic concepts, and plenty of quality instruction.

In the rest of this article, we discuss what educational researchers know about improving science education. A number of important predictor variables (i.e., variables in a statistical study that predict science achievement) have been studied thus far, and there is evidence that some of these variables are extremely important. The five most important variables are parental education, prior science achievement, instructional time, self-efficacy for learning science (i.e., the extent to which the student feels confident about learning science), and use of appropriate learning strategies.

Direct and Indirect Effects

Researchers are keenly interested in what variables are the best predictors of science achievement. To help them answer this question, researchers typically propose a *structural model* of how different predictor variables are related to each other and test the adequacy of the model using a large national sample. It is important to understand that these models are hypothetical in nature; that is, they are tentative model until they are supported by data.

There are two main types of *"effects"* in these structural models, which we refer to in this article as *direct effects* and *indirect effects*. A direct effect occurs when a change in one variable causes a direct change on a second variable. For example, a student's prior science achievement has a strong direct influence on later science achievement. The more a student has learned in the past, the better he or she will do in future science classes. This relationship holds true regardless of other variables.

An indirect effect occurs when a change in one variable causes a change in a second variable, which in turn, causes a change in a third variable. For example, gender does not have a direct influence on a student's science achievement, but it does influence instructional time, which in turn, influences science achievement. Thus, a direct effect involves two variables, where the first variable causes a change in a second variable. An indirect effect involves least three variables, where variable 1 affects variable 2, and variable 2 affects variable 3, without a direct effect between variable 1 and variable 3.

Direct Effects on Science Achievement

There are four important direct effects on science achievement. These include parental education, prior science achievement, instructional time, and learning strategies. Parental education is very important because it affects achievement in several ways. One is that parents value achievement because they have reached high levels of achievement. Second, better-educated parents may be better able to assist their children. Third, parents may be better able to afford special science opportunities for their children. Prior science achievement is important as well because it provides the informational foundation for subsequent science learning. The more you know about science, the easier it is to learn new concepts. Instructional time also plays a role. The more instructional time students have in science, the higher their learning. Generally speaking, twice as much time translates into twice as much learning. Last, learning strategies facilitate science learning, especially complex learning strategies that help students get deeper meaning. Examples of deeper strategies are integrating main concepts and relating new information to what the student already knows.

Overall multiple factors contribute directly to science achievement. Currently, there is debate about how much each variable influences science achievement. Experts really don't know, though they assume that each variable makes an important separate contribution to prediction of current science achievement. Our best guess is that the three most important direct effects are parental education, prior achievement, and instructional time.

Other Direct Effects

There are other direct effects between variables worth our attention. For example, parental education directly affects student interest, self-efficacy for learning science, and prior achievement. Many experts feel that parental education is one of the most important variables in science achievement. Highly educated parents appear to motivate and encourage their children in a manner that has many positive influences on later achievement. In addition, gender directly affects self-efficacy for learning science and instructional time. Females generally report less self-efficacy and receive less instructional time than male students. The potentially negative effects of gender can be offset through encouragement and giving equal opportunities in the science classroom.

In contrast, some variables have no effect even when we might expect them to. For example, instructional quality does not appear to affect science achievement. The lack of a relationship between these variables surprises many people, yet has been replicated many times. Experts agree that it is the amount of instruction, rather than the quality of the instruction, that is important. More research is need on this topic because sometimes statistical studies fail to detect effects that are really there (i.e., the researcher draws the wrong conclusion). Most people also are surprised to learn that interest does not affect current science achievement. Although interest makes learning more fun, it does not lead to more learning.

Indirect Effects on Science Achievement

There are three important indirect effects. These include an indirect effect of parental education on current achievement as mediated by prior achievement, an indirect effect of gender on science achievement as mediated by instructional time; and an indirect effect of self-efficacy on achievement as mediated by learning strategies. The first of these three indirect effect states that better-educated parents have children with higher levels of prior science achievement, which leads to higher levels of current science achievement. The second indirect effect suggests that gender leads to differences in instructional time, which leads to differences in current achievement. It is well known that females receive less instructional time in science than males, which decreases achievement among females. The third indirect effect indicates that students with higher self-efficacy are more likely to use effective learning strategies, which leads to higher levels of science achievement. High self-efficacy students tend to use a greater number of strategies, as well as more sophisticated strategies such as integrating main ideas.

In summary, research reveals that a number of variables affect current science achievement. Some have a direct effect; some have an indirect effect; and some have both (e.g., parental education). The most important of these variables are parental education, prior science achievement, and instructional time. Important, but secondary variables, are student self-efficacy, strategy use, and gender.

Ways to Improve Science Education

The research summarized above suggests four ways to improve science education, including parental education, early success for students who are at risk for low science achievement, more instructional time, and strategy training that enables students to generate a deeper understanding of the material. Improving parental education may sound odd at first. After all, researchers know that well-educated parents have children who do well at science. The problem, however, is with less-educated parents. Science teachers need to help these parents understand the importance of science, as well as the role that parents play in modeling science education. Helping parents feel comfortable with science might be just as important as helping their children!

Early success for at-risk students is a crucial component of science education. Students who struggle while young will not have the necessary skills and knowledge base to succeed at science as they progress through middle and high schools. Several solutions have been tried so far, including more instruction, supplemental instruction, greater use of older student tutors, and science tutorials on websites. Like other areas of education, the earlier the intervention, the more effective it is, and the better prepared the student is to succeed at each new level. Early interventions seem especially important for females who typically are given less parental support than boys.

Research highlights the need for more instructional time. Two aspects of science instruction are important. One is classroom instruction and related laboratory experiences. Research indicates that students learn to think like scientists by acting like scientists; that is, conducting experiments, analyzing data, and evaluating solutions. Students cannot learn to be scientists without laboratory experiences. Of equal importance are quality field experiences in which students can apply their science learning in real-world settings. Both components are essential for children of all age.

Strategy training is another crucial area. Many students lack an adequate strategy base and the knowledge to use these strategies effectively. This is especially true of what researchers call *shallow* versus *deeper* strategies. Shallow strategies are things like taking verbatim notes and memorizing facts. Deeper strategies are things like identifying main concepts and integrating information into a summary table or diagram. Good learners use more strategies than poor learners, and more of the strategies used by good learners are deeper strategies. Researchers know that strategy instruction is quite effective at helping low-achieving students develop a bigger repertoire of strategies. Without such a repertoire, students may lack the skills to learn science even if they are motivated and work hard.

A Brighter Future

Researchers have provided us with useful knowledge about science achievement. Thanks to public concern, more schools are emphasizing science education, and spending additional money to hire science specialists. This means more instructional time and better field experiences for students of all ages, and higher levels of science achievement. Females are finely getting a fair chance to participate on an equal footing with boys. The secret to success in science at the national level is to get parents involved and to provide all students with an excellent knowledge base and a wealth of laboratory and field experiences. Schools already are moving in that direction. As a result, the future looks bright for science education.

Appendix B
Scoring Rubric for Participant-Generated Diagrams

Outcome	Points	Rubric
Direct Effects	4	(1) Parental education, (2) prior science achievement, (3) instructional time, and (4) learning strategies.
Indirect Effects	3	(1) Parental education on current achievement as mediated by prior achievement, (2) gender on science achievement as mediated by instructional time; and (3) self-efficacy on achievement as mediated by learning strategies.
Predictor Variables	5	(1) Parental education, (2) prior science achievement, (3) instructional time, (4) self-efficacy for learning science, and (5) use of appropriate learning strategies.
Clarity	3	(1) Low, (2) medium, (3) high.
Types of Styles	3	1, 2, 3, or 4 different styles.
Amount of Information	3	(1) Low, (2) medium, (3) high.

- *Clarity* was determined by neatness, number of styles, clear labeling.
- A *style* was for example drawn as a causal diagram, a second style would be an outline and a third a tree diagram, some participants used more than one to illustrate the information from the story.
- *Amount of information* was the actual physical amount of data notated on the sheet.

REFERENCES

Ainsworth, S. (2006). DeFT: A conceptual framework for considering learning with multiple representations. *Learning and Instruction, 16*, 183-198.

Carifio, J., & Perla, R, J. (2009). A critique of the theoretical and empirical literature of the use of diagrams, graphs, and other visual aids in the learning of scientific-technical content from expository texts and instruction, *Interchange, 40*, 403-436.

Chi, M. T. H., Roscoe, R. D., Slotta, J. D., Roy, M., & Chase, C. C. (2012). Misconceived causal explanations for emergent processes. *Cognitive Science, 36*, 1-61.

Cromley, J. G., Snyder-Hogan, L. E., & Luciw-Dubas, U. A. (2010). Cognitive activities in complex science text and diagrams. *Contemporary Educational Psychology, 36*, 59-74.

DiCecco, V. M., & Gleason, M. M. (2002). Using graphic organizers to attain relational knowledge from expository text. *Journal of Learning Disabilities, 35*, 306-320.

Dunbar, K., & Fugelsang, J. (2005). Scientific reasoning and thinking. In K. Holyoak & R. Morrison (Eds.), *The Cambridge handbook of thinking and reasoning* (pp. 705-726). Cambridge, England: Cambridge University Press.

Foster, E. M. (2010). Causal inference and developmental psychology. *Developmental Psychology, 46*, 454-1480.

Gattis, M., & Holyoak, K. J. (1996). Mapping conceptual to spatial relations in visual reasoning. *Journal of Experimental Psychology: Learning, Memory, and Cognition, 22,* 231-239.

Gopnik, A., Glymour, C., Sobel, D. M., Schulz, L. E., Kushnir, T., & Danks, D. (2004). A theory of causal learning in children: Causal maps and Bayes nets. *Psychological Review, 111,* 3-32.

Inch, E. S., & Warnick, B. (1998). *Critical thinking and communication: The use of reason in argument* (3rd Ed.). Boston, MA: Allyn & Bacon.

Johnson-Laird, P. N. (2004). Mental models and reasoning. In J. Leighton & R. Sternberg (Eds.), *The nature of reasoning* (pp. 169-201). Cambridge, England: Cambridge University Press.

Jonassen, D. H., & Ionas, I. G. (2008). Designing effective supports for causal reasoning. *Educational Technology Research and Development, 56,* 287-308.

Kemp, C., Goodman, N. D., & Tenenbaum, J. B. (2010). Learning to learn causal models. *Cognitive Science, 34,* 1185-1243.

Klauer, K. J., & Phye, G. D. (2008). Inductive reasoning: A training approach. *Review of Educational Research, 78,* 85-123.

Kline, R. (2005). *Principles and practice of structural equation modeling* (2nd ed.). New York, NY: Guilford Press.

Kuhn, D. (1991). *The skills of argument.* New York, NY: Cambridge University Press.

Kuhn, D., & Dean, D. (2004). Connecting scientific reasoning and causal inference. *Journal of Cognition and Development, 5,* 261-288.

Larkin, J. H., & Simon, H. A. (1987). Why a diagram is (sometimes) worth ten thousand words. *Cognitive Science, 11,* 65-100.

Lehman, S., & Schraw, G. (2002). Effects of coherence and relevance on shallow and deep text processing. *Journal of Educational Psychology, 94,* 738-750.

Marinos, A. (2010). Handling the difficulties of technical school students in the construction and interpretation of graphic representations. *International Journal of Mathematical Education in Science and Technology, 41,* 625-648.

Mautone, P. D., & Mayer, R. E. (2007). Cognitive aids for guiding graph comprehension. *Journal of Educational Psychology, 99,* 640-652.

McCrudden, M. T., Schraw, G., & Lehman, S. (2009). The use of adjunct displays to facilitate comprehension of causal relationships in expository text. *Instructional Science, 37,* 65-86.

McCrudden, M. T., Magliano, J., & Schraw, G. (2011). The effects of diagrams on online reading processes and memory. *Discourse Processes, 48,* 69-92.

McCrudden, M. T., Schraw, G., Lehman, S., & Poliquin, A. (2007). The effect of causal diagrams on text learning. *Contemporary Educational Psychology, 32,* 367-388.

Oestermeier, U., & Hesse, F. W. (2000). Verbal and visual causal arguments. *Cognition, 75,* 65-104.

O'Donnell, A. (1993). Searching for information in knowledge maps and texts. *Contemporary Educational Psychology, 18,* 222-239.

Olivier, P. (2001). Diagrammatic reasoning: An artificial intelligence perspective. *Artificial Intelligence Review, 15,* 63-78,

Reed, S. K. (2006). Cognitive architectures for multimedia learning. *Educational Psychologist, 41,* 87-98

Scevak, J. J., Moore, P. J., & Kirby, J. R. (1993). Training students to use maps to increase text recall. *Contemporary Educational Psychology, 18*, 401-413.

Schnotz, W. (2002). Commentary: Towards an integrated view of learning from text and visual displays. *Educational Psychology Review, 14*, 101-120.

Schnotz, W., & Bannert, M. (2003). Construction and interference in learning from multiple representations. *Learning and Instruction, 13*, 141-156.

Shah, P., & Hoeffner, J. (2002). Review of graph comprehension research: Implications for instruction. *Educational Psychology Review, 14*, 47-69.

Shah, P., Mayer, R. E., & Hegarty, M. (1999). Graphs as aids to knowledge construction: Signaling techniques for guiding the process of graph comprehension. *Journal of Educational Psychology, 91*, 690-702.

Steyvers, M., Tenenbaum, J. B., Wagenmakers, E. J., & Blum, B. (2003). Inferring causal networks from observations and interventions. *Cognitive Science, 27*, 453-489.

Thagard, P. (2000). Explaining disease: Correlations, causes, and mechanisms. In F. C. Keil, & R. A. Wilson (Eds.), *Explanation and cognition* (pp. 254-276). Cambridge, MA: MIT Press.

Umoquit, M. J., Tso, P., Burchett, H. E., & Dobrow, M. J. (2011). A multidisciplinary systematic review of the use of diagrams as a means of collecting data from research subjects: application, benefits and recommendations. *Medical Research Methodology, 11*, 1471-1483.

Vekiri, I. (2002).What is the value of graphical displays in learning? *Educational Psychology Review, 14*, 261-312.

Waldmann, M. R., & Hagmayer, Y. (2005). Seeing versus doing: Two modes of accessing causal knowledge. *Journal of Experimental Psychology: Learning, Memory, and Cognition, 31*, 216-227.

Walker, C. M., Winner, E., Hetland, L., Simmons5, S., & Goldsmith, L. (2011). Visual thinking: Art students have an advantage in geometric reasoning. *Creative Education, 2*, 22-26.

Winn, W. (1991). Learning from maps and diagrams. *Educational Psychology Review, 3*, 211-247.

Wolff, P. (2007). Representing Causation. *Journal of Experimental Psychology: General, 136*, 82-111.

Yeh, H., & Cheng, Y. (2010). The influence of the instruction of visual design principles on improving pre-service teachers' visual literacy. *Computers & Education, 54*, 244-252.

Zhang, J. (2008). Causal reasoning with ancestral graphs. *Journal of Machine Learning Research, 9*,1437-1474.

CHAPTER 10

COGNITIVE MODEL OF DRAWING CONSTRUCTION

Learning Through the Construction of Drawings

Peggy Van Meter and Carla M. Firetto

ABSTRACT

Learner-generated drawing is a strategy in which learners construct representational drawings of target content. The generative theory of drawing construction (GTDC; Van Meter & Garner, 2005) is a theoretical model that describes the processes underlying drawing and is based on Mayer's (2005) model of multimedia learning. The GTDC explains drawing according to the cognitive processes of selection, organization and forced integration. In this chapter, we propose an updated model of drawing construction. This model, the cognitive model of drawing construction (CMDC), incorporates both Winne and Hadwin's (1998) self-regulation and Schnotz's (2005) integrated text and picture comprehension models. We show how principles of the CMDC can be applied to interpret existing research and to generate predictions for future studies.

Learning Through Visual Displays, pp. 247–280

Our research team was recently reading a science text for use in an upcoming study. That text described the biology of the urinary system and contained the following sentences:

> The medial surface [of the kidney] is concave and has a slit, the hilum, where it receives the renal nerves, blood vessels, lymphatics, and ureter. These structures enter through the hilum and into the renal sinus. The renal parenchyma—the glandular tissue that forms the urine—appears C-shaped in the frontal section. The Parenchyma encircles a medial cavity and is divided into an outer renal cortex and an inner renal medulla facing the sinus. Extensions of the cortex, called renal columns, project toward the sinus and divide the medulla into 6 to 10 renal pyramids. Each pyramid is conical, with a broad base facing the cortex and a blunt point called the renal papilla facing the sinus. One pyramid and the overlying cortex constitute one lobe of the kidney. The papilla of each renal pyramid is nestled in a cup called a minor calyx, which collects its urine.

One member of our team, Van Meter, read this paragraph and realized she was unable to keep track of all the named structures and their relations. She also recognized that understanding these was central to the main point of the text. She reread the paragraph but found it was still difficult to grasp all of the new information. Upon her third reading, she took out a pencil and made the drawing shown in Figure 10.1. As she drew, she was aware of how this strategy helped her to keep track of specific structures and their connections. Her drawing made clear how renal columns connect kidney tissue with the area in which blood vessels enter and urine is collected, and she wondered if these contact points would play an important role in the kidney function.

Van Meter's behavior in this scenario illustrates how the learner-generated drawing strategy facilitates content-area learning. As the scenario points out, the drawing strategy involves learner generation of a representational drawing that depicts target concepts (Van Meter & Garner, 2005). In this situation, the first characteristic of the drawing is that it is *representational*, which refers to the fact that the drawing resembles the real-world properties of the depicted objects (cf. Alesandrini, 1984; Carney & Levin, 2002). While both representational and nonrepresentational drawings, such as Euler diagrams (Grossen & Carnine, 1990) or matrix notes (Dharmananda & Kiewra, 2010), can aid learning, they should be viewed separately because the underlying cognitive processes that learners use to construct them differ. The second characteristic, that the drawings are learner-generated, means that the learner is the primary causal agent in both the construction and appearance of the drawn representation (Van Meter & Garner, 2005). In this respect, a student is using the

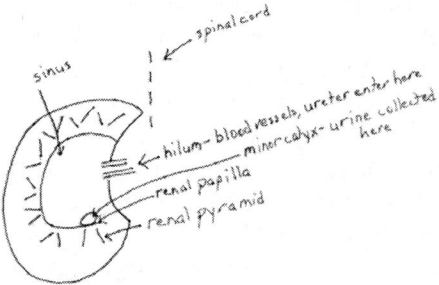

Figure 10.1.   Van Meter's drawing of the human kidney. This figure shows the drawing that resulted from Van Meter's attempt to comprehend a complex text on the anatomy of the human kidney; it provides a concrete example of both the process and the product of drawing construction.

drawing strategy when that student is responsible for determining the final product's appearance.

The drawing strategy can be as simple as the pencil-and-paper drawing shown in Figure 10.1 (e.g., Gobert & Clement, 1999; Van Meter, Aleksic, Schwarz, & Garner, 2006) or may involve the use of additional drawing aids. Examples of drawing aids include the use of cutout figures of story characters to construct representations of story events (Lesgold, Levin, Shimron, & Guttman, 1975)or modeling clay to build three-dimensional representations of anatomical systems (Waters, Van Meter, Perrotti, Drogo, & Cyr, 2005, 2011). The instructional materials from which students must learn may vary as well. The drawing strategy can support learning from provided diagrams (Waters et al., 2005, 2011), verbal text (Van Meter et al., 2006), and mathematics problems (Stylianou, 2011). Despite these recognized variations in learning materials, the emphasis throughout this chapter is on drawing when learning from verbal instructional text. This emphasis should not be understood as a limitation of the strategy but rather a convenience, which permits a straightforward presentation of cognitive drawing processes. Our hope and our intention is that the reader will think about extensions of the theoretical framework presented here and apply the principles to a broader range of instructional materials.

The theoretical framework we offer here is an extension of the generative theory of drawing construction (GTDC), which Van Meter and Garner (2005) proposed to describe the cognitive processes of drawing. The GTDC was developed by applying Mayer's (e.g., Mayer & Gallini, 1990) theoretical accounts of multimedia learning to drawing. Our thinking since that publication has developed to incorporate principles derived from additional theoretical frameworks; namely, Winne's (Winne & Hadwin, 1998) self-regulated learning and Schnotz's (2002, 2005) integrated text and picture comprehension (ITPC) model. Hence, we propose the cognitive model of drawing construction (CMDC) as a revision to the GTDC. Like the original model, the CMDC offers a framework to inform how drawing influences learning with the purpose of organizing research findings and guiding hypothesis generation. The following sections present brief descriptions of the original drawing model, Winne's model of self-regulation, and the ITPC to provide background before offering a more detailed account of the CMDC. These reviews are brief, however, and the reader is referred to original sources for greater detail.

OVERVIEW OF THEORETICAL MODELS

Generative Theory of Drawing Construction

We first proposed the GTDC (Van Meter & Garner, 2005; Van Meter et al., 2006) to describe the cognitive processes underlying drawing construction. The GTDC is based on Mayer's generative theory of textbook design (Mayer & Gallini, 1990; Mayer, Steinhoff, Bower, & Mars, 1995), which has since evolved into the cognitive theory of multimedia learning (CTML; Mayer, 2005). Though the CTML does differ from Mayer's original statement of the model, both cite Wittrock's (1974, 1989) generative learning and Paivio's (1986) dual-code (Clark & Paivio, 1991) theories as foundational. These theories also inform our perspective on the drawing strategy. First, we believe a learner benefits from the strategy, in large part, because drawing demands that the learner engage in generative learning. The learner must generate a new conceptual representations as well as connections between the new representation and prior knowledge. The drawing strategy also takes advantage of dual-coding because drawing leads to the construction of an internal nonverbal representation that is connected to the internal representation of verbal text. Taken together, we believe the drawing strategy is uniquely beneficial because drawing forces the learner to generate inferences that connect verbal and nonverbal knowledge representations.

A simple linear presentation of the cognitive progression through the GTDC begins with the learner selecting key elements from verbal instructional material. These elements are organized to form an internal verbal representation of target content. Drawing construction itself begins as the learner uses the organized verbal representation to guide construction of an internal, nonverbal representation. In this respect, the organized verbal representation plays a critical role in determining both the elements and structural relations that will be drawn.

An important feature of the GTDC is the position taken with respect to learners' integration of verbal and nonverbal representations. Integration of these internal verbal and visual representations occurs when a learner generates connections between them (Ainsworth, Bibby, & Wood, 2002; Mayer & Moreno, 2002). Theoretical accounts of multimedia learning, in which both text and visual displays are provided, claim that integration of verbal and visual internal knowledge representations is responsible for the advantage of multimedia over text alone (Azevedo, 2005; Seufert, 2003; Tabachneck-Schijf & Simon, 1998). Mayer (1993; Mayer & Sims, 1994), for instance, indicates that this integrated representation, which should also include prior knowledge, is a mental model and that this model is responsible for students' improved performance on measures of conceptual transfer when both text and visualizations are provided.

Unfortunately, learners may not construct this integrated representation when both verbal and visual materials are provided (e.g., Bodemer, Ploetzner, Feuerlein, & Spada, 2004; Seufert & Brünken, 2006). In these cases, a learner may hold both internal representations, but fail to recognize the correspondence between the two and generate the connections necessary for mental model construction (de Jong et al., 1998). This assertion is consistent with a number of multimedia research studies showing that novices do not integrate these representations (e.g., Ainsworth, Bibby, & Wood, 1998; Kozma & Russell, 1997; Tabachneck-Schijf & Simon, 1998).

Learner-generated drawing forces integration of verbal and nonverbal representations because the learner must rely on the verbal representation to construct the visual representation on which the drawing is based. In this respect, drawing requires translation between a provided verbal representation and the visual representation that underlies the constructed drawing (Cox, 1999). Integration is an automatic by-product of that construction process, and thus, the drawing strategy is more likely to lead to mental model construction than is mere inspection of provided verbal and visual representations.

Although drawing is described here as a sequential process, from the selection of verbal elements to the construction of the drawing, in reality these processes are non-linear and recursive. Drawing begins with selecting elements and organizing the verbal text, but efforts to draw will lead the learner back to the provided verbal text to identify missing elements or seek necessary clarification. This aspect of the GTDC captures the metacognitive self-monitoring that is stimulated by drawing construction (Ainsworth & Iacovides, 2005; Van Meter, 2001).

In this chapter, we propose modifications to address two specific shortcomings of the GTDC. The first shortcoming concerns limitations that arise from the focus on separate channels for internally processing verbal and visual representations. We still believe these channels are distinct, but find that this perspective alone restricts our thinking about the characteristics of knowledge representations and the ways that these representations interact and influence one another. Our drawing model addresses this limitation by incorporating principles from Schnotz's (2005) integrated text and picture comprehension (ITPC) model of multimedia learning. The second shortcoming concerns underspecification of the ways in which drawing acts within a student's system of self-regulated learning. We address this shortcoming by assimilating principles from Winne's (Winne & Hadwin, 1998) model of self-regulated learning into the GTDC. The revised drawing model, the CMDC, is presented in upcoming sections. While this presentation is focused on what is new about the revised model, the CMDC retains the basic principles of the GTDC. The sections immediately below provide brief descriptions of both Winne's self-regulation and Schnotz' ITPC models.

Self-Regulation and Learning

Self-regulation refers to control of one's learning activities and involves cognitive, metacognitive, and motivational components (Schraw, Crippen, & Hartley, 2006). A variety of theoretical models, each emphasizing different dimensions, have been proposed to account for how learners regulate their own learning. Winne (Winne & Hadwin, 1998; Winne & Perry, 2000) offers one such model, which emphasizes learners' metacognitive awareness and control mechanisms. This model begins with the learner understanding task demands, within a set of task and cognitive conditions, and setting a corresponding goal. The goal informs internal standards for performance such that a single goal can result in multiple standards. These standards correspond to the various facets of the task that a learner understands and perceives as important. Applied to drawing, for instance, a learner could set standards for the number of drawings to be constructed, the amount of detail and information to be contained in the drawings, and overall quality. Once standards have been set, the self-regulated learner devises a plan for achieving the goal. Task performance begins as the learner applies cognitive operations, such as a strategy, toward the instructional material. In high quality self-regulation, the learner's metacognitive awareness of the strategies that are best matched to task conditions will lead to the selection of specific learning strategies during the planning phase (Winne, 1995; Winne & Perry, 2000).

The execution of cognitive operations results in learning products. In complex, time-consuming tasks, multiple products are generated as the learner progresses toward the goal. Metacognitive self-monitoring is responsible for comparing these products to corresponding standards and these comparisons allow the learner to determine whether progress is being made towards the goal. When the product meets the standard, the learner continues with her plan and cognitive operations. Alternatively, if the product does not meet performance standards, the self-regulated learner will adjust the plan and corresponding cognitive operations. This metacognitive control can lead a learner to select a different strategy, repeat a previously completed part of the plan, or adjust performance standards.

This self-regulation cycle proceeds in an iterative fashion throughout the learning task. First, metacognitive awareness guides the setting of goals and standards and the selection of operations to achieve those standards. Metacognitive monitoring guides comparison of generated products to the standards. Depending on the outcome of these comparisons, metacognitive control can lead to the adjustment of plans and the selection of new strategies. For the self-regulated learner, metacognitive control oversees study behaviors until the task is complete. As will be seen in the section on the CMDC, these principles of self-regulation have implications for understanding how drawing affects learning and how it can be used most effectively.

Integrated Text and Picture Comprehension and Learning

Schnotz (2002, 2005) proposed the ITPC model to capture learning processes when both verbal text and visualizations are provided. This model shares structural similarities with Mayer's (2005) CTML, but the two emphasize different underlying cognitive processes. The ITPC, for example, focuses on the nature of internal knowledge representations and argues that a representation can, and should, be processed in either channel regardless of input modality.

The ITPC describes the comprehension of verbal text and visualizations according to levels of representations and emphasizes the descriptive or depictive nature of the representations held at each level. Descriptive representations are symbolic representations in which symbols represent content according to convention. The verbal discourse of instructional text, and the knowledge representations directly derived from this text, are descriptive because structures and relations must be represented through conventional rules for combining arbitrary symbols. Visualizations, by contrast, provide depictive representations. These representations reflect content through icons, which share structural features with the content they depict and can be either concrete or abstract. External verbal texts are descriptive and visual displays are depictive, but once information is abstracted from these external representations into the cognitive system, either external form can be constructed into either descriptive or depictive representations.

The ITPC describes different levels of internal representations, which correspond roughly to the varying levels in Kintsch's (1998) construction-integration theory of discourse processing. The first of these, the surface representation, is the only level that is tied to the form of the external verbal or visual representation. The surface representation of a provided verbal text is the set of linguistic features abstracted from the text. The surface representation of a provided visualization is a perceptual image. Similar to the surface representation of the text, this perceptual image corresponds to the surface features of the provided representation.

A propositional network is constructed at the next level. This network contains the meaning of the provided representation and may include prior knowledge. A propositional network results from semantic processing of the surface representation corresponding to either the text or the visualization. In fact, the ITPC regards semantic processing of a provided visualization as necessary if the learner is to achieve full understanding. A mental model may also be constructed from either a perceptual image or descriptive representation. In contrast to the descriptive quality of the propositional network, the mental model is a functional or structural analog that is constructed by mapping structural features of the external visualization to referential knowledge. Accordingly, the mental model is a depictive representation that is connected to prior knowledge and is more abstract than the perceptual image.

Our revised drawing model is shaped by the theoretical principles described here. Self-regulation helps us to think about drawing as a strategy that operates within a dynamic system. The execution of this strategy leads to construction of a mental model that is translated into a perceptual image and externalized as a drawing. Deeper consideration of these representations affords a better understanding of the task conditions to which drawing is best matched.

COGNITIVE MODEL OF DRAWING CONSTRUCTION

Figure 10.2 shows a graphic depiction of the CMDC. The square boxes in this figure indicate the learner's internal knowledge representations. The labels for these representations have been taken from the ITPC (Schnotz, 2002) in order to distinguish levels of descriptive and depictive representations. The CMDC claims that, when instructional material is verbal, drawing begins by forming a surface representation of linguistic features.

Semantic processing of these features leads to construction of a propositional network that describes structural elements and relations. To produce a drawing, the learner constructs a mental model from the propositional network. Thus, a learner relies on the propositional network to determine which structures to include in the mental model, what those structures look like, and how they should be related. Consistent with the ITPC, we believe this mental model is depictive, can include visuospatial information, and is more determinant than is the propositional representation (Cox, 1999; Gobert & Clements, 1999). The mental model represents structural relations in a system by analogy, which allows the learner to understand system components and how they operate together. It is this mental model that holds primary responsibility for the beneficial learning effects of drawing.

To construct a drawing, the learner must translate the mental model into a perceptual image. This perceptual image instantiates the mental model into a form the learner can translate onto the page. The learner produces a drawing by externalizing this depictive surface feature representation. Figure 10.2 shows only a single solid arrow entering the perceptual image with this arrow originating in the mental model. This is not intended to suggest that only the mental model has a direct influence on the perceptual image. Indeed, aspects of both the propositional network and the surface representation of the text may be translated directly to this image. If, for example, a learner reads, "The renal parenchyma ... appears C-shaped...," that learner can make a direct translation of the letter "C" into a perceptual image of that letter. Nonetheless, we retain the single arrow in order to highlight that the drawing strategy is most effective when it is the mental model that exerts the greatest influence on the perceptual image.

Similar to the original drawing model, prior knowledge influences both the propositional network and the mental model. Prior knowledge, in fact, plays a particularly important role when a drawing must be constructed in the absence of any provided visual representation. The learner must rely on prior knowledge, for instance, when attempting to translate a portion of text that reads, "The medial surface is concave" It is only by consulting her memory stores that this learner can determine how the words "medial" and "concave" can be translated into visual form.

Whereas the boxes in Figure 10.2 illustrate the knowledge representations underlying drawing construction, the arrows in this figure indicate cognitive processes. Arrows with solid lines reference those cognitive processes that take the learner from presentation of verbal instructional material to externalization of the drawing. For the most part, these processes are consistent with the original statement of the GTDC; namely, the selection and organization of descriptive elements and the forced integra-

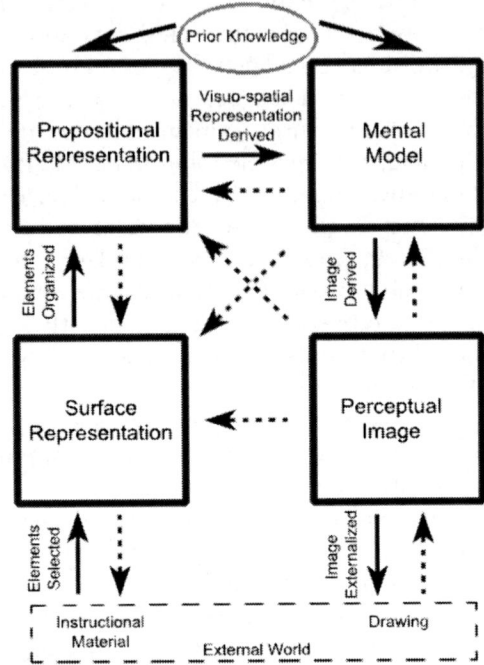

Figure 10.2.   A graphic represenation of the cognitive model of drawing construction (CMDC). The rectangular dashed box at the bottom indicates the representations present in the external world, the square black boxes indicate internal knowledge representations, and the oval indicates the influence of prior knowledge. Arrows with solid lines reference the cognitive processes that take the learner from the presentation of instructional material to externalization of the drawing; dashed arrows reference the feedback cycles resultant from metacognition and self-regulation.

tion of the descriptive and depictive representations. The CMDC, however, understands these processes in light of the learner's self-regulated learning processes. As we will explain shortly, for example, selection is influenced by the learner's task goal.

The dashed arrows in Figure 10.2 represent a clarified emphasis on the role of metacognition. Arrows indicate feedback cycles that arise when the learner's attempts to draw trigger awareness that content is not well understood. While working to construct a mental model, for instance, the learner may seek clarification of the relationship between two structures by reconsidering the propositional representation; efforts to construct a perceptual image may lead to re-inspection of the surface representation of the text to locate specific information. Of course, in both of these cases, the learner may realize that reinspection of instructional materials is necessary.

Drawing is not a simple linear sequence in the CMDC. A learner who uses the drawing strategy will undergo many recursions through the steps of the CMDC with these iterative processes driving the learner back and forth between the various internal and external representations. Although this description is consistent with the original drawing model, the need to better address these recursive processes is our motivation for incorporating self-regulation into the CMDC. The section below explains this addition with particular attention to how the mechanisms of metacognitive awareness and control manage strategy execution.

Self-Regulation and Drawing Construction as Viewed Through the CMDC

Theoretical accounts of multimedia learning, in which both verbal text and nonverbal visualizations are provided, recognize the importance of cognitive and metacognitive processes but have done little to clarify what those processes might be and how they can be taught and improved. Mayer (2005), for example, states that learners select, organize, and integrate; but does not specify how these cognitive processes are actually executed. Likewise, Schnotz (2005) indicates that semantic processing transforms a surface representation into a propositional network, but offers little explanation of what 'semantic processing' entails.

Our original drawing model described how drawing prompts metacognitive self-monitoring, but failed to account for the ways that drawing and monitoring interact with other learning mechanisms. The revised model, the CMDC, incorporates principles of self-regulated learning to address this shortcoming. This revision presents drawing as it occurs according to a three-phase self-regulation cycle[1] that drives the learner's movements between the knowledge representations described by the CMDC. This cycle reflects metacognitive control consistent with Winne's (Winne & Perry, 2000) self-regulation model and involves (1) setting standards for performance, (2) applying (strategic) operations, and (3) monitoring goal progress. Each phase holds specific implications for learners' effective use of the drawing strategy.

The first phase, the setting of standards, begins when the learner is told to "make a drawing." Upon receipt of these instructions, the self-regulated learner sets the goal to produce a drawing and establishes corresponding performance standards. These performance standards include various facets such as the amount of detail to include, the need to show how parts fit together, and overall accuracy. In addition to these drawing-specific standards, the self-regulated learner also stipulates standards regarding learning products such as understanding how the system operates or memory for specific structures. These standards reflect the learner's understanding of what it means to "make a drawing" and it is these standards that will anchor metacognitive control while executing the strategy. A learner using the drawing strategy to support learning from our kidney text, for instance, may set standards addressing inclusion of all named anatomical structures, placement of verbal labels on these structures, and depiction of how structures physically fit together.

Two predictions follow from this aspect of the CMDC. First, the CMDC predicts that the learner's understanding of what it means to make a drawing will affect strategy efficacy. We would expect, for instance, that a learner who realizes the drawing should contain details or holds herself to a standard of accuracy would benefit from the strategy to a greater degree than will a learner who does not hold these standards. Our expectation is that task instructions that support learners' understanding of how to best use the strategy can enhance their efficacy for drawing. The second prediction is that use of the drawing strategy influences learners' attention while learning. Knowing that one must make a drawing directs attention toward parts of the text that describe physical appearance and spatial relations amongst structures.

The second phase captures the cognitive operations carried out to comprehend instructional material and match task standards. These are the operations used to select elements for the surface representation of the text and to organize these elements into propositional networks. These also include drawing-specific operations such as the transformation of a verbal description into a visual depiction and determination of how two structures fit together. In order to construct the drawing shown in Figure 10.1, for example, a learner must first select the major anatomical structures from the text; such as the hilum, renal pyramids, and renal papilla; and apply comprehension strategies to determine the descriptive relations between these structures. The learner can draw only after she translates statements such as, "renal columns project toward the sinus [in] renal pyramids" and "each renal pyramid is nestled in a cup called a minor calyx" into a depictive representation.

Again, two predictions arise from this component of the CMDC. The first prediction is that drawing prompts the use of other known learning strategies and these strategies facilitate construction of a propositional network that can support drawing. To illustrate, consider a learner who constructs a drawing like that shown in Figure 10.1. This learner will apply strategies such as self-questioning (e.g., Which direction should the pyramid point?), paraphrasing (e.g., So, all of the outside structures will enter through this slit.), and prior knowledge activation (e.g., A sinus is a cavity.). Application of these strategies improves the quality of the propositional network, which supports both mental model and drawing construction. The second prediction is that drawing is affected by the same variables that affect learners' use of other learning strategies. A learner who has conditional knowledge of when to use drawing, for example, is more likely to transfer the strategy during independent study. Explicit instructions on how to use the strategy should also improve learners' strategy application.

The final phase of the drawing self-regulation cycle occurs when the learner monitors progress toward the drawing goal. During this phase, metacognitive control is triggered when the learner compares his in-progress drawing to the standards set for task performance. When drawing meets these standards, the learner will proceed to remaining portions of the task. When the standards have not been met, however, metacognitive control will direct the learner back to either the propositional network or the instructional material.

The effect of drawing on self-monitoring is a particular strength of the drawing strategy. In order to complete the "make a drawing" task, the learner must specify his understanding to such a degree that a drawing can actually be produced—a near impossible task if one cannot identify and abstract critical elements and relations. Consequently, drawing acts as a forcing function (Reason, 1990) in which forward movement is blocked if some portion of the drawing cannot be externalized. When this happens, the learner knows the instructional material has not been understood well enough and it is this forcing function that is responsible for the increased frequency of self-monitoring when the drawing strategy is used (Ainsworth & Iacovides, 2005; Van Meter, 2001). An advantage of this strategy then is that a learner is much less able to "hide" her misunderstandings when drawing than when writing (Van Meter & Riley, 1999). A learner who is studying our kidney text, for example, may overlook or misunderstand the meaning of a "sinus" as an anatomical structure and simply continue reading. She will have to specify this structure, however, or it will not be possible to create the part of the drawing that corresponds to the sentence, "two or three major calyces converge in the sinus"

In summary, the CMDC asserts that many of the benefits of the drawing strategy originate in the self-regulated learning processes that are triggered by efforts to create an external visual display that reflects internal knowledge representations. Specifically, drawing construction stimulates a three-phase self-regulation cycle that begins with a learner's understanding of the drawing task and is driven by metacognitive awareness and control. Metacognitive awareness and control in the CMDC operates similarly to Nelson and Narens' (1990) description of metacognitive control and awareness. Metacognitive control is responsible for guiding and affecting the operations a learner carries out and awareness provides the learner with information about the task and ongoing progress toward goals. These processes may act independently but are psychologically intertwined as awareness provides information that influences control mechanisms and control changes the object of which the learner is aware (Nelson & Narens, 1990, 1994). The prediction we derive from this perspective is consistent with the assertion of the original drawing model: Learners who use the drawing strategy will engage in self-monitoring more frequently than will learners who do not use this strategy. The CMDC takes this prediction one step further and adds the expectation that independent use of the drawing strategy is both possible and desirable. Specifically, we predict that a learner who is aware of the task conditions for which drawing is well-matched, knows how to execute the strategy, and is able to use drawing to drive self-monitoring can independently self-regulate her use of the strategy to achieve learning goals.

The ITPC and Drawing Construction as Viewed Through the CMDC

Whereas Winne's SRL model highlights the role of cognitive and metacognitive factors, Schnotz's (2005) ITPC draws attention to the internal knowledge representations that result from drawing construction. Like the original drawing model (Van Meter et al., 2006), the CMDC asserts drawing can exert a powerful influence on learning because this strategy forces the learner to assimilate verbal and nonverbal representations. In addition, the CMDC postulates that the drawing strategy promotes construction of knowledge representations at each level described by Schnotz's (2005) ITPC model. Namely, verbal instructional materials lead to construction of surface and propositional representations; the demand to create a drawing drives construction of a mental model and perceptual image. There are two additional principles that arise from this position and these principles implicate both the propositional network and the mental model.

First, the previous section indicated that the quality of the propositional network affects drawing efficacy. Whereas that section described the effects of learners' self-regulation on the quality of this representation, Schnotz's (2005) ITPC model brings focus to the relationship between the external and internal knowledge representations. Accordingly, the ITPC invites us to think more deeply about the influence of the instructional materials and drawing tools on how a learner uses the strategy. The

CMDC intends to subsume what is known about the text processing factors that influence the construction of propositional networks. Research on text characteristics, for instance, has demonstrated that knowledge construction is influenced by factors such as coherence (McNamara & Kintsch, 1996), surface features (Firetto & Van Meter, 2011), and text structure (Meyer, Wijekumar, & Lin, 2011).

The CMDC predicts that the efficacy of the drawing strategy is impacted by these same factors. A drawing can be more readily produced, for example, when text signals are provided. To illustrate this point, consider the sentence from our kidney text, which read, "The medial surface [of the kidney] is concave and has a slit, the hilum, where it receives the renal nerves, blood vessels, lymphatics, and ureter." The CMDC predicts that the drawing strategy could be more easily implemented if the text used signaling, such as bold print to highlight the anatomical structures: "The medial surface [of the kidney] is concave and has a slit, the **hilum**, where it receives the **renal nerves**, **blood vessels**, **lymphatics**, and **ureter**."

One factor in particular that will influence the propositional network is the degree to which the descriptive language of the text is constrained. Text can be understood as existing along a continuum from highly- to loosely-constrained text. A highly constrained text is one that limits possible interpretations by using language that is specific and detailed. A more loosely constrained text, by contrast, uses language that is less specified and lends itself to multiple determinations. In the context of the drawing strategy, a highly constrained text uses words that can be easily translated from the descriptive symbols of a propositional network into the depictive mental model. Compare, for example, what one would draw if given the sentence, "Extensions of the cortex ... project toward the sinus and divide the medulla into renal pyramids." and what one would draw from the sentence, "Extensions of the cortex ... project toward the sinus and divide the medulla into *6 to 10* renal pyramids." The constraints added by stating the number of renal pyramids that should be included makes the second sentence much easier to translate from a descriptive to a depictive representation.

The CMDC predicts that effectiveness of the drawing strategy is diminished with text that sits on either extreme of this continuum. On one extreme, when the text is highly abstract, drawing will not aid learning because the propositional network will lack sufficient detail to derive a *representational* depiction. In this case, the learner is unable to translate the abstract descriptive representation into the determinant form of a drawing. Under these conditions, a learner may be better served by constructing a visualization that is not held to the representational standard. Consider the kidney text that Van Meter read as an illustration of this point. It was possible to construct a representational drawing because the text used determinant language such as concave, conical, nestled in a cup, and project toward. Imagine if, rather than describing the appearance of these physical structures, the text had identified the physiological processes of hormones as they follow a path through the kidney. In this case, Van Meter may have been better served by constructing a flow diagram.

On the other extreme, the propositional network may be specified in such concrete, descriptive symbols that it can be directly translated into a perceptual image. In these cases, the learner does not need to engage in generative processing and mental model construction is circumvented. The CMDC allows for this superficial route by opening a path from the propositional network directly to the perceptual image. On this path, the perceptual image is constructed through piecemeal translation of individual propositions into the perceptual image. It is necessary to include this path because drawing is a resource demanding process (Leutner, Leopold, & Sumfleth, 2009) and there is no guarantee that a learner will exert the effort necessary to construct a mental model. A learner who takes this path, however, is only superficially engaged with both the instructional materials and the drawing activity. Accordingly, a learner who selects this path is unlikely to benefit from the drawing strategy. The second issue concerns the limitations of the mental model that results from drawing. Schnotz (2002) describes the mental model derived from provided illustrations as a functional or structural analog. Educational literature often cites mental model construction as the ultimate goal of learning. A learner who generates and holds such a model is more able to recall main ideas from instructional material and apply knowledge to novel problems than is a learner who does not have this model (Ainsworth, 2006; Azevedo, Cromley, & Seibert, 2004). Though this relative comparison may be true, Schnotz and colleagues' (Meyer, Rasch, & Schnotz, 2010; Rasch & Schnotz, 2009) research highlights the limitations of this knowledge representation. Schnotz and Bannert (2003), for example, tested the *structure mapping hypothesis*, which predicts that, when external representations are structurally different, these differences will be reflected in learners' mental models. Furthermore, the structural differences in mental models are revealed by better performance on posttest items that are structurally consistent with the mental model than on posttest items that are structurally inconsistent. College students in the study by Schnotz and Bannert learned about global time zones by studying a text with a carpet diagram, a text with a circular map, or a text with no diagram. The posttest included time difference tasks, which were best aligned to the carpet diagram, and circumnavigation tasks, which were best aligned to the circular diagram. Posttest scores confirmed the structure mapping hypothesis by showing that learners did have an advantage when posttest items were structurally consistent with the studied visualization.

This research demonstrates that the particular format studied affects how learners perform on posttest items. Presumably, different formats lead to different mental models and different mental models lead to different posttest performances. In the context of the CMDC, this point leads to the prediction that, when the drawing strategy is used, knowledge-based performances will be equally bound to the specific characteristics of the constructed mental model. Improved performance can only be expected when posttest assessments are well-matched to the characteristics of the specific knowledge representation that is constructed.

In summary, the CMDC offers a revised model of drawing that incorporates both the processes of self-regulation (Winne & Hadwin, 1998) and the knowledge representations of the ITPC (Schnotz, 2005). As with other theoretical models, the purpose of the CMDC is to serve as a framework that can organize and explain research findings. We demonstrate this function in the following section by using principles of the CMDC to interpret findings from existing drawing research. This review is limited, rather than exhaustive, and is organized around two themes that emerged from this research.

REVIEW OF THE RESEARCH

Improving the Effectiveness of Drawing Through Support Functions

Our initial work with the drawing strategy noted inconsistencies across studies of drawing from the 1970s through the 1990s (Van Meter & Garner, 2005). Whereas some studies reported positive effects of drawing (e.g., Alesandrini, 1981; Lansing, 1981; Lesgold et al., 1975, Experiment 2), other studies did not find a strategy advantage (e.g., Rasco, Tennyson, & Boutwell, 1975; Snowman & Cunningham, 1975; Tirre, Manelis, & Leicht, 1979). Van Meter and Garner's comprehensive review of the research identified a pattern, however, in which studies that found positive drawing effects tended to include some form of support that assisted the learners' construction of the drawing. For instance, Lesgold et al. (1975), supported first grade students' construction of a pictorial representation by providing cut-out figures of story elements. When drawing required children to select from amongst both accurate and distractor cut-outs, drawing did not improve story recall (Experiment 1). When distractor cut-outs were removed so that children only had to manipulate accurate representations, children did benefit from constructing the pictorial representation. These first grade students, it seems, could not benefit from this strategy unless given the support of the accurate cut-outs.

Van Meter (2001) tested the effect of drawing support by systematically varying support across three drawing conditions. All fifth and sixth grade participants in this study read a two-page text about the central nervous system. In the *Draw* condition, each page was followed by a blank sheet of paper and participants were told to make a drawing of the important information. Participants in the *Illustration* condition received the same instructions, but were also permitted to inspect provided illustrations after drawing. The greatest degree of support was provided in the *Prompt* condition. *Prompt* participants drew, inspected provided illustrations, and also answered prompting questions to guide drawing-illustration comparisons. Participants in the no-drawing *Control* condition read the text with both illustrations provided. Consistent with the support hypothesis, only those participants who received the greatest support, those in the *Prompt* condition, scored significantly higher on a free recall test than did *Control* participants.

Interpretation of these and other drawing studies through the framework of the CMDC clarifies the role of support during drawing construction. Theoretical principles of this model suggest that support serves one of two primary functions. The first function, the constraint function, is satisfied when support provides information about the appearance of the drawing. The second function addresses self-regulation, which is served when support influences learners' ability to use self-regulatory processes.

Constraint function. The constraint function is illustrated by drawing supports that constrain the possible depictions a learner might construct. These supports provide information about the visual characteristics of the to-be-constructed representation. An example of the constraint function can be found in the study by Van Meter et al. (2006), which was a follow up to the 2001 study. This study tested the hypothesis that learners require less external support when learning about more familiar topics than the central nervous system. Prior knowledge, we reasoned, could act as a form of support, particularly when that knowledge includes visuo-spatial relations. Participants in this study read about the primary structures of a bird wing and how those structures allow flight. We predicted that learners would require less support than did participants in the 2001 study because the students' familiarity with the shape and external structures of bird wings would constrain drawing construction.

The experimental conditions (i.e., *Draw*, *Illustration*, and *Prompt*) were identical to those of the 2001 study. *Control* participants, however, also answered questions directing comparison of the text and provided illustrations. Posttest scores on a conceptual problem solving posttest measure confirmed the prediction. Participants who received drawing support, either in the form of provided *Illustrations* after drawing or provided illustrations and *Prompting* questions, scored higher on this posttest than did participants in the *Control* condition. The provided illustrations used as support in these studies (Van Meter, 2001; Van Meter et al., 2006) serve the constraint function because these illustrations helped learners know what their own drawings should look like. A learner who inspects these illustrations after drawing receives feedback on the accuracy of their drawing and has the opportunity to revise both the drawing and their mental models.

Recent research by Schwamborn, Mayer, Thillmann, Leopold, and Leutner (2010) demonstrates how support can satisfy the constraint function during the construction of drawings rather than after drawings are completed. High school students in this study read to learn about the chemical processes of washing. A *Read* only control condition was compared to four different drawing conditions. Participants assigned to the draw condition produced six drawings, one for each of the six text paragraphs. Participants in the *Draw + Select* condition constructed these same six drawings and also underlined the most important information in the text. Participants in the *Draw + Organize/Integrate* condition generated mental images before constructing each of the six drawings. In the *Draw + Select/Organize/Integrate* condition, participants underlined text information, generated mental images, and constructed drawings.

In all drawing conditions, drawing was supported by providing drawing tools, which were graphic representations of critical elements given in a toolbar at the top of each page. Participants constructed drawings by copying each of these elements in the correct location of a partially completed background. Participants in each of the four drawing conditions obtained higher scores on transfer, retention, and drawing posttests than did participants in the no-drawing *control* condition. There were no significant differences between the four drawing conditions on any of the four posttests. These results suggest that the drawing tools provided during picture generation provided sufficient constraints for learners to benefit from this support.

The CMDC explains the constraint function by accounting for the influence of support on the contents of the perceptual image and mental model. This interpretation can be understood by placing an arrow within the depiction of the CMDC (Figure 10.2) that goes from the external world, where the support is located, in through the perceptual image. From there, the contents of the perceptual image directly inform the contents of the mental model. In this respect, the mental model receives input from both the perceptual image and the propositional network. These inputs mutually constrain the mental model and increase the likelihood that this representation will accurately depict target content.

An important caveat must be added here, which is the caution that support should not be so excessive that the learner need not engage in generative processing (Wittrock, 2010). If support provides too much information, the learner will be able to construct a perceptual image, and externalize this image as a drawing, without first generating the mental model. Evidence supporting this claim comes from a study by Hall, Bailey, and Tillman (1997). In this study, college students read an explanatory text about a hand air pump. Participants in one condition constructed drawings and participants in another condition viewed provided illustrations. This study did not find an advantage for the drawing strategy relative to studying provided illustrations. A closer look at the text used in the drawing condition, however, suggests support was too extensive. The introductory paragraph for participants in this condition gave precise directions on what to draw, such as, "In the beginning draw a cylinder which is about 2 inches ... long and 1 inch ... wide, ... in a vertical position" (p. 678). It is likely that participants reading this text engaged in piecemeal translation of propositions into perceptual images.

Self-regulation function. A second function that can be served by provided support is a self-regulation function. This form of support directly aids learners' self-regulation efforts while using the drawing strategy. These effects can be understood according to the self-regulation cycle. Specifically, drawing support can aid learners' understanding of the task and the subsequent standards that are set, as well as the self-monitoring of goal progress.

A study by Alesandrini (1981) provides evidence regarding the effects of support on task understanding. College students in this study read to learn about electrochemical concepts. Three drawing conditions were compared to three writing conditions. In two of these conditions, participants were simply told to *Draw* or *Write* a paraphrase of the content. Participants in the *Analytic Drawing* and *Analytic Writing* conditions received instructions to attend to specific components of the system while drawing or writing. Participants in the *Holistic Drawing* and *holistic writing* conditions were told to attend to how system parts fit together. These six experimental drawing and writing groups were compared to a *Read Twice Control*. A significant effect of drawing was found such that participants in drawing conditions obtained higher posttest scores than did those in writing conditions. These effects were strongest in the *Holistic Drawing* condition as this was the only condition to obtain significantly higher posttest scores than participants in any of the specific drawing groups.

Our interpretation of Alesandrini's (1981) findings is that drawing instructions influenced participants' understanding of the drawing task and, consequently, influenced the standards that were set. Participants who received holistic instructions understood that drawings should depict structural relations, and hence held a standard corresponding to this understanding. Participants who received analytic instructions, on the other hand, set a standard to match analytic instructions. Those standards directed attention so that participants focused their efforts on different parts of the text during study and different parts of the visualization during drawing. These findings suggest that support in this study served a self-regulation function by informing specific drawing standards and directing attention.

There is also evidence that drawing influences self-monitoring, the final phase of the self-regulation cycle. Research by both Ainsworth and Iacovides (2005) and Van Meter (2001) shows that engagement in the drawing strategy increases the number of self-monitoring events that occur while learning. Drawing participants in the study by Ainsworth and Iacovides, for example, generated an average of 4 monitoring statements for every 1.33 of these statements generated by participants who inspected diagrams and wrote, rather than drew, explanations. This ratio is nearly identical to the 4:1 ratio Van Meter (2001) found when comparing the frequencies of self-monitoring for participants in an unsupported drawing condition and a reading control condition. These studies show that, drawing increases learners' self-monitoring in comparison to participants who do not draw, irrespective of support.

Looking more deeply into the results of the study by Van Meter (2001) uncovers evidence that drawing support further effects self-monitoring. Recall that this study tested the drawing strategy under three conditions of varying support and learning effects were found for only those participants who drew with the most extensive support. In addition to posttest scores, Van Meter (2001) also collected think-alouds that were coded for self-monitoring events and final drawings that were scored for accuracy. Participants who drew with the most extensive support not only produced significantly more accurate drawings than did participants in the no-support drawing condition, but also engaged in a greater number of self-monitoring events. These findings indicate that drawing support increases a learner's awareness of comprehension errors and assists in the correction of these errors. We believe the provided illustrations also served the constraint function, which allowed participants who drew with support to correct detected comprehension errors and thus, to improve drawing accuracy.

The studies reviewed thus far in this section provide evidence that drawing support affects specific aspects of the self-regulation cycle. There is also evidence that support can address the more global demands that drawing places on the self-regulation system. To consider this evidence, we must first examine a study by Leutner et al. (2009). In this study, high school participants read a 13 paragraph text on the dipole character of water that contained no diagrams. Participants were directed to read the *Text-Only* for comprehension, *Draw* a corresponding diagram for each paragraph, *Mentally Imagine* a corresponding diagram for each paragraph, or *Combined* draw and mentally imagine the diagram. All participants gave cognitive load estimates after finishing the learning task. On a comprehension posttest, *Text-Only* participants obtained higher scores than did participants in the drawing conditions. Participants in both drawing conditions reported increased cognitive load, whereas participants in mental imagery conditions reported decreased cognitive load. Further analysis determined that increased cognitive load mediated the negative main effect of drawing on comprehension. Leutner et al. (2009) concluded that drawing was too effortful when the task required a number of drawings, and it was this cognitive load that eliminated the positive effects of the drawing strategy.

In contrast to the study by Leutner et al. (2009), we recently completed a study in which learners benefitted from the drawing strategy, even though this strategy required the construction of multiple drawings (Firetto & Van Meter, 2011). College student participants in our study read a 25-page text that contained 25 diagrams explaining the biology of muscle contraction. *Text + Diagram* control participants received the text and all 25 diagrams. Participants in the *Text-Only* control condition received the text, but no diagrams; which is consistent with the *text-only* condition in the study by Leutner et al. In the *Draw* condition, participants received these same materials with seven diagrams missing and were instructed to make a drawing in the blank space where the diagram should have been. Thus, similar to the study by Leutner et al., participants had to construct a number of drawings while studying a challenging text, but our participants had the other 18 provided diagrams to support drawing efforts. In contrast Leutner et al.'s findings, our *Draw* participants obtained the highest posttest scores overall. The difference between *Draw* and *Text-Only Control* participants was significant for all posttest items; the difference between *Draw* and *Text + Diagrams* participants was significant for posttest items that corresponded to drawn content.

Results of the study by Firetto and Van Meter (2011) show that learners can use the drawing strategy effectively when instructional demands are high, if adequate support is provided. Similar to the support provided in our previous drawing studies, the provided diagrams that were available served both the constraint and self-regulation support functions. Constraints were available because the 18 provided diagrams gave visual input that learners could use to inform the internal perceptual image and the mental model generated in order to support drawing. When a learner had to draw cross-bridge formation between thin and thick filaments in muscle fibers, for example, he would have the support of having seen these filaments in previous diagrams. This support effectively reduced the demands of the drawing strategy and thus, freed cognitive resources for other self-regulation processes.

Conclusion. The need for support is a fairly consistent conclusion pulled from the empirical evidence surrounding the drawing strategy (Van Meter & Garner, 2005). This evidence is found by comparing drawing methods across studies in which drawing was and was not effective (e.g., Alesandrini, 1981 vs. Tirre et al., 1979) and examining studies in which support was manipulated (e.g., Lesgold et al., 1975; Van Meter et al., 2006). The CMDC accounts for this phenomenon by proposing that support can serve a constraint function, a self-regulation function, or both. As illustrated by our research (e.g., Van Meter, 2001; Firetto & Van Meter, 2011), these functions are neither mutually exclusive nor independent. Constraints, for example, may not only inform the contents of the representations, but also support the self-regulated learning that underlies the success of the drawing strategy.

Measuring Drawing Through Well-Matched Posttests

The benefits of any strategy are most likely to be revealed when posttests are well-matched to the strategy (Kintsch, 1994; Levin & Mayer, 1993), and drawing is no exception. In our previous work, we have argued that the best matched posttests are those that assess higher-order knowledge such as comprehension (Alesandrini, 1981) and problem solving (van Essen & Hamaker, 1990, Experiment 2; Van Meter, 2001). Studies that use these higher-order assessments are more likely to report positive drawing effects than are studies that employ lower-order assessments of recognition (Van Meter & Garner, 2005; Van Meter et al., 2006).

This pattern is illustrated in the study by Van Meter (2001), which included both a multiple-choice and a free recall posttest. The multiple-choice test assessed recognition of content that was explicit in the instructional text. Free recalls were coded for expressions of individual structures and functions as well as the expression of structural connections to convey understanding of relations and systems. There were no significant differences between any of the three drawing conditions (*Draw*, *Illustration*, and *Prompt*) in this study and the read only *Control* on the recognition test. By contrast, learners who drew with the most extensive support (i.e., *Prompt*) obtained significantly higher scores on the free recall measure than did participants in the no-drawing *Control* condition. Although this was the only significant between-condition difference in this study, participants in all three drawing conditions had higher mean scores than did control participants across each of the four free recall coding categories.

Interpreting these results through the framework of the CMDC suggests that, if the benefits of the drawing strategy are to be found, the posttest must align with characteristics of the internal knowledge representations that result from drawing. We have been able to identify three such knowledge characteristics in the existing drawing research including the analog characteristics of mental models, visuo-spatial characteristics, and the limitations of knowledge that are bound to a particular internal knowledge structure.

Assessments of higher-order knowledge. Similar to the 2001 study just described, Van Meter et al. (2006) also tested the hypothesis that drawing strategy effects would be found on an assessment of higher-, but not lower, order knowledge. The two posttests included a multiple-choice recognition test and a two-item conceptual transfer problem-solving test. One problem solving item, for instance, described a problem that a bird was having in flight, and participants determined which structure was causing the problem. As expected, there were no significant differences on the recognition measure. There were significant differences on the conceptual transfer test, however. Participants who received support while using the drawing strategy received significantly higher scores on the problem solving posttest than did control participants.

These results are consistent with the characteristics of the mental model that are constructed through the drawing strategy. This mental model provides a functional analog of the bird wing, which allows the learner to reason through the implications of a disruption to this system. Because the problem solving posttest required exactly this type of reasoning, this test was well-matched to the characteristics of the knowledge representation. On the other hand, the mental model does not retain details from the instructional materials (Schnotz, 2002), accounting for the failure of the drawing strategy to improve performance on the recognition test.

Assessments of visuo-spatial knowledge. We have argued throughout this chapter that learners who use the drawing strategy are more likely to generate knowledge representations that contain visuo-spatial information than are their peers who do not use this strategy. It is not surprising then, to find that these learners are advantaged on posttests that assess visuo-spatial knowledge. Ainsworth and colleagues (Ainsworth & Iacovides, 2005; Ainsworth, Galpin, & Musgrove, 2007) provide an example of such an assessment. Their research with students' learning about the cardiovascular system includes a posttest in which participants must draw a blood-path diagram. Ainsworth et al. (2007) demonstrated significant gains on this measure for participants who constructed diagrams, regardless of whether they constructed diagrams to aid their own learning or to explain the content for someone else. Ainsworth and Iacovides (2005) found that participants who drew while studying a verbal text with no accompanying diagrams gained as much knowledge on this assessment as did participants who generated verbal self-explanations while studying a diagram.

Leutner and colleagues (e.g., Leutner et al., 2009; Schwamborn, Thillman, Opfermann, & Leutner, 2011) also found positive effects of drawing on a posttest that required participants to draw diagrams depicting key structures. Leopold and Leutner (2012), for example, included this posttest in research that compared the efficacy of the drawing strategy to either main idea selection (Experiment 1) or summarization (Experiment 2). In both instances, participants who constructed drawings obtained higher posttest scores on this visuo-spatial assessment than did participants who used either of the verbal learning strategies.

While it is not surprising that learners who construct drawings at study are better able to produce these drawings at posttest, research by Gobert and Clements (1999) suggests that this advantage may extend beyond simple replication of constructed drawings. In this research, elementary school students read a two page text on plate tectonics and were instructed to either read the text to *Understand, Draw* corresponding diagrams, or generate a *Written Summary*. The posttest included multiple-choice, short answer, and diagram questions. These questions were grouped into one of two categories so that posttest scores revealed either spatial/static or causal/dynamic knowledge. Thus, Gobert and Clements did not assess visual knowledge per se, but rather participants' understanding of visual characteristics (e.g., "Where is the thinnest part of the crust?", etc.) or causal associations (e.g., "movement of the earth's crust is caused by …?", etc.). The difference between the *Drawing* and *Written Summary* groups did not reach statistical significance, but there was a strong trend in this direction for both posttests and *Drawing* participants obtained the highest average scores on both posttests.

The CMDC points to both the mental model and perceptual image constructed while drawing to account for the pattern of findings discussed here. According to this theoretical model, a learner uses the propositional network to derive a depictive mental model. This mental model is then translated into a perceptual image to produce the drawing. It is not surprising that drawing improves performance on posttest measures of visuo-spatial knowledge because these measures directly tap the knowledge held in the mental model and perceptual image.

Assessments of local knowledge. Knowledge posttests can be designed to capture either local or global knowledge related to content. We define local knowledge as knowledge that is bound to the learning experience. This knowledge is specific to the information that a learner attends to in instructional material and is tied to the structure of these materials. Global knowledge, by contrast, falls outside of the learners' direct attention during learning and may require translation of the underlying knowledge representation (Ainsworth et al., 2002).

We found evidence that the benefits of drawing are limited to local knowledge in our study that compared *Text-Only Control* participants, those who *Drew*, and participants who viewed *Provided* diagrams (Firetto & Van Meter, 2011). Recall that this study used a text with 25 diagrams and 7 were removed in the *Draw* condition. The multiple-choice posttest included content from throughout the entire text and we grouped these into correspondent and noncorrespondent subgroups. Correspondent items measured knowledge that was directly tied to the content covered in the seven missing diagrams that participants had to draw. Noncorrespondent items, on the other hand, measured knowledge that was located elsewhere in the instructional material. Participants in both the *Provided* and *Draw* conditions performed better than *Text-Only Control* participants on both the noncorrespondent and correspondent item subgroups, a finding consistent with the multimedia effect (Mayer, 2005). Participants who constructed *Drawings*, however, also scored significantly higher on the correspondent item subgroup than did participants in either the *Text-Only Control* or *Provided* conditions. This pattern indicates that drawing improves learning of the local content for which they generated drawings, but the advantage does not generalize more globally to nondrawn content.

Other research we have done in college biology labs (Waters et al., 2005, 2011) reveals additional limitations of the drawing strategy. In these studies, students enrolled in a biology lab course were learning about the human muscular (2005, 2011), cardiovascular (2005), and digestive (2005) systems. In the 2011 study, lab sections were assigned to one of three instructional conditions, which were implemented over the course of several weeks. Students in the *Clay Modeling* condition used clay to build 3-dimensional pictorial representations of the human anatomical system and received a handout to guide construction. Students in two control conditions used a traditional *Cat Dissection* experience. In the *Cat Dissection-HO* condition, students received a handout to guide dissection consistent with the handout given in the *Clay Modeling* condition. Students in the *Cat Dissection* condition did not receive a handout.

The lab practical exams, which served as the posttests for this study, included higher-order transfer and structure identification items. Items were given in either a cat or a human format. A cat item, for example, showed a cat with a structure pinned and students had to identify the pinned structure; a human question showed a structure pinned on a human form. Thus, all students had to answer questions that matched the studied representation as well as items that did not match the studied representation. Overall, students scored significantly higher than the comparison group when the test question matched the studied representation.

Students who constructed clay models of humans scored significantly higher than did students who completed cat dissection (with or without a handout) when the question was given in human form and the reverse was true for test items that were given in the form of a cat.

A third type of test question tested students' ability to transfer knowledge to the form of a horse. Horse anatomy closely parallels that of a cat but differs significantly from that of a human. Accordingly, these items are structurally consistent for students in *Cat Dissection* conditions and structurally inconsistent for those in the *Clay Modeling* condition. Students in both *Cat Dissection* conditions obtained higher scores on these transfer items than did students in the *Clay Modeling* condition.

The results of the Firetto and Van Meter (2011) as well as the Waters et al. (2005, 2011) studies can be interpreted in light of Schnotz and colleagues' (e.g., Schnotz & Bannert, 2003) research on the ITPC. As discussed previously, this research tested the structure mapping hypothesis and demonstrated that learners' posttest performances are affected by the structure of the representation used at study. Recall, for instance, Schnotz and Bannert's (2003) demonstration that students who studied a circular diagram of global time zones were advantaged on circumnavigation posttest questions, but those who studied a carpet diagram were advantaged on time difference questions. Our research shows that the drawing strategy is also subject to structure mapping such that learners who construct visual representations are no more able to transform or extend their knowledge representations to novel forms than are learners who study provided visualizations.

Conclusions. The drawing strategy does not solve all learning problems. Instead, drawing is similar to other strategies—it is most effective when it is matched to learning goals. The studies reviewed here show that higher-order (e.g., Van Meter et al., 2006) and visuo-spatial (Schwamborn et al., 2011) assessments are sensitive to the effects of drawing. On the other hand, our research (Firetto & Van Meter, 2011; Waters et al., 2011) demonstrates that the structure mapping hypothesis (Schnotz & Bannert, 2003) should be extended to the drawing strategy as well as provided visualizations. Findings from across drawing studies are consistent with what one would expect from the knowledge representations described in the CMDC. Moreover, this pattern suggests that learners' must have metacognitive awareness of these strategy-outcome relationships if they are to self-regulate independent use of the drawing strategy.

FUTURE DIRECTIONS AND CONCLUDING REMARKS

Our purpose in proposing the CMDC is to stimulate research on the drawing strategy in order to better understand how this strategy supports learning and a number of hypotheses have been embedded in the presentation of the CMDC throughout this chapter. We close this chapter by summarizing some of these in order to highlight the main, new research questions that arise from the CMDC. These hypotheses are organized according to the self-regulation cycle and incorporate principles derived from the drawing model.

The first hypotheses are tied to the initial phase of the self-regulation cycle in which the learner is setting performance standards. In this phase, we predict that drawing will be affected by instructions that influence the learner's task understanding. According to the CMDC, when a learner is told to "make a drawing," that learner sets standards for the drawing and these standards influence task performance. Experimental manipulations to drawing instructions have the potential to impact strategy effectiveness when these instructions help a learner determine appropriate drawing standards. An example of this is Alesandrini's (1981) comparison of holistic and analytic drawing instructions, but much more research is needed to understand the characteristics of effective instructions and how these instructions influence strategy execution.

The first self-regulation phase described in the CMDC also invites hypotheses about the types of tasks for which drawing is appropriate. The CMDC retains the position of the original drawing model with respect to the match between the drawing strategy and knowledge posttests. The CMDC, however, also extends the structure mapping hypothesis (Schnotz & Bannert, 2003) from learning with provided visual displays to learning from drawing construction. Specifically, a learner who sets standards relative to the task of making a drawing will attend most closely to, and subsequently learn, aspects of the instructional material that are needed to achieve this goal. The CMDC predicts that learners who construct drawings will have an advantage on well-aligned posttests such as those that measure visuo-spatial knowledge or knowledge that is part of the constructed drawings. We also predict that no strategy benefits will be found on posttests that are not structurally-aligned. For instance, a learner who constructs a drawing that shows and labels the anatomical structures of the kidney may do well on anatomy test items but would perform more poorly on items testing knowledge of physiological processes within the kidney.

In addition to the hypotheses described above, two major hypotheses can also be located within the second self-regulation phase of the CMDC. In this phase, the learner selects operations that can be applied to reach the standards set in the first phase. If drawing is to be viewed as a strategy rather than a task, then we must begin thinking how to move learners toward independent selection and application of drawing. This thinking should be informed by the literature on effective strategy instruction, which highlights the role of metacognitive conditional knowledge in strategy maintenance and transfer. The CMDC predicts that a learner can independently select and apply the drawing strategy if she is taught about the task conditions under which drawing(s) should be constructed.

A final hypothesis derived from this self-regulation phase ties to the quality of the propositional network. According to the CMDC, a drawing is constructed when the learner derives a perceptual image from a mental model of instructional content. Because this mental model is generated from the propositional network, any improvements to the propositional network will lead to improvements in both the mental model and the drawing. As a result, we expect that drawing effectiveness will be enhanced by experimental manipulations that support construction of the propositional network such as the use of text signals, text coherence, or prompting learners to use a comprehension strategy.

Whereas the hypotheses stated thus far can be derived directly from the CMDC, there are also individual differences that should be explored and incorporated into this drawing model. Examples of these individual differences include spatial ability, drawing skill, and age. Research that includes measures of these variables is necessary to inform the degree to which the CMDC can be generalized across learners.

Despite the need for additional research, existing empirical evidence shows that the drawing strategy has great potential to support and improve student learning. Strategy benefits have been found with learners in first grade through college, across a variety of learning materials, and on different outcome assessments. Though much has been learned about this strategy over the last decade, much is still unknown. We have offered a theoretical model of drawing in this chapter and shown how existing research can be interpreted through the principles of this model. We also included a number of testable predictions here with the purpose of guiding future research. These predictions should serve to stimulate a systematic program of research, which tests model principles and points toward a better understanding of how learners can most effectively use the drawing strategy.

The perspective that underlies this chapter is our belief in how students learn and how we can best help them achieve their full potential. This belief holds that student learning occurs within a system that is driven by task goals and has the ultimate objective of constructing high quality knowledge representations. The quality of a learner's self-regulation on a given task sets the student on a trajectory toward that goal. As educators, our potential lies in the possibility that we can alter this trajectory. We can realize this potential by identifying the leverage points within that system and using those leverage points to introduce tasks or strategies that positively alter learners' paths. In the end, it is this belief that motivates the CMDC. The principles and predictions we have offered here are intended to lay bare those leverage points and direct our collective work toward those points where we can have the greatest impact.

NOTE

1. Winne identifies four phases (Winne & Perry, 2000). Our model collapses the first two phases (i.e., defining the task and goal setting/planning) into the first phase.

REFERENCES

Ainsworth, S. (2006). Deft: A conceptual framework for considering learning with multiple representations. *Learning and Instruction, 16*(3), 183-198.

Ainsworth, S.E., Bibby, P.A., & Wood, D.J. (1998). Analyzing the costs and benefits of multi-representational learning environments. In M. W. van Someren, P. Reimann, H. P. A. Boshuizen, & T. de Jong (Eds.), *Learning with Multiple Representations* (pp. 120-134). Kidlington, Oxford, England: Elsevier Science.

Ainsworth, S.E., Bibby, P.A., & Wood, D.J. (2002). Examining the effects of different multiple representational systems in learning primary mathematics. *Journal of the Learning Sciences, 11*(1), 25-62.

Ainsworth, S., Galpin, J., & Musgrove, S., (2007, August). *Learning about dynamic systems by drawing for yourself and others.* Paper presented at the 12th Biennial Conference of the European Association for Research on Learning and Instruction, Budapest.

Ainsworth, S., & Iacovides, I. (2005, August). *Learning by constructing self-explanation diagrams.* Paper presented at the 11th Biennial Conference of the European Association for Research on Learning and Instruction, Nicosia, Cypress.

Alesandrini, K. L. (1981). Pictorial—verbal and analytic—holistic learning strategies in science learning. *Journal of Educational Psychology, 73*, 358-368.

Alesandrini, K. L. (1984). Pictures and adult learning. *Instructional Science, 13*, 63-77.

Azevedo, R. (2005). Using hypermedia as a metacognitive tool for enhancing student learning? The role of self-regulated learning. *Educational Psychologist, 40*(4), 199-209.

Azevedo, R., Cromley, J. G., & Seibert, D. (2004). Does adaptive scaffolding facilitate students' ability to regulate their learning with hypermedia? *Contemporary Educational Psychology, 29*(3), 344-370.

Bodemer, D., Ploetzner, R., Feuerlein, I., & Spada, H. (2004). The active integration of information during learning with dynamic and interactive visualizations. *Learning and Instruction, 14*(3), 325-341.

Carney, R. N., & Levin, J. R. (2002). Pictorial illustrations still improve students' learning from text. *Educational Psychology Review, 14*, 5-26.

Clark, J. M., & Paivio, A. (1991). Dual coding theory and education. *Educational Psychology Review, 3*, 149-210.

Cox, R. (1999). Representation construction, externalized cognition and individual differences. *Learning and Instruction, 9*, 343-363.

de Jong, T., Ainsworth, S., Dobson, M., van der Hulst, A., Levonen, J., Reimann, P. ... & Swaak, J. (1998). Acquiring knowledge in science and mathematics: The use of multiple representations in technology-based learning environments. In M. W. van Someren, P. Reimann, H. P. A. Boshuizen, & T. de Jong (Eds.), *Learning with multiple representations* (pp. 9-40). Kidlington, Oxford, Englad: Elsevier Science.

Dharmananda, J., & Kiewra, K. A. (2010). Helping students soar to success on computers: An investigation of the Soar study method for computer-based learning. *Journal of Educational Psychology, 102*(3), 601-614.

Firetto, C., & Van Meter, P. (August, 2011). *Effects of drawing and diagram selection on learning from multiple representations in biology.* Paper presented at the 14th biannual conference of the European Association for Research on Learning and Instruction, Exeter, England.

Gobert, J. D., & Clement, J. J. (1999). Effects of student-generated diagrams versus student generated summaries on conceptual understanding of causal and dynamic knowledge in plate tectonics. *Journal of Research in Science Teaching, 36*, 39-53.

Grossen, B., & Carnine, D. (1990). Diagramming a logic strategy: Effects on difficult problem types and transfer. *Learning Disability Quarterly, 13*, 168-182.

Hall, V. C., Bailey, J., & Tillman, C. (1997). Can student-generated illustrations be worth ten thousand words? *Journal of Educational Psychology, 89*, 677-681.

Kintsch, W. (1998). *Comprehension: A paradigm for cognition.* New York, NY: Cambridge University Press.

Kozma, R. B., & Russell, J. (1997). Multimedia and understanding: Expert and novice responses to different representations of chemical phenomena. *Journal of Research in Science Teaching, 34*(9), 949-968.

Lansing, K. M. (1981). The effect of drawing on the development of mental representations. *Studies in Art Education, 22*, 5-23.

Leopold, C., & Leutner, D. (2012). Science text comprehension: Drawing, main idea selection, and summarizing as learning strategies. *Learning and Instruction, 22*, 16-26.

Lesgold, A. M., Levin, J. R., Shimron, J., & Guttman, J. (1975). Pictures and young children's learning from oral prose. *Journal of Educational Psychology, 67*, 636-642.

Levin, J. R., & Mayer, R. E. (1993). Understanding illustrations in text. In B. K. Britton, A. Woodward, & M. R. Binkley (Eds.), *Learning from textbooks: Theory and practice* (pp. 95-113). Hillsdale, NJ: Erlbaum.

Leutner, D., Leopold, C., & Sumfleth, E. (2009). Cognitive load and science comprehension:Effects of drawing and mentally imagining text content. *Computers in Human Behavior, 25*, 284-289.

Mayer, R. E. (1993). Illustrations that instruct. In R. Glaser (Ed.), *Advances in Instructional Psychology* (pp. 253-284). Hillsdale, NJ: Erlbaum.

Mayer, R. E. (2005). Cognitive theory of multimedia learning. In R. E. Mayer (Ed.), *The Cambridge Handbook of Multimedia Learning* (pp. 31-48). New York, NY: Cambridge University Press.

Mayer, R. E., & Gallini, J. K. (1990). When is an illustration worth ten thousand words? *Journal of Educational Psychology, 82*(4), 715-26.

Mayer, R. E., & Moreno, R. (2002). Animation as an aid to multimedia learning. *Educational Psychology Review, 14,* 87-99.

Mayer, R. E., & Sims, V. K. (1994). For whom is a picture worth a thousand words?: Extensions of a dual-coding theory of multimedia learning. *Journal of Educational Psychology, 86*(3), 389-401.

Mayer, R. E., Steinhoff, K., Bower, G., & Mars, R. (1995). A generative theory of textbook design: Using learning of science text. *Educational. Technology Research and Development, 43,* 31-43.

McNamara, D. S., & Kintsch, W. (1996). Learning from texts: Effects of prior knowledge and text coherence. *Discourse Processes, 22*(3), 247-288.

Meyer, B. J. F., Wijekumar, K. K., & Lin, Y. (2011). Individualizing a web-based structure strategy intervention for fifth graders' comprehension of nonfiction. *Journal of Educational Psychology, 103*(1), 140-168.

Meyer, K., Rasch, T., & Schnotz, W. (2010). Effects of animation's speed of presentation on perceptual processing and learning. *Learning and Instruction, 20,* 136-145.

Nelson. T. O., & Narens, L. (1990). Metamemory: A theoretical framework and some new findings. In G. H. Bower (Ed.), *The psychology of learning and motivation* (Vol. 26, pp. 125-173). New York, NY: Academic Press.

Nelson, T. O., & Narens, L. (1994). Why investigate metacognition? In J. Metcalfe & A. Shimamura (Eds.), *Metacognition: Knowing about knowing* (pp. 1-25). Cambridge, MA: Bradford Books.

Paivio, A. (1986). *Mental representation: A dual-coding approach.* Oxford, England: Oxford University Press.

Rasch, T., & Schnotz, W. (2009). Interactive and non-interactive pictures in multimedia learning environments: Effects on learning outcomes and learning efficiency. *Learning and Instruction, 19*(5), 411-422.

Rasco, R. W., Tennyson, R. D., & Boutwell, R. C. (1975). Imagery instructions and drawings in learning prose. *Journal of Educational Psychology, 67,* 188-192.

Reason, J. A., (1990). *Human error.* New York, NY: Cambridge University Press.

Schnotz, W. (2002). Towards an integrated view of learning from text and visual displays. *Educational Psychology, 14,* 101-120.

Schnotz, W. (2005). An integrated model of text and picture comprehension. In R.E. Mayer (Ed.) *The Cambridge Handbook of Multimedia Learning* (pp. 49-69). New York, NY: Cambridge University Press.

Schnotz, W., & Bannert, M. (2003). Construction and interference in learning from multiple representation. *Learning and Instruction, 13,* 141-156.

Schraw, G., Crippen, K., & Hartley, K. (2006). Promoting self-regulation in science education: Metacognition as part of a broader perspective on learning. *Research in Science Education, 36*(1-2), 111-139.

Schwamborn, A., Mayer, R. E., Thillman, H., Leopold, C., & Leutner, D. (2010). Drawing as a generative activity and drawing as a prognostic activity. *Journal of Educational Psychology, 102*(4), 872-879.

Schwamborn, A., Thillman, H., Opfermann, M., & Leutner, D. (2011). Cognitive load and instructionally supported learning with provided and learner-generated visualizations. *Computers in Human Behavior, 27*, 89-93.

Seufert, T. (2003). Supporting coherence formation in learning from multiple representations. *Learning and Instruction, 13*(2), 227-237.

Seufert, T., & Brünken, R. (2006). Cognitive load and the format of instructional aids for coherence formation. *Applied Cognitive Psychology, 20*(3), 321-331.

Snowman, J., & Cunningham, D. J. (1975). A comparison of pictorial and written adjunct aids in learning from text. *Journal of Educational Psychology, 67*, 307-311.

Stylianou, D. A. (2011). An examination of middle school students' representation practices inn mathematical problem solving through the lens of expert work: Toward an organizing scheme. *Educational Studies in Mathematics, 76*(3), 265-280.

Tabachneck-Schijf, H.J.M., & Simon, H.A. (1998). One person, multiple representations: an analysis of a simple, realistic multiple representation learning task. In M. W. van Someren, P. Reimann, H. P. A. Boshuizen, & T. de Jong (Eds.), *Learning with Multiple Representations* (pp. 197-236). Kidlington, Oxford, England: Elsevier Science.

Tirre, W., Manelis, L., & Leicht, K. (1979). The effects of imaginal and verbal strategies on prose comprehension by adults. *Journal of Reading Behavior, 11*, 99-106.

Van Essen, G., & Hamaker, C. (1990). Using student-generated drawings to solve arithematic word problems. *Journal of Educational Research, 83*, 301-312.

Van Meter, P. (2001). Drawing construction as a strategy for learning from text. *Journal of Educational Psychology, 69*, 129-140.

Van Meter, P., Aleksic, M., Schwartz, A., & Garner J. (2006). Learner-generated drawing as a strategy for learning from content area text. *Contemporary Educational Psychology, 31*, 142-166.

Van Meter, P., & Garner, J. (2005). The promise and practice of learner-generated drawing: Literature review and synthesis. *Educational Psychology Review, 17*, 285-325.

Van Meter, P., & Riley, S. (1999). Writing and drawing: What do we gain with different representational formats? (pp. 146-156). In T. Shanahan & F. Rodriguez-Brown (Eds.), *47th Yearbook of the National Reading Conference*. Chicago, IL: National Reading Conference.

Waters, J. R., Van Meter, P., Perrotti, W., Drogo, S., & Cyr, R. (2005). Cat dissection vs. sculpting human structures in clay: An analysis of two approaches to undergraduate human anatomy laboratory education. *Advances in Physiology Education, 29*, 27-34.

Waters, J.R., Van Meter, P., Perrotti, W., Drogo, S., & Cyr, R. (2011). Human clay models versus cat dissection: How the similarity between the classroom and the exam affects student performance. *Advances in Physiology Education, 35*, 227-236.

Winne, P.H. (1995). Inherent details in self-regulated learning. *Educational Psychologist, 30*(4), 173-187.

Winne, P. H., & Hadwin, A. F. (1998). Studying as self-regulated learning. In D. J. Hacker., J. Dunlosky, & A. Graesser (Eds.), *Metacognition in educational theory and practice* (pp. 277-304). Hillsdale, NJ: Erlbaum.

Winne, P.H., & Perry, N.E. (2000). Measuring self-regulated learning. In M. Boekarts, P. Pintrich, & M. Zeidner (Eds.), *Handbook of self-regulation* (pp. 531-566). San Diego, CA: Academic Press.

Wittrock, M. C. (1974). Learning as a generative process. *Educational Psychologist, 1*(2), 87-95.

Wittrock, M. C. (1989). Generative processes of comprehension. *Educational Psychologist, 24*, 345-376.

Wittrock, M. C. (2010). Learning as a generative process. *Educational Psychologist, 45*(1), 40-45.

CHAPTER 11

GRAPHIC ORGANIZERS AS AIDS FOR STUDENTS WITH LEARNING DISABILITIES

Douglas D. Dexter and Charles A. Hughes

ABSTRACT

In this chapter we discuss the use of graphic organizers for teaching academic content with students identified as having a learning disability (LD). This topic is of growing importance as an increasing number of students with LD are spending the majority of their school day in general education content area classes (e.g., science, social studies, English) who are expected to perform at the same level as their nondisabled peers. We begin this discussion with a review of the theoretical underpinnings of why graphic organizers (GOs) can be effective when helping students understand and remember academic content and how existing theories lead to effective design and use of GOs. These theories are then linked to certain learning problems many students with LD have (e.g., working memory, linking prior knowledge with new information). Finally, we review published investigations examining the effectiveness of GOs with students with LD, most of which show them to be effective across a variety of content areas and for both near and far recall tasks. We conclude with instructional implications based on both theoretical and applied research.

Learning Through Visual Displays, pp. 281–302

All students face greater academic demands as they progress through intermediate and secondary grades in school. This is in part because content-area material becomes more complex and the curriculum is driven by higher-order skills and advanced concepts (Fletcher, Lyon, Fuchs, & Barnes, 2007). Students do not receive as much individual attention as in primary grades (Hughes, Maccini, & Gagnon, 2003) and are often required to learn primarily through didactic lecture and expository text presentation (Gajria, Jitendra, Sood, & Sacks, 2007; Minskoff & Allsopp, 2003). This shift in learning presentation, abundant with abstract concepts, unfamiliar content, and technical vocabulary (Armbruster, 1984), may seem daunting to most students, but is especially so to students with learning disabilities (LD).

Students with LD often have difficulty with basic academic skills (e.g., reading) and organizational/study skills (Deshler, Ellis, & Lenz, 1996). Specifically, students with LD generally have difficulty connecting new material to prior knowledge, identifying and ignoring extraneous information, identifying main ideas and supporting details, drawing inferences, and creating efficient problem-solving strategies (Baumann, 1984; Dexter & Hughes, 2011; Holmes, 1985; Kim, Vaughn, Wanzek, & Wei, 2004; Johnson, Graham, & Harris, 1997; Williams, 1993). Because many textbooks are written at or above grade level reading ability and lack organizational clarity (Gajria et al., 2007), these learning difficulties make interpreting and comprehending expository text especially challenging (Bryant, Ugel, Thompson, & Hamff, 1999). Students with LD need explicit content enhancements to assist in verbal (e.g., text or lecture) comprehension and graphic organizers (GOs) have often been recommended as an instructional device to assist these students in understanding increasingly abstract concepts (Bos & Vaughn, 2002; Dexter, 2010; Dexter & Hughes, 2011; Hughes et al., 2003; Ives & Hoy, 2003; Kim et al., 2004; Nesbit & Adesope, 2006; Rivera & Smith, 1997).

WHAT ARE GRAPHIC ORGANIZERS?

GOs are intended to promote more meaningful learning and facilitate understanding and retention of new material by making abstract concepts more concrete and connecting new information with prior knowledge (Ausubel, 1968; Mayer, 1979). GOs are visual displays that present concepts or facts spatially, in a computationally efficient manner. That is, relationships between concepts are made apparent and clear by their location on the display (Hughes et al., 2003; Kim et al., 2004; Gajria et al., 2007). GOs can be used before, during, and/or after a student attends to verbal (e.g., text or lecture) stimuli (Nesbit & Adesope, 2006) and, according to Hughes et al., facts or concepts are typically presented in one of five ways: temporal (e.g., timeline), spatial (e.g., decision tree), sequential (e.g., flowchart), hierarchal (e.g., taxonomy), or comparative (e.g., Venn diagram). The choice of visual display is based upon the underlying verbal structure of the material to be learned (cf. Schraw & Paik, this volume). For instance, if the underlying text structure of a passage is comparing and contrasting two or more concepts, a comparative visual display would be utilized.

In this chapter, we will examine the theoretical framework underpinning why GOs may aid students with LD and discuss the relevant research with this population. Furthermore, through a cognitive processing perspective, we will discuss why visual displays affect learning of students with LD in such a positive way.

THEORETICAL FRAMEWORK

The research reported within this chapter draws primarily from four theories. The theory of subsumption (Ausubel, 1960) and assimilation theory (Mayer, 1979) offer direct implications about the possible benefits of GOs in learning by providing the basis for *how* GOs are able to help facilitate understanding of unfamiliar material and clarify relationships between abstract concepts. The visual argument hypothesis (Waller, 1981) and dual coding theory (Paivio, 1971) offer direct implications to the best design of effective GOs.

Why GOs May Benefit Learners

Theory of subsumption. GOs, as they are recognized today, are descended from Ausubel's (1960) theory of subsumption. Subsumption is a process in which new material is related to relevant ideas in the existing cognitive structure. The theory contains two fundamental principles: (1) the most general ideas of a subject should be presented first and then progressively differentiated in terms of detail and specificity; and (2) instructional materials should attempt to integrate new material with previously presented information through comparisons and cross-referencing of new and old ideas (Ausubel, 1968). To aid in subsumption, Ausubel advocated the use of GOs in the classroom. According to the theory, a GO presented in advance of a lesson may help incorporate and facilitate longevity of newly learned material within the cognitive structure. The GO aids retrieval of relevant prior knowledge, provides a framework for the addition of new material, and in doing so makes new information easier to understand and remember. It is important to note that Ausubel (1960) emphasized that GOs presented in advance of a lesson are different from overviews and summaries, which simply emphasize key ideas and are presented at the same level of abstraction and generality as the rest of the material. Advance GOs act as a subsuming bridge between new learning material and existing related ideas (Ausubel, 1960). An example of this kind of GO is shown in Figure 11.1. Here, the reader links new material (e.g., Hinduism) with previously learned material (e.g., Buddhism). In this example, very general ideas of the two religions (e.g., country of origin, deities, etc.) are compared and other broad similarities (e.g., belief in reincarnation, etc.) between the new and old concepts are stated. According to the theory of subsumption, this type of GO would provide a better framework for learning about Hinduism than would a nonorganizing historical introduction to the religion (Mayer, 1979).

Assimilation theory. Mayer (1979) built his assimilation theory using similar principles to the theory of subsumption. According to the assimilation theory, new information is added to the cognitive structure via (a) reception (e.g., new information is received into working memory), (b) availability (e.g., anchoring knowledge is available in long-term memory), and (c) activation (e.g., anchoring knowledge is transferred from long-term

	Previously Learned: **Buddhism**	New Material: **Hinduism**
Country of Origin:	India	India
Deity(ies):	None	Brahma, Vishnu, and Shiva
Founder(s):	Siddhartha Guatama, who later became Buddha	Unknown
Sacred Books:	None, verbal tradition	Upanishads, Vedaas, Puranas
Leadership:	Buddhist monks and nuns	Guru, Holy Man, Brahman Priests
Main Belief(s):	Nirvana is reached by following the Eight Fold Path and Four Noble Truths	Freedom from earthly desires comes from a lifetime of worship, knowledge, and virtuous acts

Similarities

–Belief in reincarnation, or the rebirth of the soul

–Happiness is achieved by eliminating all attachments to world and earthly things

–Provide explanation for the meaning of life and how to reach happiness for all eternity

Figure 11.1. Example of Subsumption

memory to working memory so that it can be actively integrated with received information). For example, when a student in geography class is learning the customs of another country, she must first process the new material through lecture or text (reception), think of similar customs in her own country (availability), and compare/contrast the new customs with those of which she is familiar (activation). Mayer surmises there are at least three sources of why GOs succeed or fail in influencing availability and activation: the material, the GO itself, and the learner. First, the material must contain a systematic overall structure. For example, a comparison of types of governments would afford an overall structure of similarities and differences, whereas if new material were a collection of isolated facts (e.g., Greek alphabet), a GO would fail because there is no inherent relationship (e.g., hierarchical, comparative, sequential, etc.) in the material. Second, the GO must provide an assimilative context to be useful. There should be a direct and explicit linkage between the content and the GO. For example, a teacher using a GO to illustrate the steps in an assembly line for making a shirt as an introduction to an industrial revolution unit must make that clear to her students. If learners do not realize the GO is related to the subsequent lesson, it is of no use. Finally, if learners lack prior knowledge, then GOs can be useful, whereas if the learner himself already possesses a plethora of past experience and knowledge, GOs may be of little or no use. Mayer, echoing Ausubel, states, "professionals and high-ability learners may not need organizers while novices and low ability learners do" (p. 376).

Discussion and implications for students with LD. The research findings of both the theory of subsumption and assimilation theory appear to have specific implications for students with LD, although neither theory focused on this group of students. Specifically, students with LD may benefit more from GOs than their nondisabled peers. A consistent pattern that emerged from the research on these theories is that students displaying lower verbal ability demonstrated larger gains than did students with average or high verbal ability, and these gains helped the students with lower verbal ability match the scores of peers with average verbal ability. As addressed earlier, students with LD typically have low verbal ability (Kim et al., 2004) that often manifests itself as difficulty in connecting new material to prior knowledge (Williams, 1993). This is because, according to Mayer (1979), the specific structure of a GO may guide construction of cognitive structures in less knowledgeable students, but may conflict with preexisting cognitive structures in more knowledgeable students. Several research groups have replicated the finding that low-ability learners gain more knowledge than average or high-ability learners from GOs (Moyer, Sowder, Threadgill-Sowder, & Moyer, 1984; Patterson, Dansereau, & Wiegmann, 1993; Stensvold & Wilson, 1990). O'Donnell, Dansereau, and

Hall (2002) posit that low ability learners gain their benefits because they can more easily understand and construct GOs than they can understand and write expository text. GOs may also offer a relatively consistent and simple syntax, making them easier to comprehend than textbooks or lecture (Amer, 1994). These ideas are all consistent with recommended content enhancements for students with LD (Deshler et al., 1996).

Students with LD also typically perform poorly on far-transfer tasks (e.g., applying knowledge to new or unusual situations) due to their inability to detect underlying concepts in verbal information (Suritsky & Hughes, 1991). Based on the above theories, this may be due to difficulty assimilating verbal information with previous knowledge. The research evidence of the assimilation theory suggests GOs may be a bridge for connecting verbal information with prior knowledge. This may dramatically assist students with LD in far-transfer tasks.

There is also some evidence that GOs may reduce the cognitive load handled in the working memory (Passolunghi & Siegel, 2004). Because GOs are a permanent product and present information in an abbreviated form compared to text or lecture, important concepts are more easily assimilated with prior knowledge in long-term memory (Hughes et al., 2003). This could help explain Mayer's (1979) findings in regard to far-transfer and near-transfer items. Students in the treatment group may have more fully realized the underlying concepts while the control group may have relied on rote memorization.

There appears to be a link between the underlying theories of GOs and students with LD. In fact, students with LD may benefit more than the average student from GOs. What these theories do not suggest is how to design GOs for maximum impact with these students. This is the theoretical base explored next.

Best Design for GOs

Two theories, visual argument hypothesis (Waller, 1981) and dual coding theory (Paivio, 1971), offer insight into the most effective and efficient design of GOs by forming the theoretical perspectives that explain the role of graphics in learning. Both of these overlapping theories describe how learners process information. Table 11.1 provides an overview of the two theories.

The main idea of each of the theories is that the presentation of graphics (e.g., GOs) has an additive effect on learning because, according to Vekiri (2002), "visual information is represented separately from verbal information in long-term memory" (p. 262).

Table 11.1   Comparison of Visual Argument and Dual-Coding

Theory	Assumptions	Design Principles
Visual Argument	1. Relationships among objects/concepts are apparent by their location in two-dimensional space.	• Static, two-dimensional representations spatially encoded • Can be used before, during, or after lesson • Minimizes cognitive processing and allows viewers to perceive relations or data patterns using visual perception.
Dual-Coding	1. Two separate, but interconnected, cognitive subsystems for verbal and visual information. 2. Verbal and visual information presented at the same time bolsters encoding.	• GOs should address goal of task and make target information apparent • GOs not effective without guiding explanations • GOs should be spatially and timely coordinated to minimize cognitive load • Explanations more effective when provided in auditory fashion

Visual argument hypothesis. Visual argument was first theorized by Waller (1981) to help explain the process by which graphics convey information. According to Vekiri (2002), the visual argument hypothesis is based on the idea that the visuospatial properties of graphics require fewer cognitive transformations (e.g., untangling implicit information to make it explicit) than does text-processing resulting in less load on working memory. Further, not only individual elements of GOs, but also the spatial arrangement of the individual elements can help facilitate learning. Larkin and Simon (1987) termed this effect *perceptual enhancement*, the ability of graphics to convey an overarching concept as well as demonstrate relationships between individual concepts. Thus, graphics could promote a cognitively easier way to perceive and make inferences about relationships among concepts than text (Robinson & Kierwa, 1995; Vekiri, 2002; Winn, 1991).

GOs developed using visual argument components use the "relative location of objects in two-dimensional space to communicate relations among those objects" (Robinson & Schraw, 1994, p. 401). For example, a tree diagram communicates hierarchical relationships by grouping smaller, related concepts under a larger, broad concept. This type of GO streamlines the process of inferring relationships between concepts. Without the tree diagram, a student would have to search through text to find a fact, retain that fact in working memory, and search for subsequent facts within the text before making an inference (Robinson & Schraw, 1994). Thus, through visual argument, students can make important inferences with much less cognitive effort (Vekiri, 2002; Winn, 1991). This apparent efficiency is echoed in the work of Larkin and Simon (1987), who concluded GOs developed using visual argument are superior to verbal descriptions in two important ways: (1) decreases search time for elements needed in making an inference; and (2) spatial arrangement of single elements eliminates the need to match symbolic labels (p. 98). For example, by viewing the GO in Figure 10.2, one can learn that Old English Sheepdogs, German Shepherds, and Australian Cattle dogs are all in the herding group. This hierarchical concept relation is communicated by locating the names of the three subordinate concepts below the name of the superordinate concept (herding group). One may also learn by viewing Figure 10.2 that the German Shepherd is the heaviest of the three dogs. This coordinated concept relation is communicated by locating the comparative attributes (e.g., weight) in a single row. The GOs spatial arrangement may help students locate coordinating concepts more quickly (Robinson & Skinner, 1996) and with less effort (Robinson & Schraw, 1994) than if viewed linearly in text or in an outline.

In summary, GOs designed using visual argument attributes can be processed in a more efficient manner than text. This supports better cognition in complex tasks (Vekiri, 2002). Not only can GOs demonstrate relationships between concepts without overloading the working memory, they can serve as memory aids, guide thinking, and help facilitate better problem-solving techniques (Larkin & Simon, 1987).

Dual-coding theory. The dual-coding theory (DCT), developed by Allan Paivio in 1971 and subsequently updated (e.g., Paivio, 1986, 1991, 2007; Sadoski & Paivio, 2001), is based on the assumption that cognition "involves the activity of two distinct cognitive subsystems, a verbal system specialized for dealing directly with language and a nonverbal system specialized for

Herding Group			
	Old English Sheepdog	*German Shepherd*	*Australian Cattle Dog*
Weight	65 lbs.	77-85 lbs.	32-35 lbs.
Height	22-24 inches	22-26 inches	17-20 inches
Temperament	Intelligent, friendly, docile	Confident, direct, approachable	Loyal, alert, courageous
Country of Origin	England	Germany	Australia

Figure 11.2   Visual argument

dealing with nonlinguistic objects and events" (Paivio, 2007, p. 13). Although these systems are both functionally and structurally independent, they are interconnected in the tasks of processing and storing information. For example, a person can associate the word "coat" with a picture of a coat, and when hearing the word coat, elicit a mental image of a coat. Thus, associative connections are formed between verbal and visual representations (Vekiri, 2002). Based on this theory, GOs can greatly benefit encoding of new information by presenting visual and verbal information concurrently.

Clark and Paivio (1991) offer two direct implications of DCT on educational outcomes. Specifically, the role concreteness, imagery, and verbal associative processes play for comprehension of knowledge and learning and memory of school material. First, the researchers claim illustrations and other visual stimuli may improve recall of verbal information (e.g., lecture or text) by "enabling students to store the same material in two forms of memory representations, linguistic and visual" (Vekiri, 2002, p. 267). According to Clark and Paivio, when verbal and visual information is presented at the same time, learners form associations between both types of material during encoding. Thus, learners may have more paths to retrieve information because subsequent verbal information may activate both linguistic and visual representations. In an applied setting, this means illustrations in text and lectures may foster greater retention because learners have two ways to encode material (Vekiri, 2002).

Second, the researchers claim learners are more likely to recall concrete over abstract information (Clark & Paivio. 1991; Paivio, 1991; Paivio, 2007). In several research studies (e.g., Paivio, 1966, 1975; Paivio, Yuille, & Madigan, 1968), Paivio and colleagues found concrete words more easily evoked a mental image than abstract words. Further, the researchers found a strong, positive correlation between mental imagery and text comprehension. According to Paivio (2007), recent work in neuroscience and brain imagery (e.g., Thompson & Kosslyn, 2000) supports DCT in that different sections of the brain are utilized during verbal encoding and visual encoding. From an applied standpoint, use of visual displays may increase the concreteness of instruction when material is abstract; and, providing a multitude of visual stimuli may bolster learners' mental representations and increase their capacity to retain abstract information (Clark & Paivio, 1991; Vekiri, 2002).

In summary, according to the DCT, GOs or other graphical displays can help facilitate learning by allowing learners to store information in two separate, but interconnected forms of memory. Also, by making abstract verbal information more concrete through visual representations, more learning may occur.

Discussion and implications for students with LD. According to both of these hypotheses, the presence of GOs along with other verbal information (e.g., text or lecture) has additive effects on learning because visual information is represented separately from verbal information in long-term memory (Vekiri, 2002). However, Larkin and Simon (1987) concluded only easily understandable displays are effective for learning. Based on research published since Larkin and Simon's seminal work, researchers have found patterns in visual argument and dual coding that support specific design principles that may achieve computational efficiency. A general principle supported by both theoretical perspectives is that GOs are effective when they address the limitations of working memory in their design. This is consistent with the work of Swanson and Kim (2007) who found students with LD performed significantly better on problem-solving tasks when the demand placed on the working memory was minimized. This principle is shown in each of the three design points below:

1. GOs are computationally efficient when they minimize the processing required for their interpretation. GOs are most efficient when their interpretation relies more on visual perception because visual perception is carried out automatically without imposing heavy cognitive load (Vekiri, 2002). This lends itself to designing GOs based on Gestalt principles (e.g., proximity and connectedness). For example, when individual pieces of important information are spatially grouped together or connected (e.g., concepts on a GO), readers are likely to perceive them as being interrelated and to draw perceptual inferences about their relationships instead of engaging in further computations (Vekiri, 2002).

2. When material is presented in multiple sources (e.g., text and GOs) cognitive processing is demanding because learners must simultaneously attend to each source and integrate their information. As a result of limitations of the working memory, this could result in students failing to integrate material from various sources coherently and negate any possible advantage of the GO. Therefore, GOs can best facilitate cognitive processing if: (a) various sources of information are presented simultaneously and are spatially close (Moreno & Mayer, 1999); (b) information is presented in different modalities, so that, according to dual coding, it is processed by different cognitive systems without overloading working memory (Moreno & Mayer, 1999). This could be accomplished by verbal information being provided in the form of auditory narration and processed by the verbal system. The GO would be processed by the visual system; and (c) GOs are not clustered with a lot of information; readers can easily perceive the phenomena or relations that are important (Vekiri, 2002).

3. When geographic or concept maps are used as reference materials to facilitate learning from text or lecture, their effectiveness is maximized when they are provided before or concurrently with the text or lecture (Vekiri, 2002), other types of GOs (e.g., sequential, hierarchical, temporal, comparative, etc.) are effective before, during, or after a lesson (Amer, 1994).

For students with LD, the design of effective and efficient GOs is paramount. In addition to the above principles for GO design, two other principles seem to have special meaning for students with LD: (1) it has been suggested that students with little prior knowledge or below-average verbal ability may not know what elements in the GO are important to attend to and consequently process information at a superficial level (Vekiri, 2002). To assist these learners, GOs need to be accompanied by explanations (e.g., labels or notes embedded in the GO) that may better cue learners to the most important graphical elements and details; and (2) each line of research for the three design theories also suggests GOs should be explicitly and directly taught (e.g., conventions of the GO) to the learners when possible. This is especially the case for students with LD, as direct instruction has consistently proven superior to other teaching methodologies (Adams & Carnine, 2003; Archer & Hughes, 2011).

RESEARCH ON GRAPHIC ORGANIZERS WITH STUDENTS WITH LD

Several research syntheses (e.g., Gajria et al., 2007; Kim et al., 2004; Moore & Readence, 1984), have reported that GOs improve the factual comprehension of upper elementary, intermediate, and secondary students with LD. Using these syntheses as a starting point, we conducted a comprehensive meta-analysis of research studies examining GOs with secondary students with LD (Dexter & Hughes, 2011). We were not only interested in factual comprehension, but also vocabulary and inference/relational comprehension, near- and far-transfer measures, and maintenance effects for students with LD.

Overall, we found a large mean effect for posttest performance ($ES = .91$, $SE = .06$) of students with LD using both a fixed effects and random effects model. The immediate posttest performance spanned multiple constructs including multiple-choice factual comprehension, vocabulary, and written recall requiring relational comprehension. This suggests that GOs are effective in not only improving basic skills (e.g., factual recall), but also higher-level skills (e.g., inference). This finding is consistent with the theories of Ausubel (1968) and Mayer (1979) that GOs may especially assist lower ability learners in both basic and higher level skills by creating an easier context to assimilate information into their memory.

There was a moderate mean effect for maintenance ($ES = .56$, $SE = .07$) of students with LD. The significant drop-off from posttest to maintenance is consistent with the other GO research syntheses. The reasoning for the drop has been attributed to lack of clarity in the duration and length of intervention sessions needed to positively affect maintenance (Gajria et al., 2007; Gersten, Fuchs, Williams, & Baker, 2001). The relatively short duration of the intervention studies (e.g., 1-7 weeks) may not have provided sufficient instruction time for students to use GOs independently. However, a component analysis revealed that visual displays with the most computationally efficient designs (e.g., simple enough for students to recognize conceptual relationships without teacher instruction) had larger effects for maintenance than posttest. This may lend support to the visual argument hypothesis (Waller, 1981) that posits GOs that are structured in a way that easily facilitate understanding and perception of concept relationships are superior to more complicated GOs that may require instruction to recognize conceptual relationships (Dexter, 2010).

Our meta-analysis also separated results into near-transfer and far-transfer measures. Near-transfer results (i.e., measures applying knowledge to situations directly covered in the text or lecture) from the analysis indicated that GOs were effective strategies for improving factual recall, factual and relational comprehension, and vocabulary knowledge. Across all near-transfer studies, the mean effect size was large ($ES = 1.07$) and maintenance effects were moderate ($ES = .78$). Students using GOs significantly outperformed their peers receiving typical classroom instruction on near-transfer measures. Interestingly, more complicated GOs requiring intensive teacher instruction resulted in the largest effects for near-transfer posttest measures. This indicates that while these GOs are difficult to understand independently, with appropriate instruction they are superior to less complicated GOs for immediate factual recall.

Far-transfer results (i.e., measures applying knowledge to situations not directly covered in the text or lecture) from this analysis indicate that GOs may also improve inference skills and relational knowledge for secondary students with LD. Across all far-transfer studies, the mean effect size was moderate ($ES = .61$) and maintenance effects were moderate ($ES = .69$). It is interesting to note that for far-transfer measure maintenance effect sizes were larger than posttest effect sizes. Previous research has indicated students with LD typically perform poorly on far-transfer tasks due to their inability to detect underlying concepts in verbal information due to difficulty assimilating verbal information with previous knowledge (Suritsky & Hughes, 1991). This analysis demonstrates that GOs may bridge the connection of verbal information with prior knowledge and assisting students with LD in far-transfer tasks. This finding supports Mayer's (1979) assimilation theory, which posits GOs that assimilate material to a broader set of past experiences allows superior transfer to new situations. This finding is also consistent with the research of Robinson and colleagues (Robinson, Katayama, DuBois, & Devaney, 1998; Robinson & Kiewra, 1995; Robinson & Schraw, 1994; Robinson & Skinner, 1996), comparing visual displays (e.g., tree diagrams, matrices, network charts) with traditional, nongraphic outlines. In each of the studies, groups of nondisabled college students using GOs and traditional outlines equally outperformed text-only groups in factual recall, but the GO groups significantly outperformed the outline and text-only groups in identifying concept relations and making far-transfer concept comparisons.

Based on our meta-analysis, the major implication for applied practice is, consistent with assimilation theory and the visual argument hypothesis; more instructionally intensive types of GOs are better for immediate factual recall while more computationally efficient GOs are better for maintenance and transfer. This knowledge can help teachers in designing GOs for initial instruction and for reteaching, studying, and retention purposes. For instance, an instructionally intensive GO for initial instruction, followed by a simpler visual display for review and study may potentially maximize the effects of recall, maintenance, and far-transfer for students with LD.

We tested these implications in a research study with several seventh grade social studies classes (Dexter, 2011). We used a semantic mapping activity as our "instructionally intensive" GO. Semantic mapping is a heuristic that enables students to recognize relevant information from lecture and text (e.g., main ideas, important supporting details) and organize that information for written or oral retell (Washington, 1988). In semantic mapping, students and/or the teacher create a visual representation of new or difficult vocabulary and any relationships existing among the different vocabulary (Bos & Anders, 1992). In addition, when teaching this type of GO, a teacher presents critical attributes of a concept along with examples and nonexamples to help promote student discrimination and generalization (Deshler et al., 1996). An example of a completed semantic map from this study is presented in Figure 10.3. A hierarchical chart was used for the visual display and can be found in Figure 10.4.

Based on the review of theory and meta-analysis of studies of GOs, both the experimental (semantic mapping + visual display) and control group (semantic mapping only) of students with LD and low achieving students should demonstrate a large effect between pretest and posttest. However, the semantic mapping + visual display condition should perform significantly higher on tests of maintenance and far transfer.

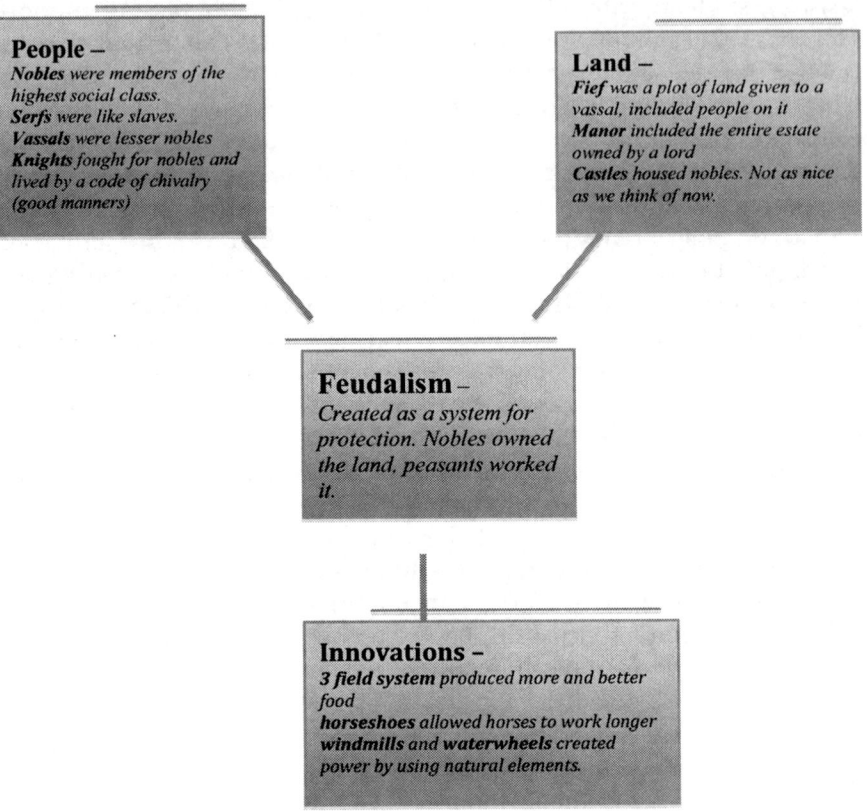

Figure 11.3.   Completed semantic map.

The results of this study supported the conclusion that semantic mapping was beneficial for factual recall, while the additive effect of a visual display significantly improved maintenance and far transfer for adolescents with LD. Results of this study also supported the conclusion that normally achieving students and low achieving students also benefit from semantic mapping and the visual display. This finding was consistent for both short-answer and multiple-choice measures.

CONCLUSION

Based on the research examining both the benefits of GOs and the effective design of GOs, as well as our own analysis and research, several key

Feudalism Hierarchy

Nobles
Kings and queens; only 10% of population
Lived in cold, drafty castles

Knights
sons of nobles;
3 stages to become a Knight =
1. Page (learned chivalry),
2. Squire (learned to ride and fight),
3. Knight

Vassals
lesser nobles;
granted fief (land) for promise to fight for the nobles

Peasants
limited rights;
could operate private business

Serfs
slaves; no rights

Figure 11.4.   Visual display.

findings are consistently replicated and may offer direct implications for applied practice. First, in general, (a) students with low verbal ability gain more from GOs than students with high verbal ability; (b) students with little or no prior knowledge in a subject gain more from GOs than students with an abundance of prior knowledge in a subject; (c) GOs are especially helpful in assisting students with far-transfer tasks in addition to near transfer tasks and factual recall; and d) GOs are effective because of their computational efficiency, which minimizes stress on the working memory.

These conclusions offer explanations for why GOs are beneficial for students with LD. Students with LD often have lower verbal ability (Deshler et al., 1996) and have difficulty connecting new material to prior knowledge (Kim et al., 2004). In addition, students with LD typically struggle with far-transfer tasks (e.g., drawing inferences; Gajria et al., 2007) and identifying and ignoring extraneous information (Johnson et al., 1997), which can strain the working memory (Bryant et al., 1999). Thus, from a cognitive psychology perspective, GOs seem to be tailor-made to assist with common difficulties shared by students with LD.

From an applied standpoint, it is crucial that teachers choose GOs based on the appropriate function, encoding or retrieval. These processes are how information is moved from short-term memory to long-term memory (e.g., encoding) or vice versa (e.g., retrieval). In the case of encoding, new information is assimilated into existing cognitive structures. Use of instructionally intensive GOs (e.g., semantic mapping) may assist with encoding. In this way, teachers can ensure only the most important and accurate information is encoded by students. As many students with LD have difficulty cuing up prior knowledge or experiences, the instructionally intensive aspect of these GOs should facilitate better encoding than by the student alone. Once students have a knowledge base in a subject, it is vital that students have efficient methods to retrieve that knowledge. Retrieval involves drawing information from the long-term memory to the short-term memory. Use of computationally efficient GOs (e.g., visual displays) may assist with retrieval. GOs that are easy to understand independently will help students review and retrieve information without the need of constant teacher supervision. From the aforementioned research, there is also evidence these types of GOs help maintain retrieval capacity for longer amounts of time than text or lecture alone.

Finally, we offer four suggestions to better facilitate the improvements described above in terms of design and delivery:

(a) GOs should be explicitly taught to students for maximum impact. Students with LD need explicit instruction to understand how concepts are related, to recognize differences between main and subordinate ideas, and to put all the pieces together to make a clear picture of the content being learned no matter how implicit a GO may seem. A teacher's use of effective instruction practices (e.g., modeling, corrective feedback, etc.) will positively impact the organizer's effectiveness.

(b) GOs should spatially group together or connect concepts so readers are more likely to perceive them as being interrelated and to draw perceptual inferences about their relationships. This will help students decrease further cognitive computations and reduce stress to the working memory.

(c) GOs should not be clustered with a lot of information; readers should easily perceive the phenomena or relations that are important. This is also known as "cutting the fluff." Eliminating nonessential information will help students focus on the biggest ideas from a lesson.

(d) GOs can be effective when used before, during, or after a lesson. Using a GO prior to a lesson can help orient the students to the material to be learned and cue up prior knowledge or experience. GOs can also be useful for note-taking during a lesson and for review of critical information after a lesson.

REFERENCES

Adams, G., & Carnine, D. (2003). Direct instruction. In H. L. Swanson, K. R. Harris, & S. Graham (Eds.), *Handbook of Learning Disabilities* (pp. 403-416). New York, NY: Guilford Press.

Archer, A. L., & Hughes, C. A. (2011). *Explicit instruction: Effective and efficient teaching.* New York, NY: Guilford.

Amer, A. A. (1994). The effect of knowledge-map and underlining training on the reading comprehension of scientific texts. *English for Specific Purposes, 13*, 35-45.

Armbruster, B. B. (1984). The problems of "inconsiderate" text. In G. G. Duffy, L. R. Roehler, & J. M. Mason (Eds.), *Comprehension instruction: Perspectives and suggestions* (pp. 202-217). New York, NY: Longman.

Atkinson, R. K., Levin, J. R., Kierwa, K. A., Meyers, T., Kim, S. I., Atkinson, L. A., Renandya, W. A., & Hwang, Y. (1999). Matrix and mnemonic text processing adjuncts: Comparing and combining their components. *Journal of Educational Psychology, 91*, 342-357.

Ausubel, D. P. (1960). The use of advanced organizers in learning and retention of meaningful material. *Journal of Educational Psychology, 51*, 267-272.

Ausubel, D.P. (1968). *Educational Psychology: A Cognitive View.* New York, NY: Holt, Rinehart, & Winston.

Ausubel, D. P., & Fitzgerald, D. (1961). The role of discriminability in meaningful verbal learning and retention. *Journal of Educational Psychology, 52*, 266-274.

Ausubel, D. P., & Fitzgerald, D. (1962). Organizer, general background and antecedent learning variables in sequential verbal learning. *Journal of Educational Psychology, 53*, 243-249.

Ausubel, D. P., & Youssef, M. (1963). Role of discriminability in meaningful parallel learning. *Journal of Educational Psychology, 54*, 331-336.

Baumann, J.F. (1984). The effectiveness of a direct instruction paradigm for teaching main idea comprehension. *Reading Research Quarterly, 20*, 93-115.

Bos, C. S., & Vaughn, S. (2002). *Strategies for teaching students with learning and behavior problems* (5th ed.). Boston, MA: Allyn & Bacon.

Bryant, D. P., Ugel, N., Thompson, S., & Hamff, A. (1999). Instructional strategies for content-area reading instruction. *Intervention in School and Clinic, 34*, 293-302.

Clark, J. M., & Paivio, A. (1991). Dual coding theory and education. *Educational Psychology Review, 3*, 149-210.

Cox, R. (1999). Representation construction, externalized cognition, and individual differences. *Learning and Instruction, 9*, 343-363.

Deshler, D. D., Ellis, E., & Lenz, B. K. (1996). *Teaching adolescents with learning disabilities: Strategies and methods.* Denver, CO: Love.

Dexter, D. D. (2010). Graphic organizers and their effectiveness for students with learning disabilities. *Thalamus, 26*, 51-67.

Dexter, D. D. (2011, April). *Graphic organizers and students with LD: Accessing intermediate and secondary content-area material.* Paper presented at the International Council for Exceptional Children Conference, National Harbor, MD.

Dexter, D. D., & Hughes, C. A. (2011). Graphic organizers and students with learning disabilities: A meta-analysis. *Learning Disability Quarterly, 34*, 51-72.

Ennis, R. H. (1997). Incorporating critical thinking in the curriculum: An introduction to some basic issues. *Inquiry, 16*, 1-9.

Fletcher, J. M., Lyon, G. R., Fuchs, L. S., & Barnes, M. A. (2007). *Learning disabilities: From identification to intervention.* New York, NY: The Guilford Press.

Gajria, M., Jitendra, A. K., Sood, S., Sacks, G. (2007). Improving comprehension of expository text in students with LD: A research synthesis. *Journal of Learning Disabilities, 40*, 210-225.

Gersten, R., Fuchs, L. S., Compton, D., Coyne, M., Greenwood, C., Innocenti, M. S. (2005). Quality indicators for group experimental and quasi-experimental research in special education. *Exceptional Children, 71*, 149-164.

Gersten, R., Fuchs, L.S., Williams, J.P., & Baker, S. (2001). Teaching reading comprehension strategies to students with learning disabilities: A review of research. *Review of Educational Research, 71*, 279-320.

Griffin, M. M., & Robinson, D. H. (2005). Does spatial or visual information in maps facilitate text recall? Reconsidering the conjoint retention hypothesis. *Educational Technology Research and Development, 53*, 23-36.

Holmes, B. C. (1985). The effects of a strategy and sequenced material on the inferential comprehension of disabled readers. *Journal of Learning Disabilities, 18*, 542 -546.

Hughes, C. A., & Archer, A. (in press). *Teaching students with learning difficulties: Effective and explicit instruction.* New York, NY: Guilford Press.

Hughes, C. A., Maccini, P., & Gagnon, J. C. (2003). Interventions that positively impact the performance of students with learning disabilities in secondary general education classes. *Learning Disabilities, 12*, 101-111.

Ives, B., & Hoy, C. (2003). Graphic organizers applied to higher-level secondary mathematics. *Learning Disabilities Research & Practice, 18*, 36-51.

Johnson, L., Graham, S., & Harris, K. R. (1997). The effects of goal setting and self-instructions on learning a reading comprehension strategy: A study with students with learning disabilities. *Journal of Learning Disabilities, 30*, 80-91.

Kim, A., Vaughn, S., Wanzek, J., Wei, S. (2004). Graphic organizers and their effects on the reading comprehension of students with LD: A synthesis of research. *Journal of Learning Disabilities, 37*, 105-118.

Krumboltz, J. D., & Nichols, C. W. (1990). Integrating the social learning theory of career decision making. In W. B. Walsh & S. H. Osipow (Eds.), *Career counseling: contemporary topics in vocational psychology* (pp. 159-192). Mahwah, NJ: Lawrence Erlbaum Associates.

Kulhavy, R. W., Lee, B. J., & Caterino, L. C. (1985). Conjoint retention of maps and related discourse. *Contemporary Educational Psychology, 10*, 28-37.

Kulhavy, R. W., Stock, W. A., & Caterino, L. C. (1994). Reference maps as a framework for remembering text. In W. Schnotz & R. W. Kulhavy (Eds.), *Comprehension of Graphics* (pp. 153-162). New York, NY: Elsevier Science.

Kulhavy, R. W., Stock, W. A., & Kealy, W. A. (1993a). How geographic maps increase recall of instructional text. *Educational Technology Research and Development, 41*, 47-62.

Kulhavy, R. W., Stock, W. A., Peterson, S. E., Pridemore, D. R., & Klein, J. D. (1992). Using maps to retrieve text: A test of conjoint retention. *Contemporary Educational Psychology, 17*, 56-70.

Kulhavy, R. W., Woodard, K. A., Haygood, R. C., & Webb, J. M. (1993c). Using maps to remember text: An instructional analysis. *British Journal of Educational Psychology, 63*, 161-169.

Larkin, J. H., & Simon, H. A. (1987). Why a diagram is (sometimes) worth ten thousand words. *Cognitive Science, 11*, 65-99.

Mayer, R. E. (1975a). Information processing variables in learning to solve problems. *Review of Educational Research, 45*, 525-541.

Mayer, R. F. (1975b). Different problem solving competencies established in computer programming with and without meaningful models. *Journal of Educational Psychology, 67*, 725-734.

Mayer, R. E. (1977a). Different rule systems for counting behavior acquired in meaningful and rote contexts of learning. *Journal of Educational Psychology, 69*, 537-546.

Mayer, R. E. (1977). The sequencing of instruction and the concept of assimilation-to-schema. *Instructional Science, 6*, 369-388.

Mayer, R. E. (1979). Can advanced organizers influence meaningful learning? *Review of Educational Research, 49*, 371-383.

Mayer, R. E. (1989a). Models for understanding. *Review of Educational Research, 59*, 43-64.

Mayer, R. E. (1989b). Systematic thinking fostered by illustrations in scientific text. *Journal of Educational Psychology, 81*, 240-246.

Mayer, R. E., & Anderson, R. B. (1991). Animations need narrations: An experimental test of a dual coding hypothesis. *Journal of Educational Psychology, 83*, 484-490.

Mayer, R. E., & Anderson, R. B. (1992). The instructive animation: Helping students build connections between words and pictures in multimedia learning. *Journal of Educational Psychology, 84*, 444-452.

Mayer, R. E., Bove, W., Bryman, A., Mars, R., & Tapanengco, L. (1996). When less is more: Meaningful learning from visual and verbal summaries of science textbook lessons. *Journal of Educational Psychology, 88*, 64-73.

Mayer, R. E., & Gallini, J. K. (1990). When is an illustration worth ten thousand words? *Journal of Educational Psychology, 82*, 715-726.

Mayer, R. E., & Moreno, R. (1998). A split-attention effect in multimedia learning: Evidence for dual processing systems in working memory. *Journal of Educational Psychology, 90*, 312-320.

Mayer, R. E., & Sims, V. K. (1994). For whom is a picture worth a thousand words? Extensions of a dual coding theory of multimedia learning. *Journal of Educational Psychology, 86*, 389-401.

Mayer, R. E., Steinhoff, K., Bower, G., & Mars, R. (1995). A generative theory of textbook design: Using annotated illustrations to foster meaningful learning of science text. *Educational Technology Research and Development, 43*, 31-43.

Mayer, R. E., Stiehl, C. C., & Greeno, J. G. (1975). Acquisition of understanding and skill in relation to subjects' preparation and meaningfulness of instruction. *Journal of Educational Psychology, 67*, 331-350.

McCrudden, M. T., Schraw, G., Lehman, S., & Poliquin, A. (2007). The effect of causal diagrams on text learning. *Contemporary Educational Psychology, 32*, 367-388.

Merrill, M. D., & Stolurow, L.M. (1966). Hierarchical preview vs. problem oriented review in learning an imaginary science. *American Educational Research Journal, 3*, 251-261.

Minskoff, E., & Allsopp, D. (2003). *Academic success strategies for adolescents with learning disabilities and ADHD.* Baltimore, MD: Brookes.

Moore, D. W., & Readence, J. F. (1984). A quantitative and qualitative review of graphic organizer research. *Journal of Educational Research, 78*, 11-17.

Moreno, R., & Mayer, R. E. (1999). Cognitive principles of multimedia learning: The role of modality and contiguity. *Journal of Educational Psychology, 91*, 358-368.

Moyer, J. C., Sowder, L., Threadgill-Sowder, J., & Moyer, M. B. (1984). Story problem formats: Drawn versus verbal versus telegraphic. *Journal for Research in Mathematics Education, 15*, 342-351.

Nesbit, J. C., & Adesope, O. O. (2006). Learning with concept and knowledge maps: A meta-analysis. *Review of Educational Research, 76*, 413-448.

O'Donnell, A. M., Dansereau, D. F., & Hall, R. H. (2002). Knowledge maps as scaffolds for cognitive processing. *Educational Psychology Review, 14*, 71-86.

Paivio, A. (1966). Latency of verbal associations and imagery to noun stimuli as a function of abstractness and generality. *Canadian Journal of Psychology, 20*, 378-387.

Paivio, A. (1971). *Imagery and verbal processes.* New York, NY: Holt, Rinehart, & Winston.

Paivio, A. (1975). Neomentalism. *Canadian Journal of Psychology, 29*, 263-291.

Paivio, A. (1983). The mind's eye in arts and science. *Poetics, 12*, 1-18.

Paivio, A. (1986). *Mental representations: A dual coding approach*. New York, NY: Oxford University Press.

Paivio, A. (1991). *Images in mind: The evolution of a theory*. Sussex, England: Harvester.

Paivio, A. (2007). *Mind and its evolution: A dual coding theoretical approach*. Mahwah, NJ: Lawrence Erlbaum Associates.

Paivio, A., Yuille, J. C., & Madigan, S. A. (1968). Concreteness, imagery, and meaningfulness values for 925 nouns. *Journal of Experimental Psychology Monograph Supplement, 76*(1, Pt. 2), 1-25.

Passolunghi, M. C., & Siegel, L. S. (2004). Working memory and access to numerical information in children with disability in mathematics. *Journal of Experimental Child Psychology, 88*, 348-367.

Patterson, M. E., Dansereau, D. F., & Wiegmann, D. A. (1993). Receiving information during a cooperative episode: Effects of communication aids and verbal ability. *Learning and Individual Differences, 5*, 1-11.

Pressley, M. & Harris, K.R. (1994). More about increasing the quality of educational intervention research: A synthesis. *Educational Psychology Review, 6*, 271-289.

Rivera, D. P., & Smith, D. (1997). *Teaching students with learning and behavior problems* (3rd ed.). Boston, MA: Allyn & Bacon.

Robinson, D. H., Katayama, A. D., DuBois, N. F., & Devaney, T. (1998). Interactive effects of graphic organizers and delayed review on concept acquisition. *Journal of Experimental Education, 67*, 17-31.

Robinson, D. H., & Kierwa, K. A. (1995). Visual argument: Graphic organizers are superior to outlines in improving learning from text. *Journal of Educational Psychology, 87*, 455-476.

Robinson, D. H., & Schraw, G. (1994). Computational efficiency through visual argument: Do graphic organizers communicate relations in text too effectively? *Contemporary Educational Psychology, 19*, 399-415.

Robinson, D. H., & Skinner, C. H. (1996). Why graphic organizers facilitate search processes: Fewer words or computationally efficient indexing? *Contemporary Educational Psychology, 21*, 166-180.

Sadoski, M., & Paivio, A. (2001). *Imagery and text: A dual coding theory of reading and writing*. Mahwah, NJ: Lawrence Erlbaum Associates.

Stensvold, M. S., & Wilson, J. T. (1990). The interaction of verbal ability with concept mapping in learning from a chemistry laboratory activity. *Science Education, 74*, 473-480.

Suritsky, S. K., & Hughes, C. A. (1991). Benefits of notetaking: Implications for secondary and postsecondary students with learning disabilities. *Learning Disability Quarterly, 14*, 7-18.

Swanson, L., & Kim, K. (2007). Working memory, short-term memory, and naming speed as predictors of children's mathematical performance. *Intelligence, 35*, 151-168.

Thompson, W. L., & Kosslyn, S. M. (2000). Neural systems activated during visual mental imagery. In A. W. Toga, & J. C. Mazziotta (Eds.), *Brain mapping: The systems* (pp. 535-560). San Diego, CA: Academic Press.

Vekiri, I. (2002). What is the value of graphical displays in learning? *Educational Psychology Review, 14*, 261-313.

Waller, R. (1981, April). *Understanding network diagrams.* Paper presented at the annual meeting of the American Educational Research Association, Los Angeles, CA.

Washington, V. M. (1988). Semantic mapping: A heuristic for helping learning disabled students write reports. *Reading, Writing, and Learning Disabilities, 4*, 17-25.

Wiegmann, D. A., Dansereau, D. F., McCagg, E .C., Rewey, K. L., & Pitre, U. (1992). Effects of knowledge map characteristics on information processing. *Contemporary Educational Psychology, 17*, 136-155.

Williams, J. P. (1993). Comprehension of students with or without learning disabilities: Identification of narrative themes and idiosyncratic text representations. *Journal of Educational Psychology, 85*, 631-641.

Winn, W. (1991). Learning from maps and diagrams. *Educational Psychology Review, 3*, 211-247.

CHAPTER 12

CONCEPT MAPS FOR LEARNING

Theory, Research, and Design

John C. Nesbit and Olusola O. Adesope

ABSTRACT

Concept maps are node-link diagrams that represent verbal information. Serving as an alternative medium to written text, they typically have nodes labeled with noun phrases to denote concepts and arrows labeled with verb phrases to denote relationships between concepts. Like text, concept maps are used (a) as way for students to represent their knowledge in collaborative and individual learning activities, (b) to present information to students, and (c) to assess what students know. In this chapter we summarize the theory and research relating to the use of concept maps for these three instructional functions and consider their implications for design and practice. We conclude that concept maps should be viewed as tools for representing information whose instructional value hinges on the learning and assessment activities within which they are deployed and on characteristics of the learners who use them.

Learning Through Visual Displays, pp. 303–328
Copyright © 2013 by Information Age Publishing
All rights of reproduction in any form reserved.

Researchers and practitioners have used varying definitions of concept maps. For the purposes of this chapter, *concept maps* are diagrams that represent concepts as labeled nodes and represent relationships between the concepts as labeled links that connect the nodes. The small concept map shown in Figure 12.1 was constructed by a student reading about climate change.

Node labels are usually noun phrases (e.g., greenhouse gas), and link labels are usually verb phrases (e.g., causes). Thus, node-link-node structures can be read as propositions (e.g., greenhouse gas causes global warming). An important property of concept maps is that a concept is represented by a single node, and therefore propositions that refer to the same concept are always visually connected.

Node-link maps that use unlabeled links to connect nodes are sometimes referred to as concept maps, but in this chapter we consider such maps to be only borderline instances because they lack specification of the relationship between concepts and reflection on the relationship between concepts is thought to be an important source of learning when students read or construct maps.

Some theorists place further restraints on the structure of concept maps. Novak and Cañas (2008), for example, specify that concept maps should be hierarchical in the sense that concepts placed near the top of the map are more general (e.g., greenhouse gas), whereas those placed lower in the map are more specific (e.g., methane).

Knowledge maps are a type of concept map devised by Dansereau and his colleagues in which links are labeled with a canonical vocabulary of nine symbols representing relationships between concepts (O'Donnell, Dansereau, & Hall, 2002). We use the term "knowledge maps" only to denote this sub-category of concept maps. Figure 12.2 lists the nine types of relationships in knowledge maps and gives examples of how they are used. The research involving knowledge maps has mostly investigated the learning effects of studying preconstructed maps.

HISTORICAL ANTECEDENTS

Although the terminology and instructional theory of concept maps were developed by Novak and his colleagues in the 1970s (Novak & Cañas, 2008; Novak & Gowin, 1984), the essential infographic form of the concept map has a longer history. Classical and medieval philosophers drew hierarchical diagrams that bear similarities to today's concept maps (Sowa, 2000), and, to capture and compute the meaning of sentences, logicians and machine translation researchers constructed systematically-defined diagrams in which the sentences were parsed into line-connected

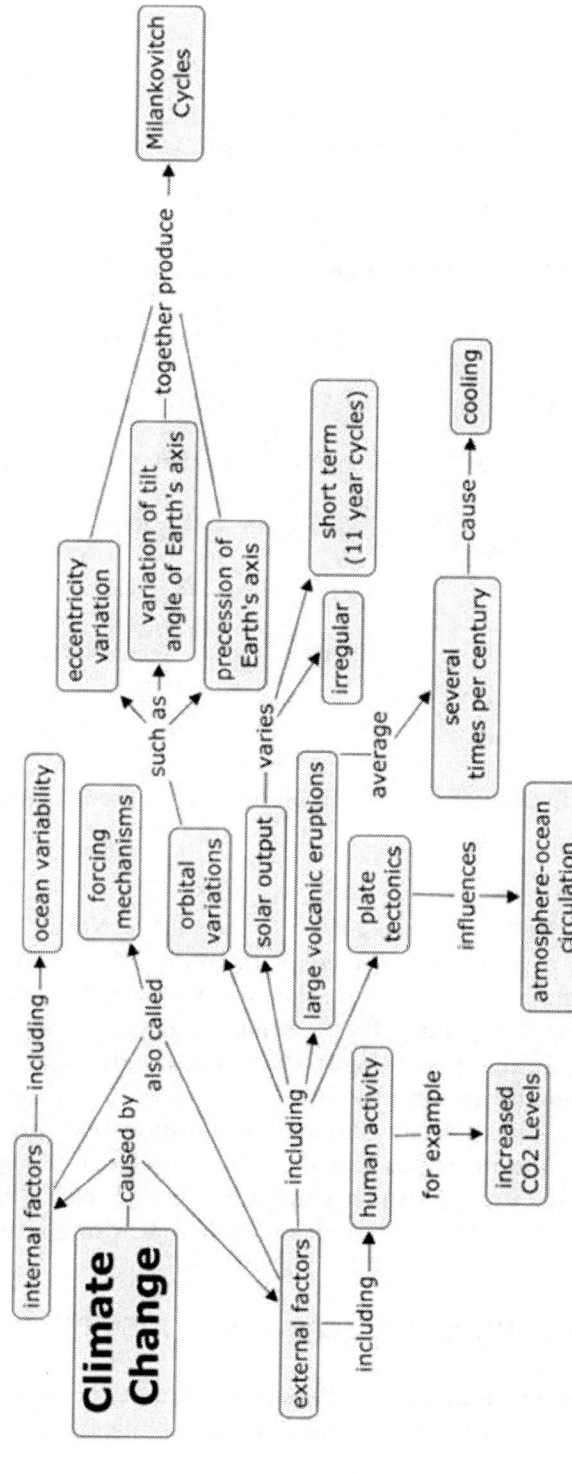

Figure 12.1.   A concept map constructed by a student using CmapTools (software developed by the Institute of Human and Machine Cognition, 2011).

Relationship	Symbol	Example
type	T	planet —T→ gas giant
part	P	comet —P→ tail
characteristic	C	orbit —C→ ellipse
leads to	L	magnetic activity —L→ sunspots
influences	I	mass —I→ force
definition	D	comet —D→ orbiting body with tail
analogy	A	solar system —A→ family
example	EX	dwarf planet —EX→ Pluto
next	N	Mercury —N→ Venus —N→ Earth

Source: O'Donnell et al. (2002).

Figure 12.2.   The fixed vocabulary of relationship symbols used in knowledge maps.

elements (Peirce, 1909; Richens, 1956). But second to Novak's work, the most prominent of the early influences on our understanding of the nature of concept maps is research on semantic networks by cognitive psychologists (Collins & Quillian, 1969). Semantic networks are node-link diagrams that cognitive psychologists have used with some success to model human memory and attention.

Throughout this chapter we develop the position that, no less than written text, the concept map is a medium for knowledge representation with properties that make it, under conditions that are being discovered by research, a tool that can add significant value to learning activities.

OVERVIEW OF RESEARCH AND THEORY

Figure 3 shows trends from 1980 to 2011 in the number of articles on concept maps and knowledge maps indexed in three bibliographic databases

(PsycINFO, ERIC, and Web of Science). The graph was constructed by searching for the subject terms "concept map" and "knowledge map." It shows that scholarly interest dramatically increased from the early 1980s, when only a few technical reports and conference summaries were indexed, and peaked in 2008 with over 200 articles and book chapters indexed by the Web of Science database.

Although not all the articles returned by our search were related to instructional applications, our examination of a sample of the articles indicated that the data shown in Figure 12.3 provides a generally accurate estimate of the number of publications related to instructional applications. Reviewing the hundreds of published research articles on the uses of concept maps is a project beyond the reach of this chapter. Instead, we have used existing reviews and selected research to examine fundamental questions about the instructional uses and design of concept maps.

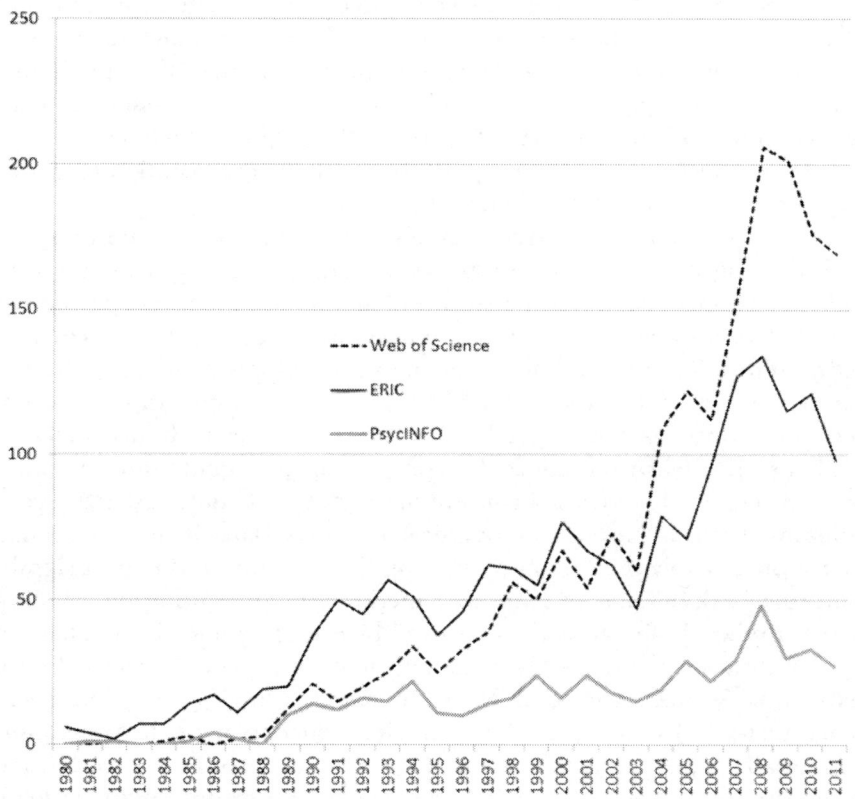

Figure 12.3.   Number of academic articles on concept maps and knowledge maps from 1980 to 2011 indexed by three bibliographic databases.

How Effective are Concept Maps as Tools for Learning?

In a meta-analysis conducted some years ago, we aggregated the results from 55 studies in which participants learned by constructing, modifying or studying concept maps (Nesbit & Adesope, 2006). We found achievement was substantially higher when learners constructed concept maps rather than attended a lecture or discussion about the same information ($d = .74$).[1] However, achievement was only slightly higher for learners who constructed concept maps compared with others who wrote texts or outlines ($d = .19$). Learners who studied concept maps had higher achievement than learners who studied equivalent text passages ($d = .39$) and those who studied lists or outlines ($d = .28$).

One appealing explanation for why learners who study researcher-constructed concept maps might achieve higher posttest scores than learners who study text is that concept maps and posttests might similarly emphasize main ideas, and text might place relatively greater emphasis on detail ideas which may not be assessed in posttests. However, a meta-analysis of six studies contradicted this explanation. In these studies, the same information was presented in maps and texts, and posttests assessed main ideas and detail ideas (Nesbit & Adesope, 2006). The meta-analysis found that learners who studied concept maps recalled significantly more central ideas ($d = .60$) and detail ideas ($d = .20$).

Despite the demonstrated success of concept maps as tools for teaching and learning they do have drawbacks. A concept map typically requires much more space on a viewing surface than an equivalent text passage or list of propositions. Also, because nodes may have to be erased and redrawn in different locations as the map is developed, concept mapping can be onerous unless the learner has access to an easily erased medium such as a whiteboard or specialized software. And, as with any medium, students must learn the particular conventions that guide interpretation and expression. The types of concept maps that have more restrictive conventions, such as Novak's hierarchical maps or Dansereau's knowledge maps, presumably require more training time. However, the most significant drawback of concept maps as a medium for presenting information is that the level of complexity conveyed by even medium-sized maps can be daunting for viewers. When reading text on a page, learners do not have to make decisions about where to start reading or which next sentence to read. In contrast, when studying concept maps, learners must continually make decisions about the reading order of the connected propositions, a process which may introduce extraneous cognitive load. As we will discuss later, alternate designs have been implemented to address this disadvantage.

Seven Possible Reasons for the Effectiveness of Concept Maps

Although a considerable body of research has assessed the instructional application of concept maps, very little research has examined the cognitive processes that underlie their effects on learning. In this section, we identify the main reasons that theorists have proposed to explain the findings we summarized in the previous section.

Dual-Coding. Studying or drawing concept maps while reading text passages that represent similar meaning may enable learners to encode corresponding elements from the different media in separate, but linked verbal and visuospatial long term memories. Even when working with concept maps without corresponding text passages, the learner may encode the textual and visuospatial components of the map separately (Bahr & Dansereau, 2001). Paivio's dual coding theory (Paivio, 1986) proposes that pictures and words are represented as separate, distinct types of memory and when instances of the two types of memory are interlinked, they are more easily retrieved. For this mechanism to come into play, learners need to retain and retrieve memories of the visuospatial properties of concept maps. Besides the sparse research that has found learners can recall these properties (e.g., Bahr & Dansereau, 2001), no research has specifically demonstrated that recall of verbal information from concept maps is mediated by long term visual memories.

Balancing visual and verbal processing. When reading text passages, learners first convert the visual information presented by written words into verbal information and then engage verbal working memory intensively to extract meaning (Baddeley, 2003). A possible advantage of studying concept maps is that they might alleviate overloaded verbal working memory by enabling the learner to offload some processing onto the cognitive resources available for visual processing (Nesbit & Adesope, 2006). For example, a text reader might normally load a series of words into verbal working memory and expend cognitive resources to parse them into noun phrases, verb phrases, and so on. Because the nodes and links in concept maps separate and connect meaningful syntactic units spatially, they may enable some of the parsing to be performed in visual working memory.

Integrating multiple occurrences of a concept. When a concept reoccurs in a page of text, typically because it is central to the meaning of the text, the locations of the multiple occurrences tend to be unpredictably scattered. In contrast, a concept map represents each concept by a single node even when the concept participates in many propositions. By visually integrating concepts, concept maps may reduce the visual search that learners require to cognitively integrate related ideas when studying verbal information.

Concept maps not only integrate multiple occurrences of a concept, but also locate related concepts closer together, which would also assist the process of cognitive integration. Because cognitive integration of ideas is thought to be a key process for constructing new ideas, the ability to reduce the extrinsic cognitive load imposed by visual search may be a crucial advantage of concept maps.

Attending to macrostructure and relationships among concepts. Printed text uses paragraph breaks and hierarchically-related headings to indicate how sentences are organized into higher-level structures. Concept maps also communicate macrostructure, but they do so using different and possibly more effective means (O'Donnell, Dansereau, & Hall, 2002). In addition to representing hierarchical structures, concept maps can represent lattice-like structures, for example "mammal" could be linked to "dog" and "human" and there could be a cross-link from "human" to "dog." The prominence of labeled links in concept maps may make the relationships among concepts more salient than in text. Concept maps also show the centrality or importance of each concept by the number of its connected links. Thus, using concept maps may be advantageous in situations where the learner can benefit from strong visual cueing of the pattern of relationships among concepts, the relative importance of concepts, and lattice-like content structure.

Simplifying language. The node-link-node syntax of the concept map language is much simpler and obviously has less expressive capacity than natural language in text, especially when a fixed relational vocabulary like the one shown in Figure 12.2 is used. This suggests that studying or constructing concept maps instead of text may be especially helpful for learners who have difficulties reading or writing at advanced levels. Indeed there is substantial evidence that learners with lower verbal ability or poor literacy skills obtain greater benefit from using concept maps (Nesbit & Adesope, 2006; O'Donnell et al., 2002; Thiede, Griffin, Wiley, & Anderson, 2010). This advantage of concept maps is presumably the same as that offered by a textual list of equivalent noun-verb-noun propositions. We are not aware of any research that has compared the effects of learning from concept maps and equivalent lists of simple propositions.

Elaborative processing. When learners translate a text passage into concept map form, the task may demand that they process the text more deeply than they normally do when studying. The learners discover that they must judge which concepts are closely related so those concepts can be placed closer together in the map. When students construct the type of hierarchically arranged map advocated by Novak, they must distinguish among the levels of generality of the concepts so that more general concepts can be placed higher in the map. To create clean-looking maps, learners often must determine which concepts are multiply-connected so they can be placed in more central locations to reduce link length and link crossings. If they are constructing a map with a fixed vocabulary of relationship symbols (like those in Figure 12.2), learners must select which of the symbols is the best match to what may be a complicated predicate in the text. These types of decisions are theorized to promote meaningful learning because they demand close attention to the meaning of concepts and the relationships among them, and learners must activate associations with prior knowledge to attend to meaning.

Summarizing. Concept mapping may also promote elaborative processing by encouraging a high degree of summarization. Because concept maps take up much more space than text, learners discover that when translating from a one-page text to a one-page concept map they must select only the most important information. There is evidence that summarization, normally the translation of detailed documents into concise summary texts, is an effective learning strategy (King, Biggs, & Lipsky, 1984).

LEARNING BY CONSTRUCTING CONCEPT MAPS

Theorists usually point to elaborative cognitive processing or Ausubel's related theory of meaningful learning to explain the effects of concept mapping (Novak, 2010). These theories claim that cognitive operations that activate more associations between new information and prior knowledge will more strongly promote retention and understanding of the new information. They predict that more generative activities such as constructing a concept map will be more instructionally effective than less generative activities such as filling in a partially complete map, and, similarly, filling in a partially complete map will be more instructional effective than reading the map. In research comparing these three learning activities, Lim, Lee, and Grabowski (2009) found a trend in the predicted direction with a significant difference between participants who constructed maps and those who only read maps. The processes of elaborative processing and meaningful learning are theorized to result in greater comprehension and transferable knowledge than non-elaborative rehearsal and provide a better foundation for critically analyzing and drawing inferences from the new information. Indeed, there is evidence that concept mapping promotes critical thinking (Vacek, 2009; Wheeler & Collins, 2003).

Translating text passages into concept maps is not necessarily an optimal study strategy. Karpicke and Blunt (2011) compared posttest performance of participants randomly assigned to (a) an "elaborative" studying task in which they constructed concept maps while viewing source texts or

(b) a retrieval practice task in which they summarized source texts from memory. Although total learning time was the same, the retrieval practice condition involved two study-recall cycles. The retrieval practice groups outperformed concept mapping groups on posttests by over one standard deviation, even when the posttests consisted of concept mapping. This finding makes a powerful point about the effectiveness of retrieval practice, and, as the authors commented, it does not indicate a deficiency of concept mapping per se. Instead of challenging the value of concept mapping, we believe the finding shows the inadequacy of study strategies in which learners are not obliged to retrieve or generate information.

Concept mapping is a way of expressing and building knowledge and, and, like writing, can be used as an element in many different types of study strategies. Karpicke and Blunt (2011) used concept mapping as part of a studying task in which learners converted information from a text passage into a concept map format. It is possible to carry out that task by a nearly algorithmic process in which two noun phrases in a sentence are parsed and copied into the map to create two linked nodes, and a verb phrase from the sentence is similarly copied into the map as the link label. Performed in this way, concept mapping requires little elaborative processing and would not be expected to result in high levels of information recall or knowledge transfer. Fortunately, there are many ways to alter the task to promote elaborative processing. Theoretically, if learners were required to convert text into the type of hierarchical concept maps advocated by Novak and Cañas (2008) they would engage in elaborative processing as they compared the semantic scope of noun phrases in the text to determine where to place them in map. Similarly, if the learners were required to construct a concept map that summarized the source text they would engage in elaborative processing as they compared the importance of propositions in the text and selected those to include in the summary. We believe that the degree of elaborative encoding prompted by concept mapping depends on the type of concept mapping performed and the specific features of the study strategy in which the concept mapping is embedded.

Prewriting

Writing is a complex activity that can be challenging for even high-achieving students, and strategies that support novice writers could bring far-reaching benefits. Although concept mapping has often been recommended as a planning or prewriting strategy (e.g., Anderson-Inman & Horney, 1996), there is little research investigating its efficacy for that purpose. In a repeated-measures design, Sturm and Rankin-Erickson (2002) taught eighth grade students with reading difficulties how to use concept mapping as a prewriting strategy and then instructed three treatment groups to use computer-aided mapping, hand-drawn mapping or no mapping prior to writing. In comparison to baseline writing performance measured at the start of the study, all groups improved their writing after learning the concept mapping strategy. However, actually using concept mapping as a prewriting strategy was not observed to have a significant effect on the quality of writing. Liu (2011) found that mapping was highly effective as a prewriting strategy, but the maps that learners constructed in Liu's research had no link labels and were more similar to hierarchical outlines than the concept maps discussed in this chapter. Considering its potential value to learners, we believe that more research is needed to evaluate the effectiveness of concept mapping as a prewriting strategy.

Collaborative Mapping

When used for collaborative learning, concept maps can be drawn on large paper sheets or whiteboards and may be concurrently edited, extended or corrected by group members without reorganizing the entire map (Nesbit & Adesope, 2006). Researchers have investigated the extent to which collaborative construction of concept maps can promote social interactions and sustain critical thinking (Okebukola & Jegede, 1988; Roth & Roychoudhury, 1993, 1994; Stoyanova & Kommers, 2002; van Boxtel, van der Linden, Roelofs, & Erkens, 2002). For example, Stoyanova and Kommers (2002) reported that collaborative construction of a concept map brought out the conceptual structure of a given topic, assisted group negotiation of meaning, and promoted deeper mutual understanding among group members.

Haugwitz, Nesbit, and Sandmann (2010) compared collaborative concept mapping and collaborative writing as ways to summarize and reflect on a collaborative learning activity in high school biology. While the treatment variation had no significant effect on the achievement of students with higher cognitive ability, students with lower cognitive ability who self-selected into groups with others having lower cognitive ability learned much more in the concept mapping condition ($d = 1.04$).

Other studies have suggested that collaborative concept mapping might be deleterious to learning. van Boxtel et al. (2002) found that participants in collaborative concept mapping rarely offer explanations for selecting some propositions. Similarly, Roth and Roychoudhury (1994) observed several instances where misconceptions among members became ingrained, purportedly because they were not challenged. Other studies have found that collaborative mapping may engender off-task

interaction and inadvertently lead discussion away from important con-
tent-oriented concepts (Chiu, 2003). It appears that many of the pitfalls
of collaborative concept mapping can be traced to participants' lack of
training. We see no reason to believe that collaborative concept mapping
is any more susceptible than other collaborative learning strategies to
being thwarted by insufficient training. Collaborative concept mapping
research might be improved substantially by giving greater attention to
the pretraining of participants in collaborative as well as concept mapping strategies (Adesope & Nesbit, 2009; O'Donnell et al., 2002).

LEARNING BY STUDYING CONCEPT MAPS

A preconstructed concept map can be used at any stage of a learning
activity where information might otherwise be provided by text; for
instance as a graphic organizer to initiate a learning activity or as a clos-
ing summary. Dansereau and his colleagues conducted extensive research
on the instructional use of preconstructed knowledge maps, much of
which focused on the effects of map design, prior knowledge and their
interactions (O'Donnell et al., 2002). They found that participants learn
more from maps designed so that similar concepts are grouped together
or marked with the same color or shape. For example, Wallace, West,
Ware, and Dansereau (1998) found that learners who studied black and
white knowledge maps attained only a moderate benefit ($d =.35$) over
learners who studied a text passage, while learners who studied a knowledge map enhanced with colors, node shapes and structural arrange-
ments to represent semantic relatedness attained a much larger
comparative benefit ($d =1.1$). Although Nesbit and Adesope (2011) found
the use of color to signal semantic relatedness of nodes did not significantly enhance learning outcomes over the use of a black and white map
($d = .34, p > .05$), the weight of evidence seems to favor the use of proximity, color or shape to signal semantic similarity of concepts.

The macrostructure of concept maps is an instructionally important
design feature. Research that compared learning from hierarchically-
structured and network-structured maps found learners who studied
hierarchically-structured maps scored higher on a posttest of conceptual
knowledge (Amadieu, van Gog, Paas, Tricot, & Mariné, 2009). Contrary to
the researchers' hypothesis, both low prior knowledge and high prior
knowledge learners benefited from studying the hierarchically structured
maps. One explanation for these results is that the hierarchically structured
map provided more information about the superordinate-subordinate
relationships among concepts. Another explanation is suggested by the
researchers' observation that the hierarchical map "tended to induce a

more systematic reading path" (p. 383). It may be that learners in the network-structured map condition needed to devote more cognitive resources to deciding how to the traverse the map.

Several studies found that studying knowledge maps rather than text offers greater advantages for students having low prior knowledge compared with those having high prior knowledge (O'Donnell et al., 2002). Concept maps can be used as source materials for collaborative studying, and, in parallel with the finding that collaboratively *constructing* concept maps rather than text seems especially beneficial for students having lower cognitive ability (Haugwitz et al., 2010), there is evidence that collaboratively *studying* knowledge maps rather than text offers greater benefits to those having lower verbal ability (Patterson, Dansereau, & Wiegmann, 1993). These similar findings provide backing for the hypothesis that the advantages of learning with concept maps, whether by constructing or studying them, are due to their simpler syntax. One would expect that an easier-to-apprehend medium for representing verbal information would offer some benefit to all learners but would be especially advantageous to those who have less knowledge of the topic or lower verbal ability.

What Eye Movement Data Can Tell Us

Eye-tracking technology is used in educational research because it has potential to identify what information learners are attending to and the order of cognitive operations (Hegarty, 2006; Henderson, 2003; Rayner, 1998; van Gog & Scheiter, 2010). Recently, researchers have begun using eye movement data to build an understanding of how learners visually process concept maps. In research that tracked eye-movements to examine the order of learners' initial processing of nodes in studying concept maps, we observed widely varying sequential patterns of map reading (Nesbit, Larios, & Adesope, 2007). We found that participants gave early attention to nodes in the upper left region of concept maps, which we proposed may be transfer from acquired reading skills. We also found that participants gave early attention to centrally located nodes, which we proposed may reflect a search for highly interconnected hub nodes that offer superordinate information. These findings suggest that students may more easily read maps in which hub nodes are consistently located in the map centre and links are directed from left-to-right. Amadieu et al. (2009) used pupil dilation, fixation duration and navigational data to examine the effects concept map structure on disorientation, cognitive load, and learning from nonlinear documents. They concluded that "the eye tracking and navigation data provided more detailed insight" that helped them interpret their findings (p. 376).

Ideally, eye movement data would be used to make inferences about learners' cognitive activity while studying concept maps. But how much does the eye tell us about what the mind is thinking? To make inferences about cognitive activity, we need to know that eye movements are correlated with the contents of working memory and with learning outcomes. Bisra and Nesbit (2012) measured participants' eye movements while they were searching concept maps to gather information for argumentation. They found that participants' eyes fixated more on task-relevant nodes and more on nodes they later recalled correctly. These results indicated that, at least for similar research settings, eye movement data can be used to make valid inferences about cognitive activity.

Concept Maps as Interactive Multimedia

The effectiveness of concept maps as instructional media may be limited by the visual complexity they present as their nodes and links increase in number. Unlike text, which in most languages has only one conventional processing sequence (e.g., left to right and top to bottom in European languages), concept maps have no conventional processing sequence. Consequently, as we have noted, the sequence of nodes and links by which learners traverse concept maps is extremely varied (Nesbit et al., 2007). When learners first approach a concept map of even moderate complexity they may find it difficult to process the entire map in a coherent order. Indeed, Blankenship and Dansereau (2000) used the term "map shock" for the "bewilderment of not knowing where to start or how to penetrate the topography of the map" (p. 294). In addition to learners possibly experiencing a negative affective reaction to complex concept maps (Dansereau, Dees, & Simpson, 1994), the lack of a systematic order of processing may cause them to miss or redundantly revisit nodes and links. However, as we discuss in the next section, by presenting concept maps as interactive multimedia and using multimedia features to guide order of node visitation it may be possible to mitigate the negative effects of map complexity.

Animation and Audio Narration

Animating a concept map may remediate the inherent difficulty of processing complex maps if the animation effectively signals a sequence for visiting nodes and links (Blankenship & Dansereau, 2000; Nesbit & Adesope, 2011). A concept map could be animated in a variety of ways, for example by successively highlighting individual node-link-node structures while dimming other areas of the map. Although different in several respects from the more common type of instructional animation that shows the action of physical systems, concept map animation uses the same general technique of signaling a sequence of changes by apparent movement. For this reason one might expect that the enhanced learning outcomes due to other types of animation reported in a meta-analysis by Hoffler and Leutner (2007) might also be produced by concept map animation.

Blankenship and Dansereau (2000) designed an animated knowledge map that was built up gradually by adding a new link-node pair approximately every 3 seconds. One comparison treatment used a "static map" which presented the same knowledge map all at once. There were two comparison treatments that presented text versions of the knowledge map content: a "static text" condition that presented the text all at once and an "animated text" condition that built up the text by adding one word at a time. Participants who learned from the animated map recalled more main ideas than those who learned from the static map or the animated text. Blankenship and Dansereau theorized that the animated knowledge map offered better support for learning than the static map "by directing viewers' attention along a coherent processing route, by illustrating relevant information clusters (chunks), and by slowly revealing complexity, thereby reducing map shock" (p. 305).

In our research on animated concept maps, a series of learner-paced slides is ordered so that the first slide shows a blank map, subsequent slides show the progressively developing map and the last slide shows the complete map. Each slide presents all the nodes and links of the preceding slides and introduces a few new nodes and links. In two separate studies, we found that participants who studied animated concept maps recalled more main ideas and detail ideas than others who studied semantically equivalent animated texts which introduced a single new sentence in each slide (Adesope & Nesbit, 2011; Nesbit & Adesope, 2011). In one of these studies (Adesope & Nesbit, 2011) we failed to find a significant difference between animated and static map conditions, an outcome which we attribute to the use of audio narration in all conditions. We speculate that learners viewing a static concept map while listening to semantically equivalent audio synchronize their visual processing of the map to the audio narration. If this is the case then audio narration would, like animation, cue a sequence for traversing the map and reduce the negative effects of map complexity. In a recent meta-analysis of instructional research on the concurrent presentation of audio and text (Adesope & Nesbit, 2012), we found that visually presenting only key words or phrases from a concurrent audio narration was a highly efficacious way to combine text and speech ($d = .99$ over three studies). This finding suggests that augmenting audio narrations with animated concept maps that present only key terms and their relationships could significantly boost what students learn from the narrations.

Hypermaps

Using common web authoring techniques, it is a simple matter to implement web-based concept maps which double as navigation menus. Called hypermaps these concept maps contain hyperlinks to other instructional materials and can be hyperlinked with other hypermaps to create an interconnected network of web-based concept maps (Chang, Sung, & Chiou, 2002). Hypermaps present a potential solution to the previously mentioned problem that a concept map, compared to an equivalent text passage, takes up much more space on a page or screen. A page of text can be translated to several interconnected hypermaps such that a concept on one hypermap can be hyperlinked to another hypermap which decomposes the concept into its constituent propositions.

On the premise that concept maps can represent the macrostructure of a topic with greater fidelity than indented outlines or text, researchers have hypothesized that using hypermaps rather than hyperlinked lists or hypertext as navigation tools might foster deeper learning about the topic (Reynolds, Patterson, Skaggs, & Dansereau, 1990). Across six studies, Nesbit and Adesope (2006) found no significant increase in posttest scores due to learning with hypermaps compared to hypertext and hyperlinked outlines. Research by Reynolds et al., which compared learning from hyperlinked knowledge maps to learning from hypertext, failed to detect an effect on posttest scores but did find that the participants learning from hypermaps reported greater satisfaction and less frustration with the learning experience. A study by Potelle and Rouet (2003), which compared navigating instructional materials with a hierarchical hypermap to navigating them with a hyperlinked alphabetical list, found only participants with low prior knowledge obtained additional benefit by using the hypermap. One reason that few advantages have been found for learning from hypermaps is that the hyperlinked lists and hypertext used for comparison conditions in the research may be easier to comprehend than the instructional texts used as comparison conditions in the research on nonhyperlinked materials. Transforming text into hypertext requires that the hyperlinked terms be underlined or otherwise highlighted, and prior research has established that providing readers with highlighted key terms boosts their posttest scores (e.g., Hartley, Bartlett, & Branthwaite, 1980). We propose that learners studying hypertext benefit from this highlighting effect and therefore hypertexts are able to compete more favorably with hypermaps.

CONCEPT MAPPING FOR ASSESSMENT

Demonstrating the feasibility of concept mapping assessment in postsecondary education, Thompson and Licklider (2011) described how concept mapping was used over a 5-year period as a final examination in a university course in forestry. The rubric developed to assess the maps, which was given to students at the beginning of the course, did not specify which concepts must be included but instead emphasized comprehensiveness, accuracy, hierarchical ordering, and evidence of revision. The students were given several opportunities to practice concept mapping throughout the course and constructed maps with varying organizational schemes. It was reported that most developed "very creative and comprehensive representations of their learning" suggesting "deeper learning" (Thomson & Licklider, 2011, p. 407).

In an early example of the use of concept maps to produce outcome measures in educational research, Novak and colleagues coded interviews with students as concept maps and scored the maps to obtain an outcome variable (Novak & Musonda, 1991). The researchers found that the concept maps demonstrated, qualitatively and quantitatively, long term differences between treatment groups in cognitive structures representing scientific knowledge. Novak and others have claimed that concept mapping is a form of assessment that is especially good at detecting scientific misconceptions because the spatial structure of concept maps can more explicitly reveal incorrect or missing relationships between concepts (Novak, 2002; Schroeder & Adesope, 2011).

Across a wide variety of subject domains, research has evaluated the utility of concept mapping for classroom assessment and as an instrument for measuring the effectiveness of educational interventions. What does this research tell us about the nature of concept map assessments and their validity and reliability?

Ruiz-Primo and Shavelson (1996) observed that concept mapping assessments consist of a task, a response format, and a scoring system, and they found that published research shows variation across all three elements. The task may involve students filling in a partially completed map, constructing a map using given concept terms, collaborative mapping and so on. The response format may require that maps be drawn on paper or constructed using software that constrains students' input to varying degrees. According to Ruiz-Primo and Shavelson, concept map scoring systems measure (a) structural and semantic properties of the student's map, (b) the similarity of the student's map to a criterion map prepared by an expert, or use a combination of these two methods. Novak and Gowin (1984) developed a widely used system of the first kind for scoring hierarchically structured concept maps. Their system gives point credit for valid propositions, depth of the hierarchy, crosslinks, and examples.

There is plentiful evidence, mostly from science classrooms at the secondary and postsecondary levels, that concept map assessments have high interrater reliability, correlate moderately with other assessments, and are sensitive to knowledge gains that result from instruction (Lopez et al., 2011; Szu et al., 2011; Vachliotis, Salta, Vasiliou, & Tzougraki, 2011). In a review of their research on the psychometric properties of different types of concept map assessments with high school science students, Shavelson and Ruiz-Primo (2000) concluded that "map scores can consistently rank students relative to one another as well as provide a good estimate of a student's level performance regardless of how well his or her classmates performed" (p. 330). More specifically, they observed:

- The interrater reliability of trained raters scoring concept maps tends to be high.
- "Concept maps and multiple-choice tests measure overlapping yet somewhat different aspects of declarative knowledge" (p. 326).
- Compared to having students fill in blank nodes and links, having students construct a complete map using assessor-provided concepts is a more sensitive measure of differences among students.
- Filling in blank nodes and filling in blank link labels express measurably different types of knowledge.

Software systems have been created that can automatically score concept maps (Harrison, Wallace, Ebert-May, & Luckie, 2004; Park & Calvo, 2008), and in some cases have been shown to produce scores that strongly correlate with the scores of human raters (Koul, Clariana, & Salehi, 2005). The Concept Mapping Tool (CMT) developed by Cline, Brewster and Fell (2010) is a system in which a student can construct a map, have it immediately evaluated, and receive feedback that helps them iteratively improve it. To make the automatic scoring problem tractable, the instructor inputs a criterion map along with a set of allowable concepts and relations. The student's completed concept map is evaluated by comparing it with the map input by the instructor. As part of an evaluation of CMT by Cline et al., university students studying entomology drew concept maps on paper that were scored by their instructor and also input to CMT for automatic scoring. There was a high correlation between the instructor's scores and CMT's scores ($r = 0.80$). A high correlation ($r = 0.94$) was also obtained when students constructed a second set of maps directly in CMT. When students were given the option to revise and resubmit their maps, most of them did so repeatedly and raised their scores significantly. The researchers inferred that for supporting formative assessment, the speed and convenience of automatic concept map scoring are important advantages.

Self-Monitoring Writing

Another way that concept maps can support learning is as feedback for self-assessment during the writing process. Software that provides this functionality must be able to extract concept maps from text, a problem that has attracted attention from computer scientists (Chen, Kinshuk, Wei, & Chen, 2008; Lee, Lee, & Leu, 2009; Tseng, Sue, Su, Weng & Tsai, 2007). Villalon and Calvo (2011) developed an instructional system that converts students' essays into concept map summaries they can use to reflect on the quality and completeness of their work. Because it is a significant technical challenge to automatically generate meaningful concept maps from text and, for the time being, computer-generated map summaries will tend to be less meaningful than human-generated summaries, the map summaries need to be used in ways that are not heavily reliant on their semantic accuracy. In Villalon and Calvo's system, after displaying a concept map to the student the system asks questions designed to prompt reflection about content of the essay such as "do you thing the most relevant topics you covered in the essay are present in the map" and "could you improve the map by adding or removing concepts." There is no research evaluating the instructional effectiveness of this feature.

IMPLICATIONS FOR DESIGNERS, TEACHERS AND STUDENTS

The research we have discussed in this chapter supports the claim that concept maps can be a useful component of learning and assessment activities in a range of instructional contexts. Concept maps should be regarded as tools for representing information whose instructional value is contingent on the type of information they are intended to represent, how they are structured, the learning activities within which they are deployed and on the characteristics of the learners who use them.

Concept maps have been successfully used in primary, secondary, and postsecondary levels of education in subjects within the humanities, social sciences, biosciences, physical sciences, and other domains. Because they represent verbal information, concepts maps are best suited to learning verbal and conceptual knowledge within these domains.

Although there is insufficient research on how concept maps should be structured, theories of meaningful learning and elaborative processing indicate that learners should construct concept maps according to constraints that prompt reflection on the meaning of concepts. For example, constructing a hierarchical concept map in which a more general concept appears higher on the map than a concept it subsumes is theorized to promote a deeper understanding of both concepts. Constructing a concept map in which related concepts (whether connected or unconnected) are grouped together or given the same color is also theorized to promote elaborative processing. When using concept maps to present information to students, there is some evidence that orderly designs which eliminate unnecessary complexity (e.g., lengthy links, crossed links) are beneficial. When it is necessary to present a larger concept map, especially one with complex linkage patterns, designers should consider using multimedia features such as animation or audio to signal an order in which the student might first navigate the map.

Concept maps can be used to advantage in learning activities that would more commonly use text or speech. But the mere adoption of concept maps in place of other modes of representation is not enough to ensure that a learning activity will be effective. Instead, instructional designers should combine the use of concept maps with learning strategies that are supported by theory and evidence. For instance, rather than copy information directly from a page of text to a concept map, to promote elaborative processing a student might draw a concept map that consists of self-constructed explanations or examples for the main ideas on the page. Or, to obtain the benefits of retrieval practice, the student might read the page of text, remove it from sight, and then create a concept map that summarizes it.

Because the use of concepts maps seems to be especially advantageous for students who have lower verbal ability, teachers should consider substituting concept maps for text in learning activities designed for such students.

RESEARCH PRIORITIES

Much of the research on concept maps has compared learning with concept maps and text. Although this work has established that the instructional use of concept maps can offer measurable improvement in learning outcomes, the significant heterogeneity found in our meta-analysis (Nesbit & Adesope, 2006) suggests that research should now focus on delineating the conditions under which the use of concept maps is effective and explaining why those conditions are important.

In our view, the greatest need is for research that assesses the learning outcomes from different concept mapping strategies. Novak and his colleagues have long claimed that more can be learned by constructing hierarchical concept maps. Indeed, a key objection by Mintzes et al. (2011) to the research by Karpicke and Blunt (2011) which found that concept mapping produced learning outcomes inferior to retrieval practice, was that the hierarchical structure of the participants' maps was not reported. To resolve such debates, research is needed that investigates whether and to what degree hierarchical mapping and other task features such as instructor-provided concept terms and summarization promote learning.

There is already evidence that students' prior ability moderates the degree to which they can benefit from using concept maps: Lower ability students appear to obtain greater benefit. Research is needed to pinpoint which of the complex of correlated individual differences factors that include general cognitive ability, verbal ability, target language competence, and prior subject knowledge play a causative role in this interaction. Beyond the practical need to know who can benefit from using concept maps so they can be appropriately deployed, this research will contribute to our understanding of why concept maps are effective tools for learning.

Another priority for research, in our opinion, is the project of determining whether the eye movements of learners studying concept maps might help in assessing the quality of their cognitive engagement with presented information. Researchers investigating self-regulated learning and meta-cognition have discussed at length the shortcomings of post-hoc and summative self-reports of study strategies, motivation, and other self-regulatory constructs, and have emphasized the need for sequential data that more immediately reflect learners' mental processes (Winne, 2010). The eye movements of learners studying concept maps are much more variable than the eye movements of learners studying printed text because after fixating on one node the learner typically has several nearby nodes and links that offer targets for the next fixation. The key research question is what to degree the decision about that next fixation is dependent on metacognitive and motivational processes. If those processes do play a significant role in determining fixation order, then analyses of the eye movements of learners studying concept maps could present a picture of self-regulatory processes at a much finer grain size than currently available methods.

THE FUTURE OF CONCEPT MAPS

As eye-tracking, brain imaging, and behavioral data-mining technologies become more accessible to researchers, we anticipate an expansion of research investigating how learners interact with concept maps at cognitive and neurological levels. The detailed, new knowledge generated by this research will indicate how and under which conditions concept maps should be used and will more fully inform design principles needed to develop comprehensive instructional systems.

By extrapolating current research and development in fields such as intelligent tutoring systems, information visualization, natural language processing and instructional psychology, it is possible to imagine how learners at all levels of education will be interacting with concept maps a decade from now, and, broadly, what theoretical understanding and research will inform the designs of the systems they will be using to do so. In this chapter we have presented research on the instructional uses of concept maps for the separate functions of construction, study, and assessment. We imagine that future research and practice will be marked by convergence across these functions and a corresponding integration of features in the software environments that support them. That is, it will be possible within one software application for a student working individually or collaboratively to construct a concept map, receive feedback on the quality of that map, and study concept maps created by an instructor, other students, or the software system. As software becomes more adept at translating text into concept maps and recognizing the meaning in student-constructed concept maps, it seems likely that instructional concept mapping systems will become incorporated within other types of instructional systems that provide intelligent tutoring and support collaborative learning. The inclusion of support for concept maps in comprehensive instructional software systems will help to promote their use.

Concept maps are not an instructional panacea. Neither do they offer a more accurate picture of the mind of a learner than other representational media. They are a widely used format for studying, expressing and sharing verbal information that complements text, lists, and other verbal formats. They will continue to be used, and will be supported in future instructional systems, because in some learning activities and for some learners they offer fewer barriers to comprehending and expressing ideas than alternative media.

NOTE

1.   Throughout this chapter we use Cohen's d to report effect sizes.

REFERENCES

Adesope, O. O., & Nesbit, J. C. (2009). A systematic review of research on collaborative learning with concept maps. In P. L. Torres & R. C. V. Marriott (Eds.), *Handbook of research on collaborative learning using concept mapping* (pp. 238-255). Hershey, PA: IGI Global.

Adesope, O. O., & Nesbit, J. C. (2011). *The effects of animated concept maps on transfer of learning.* Paper presented at the annual meeting of the American Educational Research Association, New Orleans, LA.

Adesope, O. O., & Nesbit, J. C. (2012). Verbal redundancy in multimedia learning environments: A meta-analysis. *Journal of Educational Psychology, 104,* 250-263.

Amadieu, F., van Gog, T., Paas, F., Tricot, A., & Mariné, C. (2009). Effects of prior knowledge and concept-map structure on disorientation, cognitive load, and learning. *Learning and Instruction, 19,* 376-386.

Anderson-Inman, L., & Horney, M. (1996). Computer-based concept mapping: Enhancing literary with tools for visual thinking. *Journal of Adolescent & Adult Literacy, 40,* 302.

Baddeley, A. (2003). Working memory: Looking back and looking forward. *Nature Reviews Neuroscience, 4,* 829-839.

Bahr, G. S., & Dansereau, D. F. (2001). Bilingual knowledge maps (BiK-Maps) in second-language vocabulary learning. *Journal of Experimental Education, 70,* 5-24.

Bisra, K., & Nesbit, J. C. (2012). *How learners visually navigate concept maps: An analysis of eye movement single transitions.* American Educational Research Association Annual Conference. Vancouver, BC, Canada.

Blankenship, J., & Dansereau, D. F. (2000). The effect of animated node-link displays on information recall. *Journal of Experimental Education, 68,* 293-308.

Chang, K., Sung, Y., & Chiou, S. (2002). Use of hierarchical hyper concept map in web-based courses. *Journal of Educational Computing Research, 27,* 335-353.

Chen, N. S., Kinshuk, Wei, C. W., & Chen H. J. (2008). Mining e-learning domain concept map from academic articles. *Computers & Education, 50,* 1009-1021.

Chiu, C. H. (2003). Exploring how primary school students function in computer supported collaborative learning. *International Journal of Continuing Engineering Education and Lifelong Learning, 13,* 258-267.

Cline, B. E., Brewster, C. C., & Fell R. D. (2010). A rule-based system for automatically evaluating student concept maps. *Expert Systems with Applications, 37,* 2282-2291.

Collins, A. M., & Quillian, M. R. (1969). Retrieval time from semantic memory. *Journal of Verbal Learning and Verbal Behavior, 8,* 240-247.

Dansereau, D. F., Dees, S. M., & Simpson, D. D. (1994). Cognitive modularity: Implications for counseling and the representation of personal issues. *The Journal of Counseling Psychology, 41,* 513-523.

Harrison, S. H., Wallace, J. L., Ebert-May, D., & Luckie, D. B. (2004). C-Tools automated grading for online concept maps works well with a little help from WordNet. In A. Cañas, J. Novak, & F. González (Eds.), *Concept maps: Theory, methodology, technology, proceedings of the first international conference on concept mapping* (Vol. 2, pp. 211-214). Pamplona, Spain: Universidad Pública de Navarra.

Hartley, J., Bartlett, S., & Branthwaite, A. (1980). Underlining can make a difference—sometimes. *The Journal of Educational Research, 73,* 218-224.

Haugwitz, M., Nesbit, J. C., & Sandmann, A. (2010). Cognitive ability and the instructional efficacy of collaborative concept mapping. *Learning and Individual Differences, 20,* 536-543.

Hegarty, M. (2006). Eye fixations and diagrammatic reasoning. *Lecture notes in Computer Science, 4045,* 13-15.

Henderson, J. M. (2003). Human gaze control during real-world scene perception. *Trends in Cognitive. Sciences, 7,* 498-504.

Hoffler, T. N., & Leutner, D. (2007). Instructional animation versus static pictures: a meta-analysis. *Learning and Instruction, 17,* 722-738.

Institute for Human & Machine Cognition. (2011). CmapTools v5.04.02. Retrieved from http://cmap.ihmc.us/

Karpicke, J. D., & Blunt, J. R. (2011). Retrieval practice produces more learning than elaborative studying with concept mapping. *Science, 331,* 772-775.

King, J. R., Biggs, S., & Lipsky, S. (1984). Students' self-questioning and summarizing as reading study strategies. *Journal of Reading Behavior, 16,* 205-218.

Koul, R., Clariana, R. B., & Salehi, R. (2005). Comparing several human and computer-based methods for scoring concept maps and essays. *Journal of Educational Computing Research, 32,* 227-239.

Lee, C. H., Lee, G., & Leu, Y. (2009). Application of automatically constructed concept map of learning to conceptual diagnosis of e-learning. *Expert Systems with Applications, 36,* 1675-1684.

Lim, K. Y., Lee, H. W. & Grabowski, B. (2009). Does concept-mapping strategy work for everyone? The levels of generativity and learners' self-regulated learning skills. *British Journal of Educational Technology, 40,* 606-618.

Liu, P. (2011). A study on the use of computerized concept mapping to assist ESL learners' writing. *Computers & Education, 57,* 2548-2558.

Lopez, E., Kim, J., Nandagopal, K., Cardin, N., Shavelson, R. J., & Penn, J. H. (2011). Validating the use of concept-mapping as a diagnostic assessment tool in organic chemistry: Implications for Teaching. *Chemistry Education Research and Practice, 12,* 133-141.

Mintzes, J. J., Canas, A., Coffey, J., Gorman, J., Gurley, L., Hoffman, R., ... & Wandersee, J. H. (2011). Comment on "Retrieval practice produces more learning than elaborative studying with concept mapping." *Science 334,* 453.

Nesbit, J. C., & Adesope, O. O. (2006). Learning with concept and knowledge maps: A meta-analysis. *Review of Educational Research, 76,* 413-448.

Nesbit, J. C., & Adesope, O. O. (2011). Learning from animated concept maps with concurrent audio narration. *Journal of Experimental Education, 79,* 209-230.

Nesbit, J., Larios, H., & Adesope, O. (2007). How students read concept maps: A study of eye movements. *Proceedings of World Conference on Educational Multimedia, Hypermedia and Telecommunications, 2007,* 3961-3970.

Novak, J. D. (2002). Meaningful learning: The essential factor for conceptual change in limited or inappropriate propositional hierarchies leading to empowerment of learners. *Science Education, 86,* 548-571.

Novak, J. D. (2010). *Learning, creating, and using knowledge: Concept map as facilitative tools in schools and corporations* (2nd ed.). New York, NY: Routledge.

Novak, J. D., & Cañas, A. J. (2008). *The theory underlying concept maps and how to construct them.* Technical Report IHMC CmapTools 2006-01. Retrieved from http://cmap.ihmc.us/Publications/ResearchPapers/ TheoryUnderlyingConceptMaps.pdf

Novak, J. D., & Gowin, D. (1984). *Learning how to learn.* New York, NY: Cambridge University Press.

Novak, J. D., & Musonda, D. (1991). A twelve-year longitudinal study of science concept learning. *American Educational Research Journal, 28,* 117-153.

O'Donnell, A. M., Dansereau, D. F., & Hall, R. H. (2002). Knowledge maps as scaffolds for cognitive processing. *Educational Psychology Review, 14*, 71-86.

Okebukola, P. A., & Jegede, O. J. (1988). Cognitive preference and learning-mode as determinants of meaningful learning through concept mapping. *Science Education, 72*, 489-500.

Paivio, A. (1986). *Mental representations: A dual coding approach*. New York, NY: Oxford University Press.

Park, U., & Calvo, R. (2008). Automatic concept map scoring framework using the semantic web technologies. In *Proceedings of the 2008 eighth IEEE international conference on advanced learning technologies* (pp. 238–240).

Patterson, M. E., Dansereau, D. F., & Wiegmann, D. A. (1993). Receiving information during a cooperative episode: Effects of communication aids and verbal ability. *Learning and Individual Differences, 5*, 1-11.

Peirce, C. S. (1909) *Manuscript 514* (with commentary by J. F. Sowa). Retrieved from http://www.jfsowa.com/peirce/ms514.htm

Potelle, H., & Rouet, J. (2003). Effect of content representation and readers' prior knowledge on the comprehension of hypertext. *International Journal of Human–Computer Studies, 58*, 327-345.

Rayner K. (1998). Eye movements in reading and information processing: 20 years of research. *Psychological Bulletin, 124*, 372-422.

Reynolds, S. B., Patterson, M. E., Skaggs, L. P., Dansereau, D. F. (1990). Knowledge hypermaps and cooperative learning. *Computers & Education, 16*, 167-173.

Richens, R. H. (1956). Preprogramming for mechanical translation. *Mechanical Translation, 3*, 20-25.

Roth, W. M., & Roychoudhury, A. (1993). The concept map as a tool for the collaborative construction of knowledge: A microanalysis of high school physics students. *Journal of Research in Science Teaching, 30*, 503-534.

Roth, W. M., & Roychoudhury, A. (1994). Science discourse through collaborative concept-mapping: New perspectives for the teacher. *International Journal of Science Education, 6*, 437-455.

Ruiz-Primo, M., & Shavelson, R. J. (1996). Problems and issues in the use of concept maps in science assessment. *Journal of Research in Science Teaching, 33*, 569-600.

Schroeder, N. L., & Adesope, O. O. (2011). Concept maps as tools for learning scientific language. In L. Lennex & K. Nettleton (Eds.), *Cases on inquiry through instructional technology in math and science: Systemic approaches* (pp. 52-73). Hershey, PA: IGI Global.

Shavelson, R. J., & Ruiz-Primo, M. (2000). On the psychometrics of assessing science understanding. In J. J. Mintzes, J. H. Wandersee, J. D. Novak, J. J. Mintzes, J. H. Wandersee, & J. D. Novak (Eds.), *Assessing science understanding: A human constructivist view* (pp. 303-341). San Diego, CA: Academic Press

Sowa, J. F. (2000). *Knowledge representation: Logical, philosophical, and computational foundation*. Pacific Grove, CA: Brooks Cole.

Sturm, J. M., & Rankin-Erickson, J. L. (2002). Effects of hand-drawn and computer-generated concept mapping on the expository writing of middle school students with learning disabilities. *Learning Disabilities: Research & Practice, 17,* 124-139.

Stoyanova, N., & Kommers, P. (2002). Concept mapping as a medium of shared cognition in computer-supported collaborative problem solving. *Journal of Interactive Learning Research, 13,* 111-133.

Szu, E., Nandagopal, K., Shavelson, R. J., Lopez, E. J., Penn, J. H., Scharberg, M., & Hill, G. W. (2011). Understanding academic performance in organic chemistry. *Journal of Chemical Education, 88,* 1238-1242.

Thiede, K. W., Griffin, T. D., Wiley, J., & Anderson, M. M. (2010). Poor metacomprehension accuracy as a result of inappropriate cue use. *Discourse Processes, 47,* 331-362.

Thompson, J. R., & Licklider, B. L. (2011). Visualizing urban forestry: Using concept maps to assess student performance in a learning-centered classroom. *Journal of Forestry, 109,* 402-408.

Tseng, S. S., Sue, P. C., Su, J. M., Weng, J. F., & Tsai, W. N. (2007). A new approach for constructing the concept map. *Computers in Education Journal, 49,* 691-707.

Vacek, J. E. (2009). Using a conceptual approach with concept mapping to promote critical thinking. *Journal of Nursing Education, 48,* 45-48.

Vachliotis, T., Salta, K., Vasiliou, P., & Tzougraki, C. (2011). Exploring novel tools for assessing high school students' meaningful understanding of organic reactions. *Journal of Chemical Education, 88,* 337-345.

van Boxtel, C., van der Linden, J., Roelofs, E., & Erkens, G. (2002). Collaborative concept mapping: Provoking and supporting meaningful discourse. *Theory into Practice, 41,* 40-46.

van Gog, T., & Scheiter, K. (2010). Eye tracking as a tool to study and enhance multimedia learning. *Learning and Instruction, 20,* 95-99.

Villalon, J., & Calvo, R. A. (2011). Concept maps as cognitive visualizations of writing assignments. *Journal of Educational Technology & Society, 14,* 16-27.

Wallace, D. S., West, S. W. C., Ware, A., & Dansereau, D. F. (1998). The effect of knowledge maps that incorporate gestalt principles on learning. *Journal of Experimental Education, 67,* 5-16.

Wheeler, L., & Collins, S. (2003). The influence of concept mapping on critical thinking skills in baccalaureate nursing students. *Journal of Professional Nursing, 19,* 6, 339-346.

Winne, P. H. (2010). Improving measurements of self-regulated learning. *Educational Psychologist, 45,* 267-276.

CHAPTER 13

ARGUMENT DIAGRAMS AND LEARNING

Cognitive and Educational Perspectives

Jerry Andriessen and Michael Baker

ABSTRACT

Argument diagrams are visual representations of interlinked claims, arguments and counterarguments that can be created and modified by small groups of students interacting on the same screen. Such elements of argument diagrams commonly take the form of small text boxes. Mostly, these diagrams are constructed by participants working on a computer using dedicated software. Rather than making an inventory of argument diagram software, the focus in our chapter will be on learning outcomes associated with use of such software, and the processes that lead to them. It is assumed that constructing these argument representations in collaboration has several advantages over arguing without the use of argument diagrams. However, whether such advantages result in significant gains in terms of learning is a consequence of complex interplay between various aspects of the learning situation such as the type of assignment, the way diagrams are precisely exploited within the assignment, and the learning gains envisaged. We distinguish four different types of learning outcomes associated to the use of argument diagrams in learning contexts: (1) knowledge acquisition; (2) improving collaboration; (3) knowledge management; and (4) knowledge building/creation. These learning outcomes are not mutually exclusive, but indicate the main focus of learning goals of students, the instructional design by teacher or researcher as well as the assessment of the outcomes. Our claim is that research on argument maps should ask questions that take into account the type of learning that is at stake, which will thus determine the methodology applied for experimentation and analysis.

INTRODUCTION

Defining Argument Diagrams

Argument diagrams allow arguments to be mapped visually. Argument diagrams consist of text boxes representing claims, arguments, and data for or against the claim. The text boxes are often linked by arrows that indicate positive or negative argumentative relations (for or against) between the arguments in the text boxes with respect to the main claim. In general, an argument diagram is textual, hierarchical, structured, and maps some argumentative ontology (description language of argumentation) to statements and their (inferential) connections. In this chapter we discuss the collaborative use of argument maps for learning, a situation that always requires computers, and is principally studied within the CSCL (computer supported collaborative learning) research community. For example, Lund, Molinari, Séjourné, and Baker (2007) used a tool called JigaDREW (Figure 13.1) which can be used by up to eight participants at the same time, sitting behind different or the same computers, to synchronously construct an argument map in one window (i.e., the graphical space for argumentation) and chat in another window (i.e., the chat area). In the graphical space, participants can add *boxes* and *relations*, whereby boxes can be filled with text, and relations (between boxes) can be qualified as positive or negative. The argumentative ontology in this case would be box (or argument), and relation (pro/contra). The ontology does not distinguish between "claim" and "(counter-)argument" since any element (box) can have either function. However, once an argument has arguments for or against it, it can become a new claim, to be attacked or defended. In the chat area, participants can add text which is displayed below the previous addition. Not seen in the figure is the collaborative text editor, a window with a text editor to be jointly used by participants to write a synthesis text. In addition, participants can freely add *comments* and indicate *opinions* (for/against) to the boxes and the relations, by clicking on them and opening a separate window which closes after editing.

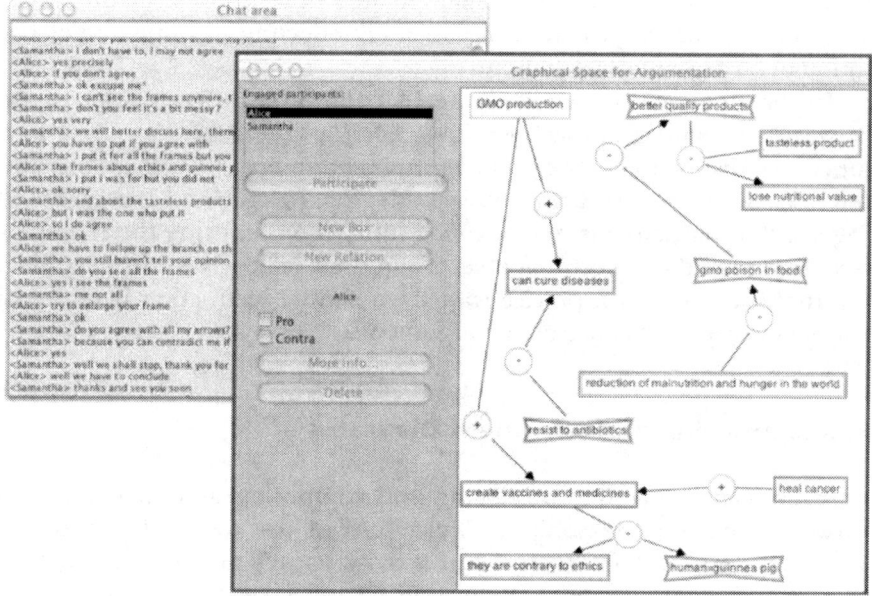

Figure 13.1. JigaDREW interface.

The distinction between argument and opinion is particularly important, since it can be difficult to understand. For example, the expression of a counterargument for a claim might be seen as expressing an opinion against it. But this is not necessarily so, since one might be simply evoking a possible counterargument, that one might oneself not agree with. Argument and opinion are often aligned, although this is not required, especially when we consider cooperative kinds of argumentation, involving exploring possible arguments for and against an idea, in order to search for what is most acceptable. These *comments* are displayed on screen when the mouse goes over the box or relation to which the comment was added. Different *attitudes* (for/against) indicated by different participants concerning the same box results in a dented box (e.g. the box called *better quality products* in figure 1).

Argument diagrams are used for representing networks of arguments. Argumentation is considered essential for learning, especially for understanding open and complicated subject matter (Andriessen, 2006). Representing argumentation as arguments in a diagram ought to help learning as well. For example it could be useful during a debate or discussion to keep track of what was contributed, and to have an easy overview after the debate is over. Diagrams can be manipulated in terms of structure, links, and content, allowing room for organizing, reflecting, relating and elaboration of (argumentative) content.

The arrangement shown in Figure 13.1 allows for differentiation of use between chat and graphical windows. Such a differentiation refers to a functional distinction between the representation map (of arguments) and the discussion itself. Suthers, Vatrapu, Medina, Joseph, and Dwyer (2008) suggest that participants need explicit instruction on using the representations to map the conceptual objects and their relations constructed during the discussion in a precise way. Even simple instruction is useful to learners in terms of constructing arguments.

Argumentation and Argument Diagrams

Argumentation involves producing and comparing arguments using a variety of types of reasoning. The nature of the topic, the media of expression, the wider situation and activity, as well as the local goals of argumentation all influence the overall form it takes (Andriessen, Baker, & Suthers, 2003). WE define an argument as a statement (utterance, piece of text) that is *linked* to another statement (the "claim," or "thesis") that is not accepted outright (by the hearer, reader, audience). When a statement is linked to another statement, it becomes an argument when it makes the latter more or less acceptable from some point of view (normative or subjective). For example, the statement "the stock market will go up" (A) is not, in itself an argument, but it's just a statement. It could become an argument when put in relation to another statement that is not an object of consensus, such as, "candidate XYZ would make the best president" (B). In this case, the link between statements "A" and "B" must be such that acceptance of "A", the argument, would make statement "B" more or less acceptable, from the point of view of the people concerned by the debate.

Arguments and argumentation (the process of producing arguments) also depend on *links* between statements or ideas. Argument diagrams make these links explicit. Everything in argumentation depends on the link, one might say. It is therefore regrettable that most argument diagram tools do not enable or support explicitly such discussions about the meaning of argumentative links, but often are reduced to a simple link on the screen, perhaps with a "+" or "-"label. It is important to discuss what the link means, because this leads to generalization, making reasoning explicit, working on understanding conceptual underpinnings and, more generally, negotiation of meaning.

A large number of argumentation ontologies, or description languages of argumentation, have been based on very restricted versions of the work of Toulmin (1958). Such a common choice of argument diagrams for collaborative learning, involving dialogue, merits comment, since the Toulmin maps are inherently monological (i.e., for representing texts or an individuals' discourse). It is possible, however, to imagine that the different elements of these diagrams—for example, "conclusion," "datum," "warrant," "qualifier"—could be uttered successively by different participants in dialogue. Another issue raised by Toulmin's diagramming method is the extent to which collaborative learning associated with argument diagrams involves or should involve the learning of such an ontology, or metalanguage of argumentation.

Such an ontology and structure makes argument mapping different from mind-mapping (map ideas and random links), concept mapping (focus on structure of links between ideas) or causal mapping (cause-consequence links), and therefore should be discussed as a separate type. Indeed, students often confuse conceptual, causal and argumentative links because their underlying fuzzy conceptions of relations between statements seem to be that certain concepts generally "go together," regardless of the type of relation between them. We should also highlight that argument maps are mixtures of textual and diagrammatic/structural visual representations, and therefore can be understood in terms of learning from multiple representations (Ainsworth, 1999, 2006).

Six Assumptions About Argumentation

We make six assumptions about argumentation: (1) Argumentation in learning situations refers to a broad range of learning activities in which arguments are produced and used as a source for reflection; (2) There is no particular argument schema (ontology) that we adhere to, unless the acquisition of such a schema is the objective of a learning situation; (3) It is the objective of the learning situation that is primary to us (i.e., the advantages of the use of argument maps, as mediators of some learning processes, depend on what they are used for in a particular learning situation); (4) Our results and conclusions about using argument maps for learning depend to a large extent on what we know and understand about argumentation and learning; (5) Because we focus on collaborative learning situations, we need to include interactive and collaborative activities in our understanding of the role of argument maps in learning, and (6) Asking participants to argue, or to construct an argument map does not by default produce effective learning; therefore it is imperative to consider explanations taking into account the domain of reasoning, the type of medium, and the local situation and activity of which the assignment is part, and especially consider how these aspects shape the learning objectives over time.

Goals of This Chapter

In this chapter, we provide a conceptual framework, based the objectives of a learning situation for discussing the merits of argumentation maps in different types of learning situations. We focus here on the objectives of the learning situation as well as the collaborative processes involved, rather than on the features of the software, because it is not the introduction of the software into an educational situation that in itself produces learning, but the way the newly introduced tool is actually *appropriated* by the students and teacher (Baker, Bernard, & Dumez-Féroc, 2012; Overdijk, van Diggelen, Kirschner & Baker, 2012; Rabardel, 1995). In other words, the learning outcomes of using argument diagram tools depend on the precise ways that students actually use them, often despite the designers' and teachers' intentions.

In this chapter we take a learning perspective, not a technological or a design viewpoint. What we mean by a learning perspective is that we look at the learning outcomes of the use of the software, combined with appropriate instruction, in a learning context. Within this perspective, we started out asking ourselves *what are the particular collaborative learning processes and outcomes belonging to the use of argument diagrams in learning settings, and how can these processes and outcomes be facilitated by instruction?* A summary of most relevant work can be found in recent reviews such as Andriessen and Schwarz (2009), McLaren, Scheuer, and Mikšátko (2010), Newell, Beach, Smith, and VanDerHeide (2011), Noroozi, Weinberger, Biemans, and Mulder (2012), and Scheuer, Loll, Pinkwart, and McLaren (2010). These studies provide us with different perspectives on the use of argument diagrams for learning on the design of computer supported argumentation, the use of artificial intelligence techniques, teaching and learning effective argumentative reading and writing, effective teaching and learning of argumentation, and computer-support of argumentation, respectively.

Unfortunately, the outcomes of many studies with argument graphs in learning situations do not allow us to answer our question because they do not provide us with sufficient detail to be able to explain the results or the lack of them, especially because no analysis of the arguments themselves is provided. In the next section, we discuss a detailed example of a study so readers may grasp the issues involved. In order to get better answers to our question, we propose that the analysis of outcomes, the instructions for participants, and the research questions of studies about using argument graphs in for learning should be tuned in a more coherent way than has been the case so far, to the constraints of the actual learning context, in particular to the (learning) activities the participants engage in as a consequence of their interpretation (their learning goals) of that context. We then propose four general types of learning objectives (knowledge of a domain, knowledge of collaboration, knowledge management, and knowledge building) and discuss the research needed to answer questions about the possible roles of argument maps.

SOME ISSUES CONCERNING THE COLLABORATIVE USE OF ARGUMENT DIAGRAMS

Argument diagrams have been used for various learning purposes, which come under various labels, such as:

- representing arguments from difficult texts (Harrell, 2005),
- mediating a debate though computer based communication (Andriessen, Baker, & Suthers, 2003),
- teaching (legal) argumentation (Carr, 2003),
- deciding where we stand (van Gelder, 2003),
- scientific reasoning and problem solving (Baker, 2003),
- creative thinking (Wegerif et al., 2010),
- evidential reasoning and collaborative inquiry (Suthers, 2003),
- critical thinking (Davies, 2011).

The *pedagogical objectives* of assignments using argument maps can be diverse. We can distinguish argument maps used for planning argumentative texts (van Amelsvoort, Andriessen, & Kanselaar, 2007; Van Drie, Van Boxtel, Jaspers, & Kanselaar, 2005), representing the main issues and arguments in a particular debate (Baker, 2003), representing an integration of viewpoints (Veerman, Andriessen, & Kanselaar, 2000), representing a historical debate (Muller Mirza, Tartas, Perret-Clermont, & de Pietro, 2007), and many others. In addition, the *argumentation* that is supposed to be represented in the argument maps can be of a quite different nature between various uses, such as summarizing, analyzing, integrating, coordinating, re-representing, translating (in the sense of from one representation into another), organizing, and reflecting.

An Extended Example

Lund et al. (2007) examined the difference between student dyads using an argumentation graph (JigaDREW, see Figure 13.1) as a *medium* of debate and students using a graph as a way of *representing* their ongoing chat debate. In condition one (graph for debating) students used chat and graph simultaneously. In condition two (graph for representing chat), students were first asked to discuss using chat, and then to re-present their chat-debate in a graph. Lund et al. characterized the research objective as an experimental comparison between coordinating versus translating representations (chat and graph versus from chat to graph). This study is important because it elaborated the research objectives into pedagogical objectives. To this end, the authors developed a pedagogical three-phase sequence in collaboration with a classroom teacher. The pedagogical goal was the collaborative elaboration of knowledge on a particular subject of debate, genetically modified organisms (GMOs). The pedagogical sequence (4 sessions on 4 days) started with 15- to 16-year-old student participants being told the elementary principles of argumentation and being provided limited training in using the argumentation tools. Tthe students then were asked to construct their own opinion on the debate, supported by materials (texts on a website) that were assembled by researchers and teachers summarizing the viewpoints of the main societal actors in the debate on GMO. Students first drew an individual argument graph, then studied the materials and were subsequently asked to revise their graph. All of this occurred during the *preparation phase*. Then, on day 4, there was a *collaborative debate phase*. In the "graph for debating" condition students studied their *own* graph (and consulted it during the debate), and then discussed using chat and JigaDREW for about 60 minutes. In the "graph for representing chat" class, students also studied their graphs, and then debated through chat for 30 minutes, but were also asked to represent their own chat debate in JigaDREW while using chat for interaction management. Both groups ended their debate with a synthesis in chat summarizing what they agreed and disagreed during debate. Finally, there was a *consolidation phase* during which individuals revised their graphs in the light of all activity. Dyads were constituted by the teacher, based on students' records of working well together.

The theoretical assumption was that argumentation in both situations would favour elaboration of the space of debate (Baker, Quignard, Lund, & Séjourné, 2003). This means that the learning objective was not the acquisition of concrete facts or argumentation skill per se, but for students to become better acquainted with societal and epistemological points of view, for their associated arguments and value systems to go deeper into argument chains, and to elaborate upon the meaning of arguments, and to better understand the argumentation processes involved. This was accomplished by creating situations that would favour cooperative exploration of a dialogical space of debate (Baker, 1999; Nonnon, 1996).

In an influential paper, Baker, Andriessen, Lund, van Amelsvoort, and Quignard (2007) proposed a method (called Rainbow, see Figure 13.2) for

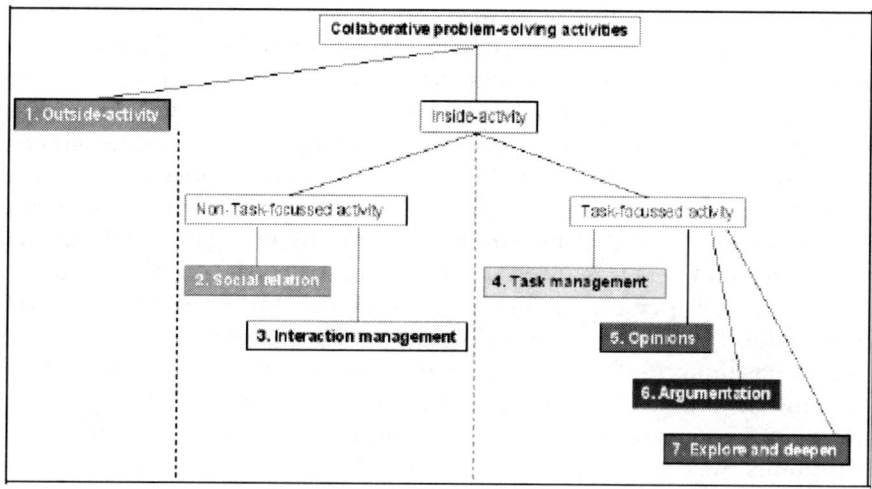

Figure 13.2. Principal categories of the Rainbow functional analysis of computer-mediated pedagogical debates.

the analysis of contributions to collaborative dialogues based on the learning goal of *elaboration of a space of debate* by argumentation. The reasoning was that contributions could be classified by their main function (relational or task oriented, and within task orientation, task management or argumentative), and that content elaboration was the case when learners produced arguments and elaborated on those arguments (see figure 13.2). A Rainbow analysis was applied in many studies for the classification of oral or written contributions to a learning dialogue (e.g., Laurinen & Marttunen, 2007; Munneke, Andriessen, Kanselaar, & Kirschner, 2007).

The outcome measure in the Lund et al. (2007) study, however, was not the chat itself, but the argument diagram. To analyze the diagram, the authors developed the Argumentation diagram analysis method (ADAM). Six characteristics of diagrams were included in ADAM: (1) the form of the diagram (type of branching: list or tree, or both); (2) quantity of arguments and relations (including comments); (3) quantity and nature of opinions (for, against); (4) quantity of topics within the space of debate (health, welfare, environment, world-view, other); (5) Elaboration of arguments (number of propositions); and (6) Correctness of relations.

The expectation in this study was that participants would extend their space of debate by debating the issue using one of two graph conditions described below. Broadening and deepening of the space of debate was assessed indirectly by counting the numbers of arguments and links in the graphs. If we look at this particular comparison of graph use, one would expect participants in condition 1 to express their issues directly in the graph, while in second condition the graph would be constructed after somewhat more reflection. In condition 1, the graph would be the main mediator of ongoing meaning making, while in condition 2, it would be a translation of the main issues in the chat. As a consequence, we would expect more elaboration in condition 1, but more coherent structure and content in condition 2. All of this is based on the implicit hypothesis that epistemic awareness is realized during the particular interactions and that the interaction medium is affecting this. In the ADAM analysis method, elaboration would be reflected in quantity of arguments, opinions, topics and elaborations (2, 3, 4, 5), especially elaborations (5), and better structure and content could be seen as the tree structure (1) and the quality of ideas (6). Unfortunately, only one significant difference for experimental conditions was obtained: for "opinions" scores. Students who were instructed to represent their chat debate in an argument graph (condition 2) were *less* inclined to state their respective opinions about the same elements of their collaborative graph. In addition, there was an effect on the consolidation phase, during which participants revised their initial graph as a result of the debate. Students in the representing condition (2) added more non-argumentative relations (causal, examples, semantic).

What is most surprising about this study is the lack of significant differences on most measures. This raised questions concerning the way the task was presented to the participants, the method for analyzing effects, the lack of sufficient numbers of participants, or the way the participants actually understood the instructions, and, most importantly, more detail about what participants actually did. Several of these issues were examined in a related study, by van Amelsvoort, Andriessen, and Kanselaar (2007), who investigated the conditions under which diagrammatic representations supported collaborative argumentation-based learning in a computer environment. They applied Rainbow and used content analysis to examine the breadth and depth of arguments. Thirty dyads of 15- to 18-year-old students participated in a writing task consisting of 3 phases. Students *prepared* by constructing a representation (text or diagram) individually. Then they discussed the topic and wrote a text in dyads. As a source of reference for this discussion, students used either: (a) the individual texts they wrote, (b) the individual diagrams they constructed, or (c) a diagram that was constructed for them based on the text they wrote. Results showed that students who constructed a diagram themselves (condition (b) explored the topic more (collaboratively) than students in the other conditions. No other significant comparisons were obtained. Then, in further exploration of this disappointing result, the authors found differences in the way collaborating dyads used their representations. Dyads who engaged in deep discussion used their representations as a basis for knowledge construction. In contrast, dyads that engaged in only shallow discussion used their representations solely to copy information to their collaborative text. These approaches were independent of experimental conditions. The authors concluded that diagrammatic representations can improve collaborative learning, but only when they are used in a co-constructive way.

The Role of Learning Goals

The conclusion with which we ended the previous section suggests that students may benefit from using argumentative graphs, but they have to learn to use them in an appropriate way, and preferably in the way that the experimenter or teacher intended. This could be read by some as a call for "scripting." Scripting implies influencing student behavior by specific communication interfaces (Scheuer et al, 2010) and a limited range of options for action. Appropriate designs of the interface, in combination with more strictly defined activities may cause students to produce more relevant claims (Cho & Jonassen, 2002; Schwarz & Glassner, 2007), or more disagreements (McAlister, Ravenscroft, & Scanlon, 2004), or argumentation of better formal quality (Stegmann, Weinberger, & Fisher, 2007). But what scripting mainly does is to restrict the activities of participants to make them more similar. This may be an accepted strategy for experimentation, and may even be an appealing approach to education by some, but it can only be applied to a limited number of tasks, that is, those for which the options can be determined for every move beforehand.

The assignments described in the Lund et al (2007) and van Amels-voort et al. (2007) studies discussed in the previous section were relatively open-ended, but also had a clear scenario of subtasks with particular learning purposes that included orientation (understand the basics), reading comprehension (study the materials), create an opinion (a graph, or a text, or a dialogue), collaborative argumentation (create a joint graph), and consolidation (revise first ideas based on collaborative session). These five subgoals imposed high processing demands on learners, and although the work was dispersed over several sessions, one might expect consistent results only after more thorough familiarization of both students and teachers with the full scenario.

There are surprisingly few studies such as those discussed above in which the researchers, in addition to comparing experimental conditions, try to track what participants are actually doing while they construct and use argument maps. We think studying these processes is crucial for better understanding the roles of graphs in various educational assignments and that counting the number of arguments does not help us understanding why these arguments were generated. Arguments in complex learning scenarios can be produced for several reasons, not always related to the researcher's experimental manipulations. Conclusions from several review studies support our argument.

Andriessen and Schwarz (2009) concluded that the extended pedagogical designs, implying several phases and various learning activities, do not always lead to participants engaging into the desired activities. As a consequence, learning outcomes with argument diagrams are variable, and may depend on the degree of integration of a particular way of argument diagram used in educational practice. One instructional consequence is that both teachers and students need support with assignments employing argument diagrams. The work described by McLaren, Scheuer, and Mikšátko (2010) with an argument diagram called Argunaut reports ongoing research on designing advanced techniques for capturing and interpreting student activities in chat and diagrams, to support teachers and students. It concludes that it still remains to be shown "how useful the provided alerts are for teachers in actual, fast-paced moderation scenarios" (p. 36). Similarly, the section on argument tools in the review study by Newell et al. (2011) concludes with "all of this points to the importance of defining specific purposes for using mapping or graphing tools to foster representations of arguments" (p. 286). And, to further illustrate the point we make: "Although the use of maps of graphic organizers may serve to effectively scaffold students' representations of aspects of arguments and use of argumentative strategies, maps and graphic organizers may not necessarily enhance critical understanding of complex issues" (Scheuer et al., 2010).

All these conclusions warrant the idea that while argument graphs may do a good job in suggesting argument representations for various educational goals, their actual use seems to be more of a problem then their technical design. This means that for teachers as well as for students, in experimental as well as in real practice, the precise purpose of using argument diagrams seems to be escaping them, and even if this purpose is more or less clear, then they do not really know how to use argument diagrams for effective learning. These problems may occur because argument diagrams are complicated tools, but more so because their use involves specific types of collaboration and argumentation. Learners using argument maps collaboratively require appropriate instructions and assignments, and criteria by which they can estimate good progress, in terms of collaboration and argumentation and their need for supports that allow them to develop better understanding of what they are doing.

From an instructional perspective, using an argument map successfully is more important than constructing the map. As is the case with all production activities, such as writing or designing, one is producing a representation to enhance understanding rather than to produce something per se. Scientific authors produce scientific texts for sharing their ideas in their community. However, in the end, the main criterion for success would be the acceptance of the ideas within the community. What we propose is that when argument graphs are introduced at some point, to support scientific text production, it is not the number of arguments that is a measure of success, but rather how these arguments relate to ideas within the scientific community in terms of completeness of ideas, coverage of various positions, accuracy of formulation, and persuasiveness. Additional norms and criteria need to be derived from the educational context such as the desired level of quality, the level of the learners, and the moment in their learning trajectories. In the next section, we introduce four types of learning objectives for collaboration in constructive tasks. Our main claim is that this is the level of description that is most important for explaining learning outcomes with argument graphs.

A CONCEPTUAL FRAMEWORK BASED ON FOUR LEARNING OBJECTIVES

One challenge of argumentation design is that it involves new modes of communication and their structure, the elaboration of new tools for sustaining productive collective argumentation, and new ways of learning (Andriessen & Schwarz, 2009). What does a tool bring to learning? At a minimum, it brings a medium for expression in which things can be presented in a different way. What is expressed and how it is expressed may imply different ways of thinking, and may engage learners in a process of appropriation in which hey develop their own unique ways of working with the tools.

Many studies with argument diagrams address issues of collaboration and argumentation, not the use of diagrams per se. We believe that the results of using argument diagrams for collaborative learning are highly linked to the learning goals of the participants. Furthermore, we think that research has not been able to link details of the design of argument graphs to learning activity itself or the learning result. It is important to identify general links between uses of argument graphs and learning processes. To this end, we propose four types of learning that have generally been associated with collaboration, including: *(1) knowledge acquisition; (2) knowledge of collaboration; (3) knowledge management; and (4) knowledge building/creation*. Participants' learning goals may be associated with these four types of learning; thus, it is important to distinguish qualitatively different goals and types of collaboration that are characteristic of very different learning situations. Any collaborative learning situation may include all four types of learning, but for research to grasp each of them, different assessments of learning would be required, including experimental design, participant instruction and pedagogical design.

(1) Knowledge of a Domain: Acquisition of Individual Knowledge and Understanding in a Learning Domain

Studies often address the extent to which the knowledge and understanding in a domain have been affected through some pedagogical approach and/or some innovative use of technology. The goal of collaboration in these studies is, just as in the case of individual learning, the growth of knowledge and understanding in some learning domain. We assume that different design principles will apply for different pedagogical functions (Ainsworth, 2006). Pedagogical methods for knowledge acquisition will be based on what is known in the respective field of expertise as the most efficient approach. For example, collaborative problem solving in order to better understand principles of energy in physics (e.g. Baker, 1999, 2003) may have different pedagogical requirements from collaborative discussion of some event in history in order to better grasp its causes and consequences (e.g., Muller Mirza et al., 2007). The nature of knowledge in a domain (e.g. physics vs. history) or core assumptions (e.g., principles versus event chains) may constrain the pedagogical approach as well as the specific learning goals of instruction. The aim in physics may be to understand a concept underlying a theory (e.g., energy), whereas in history, it may be to understand the complexity of forces at work during a particular period of time, and the impossibility of simple linear, causal and deterministic explanations. While the former pedagogical goal may be achieved with direct instruction and demonstration, or by practical activities oriented towards individual or collaborative knowledge-construction, it seems that the very nature of knowledge in open domains such as history calls for a dialogical approach to learning the viewpoints of different social actors.

The same reasoning applies to designing and using argument graphs. The ontology of the graphical interface should to some extent be inspired by the ontology of the knowledge in the learning domain in question. Issues discussed should be inspired by this ontology, and, more importantly, by the known problems of learners with knowledge acquisition in the domain. Precisely because the goal is knowledge acquisition, we need experimental design to address the ideas, concepts and relations that are produced and these need to be compared against some desired level of expertise. Indeed, many studies about argument graphs confuse the mere use of graphs with a specific pedagogical approach, ignore explicit learner needs, and lack an adequate method for analyzing knowledge acquisition in (interactive) processes and outcomes. Although these studies may address knowledge acquisition as an outcome of using argumentation graphs, it is very rare that this knowledge is addressed explicitly in the analyses of processes and outcomes. Arguments are usually counted, but not examined.

The goal in the Lund et al. (2007,) study discussed above was knowledge acquisition in the domain of genetically modified organisms, so the outcome would be the number of relevant ideas and concepts that were produced in the two conditions. Distinctions between arguments, opinions or other types of ideas and relations would not be relevant, but in this case the researchers have particular ideas about the nature of the knowledge as being argumentative. The difference in numbers of opinions between the two conditions reflects the difference in task goals, either in terms of representing a debate or carrying out the debate. The experimental comparison did not really address the design and use of the argument graph, but rather, the instructional scenario of which it was a part. If we agree that revising an individual graph to reflect ideas grasped during the discussion indicates transfer of knowledge, then the task of representing a debate leads to more ideas, but not necessarily to argumentative ones. Moreover, the task itself of updating one's own argument graph in the light of a previous debate may be a constructive/reflective task in itself that leads to elaboration of further ideas that were not in fact at stake in the debate. Closer inspection of these outcomes would be needed to determine the types and depth of knowledge acquisition. In addition, the Lund et al. study used computer mediated chat as the medium for conversation. Participants who used Belvedere on a shared desktop revealed that the most interesting argumentation was not within the diagrams, but in the oral dialogues among participants (Suthers, 2003). The diagrams were later redesigned to encourage focus on evidential relations between data and hypotheses. However, rather than serving as a medium of communication or a formal record of the argumentation process, the representations were now viewed as resources (stimuli and guides) for stimulating conversation and reasoning 'around' the diagrams.

As we see it, argument graphs serve knowledge acquisition most importantly as *resources for reflection* on the argumentive structure of a domain under discussion. The underlying structure is not necessarily an argumentative schema, but relates to the knowledge of the domain under discussion. The ontology that is used for the structuring of the ideas may have a strong constraining effect on thinking and learning activities, but we have seen cases where instructions were completely overruled by users (e.g., van Amelsvoort et al., 2007). What learners take away from the activity is contingent on the extent to which the instructional design addresses conceptual difficulties in the domain, and the nature of the support and feedback on the adequacy of their activity, within the rules and norms of the educational context. Concerning argument graphs, it seems that integration of graph construction activity with other modes of communication is a crucial factor, for technical as well as pedagogical design.

(2) Knowledge of Collaboration: Groups Improving Collaboration by Participating in Joint Activity

The type of collaborative learning that most people engage in—and for many people, the only type of collaborative learning they ever engage in—is the collaborative learning involved in becoming part of a group. In daily life, people are part of work, home, leisure communities. Members of a community share aspects of common identity and viewpoints with respect to some issue or activity (Wenger, McDermott, & Snyder, 2002). Becoming and being part of a community is an ongoing interactive and collaborative process. It cannot be done by individuals alone, nor is it a purely cognitive process. It involves activities in which relational and emotional involvement of people is at stake. Finally, it is a slow process of long duration that may take several years, and may truly never end as groups change and new members and developments affect the community. With respect to collaborative learning processes, two general types of questions may be posed here: (1) how does a community learn and change? and (2) how do we characterise the process of becoming part of it?

The first question does not seem to concern cognitive psychology directly, although there is substantial research about the role of argument graphs in changing how people think and learn (e.g., Schwarz, Schur, Pensso, & Tayer, 2011). In the next section, on knowledge management, we discuss studies about groups changing and learning as a consequence of sharing each other's ideas. In the current section, however, we focus on the social aspects of collaboration. The question is how collaborative groups develop and how collaboration itself changes as a result of collaborative activities (Stahl, 2011). The main issue for education is how to design appropriate learning scenario's (and tools) matching a communities interests and learning needs (Baker, Bernard, & Dumez-Féroc, 2012).

Crook (2013) discusses the current trend of many theorists turning away from perspectives that center on individual minds towards perspectives that highlight social interaction and social practice (e.g., Wenger, McDermott, & Snyder, 2002). Intersubjectivity, or the ability to coordinate with other people, involves the ability of people to "mindread" each other (Byrne & Whiten, 1991), including their desires, beliefs, intentions, perceptions, and so on (Tomasello, Kruger, & Ratner, 1993). When this ability to understand the psychological states of others turns into the motivation to share those states within interactions, we may have a powerful drive towards collaboration as a specific and rewarding experience (Crook, 2013). This type of learning involves the relatively slow learning processes of groups, and especially relationships and practices changing within groups, as an outcome of social activity, or what Crook (2013) refers to as *motivated coordination*.

It is important to consider how community building—or group development and its corresponding quality of collaborative practices around it (see Détienne, Baker, & Burkhardt, 2010)—is *mediated* by activities involving argument maps. By jointly constructing an argument diagram and representing relations between individuals' ideas and reasons, some kind of "intercognitive bond" may be created between people. Discussions based on the diagram may lead to the creation or maintenance of interpersonal and affective relations (Andriessen, Baker, & van der Puil, 2011). There may be multiple timescales involved in these processes (Lemke, 2000) in which the long term process of tools becoming part of daily practice, thereby changing this practice (Säljö, 1991), while in the short term, learners may work with an argument map for the first time. When we ask ourselves how collaboration and community building is affected by using argument maps as an example of a social medium, we may have to incorporate more than one timescale.

One might inquire as to the effects of using argument graphs on collaboration. This is an important issue because the effect of any multimedia representational tool depends on the learners having mastered the cognitive tasks associated with their use (Ainsworth, 2006), and because argument graphs typically are used in collaboration. As far as we know, there have not been any explicit research findings linking argument graphs to improving collaboration, but especially studies investigating the effects on collaboration of different roles assigned to learners, the awareness of group activity during collaborative argumentation, or comparing effects of use of tools on collaboration.

However, some indirect evidence may be worth discussing. Strijbos (2004) showed that the main result of assigning roles to collaborative groups involved in a learning assignment was increased awareness of group efficiency and more task coordination. Research by Janssen (2008) likewise used argument maps in combination with a participation tool to study collaborative text production in the domain of history. This participation tool provided information about the amount and length of messages by each participant and by the group. The coding scheme for collaborative activities distinguished task-related and social activities, as well as performance and regulation activities. Awareness of group activities was assessed by a questionnaire. Treatment group students sent more long (five words or more) messages, and there was some evidence for higher equality of participation. Similar levels of group awareness were reported from the questionnaire. Also, there were indications that the tool stimulated students to spend more time on regulation of social activities (p. 62). Each of these outcomes indicated that working with argument graphs improved collaboration. In contrast, Janssen compared an argument graph to a linear textual representation with the same coding scheme for collaborative activities. The students' task was to provide a complete representation of a historical debate. No clear differences on social aspects of collaboration were obtained.

We think that research about the social processes of group work, CSCL, and collaborative argumentation is the basis for understanding how tools change learning in the long term. Perhaps because effects on such processes only show up after longer periods of work rather than a single experimental session, there is little cognitive research concerning this. One possible exception is the related research on the positive effects of explicitly teaching students "ground rules" of different types of "talk" (e.g. exploratory, inquiry, knowledge building) on collaboration that is described in Wegerif, Mercer, and Dawes (1999) and Mercer (2000). Similarly, within the framework of developing a method for analyzing the quality of collaboration in groups of learners, Spada and colleagues (Meier, Spada, & Rummel, 2007) showed that groups improved their collaboration and learning outcomes when they were explicitly taught the same criteria for good quality collaboration (e.g., grounding, building on each other's ideas, and trying to resolve conflicts constructively). There is every reason to believe that teaching rules for how to collaborate would also be beneficial in the case of argument diagrams.

A starting case for this point is the study by Wegerif et al. (2010), using an argument mapping tool called Digalo, in which an awareness system for creative and critical thinking was implemented. Instead of looking for formal indicators of deepening of the space of debate by testing proposed ideas, these researchers looked for "new ways of seeing problems" by integrating multiple perspectives. Graphical interfaces may be more suitable for this purpose than linear threaded discussions (Wegerif, 2007, p. 259). It appeared that such "widening" moves could be coded by artificial intelligence techniques, and fed back to the moderators of the dialogues. The algorithm identifies clusters of contributions made by different students that indicate critical deepening or creative widening of a conversation. The algorithm is based on the idea of using cluster examples to find similar clusters in new discussions, which is similar to the ideas from the subfield of artificial intelligence known as case-based reasoning (Kolodner, 1993; McLaren, 2003). The study reports results supporting the validity of the algorithm, but not about its effects on collaboration and development of creative thinking.

(3) Knowledge Management: Sharing and Using Each Other's Knowledge in a Network

The types of learning discussed so far are each typical of different contexts. Knowledge acquisition within in a domain mainly takes place in a school context, while learning to collaborate takes place as part of the daily social contexts in which individuals participate. The type of learning discussed in the current section—knowledge management—is most relevant for professional contexts, especially those in which knowledge is rapidly changing (Andriessen, Baker, & Suthers, 2003).

The term "knowledge management" refers to the process of strategically moderating shared ideas and experiences within a professional context such as a knowledge organization (Nonaka, 1991). Knowledge management research is carried out in a specific community called CSCW (computer supported collaborative work). Tools for collaboration, deliberation, and decision support, also known as tools for collective intelligence, are being designed to manage ideas and knowledge. People need to be managed in order for them to share their knowledge, and do not do so spontaneously, out of generosity, but out mutual best-interest. Sharing knowledge is difficult, but its benefits can be huge. Many organizations, including universities, would perform better if their members would be able to efficiently and effectively share what they know. This would allow quick identification of new ideas and important experiences, allow these ideas and experiences to travel fast within the organization, prevent knowledge from disappearing when individual workers leave, improve the quality of work and innovation because more people can be relied on to know, and understand what would be relevant for a job or problematic situation. The mutuality of what is known makes it increasingly less necessary to articulate the contexts, premises and assumptions of reasoning—these are implicitly known by the partners, and are understood to be known (Ainsworth, 2006). Nevertheless, the main point about shared knowledge as an output of collaboration is not that it is simply knowledge that is more extensive (in the simplest sense of "two heads are better than one"), but that the shared nature of the knowledge creates a platform for the sustained process of knowledge construction.

Supporting the sharing of knowledge alone is insufficient; it needs management as well. Internet technology is very successful in capturing many loose ideas, by many people, and there is a lot of knowledge being shared. But many contributions have insufficient quality, discussions are unsystematic, group discussions wander off, are strongly influenced by some loud voices, and are rarely evidence-based or based on valid argumentation. This is where argumentation tools may help (Kirschner, Buckingham-Shum, & Carr, 2003). Most researchers studying the use of argument graphs would agree that these tools are platforms for sharing understanding. For example, Suthers (2003) listed three general advantages of using argument maps in learning situations: (1) Initiating negotiation of meaning; (2) serving as a representational proxy for gestures; and (3) providing a foundation for shared awareness.

For collective knowledge management and sharing, argument diagrams have the advantage of making explicit, visible, relations between "pieces of knowledge" (to paraphrase DiSessa, 1988), between people and knowledge, and between people themselves, in a knowledge-mediated way. The disadvantage of such diagrams—at least if they are considered in isolation—is that their restriction to small text-box statements makes them less suitable as means for keeping a trace of the interactive negotiation of knowledge in the surrounding discussion. Thus, one reason why argument diagram tools are rarely used alone is that they could be considered as enabling creation of maps or relations between ideas or statements which serve as a basis for subsequent collaborative text writing in which extended knowledge negotiation can be summarized.

However, collaborative argument maps usually are highly effective. Ligorio, Andriessen, Baker, Knoller & Tateo (2009) introduce a tool called CoFFEE (collaborative face-to-face educational environment), the design of which is based on group systems used in professional communities for sharing ideas and collective decision making (e.g., van Gelder, 2003). Both CoFFEE and other tools for argumentative discussion, such as chat, discussion forum, voting, and an argument graph, can be combined in a scenario in which sharing and elaborating ideas through collaborative argumentation is central. Users work together in the same room, while speaking orally as well as communicating with the computer. This allows a group working with the same ideas using several tools, and exploiting the benefits of written as well as oral communication.

(4) Knowledge Creation: Construction and Application of Innovative Designs, Solutions, and Other Artifacts by Group Activity

Advancing the frontiers of knowledge has been the goal of all scientific endeavour. Knowledge building, as it has been coined by Scardamalia and Bereiter (2006), is an attempt to create a knowledge-creating civilization, by initiating students into a knowledge creating culture. Hence, the purpose of learning activities is creating a way of knowing and thinking most conducive to knowledge creation. This is accomplished by a pedagogy in which learners engage in creative work significantly advancing the state of knowledge in the classroom and situating this activity with respect to larger societal knowledge building effort. Learners are honoured for the contributions they make to this effort. An important component of knowledge building is the creation of epistemic artifacts such as theories and models, concrete models and setups. These artifacts serve as tools in the further advancement of knowledge, in the sense that others can further build on them. Discourse in knowledge building activities do not merely serve to share and criticize ideas, but also to advance common understanding rather than mere agreement, and to expand the base of accepted facts (Bereiter, 1994). This is why, according to Bereiter (2002) argumentation, with its focus on logic, evidence and persuasion is not a suitable knowledge-building activity. We take issue with this statement because particular forms of argumentation, but especially those oriented towards the cooperative exploration of a dialogical space (see e.g., Nonnon, 1996.), can precisely serve to create consensus that may be all the more solid since it has been put to critical test. Software supporting knowledge building such as CSILE is a complex environment in which many participants can work on several projects, and ideas are part of a multilayered, multimedia, and asynchronous system by which much more precision (and complexity) could be achieved in linking ideas.

In spite of this caution against the practice of argumentation in learning situations, many researchers working with argumentation and argument maps have linked their work with knowledge building (e.g., Leitão, 2000). It may be fruitful in the future to broaden our definition to include this. Perhaps it is by cooperative critical exploration of issues that do not form the object of consensus, that knowledge-building can better delineate the space of shared knowledge? In our view of argumentation and knowledge building, we think the work by Suthers and colleagues is very relevant (although these authors deliberately avoid exploiting the terms argumentation and knowledge building). For example, Suthers, Dwyer, Medina, and Vatrapu (2010) propose a framework for conceptualizing, representing and analyzing distributed interaction. This research goes beyond the affordances of argument graphs, and aims to develop a (media-independent) methodology for relating interaction and learning as the construction of (new) knowledge.

DISCUSSION

As researchers, the authors of this chapter have worked for more than fifteen years on the development and evaluation of argument graphs for learning. Like other researchers in the field (e.g., Schwarz et al., 2011;

Suthers & Chu, 2012), we see the use of argument graphs as part of a larger research program, which supports teachers and students, promotes understanding of the social dynamics of collaborative learning, improves sharing of ideas between professionals, and sustains knowledge creation. Our underlying message, for research as well as for practice, is to shift from individual perspectives on learning to perspectives that explain learner behavior based on the goals of the educational situation. Our division of types of learning is a division based on types of contexts and essential goals of four main types of learning situation. This does not mean that goals of a learning situation fixate those of learners. In our own research we have found that learning goals for groups are not constant, but fluctuate during various phases and as a consequence of social and cognitive events during collaboration (Andriessen, Pardijs, & Baker, 2013). What is required is a long-term, developmental approach to the study of the appropriation of artifacts such as argument diagrams, taking into account the general learning purposes with which their creation and critical examination may be associated. Cognitive research with argument graphs should go deeper into analyzing learning activities and eschew merely counting arguments or other loose activities.

Our work has taught us something else as well, which seems equally important for our current purpose. Argument diagrams as tools can be used for a variety of activities. These activities should be studied under various forms of learning. But it also seems that the results relating to their use give rise to an integrated conclusion about the use of argument graphs in learning situations. Argument graphs used in collaboration allow linking and categorizing pieces of knowledge together. Our claim is that the simple quality of explicitness in terms of such links makes them quite special, and more suitable than mind maps, concept maps, or causal maps for a particular form of collaborative activity involving the *construction of coherence* between participants involved in the learning activity. This coherence can be in terms of individual knowledge, knowledge of people functioning in a group or community and of the group itself, knowledge about what others know and how they understand things, and knowledge about their goals, ambitions, and trajectories of progress. This is because the social activity of engaging in the construction of argument diagrams requires participants to get together and produce a joint outcome.

We believe that argument maps provide an optimal form of collaborative learning. More than with mind maps and concept maps, the essential learning activity is shared in the sense of mutual understanding and mutual agreement, and also joint ownership. More than with causal maps or pictorial representations, users are free to produce according to their own constraints. Argument diagrams appear to be situated within a middle ground between relatively free and unconstrained on the one hand,

and scripted and restricted to only particular types of links and ideas on the other. This is also the case because we have seen that participants do not really argue all the time, but they do relate ideas, which requires reflection on what the others say and do, and on how they behave.

Argumentation, as a social activity, also allows participants in a group or community to discuss more freely and openly when they know each other better, or become better at discussing in a specific way, according to particular norms and rules that appear to exist in a community. Arguing to learn in school situations is no exception. Because argumentation has a personal component there is more at stake, and more diversity involved, than in cases of reproducing knowledge. Indeed, one of the goals of such an argumentative activity can in fact be to form and elaborate an argued, reasonable opinion that takes others' opinions into account, as in the case where one does not really know what one thinks in the first place. This diversity, in which one person takes on the idea of the other, makes it explicit by creating the argument diagram, helps to create the knowledge acquisition, social bonding, knowledge management and/or knowledge building.

In contrast, we assume that creating argument maps requires its users to reflect and create more coherence in the diverse ideas that come to mind, compared with argumentation without software support. We should not forget here the simple advantages of ease of modifiability of diagrams on a screen, facilitation of joint work, the possibility of integrating diagrams into other texts and obtaining a neat printout that diagrams have over pencil and paper. Hence, we suppose that more than in the canonical case of individual writing, the mere process of linking and adding to an argument map involves creating overlap with what is already there, on a local, but maybe even on a global level.

REFERENCES

Ainsworth, S. (2006). DeFT: A conceptual framework for considering learning with multiple representations. *Learning and Instruction, 16*, 183-198.

Ainsworth, S. E. (1999). A functional taxonomy of multiple representations. *Computers and Education, 33*, 2-3, 131-152.

Andriessen, J. (2006). Arguing to learn. In K. Sawyer (Ed.), *Handbook of the Learning Sciences, first edition* (pp. 443-460). New York, NY: Cambridge University Press.

Andriessen, J., Baker, M., & Suthers, D. (2003). Argumentation, Computer Support, and the Educational Context of Confronting Cognitions. In J. Andriessen, M. Baker & D. D. Suthers (Eds.), *Arguing to Learn: Confronting cognitions in computer supported argumentation* (pp. 1-25). Dordrecht, The Netherlands: Kluwer.

Andriessen, J., Baker, M., & Pardijs, M. (2013). Getting on and getting along: tension in the development of collaborations. In M. Baker, J. Andriessen & S. Järvelä (Eds.), *Affective Learning Together: The socio-emotional turn in collaborative learning research* (pp. 205-230). London, England: Routledge.

Andriessen, J., Baker, M., & van der Puil, C. (2011). Socio-cognitive tensions in collaborative working relations. In S. Ludvigsen, A. Lund, I. Rasmussen, & R. Saljo (Eds.), *Learning across sites: New tools, infrastructures and practices* (pp. 222-242). London, England: Routledge.

Andriessen, J. E. B., & Schwarz, B. B. (2009). Argumentative design. In N. Muller Mirza & A.-N. Perret-Clermont (Eds.), *Argumentation and education: Theoretical foundations and practices* (pp. 145-176). Dordrecht, The Netherlands: Springer.

Baker, M. J. (1999). Argumentation and Constructive Interaction. In G. Rijlaarsdam & E. Espéret (Series Eds.) & P. Coirier & J. Andriessen (Vol. Eds.), *Studies in Writing: Foundations of argumentative text processing* (Vol. 5., pp. 179–202). Amsterdam, The Netherlands: University of Amsterdam Press.

Baker, M. (2003). Computer-mediated argumentative interactions for the co-elaboration of scientific notions. In J. Andriessen, M. Baker, & D. Suthers (Eds.), *Arguing to learn: Confronting cognitions in computer-supported collaborative learning environments* (pp. 47-78). Dordrecht, the Netherlands: Kluwer Academic.

Baker, M. (2009). Argumentative interactions and the social construction of knowledge. In N. Muller Mirza & A.-N. Perret-Clermont (Eds.), *Argumentation and Education: Theoretical foundations and practices* (pp. 127-144). Dordrecht, The Netherlands: Springer.

Baker, M., Andriessen, J., Lund, K., Van Amelsvoort, M., & Quignard, M. (2007). Rainbow: A framework for analyzing computer-mediated pedagogical debates. *International Journal of Computer-Supported Collaborative Learning*, *2*(3), 315-357.

Baker, M., Bernard, F.–X. & Dumez-Féroc, I. (2012). Integrating Computer-supported collaborative learning into the classroom: the anatomy of a failure. *Journal of Computer Assisted Learning*, *28*(2), 161-176.

Baker, M. J., Quignard, M., Lund, K., & Séjourné, A. (2003). Computer-supported collaborative learning in the space of debate. In B. Wasson, S. Ludvigsen, & U. Hoppe (Eds.), *Designing for change in networked learning environments: Proceedings of the international conference on computer support for collaborative learning 2003* (pp. 11-20). Dordrecht, The Netherlands: Kluwer Academic.

Bereiter, C. (1994). Implications of postmodernism for science, or, science as a progressive discourse. *Educational Psychologist*, *29*(1), 3-12.

Bereiter, C. (2002). *Education and mind in the knowledge age*. Mahwah, NJ: Erlbaum.

Byrne, R., & Whiten, A. (1991). Computation and mindreading in primate tactical deception. In A. Whiten (Ed.), *Natural theories of mind* (pp. 127-141). Oxford, England: Basil Blackwell.

Carr, C. S. (2003). Using computer supported argument visualization to teach legal argumentation. In P. A. Kirschner, S. J. Buckingham-Shum, & C. S. Carr (Eds.), *Visualizing argumentation: software tools for collaborative and educational sense-making* (pp 75-96). Berlin, Germany: Springer.

Cho, K. L., & Jonassen, D. H. (2002). The effects of argumentation scaffolds on argumentation and problem solving. *Educational Technology Research and Development, 50*(3), 5-22.

Crook, C. (2013). Varieties of "togetherness" in learning—and their mediation. In M. Baker, J. Andriessen, & S. Järvelä (Eds.), *Affective Learning Together: the social turn in collaborative learning research* (pp. 33-51). London, England: Routledge.

Davies, M. (2011). Concept mapping, mind mapping and argument mapping: what are the differences and do they matter? *Higher Education, 62,* 279-301.

Détienne, F., Baker, M. J. & Burkhardt, J.-M. (Eds.) (2010). *Proceedings of the International Workshop on Quality of Collaboration. COOP 2010 Conference* (Aix-en-Provence, 18 May 2010). International Reports on Socio-informatics, vol. 7, issue 1. Bonn: International Institute for Socio-informatics Publishers (ISSN 1861-4280). Retrieved from http://www.iisi.de/102.0.html

DiSessa, A. (1988). Knowledge in pieces. In G. Forman & P. Pufall (Eds.), *Constructivism in the computer age* (pp. 49–70). Hillsdale, NJ: Lawrence Erlbaum Associates.

Harrell, M. (2005). *Using argument diagramming software in the classroom* (Paper 348). Pittsburgh, PA: Carnegie Mellon University, Department of Philosophy. Retrieved from http://repository.cmu.edu/philosophy/348

Janssen, J. (2008). *Using visualizations to support collaboration and coordination during computer-supported collaborative learning* (Doctoral dissertation). Print Partners Ipskamp.

Kirschner, P. A., Buckingham-Shum, S. J., & Carr, C. S. (Eds.), *Visualizing argumentation: Software tools for collaborative and educational sense-making.* Berlin, Germany: Springer.

Kolodner, J. (1993). *Case-based reasoning.* San Francisco, CA: Morgan Kaufman.

Laurinen, L. I., & Marttunen, M. J. (2007). Written arguments and collaborative speech acts in practicing the argumentative power of language through chat debates. *Computers & Composition, 24,* 3, 230-246.

Leitão, S. (2000). Knowledge building in discourse communities. *Human Development, 43,* 364-368.

Lemke, J. (2000). Across the scales of time: Artifacts, activities, and meanings in ecosocial systems. *Mind, Culture, and Activity 7*(4), 273-290.

Ligorio, M. B., Andriessen, J., Baker, M., Knoller, N., & Tateo, L. (2009). *Talking over the Computer. Pedagogical scenarios to blend computer and face to face interaction.* Napoli, Naples: Scriptaweb.

Lund, K., Molinari, G., Séjourné, A., & Baker, M. (2007). How do argumentation diagrams compare when student pairs use them as a means for debate or as a tool for representing a debate? *Computer-Supported Collaborative Learning, 2,* 273-295.

McAlister, S., Ravenscroft, A., & Scanlon, E. (2004). Combining interaction and context design to support collaborative argumentation using a tool for synchronous CMC. *Journal of Computer Assisted Learning, 20*(3), 194-204.

McLaren, B. M. (2003). Extensionally defining principles and cases in ethics: An AI model. *Artificial Intelligence, 150,* 145-181.

McLaren, B. M., Scheuer, O., & Mikšátko, J. (2010). Supporting collaborative learning and e-discussions. Using artificial intelligence techniques. *International Journal of Artificial Intelligence in Education, 20,* 1-46.

Mercer, N. (2000) Words and minds: How we use language to think together. London, England: Routledge.

Meier, A., Spada, H., & Rummel, N. (2007). A rating scheme for assessing the quality of computer-supported collaboration processes. *International Journal of Computer-Supported Collaborative Learning, 2*(1), 63-86.

Muller Mirza, N., Tartas, V., Perret-Clermont, A.-N., & De Pietro, J.-F. (2007). Using graphical tools in a phased activity for enhancing dialogical skills: An example with Digalo. *International Journal of Computer-Supported Collaborative Learning, 2,* 247-272.

Munneke, L., Andriessen, J., Kanselaar, G., & Kirschner, P. (2007). Supporting interactive argumentation: influence of representational tools on discussing a wicked problem. *Computers in Human Behavior 23*(3), 1072-1088.

Newell, G. E., Beach, R., Smith, J., & VanDerHeide, J. (2011). Teaching and learning argumentative reading and writing: A Review of Research. *Reading Research Quarterly, 46*(3), 273-304.

Nonaka, I. (1991). The knowledge creating company. *Harvard Business Review 69,* 96-104.

Nonnon, E. (1996). Activités argumentatives et élaboration de connaissances nouvelles: le dialogue comme espace d'exploration [Argumentative activities and the elaboration of new knowledge: dialogue as a space of exploration]. *Langue Française, 112,* 67-87.

Noroozi, O., Weinberger, A., Biemans, H. J. A., Mulder, M., & Chizari, M. (2012). Argumentation-based computer supported collaborative learning (ABCSCL): A synthesis of 15 years of research. *Educational Research Review, 7*(2), 79-106.

Overdijk, M., van Diggelen, W., Kirschner, P., & Baker, M. (2012). Connecting agents and artifacts in CSCL: Towards a rationale of mutual shaping. *International Journal of Computer-Supported Collaborative Learning, 7*(2), 193-210.

Rabardel P. (1995). *Les Hommes et les technologies: Approches cognitives des instruments contemporains* [Humans and technologies: Cognitive approaches to contemporary instruments]. Paris, France: Armand Colin.

Säljö, R. (1991). Learning and mediation: Fitting reality into a table. *Learning and Instruction, 1,* 261–272.

Scardamalia, M., & Bereiter, C. (2006). Knowledge building. In K. Sawyer (Ed.), *Handbook of the learning sciences* (1st ed., pp. 97-115). New York, NY: Cambridge University Press.

Scheuer, O., Loll, F., Pinkwart, N., & McLaren, B. M. (2010). Computer-supported argumentation: A review of the state of the art. *International Journal of Computer-Supported Collaborative Learning, 5*(1), 43-102.

Schwarz, B. B., & Glassner, A. (2007). The role of floor control and of ontology in argumentative activities with discussion-based tools. *International Journal of Computer-Supported Collaborative Learning, 2*(4), 449-478.

Schwarz, B. B., Shur, Y., Pensso, H., & Tayer, N. (2011). Perspective taking and synchronous argumentation for learning the day/night cycle. *International Journal of Computer-Supported Collaborative Learning, 6*(1), 449-478.

Stahl, G. (2011). How to study group cognition. In S. Puntambekar, G. Erkens, & C. Hmelo-Silver (Eds.), *Analyzing interactions in CSCL: Methodologies, approaches and issues* (pp. 107-130). New York, NY: Springer.

Stegmann, K., Weinberger, A., & Fischer, F. (2007). Facilitating argumentative knowledge construction with computer-supported collaboration scripts. *International Journal of Computer-Supported Collaborative Learning, 2*(4), 421-447.

Strijbos, J.-W. (2004, April). *The effect of roles on computer-supported collaborative learning* (Doctoral dissertation). Maastricht, The Netherlands: Datawyse.

Suthers, D. D. (2003). Representational guidance for collaborative learning. In H. U. Hoppe, F. Verdejo, & J. Kay (Eds.), *Artificial intelligence in education* (pp. 3-10). Amsterdam, The Netherlands: IOS Press.

Suthers, D. D., & Chu, K-H. (2012). Identifying mediators of socio-technical capital in a networked learning environment. In L. Dirckinck-Holmfeld, V. Hodgson, & D. McConnell (Eds.), *Exploring the theory, pedagogy and practice of networked learning* (pp. 61-74). New York, NY: Springer.

Suthers, D. D., Dwyer, N., Medina, R., & Vatrapu, R. (2010). A framework for conceptualizing, representing, and analyzing distributed interaction. *International Journal of Computer Supported Collaborative Learning, 5*(1), 5-42.

Suthers, D., & Hundhausen, C. (2003). An empirical study of the effects of representational guidance on collaborative learning. *Journal of the Learning Sciences, 12*(2), 183-219.

Suthers, D. D., Vatrapu, R., Medina, R., Joseph, S., & Dwyer, N. (2008). Beyond Threaded discussion: representational guidance in asynchronous collaborative learning environments. *Computers & Education, 50*(4), 1103-1127.

Tomasello, M., Kruger, A., & Ratner, H. (1993). Cultural learning. *Behavioral and Brain Sciences, 16*, 495-552.

Toulmin, S. E. (1958). *The uses of argument.* Cambridge, England: Cambridge University Press.

Van Amelsvoort, M., Andriessen, J., & Kanselaar, G. (2007). Representational tools in computer-supported collaborative argumentation-based learning: How dyads work with constructed and inspected argumentative diagrams. *Journal of the Learning Sciences, 16*(4), 485-521.

Van Gelder, T. (2003). Enhancing deliberation through computer supported argument visualization. In P. A. Kirschner, S. J. Buckingham-Shum, & C. S. Carr (Eds.), *Visualizing argumentation: Software tools for collaborative and educational sense-making* (pp. 97-116). Berlin, Germany: Springer.

Van Drie, J., Van Boxtel, C., Jaspers, J., & Kanselaar, G. (2005). Effects of representational guidance on domain-specific reasoning in CSCL. *Computers in Human Behavior, 21*(4), 575-602).

Veerman, A. L., Andriessen, J. E. B., & Kanselaar, G. (2000). Enhancing learning through synchronous electronic discussion. *Computers & Education, 34*(2-3), 1-22.

Wegerif, R. (2007). *Dialogic, educational and technology: Expanding the space of learning.* New York, NY: Springer-Verlag.

Wegerif, R., McLaren, B. M., Chamrada, M., Scheuer, O., Mansour, N., Mikšátko, J., & Williams, M. (2010). Exploring creative thinking in graphically mediated synchronous dialogues. *Computers & Education, 54*, 613-621.

Wegerif, R., Mercer, N., & Dawes, L. (1999). From social interaction to individual reasoning: An empirical investigation of a possible socio-cultural model of cognitive development. *Learning and Instruction, 9*(6), 493-516.

Wenger, E., McDermott, R., & Snyder, W. (2002). *Cultivating communities of practice: a guide to managing knowledge.* Cambridge, MA: Harvard Business School Press.

SECTION IV

USING VISUAL DISPLAYS TO IMPROVE RESAERCH

CHAPTER 14

A TYPOLOGY OF VISUAL DISPLAYS IN QUALITATIVE ANALYSES

Lori Olafson, Florian Feucht, and Gwen Marchand

ABSTRACT

This chapter describes how visual displays are used in qualitative analysis and how the use of different analysis tools of computer aided qualitative data analysis software (CAQDAS) programs that enhance the visual displays of qualitative analyses. A brief overview of qualitative analysis is provided, and the use of visual displays in qualitative research is outlined. A 3 x 2 typology of visual displays is introduced that is used to categorize visual displays by the type of display (text, table, graphic) and its intended function (process, product). This typology is then utilized to provide specific examples of visual displays derived from ATLAS.ti, a software program that is one type of CAQDAS designed to support qualitative analysis. We describe how ATLAS.ti can be used to visually capture processes and products of data analysis, and discuss ways in which using visual displays facilitates a variety of activities related to managing, coding, and interpreting data.

Learning Through Visual Displays, pp. 359–385
Copyright © 2013 by Information Age Publishing

The use of visual displays, such as graphs, charts, and histograms has a long history in quantitative research. Their use goes back to the time of Shakespeare, as described by Wainer and Thissen (1981): "The use of visual displays to present quantitative material is very old indeed. As Shakespeare noted (Henry VI, Act IV), 'Our forefathers had no other book but the score and tally' " (p. 194). The appeal of visual displays for quantitative data is that they communicate complex ideas with clarity, precision, and efficiency. Tufte (2001) outlined three broad purposes for creating data displays in quantitative research: (1) they "induce the viewer to think about substance rather than methodology," (2) they "encourage the eye to compare different pieces of data," and, (3) they "reveal the data at several levels of detail, from a broad overview to the fine structure" (p. 13).

On the other hand, the use of visual displays in qualitative research has been limited. Grounded theory is the only qualitative methodology that explicitly advocates for the use of graphics to visually present results. These grounded theory visual displays may take the form of integrative diagrams (Corbin & Strauss, 2007; Harry, Sturges, & Klingner, 2005) or paradigm models (Schraw, Wadkins, & Olafson, 2007). An integrative diagram provides a visual model of interrelated explanations of themes and represents a plausible explanatory framework at the end of analysis (Corbin & Strauss, 2007). Similarly, a paradigm model visually relates themes into an integrated storyline that describes a phenomenon by systematically linking antecedents, contexts and conditions, and consequences related to the phenomenon under study (Schraw et al., 2007). Although grounded theory has utilized visual displays, the need for qualitative data displays across methodologies has been recognized for at least 30 years. In 1984, Miles and Huberman published the first edition of their book on qualitative analyses in which they described their approach as involving three analytic activities: data reduction, data display, and conclusion drawing. The second edition of their book in 1994 continued to press the need for using data displays in qualitative research, noting that a data display is "a visual format that presents information systematically" (Miles & Huberman, 1994, p. 91). Others have extended this argument by stating that a visual presentation in a qualitative study, "is dramatically easier to use than is a textual description or a spoken report" (Schneiderman, 1996, p. 336).

The purpose of this chapter is to describe how visual displays are used in qualitative analysis and how the use of computer aided qualitative data analysis software (CAQDAS) enhances the visual displays resulting from qualitative analyses. Software, such as MAXQDA, ATLAS.ti, NVivo, and HyperRESEARCH, are categorized as falling under the CAQDAS umbrella because they are packages that take an explicitly qualitative approach to qualitative data (Lewins & Silver, 2004). We begin with a brief overview of qualitative analysis, and outline how visual displays have been used in qualitative research. Then we describe how these techniques are used in CAQDAS. Drawing from our own research projects, we provide specific visual display examples from ATLAS.ti, a software program belonging to the genre of CAQDAS that is designed to support the process of discovering patterns with numerous output options and collaboration tools (Friese, 2010).

QUALITATIVE ANALYSIS

Qualitative analysis is "a process of reviewing, synthesizing, and interpreting data to describe and explain the phenomena or social worlds being studied" (Fossey, Harvey, McDermott, & Davidson 2002, p. 728). It is the search for patterns in the data and the development of ideas to explain these patterns (Bernard & Ryan, 2010). There are several levels of analysis, described by Creswell (2013) as a data analysis spiral that are representative of most qualitative analyses. Analysis begins with organizing data for analytic procedures, then moves to reading and memoing, describing and classifying, and to visualizing and representing (Creswell, 2013). The first three phases of analysis are analytic processes, or procedures, in which the researcher actively works with the data in order to organize, describe, classify, and interpret. In the final phase of analysis, visualizing and interpreting, "researchers present the data, a packaging of what was found in text, tabular, or figure form" (p. 187). These final products, the outcomes of the analysis processes, may be in the form of paradigm model as in a grounded theory study, or primarily as a narrative augmented by tables and figures (Creswell, 2013). Table 14.1 illustrates how we interpreted Creswell's data analysis spiral as consisting of analytic processes and products.

A TYPOLOGY OF VISUAL DISPLAYS IN QUALITATIVE RESEARCH

Onwuegbuzie and Dickinson (2008) presented a taxonomy of visual displays for representing data in mixed methods research. Since visual displays can be used for both qualitative and quantitative data, Onwuegbuzie and Dickinson reasoned that graphical methods could be used in mixed methods research, involving the mixing of quantitative and qualitative approaches within the same study (p. 205). They developed a five-level taxonomy of visual display pertinent to both quantitative and qualitative analysis based on Tufte's (2001) description of methods for displaying quantitative data. In our reading of Tufte, we

Table 14.1.   Functions of Qualitative Analysis

Analytic Processes (Procedures)	Analytic Products (Outcomes)
Sorting and organizing data	Thick description (i.e., ethnography)
Identifying codes and developing a coding system.	Paradigm model (i.e., grounded theory)
Applying a coding system to a data set (interviews, observations, documents)	Patterns and themes (i.e., case study)
Comparing and grouping categories and codes	Description of the "essence" (i.e., phenomenology)
Writing analytic memos.	

found there were three primary levels: "The basic structures for showing data are the sentence, the table, and the graphic" (p. 178). We suggest that a three level taxonomy is appropriate for classifying visual displays of qualitative data.

The sentence, or text, is the lowest level of visual data and is the most common way of presenting qualitative data (Onwuegbuzie & Dickinson, 2008). However, the use of lengthy excerpts from interviews is "dispersed, sequential rather than simultaneous, poorly structured, and extremely bulky" (Miles & Huberman, 1994, p. 11). Providing interview excerpts in the form of quotations (the actual words of the participants) is an example of a level one data display.

The second level of data display is a table or matrix. Tufte (2001) referred to tables that included labels and explanatory sentences as "text-tables." An example of a text-table is a time-ordered display, described by Onwuegbuzie and Dickinson (2008) as a visual representation ordering data by time and sequence.

The third level of data display is a graphic, defined by Tufte (2001) as the integration of words and pictures. Mapping in graphic form, or in a network as described by Miles and Huberman (1994), shows "the interrelationships among groups and roles that underlie the context of individual behavior" (Onwuegbuzie & Dickinson, 2008, p. 207) and is an example of a level three data display.

In addition to modifying Onwuegbuzie and Dickinson's (2008) taxonomy of types of visual displays, we added the intended function of visual display (process and product) to our framework based on the work of Creswell (2013). Distinguishing between the function of a visual display as process or product was noted by Tufte (2001) in his description of a level three display:

the use of words and pictures together requires a special sensitivity to the purpose of the design—in particular, whether the graphic is primarily for communication and illustration of a settled finding, or, in contrast, for the exploration of a data set. (p. 182)

Our framework yields a 3 x 2 matrix that allows us to look at how level one, two, and three visual displays are used in the processes of qualitative analysis and how they are used to create products of analysis (see Table 14.2). We believe that the six cells of this matrix provide a more complete representation of the uses of visual displays in qualitative analyses.

In the next section of the chapter we provide examples from qualitative research to describe how visual displays are used for graphical representations of processes and products of qualitative analyses.

FUNCTIONS OF VISUAL DISPLAYS IN QUALITATIVE RESEARCH

In qualitative research, visual displays can be used in a variety of ways to represent processes and products of qualitative analysis. Miles and Huberman (1994) described process and product functions when they noted that data displays

are designed to assemble organized information into an immediately accessible, compact form so that the analyst can see what is happening and either draw justified conclusions or move on to the next step of analysis the display suggests might be useful. (p. 11)

A general strategy is to begin with descriptive display formats in which "coded data are entered, and, from them, conclusions of a descriptive sort are drawn and verified" (p. 307). Next, explanatory displays can be built and explanatory conclusions can be drawn (Miles & Huberman, 1994). In this way, data displays support reasoning about data and results by providing researchers with representational tools to move from description to explanation (Lyons, 2000).

More sophisticated data displays such as those that are designed "to permit careful comparisons, detection of differences, noting of patterns

Table 14.2.   Types of Visual Display by Function

	Process	Product
Level 1: Text	Text: Process	Text: Product
Level 2: Table	Table: Process	Table: Product
Level 3: Graphic	Graphic: Process	Graphic: Product

and themes, seeing trends" are advocated by Miles and Huberman (1994, p. 92). Formats for more sophisticated data displays fall into two major families: "matrices, with defined rows and columns, and networks, with a series of 'nodes' with links between them" (p. 93). For all their appeal, however, Onwuegbuzie and Dickinson (2008) note the challenge of using visual displays in qualitative research to effectively translate qualitative data into a visual format.

Visual Displays for Process

The creation and use of displays are analytic activities, according to Miles and Huberman (1994). Even the selection of participant quotes from lengthy interview transcripts, for example, is a form of data reduction. Yet, as Miles and Huberman note, displaying data in this format alone is "a weak and cumbersome form of display" (p. 91). Table and graphical data displays (levels two and three) are more likely to fulfill the goals of showing how data were reduced, detailing analytic steps, and making comparisons between categories and codes.

Tables can be utilized in a variety of ways. In their grounded theory study of academic procrastination, Schraw et al. (2007) used a table to identify and display to the reader five major categories and codes related to each category during the first phase of their analysis. Preliminary themes were then developed on the basis of these categories and codes (Schraw et al., 2007). Using the Type of Visual Display by Function matrix (Table 14.2), the table showing the analytic processes involved in coding and categorizing their interview data would be considered *Table: Process*.

An excellent example of a visual display that describes analytic procedures is provided by Harry et al. (2005) who included a data analysis map in their grounded theory study. They presented a visual model of the six levels of analysis they undertook, moving from open coding (level 1) to the theory that was generated (level 6). As described by Harry et al., "The numbers at far left represent the six levels of analysis, moving upward from the bottom of the figure" (p. 6). This graphical model of analytic processes is an example of a data display that would be categorized as *Graphic: Process* according to the Type of Visual Display by Function matrix.

An overview display, or "information visualization," is another example of a visual display related to the processes of analyses (*Graphic: Process*). These displays provide an overview of a data set, showing the structure of a data set and relations among data (Hornbaek & Hertzum, 2011). Overviews "should not only broadcast information but also aim to integrate multiple pieces of information" (p. 520).

Feucht (2011) also provided an example of a level three visual display used to communicate his analytic procedures (*Graphic: Process*). In his case study on the epistemic climate of a fourth grade English unit on drawing conclusions from text Feucht engaged in interviews, observations, and document collection. He created a map (see Figure 14.1) to illustrate the data collection methods/data sources, their triangulation, and the element of the model they informed succinctly and, therefore, functioned as a visual display of the data analysis process in the method section of the publication.

Visual Displays for Products

Visual displays are also used to graphically represent major findings, or products, of a qualitative study. As described previously, providing an excerpt from an interview with a participant would be considered a display of *Text: Product* using the Type of Visual Display by Function matrix (see Table 14.2).

Visually displaying the main themes resulting from data analysis procedures can be accomplished through the creation of a table (*Table: Product*). Schraw et al. (2007) used a table to summarize themes and macrothemes in their study of academic procrastination. These macrothemes were fully described in the main body of their article, but the summary table provided a clear overview. The table also demonstrated how themes were grouped into macrothemes and how they were related to final paradigm model.

Most common, however, are product displays in the form of matrices or networks (Miles & Huberman, 1994). The columns and rows of a matrix display draw attention to overall trends across categories (Averill, 2002). Additionally, a matrix can make "the synthesis and summary of important findings accessible to audiences who might otherwise never take the time to examine the voluminous data generated by the interview process" (p. 864).

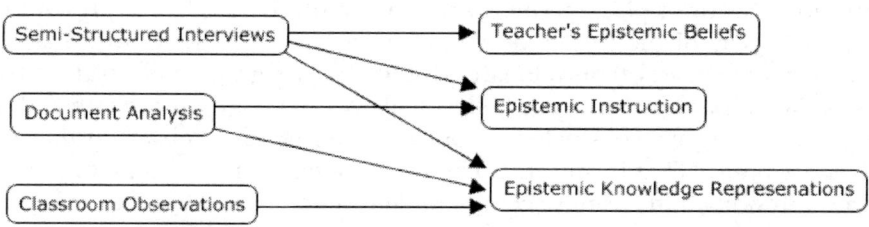

Figure 14.1.   Data collection, sources, and triangulation.

Lacey and Luff (2001) described framework analysis as developing and applying a coding framework to a data set, resulting in a matrix. Findings were represented in columns and rows by using headings from the thematic framework to create charts: "Charts can be either *thematic* for each theme across all respondents (cases) or *by case* for each respondent across all themes" (p. 10). These two matrix examples are displays categorized as *Graphic: Product*. Any choice of matrix type (i.e., thematic or case) utilized is dependent upon the researcher's purpose for the graphic.

Networks can take the form of maps and models, and in either map or model form a network is considered a graphical display (level 3). A common use of a network in a map form is a concept map (see Nesbit & Adesope, this volume). Concept maps have several uses in qualitative analysis. They can be used to reduce data, create a coding system, and analyze themes (Daley, 2004). These uses are all related to processes of analyses. However, the strength of concept mapping is seen in their utility in creating products of analysis, by visually displaying the associations between multiple themes and ideas (Burke et al., 2005).

Another example of a more sophisticated visual display is a conceptual model. These are described by Bernard and Ryan (2010) as a major part of qualitative analysis, involving "building, testing, displaying, and validating models" (p. 121). Examples of conceptual models provided by Bernard and Ryan include a process model that visually displays how events unfold over time, and an actor interaction model showing how each individual acts and behaves before and during an event. These are both presented graphically and would therefore be considered *Graphic: Product*.

Another example of a *Graphic: Product* display was provided in Feucht's (2011) case study on the epistemic climate of Mrs. M's fourth grade lesson on drawing conclusions from text. At the outset of the study the educational model for personal epistemology was used to theoretically frame and methodologically operationalize the study. The model describes the epistemic climate of classrooms based on four interrelated components: epistemic instruction, epistemic knowledge representations, epistemic beliefs of the teacher and students. In the results section, the educational model for personal epistemology was reprinted with alterations made to include a synopsis of the results of the case study. Figure 14.2 represents a visual display of the results pertaining to each of the three investigated elements of the epistemic climate. Essentially, the graphic illustrates that Mrs. M's espoused epistemic beliefs (solicited through an interview) did not match her enacted beliefs about teaching reading (observed during her teaching). That is, her instruction to students on what sources to use when drawing conclusions seemed to contradict each other and resulted in mixed epistemic messages. The model allowed the authors to theoretically speculate on the potential relationships among the teacher's epis-

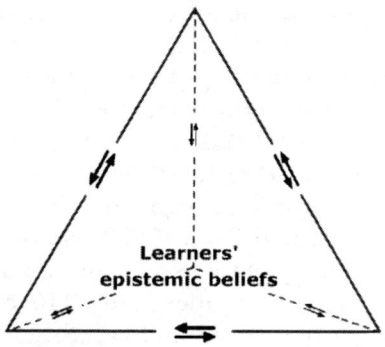

Epistemic instruction:
Teaching instruction have absolutistic &
multiplistic underpinnings of drawing
conclusions

**Learners'
epistemic beliefs**

**Epistemic knowledge
representations:**
Curriculum, textbook, and worksheets
have an absolutistic underpinning of
drawing conclusions

**Mrs. M's
epistemic beliefs:**
Teacher has absolutistic & evaluativistic
beliefs about drawing conclusions

Figure 14.2.   Mrs. M's epistemic beliefs, instruction, and knowledge representations about drawing conclusions.

temic beliefs, and the epistemic underpinnings of instruction and educational materials used in the observed lesson.

In qualitative research, visual displays can be created to illustrate the processes and products of analysis. As qualitative analysis rarely occurs as a fixed linear approach (Creswell, 2013) creating visual displays for process and product can occur at any point during the analysis. These can take the form of text, tables, or graphics. In the next section of the chapter, we consider how the use of a CAQDAS package can be used to create visual displays for the processes and products of qualitative analysis. We begin this section by providing a general overview of data analysis software.

COMPUTER AIDED QUALITATIVE DATA ANALYSIS SOFTWARE

Computer aided qualitative data analysis software (CAQDAS) programs have been available since the late 1980s and their use has expanded significantly. There are more than 30 different software applications for qualitative data analysis (Marshall & Rossman, 2011). Creswell (2013) notes that four of these programs are popular: MAXQDA, ATLAS.ti, NVivo, and HyperRESEARCH. A common misconception about software packages is that qualitative analysis is automated, which it is not. The programs are primarily responsible for data management while the tasks of analysis are the responsibility of the researcher who can use the software's tools to aid in analytic processes (Bernard & Ryan, 2010; Creswell, 2013; Friese, 2012). For example, the underlying analytic processes are the same for hand coding or using a computer (Creswell, 2013). In both cases, the researcher must identify text segments, develop codes, and assign codes to the text segments. One technique for hand coding outlined by Bernard and Ryan (2010) is cutting and sorting. In this method, text segments (quotations) are physically cut out from the interview transcript and pasted on index cards. The index cards are then sorted into piles of similar quotations and are assigned labels developed by the researcher. Similarly, when coding on the computer, the researcher decides on the text segments that are relevant for analysis, and assigns codes. CAQDAS programs do not identify quotations, develop codes or assign codes to text segments.

However, there are advantages to using CAQDAS related to both mechanical and conceptual data-analysis tasks (Thompson, 2002). The mechanical tasks of data management (i.e., storage and retrieval of qualitative data), for example, are superior to paper-based systems (Fielding & Lee, 2002). In these virtualized environments, "we can not only do all the operations available to the pre-CAQDAS researcher equipped with paper, scissors and pencils, but much more" (Konopásek, 2008, p. 7). Conceptual level processes are those in which the meanings, patterns, or connections among the data are explored by the researcher (Fossey et al., 2002). Software packages "can offer substantial support in the development of concepts and analytic frameworks, theoretical elaboration and hypothesis testing" because it makes the data-management process much less resource demanding (Garcia-Horta & Guerra-Ramos, 2009, p. 153).

Most qualitative software also facilitates an orderly and accountable practice of analysis (Fielding & Lee, 2002), allowing the processes of analyses to be more transparent and the analytical steps more systematically built into each other (Hwang, 2008). Transparency is described by Fossey et al. (2002) as the extent to which the processes of analysis are systematic, explicit, and visible and the extent to which these processes are shared in the written report. As Friese (2012) notes, "The steps of analysis can be traced and the entire process is open to view" (p. 2). This function is also described by Bringer, Johnston, and Brackenridge (2006): "Another benefit of consistent use of CAQDAS is that it doubles as an audit trail" (p. 246).

In this chapter, we focus on the use of ATLAS.ti, one of the many CAQ-DAS programs commercially available, as it is the program with which we are most familiar, having used it in our own research projects. It is not our intention to provide step-by-step directions for creating visual displays as these can be found in the user's guide to the software. Our goal is to draw attention to the ways in which visual displays can be utilized in qualitative analyses and how these can be represented in written accounts of the research.

ATLAS.ti has tools to assist with the development of visual displays for both the processes and products of analyses. According to Friese (2012), the software "allows you to explore your data visually. It can be used throughout the analysis and toward the end as a tool to integrate all your findings" (p. 191). The visualization component of the program helps researchers by enabling them to organize and visualize complex relationships and processes in the data. The ability of ATLAS.ti to capture complexity was noted by Muhr (2004), who concluded that "Tools are offered to visualize complex properties and relations between the objects accumulated during the process of eliciting meaning and structure from the analyzed data" (p. 3). Indeed, anything done in ATLAS.ti can be visualized (Friese, 2012).

Visual Displays for Process

The process of forming codes or categories represents the heart of qualitative data analysis, according to Creswell (2013). In the coding process, key words or tags are attached to segments of text for later retrieval (Miles & Huberman, 1994, p. 44). There are a variety of paper-and pencil methods to develop codes and coding systems described by Bernard and Ryan (2010), such as writing codes in the margins of the text, highlighting text segments with different colors, and cutting and sorting multiple copies of transcripts. As Friese (2012) explains, however, "software changes the way we build up coding systems. The process becomes much more exploratory due to the ease of renaming and modifying codes" (p. 3). One of the greatest advantages to using CAQDAS is "the visualization of data in the analytic process" and the ability to easily retrieve and visualize data, codes, categories and the ways in which these are linked (Garcia-Horta & Guerra-Ramos, 2009, p. 163). The search and retrieval functions of CAQDAS allow relevant segments of text to be quickly located, "making them available for inspection" (Miles & Huberman, 1994, p. 44). In ATLAS.ti, simple retrieval of coded data is performed by double-clicking on a code to generate a list of the code's quotations. The quotation can be viewed in its original context. More complex retrieval functions are also available, including retrieving multiple codes with a variety of output options.

As noted by Weitzman and Miles (1995) the text output options in ATLAS.ti are extremely rich. From the codes menu, it is possible to print a code list, a complete code hierarchy, or a list of codes with their immediate neighbors. Also available as output (to a printer or to a text editor) are code "trees" and code "forests" which are "graphical representations of the hierarchical relationships among codes" (Weitzman & Miles, p. 226). Additional outputs can be created that include coded documents, and a list of all codes used in a project. Groundedness (i.e., how many times the code has been used) and density (i.e., number of links to other codes) can be displayed for each code showing how relevant the code is in the data (Friese, 2012). A code that is used repeatedly within and across text files and that is linked to a number of other codes, is seen as potentially pertinent for additional analyses.

In the ATLAS.ti environment, text segments (referred to as quotations) and codes are displayed both textually in a drop-down list and graphically in the margin area (Friese, 2012). Definitions for codes can be written as comments that are attached to each code," making it easier to track changing meanings or associations, since you see the code definition right in front of you" (p. 79). Code definitions are also needed in a paper and pencil environment in order to assist with the coding process. For each code, Bernard and Ryan (2010) recommend providing a short description, a detailed description, a list of inclusion and exclusion criteria, and some typical and atypical examples from the text. This cumbersome document, known as a codebook, is needed by the analyst when coding to ensure consistency.

Comparing codes can be accomplished in a short amount of time, and viewing a list of codes after they have been grouped together can assist with the development of a theme (Leech & Onwuegbuzie, 2011) and in the development of categories. The quick comparison can also be utilized in the development of a coding hierarchy. The sorting and structuring of codes helps to bring order to the code list, as the researcher begins to realize that some codes would be good candidates for categories (Friese, 2012). From the code list, the researcher can "look for codes that are similar and might fit together under a more abstract category name" (p. 107). The newly developed category can then be linked to existing codes, and the linking feature of ATLAS.ti is another powerful application. In data linking, relevant data segments are connected with each other, "forming categories, clusters, or networks of information" (Miles & Huberman, 1994, p. 44). In these ways, software provides "powerful capabilities to develop hierarchically organized groups of codes (from categories to subcategories)" (Garcia-Horta & Guerra-Ramos, 2009, p. 153).

Tables can also be created that show the frequency of all codes by document. Graphs and tables of code counts can be used to give a sense of magnitude in the search for an underlying structure (Peters & Wester, 2007). It is also possible to create a matrix in which co-occurrences of codes are shown, and these "may reveal which codes take a central position and with which other codes these codes co-occur frequently" (p. 650). The *Co-occurrence Explorer* in ATLAS.ti shows "all codes that co-occur across all of your primary documents. The result is a cross-tabulation of all codes" (Friese, 2010, p. 31). This output can be displayed in a tree view or matrix.

Writing research memos can assist in the processes of data analysis and these can be attached to other objects (Friese, 2012). For example, "You could call up all text segments pertaining to characteristics of the victims and analyze these commonalities in a memo" (p. 22). Writing memos is described by Hutchison, Johnston, and Breckon (2010) as providing a workspace reflect on analytic techniques. They wrote conceptual memos attached to nodes that contained information about concepts or categories and about their analytical procedures (Hutchison et al., 2010).

Creating networks allows the researcher to explore and visualize relationships among different objects (Weitzman & Miles, 1995). In ATLAS.ti, the tool used to create a network is called the Network view. These graphical illustrations can be used to explore the data, discovering connections between concepts and interpreting findings, and to "aid creativity and to help in detailing the entire structure of an idea or a line of argument" (Friese, 2012, p. 191). Network views allow you to "conceptualize the structure by connecting sets of similar elements together in a visual diagram. With the aid of network views you can express relationships between codes, quotations, and memos" (Muhr, 2004, p. 33). Within the network view, the researcher decides on the quotations, codes, or memos to be included and the software quickly places these within the network view screen. Exploring the meanings, patterns or connections among the data and creating links, however, cannot be relegated to the software: "computer software cannot replace the conceptual level processes required of the researcher" (Fossey et al., 2002, p. 729). To express relationships between codes, quotations, or memos the researcher clicks on the linking feature and chooses from a list of possible relations such as "is associated with," "is a cause of," or "is a property of."

Visual Displays for Product

There are many kinds of visual displays that can be created using qualitative software for theory building and for the presentation of findings.

The network view, described above as a tool for ongoing conceptual work, can also be used to create a visual display of the product of the analysis as well as to describe the process.

Within ATLAS.ti there are two layout options for networks, the semantic layout and the topological view. The semantic layout evenly distributes all nodes in a network view, whereas the topological view "arranges your codes from the upper left-hand corner to the lower right-hand corner ... this is useful when you want to visualize a sequence of events or activities" (Friese, 2012, p. 198). Figure 14.3 shows how the software arranges the codes in a topological view.

Both the semantic and topological network views can be used as products and are selected on the intended purpose of use by the researcher. Graphics editing is also possible within ATLAS.ti as nodes and links can be dragged and dropped anywhere in the network (Weitzman & Miles, 1995). Additionally, there are various ways to use colors in network views.

The network view can be used for model building. "By producing visual representations of these increasingly complex observations, (e.g.

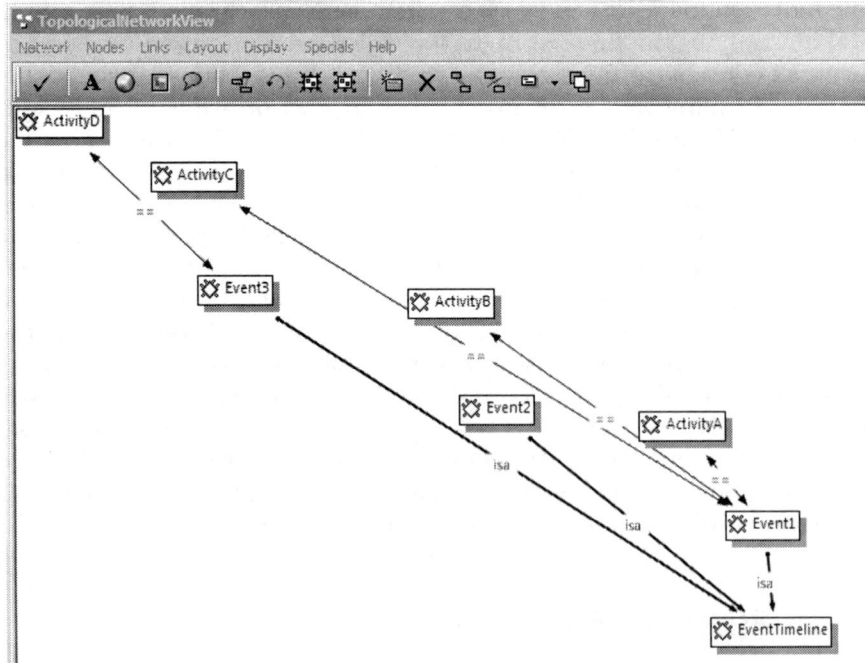

Figure 14.3.   Topological network view.

showing the various dimensions of a particular category and how they interact/relate to other concepts and categories), it became easier to explore relationships which may otherwise have been difficult to conceptualise" (Hutchison, Johnston, & Breckon, 2010, p. 298).

Theory building is also possible within the network view. In ATLAS.ti "You can create links among quotations, codes, and memos; give the links different logical properties; graphically view, manipulate, and print the resulting networks; and conduct searches based on the logical relations in the networks" (Weitzman & Miles, 1995, p. 222). Developing plausible explanations, or interpretations, involves making sense of the data and using software helps the researcher visually conceptualize levels of abstraction (Creswell, 2013). Within a network view, codes and themes are less abstract, but developing patterns and associations through linking is conceptually more difficult. The network view allows graphic, meaningful links to be created as codes can be linked together to express connections (Lewins & Silver, 2004). Within the network view, the researcher can create a visual display that integrates the findings and presents a theoretical model (Friese, 2012, p. 235).

The preceding descriptions of how visual displays are used in qualitative analysis are summarized in Table 14.3. In this table we extend the 3 x 2 matrix showing type of display by function (Table 14.2) to include how visual displays are used generally in qualitative research and how they are used more specifically in the ATLAS.ti environment. In the next section of the chapter, we provide extended examples of visual displays that can be created using ATLAS.ti.

EXAMPLES OF VISUAL DISPLAYS IN QUALITATIVE RESEARCH

In this section of the chapter, we provide illustrative examples for the "Typology of Visual Displays in Qualitative Research" (see Table 14.3) introduced above. These examples map onto the three different levels of *Text*, *Table*, and *Graphic* as well as the intended function of *Process* and *Product*, respectively. The examples are taken from a cross-cultural research project investigating similarities and differences of German and U.S. elementary school teachers' beliefs about the nature of knowledge and processes of knowing (Feucht & Bendixen, 2010). The beliefs were solicited with semistructured interviews from a sample of 20 teachers representing both countries proportionately. ATLAS.ti was used as computer aided qualitative data analysis software to efficiently support the completion of this project.

Table 14.3.   Typology of Visual Displays in Qualitative Research

	Process: Generic	*Process: ATLAS.ti*	*Product: Generic*	*Product: ATLAS.ti*
Text (Level 1)	• Contact summary form (Miles & Huberman, 1994)	• Creating quotations (Feucht & Bendixen, 2010)	• Interview excerpts • Case summary outline (Miles & Huberman, 1994)	• Interview excerpts (Feucht & Bendixen, 2010)
Table (Level 2)	• Qualitative Analysis Documentation Form (Miles & Huberman, 1994) • Code/category list (Shraw, Wadkins, Olafson, 2007)	• Code hierarchy (Feucht & Bendixen, 2010)	• Summary table of themes (Shraw, Wadkins, Olafson, 2007)	• Code hierarchy and code occurrence across participants (Feucht & Bendixen, 2010)
Graphic (Level 3)	• Data analysis map (Harry, Sturges, & Klingner, 2005) • Causal display (Miles & Huberman, 1994)	• Network view: showing relationships between categories (Feucht & Bendixen, 2010)	• Concept map • Matrix analysis (Miles & Huberman, 1994) • Framework analysis (Lacey & Luff, 2001) • Process model (Bernard & Ryan, 2010) • Paradigm Model (Shraw, Wadkins, Olafson, 2007)	• Network view: presenting a theory, key findings, model building

Level 1: Text

As discussed above, Level 1 of the typology focuses on textual displays of qualitative data. In the following example, Figure 14.4 depicts a screen shot from ATLAS.ti that includes the software's interface, an uploaded transcript (textual data) of a U.S. teacher on the left side, and the assigned code to the selected quotation in the transcript on the right side. This screen shot represents the function of the process at the textual data level. It displays a section of an interview transcript in which a teacher responds to the interviewer question on the origin of knowledge; where does knowledge come from? In the software, the researcher highlighted the relevant quotation in the transcript and assigned the code *Origin of Knowledge*.

A product at the textual level of the typology can be a simple quotation that was assigned to a code and later retrieved from ATLAS.ti. That is, a line from the interview transcript in Figure 14.4 was used to illustrate a theme that was found in U.S. teachers only. This interview excerpt could be included as a data display (*Text: Product*) within an article in the following manner:

> Knowledge was predominately perceived as an externally residing entity and barely considered as an internally derived human construct. This belief was also reflective in the U.S. teachers' beliefs about the origin of knowledge. That is, "Knowledge is coming from everything around me. (US5 P15:5. This quotation is exemplary for the theme *Knowledge Embedded Within Community*)

Level 2: Table

Level 2 of the typology focuses on the use of tables to display qualitative analysis. In the process of data analysis, there is a fluid transition from assigning free text segments as quotations to operationalized codes. This categorization of quotations along codes and subcodes that are qualitatively distinct from each other forces the data naturally into hierarchies that can be captured in the format of a table. These hierarchical coding schemes permit a systematic reduction of the data and a methodological identification of evidence and themes to support emerging or existing theories from the data. Figure 14.5 is a screen shot of a segment of a code forest, representing the hierarchical structure of

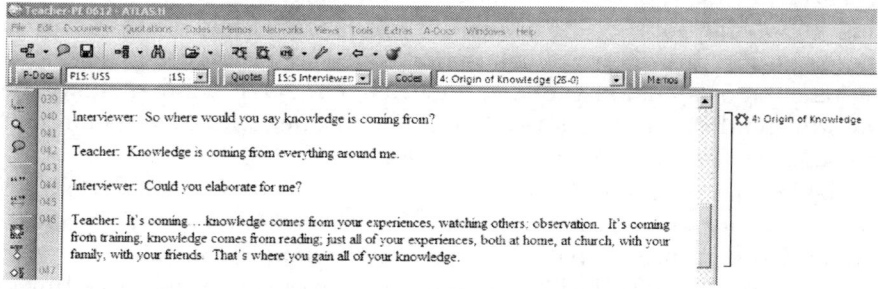

Figure 14.4.   A coded transcript in ATLAS.ti (*Text: Process*).

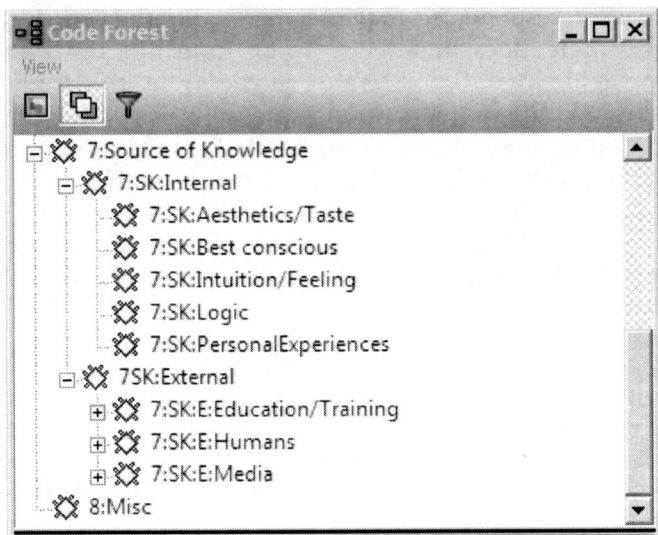

Figure 14.5.   Segment of a coding scheme in ATLAS.ti (*Table: Process*).

the coding scheme. Depicted is the code *Sources of Knowledge* which includes three additional layers of subcodes. After the researchers have built the coding scheme in ATLAS.ti, quotations can be systematically assigned to the given codes, which is often an iterative process. This process permits (a) systematically dividing the data into meaningful units that are distinct from each other (e.g., *Origin of Knowledge* versus *Source of Knowledge*) and (b) moving from specific, applied, and concrete aspects of the data to more general, theoretical, and abstract concepts and themes to support emerging or existing theories.

Table 14.4 provides an example of a visual display that represents a *Table: Process* according to our matrix. In this table, each interview participant, labeled P1 to P20, is represented along with the number of occurrences for two subcodes (internal and external) of the code learning knowledge sources. Participant 5, for example, had 16 instances of quotations in her interview transcript coded as external and only one instance of a quotation coded as internal. The totals column shows the overall trend that the majority of teachers in the sample were more apt to describe external sources of knowledge.

Table 14.5 represents a visual display categorized as *Table: Product.* The main purpose of the table was to effectively demonstrate the cross-cultural occurrence of patterns across the sample. To make the table easier to read, it was decided to switch the interviews transcripts (lines) with the codes (columns) using the axis transpose function in Excel.

More detailed information was added to the table, such as clearer labels for the participants, subtotals, and exemplary quotations to illustrate the different codes. Furthermore, it was decided that the code occurrence was a sufficient provision of evidence to make the claim of a cross-cultural pattern about internal and external sources of knowledge. That is, the code density count was replaced with a simple "X" to represent the occurrence of codes only. This decision was made to avoid potential confusion among the readership by providing too much information that essentially was not needed to support the emerging theory. In other words, although code density was an easily available software output feature, the decision was made not to use it for the sake of clarity.

Table 14.4.   Codes-Primary-Documents-Table (*Table: Process*)

CODES-PRIMARY-DOCUMENTS-TABLE [Super - 06/12/09 01:41:13 PM]
HU: [C:\Documents and Settings\Owner\Desktop\Most current HU\TeacherPe06212.hpr5]
Code-Filter: Code Family 0:CategoryTree
PD-Filter: All

	Learning of Knowledge (LK)	LK:Sources	LK:So:External	LK:So:Internal	(...)		
P1		0	5	1			
P2		0	3	3			
P3		0	6	1			
P4		0	8	4			
P5		0	16	1			
P6		0	6	3			
P7		0	2	1			
P8		0	8	1			
P9		0	12	0			
P10		0	7	2			
P11		0	5	0			
P12		0	4	0			
P13		0	5	0			
P14		0	7	0			
P15		0	3	1			
P16		0	2	0			
P17		0	4	0			
P18		0	3	0			
P19		0	3	0			
P20		0	7	2			
TOTALS:		0	116	20			

Table 15.5. Code hierarchy, Code Occurrence Across Participants, and Example Quotations (*Table: Product*)

Categories Codes/Subcodes	German participants										G Total	US participants										US Total	TOTALS	Example quotations
	G1	G2	G3	G4	G5	G6	G7	G8	G9	G10		US1	US2	US3	US4	US5	US6	US7	US8	US9	US10			
Definition of knowledge (DK)																								
(…)																								
Learning of knowledge (LK)																								
(…)																								
LK:Sources (LK:So)																								
LK:So:External	X	X	X	X	X	X	X	X	X	X	10	X	X	X	X	X	X	X	X	X	X	10	20	So I read **books** and also went to **workshops** with people.
LK:So:Internal	X	X	X	X	X	X	X	X	X	X	9					X					X	2	11	The **experience** (…) with children (…) has taught me a lot (…).
(…)																								

378

Level 3: Graphic

Level 3 of the typology focuses on the use of graphics as visual displays of qualitative research. ATLAS.ti encourages the use of graphics in the process of data analysis by providing a network view feature. The network view feature can be roughly compared to a concept mapping editor; however, the building of the "concept map" is grounded within the data. That is, codes, subcodes, and memos can be graphically displayed as nodes and linked with each other with a choice of qualifying link labels theory building stage of the data analysis. Figure 14.6 displays an analysis on the earlier reported theme of German teachers accessing internal sources of knowledge. From a conceptual perspective, there was interest in understanding what types of codes supported the theme. The network view *Theme: Internal Sources of Knowledge* was used to systematically generate a graphical overview of the underlying main codes and to display one of the major findings of the study. The network view includes a graphical representation of the code hierarchy of the code *Internal Sources* (SK: Internal), and is therefore an example of a *Graphic: Process* visual display. A memo that described in words the graphically depicted relationship and groundedness of the emerging theme (*Memo: Internal Source*) was also created in ATLAS.ti and linked to the network view. The main codes of *Defining Knowledge* (DK), *Learning of Knowledge* (LK), and *Justifying Knowledge* (JK) are displayed as nodes in the network view and demonstrate the manner in which nodes can be integrated and linked in a theory-building graphical representation.

As illustrated by the tables and figures created in ATLAS.ti, the tools within CAQDAS can be used to create visual displays that function to graphically represent processes and products of qualitative analysis. Any analysis task, whether at the level of assigning codes to interview segments or creating a process model for a particular phenomenon, can be visually represented in the ATLAS.ti environment.

CONCLUSION

In this final section we provide a summary of the chapter and conclude with recommendations for using visual displays. Generally speaking, visual displays in qualitative research can be powerful devices for representing data reduction, data display, and conclusion-drawing. Text, tables, and graphics are types of visual displays that can be created to represent the processes and products of qualitative analysis. Some visual displays are automatically generated at the request of the researcher; for example, double clicking on a code will produce a list of all occurrences of that code. Creating other types of visual displays, such as a network view,

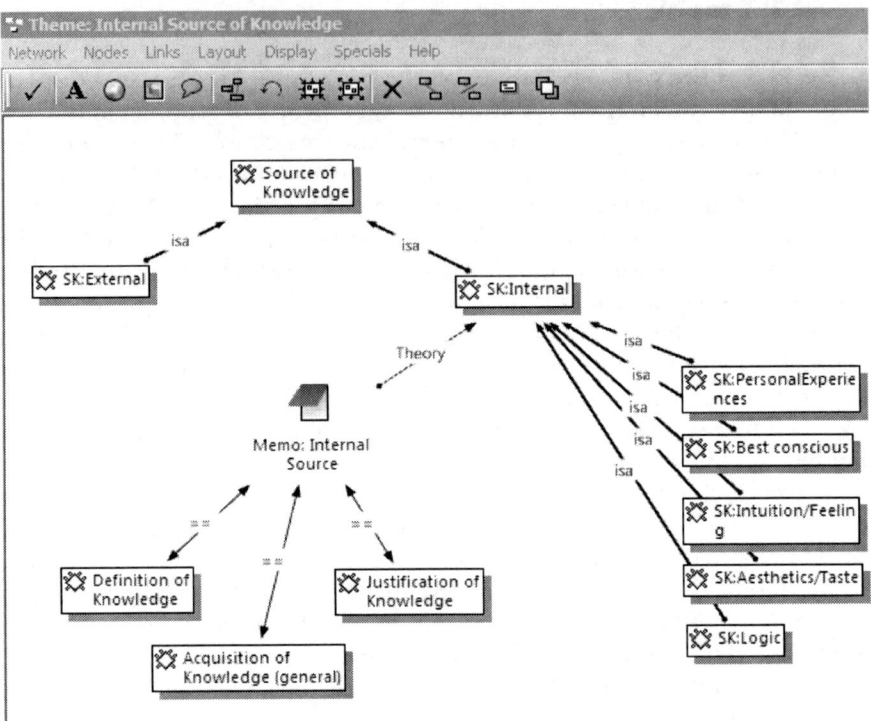

Figure 14.6. Theme: Internal sources of knowledge (*Graphic: Process and Product*).

require more input from the researcher. Although the network view provides a convenient space for exploring the data, it is the researcher's responsibility to decide upon the data that is included, the way that it is displayed, and to create links between data elements.

The 3 x 2 matrix that we introduced demonstrated how types of displays (i.e., text, table, graphic) could be considered along with their function (i.e. process, product). The resulting typology consisted of six variations of type by function that we termed *Text: Process*, *Text: Product*, *Table: Process*, *Table: Product*, *Graphic: Process*, and *Graphic: Product*. Each of these six variations can be created with or without the use of CAQDAS. Although translating qualitative data into effective visual formats can be challenging (Onwuegbuzie & Dickenson, 2008), utilizing the tools provided by CAQDAS packages to create visual displays is one way to address the challenges associated with analyzing what Patton (2002) described as the voluminous amount of data generated by qualitative methods.

There are drawbacks associated with the use of CAQDAS. Learning the software, for example, can be a daunting task for the researcher (Creswell,

2013), and can quickly become overwhelming for novice qualitative researchers. Although user's guides are provided with the software, these might not be very user-friendly. The user guide for ATLAS.ti is over 400 pages. Additional resources are few. Introductory qualitative methods text-books (e.g. Bogdan & Biklen, 2007; Creswell, 2013; Marshall & Rossman, 2011) typically provide limited discussion of available software and their basic functions; however, they do not address how to conduct an analysis. Or, as noted by Friese (2012), "What is fundamentally lacking in the liter-ature is a data analysis method for computer-assisted software" (p. 2).

Once the software is learned, it provides a number of advantages. One advantage is that analysis becomes more systematic (Friese, 2012), both with mechanical analysis tasks and analytic tasks that are more conceptual in nature. The software can be used throughout the analysis at all levels of analysis and can be used after these analyses to integrate findings (Friese, 2012). As demonstrated by the examples provided in this chapter, the software tools can be used to create visual displays of the analytic activi-ties. The six variations of visual display by type and function that can be created using qualitative software are powerful representations of the pro-cesses and products of analysis.

Table 14.6 provides an overview of common analytic and interpretive processes that are assisted through the use of qualitative software and visual displays in CAQDAS. Qualitative software offers many general functions for the handling and analysis of qualitative data. From these general activities, visual displays may be created. In other words, research-ers may use qualitative software for many activities of qualitative pro-cesses, yet use few of the visual display tools as outputs specifically designed to enhance analysis and interpretation. Thus, Table 14.6 dem-onstrates examples of both general ways that qualitative software is used

Table 14.6.   Overview of Common Analytic and Interpretive Processes

	Qualitative Software	*Use of Visual Displays*
Data organization	Consolidate multiple data types, including photos, text, and video into a single ana-lytic location	Create list of all data files Generate list of descriptive comments for cataloging sources and "at a glance" access during analyses
	Group documents according to specified criteria	
	Attach comments to individ-ual documents for quick summary of document con-tent	

(Table continues on next page)

Table 14.6.   **(Continued)**

	Qualitative Software	*Use of Visual Displays*
Data reduction	Select data segments	Create output of data segments (e.g. list of all quotations from a single data source) Create output of particular subset of data
Coding	Develop codes from the data or import predetermined codes Write coding criteria for each code Assign codes to quotations using a drop down list of coding options	Generate table of codes and code descriptions Produce output of all quotations for individual codes
Linking data	Develop code hierarchies by creating and specifying relations between codes Create network views to link quotations, codes, memos	View and print code list to see how many times each code is linked to another code Print network view showing relationships within data
Interpretation processes	Compare networks and tables to determine code prevalence and relationships across cases	Link interpretive memos to quotes, codes, or other memos as a way to assign meaning and reflection Show quotes illustrating specific memos as a visual display product Use visual displays of networks to determine similarities and differences across cases Create network view of identified themes to explore meanings and patterns
Theory construction	Create alternate semantic networks or use data exploration tools (such as code co-occurrence) to generate possible theory derived from the data	Create networks and tables showing several alternative ways of viewing data to demonstrate the theoretical development process as visual display product

as well as specific types of visual displays that enhance analysis and interpretation during qualitative research activities.

Across the steps of the qualitative research process, there may be certain points where visual displays of process or product may be more commonly utilized; however, we encourage readers to consider trying new visual display outputs at various stages in the process to enhance methodological rigor. For example, researchers may most often think of visual displays in terms of process during the coding stage of analyses, however, visual displays of code descriptions may be quite useful as a product in written documentation.

In conclusion, one of the greatest benefits of CAQDAS is that "Qualitative software enhances the legitimacy of qualitative research" (Fielding & Lee, 2002, p. 205). Critics of qualitative research have noted its lack of formality, yet the use of CAQDAS allows the researcher to operationalize procedures and approaches (Fielding & Lee, 2002). The use of qualitative software to create visual displays resulting from qualitative analyses further enhances the methodological and interpretive rigor of qualitative research. These visual displays can serve as evidence for the analysis, showing how researchers moved from the raw data to their findings. For these reasons we recommend increased inclusion of visual displays in reports of qualitative research. Although such displays can be created without the use of software, using CAQDAS enhances these visual displays.

REFERENCES

Averill, J. (2002). Matrix analysis as a complementary analytic strategy in qualitative inquiry. *Qualitative Health Research, 12*(6), 855-866.

Bernard, H. R., & Ryan, G. W. (2010). *Analyzing qualitative data: Systematic approaches*. Los Angeles, CA: SAGE.

Bogdan, R., & Biklen, S. (2007). *Qualitative research for education*. Thousand Oaks, CA: SAGE.

Bringer, J., Johnston, L., & Brackenridge, C. (2006). Using computer-assisted qualitative data analysis software to develop a grounded theory project. *Field Methods, 18*(3), 245-266.

Burke, J., O'Campo, P., Peak, G., Gielen, A., McDonnell, K., & Trochim, W. (2005). An introduction to concept mapping as a participatory public health research method. *Qualitative Health Research, 15*(10), 1392-1410.

Corbin, J., & Strauss, A. (2007). *Basics of qualitative research: Techniques and procedures for developing grounded theory* (3rd ed.). Thousand Oaks, CA: SAGE.

Creswell, J. (2013). *Qualitative inquiry and research design: Choosing among five approaches* (3rd ed.). Los Angeles, CA: SAGE.

Daley, B. J. (2004). Using concept maps in qualitative research. In *Proceedings of the First International Conference on Concept Mapping* (pp. 14-17). Universidad Publica de Navarra, Spain.

Feucht, F. C. (2011). The epistemic underpinnings of Mrs. M's reading lesson on drawing conclusions. A classroom-based research study In J. Brownlee, G. Schraw, & D. Berthelsen (Eds.), *Personal epistemology in teacher education* (pp. 227-245). London: Rutledge.

Feucht, F. C. (2010). Epistemic climate in elementary classrooms. In L. D. Bendixen & F. C. Feucht (Eds.), *Personal epistemology in the classroom: Theory, research, and educational implications* (pp. 55-93). New York, NY: Cambridge University Press.

Feucht, F., & Bendixen, L. (2010). Exploring similarities and differences in personal epistemologies of U.S. and German elementary school teachers. *Cognition and Instruction, 28*(1), 39-69.

Fielding, N., & Lee. R. (2002). New patterns in the adoption and use of qualitative software. *Field Methods, 14*(2), 187-216.

Fossey, E., Harvey, C., McDermott, F., & Davidson, L. (2002). Understanding and evaluating qualitative research. *Australian and New Zealand Journal of Psychiatry, 36*, 717-732.

Friese, S. (2012). *Qualitative data analysis with ATLAS.ti*. Los Angeles, CA: SAGE.

Garcia-Horta, J. B., & Guerra-Ramos, M. T. (2009). The use of CAQDAS in educational research: Some advantages, limitations and potential risks. *International Journal of Research and Methods in Education, 32*(2), 151-165.

Harry, B., Sturges, K., & Klingner, J. (2005). Mapping the process: An exemplar of process and challenge in grounded theory analysis. *Educational Researcher, 34*(3), 3-13.

Hornbaek, K., & Hertzum, M. (2011). The notion of overview in information visualization. *International Journal of Human-Computer Studies, 69*, 509-525.

Hutchison, A. J., Johnston, L. H., & Breckon, J. D. (2010). Using QSR-NVivo to facilitate the development of a grounded theory project: An account of a worked example. *International Journal of Social Research Methodology, 13*(4), 83-302.

Hwang, S. (2008). Using qualitative data analysis software: A review of ATLAS.ti. *Social Science Computer Review, 26*(4), 519-527.

Konopásek, Z. (2008). Making thinking visible with ATLAS.ti: Computer assisted qualitative analysis as textual practices [62 paragraphs]. *Forum Qualitative Sozialforschung/ orum: Qualitative Social Research, 9*(2), Art. 12. Retrieved from http://nbn-resolving.de/urn:nbn:de:0114-fqs0802124

Lacey, A., & Luff, D. (2001). *Trent focus for research and development in primary health care: An introduction to qualitative analysis*. Sheffield, England: Trent Focus.

Leech, N. L., & Onwuegbuzie, A. J. (2011). Beyond constant comparison data analysis: Using NVivo. *School Psychology Quarterly, 26*(1), 70-84.

Lewins, A., & Silver, C. (2004). *Choosing a CAQDAS package: A working paper*. University of Surry, England: CAQDAS Networking Project.

Lyons, E. (2000). Qualitative data analysis: Data display model. *Research methods in psychology, 2*, 269-280.

Marshall, C., & Rossman, G. (2011). *Designing qualitative research* (5th ed.). Los Angeles, CA: SAGE.

Miles, M., & Huberman, A. (1994). *Qualitative data analysis: An expanded sourcebook* (2nd ed.). Thousand Oaks, CA: SAGE.

Muhr, T. (2004). *ATLAS.ti v.5.0 User's guide and reference* (2nd ed.). Berlin, Germany: Scientific Software Development.

Onwuegbuzie, A. J., & Dickinson, W. B. (2008). Mixed methods analysis and information visualization: Graphical display for effective communication of research results. *The Qualitative Report, 13*(2), 204-225.

Patton, M. (2002). *Qualitative research and evaluation methods* (3rd ed.). Thousand Oaks, CA: SAGE.

Peters, V., & Wester, F. (2007). How qualitative data analysis software may support the qualitative analysis process. *Quality and Quantity, 41*, 635-639.

Schneiderman, B. (1996). The eyes have it: A task by data type taxonomy for information visualizations. *IEEE*, 336-343.

Schraw, G., Wadkins, T., & Olafson, L. (2007). Doing the things we do: A grounded theory of academic procrastination. *Journal of Educational Psychology, 99*(1), 12-25.

Thompson, R. (2002). Reporting the results of computer-assisted analysis of qualitative research data. *Forum Qualitative Sozialforschung/Forum: Qualitative Social Research, 3*(2), Art. 12. Retrieved from http://nbn-resolving.de/urn:nbn:de:0114-fqs0802124.

Tufte, E. (2001). *The visual display of quantitative information* (2nd ed.). Chelshire, CT: Graphics Press.

Wainer, W., & Thissen, D. (1981). Graphical data analysis. *Annual Review of Psychology, 32*, 191-241.

Weitzman, E., & Miles, M. (1995). *Computer programs for qualitative data analysis: A software sourcebook*. Thousand Oaks, CA: SAGE.

CHAPTER 15

USING VISUAL DISPLAYS TO ENHANCE UNDERSTANDING OF QUANTITATIVE RESEARCH

Dena A. Pastor and Sara J. Finney

ABSTRACT

It is not uncommon for students new to statistics to experience difficulty comprehending basic statistical concepts. Even seasoned researchers may struggle to understand statistical techniques with which they have little experience. To facilitate comprehension, it is important for statistical concepts to be presented in a manner that aligns with the principles of cognitive processing. Several cognitive theories suggest that visual displays can be used to enhance comprehension. In this chapter we describe why visual displays are useful and illustrate their effectiveness in quantitative research by providing the results from a multiple regression model, a latent profile analysis model, and a latent growth model twice—once with visual displays and once without. Although visual displays enhance understanding and facilitate more accurate interpretations of statistical analyses, their presence in published research is limited. Possible reasons for the scarcity of visual displays are provided along with a call for their increased use.

Learning Through Visual Displays, pp. 387–415

Imagine yourself in two situations. In the first, you have been asked to explain the differences among a positive correlation, a negative correlation, and no correlation to students unfamiliar with the correlation coefficient. In the second scenario, you have been asked to write the results section of a study in which the strength of a positive correlation between two variables differs by gender. Again, assume that the readers of the study are unfamiliar with the correlation coefficient. In each situation, would a verbal or written explanation suffice? In other words, do you believe the students in the first situation or the readers in the second situation would be able to understand the distinction among these correlations through a verbal description alone? We suspect that most people would disagree and as an alternative, would suggest pairing the verbal description with a visual display, such as a scatterplot.

These two situations, as simple as they are, demonstrate how visual displays can be used to enhance comprehension of statistical concepts and techniques that are unfamiliar to learners. Although most students are familiar with a statistic as common as the correlation coefficient, advanced statistical techniques, such as latent profile analysis (LPA) and latent growth models (LGMs), are typically much less familiar. Thus, the use of visual displays with these more advanced statistical techniques might be incredibly beneficial not only when teaching students these techniques, but also when communicating the results of research in which these techniques were employed.

In the sections that follow, we first highlight four ways in which visual displays can enhance cognitive processing. Specifically, we describe how visual displays reduce cognitive load, organize information into a coherent representation, provide novel information that text alone cannot communicate, and activate prior knowledge. Second, we argue for the use of visual displays when presenting the results of advanced statistical techniques given the nature of the material and its likely unfamiliarity in most audiences. We then demonstrate the utility of visual displays by presenting the results from three statistical techniques without and then coupled with visuals displays, with the latter enabling more accurate interpretations of the results and understanding of the techniques.

THE USE OF VISUAL DISPLAYS TO
ENHANCE COGNITIVE PROCESSING

Working memory refers to the ability to hold and process information (Baddeley, 2001). It is well known that a very limited amount of information can be stored and processed in working memory. To prevent overloading working memory, care needs to be taken when providing instruction on novel and complex topics, such as unfamiliar statistical concepts. Similarly, the results from a statistical procedure should be presented in such a way that it does not burden the audiences' limited working memory capacities, particularly if they have little experience with the technique.

According to cognitive load theory (e.g., Sweller, 2005; van Merriënboer & Sweller, 2010) and the cognitive theory of multimedia learning (e.g., Mayer, 2005; Mayer, 2008), one way to reduce the load on working memory is to present information both verbally and visually. The advantage of presenting information in different formats is based on the idea that working memory consists of different channels: a visual channel for processing visual imagery and a verbal channel for processing words. By accessing both channels during instruction, as opposed to accessing just one channel, the burden on any one channel is reduced and the resources in working memory are more fully utilized. Within both channels relevant information needs to be selected and organized, and then integrated across channels. According to Mayer (e.g., 2005, 2008), it is the act of integrating information across the different channels in working memory that results in increased and deeper learning of the material.

Given successful processing in working memory, the new information is then linked with prior knowledge in long-term memory and stored as schemas (Mayer, 2008; Mayer & Moreno, 2003). Schemas can be thought of as knowledge stored in long-term memory or, as defined by Sweller (2005), "cognitive constructs that allow multiple elements of information to be categorized as a single element" (p. 21). In addition to reducing cognitive load, a second advantage of visual displays is their ability to assist in the creation of schemas by essentially "schematizing" the information for the learner. For instance, a visual display for a statistical technique is effective if it enables learners to select and organize the relevant information, minimizing the need for learners to do these tasks themselves, and enabling them to use their working memory resources for integration. In effect, an effective visual display promotes essential processing and minimizes nonessential processing.

A third advantage of visual displays is their ability to convey information in a manner that is not redundant with a verbal description. That is, visual displays can present information that might be too cumbersome or even impossible to convey using words. In these situations, visual displays provide unique, value-added information that is essential for a complete understanding of the material.

Finally, a visual display for an advanced technique can also enhance understanding if it resembles a visual display that is already familiar to the learner. For instance, consider the use of a visual display for an advanced technique that is similar to a display used with more conventional techniques (e.g., ANOVA, correlation). In this situation, the visual display for the advanced technique serves to activate pre-existing schemas associated with more familiar statistical methods. The activation of pre-existing schemas not only deepens understanding of the advanced technique through the integration of novel information with prior knowledge, but it also reduces the burden on working memory (van Merriënboer & Sweller, 2010).

When discussing the benefits of visual displays, Hannafin, Hannafin, Hooper, Rieber, and Kini (1996) explained that visual displays highlight the important concepts, structure the concepts, and facilitate connections with previously learned concepts. These benefits clearly align with our description of how visual displays assist in comprehension. In sum, an effective visual display for a statistical technique reduces cognitive load, selects and organizes relevant information, provides unique information not afforded by text alone, and helps learners connect the information with traditional techniques that are more familiar.

The Need for Visual Displays in Quantitative Research

The benefits of pairing visual displays with text or oral explanations span across domains (e.g., history, mathematics, chemistry; see Mayer, 2005). Here we make the argument that this coupling of visual displays with verbal information is essential to understanding results from quantitative data analyses for two main reasons: the nature of the material and the limited prior knowledge of many who need to interpret and understand this information.

First, statistical analyses produce numerical values that represent the relationships among variables. However, the relationships being modeled are inherently spatial and the numerical values are simply an efficient way to represent the relationships. For example, the correlation coefficient is a single numerical value used to represent the linear relationship between two variables. That is, the coefficient condenses the information from a large collection of data points in two-dimensional space into a single number. Obviously, providing a visual display of these relationships reflects, in much more detail, the phenomenon under study.

Second, the importance of visual displays is amplified given frequent methodological advances, which results in consumers of research being unfamiliar with the data analysis techniques. That is, cognitive load and multimedia learning research has shown that novices or those with limited prior knowledge benefit the most from the coupling of verbal information and visual displays (Fletcher & Tobias, 2005; Mayer, 1999). Advances in quantitative methods in recent years, such as LGM and mixture modeling, have fortunately allowed researchers to investigate a wide array of research questions. However, training in statistical analyses has not kept pace with the ever-increasing number of new (and complex) techniques. In a review of 201 psychology PhD programs in the U.S. and Canada, Aiken, West, and Millsap (2008) reported that approximately 50% or fewer programs regularly provided instruction on techniques such as structural equation modeling and longitudinal modeling. When instruction was provided, it often was not in the form of a full course devoted to the topic. Thus, it is questionable whether recent graduates of psychology doctoral programs have the proper training that would allow them to fully understand the results of studies using more advanced techniques. Less recent graduates may similarly struggle, given it is reasonable that other career goals may have taken priority over keeping current with advances in statistical methodology. For these reasons, it is imperative that users of these more sophisticated methods make every effort to communicate their results in accurate and understandable ways. We argue that visual displays are a particularly useful and effective approach for making the results of complex statistical analyses interpretable, especially for those consumers unfamiliar with the techniques.

Thus, below we demonstrate how graphics aid interpretation of statistical analyses by describing the results of studies using three different techniques: multiple regression with interactions, LPA and LGM. For each technique, two different approaches to presenting the results are provided: (1) text only, where the size, direction, practical significance, and statistical significance of parameter estimates are described; and (2) text plus visual display of the results. For each technique, we illustrate how both the understanding of a technique and the interpretability of its results are greatly enhanced through the addition of visual displays.

Visually Depicting Interactions Between Continuous Predictors in Multiple Regression

A researcher wishes to examine the effects of two continuous predictors, X and Z, on the continuous outcome variable, Y. A large sample of participants provided data using psychometrically sound measures of the variables. As is common, the researcher is interested in the joint effects of X and Z. In particular, the researcher is interested in examining if Z buffers the effect of X on Y. That is, the basic question under study is if the relationship between X and Y is moderated (weakened or amplified) by a third variable.

When discussing the utilization of multiple regression to answer research questions involving the interaction between two continuous predictors, Aiken and West (1991) noted, "One main impediment to the use of MR has been that procedures for displaying and probing significant interactions have not been readily available" (p. 5). If researchers are not aware of the appropriate way to communicate these results visually, they may avoid these techniques altogether. In fact, the literature is thick with examples of multiple regression models with main effects only. If the effect of a predictor on the criterion is moderated by another predictor, the regression model is misspecified when the interaction term is not included in the model, resulting in biased estimates. Just as concerning, some researchers' desire to model the interaction, coupled with a lack of understanding of how this is accomplished via multiple regression, results in the categorization of continuous predictors to force the data into an ANOVA framework. The negative effects of dichotomizing continuous predictors have been long established: loss of information, biased effect sizes, decreased reliability, and arbitrary groups (e.g., MacCallum, Zhang, Preacher, & Rucker, 2002). Thus, to alleviate these poor practices, Aiken and West (1991) wrote a book that demonstrated the graphical approaches one could use to appropriately model and display interactions between continuous predictors.

To highlight the effects of cognitive load, and, thus constraints on comprehension (van Merriënboer & Sweller, 2010), we first present an example of an interaction between continuous variables without a visual display. We then demonstrate how adding the visual display increases efficiency in processing and directs the reader to the important information (Mayer, 2008).

Using artificial data, we predicted time spent on a difficult cognitive task from age and need for cognition (NFC). Specifically, imagine 245 adults ranging from 19 to 82 years old participating in a study that measured the number of minutes each individual engaged in a difficult math problem. When presenting the difficult task to each individual, the investigators tried to persuade each individual to engage in the task as long as possible. Suppose that one developmental theory claims that as age increases, time spent on a difficult cognitive task decreases; older adults are less likely to be persuaded to engage in the taxing activity than younger adults. However, cognitive scientists believe that NFC moderates this relationship. That is, given that individuals high in NFC enjoy engaging in effortful cognitive endeavors and are more likely to be persuaded by convincing arguments (Cacioppo, Petty, & Morris, 1983), whereas individuals low in NFC tend to avoid or minimize cognitive effort, it was predicted that the slope of time regressed on age would change as NFC changed, with the slope becoming less negative as NFC increased.

Tables 15.1 and 15.2 include the typical descriptive statistics and regression coefficients authors would present and interpret to assess the presence of an interaction between age and NFC. Recall that learning depends on the learner (the reader in this case) selecting or attending to relevant material, organizing the material into a coherent representation, and integrating the new material with knowledge in long-term memory (Mayer, 2008). A novice may find it difficult to identify which values in Table 15.2 are relevant to interpret the interaction and may focus on extraneous information. A helpful author may signal or highlight the coefficients that are most essential. That is, the sign of the slope associated with the interaction indicates that as NFC increases, the slope of time on age becomes less negative. Even if a novice was provided with this statistical information and interpretation, it would be difficult to organize the information into a mental representation of this interaction. Those savvy with multiple regression could argue that more information can be extracted from Table 15.2. In particular, given NFC was mean centered, the slope associated with age (−.23) represents the change in time spent on task for every unit increase in age when NFC is at the mean (2.80). We would argue that although this signaling of the essential coefficients is helpful and the interpretations are correct, it remains difficult to form a coherent representation of the form of the interaction with just this information.

According to the multimedia principle, the reader should better understand the interaction of age and NFC on time if presented with a verbal description, like that above, *and* a visual display. Figure 15.1 clearly depicts the form of the interaction (i.e., organizes the relevant information into a coherent representation) and directs readers to important information. As reported in Table 15.2, the interaction accounts for 4% of the variance in time on task. Some researchers may consider this effect size small. However, the visual display clearly depicts the powerful buffering effect of NFC. Specifically, with a NFC of 2.80 (the mean) time on task decreases .23 minutes for each yearly increase in age. Moreover, with a NFC of 1.69 (1 *SD* below the mean) time on task decreases .44 minutes for each yearly increase in age. However, with a NFC of 3.91 (1 *SD* above

Table 15.1. Means, Standard Deviations, and Correlations for Age, Need for Cognition, and Time on Task

Variable	M	SD	Min	Max	Age	NFC	Time on Task
Age in Years	49.18	10.11	19	82.00	1.00	0.23*	−0.13*
Need for Cognition	2.80	1.11	1	6.50	–	1.00	0.36*
Time on Task	26.53	10.82	0	55.00	–	–	1.00

Note: Need for Cognition (NFC) was scaled from 1-7. Time on task is measured in minutes.

*p <.05

Table 15.2.   Regression Analysis Predicting Time From Age, Need for Cognition, and Their Interaction

Model and Predictor Variables	R^2	95% CI of R^2	ΔR^2	b	95% CI of b
Model 1	0.17*	[0.09, 0.26]	0.17*		
Age				−0.24*	[−0.36, −0.11]
NFC				3.97*	[2.81, 5.13]
Model 2	0.21*	[0.12, 0.30]	0.04*		
Age				−0.23*	[−0.35, −0.10]
NFC				4.12*	[2.98, 5.26]
Interaction				0.186*	[0.073, 0.30]

Note: NFC = need for cognition. b = raw score regression coefficient.
Age and NFC have been mean centered.

*$p < .05$

the mean), there is no statistically significant decrease in time on task as age increases (slope = −.02). Noticeably, the visual display represents the powerful joint effects of NFC and age on time spent on task much better than simply the percentage of variance associated with the interaction term.

In addition, notice that the graph clearly illustrates the point of intersection or the age at which differing levels of NFC results in the same amount of time on task. Recall that age is mean centered to reduce multicollinearity between the predictors and the interaction. The point of intersection is −22.14, or 22.14 units below the mean of zero. By creating a graphic and incorporating the values of age both centered and uncentered on the x-axis, a reader can easily see that at an age of 27.04 (22.14 units below the mean of zero), time on task does not vary as a function of the level of NFC.

Moreover, plotting the three simple regression lines plainly illustrates the symmetrical pattern that is characteristic of a significant linear interaction. It would be extremely difficult to mentally represent this symmetry given a verbal description of the regression coefficient associated with the interaction term. That is, one would have to consider the value of the slope for the regression of time (Y) on age (X) coupled with the value of the slope associated with the interaction and then visualize how the regression of time on age would change for each unit change in NFC (Z), essentially the value of the interaction term. According to cognitive load theory, working memory can actively process no more than two to four elements simultaneously (van Merriënboer & Sweller, 2010). When trying

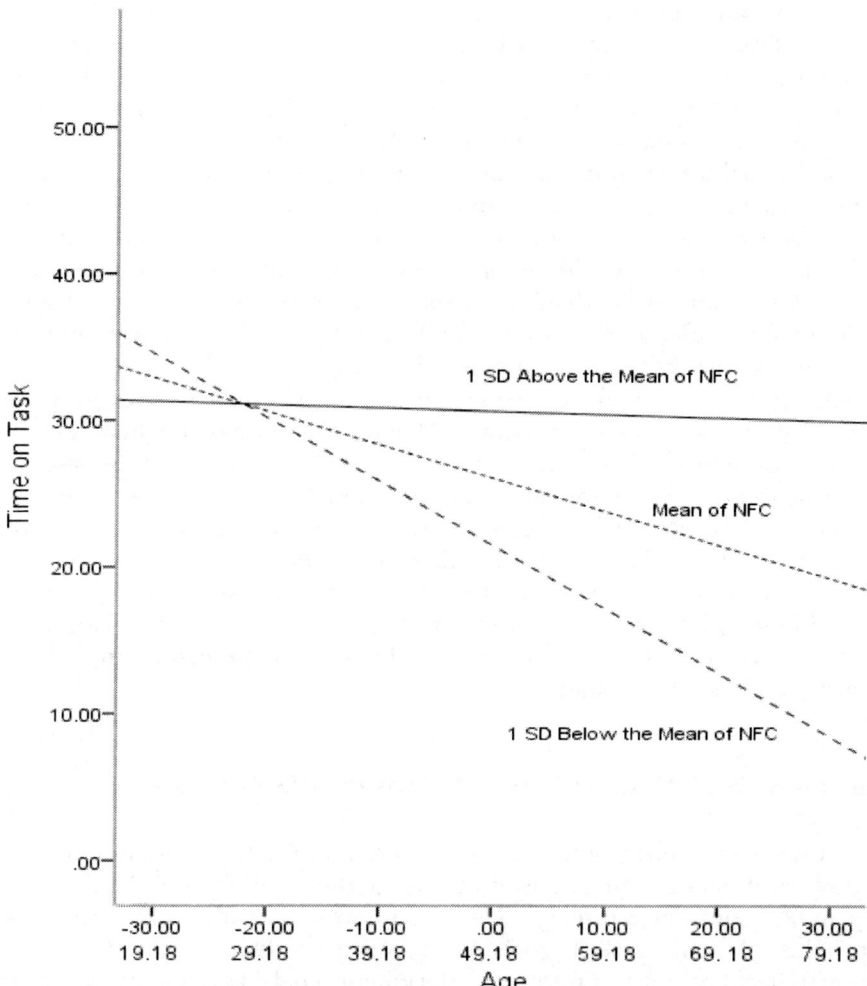

Note: The regression of Time on Age was estimated and plotted at three levels of NFC: 1 SD below the mean (1.69), at the mean (2.80), and 1 SD above the mean (3.91; see Aiken & West, 1991 for procedures). The slope of Time on Age was statistically significantly different from zero when NFC was 1 SD below the mean ($b = -.44$) and when NFC was at the mean ($b = -.23$); however, the slope of Time on Age was not statistically significantly different from zero when NFC was 1 SD above the mean ($b = -.02$). The point of intersection equaled -22.14 when age was centered (upper values along x-axis), which corresponded to 27.04 years old when age was uncentered   (lower values along x-axis). The point of intersection is computed as $-b_{NFC}/b_{Interaction}$, which for this data corresponds to $-4.12/.186$.

Figure 15.1.   Regression of Time on Age at three levels of need for cognition.

to understand something complex, such as the linear interaction between two continuous predictors, working memory may be overloaded. The figure reduces this cognitive load (i.e., burden on working memory) by integrating elements (e.g., the interaction slope, the age slope) into one cohesive representation. As noted by Vekiri (2002) and demonstrated here, "Visual information has the advantage that it is organized in a synchronous manner, which allows many parts of a mental image to be available for simultaneous processing" (p. 267). A verbal description alone, although accurate, would be massively more difficult to process and extract meaning from than the visual display. Thus, the visual display offers value-added information not afforded by the verbal description (no matter how extensive the verbal description).

An additional benefit of Figure 15.1 is its potential to activate prior knowledge regarding interactions. That is, the interaction between the two continuous predictors is plotted in much the same way as the interaction between two categorical predictors modeled via ANOVA. Although readers might not be familiar with interactions between continuous predictors, it is likely that they are familiar with interactions between categorical predictors and the plots used to characterize such interactions. By providing a plot similar to one with which they are already familiar, novel information is linked with prior knowledge and understanding of the regression results is enhanced.

Visually Depicting Profiles in Latent Profile Analysis

A researcher has a set of variables and is interested in identifying the most common configurations or profiles of these variables in the data. For example, consider a researcher who is interested in identifying common profiles of achievement goals in a college student population. The researcher has four different achievement goals and is interested in whether there are groups of students who endorse all goals and other groups who endorse some goals, but not others. Because these groups with their differing profiles are unknown prior to data analysis, they are often described as latent classes. As shown below, understanding the form of the latent class profiles is exceedingly difficult if represented by only words and numerical values. A visual display, on the other hand, provides a coherent representation of not only each class' profile but highlights the differences among them.

Although cluster analysis could be used to identify classes, an increasingly popular method is LPA (Gibson, 1959; Lazarfield & Henry, 1968), which differs from most applications of cluster analysis in that it is based upon a statistical model of the latent class structure. LPA is subsumed under a larger set of statistical models known as finite mixture models (McLachlan & Peel, 2000), which assume that the data (achievement goal scores in the current example) have been sampled from a population that contains several unobserved classes, each described by its own set of distributional parameters (e.g., mean, variance). In LPA, the multivariate normal distribution is assumed for each class and classes are allowed to differ in their variable means and variances.[1] In the context of the achievement goal example, the analysis would begin by fitting a 1-class model, which assumes that all individuals belong to the same class. For a single class model, the estimated parameters include the means and variances of each of the four achievement goals. Next, the analysis would proceed by fitting a 2-class model. The estimated parameters would include the means and variances of the achievement goals in each class, as well as the percentage of the population in each class. The process would continue by fitting additional models with an increasing number of classes and various statistical indices would be used, along with substantive considerations, to choose the most appropriate model from those estimated.

To illustrate, a series of LPA models were fit to achievement goal data collected from a large sample of college students. A 5-class model was championed indicating that the population consists of five unobserved groups or classes, each with a unique goal orientation profile. The estimated parameters associated with the five achievement goal profiles are shown in Table 15.3. Of particular interest in Table 15.3 are the class-specific means, which convey the achievement goal profile in each class, and the class percentages, which capture the prevalence of each profile in the population. Although all the information needed to understand the profiles is contained in Table 15.3, it is quite difficult to visualize each profile and to ascertain how similar or different the profiles are from one another. The researcher's verbal explanation of the results, which is likely to direct readers' attention to the within-class averages of Classes 2, 4, and 5 (i.e., selection of relevant information), could enhance understanding of the profiles. For instance, the researcher may point out that within these classes, the four goal means are fairly similar in value. Similarly, the researcher might also direct readers' attention to the fact that these three classes primarily differ from one another in how strongly the goals are endorsed and draw attention to the unique profiles of Classes 1 and 3, which differ from the other three classes in that some goals are more strongly endorsed than others.

Although it is possible to select important information about the profiles from Table 15.3, coupled with direction from the researcher, it is nearly impossible to consider all profiles simultaneously due to the load imposed on working memory. For example, to compare profiles to one another, the reader would need to hold each profile in working memory

Table 15.3.   Estimated Parameters for the 5-Class LPA Model

Class	Estimated Class Proportions	Estimated Achievement Goal Means			
		MAP	PAP	PAV	MAV
1	6%	6.07	2.23	2.70	4.52
2	42%	5.06	5.11	4.76	4.12
3	9%	6.09	5.78	2.77	3.83
4	5%	3.51	3.22	3.30	2.99
5	38%	6.29	6.16	5.71	5.13

Note: The four achievement goals are mastery-approach (MAP), mastery-avoidance (MAV), performance-approach (PAP), and performance-avoidance (PAV). For further information on achievement goals, see Elliot (2005).The possible range for all goals is 1-7. The variances, which were fixed to be equal across classes, were estimated as 0.53 for MAP, 0.89 for PAP, 0.88 for PAV, and 0.67 for MAV.

(i.e., envision the form of the four goal means for each of the five classes) and then attempt to compare these profiles for differences in form and magnitude. Because it is also important to consider the means in relation to the achievement goal scale, the scale range would also need to be held in working memory, burdening its resources even further.

By comparison, a visual display of the profiles, such as the one provided in Figure 15.2, very easily and effectively conveys the form of each profile, the differences among the profiles, and how the profiles relate to the achievement goal scale. For instance, the unique patterns of achievement goals represented by Classes 1 and 3 are readily apparent. As well, it is clear from this figure that Classes 2, 4, and 5 have similar patterns and only differ in their achievement goal levels. Moreover, because the full range of the achievement goal scale is available on the y-axis, it is evident that although Class 4 has "low" means in relation to Classes 2 and 5, its means would not be considered "low" in relation to the achievement goal scale.

Figure 15.2 greatly eases cognitive processing of the results by organiz-ing the information about the profiles into a coherent representation, enabling the reader to identify relations within the data without having to construct such a representation mentally. It is incredibly important in LPA to present the findings in such a way that a clear understanding of how the profiles differ from one another is ascertained. If profiles differ in ele-vation and not pattern, it suggests that a single factor model (a more sim-plistic model with a very different interpretation than LPA) is a plausible model for the data (Vermunt, 2001). For instance, had only a 3-class solu-tion been obtained with profiles similar to Classes 2, 4, and 5, it would have suggested that a single continuous factor may underlie the relation-ships among the four achievement goals. In other words, the three classes

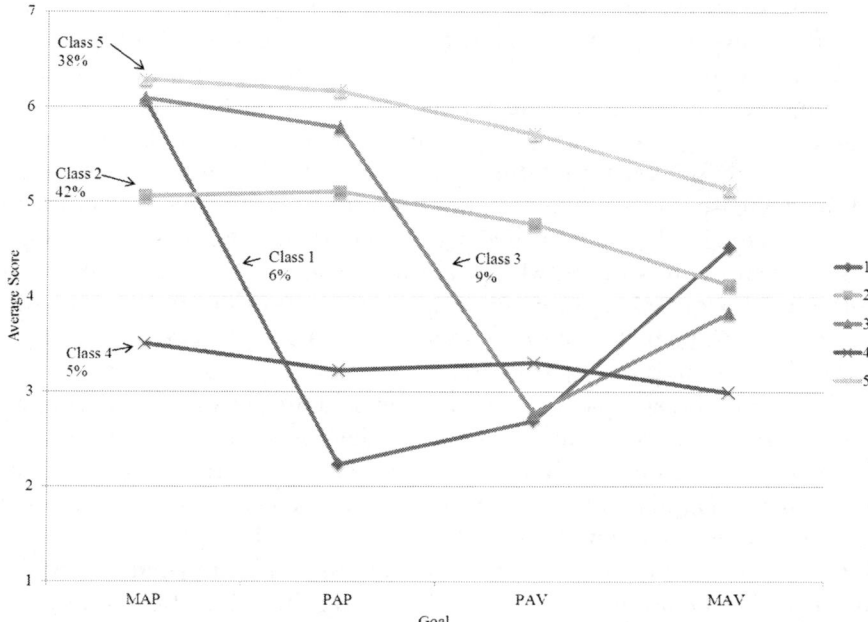

Note: The goal profiles of Classes 1 and 3 have unique patterns and only differ from one another in their levels of PAP. Classes 2, 4, and 5 have similar patterns and only differ from one another in elevation, with Class 5 being the highest, Class 4 being the lowest, and Class 2 falling in between. Although Class 4 is "low" relative to Classes 2 and 5, its goal values would not be considered "low" relative to the achievement goal scale, which ranges from 1 to 7.

Figure 15.2.   Estimated means and class percentages for the 5-class LPA model.

might simply represent low, medium, and high levels of the factor. Through the use of a visual display, profiles can be considered simultaneously, facilitating the identification of differences among profiles or lack of differences, which may suggest more appropriate models for the data.

Visually Depicting Growth in Latent Growth Modeling

Most researchers are familiar with traditional techniques, such as repeated measures ANOVA or MANOVA, which allow for the examination of mean differences in a variable over time. A more modern technique known as LGM (Bryk & Raudenbush, 1987; McArdle & Epstein, 1987; Meredith & Tisak, 1990) allows researchers to model not only overall (mean) change in a variable over time, but also individual differences in change. As an example, consider an artificial longitudinal data set used for illustrative purposes by Willett (1988) and Singer and Willet (2003). This data set was created to capture persons' scores on a timed "opposites naming" task across four time points, with each measurement occasion separated by 1 week.[2] With practice, performance on this task is considered to increase over time, although individual differences are expected in this increase. LGM aligns with this research scenario given its ability to estimate an overall (mean) trajectory of change in scores over time along with variance components, which capture the extent to which individuals differ in the growth parameters (e.g., intercepts, slopes). Additionally, predictors can be included in the model in an attempt to explain individual differences in growth parameters.

Through this example, we illustrate the benefits of using visual displays during three different phases of the modeling process: (a) preliminary inspection of the data, (b) growth models without predictors (i.e., unconditional LGMs), and (c) growth models with predictors (i.e., conditional LGMs). We describe how the use of visual displays throughout the modeling process can greatly enhance understanding and interpretation of the results, with the additional benefit of assisting the researcher in identifying violations of model assumptions and outlying trajectories.

Preliminary inspection of the data. Because the purpose of LGM is to capture overall and individual differences in change over time, it is important to consider the appropriate functional form (e.g., linear, quadratic) for the trajectories prior to fitting models to the data. Although theory and prior research should guide this decision, empirical results can also be consulted and are often derived from fitting ordinary least squares (OLS) regression models to each individual's data. Descriptive statistics summarize the OLS parameter estimates obtained from fitting both linear and quadratic models to each individual's scores (see Table 15.4). For example, the average intercept across individuals is 164.39 and the average slope is 28.20 when linear models are fit to individual's scores. These values indicate that on average, individuals are scoring fairly low on the opposites-naming task at the initial time point and increasing in their scores with each measurement occasion by about 28 points. However, the sizeable variances associated with the individual intercepts and linear slopes imply that the overall trajectory may not characterize growth well for all individuals. These variances suggest that individuals differ from one another not only in their scores at the initial measurement occasion, but also in how their scores change linearly over time. In fact, for both the linear and quadratic models, there appears to be substantial variability in the growth parameters suggesting that LGMs are needed to model the data.

To choose between the linear and quadratic models, the average R^2 values are often consulted as these values capture the fit of the model to the data. Because the average R^2 value for the quadratic model (.93) is slightly higher than the linear model (.86), a researcher might decide that a latent growth model specifying quadratic trajectories is needed. However, visual inspection of the linear and quadratic trajectories plotted against the observed scores for each individual suggests otherwise. As shown in Figure 15.3, the observed scores for a random sample of eight individuals appear to change linearly over time, with little benefit obtained by the more complex quadratic model.

The same conclusion holds for most individuals in the data, as conveyed by Figure 15.4, which consists of the observed trajectories[3] for a random sample of 35 individuals. There are three important features of the data conveyed in Figure 15.4. First, the individual trajectories appear linear in form. Second, individuals appear to differ in their intercepts or their opposites-naming scores at the initial measurement occasion (i.e., Time 0). Third, most individuals appear to be increasing in their scores over time; however, the rates of increase appear to vary across individuals. Although Table 15.4 conveys some of this information, unlike Figures 15.3 and 15.4, it does not allow the researcher to fully consider the appropriate functional form for the relationship between scores and time. Importantly, the information in Table 15.4 only allows the researcher to consider two forms for growth (i.e., linear and quadratic), whereas the trajectories in Figures 15.3 and 15.4 might suggest other representations of change over time are needed (e.g., cubic, hyperbolic, exponential).

Figures 15.3 and 15.4 are incredibly important visual displays in the analysis of longitudinal data. Not only can they be used to determine the nature of the individual trajectories, but they can also be used to identify unusual trajectories that might be considered outliers. Although these figures may not be featured in the final research product, it is essential that they are consulted prior to fitting LGMs to the data. Given the importance of these visual displays in longitudinal data analysis, it is not surprising that full

Table 15.4. OLS Regression Parameter Estimates for the Linear and Quadratic Models

	Linear Model			Quadratic Model			
	Intercept	Linear	R^2	Intercept	Linear	Quadratic	R^2
Mean	164.39	28.20	0.86	164.80	29.14	−0.32	0.93
Variance	1,582.83	199.81	0.04	1,664.57	580.60	43.06	0.02

Note: Scores on the opposite naming task across the four time points ranged from 38.72 to 350.95.

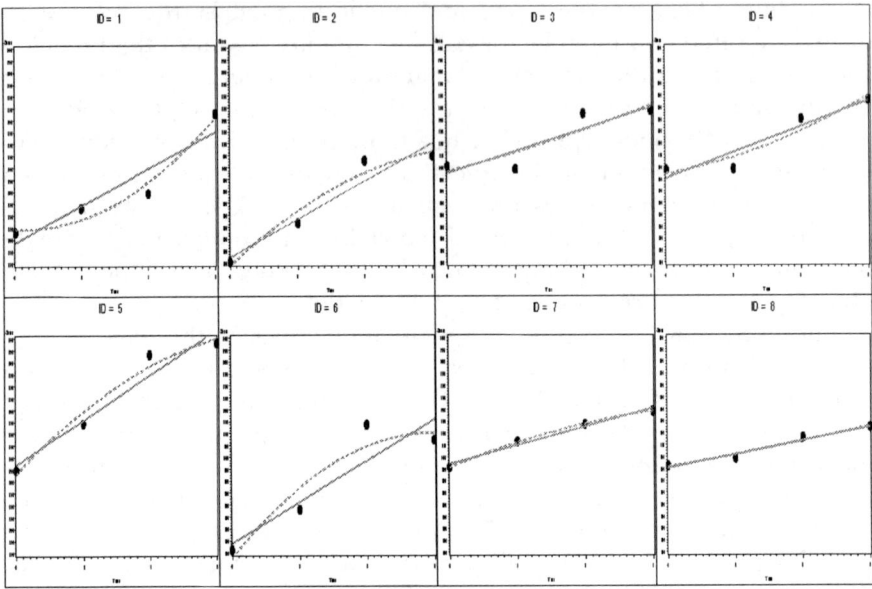

Note: In each graph, *time* is on the *x*-axis and *score* is on the *y*-axis. Dots represent observed scores, solid trajectories are from OLS regression linear models and dotted trajectories are from OLS regression quadratric models. Because observed scores appear to follow a linear rather than nonlinear pattern, support is garnered for estimating a linear LGM.

Figure 15.3.   Change in opposites-naming scores over time for a random sample of eight individuals.

chapters have been devoted to the topic (e.g., Chapter 2 of Singer & Willett, 2003) and programs have been written to assist in their creation (e.g., Carrig, Wirth, & Curran, 2004).

Unconditional latent growth model. After a preliminary inspection of the data, the first model considered is the unconditional LGM. Because a linear model was deemed appropriate for the data, a linear form was specified. The results of the unconditional growth model are shown in Table 15.5 and include the overall intercept (β_{00}) and slope (β_{10}), the variance of the individual intercepts (τ_{00}), the variance of the individual slopes (τ_{11}), and their covariance (τ_{10}). The findings likely to be highlighted by the researcher include the overall intercept and slope, which indicate that on average, participants' scores at the initial measurement occasion are 166, a fairly low value, and increase significantly by 27.19 points with each subsequent testing. The researcher would also draw attention to the intercept and slope variance, which indicate significant variability across individuals not only in their scores at the initial measure-

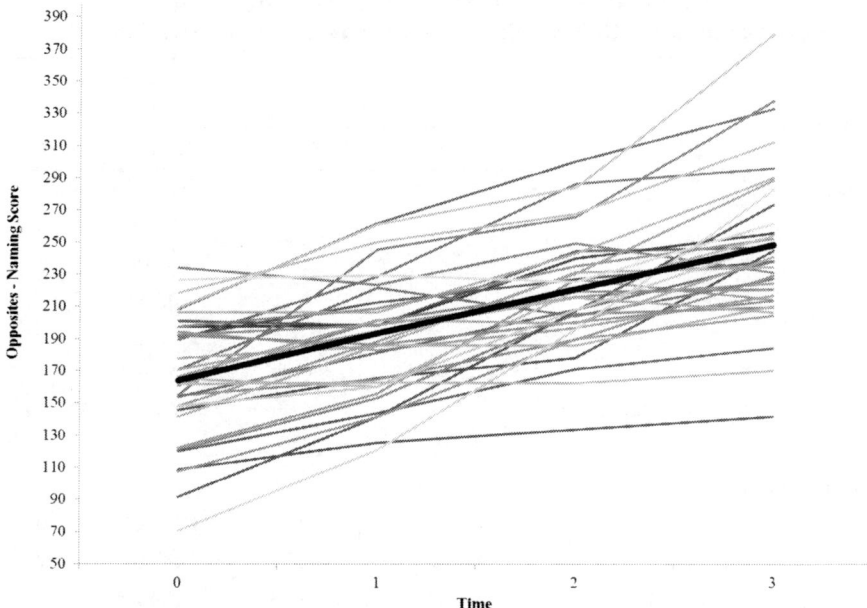

Note: The solid black line connects the average opposites-naming score at each time point. All other lines connect the opposites-naming score at each time point for a random sample of 35 individuals. Both overall and individual observed trajectories appear linear in form, supporting the use of a linear LGM. Scores at the initial time point and changes in scores over time appear to differ across individuals, supporting the use of a LGM to capture individual differences in trajectories.

Figure 15.4.   Observed trajectories of change in opposites-naming scores over time.

ment occasion, but also in how their scores change over time. Because the estimates of these variance components are difficult to interpret, the researcher might facilitate understanding by converting them to standard deviations or by providing plausible value ranges for the parameters. For instance, the 95% plausible value range for the intercepts is 99.77 to 232.23, indicating that individual predicted scores at the initial measurement occasion are fairly low in the population and range from 99.77 to 232.23. The 95% plausible value range for the slopes is 4.14 to 50.24. Thus, slopes in the population are positive with the majority of individual slopes ranging from a low of 4.14 to a high of 50.24.

In order for a reader to create a coherent mental representation of the trajectories in the population, several of pieces of information would have

Table 15.5.   Results for Unconditional and Conditional Growth Models: Opposites-Naming Scores Over Time

Parameter	Unconditional Growth Model		Conditional Growth Model	
	Estimate	SE	Estimate	SE
Fixed Effects				
Intercept				
Base (β_{00})	166.00**	2.04	166.00**	2.05
Cognitive Skill (β_{01})	–	–	–0.15	0.21
Slope				
Base (β_{10})	27.19**	0.75	27.19**	0.71
Cognitive Skill (β_{11})	–	–	0.45**	0.07
Variance Estimate				
Level one (σ_2)	159.12**	9.19	159.12**	9.19
Intercept (τ_{00})	1,141.82**	102.7	1,143.68**	102.7
Slope (τ_{11})	138.34**	4.04	118.46**	12.45
Intercept, Slope (τ_{10})	–208.26**	30.66	–202.19**	29.16

$** p < .001$

to be held and synthesized in working memory. For instance, the overall intercept and slope parameters would have to be selected and translated into an overall trajectory. Although it is possible that a reader might be able to generate their own mental representation of the overall trajectory from Table 15.5, the task of also visualizing differences among individuals in their trajectories is likely too cumbersome, even if the plausible value ranges for the growth parameters are provided. A visual display is needed to not only reduce the burden on working memory, but also to organize the information.

A useful visual display would include the model-implied overall and individual trajectories, as shown for the present example using a random sample of 35 individuals in Figure 15.5. Not only does Figure 15.5 nicely display the overall trajectory, but it also clearly conveys the substantial individual variation in intercepts and slopes. It is evident that individual's initial scores are quite different from one another, and as suggested by the 95% plausible value range for the slopes, all individual slopes shown appear to be positive, with some being steeper than others. Pairing the numerical values presented in Table 15.5 with Figure 15.5 is essential to clearly communicating the results of an unconditional LGM.

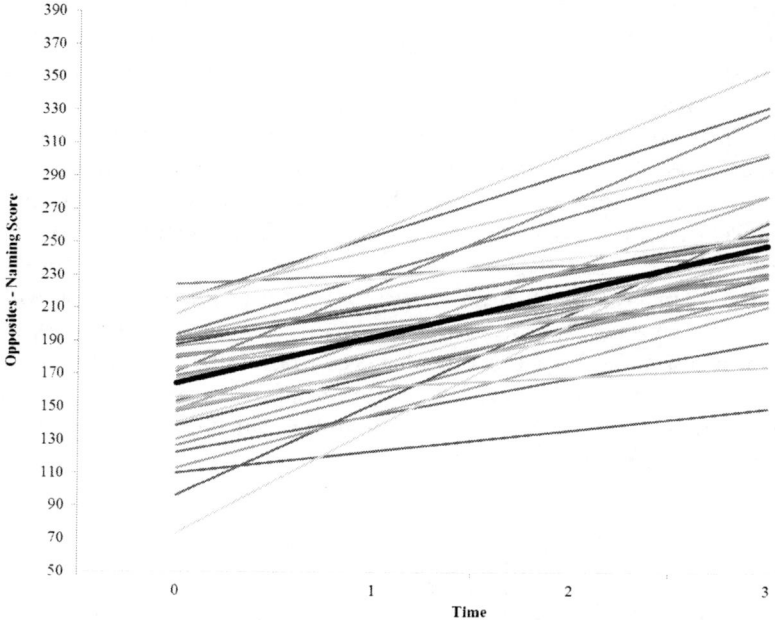

Note: The solid black line represents the model-implied overall trajectory. All other lines represent individual model-implied trajectories for a random sample of 35 individuals. All trajectories are in linear in form because the model was specified to characterize change over time as linear. Overall, scores are fairly low at the initial time point and increase gradually over time. Individuals differ in their intercepts with some individuals scoring higher than others at the initial time point. All slopes appear to be positive, although there are individual differences in slopes, with some individuals increasing in their scores at a faster rate than others.

Figure 15.5.   Model-implied trajectories of change in opposites-naming scores over time: Unconditional LGM.

Although the primary benefit of Figure 15.5 is its ability to elucidate the results of the LGM, there are other benefits associated with this visual display. For instance, the act of integrating the verbal explanation of the results with the graphical depiction in Figure 15.5 may very well deepen one's understanding of LGM in general. Additionally, because Figure 15.5 is similar to figures commonly used to display results in regression (e.g., Figure 15.1), its presence might activate schemas associated with regression, thereby reducing the load on working memory and enabling connections between LGMs and models more familiar to the reader. Specifically, the figure might help the reader conceptualize LGMs as complex regression models in which scores are regressed on time and the coefficients capturing this relationship are allowed to vary across individuals.

Unfortunately, an important aspect of the results is not readily apparent in Figure 15.5. Specifically, the significant covariance between intercepts and slopes (−208.26) is not clearly evident. Interpretation of this relationship can be facilitated by converting the covariance to a correlation ($r = -.52$). This negative, moderate correlation implies that relatively higher intercepts are associated with relatively lower slopes and vice versa. An even deeper understanding of the correlation can be obtained through a scatterplot consisting of the empirical Bayes estimates[4] of the individual intercepts and slopes (see Figure 15.6). As seen in the figure, individuals scoring relatively high at the first time point (i.e., those with relatively high intercepts) are increasing in their scores over time, although not much of an increase is observed. This is in contrast to individuals who are scoring relatively low at the initial measurement occasion. These individuals have steeper slopes, meaning that larger increases are seen in their scores over time.

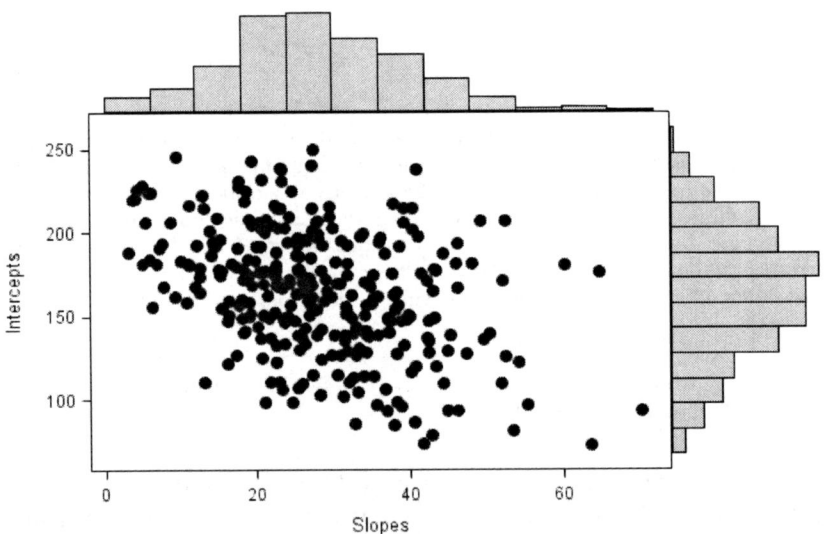

Note: The histogram on top of the scatterplot represents the distribution of the slopes across individuals and illustrates how slopes are positive, with the majority having values between 20 and 40. The histogram on the right represents the distribution of the intercepts across individuals and illustrates how the frequently occurring values for the intercepts are in the range of 150 to 200. Both histograms indicate fairly normal distributions for the growth parameters. Each dot within the scatterplot represents the intercept and slope for an individual. This scatterplot reflects a negative relationship between initial performance (intercept value) and change in performance over time (slope value).

Figure 15.6.   Scatterplot and marginal distributions of empirical Bayes estimates of intercepts and slopes: Opposites-naming example.

The marginal distributions in Figure 15.6 are also incredibly informative as they visually convey information about the distributions of each growth parameter. Although Table 15.5 provides information about the typical values of each growth parameter (β_{00} and β_{10}), and the extent to which they vary across individuals (τ_{00} and τ_{11}), Figure 15.6 also conveys this information and offers the additional advantage of indicating whether the distributions are normally distributed. It is important in LGM to inspect the univariate distributions of the growth parameters in order to assess the extent to which the assumption of multivariate normality of these parameters has been satisfied (Raudenbush & Bryk, 2002).

There may be situations in LGM where a scatterplot of the empirical Bayes estimates of the individual intercepts and slopes is not needed. For instance, if the covariance is not significant or the variance of one or both of the growth parameters is not significant, then a scatterplot is not necessary and may even be misleading. However, there are other times when a scatterplot is needed to avoid misinterpretation of the results. For example, consider another example used by Singer and Willett (2003) based on data from 254 individuals collected by Ginexi, Howe, and Caplan (2000) in their study of change in depression levels after unemployment. Individuals were measured three times during the 16 months that followed their unemployment using the Center for Epidemiological Studies' Depression (CES-D) scale (Radloff, 1977), which has scores ranging from 0 to 60 with higher scores associated with higher depression. Results for the unconditional linear growth model are shown in Table 15.6 and a scatterplot of the empirical Bayes estimates of the individual intercepts and slopes in Figure 15.7.

There are several important features of the results that might be missed or interpreted incorrectly if only Table 15.6 were consulted. First, note the change in depression scores over time. A reader limited to Table 15.6 might accurately conclude that on average, CES-D scores decrease over time (−.42) and that there is significant variation in how individuals are changing in depression (.36). The reader might not realize, however, how individuals differ in their slopes. For instance, the reader may wonder whether all slopes are negative or if there are some that are positive. The 95% plausible value range for the slopes could be provided to assist in the interpretation of the slope variability (−1.60 to 0.76); however, this range does not emphasize the infrequency with which positive slopes occur, which is readily apparent in Figure 15.7.

The significant negative covariance between intercepts and slopes might also be misinterpreted if a reader were only given access to Table 15.6. If the covariance is converted to its correlation of $r = -.55$, the reader may accurately conclude that higher CES-D scores soon after employment are associated with a more pronounced decreases in scores

Table 15.6.   Results for the Unconditional Growth Model: CES-D Scores Over Time

Parameter	Estimate	SE
Fixed Effects		
Intercept		
Base (β_{00})	17.67**	0.78
Slope		
Base (β_{10})	−0.42**	0.08
Variance Estimate		
Level one (σ_2)	68.85**	6.60
Intercept (τ_{00})	86.85**	14.96
Slope(τ_{11})	0.36*	0.19
Intercept, Slope (τ_{10})	−3.06*	1.39

$* p < .05;$ $** p < .001$

over time (and vice versa). It is important, however, that the reader consider what values characterize "higher" CES-D scores in this interpretation. Although the highest possible CES-D score that could be obtained is 60, as shown in Figure 15.7 the highest scores in the population at the initial measurement occasion are between 30 and 40. Similarly, the plausible range of slopes needs to be considered when interpreting the correlation. For instance, in the interpretation of the correlation, it was said that "higher CES-D scores soon after employment are associated with a *more pronounced decreases in scores over time*," but what slope values characterize this "more pronounced decrease?" As shown in Figure 15.7 the "more pronounced decrease in scores" associated with individuals with relatively high CES-D scores at the initial measurement is equal to a mere 1 to 1.5 point decrease in scores per month. Scatterplots, therefore, are essential in maintaining the interpretation of the intercept and slope correlation within the range of plausible values for the growth parameters, which would be difficult to accomplish with a verbal description alone.

Another benefit of presenting the scatterplot to convey the relationship between intercepts and slopes is that this graphic is a familiar visual display. That is, even though readers might not be familiar with LGM, they are likely familiar with the use and interpretation of scatterplots to illustrate how variables are related. The visual display may therefore demystify the LGM somewhat and help the reader connect it with more common statistical techniques (i.e., integration).

Conditional latent growth model. The figures we have described thus far are useful in conveying several important features of the unconditional

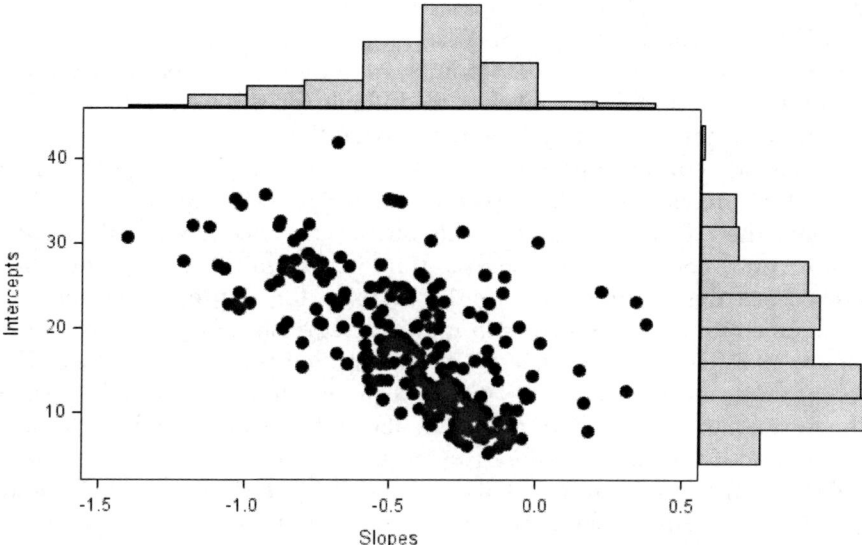

Note: The histogram on top of the scatterplot represents the distribution of slopes, which is fairly normal and indicates the greater frequency of decreases as opposed to increases in depression over time. The histogram on the right represents the fairly skewed distribution of the intercepts across individuals, which indicates most individuals have fairly low levels of depression (CES-D scores below 30) at the initial measurement occasion. Each dot within the scatterplot represents the intercept and slope for an individual. This scatterplot reflects a negative relationship between depression levels immediately after unemployment (intercept value) and change in depression levels over time (slope value).

Figure 15.7.   Scatterplot and marginal distributions of empirical Bayes estimates of intercepts and slopes: CES-D example.

LGM, including the overall trajectory, individual variability in growth parameters, and relationships among growth parameters. Indeed, such visual displays can greatly enhance understanding of the results, which is likely to promote theory development in the substantive area. For example, illustrating individual differences in growth trajectories may lead researchers to consider the reasons *why* individuals vary. In our initial example, the researcher may speculate that performance on the opposites-naming task would increase at a faster rate for those with higher cognitive skills. To explore this hypothesis, scores on a cognitive skills measure collected at the initial measurement occasion were used to explain individual differences in both intercepts and slopes.

The results of this conditional LGM, provided in Table 15.5, indicate that cognitive skill is not a significant predictor of intercepts (–.15), but it is a significant predictor of slopes (.45). Specifically, the cognitive skill coefficient for the slopes (β_{11}) indicates that as cognitive skill increases by 1 point, slopes increase by 0.45 points. Although this verbal explanation of the effect is useful, it is likely still difficult for the reader to visualize how trajectories change as a function of cognitive skill.

To facilitate understanding, a plot of the model-implied trajectories for individuals having various levels of cognitive skill can be provided. Because the effect of cognitive skills on slopes is actually an interaction between two continuous predictors (time and cognitive skills), the same procedures described earlier in the chapter for graphing interactions between continuous predictors in multiple regression were used to create Figure 15.8. Figure 15.8 plots the model-implied trajectories at three different values of cognitive skill: at the mean, one standard deviation below the mean, and one standard deviation above the mean. The figure clearly conveys both the lack of differences in the intercepts for individuals with different levels of cognitive skills and the steeper slopes for individuals with higher cognitive skills. However, the differences in slopes among the three levels of cognitive skills appear to be quite small. Figure 15.8 makes it evident that the statistically significant effect of cognitive skills on slopes is actually of minor practical significance. Without the use of a visual display, a different conclusion may have been reached about the effect's importance.

The similarities between Figure 15.1 and Figure 15.8 can be used to illustrate a benefit of visual displays emphasized throughout this chapter. As aforementioned, visual displays can deepen understanding and reduce the load on working memory through the activation of preexisting schemas. By providing Figure 15.8, a visual display very similar to Figure 15.1, the schema associated with interactions between continuous predictors in multiple regression should be activated in persons reading this chapter. Figure 15.8 should therefore reduce the load on working memory and deepen readers' understanding of interactions in LGM by connecting it to a topic with which they are already familiar.

CONCLUSIONS

When communicating the results of quantitative methods, whether as an instructor or author of an empirical article, we should actively and intentionally engage in strategies that facilitate comprehension. Several cognitive theories suggest that pairing a visual display with a verbal description is an effective strategy for enhancing understanding. Our review of relevant cognitive theories provided four reasons why visual displays are effective. In essence, an effective visual display for a statistical technique:

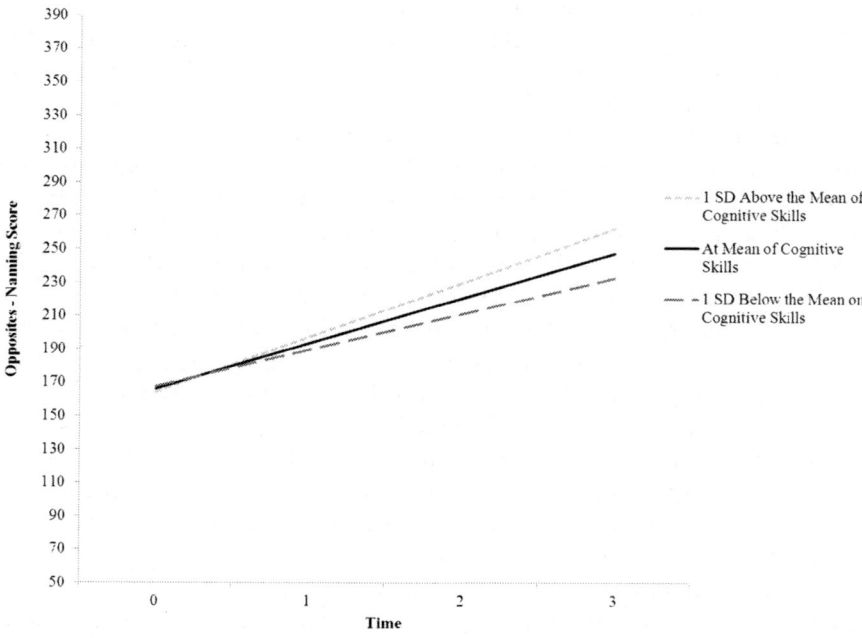

Note: To illustrate the relationship between cognitive skills and individual growth parameters in an LGM model capturing change in opposites-naming scores over time, the model-implied trajectories are shown for three levels of cognitive skills: 1 SD below the mean, at the mean, and 1 SD above the mean. There are no differences in intercepts among individuals with different levels of cognitive skills. There are somewhat steeper slopes for individuals with higher cognitive skills, but the differences among the slopes appear to be quite small.

Figure 15.8.   Model-implied trajectories of change in opposites-naming scores over time at three levels of cognitive skills: Conditional LGM model.

(a) reduces cognitive load, (b) selects and organizes relevant information, (c) provides unique information not afforded by text alone, and (d) helps learners connect the information with traditional techniques that are more familiar. To illustrate the benefits of visual displays in quantitative research, the results from three different advanced statistical techniques were presented with and without visual displays. Contrasting these two different representations of results clearly demonstrated how the core cognitive processes of selecting, organizing, and integrating relevant material can be facilitated by visual displays. Unquestionably, these visual displays are most effective when the text explicitly references the displays and directs readers to specific elements of the visual (Vekiri, 2002).

Given the important role of visual displays in understanding statistical information, why do we not encounter more figures embedded in articles presenting empirical research? The scarcity of visual displays is not due to a lack of recommendations for their inclusion in publications of research. For example, the APA Publication Manual (2010) notes the importance of presenting visual displays of results. Moreover, editors of journals have called for authors to present results using graphics (e.g., Loftus, 1993). Nevertheless, even those making the recommendations for graphics are not presenting visual displays of results: "Statisticians recommend graphical displays but often do not follow this recommendation in presenting their own research" (Gelman, Pasarica, & Dodhia, 2002, p. 121). Why?

One possible reason for the lack of visual displays is space restrictions in journals. That is, visual displays and their explanations require space. When examining the author instructions accompanying journals, one commonly observes a limit to the number of figures that can be included in an article. This limit on the number of figures conflicts with the importance of figures for comprehension and, as noted above, the call from some editors to include more graphics.

A second possible reason visual displays are not included, and a more likely culprit, is the amount of effort needed to create a high quality graph (Feinberg & Wainer, 2011; Kastellec & Leoni, 2007; Lane & Sándor, 2009; Schriger, Sinha, Schroter, Lui, & Altman, 2006). As all graphs involve a comparison of some sort, creating a graphic requires the researcher to identify what comparison is of interest and the identification of the best way to showcase that comparison. As Gelman et al. (2002) so clearly noted when discussing the effectiveness of graphs versus tables, "One thing we have learned in this research is there is a good reason to be lazy—it takes a lot of work to make nice graphs!"

Third, researchers may believe that visual displays of data are for exploratory data analyses only, especially given the emphasis on using graphs for this purpose (see Tukey, 1977). When applying a statistical model to the data, the focus often shifts to the (efficient and precise) numerical values produced. Although we agree that graphics are extremely helpful for exploring data, we hope we have demonstrated the utility of visual displays for extracting meaning from the numerical values produced by statistical models (see also Lane & Sándor, 2009).

Finally, we agree with Gelman (2011) that some researchers may (erroneously) believe that graphs distance the reader from the numerical values "that are the essence of rigorous scientific inquiry" (p. 4). As we discussed above, understanding the information represented by these numerical values requires mentally manipulating these values, which necessitates a great deal of working memory resources. We contend it is naïve to believe the numerical values on their own are intuitive, easy to interpret entities that carry great insight into the phenomenon under study. Instead, we hope we have successfully demonstrated that visual displays of statistical information illuminate the phenomenon much more clearly, potentially highlighting aspects that would have gone unnoticed, or worse been misinterpreted, without the use of visual displays, and encourage researchers to use them when reporting their findings.

NOTES

1. In a classical LPA, covariances among variables are constrained to be zero within class and variances are constrained to be equal across classes. Although within classes the covariances are constrained to be zero, nonzero relations among variables in the population are anticipated and considered to be the result of mixing classes together which have differing means on the variables. If the classical LPA within class specification is considered too restrictive, other multivariate mixture models with more flexible specifications of the within class covariance matrix can be used (e.g., Pastor, Barron, Miller, & Davis, 2007).
2. Although the original data for this example consisted of 35 individuals, we generated data for a larger sample of 300 individuals for illustration purposes. Simulated scores on the opposite naming task across the four time points ranged from 38.72 to 350.95.
3. Although the trajectories in Figure 15.4 were formed by joining adjacent observed scores with lines, a variety of methods exist for creating observed trajectories (e.g., nonparametric smoothing). As well, the linear or quadratic trajectories implied by the OLS regressions can also be used.
4. Further information regarding the empirical Bayes estimates of growth parameters can be found in Raudenbush and Bryk (2002).

REFERENCES

Aiken, L. S., & West, S. G. (1991). *Multiple regression: Testing and interpreting interactions*. Thousand Oaks, CA: SAGE.

Aiken, L. S., West, S. G., & Millsap, R. E. (2008). Doctoral training in statistics, measurement, and methodology in psychology: Replication and extension of Aiken, West, Sechrest, and Reno's (1990) survey of PhD programs in North America. *American Psychologist, 63*, 32-50.

American Psychological Association. (2010). *Publication manual of the American Psychological Association* (6th ed.). Washington, DC: Author.

Baddeley, A. D. (2001). Is working memory still working? *American Psychologist, 56*, 851-864.

Bryk, A. S., & Raudenbush, S. W. (1987). Application of hierarchical linear models to assessing change. *Psychological Bulletin, 101*, 147-158.

Cacioppo, J. T., Petty, R. E., & Morris, K. J. (1983). Effects of need for cognition on message evaluation, recall, and persuasion. *Journal of Personality and Social Psychology, 51*, 805-818.

Carrig, M. M., Wirth, R. J., & Curran, P. J. (2004). A SAS macro for estimating and visualizing individual growth curves. *Structural Equation Modeling, 11*, 132-149.

Elliot, A. J. (2005). A conceptual history of the achievement goal construct. In A. J. Elliot & C. S. Dweck (Eds.), *Handbook of competence and motivation* (pp. 52-72). New York, NY: Guilford Press.

Feinberg, R. A. & Wainer, H. (2011). Extracting sunbeams from cucumbers. *Journal of Computational and Graphical Statistics, 20*, 793-810.

Fletcher, J. D., & Tobias, S. (2005). The multimedia principle. In R. E. Mayer (Ed.), *The Cambridge handbook of multimedia learning* (pp. 117-134). New York, NY: Cambridge University Press.

Gelman, A. (2011). Why tables are really much better than graphs. *Journal of Computational and Graphical Statistics, 20*, 3-7.

Gelman, A., Pasarica, C., & Dodhia, R. (2002). Let's practice what we preach: Turning tables into graphs. *The American Statistician, 56*, 121-130.

Gibson, W. A. (1959). Three multivariate models: Factor analysis, latent structure analysis, and latent profile analysis. *Psychometrika, 24*, 229-252.

Ginexi, E. M., Howe., G. W., & Caplan, R. D. (2000). Depression and control beliefs in relation to reemployment: What are the directions of effects? *Journal of Occupational Health Psychology, 5*, 323-336.

Hannafin, M. J., Hannafin, K. M., Hooper, S. R., Rieber, L. P., & Kini, A. S. (1996). Research on and research with emerging technologies. In D. H. Jonassen (Ed.), *Handbook for education communications and technology* (pp. 378-402). New York, NY: Macmillan.

Kastellec, J. P., & Leoni, E. L. (2007). Using graphs instead of tables in political science. *Perspectives on Politics, 5*, 755-771.

Lazarfield, P. F., & Henry, N. W. (1968). *Latent structure analysis*. New York, NY: Houghton-Mifflin.

Lane, D. M., & Sándor, A. (2009). Designing better graphs by including distributional information and integrating words, numbers, and images. *Psychological Methods, 14*, 239-257.

Loftus, G. R. (1993). Editorial comment. *Memory and Cognition, 21*, 1-3.

MacCallum, R. C., Zhang, S., Preacher, K. J., & Rucker, D. D. (2002). On the practice of dichotomization of quantitative variables. *Psychological Methods, 7*, 19-40.

Mayer, R. E. (1999). Multimedia aids to problem-solving transfer. *International Journal of Educational Research, 31*, 611-623.

Mayer, R. E. (Ed.) (2005). *The Cambridge handbook for multimedia learning*. Cambridge, England: Cambridge University Press.

Mayer, R. E. (2008). Applying the science of learning: Evidence-based principles for the design of multimedia instruction. *American Psychologist, 63*, 760-769.

Mayer, R. E., & Moreno, R. (2003). Nine ways to reduce cognitive load in multimedia learning. *Educational Psychologist, 38*, 43-52.

McArdle, J. J., & Epstein, D. (1987). Latent growth curves within structural equation models. *Child Development, 58,* 110-133.

McLachlan, G., & Peel, D. (2000). *Finite mixture models.* New York, NY: Wiley.

Meredith, W., & Tisak, J. (1990). Latent curve analysis. *Psychometrika, 55,* 107-122

Pastor, D. A., Barron, K. E., Miller, B. J., & Davis, S. L. (2007). A latent profile analysis of college students' achievement goal orientation profiles. *Contemporary Educational Psychology, 32,* 8-47.

Radloff, L. S. (1977). The CES-D scale: A self report major depressive disorder scale for research in the general population. *Applied Psychological Measurement, 1,* 385-401.

Raudenbush, S. W., & Bryk, A. S. (2002). *Hierarchical linear models: Applications and data analysis methods* (2nd ed.). Thousand Oaks, CA: SAGE.

Schriger, D. L., Sinha, R., Schroter, S., Liu, P. Y., & Altman, D. G. (2006). From submission to publication: A retrospective review of the tables and figures in a cohort of randomized controlled trials submitted to the *British Medical Journal. Annals of Emergency Medicine, 48,* 750-756.

Singer, J. D., & Willett, J. B. (2003). *Applied longitudinal data analysis: Modeling change and event occurrence.* New York, NY: Oxford University Press.

Sweller, J. (2005). Implications of cognitive load theory for multimedia learning. In R. E. Mayer (Ed.), *The Cambridge handbook for multimedia learning* (pp. 19-30). Cambridge, England: Cambridge University Press.

Tukey, J. W. (1977). *Exploratory data analysis.* New York, NY: Addison-Wesley.

van Merriënboer, J.J.G. & Sweller, J. (2010). Cognitive load theory in health professional education: Design principles and strategies. *Medical Education, 44,* 85-93.

Vekiri, I. (2002). What is the value of graphical displays in learning? *Educational Psychology Review, 14,* 261-312.

Vermunt, J. K. (2001). The use of restricted latent class models for defining and testing nonparametric and parametric item response theory models. *Applied Psychological Measurement, 25,* 283-294.

Willett, J. B. (1988). Questions and answers in the measurement of change. In E. Z. Rothkopf (Ed.), *Review of research in education* (Vol. 15, pp. 345-422). Washington, DC: American Educational Research Association.

CHAPTER 16

USING VISUAL DISPLAYS TO INFORM ASSESSMENT DESIGN AND DEVELOPMENT

Brett P. Foley and Chad W. Buckendahl

ABSTRACT

The development of an assessment program draws on the expertise of testing professionals for procedural guidance and the judgment and knowledge of subject matter experts (SMEs) who are familiar with the content and testing population of interest. In addition to development, consumers of test results (e.g., students, parents, candidates, policymakers), rely on score reports and related documentation to help interpret test scores. In this chapter, we discuss how visual displays can help inform steps of the test development and validation process, from program design to item writing and review to score reporting. Relevant examples of visual displays are provided for various development activities in a range of testing settings (e.g., education, licensure, certification). We conclude with three general recommendations to improve the test development process using visual displays.

Learning Through Visual Displays, pp. 417–445
Copyright © 2013 by Information Age Publishing
417

As demand for data-driven accountability proliferates across educational and industry arenas, there is a concomitant call for "valid assessments." However, assessment professionals do not view tests as either valid or invalid. Validity is judged based on whether or not sufficient evidence exists to support a particular interpretation and use of a set of test results (Kane, 2006; Messick, 1989). Such evidence should be gathered and documented at each phase of the test development and delivery cycle. The interpretability and clarity of this evidence can be enhanced through the use of visual data displays and graphic organizers. Visual displays can also help facilitate understanding in activities conducted during the test development process that form the basis of evidence collection and evaluation. The purpose of this chapter is to illustrate types of visualization tools in the context of a validity-centered assessment development framework. For each step in this process we will summarize the relevant test development activities, present examples of relevant visual displays, and discuss how these tools (and others like them) can support and enhance the assessment development process (Downing & Haladyna, 2006; Schmeiser & Welch, 2006; Shrock & Coscarelli, 2007).

At the outset, it is helpful to illustrate the test development process that we will be discussing throughout this chapter. A visual display that we regularly use for conceptualizing the assessment development process is shown in Figure 16.1.[1] This flow chart shows each step, beginning with *Design Program* at the top of the figure and cycling clockwise through *Maintain Test*, with each step connected to a central hub conceptually representing *Validity*. Validity is a central tenet of assessment. Simply put, test results have validity if a preponderance of evidence supports their intended interpretations and uses (Kane, 2006; Messick, 1989; Lissitz, 2009). The flow chart clearly identifies each step in the test development process and that each of these steps contributes to the accrual of validity evidence. Displays like this, along with professional standards, such as the *Standards for Educational and Psychological Testing* (hereafter, *The Standards*; AERA, APA, & NCME, 1999), can help organizations understand the connection between the amount of effort and consideration of validity through the assessment development process. These steps are common to many testing programs, including those in education, licensure, and professional certification. The flow chart shown in Figure 16.1 also serves as a map of the layout of this chapter. We will provide examples of how visual displays can be used to enhance the early stages of program design (i.e., Design Program, Design Test, Analyze Domain, Develop Blueprint), content development, testing, and assembly (i.e., Develop Content, Review Content, Pretest & Analyze, Assemble Operational Test), and postadministration activities (i.e., Conduct Standard Setting, Maintain Test).

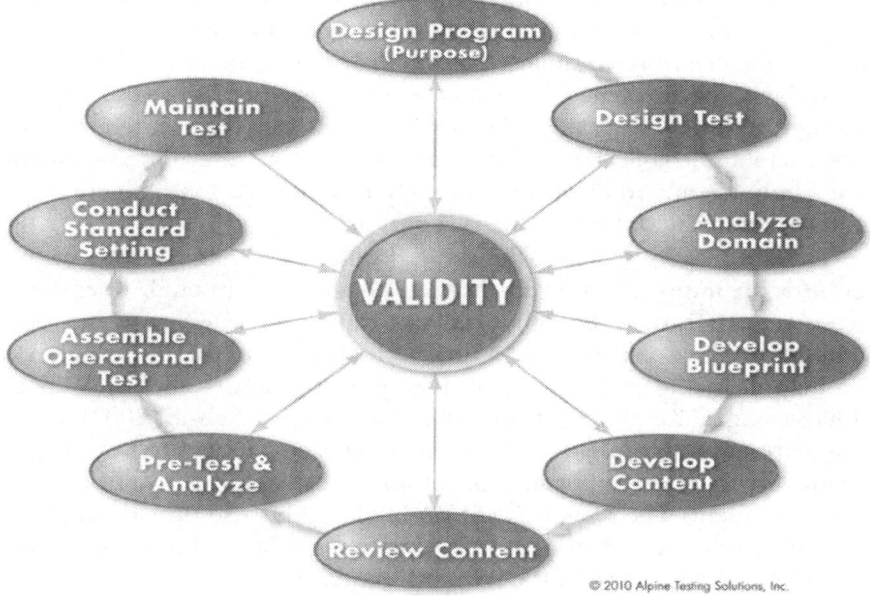

Figure 16.1.   Flow chart illustrating the steps in validity-centered assessment development.

DESIGN PROGRAM

The initial design stage of an assessment program is when fundamental questions about the program must be answered, for example:

- What is the purpose of the test?
- What question(s) is the test designed to answer?
- Who will take the test?

Answers to these and similar questions influence all subsequent assessment development activities. Careful consideration of the assessment's purpose and ways to collect evidence supporting this purpose is essential to valid interpretation and use of results. One way to organize this information is through a validation framework. A validity framework (e.g., agenda, plan) is an organizing tool that guides collection and prioritization of the evidence needed to evaluate the proposed uses and interpretations of a test (Buckendahl et al., 2009). Visual displays can help make a validation framework more concrete and communicate it to stakeholders.

For example, a licensure organization may wish to create an assessment program with two primary purposes: (1) Identify minimally qualified candidates for licensure eligibility, and (2) Provide summary feedback about candidates' performance to training programs (e.g., medical schools, teacher training programs). Evidence supporting these intended purposes should be collected and evaluated before and after the assessments are administered. To illustrate how such a framework could be organized and communicated, Figure 16.2 is shown below.

Thinking critically about the desired outcomes of an assessment program is an important step in the design process. Although operational score reports cannot be produced until after an assessment has been administered, visualizing what a finalized score report might look like can be helpful in the early stages of a testing program (Cohen & Wollack, 2006; Deng & Yoo, 2009; Ryan, 2006; Ysseldyke & Nelson, 2002). Creating score report templates early in the process encourages test developers to identify the most important conclusions they want to derive from use of the assessment. The *Standards* (AERA et al., 1999) also provide guidance regarding score report design. Following that guidance, we address strategies to comply with two of the relevant standards.

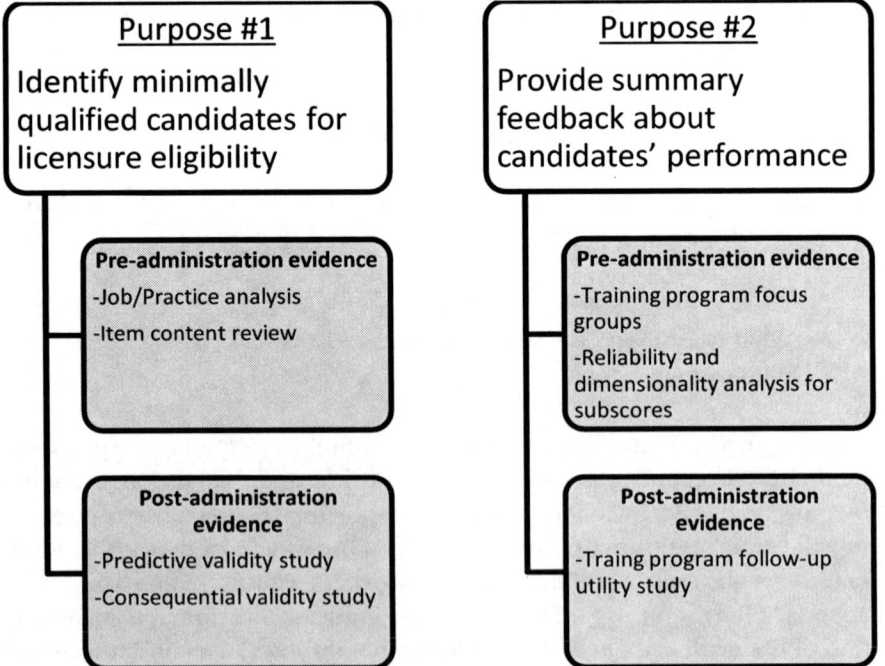

Figure 16.2.   Summarizing two purposes within a validity framework.

Figure 16.3 shows an excerpt from an example score report based on a eighth grade mathematics test. First, *Standard 13.14* states, "In educational settings, score reports should be accompanied by a clear statement of the degree of measurement error associated with each score or classification level and how to interpret the scores" (AERA et al., 1999, p. 148). This is addressed in the score report by the statement in the upper right, which presents a score error band around the hypothetical student's score in layman's terms. Additionally, although not shown here, instructions in the report direct the reader where they can find more information about the student's proficiency level (i.e., "Please refer to page X for some of the knowledge and skills a student at the Proficient level has learned in Math..."). Second, *Standard 11.6* states, "the test user is obligated to provide a timely report of the results that is understandable to the test taker and others entitled to receive this information" (AERA et al., 1999, p. 114). The report in Figure 16.3 attempts to meet this standard by presenting the student's results numerically and graphically. It also provides both norm-referenced information (i.e., school district, state averages) to help the student interpret their performance with respect to his/her peers and criterion-referenced information (i.e., proficiency level) to let report users identify the specific math skills typical of a student with that particular score. The report also includes strand-level information (e.g., number sense, measurement). This information is important to know at the outset of the assessment design process because including meaningful feedback at the strand level will affect later test design decisions. One of these decisions includes the need to make sure there are a sufficient number of items from each strand on the operational test.

DESIGN TEST

Once decisions have been made regarding the purpose of an assessment, appropriate interpretation and use of scores, and the intended population of examinees, developers can move forward with specific test design decisions. For example, questions one could ask at this stage include:

- What format should the test be (e.g., constructed response, selected response)?
- How will the test be administered (e.g., paper and pencil, computer based, adaptive)?
- How many test forms, if appropriate, are necessary?

Again, answers to questions like these will affect subsequent decisions in the assessment development process (Davey & Pitoniak, 2006; Green,

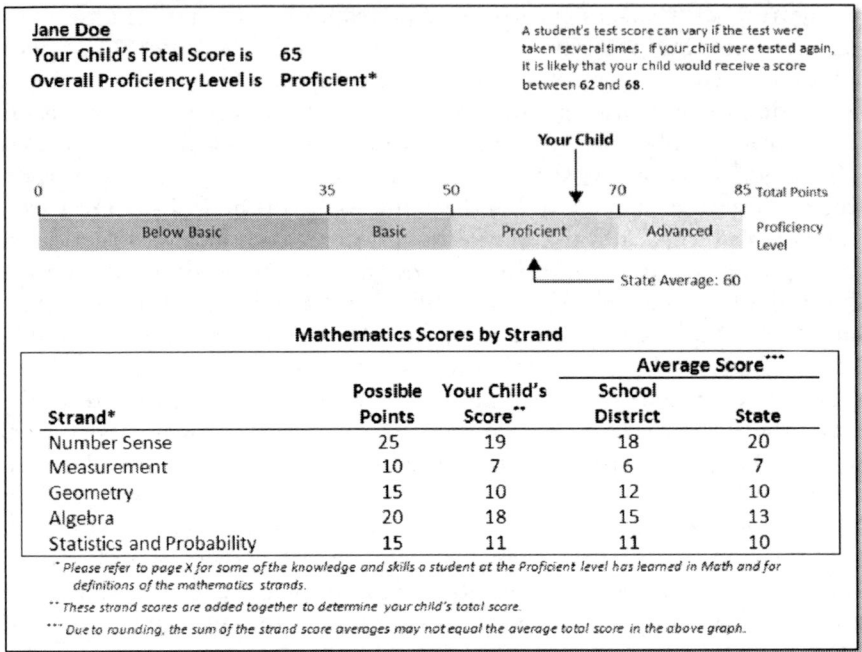

Figure 16.3.   Excerpt from a sample score report.

2000; Roid, 2006; Nitko & Brookhart, 2011). One area of design consideration relates to security. Test developers may decide that to improve test security and reduce item exposure (i.e., the number of examinees that have seen each item), that multiple forms of the assessment will be created. To ensure fairness, steps need to be taken to make sure that results from the different test forms have the same meaning. In other words, it should not matter to the examinee's performance which of the forms he/she is assigned. One way to accomplish this is through a statistical process called equating. In equating, test scores are adjusted to account for differences in difficulty across test forms (Dorans, Pommerich, & Holland, 2004; Kolen & Brennan, 2004; von Davier, 2011). Although psychometric analysis like equating occurs at a later stage in the development and validation process, the consideration of appropriate designs should be considered at the outset of program development.

Visual displays can illustrate equating designs. Figure 16.4 shows an example of an organization's 4 year equating plan. In this example, for the 2008 program year, the organization plans to develop four test forms (i.e., 2008A, 2008B, 2008C, and 2008D). To be able to compare the difficulty across forms, the organization includes sets of common "linking" items in the test forms (i.e., Set 1, Set 2, and Set 3). Linking sets are subsets of test items that are common across multiple test forms for adjacent years. For example, Set 1 is used to link the four 2008 forms to each other. Set 1 is also used to link 2008 forms to the 2009 forms. All of the 2009 forms contain two linking sets (i.e., Set 1 and Set 2) so the forms can be linked to the 2008 forms and the 2010 forms. In this way, the relative difficulty of the forms can be determined and used to ensure that scores have the same meaning regardless over time and across forms within years. The diagram illustrates a concise way of summarizing the equating design. The three linking sets may contain the same items or may be completely different sets of items. For example, if the linking sets are the same, the 2011 forms could be directly linked to the 2008 scale. However, if the linking forms are different, the 2011 forms could still be linked to the 2008 scale, but only indirectly through the intermediate testing years. In this example, because the linking sets are given different labels, the visual display for this design implies that the linking sets contain different items.

ANALYZE DOMAIN/DEVELOP BLUEPRINT

After purpose and design considerations, test developers must consider the details of the domain representation (e.g., content, cognitive processes) on the test (Raymond & Neustal, 2006; Shrock & Coscarelli, 2007). Questions asked at this assessment development stage may include:

- What knowledge/skills/abilities should the test address and at what level of cognitive complexity?
- How many test items or score points should be devoted to each content area and cognitive complexity level?
- What item format and scoring method are most appropriate for measuring each content area?

One way to begin to identify the content that should appear on the assessment is to work with a panel of subject matter experts (SMEs). The SMEs typically are professionals in the field of interest who have a strong understanding of the content as well as familiarity with the abilities of the intended population of examinees. One strategy for evaluating domain representation is called a practice analysis (Knapp & Knapp, 1995). In these types of studies, the SME panel might start by listing topics believed to be important and related to the purpose of the assessment. The panel then can work with the listed topics organizing them

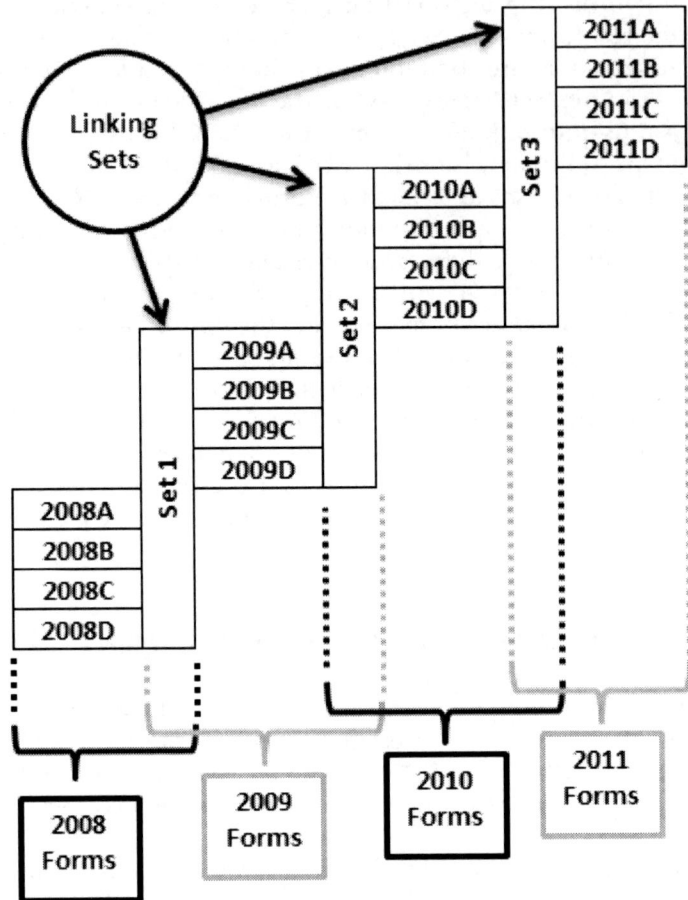

Figure 16.4.   Diagram illustrating an equating design with linking sets of items.

into meaningful groups, identifying the relationships among the groups, and identifying assessment objectives. The cluster diagram shown in Figure 16.5 illustrates a helpful visual display that can be used to assist the SMEs with this process. This example is based on the economics assessment framework for the *National Assessment of Educational Progress* (National Assessment Governing Board, 2006), a test designed to measure the economic literacy of Grade 12 students in the United States. The diagram clearly shows a design focused on three primary content areas (i.e., The Market Economy, The National Economy, and The International Economy), as well as a series of topics linked to one or more of these content areas. After SMEs identify primary content areas for the assessment (sometimes called "objectives" or "content standards") it is necessary to identify in what proportions these content areas will appear on the assessment. One might accomplish this by surveying a large number SMEs in the field, asking them to rate the importance of each of the objectives and identifying ones the earlier SME panel may have omitted. The survey results can be used to ensure the content coverage of the assessment matches what SMEs in the field view as important for examinees to know (Raymond, 2001). The document that summarizes the distribution of test content across assessment objectives is referred to as a test blueprint.

Test blueprints are often shown visually in a tabular format. Table 16.1 shows an example of a three-dimensional test blueprint for a test with 100 selected response (e.g., multiple choice) items and 5 constructed response (e.g., short answer, extended response, performance task) items. The three dimensions referred to are content, cognitive complexity, and item type. The content is merely the assessment objectives. Cognitive complexity is a

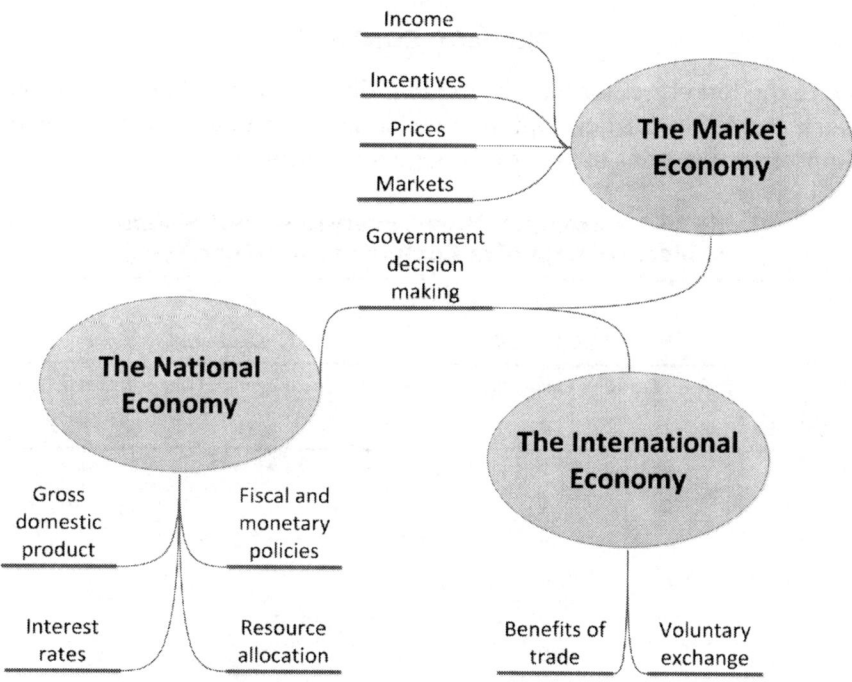

Source: Adapted from National Assessment Governing Board (2006).

Figure 16.5.   Cluster diagrams for representing the content domain of Grade 12 economics.

description of the cognitive processes examinees must use to answer a given test question. Cognitive complexity represents a continuum of processes, ranging from simple recall of facts at the low end to extended reasoning, creation of new products and processes, and evaluation a the high end. Several different classification strategies have been suggested to help break this continuum into meaningful ranges (Anderdos & Krathwohl, 2001; Bloom, 1956; Webb, 1997). In our experience, item writers tend to find items with at higher cognitive complexity levels more difficult to create, therefore it is important to explicitly include cognitive complexity in the test blueprint if the assessment objectives include higher order thinking skills. Because some content is more appropriately assessed by constructed response items than multiple choice (and vice versa), it is useful to include item type in the assessment blueprint to guide development. The example in Table 16.1 shows how these three dimensions are integrated by showing concisely the intended number of items or score points for each objective/cognitive complexity/item type combination.

DEVELOP CONTENT

Once the test objectives have been identified and a test blueprint created, work can begin on developing content (i.e., items) for the assessment. Important questions to ask at this stage may include:

Table 16.1.   Example Three-Dimensional Test Blueprint (Objective, Cognitive Complexity, and Item Type)

	Item Type					
	Multiple Choice			Constructed Response		
	Cognitive Complexity Level			Cognitive Complexity Level		
Objective	1	2	3	1	2	3
1	8	1	1			
2	2	7	1			1
3	1	6	3			1
4	8	1	1			
5	2	3	5			2
6	5	2	3			
7	5	2	3			
8	2	8	0			
9	1	2	7			1
10	8	1	1			

- How will items be created and evaluated?
- Who will create them?
- How many items should be written?

Items are often constructed during an in-person or remotely attended item development workshop. Items typically are drafted by panels of either SMEs or professional item writers. At an item development workshop, panelists are trained in item writing practices and assigned to write items targeted at the test blueprint (Haladyna, 2004; Haladyna, Downing, & Rodriguez, 2002; Flaughter, 2000; Rodriguez, 2011). Typically, more items are developed than are needed for the operational test forms because some items will be removed during the review and pilot testing stages. If given a choice, item writers will tend to write items for the objectives that are easier to write to, often content targeting lower levels of cognitive complexity.

Figure 16.6 is an example of a table with embedded graphics that can be displayed during an item writing meeting to help ensure each objective receives attention from the item writers. In addition to counts of the number of needed items and the number currently written, the visual display uses conditional formatting functionality that spreadsheet software such as Microsoft Excel offer to embed cell-sized bar graphs in the table. This display draws from principles in Tufte's (2006) discussion of sparklines, which are "small, high-resolution graphics usually embedded in a full context of words, numbers, images" (p. 47). These small graphs allow item writers to see, at a glance, which objectives are most in need of items. In this example, small graphics have also been included to indicate when item writing for an objective is complete (e.g., check mark) and when an objective is in great need of additional items (e.g., exclamation point).

REVIEW CONTENT

After items have been drafted, they proceed through a review process. Questions asked at this stage of the item development process may include:

- What steps should be taken to make sure items are not biased against certain subgroups?
- How can we ensure the items are technically accurate?
- How can we ensure that items meet published criteria for quality?
- Are there sufficient items to create the forms required by our test blueprint and program design?

Section	Objective	Needed	Written	Progress
Section 1	1.1	9	4	
	1.2	7	0	
	1.3	7	5	
Section 2	2.1	7	1	
	2.2	6	1	
	2.3	7	0	
Section 3	3.1	10	10	
	3.2	7	1	
	3.3	10	10	
Section4	4.1	9	5	
	4.2	7	6	
	4.3	8	4	
	Total:	94	47	

Figure 16.6.   Conditional formatting for illustrating real-time item development progress.

A critical step in the collection of validity evidence is ensuring that the assessment items align with the domain (e.g., objectives, content standards) in terms of content and cognitive complexity. Depending on the field in question (e.g., education, licensure, professional certification), this evaluation may take place in an aptly named alignment study or a congruence and accuracy review. In some alignment study methodologies (e.g., Frisbie, 2003; Webb, 1997), SMEs are asked to make judgments about how the content necessary to answer an item correctly overlaps with the content of an objective. Panelists may make qualitative decisions about whether a content match is complete, partial, slight, or no match. The Venn diagrams in Figure 16.7 help to illustrate this judgment by representing the relationship of the item with the objective. The diagram for a "Complete Match" makes it clear that an item does not have to cover the full breadth of an objective to be considered a complete match. Rather, the content of the item may be a subset of the content indicated by the objective. For example, if an objective stated, "The qualified examinee should be able to multiply and divide whole numbers," a test item that required an examinee to multiply, but not divide whole numbers would still be considered a complete match with respect to the content of that item and the objective.

Thus far, we have discussed how visual displays can inform the assessment design and development process. Visual displays can also be used to clarify individual test items. Consider the two versions of the same test item targeting understanding of computer networking structure shown in Figure 16.8. The version of the item without the diagram is unnecessarily wordy

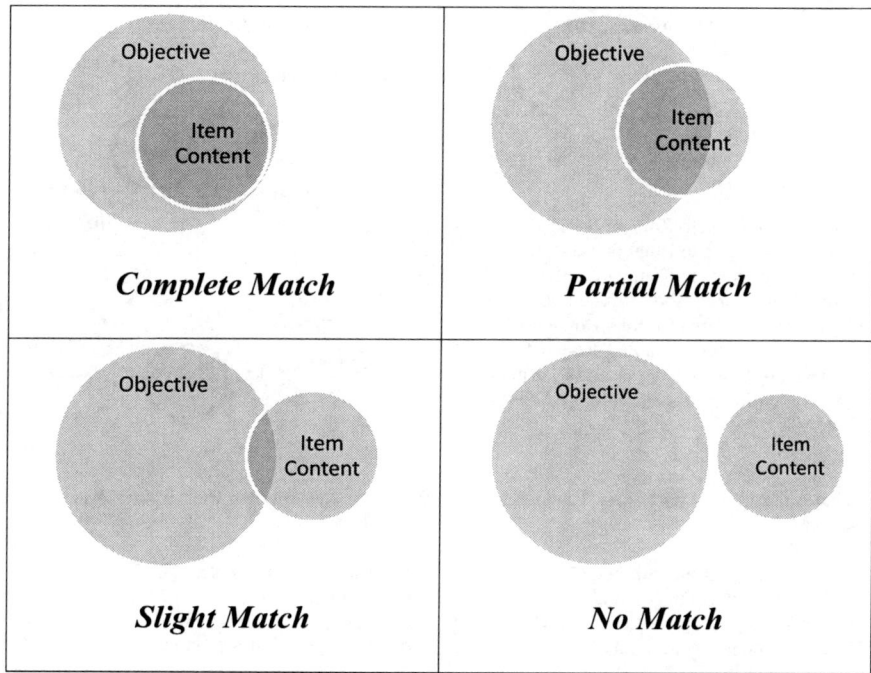

Figure 16.7.   Venn diagrams use for alignment study training to illustrate degrees of relationship between the content of a test item and the content of an objective.

and complicated; it presents a heavy cognitive burden for the test taker just to follow the passage preceding the question, which is a source of difficulty likely not intended by the item writer or indicated in an objective. The item with the diagram presents the same information much more succinctly. The example from Figure 16.8 illustrates the need for test developers to think critically about the inclusion of visual displays in items. In this example, the item benefited from the addition of a diagram and is likely a better representation of the content as it occurs in practice as opposed to the text-based format. In other situations, however, an unnecessary diagram may add an additional cognitive burden for the test taker and distract from the intended measurement (Kalyuga, this volume).

In order to help ensure fairness for all test takers, researchers have identified ways to evaluate and modify items to help ensure they are accessible to as broad an audience as possible (Beddow, Elliott, & Kettler, 2009; Beddow, Kettler, & Elliott, 2008; Beddow, Kurx, & Frey, 2011). This research was originally focused on accessibility for examinees with disabilities. However, the design guidance represents good practice for any program. With respect to visual displays in test items, Beddow et al. (2011) argue that they are optimally accessible if they,

Item without diagram	*Item with diagram*
	Refer to the Exhibit.
Router A connects to Routers B and E. Router B connects to Routers A and E. Router C connects to Routers B and D. Router D Routers C and G. Router G connects to Routers D and F. Router F connects to Routers G and E. Router E connects to Routers A, B, C, and F. Rip is the only routing protocol configured on the routers.	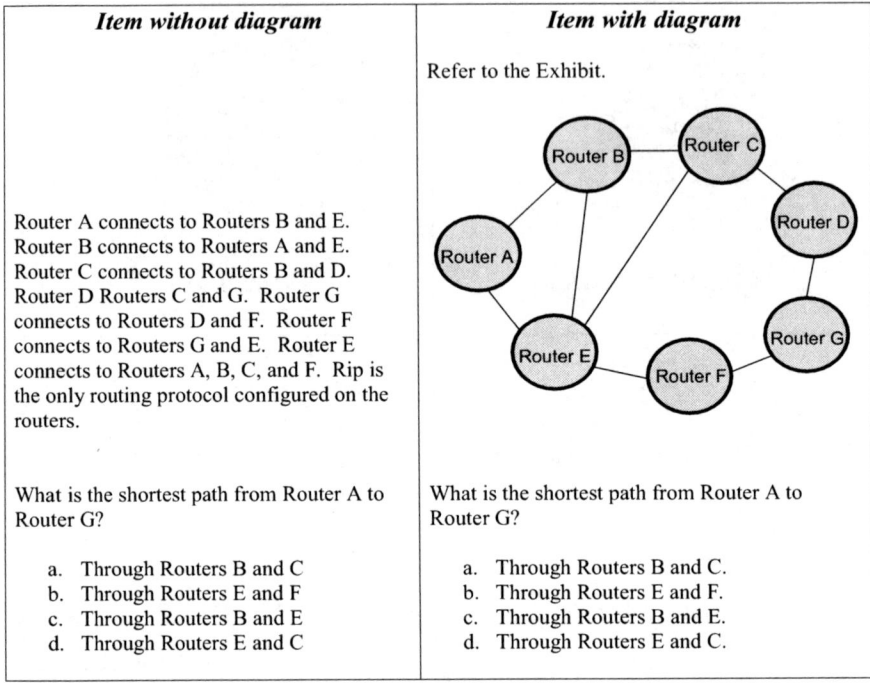
What is the shortest path from Router A to Router G?	What is the shortest path from Router A to Router G?
a. Through Routers B and C b. Through Routers E and F c. Through Routers B and E d. Through Routers E and C	a. Through Routers B and C. b. Through Routers E and F. c. Through Routers B and E. d. Through Routers E and C.

Figure 16.8. Example of graphic inclusion review as part of the item review process.

- Are necessary for responding to the item.
- Clearly depict the intended images and are as simple as possible.
- Contain only text that is necessary for responding.
- Are unlikely to distract test-takers (p. 169)

PRETEST AND ANALYZE

Now that items have been developed and reviewed, items should be tried out on a sample of the intended population before creating the operational test form. The purpose of this pretesting is to empirically evaluate the psychometric properties of the test items.

- What kind of analyses should be performed (Haladyna, 2004; Livingston, 2006)?
- How large of a pretest sample should we have?

Visual displays can help to simplify the interpretation of pretest data. Consider the example in Figure 16.9. Figure 16.9. shows a summary for 10 test items taken by 150 examinees. The test items are polytomously scored in which an examinee can get a score of 0, 1, 2, or 3 on each item. For completeness, the figure includes four columns that show the number of examinees who received each score level for each item. There are four additional columns that convert these numbers to percentages. Even with only 10 items, interpretation of the eight aforementioned columns becomes cumbersome. However, the column labeled "Distribution of Scored Responses" employs Tufte's (2006) constructs of sparklines and small multiples (1990). "Small multiples" refers to a type of visual display design in which several small, related displays are included together in a compact area. In this way, "Information slices are positioned within the eyespan, so that viewers make comparisons at a glance—uninterrupted visual reasoning. Consistency of design pits the emphasis on changes in the data, not changes in data frames" (Tufte, 1990, p. 67). This column uses Microsoft Excel 2010's sparkline functions to create cell-sized bar graphs that summarize visually the data in the previous eight columns. These graphs make it easy to see, at a glance, the spread of scores for each item. Additionally, the most common score for each item is shaded more darkly, further enhancing interpretability. The "Average Score" column can serve as a measure of item difficulty: items with lower average scores are more difficult than items with higher average scores. Conditional formatting is also used in this column, while Lorch (1989) and Meyer's (1975) principal of *signaling* (summarized in Mayer & Moreno, 2003) is used to place emphasis on the easiest and most difficult items. This is accomplished by applying a grayscale gradient to each cell in the column, whereby easier items are darker shades and more difficult items are lighter. Taken together, these two columns make it easier to identify important features of the data. For example, it is immediately apparent that item 2 is the most difficult item of this set and items 3-5 are the easiest. Simple augmentations to tables of item statistics, like those discussed here, can greatly improve the interpretability and effectiveness of item analysis results.

When evaluating pretest data, it is often of interest to identify items that may disadvantage one group or another. Differential item functioning (DIF) refers to a set of statistical procedures that attempt to identify items where examinees of similar abilities, but from different groups (e.g., gender, race, socioeconomic status), have different probabilities of getting an item correct. This, combined with qualitative bias reviews conducted during item reviews, helps to ensure fairness (however, it should be noted that although DIF is a useful tool for flagging items for further study, an item demonstrating DIF may not necessarily be biased). One way to evaluate items for

Item	Number of responses at scorepoint...				Percent of responses at scorepoint...				Distribution of scored responses	Average score
	0	1	2	3	0	1	2	3		
1	12	46	33	59	8%	31%	22%	39%		2.9
2	71	38	35	6	47%	25%	23%	4%		1.3
3	0	59	6	85	0%	39%	4%	57%		3.3
4	18	6	67	59	12%	4%	45%	39%		3.2
5	1	41	23	85	1%	27%	15%	57%		3.4
6	52	12	54	32	35%	8%	36%	21%		2.2
7	45	57	15	33	30%	38%	10%	22%		1.9
8	25	48	45	32	17%	32%	30%	21%		2.3
9	3	49	49	49	2%	33%	33%	33%		2.9
10	44	1	77	28	29%	1%	51%	19%		2.4

Figure 16.9.   Example of conditional formatting and spreadsheet-embedded sparklines for evaluation of item level pretest data.

DIF is to calculate and compare separate item characteristic curves (ICCs) each item based on the subgroups of interest. ICCs are graphs that show the probability of an examinee answering an item correctly across the range of examinee abilities. Figure 16.10 shows two ICCs for a test item, one based on examinees from a subgroup labeled "Group A" and another for a subgroup labeled "Group B." These graphs show that the probability of responding correctly to the item varies depending on what group an examinee is in. For example, an examinee from Group A with an ability of 0.5 has a 50% chance of answering the question correctly. An examinee with the same ability from Group B has only a 38% chance of answering the item correctly. This information may be indicative that this item is exhibiting DIF favoring examinees from Group A.

ASSEMBLE OPERATIONAL TEST

Once item development, review, and pilot testing are complete, the next step in the process is to assemble one or more operational test forms (Drasgow, Luecht, & Bennett, 2006; Wendler & Walker, 2006). The primary

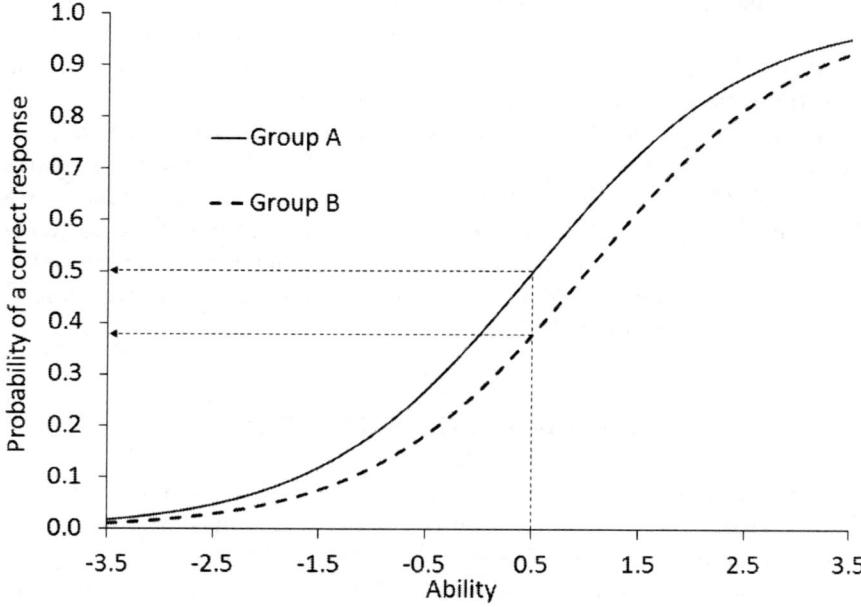

Figure 16.10.   Example of using item characteristic curves to show the effect of differential item functioning.

driver of this process will be the test blueprint that specifies the number and type of items across content areas and cognitive complexity levels. Additional questions asked at this stage may include:

- How are pretest data used to assemble operational tests?
- How do we make sure results from different forms are comparable?

If the test design calls for multiple test forms, as discussed earlier in the design section of this chapter, an equating plan should be in place to ensure comparability of results across forms. If, however, adequate pretest data are available, another option is to build pre-equated test forms. That is, forms that are built to the same test blueprint for content representation and have equivalent statistical characteristics. A common way of building equivalent forms is to use test information function (TIF) targets (Drasgow, Luecht, & Bennett, 2006). Each item on a test contributes to the amount of information we have about examinees. TIFs summarize the amount of information and consequently the precision of measurement across the range of examinee abilities. TIFs can be described numerically, but are often shown through a visual display. Similarly, although the differences between two

TIFs can be described with numbers, the differences can also be examined visually as in Figure 16.11. Consider a testing program that builds a single test form, Form A, through either a manual or an automated test assembly procedure. Now consider the same testing program wants to build a second, pre-equated test form. Two competing forms (i.e., Form B and Form C) are created using the same blueprint and the TIFs of these forms are compared to the TIF of Form A. It is easy to see in Figure 16.11 that Form B has nearly the same TIF as Form A, indicating that they have similar statistical properties. Form C is shifted to the left, and consequently provides more information about lower ability examinees. However, based on our goal of creating pre-equated forms, Form B is clearly the better choice.

CONDUCT STANDARD SETTING

If assessment results are used to classify examinees into two or more groups (e.g., pass/fail, basic/proficient/advanced, masters/nonmasters, qualified/unqualified) steps need to be taken to choose a cut score (or scores) that can be used to determine the point on the test score scale

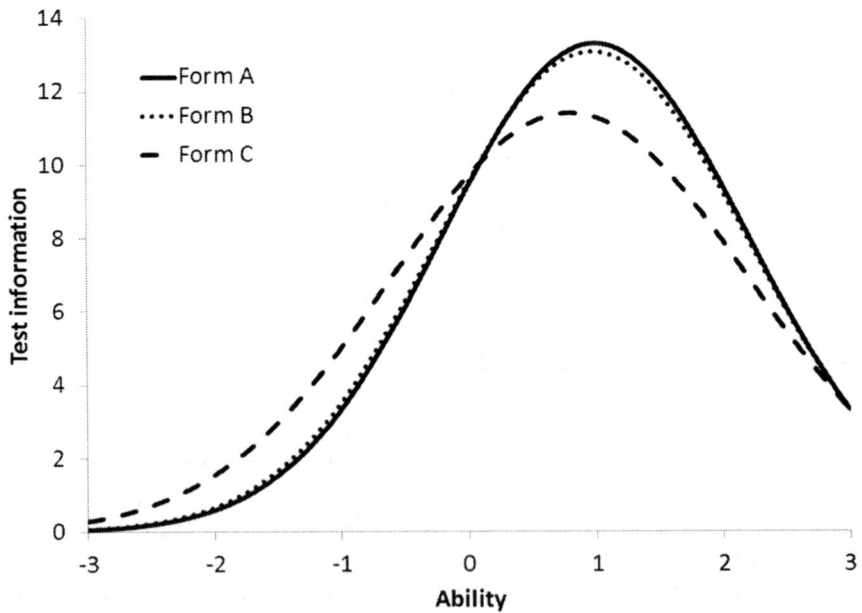

Figure 16.11.   Example of using test information functions to evaluate form comparability.

where the transition between these classifications will take place. Standard setting refers to the family of methodologies used to link test scores to performance categories (Cizek, 2012; Cizek & Bunch, 2007; Hambleton & Pitoniak, 2006; Zieky, Perie, & Livingston, 2008). Many standard setting methodologies rely on the judgments of subject matter experts (SMEs). The SMEs typically are chosen for their expertise in the field and knowledge of the target population of test takers. Several standard setting methodologies use multiple rounds of judgments, with feedback to SMEs occurring between rounds. One type of feedback provided to SMEs is a comparison of their initial cut score recommendations with that of their peers on the standard setting panel. This information is typically presented in terms of summary statistics using some combination of panel means, medians, ranges, and standard deviations. The utility of this feedback is limited, however, if the field does not place an emphasis on numeracy. In other words, if the SMEs are not comfortable interpreting these statistics, they may be of little use in evaluating the reasonableness of their own ratings.

For SMEs who are not as quantitatively adept, it is often more useful to provide a visual display to summarize the distribution of the cut score recommendations. For example, a testing program would like to use a 25-point mathematics test to classify examinees into four performance categories: *Below Basic, Basic, Proficient,* and *Advanced*. To do this, we need to set three cut scores along the 25-point scale at the *Below Basic/Basic, Basic/Proficient,* and *Proficient/Advanced* thresholds. Using a standard setting methodology, 17 SMEs provide initial cut score recommendations. To show each SME how their recommendations compare with the rest of the panel, we have found it useful to show the SMEs the distribution of their recommendations graphed on a stacked dot plot, like that shown in Figure 16.12.

In this graph, each dot represents each panelist's initial cut score recommendation. These graphs allow SMEs to quickly see both a typical recommendation for the group and the variability of the group's recommendations. Additionally, by showing graphs for each of the tree cut points in a stacked manner, SMEs can see how the group's expectations change across the different performance categories. For example, Figure 16.12 illustrates that seven SMEs recommended a *Proficient* cut score of 15, with the other recommendations distributed fairly symmetrically around the mode. On the other hand, the distribution of cut scores for the *Advanced* performance category begins at 19 and is positively skewed. We can also see that one SME appears to have very high expectations for the *Proficient* cut score. Specifically, this SME recommended a *Proficient* cut score of 20 which was at or above the majority of the other panelists' *Advanced* cut score recommendations. This type of graph is useful for communicating to SMEs how their expectations compared to their peers.

Distribution of Panelist Cut Score Recommendations

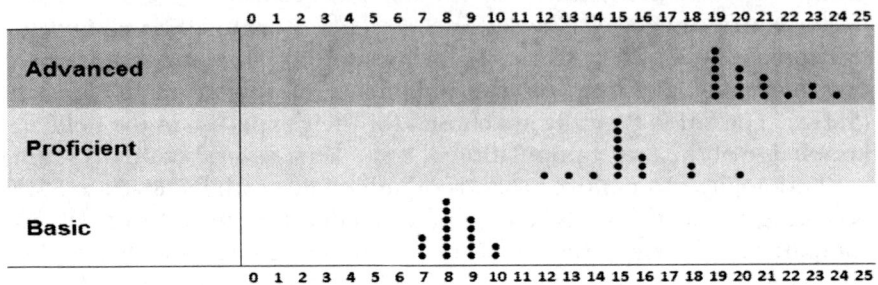

Figure 16.12.   Example of stacked dot plots for standard setting panelist feedback.

Another way visual displays can help with standard setting is by aiding the process of vertical moderation. In K-12 education testing, cut scores often are set for multiple grade levels; for example, there are federal requirements that reading be tested and proficiency rates calculated for students in Grades 3 through 8 and once in high school. Some suggest that when standards are set across grades, it is reasonable to expect relatively smooth transitions in proficiency rates across grades and therefore acceptable to adjust cut scores to help ensure these smooth transitions (Huynh & Schneider, 2005; U.S. Department of Education, 2007). This process of smoothing across grades is referred to as vertical moderation.

As mentioned before, cut score recommendations derived from a standard setting study are based on the judgments of group of SMEs. These SMEs represent a sample of the entire population of possible SMEs who could have participated in the study. If a different group of similarly-qualified SMEs had participated instead, one would expect that the results would be similar, but not necessarily identical. This uncertainty due to sampling should be accounted for in the cut score recommendations, and is typically integrated into the process by calculating confidence intervals around each cut score. These confidence intervals then can be considered a range of defensible cut scores.

Combining a visual display with the confidence intervals described above can be a useful tool when trying to vertically articulate proficiency rates. Vertical articulation often appears in the context of K-12 education assessment programs and refers to the coherency of expectations across grades within a content area. In other words, there is a general expectation that there should not be large swings in proficiency rates across grades when scores are aggregated across large populations (e.g. the state level). Consider Figure 16.13 as an example. Figure 16.13 the solid line represents the trend in proficiency rates across grades that might result if we used the mean SME recommendation from a standard setting panel as the final cut scores. The vertical error bars represent confidence intervals about the mean SME recommendations for each grade. One way to produce vertically articulated proficiency rates is to attempt to draw a line that passes through all of the confidence intervals (see the dotted line in the graph). The points at which this dotted line lines up with each grade level represent a set of vertically aligned proficiency rates. As a result, the rates may be interpreted by policymakers as psychometrically reasonable, because they fit within the confidence intervals estimated from the judgments of the SMEs and smoothly transition from grade to grade.

MAINTAIN TEST

At this point in the test development process, one or more test forms have been created and are being used operationally. Questions assessment developers need to ask at this point may include:

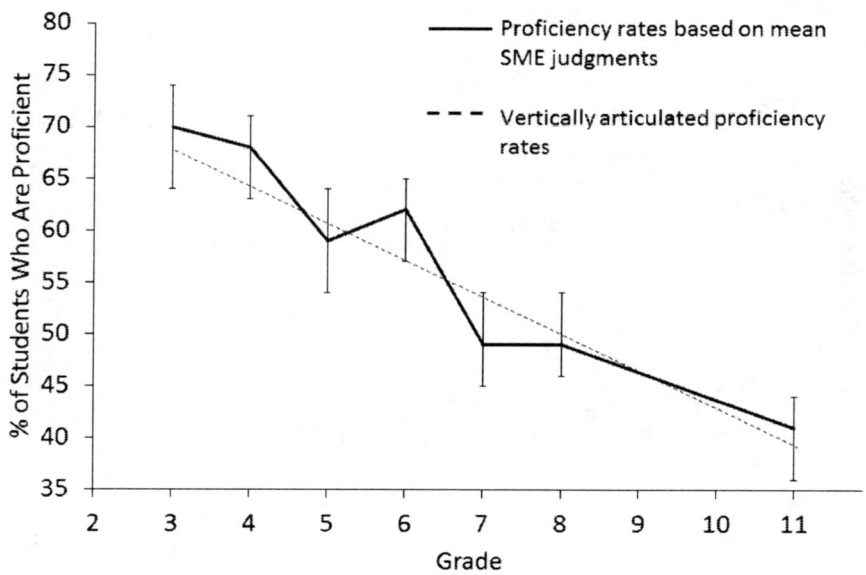

Figure 16.13.   Example of a line graph with confidence intervals for vertical articulation in standard setting.

- Once a test is created, what are the test developers' ongoing responsibilities?
- What additional validity studies are necessary to support test use?

As the stakes of defined test uses increase, so too do the incentive for examinees to cheat. Cheating and breaches in test security threaten the validity of test results by allowing otherwise unqualified examinees to pass. Therefore, an ongoing responsibility of testing organizations is maintaining test security. Visual displays can be useful in the evaluating item exposure and identifying potential cheaters. For example, Figure 16.14 shows the examinee passing rates each week for the first 6 months of a new testing program. For the first 15 weeks of test administration, passing rates hover around 60%. After week 15, we see an abrupt jump in passing rates up to near 90%. The abruptness of the jump may indicate a security breach (e.g., items from the test form getting published on the Internet).

Figure 16.15 shows the test results of 245 examinees on a 100-point test (consisting of 100, dichotomously scored, four-option multiple choice items). Each examinee's score is plotted against the time (in minutes) it

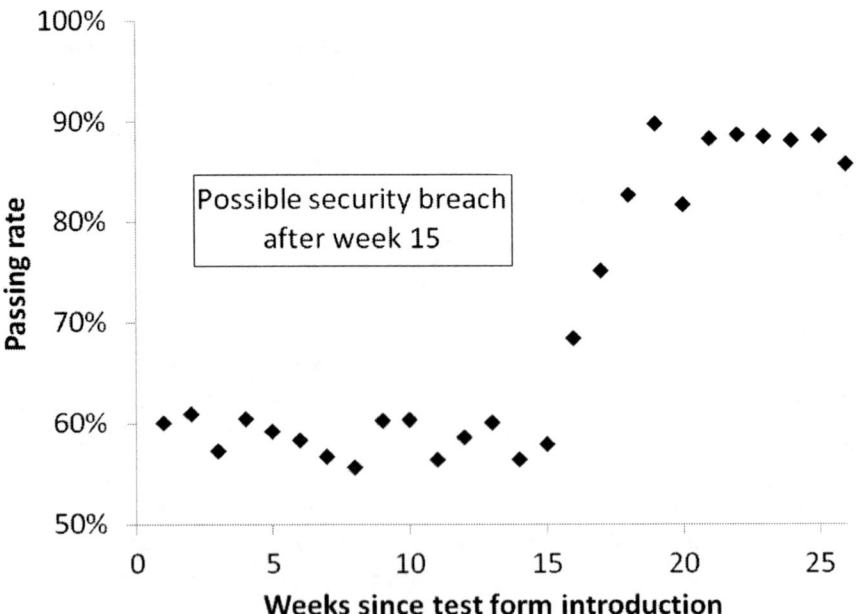

Figure 16.14.   Example of a scatter plot showing passing rates over time.

took them to complete the test (up to the one hour maximum time allowed). There is a trend showing a gradual increase in scores as examinees use more time to finish the test. Another interesting feature seen clearly in this graph is the presence of five observed examinees' scores that were very high in very little time (see top left corner of Figure 16.15). One examinee received a score of 99 after finishing in only 5 minutes. Given that the test is 100 items long, it is unlikely that someone could read through all of the questions in five minutes. It is also unlikely that one would score this high based on guessing. Therefore it may be reasonable to investigate the possibility that the examinees in the upper left of the graph for possible cheating behavior.

In the *Design Program* section of this chapter, we discussed issues related to individual score reporting. At this stage in the assessment process, another type of score report that can be examined is at an aggregate level. Score reports on their own may be considered visual displays, and they may also contain additional visual displays. For example, Figure 16.16 is a state level Snapshot report for the 2002 *National Assessment of Educational Progress* for Grade 8 writing in Nebraska (U.S. Department of Education, Institute of Education Sciences, National Center for Education Statistics, 2003).

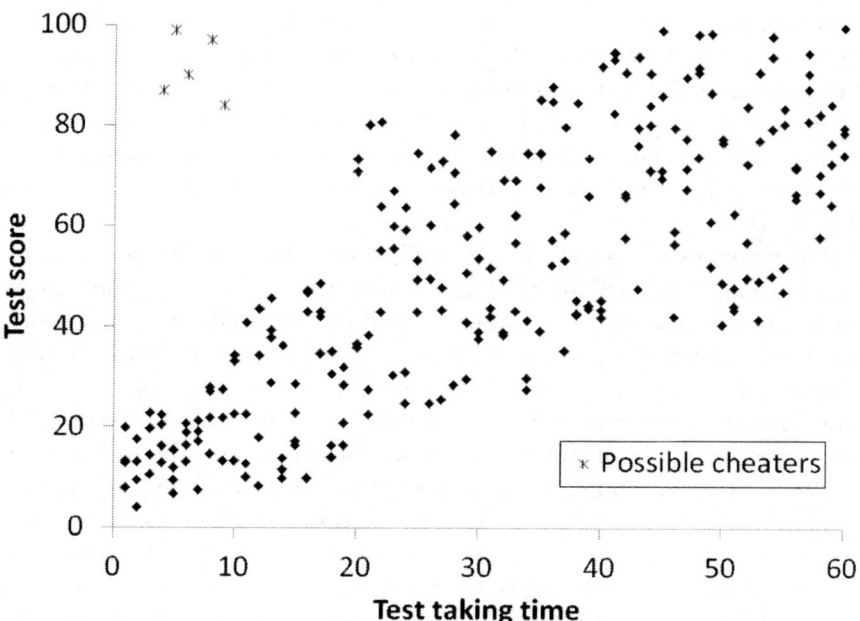

Figure 16.15.   Example of a scatter plot comparing test score for different test-taking times.

Rather than reporting data for an individual student this report provides data at the state level. Data are also disaggregated by gender, race/ethnicity, and free/reduced price lunch status. The report provides a wealth of data about the test results and the assessment itself. Like the student-level score report discussed earlier, this report explicitly acknowledges the error/variability in test scores by presenting the results of significance tests, indicating when differences are larger than would be expected by chance. This report also address another one of *The Standards*: Standard 11.14 states, "Test users are obligated to protect the privacy of examinees and institutions that are involved in a measurement program" (1999, p. 116). If subgroups are very small reporting statistics for that subgroup may allow scores for individuals in that group to be determined, violating their confidentiality. It can be seen in the report that scores for Asians/Pacific Islanders and American Indians/Alaskan Natives are not reported due to small group sizes.

CONCLUSIONS

The purpose of this chapter was to identify examples of visual displays that help to inform the assessment development process. Clearly, each stage of the assessment development process can benefit from the use of well thought-out visual displays. This chapter does not purport to be an exhaustive list of all visual displays used in testing or a comprehensive explication of the test development process. Instead, we hope that this chapter serves to motivate practitioners to seek out innovative ways to integrate useful visual displays into their own assessment development activities to communicate important concepts and results to a range of audiences.

For many testing programs, the individuals who help design the assessment are not SMEs. Similarly, SMEs only rarely are testing professionals. Although it is important to involve testing professionals when designing a testing program, the judgments, input, and expertise of SMEs are indispensable for creating a quality assessment. These test development activities present different levels of cognitive burden for the SMEs. The cognitive challenge of the specific tasks combined with the unfamiliarity of the test development and validation process can result in especially difficult and mentally taxing activities. In the same way, test takers and other consumers of test results (e.g., students, parents, candidates, policymakers) who lack understanding of the nuances of test design may struggle to correctly interpret test results. It is a professional and ethical responsibility of test users to provide results in ways that test takers can understand. Well thought out visual displays can help address both of the above issues.

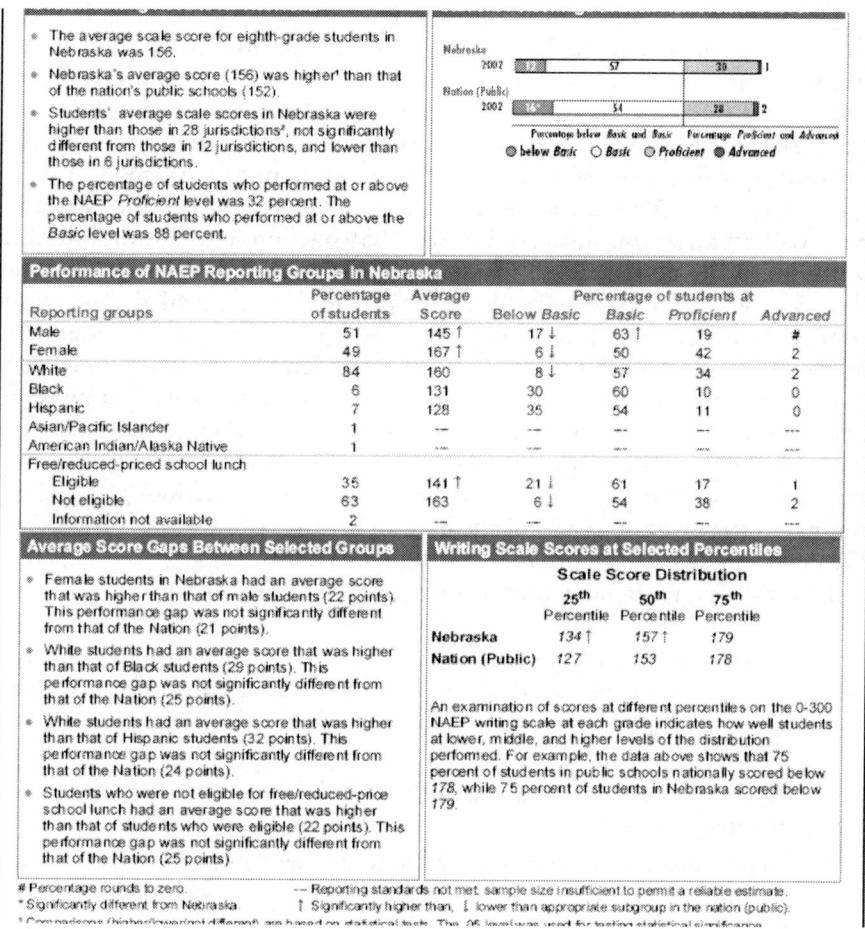

- The average scale score for eighth-grade students in Nebraska was 156.
- Nebraska's average score (156) was higher¹ than that of the nation's public schools (152).
- Students' average scale scores in Nebraska were higher than those in 28 jurisdictions², not significantly different from those in 12 jurisdictions, and lower than those in 6 jurisdictions.
- The percentage of students who performed at or above the NAEP *Proficient* level was 32 percent. The percentage of students who performed at or above the *Basic* level was 88 percent.

Performance of NAEP Reporting Groups in Nebraska

Reporting groups	Percentage of students	Average Score	Below *Basic*	*Basic*	*Proficient*	*Advanced*
Male	51	145 ↑	17 ↓	63 ↑	19	#
Female	49	167 ↑	6 ↓	50	42	2
White	84	160	8 ↓	57	34	2
Black	6	131	30	60	10	0
Hispanic	7	128	35	54	11	0
Asian/Pacific Islander	1	--	--	--	--	---
American Indian/Alaska Native	1	---	---	---	---	---
Free/reduced-priced school lunch						
Eligible	35	141 ↑	21 ↓	61	17	1
Not eligible	63	163	6 ↓	54	38	2
Information not available	2	---	---	---	---	---

Average Score Gaps Between Selected Groups

- Female students in Nebraska had an average score that was higher than that of male students (22 points). This performance gap was not significantly different from that of the Nation (21 points).
- White students had an average score that was higher than that of Black students (29 points). This performance gap was not significantly different from that of the Nation (25 points).
- White students had an average score that was higher than that of Hispanic students (32 points). This performance gap was not significantly different from that of the Nation (24 points).
- Students who were not eligible for free/reduced-price school lunch had an average score that was higher than that of students who were eligible (22 points). This performance gap was not significantly different from that of the Nation (25 points).

Writing Scale Scores at Selected Percentiles

Scale Score Distribution

	25th Percentile	50th Percentile	75th Percentile
Nebraska	134 ↑	157 ↑	179
Nation (Public)	127	153	178

An examination of scores at different percentiles on the 0-300 NAEP writing scale at each grade indicates how well students at lower, middle, and higher levels of the distribution performed. For example, the data above shows that 75 percent of students in public schools nationally scored below 178, while 75 percent of students in Nebraska scored below 179.

\# Percentage rounds to zero.   --- Reporting standards not met; sample size insufficient to permit a reliable estimate.
* Significantly different from Nebraska.   ↑ Significantly higher than, ↓ lower than appropriate subgroup in the nation (public).

Source: U.S. Department of Education. Institute of Education Sciences, National Center for Education Statistics (2003).

Figure 16.16.   Example state-level score report.

It makes sense to reduce the cognitive burden for SMEs whenever feasible. In this chapter, we have shown examples of how testing professionals can integrate visual displays into the test development process with an aim of providing additional clarity for SMEs. We have also shown examples of using visual displays to help with the interpretability of score reports. We recommend that testing professionals continue to work to identify new ways of using visual displays to decrease the cognitive burden for SMEs and consumers of test results.

However, it is unlikely that a given visual display will be equally effective in all contexts. With this in mind, testing professionals should take steps to monitor the comprehension of SMEs and consumers of test results and evaluate the utility of various visual displays in multiple contexts. For example, Zieky et al. (2008) recommend the inclusion of a mid-workshop evaluations of training and "agreements to proceed" (i.e., a form by which SMEs indicate that they have understood the training, have had all questions answered to their satisfaction, and are prepared to move on to the next activity). Testing professional should integrate questions about the effectiveness and interpretability of visual displays into similar tools in order to monitor SME understanding and evaluate the utility of the displays. Similarly, Zenisky and Hambleton (2009) have conducted research where various test consumers are interviewed in order to better understand how they use and interpret testing score reports. Such research helps testing professionals identify effective score reporting practices. This also leads to a third recommendation: when researchers evaluate effectiveness of visual displays in testing, these results should be disseminated across the broader testing community.

In summary, we believe that testing professionals should

1. explore the expanded use of visual displays throughout the test development and validation process to reduce the cognitive burden for SMEs and increase interpretability for consumers of test results,
2. evaluate the effectiveness of different data visualizations in various testing contexts, and
3. disseminate the results of such inquiries to the broader testing community.

In this way SMEs can focus on assessment content rather than testing concepts and consumers of test results can be encouraged and guided with tools to make more valid use and interpretations of test results.

NOTE

1.   Copyright 2010 Alpine Testing Solutions. Reprinted with Permission.

REFERENCES

American Educational Research Association, American Psychological Association, and National Council on Measurement in Education (1999). *Standards for*

Educational and Psychological Testing. Washington, DC: American Educational Research Association.

Anderson, L. W., & Krathwohl, D. R. (Eds.). (2001). *A taxonomy for learning, teaching and assessing: A revision of Bloom's Taxonomy of Educational Outcomes*. New York, NY: Longman.

Beddow, P. A., Elliott, S. N., & Kettler, R. J. (2009). *TAMI accessibility rating matirix*. Nashville, TN: Vanderbilt University.

Beddow, P. A., Kettler, R. J., & Elliott, S. N. (2008). *Test accessibility and modification inventory*. Nashville, TN: Vanderbilt University.

Beddow, P. A., Kurz, A., & Frey, J. R. (2011). Accessibility theory: Guiding the science and practice of test item design with the test-taker in mind. In S. N. Elliott, R. J. Kettler, P. A. Beddow, & A. Kruz (Eds.), *Handbook of accessible achievement tests for all students* (pp. 201-216). New York, NY: Springer.

Bloom, B. S. (Ed.) (1956). *Taxonomy of educational objectives, the classification of educational goals—Handbook I: Cognitive Domain*. New York, NY: McKay.

Buckendahl, C. W., Davis, S. L., Plake, B. S., Sireci, S. G., Hambleton, R. K., Zenisky, A. L., & Wells, C. S. (2009). *Evaluation of the National Assessment of Educational Progress: Final Report*. Washington, DC: U.S. Department of Education.

Cizek, G. J. (Ed.). (2012). *Setting performance standards: Foundations, methods, and innovations* (2nd ed.). New York, NY: Routledge.

Cizek, G. J., & Bunch, M. B. (Eds.). (2007). *Standard setting*. Thousand Oakes, CA: SAGE.

Cohen, A. S., & Wollack, J. A.. (2006). Test administration, security, scoring, and reporting. In R. L. Brennan (Ed.), *Educational measurement* (4th ed., pp. 345-386). Westport, CT: Praeger.

Davey, T., & Pitoniak, M. J. (2006). Designing computer adaptive tests. In S. M. Downing & T. M. Haladyna (Eds.), *Handbook of test development* (pp. 543-574). Mahwah, NJ: L. Erlbaum.

Deng, N., & Yoo, H. (2009). *Resources for reporting test score: A bibliography for the assessment community*. Madison, WI: National Council on Measurement in Education.

Dorans, N. J., Pommerich, M., & Holland, P. W. (Eds.) (2004). *Linking and aligning scores and scales*. New York, NY: Springer.

Downing, S. M., & Haladyna, T. M. (Eds.) (2006). *Handbook of test development*. Mahwah, NJ: L. Erlbaum.

Drasgow, F., Luecht, R. M., & Bennett, R. E. (2006). Technology and Testing. In R. L. Brennan (Ed.), *Educational measurement* (4th ed., pp. 471-515). Westport, CT: Praeger.

Flaughter, R.. (2000). Item pools. In H. Wainer (Ed.), *Computer adaptive testing: A primer* (2nd ed. pp. 37-59). Mahwah, NJ: L. Erlbaum.

Frisbie, D. A. (2003). Checking the alignment of an assessment tool and a set of content standards. Iowa Technical Adequacy Project (ITAP). Iowa City, IA: University of Iowa.

Green, B. F. (2000). System design and operation. In H. Wainer (Ed.), *Computer adaptive testing: A primer* (2nd, ed. pp. 23-35). Mahwah, NJ: L. Erlbaum.

Haladyna, T. M. (2004). *Developing and validating multiple-choice test items*. Mahwah, NJ: L. Erlbaum.

Haladyna, T. M., Downing, S. M., & Rodriguez, M. C. (2002). A review of multiple-choice item-writing guidelines for classroom assessment. *Applied Measurement in Education, 15*, 309-334.

Hambleton, R. K., & Pitoniak, M. J. (2006). Setting performance standards. In R. L. Brennan (Ed.), *Educational measurement* (4th ed., pp. 433-470). Westport, CT: Praeger.

Huynh, H., & Schneider, C. (2005). Vertically moderated standards: Background, assumptions, and practices. *Applied Measurement in Education, 18*, 99-113.

Kane, M. T. (2006). Validation. In R. L. Brennan (Ed.), *Educational measurement* (4th ed., pp. 17-64). Westport, CT: Praeger.

Knapp, J., & Knapp, L. (1995). Practice analysis. In J. C. Impara (Ed.), *Licensure testing: Purposes, procedures and practices* (pp. 93-116). Lincoln, NE: Buros Institute of Mental Measurements.

Kolen, M. J., & Brennan, R. L. (2004). *Test equating, scaling, and linking: Methods and practices* (2nd ed.). New York, NY: Springer.

Lissitz, R. W. (Ed.). (2009). *The concept of validity: Revisions, new directions, and applications.* Charlotte, NC: Information Age Publishing.

Livingston, S. A. (2006). Item Analysis. In S. M. Downing & T. M. Haladyna (Eds.), *Handbook of test development* (pp. 421-441). Mahwah, NJ: L. Erlbaum.

Lorch, R. F., Jr. (1989). Text signaling devices and their effects on reading and memory processes. *Educational Psychology Review, 1*, 209-234.

Mayer, R. E., & Moreno, R. (2003). Nine ways to reduce cognitive load in multimedia learning. *Educational Psychologist, 38*, 43-52.

Messick, S. (1989). Validity. In R. L. Linn (Ed.), *Educational measurement* (3rd ed., pp. 13-103). New York, NY: Macmillan.

Meyer, B. J. F. (1975). *The organization of prose and its effects on memory.* New York, NY: Elsevier.

National Assessment Governing Board. (2006). *Economics framework for the 2006 National Assessment of Educational Progress.* Retrieved from http://www.nagb.org/publications/frameworks/economics_06.pdf

Nitko, A. J., & Brookhart, S. M. (2011). *Educational assessment of students* (6th ed.). Upper Saddle River, NJ: Pearson.

Raymond, M. R. (2001). Job analysis and the specification of content for licensure and certification examinations. *Applied Measurement in Education, 14*, 369-415.

Raymond, M, & Neustel, S. (2006). Determining the content of credentialing examinations. In S. M. Downing & T. M. Haladyna (Eds.), *Handbook of test development* (pp. 181-244). Mahwah, NJ: L. Erlbaum.

Rodriguez, M. C. (2011). Item-writing practice and evidence. In S. N. Elliott, R. J. Kettler, P. A., Beddow, & A. Kruz (Eds.), *Handbook of accessible achievement tests for all students* (pp. 201-216). New York, NY: Springer.

Roid, G. H. (2006). Designing ability tests. In S. M. Downing & T. M. Haladyna (Eds.), *Handbook of test development* (pp. 527-542). Mahwah, NJ: L. Erlbaum.

Ryan, J. M. (2006). Practices, issues, and trends in student test score reporting. In S. M. Downing & T. M. Haladyna (Eds.), *Handbook of test development* (pp. 677-710). Mahwah, NJ: L. Erlbaum.

Schmeiser, C. B., & Welch, C. J. (2006). Test development. In R. L. Brennan (Ed.), *Educational measurement* (4th ed., pp. 307-344). Westport, CT: Praeger Publishers.

Shrock, S. A., & Coscarelli, W. C. (2007). *Criterion-referenced test development: Technical and legal guidelines for corporate training* (3rd ed.). San Francisco, CA: Pfeiffer.

Tufte, E. R. (1990). *Envisioning Information.* Cheshire, CT: Graphics Press.

Tufte, E. R. (2006). *Beautiful evidence.* Cheshire, CT: Graphics Press.

U.S. Department of Education. (2007, December 21). *Standards and assessments peer review guidance: Information and examples for meeting the requirements of the No Child Left Behind Act of 2001.* Washington, DC: U.S. Department of Education, Office of Elementary and Secondary Education.

U.S. Department of Education. Institute of Education Sciences, National Center for Education Statistics. (2003). *The Nation's Report Card state writing 2002: Nebraska grade 8 public school snapshot report (NCES 2003-532NE8).* Retrieved from http://nces.ed.gov/nationsreportcard/pdf/stt2002/writing/2003532NE8.PDF

von Davier, A. A. (Ed.) (2011). *Statistical models for test equating, scaling, and linking.* New York, NY: Springer.

Webb, N. L. (1997). Criteria for alignment of expectations and assessments in mathematics and science education (NISE Research Monograph No. 6). Madison, WI: University of Wisconsin-Madison, National Institute for Science Education.

Wendler, C. L. W, & Walker, M. E. (2006). Practical issues in designing and maintaining multiple test forms for large-scale programs. In S. M. Downing & T. M. Haladyna (Eds.), *Handbook of test development* (pp. 445-468). Mahwah, NJ: L. Erlbaum.

Ysseldyke, J., & Nelson, J. R. (2002). Reporting results of student performance on large-scale assessments. In G. Tindal & T. M. Haladyna (Eds.), *Large-scale assessment programs for all students: Validity, technical adequacy, and implementation* (pp. 467-480). Mahwah, NJ: L. Erlbaum.

Zieky, M. J., Perie, M., & Livingston, S. A. (2008). *Cutscores: A manual for setting standards of performance on educational and occupational tests.* Princeton, NJ: Educational Testing Service.

Zenisky, A. L., & Hambleton, R. K. (2009). Getting the message out: An evaluation of NAEP score reporting practices with implications for disseminating test results. *Applied Measurement in Education, 22,* 359-375.

ABOUT THE AUTHORS

EDITOR BIOS

Matthew T. McCrudden is an associate professor in the School of Educational Psychology and Pedagogy at Victoria University of Wellington (VUW). He received his PhD in learning and technology in 2005 from the University of Nevada-Las Vegas. He has held academic appointments at the University of North Florida (2005-2008) and VUW (2008-present). He teaches educational psychology, research methods, and text learning courses at VUW, and serves on five editorial boards. His research interests include how task characteristics (e.g., prereading instructions), reader characteristics (e.g., prior knowledge/beliefs), and text characteristics (e.g., visual displays; refutational text) are related to readers' cognitive processes while they read and the mental products that result from reading.

Dan Robinson is director and professor of the School of Education at Colorado State University. He received his PhD in educational psychology in 1993 from the University of Nebraska where he majored in both learning/cognition and statistics/research. He has taught at Mississippi State University (1993-1997), the University of South Dakota (1997-1998), the University of Louisville (1998-1999), and the University of Texas (1999-2012). Dr. Robinson has served as the editor of *Educational Psychology Review* since 2006, and as an editorial board member of nine journals. He has published over 100 articles, books, and book chapters, presented over 100 papers at research conferences, and taught over 100 college courses. His research interests include educational technology innovations that may facilitate learning, team-based approaches to learning, and examining trends in articles published in various educational journals and societies.

Gregory Schraw is Barrick distinguished professor of educational psychology at the University of Nevada, Las Vegas. Dr. Schraw holds a Ph.D. in learning and an MS in applied statistics. He has published widely in both the areas of human learning and testing, including eight textbooks and edited volumes. He teaches statistics, human measurement, research methods, and evaluation courses at UNLV, and serves on eight editorial boards. He is the recipient of several teaching and research awards, as well as the American Psychological Association's early career achievement award and AERA fellow. He currently serves on the Nevada Technical Advisory committee which oversees the state testing programs, several Institute of Educational Science evaluation panels, and recently served three years on the NAEP Technical Working Group. Dr. Schraw coordinated the alternate assessment testing and accountability program for four years under contract to the Nevada department of Education, which assessed math, reading, and science. He also has consulted extensively with a number of state testing programs. He is a fellow of the American Educational Research Association.

AUTHOR BIOS

Jerry Andriessen is a psychologist and senior researcher now serving as a private consultant and project manager at Wise & Munro Learning Research (www.wisenmunro.org). For many years his research is about computer support of collaborative learning, especially focused on the interactions and discussions (argumentation) as part of the learning activities. He is a reviewer and member of the board of many international research journals, such as *Cognitive Science, Cognition & Instruction* and the *International Journal of Computer Assisted Collaborative Learning*. He coedited books on argumentative writing (1999), computer support of argumentation (2003) and on the role of affect in collaborative learning (2013).

Michael Baker is a tenured research professor of the French National Scientific Research Centre (www.cnrs.fr), working in Paris in the economic and social sciences department of France's premier graduate telecom engineering school (Telecom ParisTech). After his PhD in cognitive science (1989) at the Open University (United Kingdom), his research has concentrated on computer-supported collaborative learning, and particularly on how students coelaborate new knowledge as a result of engaging in argumentative interactions. The book *Arguing to Learn* (Kluwer Academic, 2003), coedited with J. Andriessen and D. Suthers, was on this theme. More recently, his work has focussed on the role of affect in collaborative learning, as evidenced by the book *Affective Learning Together* (Routledge, 2013), coedited by M. Baker, J. Andriessen and S. Järvelä. He is member of the editorial boards of the *International Journal of Computer Supported Collaborative Learning* and *Journal of Computer Assisted Learning*.

Chad W. Buckendahl, PhD, is a senior psychometrician and director of Education, Licensure, and Professional Certification Services with Alpine Testing Solutions. He provides psychometric and testing policy consultation and leads validation and research projects for a range of testing programs. Dr. Buckendahl's research interests are applied psychometrics including alignment, legal/policy issues, standard setting, test evaluation, and validity. He was a coprincipal investigator for the *Evaluation of the National Assessment of Educational Progress* (2009), a chapter coauthor for *Setting Performance Standards: Foundations, Methods, and Innovations* 2nd ed. (2012), *Assessment of Higher Order Thinking Skills* (2011), *Handbook of Test Development* (2006), and *Defending Standardized Testing* (2006), and coeditor and chapter coauthor for *High Stakes Testing in Education: Science and Practice in K-12 Settings* (2011). Dr. Buckendahl has also served on committees for membership, outreach, and program for the National Council on Measurement in Education (NCME) and as an associate editor for *Applied Measurement in Education* (AME). He currently serves as cochair and a psychometric reviewer for the National Commission for Certifying Agencies (NCCA) and coeditor of the *Journal of Applied Testing Technology* (JATT).

Douglas D. Dexter is an assistant professor of special education at The Pennsylvania State University. His research interests include effective instruction and successful inclusion practices for adolescents with learning disabilities. He is currently associate editor of the journal, *Insights on Learning Disabilities: From Prevailing Theories to Validated Practices*.

Sara J. Finney has a dual appointment at James Madison University as associate professor in the Department of Graduate Psychology and as associate assessment specialist in the Center for Assessment and Research Studies. In addition to teaching multivariate statistics and structural equation modeling for the assessment and measurement PhD program, she is coordinator of the quantitative psychology concentration within the psychological sciences MA program. Much of her research involves the application of structural equation modeling to better understand the functioning of self-report instruments. Her research has appeared in such journals as *Educational and Psychological Measurement, Contemporary Educational Psychology,* and *International Journal of Testing*.

Brett P. Foley, PhD, is a psychometrician with Alpine Testing Solutions. He has worked with many types of testing programs, including licensure, educational and information technology certification testing. Additionally, he has provided general educational measurement and related policy consultation and has led validation research in alignment and standard setting. Dr. Foley received his PhD in quantitative, qualitative, and psychometric methods from the Department of Educational Psychology at the University of Nebraska-Lincoln. He is a past president of the Northern Rocky Mountain Educational Research Association. His research interests include alignment, standard setting, policy considerations in testing, and using visual displays to inform the test development process.

Tim Höffler is an instructional psychologist. He graduated at the University of Kiel and received his PhD at the University of Duisburg-Essen in the research group of Detlev Leutner and colleagues. Currently, he is working as a post-doc at the Leibniz-Institute for Science and Mathematics Education (IPN). Apart from multimedia learning in general and individual learning differences with visualizations in particular, his research interests include the development of supportive measures for science learning and research on students' interests and self-concepts in science.

Charles Hughes is professor of special education at the Pennsylvania State University and an adjunct senior scientist at the University of Kansas Center for Research in Learning. His research interests center on helping students with learning disabilities succeed academically in general education classrooms. He has served as both president and executive director of the Council for Exceptional Children's Division for Learning Disabilities and was editor-in-chief of the journal, *Learning Disabilities Research and Practice.*

Putai Jin obtained his PhD in psychology from La Trobe University in 1992. His research interests are in health and educational psychology with special emphasis on learning, stress management, and quantitative research methods.

Slava Kalyuga is professor of educational psychology at the School of Education, the University of New South Wales, where he received a PhD and has worked since 1995. His research interests are in cognitive processes in learning, cognitive load theory, and evidence-based instructional design principles. His specific contributions include detailed experimental studies of the role of learner prior knowledge in learning (expertise reversal effect); the redundancy effect in multimedia learning; the development of rapid online diagnostic assessment methods; and studies of the effectiveness of different adaptive procedures for tailoring instruction to levels of learner expertise. He is the author of three books and many research articles and book chapters.

Renae Low received a PhD in psychology from La Trobe University, Australia in 1990. Her research interest is in features of science of learning that are relevant to education.

Richard E. Mayer is professor of psychology at the University of California, Santa Barbara, where he has served since 1975. His research interests are in applying the science of learning to education, with a focus on multimedia learning and computer-supported learning. He served as president of division 15 (educational psychology) of the American Psychological Association and vice president of the American Educational Research Association for Division C (learning and instruction). He is the winner of the Thorndike Award for career achievement in educational psychology, the Scribner award for career research in learning and instruction, and the distinguished contribution of applications of psychology to education and training award from the American Psychological Association. He is ranked #1 as the most productive educational psychologist in the world in contemporary educational psychology. He serves on the editorial boards of 12 journals mainly in educational psychology. He is the author of more than 400 publications including 25 books, such as *Applying the Science of Learning, e-Learning and the Science of Instruction: Third Edition* (with R. Clark), *Multimedia Learning: Second Edition, Learning and Instruction: Second Edition, Handbook of Research on Learning and Instruction* (coeditor with P. Alexander) and the *Cambridge Handbook of Multimedia Learning* (editor).

Maria Opfermann has studied psychology at the University of Bielefeld. After working at an epilepsy centre for 2 years, she started her PhD at the Knowledge Media Research Centre in Tuebingen. She is currently working as an assistant professor at the department of Instructional Psychology at the University of Duisburg-Essen. Her main research interest concern multimedia learning, in particular the benefits of text-picture combinations and the impact of individual learner characteristics, cognitive load and its measurement, and the support of metacognitive and self-regulated learning activities.

Dena Pastor (pastorda@jmu.edu) has a dual appointment at James Madison University as associate professor in the Department of Graduate Psychology and as associate assessment specialist in the Center for Assessment and Research Studies. She teaches courses in hierarchical linear modeling, categorical data analysis, and data management. Her research applies statistical and psychometric techniques to the modeling and measurement of college student learning and development. Her publications have appeared in *Contemporary Educational Psychology, Applied Psychological Measurement*, and *Applied Measurement in Education*. She serves on the editorial board for *Educational and Psychological Measurement* and the statistical and methodological advisory board for *Journal of School Psychology*.

Alexander Renkl studied psychology in Aachen and Marburg (Germany) and finished his diploma degree in 1987. From 1988 to 1990 he worked as a graduate student at the Max-Planck Institute of Psychological Research, Munich (Germany), and received his doctoral degree from the University of Heidelberg in 1991. As assistant professor, he spent several years (1991 to 1997) at the University of Munich before he became a full professor of educational psychology at the University of Education in Schwäbisch Gmünd (Germany). Since 1999, he is working at the University of Freiburg as professor of educational and developmental psychology. His main research areas are cognitive learning processes, learning from examples, learning and communicating with new media, and learning by journal writing.

Annett Schmeck (nee Schwamborn) has studied psychology at the Ruhr-University in Bochum and received her PhD at the Research Group & Graduate School "Teaching & Learning of Science" at the University of Duisburg-Essen. She is currently working as a post-doc at the department of Instructional Psychology at that university. Her main research interests concern multimedia learning, the benefits of self-generated visualizations, self-regulated learning and cognitive load and its measurement.

John Sweller is an emeritus professor of education at the University of New South Wales. His research is associated with cognitive load theory. The theory is a contributor to both research and debate on issues associated with human cognition, its links to evolution by natural selection, and the instructional design consequences that follow.

Lightning Source UK Ltd.
Milton Keynes UK
UKOW03f1834031013

218459UK00007B/479/P